EIGHTH EDITION

An Introduction to Human Services

Policy and Practice

BETTY REID MANDELL

Bridgewater State College, Emerita

BARBARA SCHRAM

Northeastern University, Emerita

PEARSON

Boston   Columbus   Indianapolis   New York   San Francisco   Upper Saddle River
Amsterdam   Cape Town   Dubai   London   Madrid   Milan   Munich   Paris   Montreal   Toronto
Delhi   Mexico City   São Paulo   Sydney   Hong Kong   Seoul   Singapore   Taipei   Tokyo

Editorial Director: *Craig Campanella*
Editor in Chief: *Dickson Musslewhite*
Executive Editor: *Ashley Dodge*
Editorial Product Manager: *Carly Czech*
Director of Marketing: *Brandy Dawson*
Executive Marketing Manager: *Jeanette Koskinas*
Senior Marketing Manager: *Wendy Albert*
Marketing Assistant: *Jessica Warren*
Media Project Manager: *Felicia Halpert*

Production Manager: *Meghan DeMaio*
Creative Director: *Jayne Conte*
Cover Designer: *Suzanne Duda*
Cover Design: *Vetta Collection/iStockphoto*
Photo Researcher: *Martha Shethar*
Editorial Production and Composition Service:
  Revathi Viswanathan / PreMediaGlobal
Printer/Binder/Cover Printer: *Courier*
Companies

Credits appear on Page 622, which constitutes an extension of the copyright page.

Library of Congress Cataloging-in-Publication Data
Mandell, Betty Reid.
  An introduction to human services : policy and practice / Betty Reid Mandell,
Barbara Schram. — 8th ed.
    p. cm.
  Includes bibliographical references and index.
1. Social service. 2. Social case work. I. Schram, Barbara, II. Title.
  HV40.M3137 2012
  361—dc23

                                                                2011017796

10 9 8 7 6 5 4 3   CRW 15 14 13

PEARSON

ISBN-10:   0-205-83885-5
ISBN-13: 978-0-205-83885-1

Contents

CHAPTER 3

CHAPTER 4

Attitudes/Values, Skills, and Knowledge   *105*

SECTION TWO

Implementing Human Service Interventions

CHAPTER 7

Poverty   225

CHAPTER 9

Interviewing   *323*

CHAPTER 10
Case Management/Counseling   *358*

Preface

In the previous seven editions of this text, we have used the analogy of taking a ride on a seesaw to describe how we learn and teach about the human service field. When we sit on the end of the seesaw closest to the ground, we can observe in vivid detail a troubled individual struggling with his or her particular life circumstance. Based on this observation, we can describe the options that might be available to that individual in a human service network. Then we might map out the steps that need to be taken to provide him or her with the most appropriate social services and emotional support.

But as we soar high above the ground on our seesaw, we see that individual in less detail. Now we can see how that single life situation complements or conflicts with others in the community. From our vantage point, we can also learn about the world events and cultural or sociopolitical forces that might influence an individual's fate. At this height, we focus less on one person's struggle and think instead about the ways in which a community or a whole society can tackle the vexing problems of violence, abuse, poverty, or lack of opportunity. Looking at individuals in the context of society also helps us sort out, among many conflicting schools of thought, how their problems came about and how their problems should be prevented or solved. As human service providers, we are always looking at both the intimate portrait and the big picture. Both are equally important. In this text, we place more emphasis on social systems than on individual psychology because we believe it is important for beginning students to understand the context of the field before they take specialized courses in psychology and intrapsychic development.

Our understanding of social problems and the social services they require is made far richer but much more ambiguous by this dual set of perspectives. It also prevents us from accepting simplistic, one-size-fits-all solutions to complex social problems.

The seesaw analogy also expresses our feelings about the vast changes we have all experienced since the first edition of our book. As we look back, we realize with surprise, that in our first edition the word *AIDS* did not appear anywhere in the text. It is hard to believe that a disease that has spread so quickly and taken such a high toll was barely recognized as a major social problem when our book first went to the printer in 1983. After many years in which AIDS was a death sentence, things are finally improving in developed countries. Many people with AIDS are now living many years beyond the one to two years that used to be their predicted life expectancy. New medications, a societal increase in condom use, and the postponing of early sexual activity appear to be helping to contain this devastating medical and social problem. This help, however, has still not become widely available to people in poor countries. In fact, AIDS now claims the lives of increasingly large numbers of persons in Africa and Asia.

In the seventh edition, we noted with regret that the problem of affordable housing and homelessness had steadily risen to alarming proportions. Temporary shelters have become permanent institutions, and most of us have become used to seeing people sleeping on the streets. Previous solutions to the housing crises, such as subsidized public housing, have virtually been abandoned, but neither new ideas nor the will to implement them has surfaced. We have worried that the entitlements and social services designed to help people through hard times seemed to be diminishing as the cries for tax relief were becoming louder and more insistent. Now it is clear that the restructuring of welfare in the United States has done nothing to solve this thorny problem.

Since our first edition, some awesome positive changes have occurred in the rest of the world. The tearing down of the Berlin Wall and the breaking up of the Soviet empire have lifted the ominous threat of nuclear destruction. We have noted with pleasure the dismantling of the racial-segregation system in South Africa and the rising interest in the positive rewards of diversity in our own country. We have applauded the increased spirit of volunteerism that has been spreading across the land and the continued healthy growth of the self-help movement.

In the preface to our seventh edition, we predicted that there would soon be a congressional solution to the vexing problems of delivering adequate physical and mental health care for all our citizens. We anticipated then that we would soon be writing about some new form of universal national health insurance. But we proved to be poor prophets. During the two terms of President Clinton, followed by the two terms of President George W. Bush, universal health care proposals were completely wiped off Congress's agenda. Private, managed health care schemes, most of them sponsored by for-profit companies, proliferated, leaving many citizens uncovered. Finally, in 2010, after countless revisions and compromises as well as unprecedented partisan wrangling, a health care bill was passed by both houses of Congress. But, as we go to press, there are several lawsuits pending that seek to repeal or greatly weaken the health care bill. Students of human services need to closely follow the news about the current status of health care coverage, since the provisions for mental and physical care are likely to impact all of the people we serve (as well as ourselves and our families).

As we write the preface to our eighth edition, we cannot help but note the alarming rise in violence in the world in which we live and deliver human services. Although crime statistics showed a remarkable decrease in many of our cities as we entered the new millennium, high school and workplace shootings and similar violent acts shattered many lives and occupied the worried attention of pundits and parents. The secure world of the middle-class schoolyard and work place has been irretrievably altered.

After thinking there could not be many things worse for our country than disaffected young people turning on their classmates, we now face even greater escalations of violence. Since the World Trade Center Towers were demolished; Hurricane Katrina destroyed much of a large city; and a massive oil spill fouled a large portion of the Gulf of Mexico, forcing thousands from their homes and jobs; all of our lives have been touched. Along with the loss of life and property has gone a substantial amount of our sense of security and comfort.

Many of the gains made in civil liberties, in communication technology, and in the embrace of a multicultural society may be whittled back as our government attempts to stop further terrorist acts and has embarked on two seemingly endless wars. We cannot even begin to estimate what losses this will bring to our clients. Obviously, with the defense buildup and downward spiral in the economy, there is less and less money available to house the victims of natural disasters, build homes for the homeless, educate the disabled, and provide solutions for a host of other human service problems.

Perhaps the most important message of this text in all its editions is that our work is always intimately connected with the history, current events, and future of society. Every shift in the social fabric impacts hugely on the daily life of the people you are learning to serve. In our many years in the field, there has never been a time when knowledgeable, skillful human service workers have been so needed. To act with and on behalf of clients and communities, students need to understand the root causes that underpin social service interventions and social policy. As new workers enter this field, they will be called on to be generalists—able to interview and counsel an elderly citizen so he or she can obtain the services that will sustain him in his home and then advocate for him when a faceless bureaucrat decides the services are no longer needed. When day care facilities or job-training programs for teen parents lose their funding, you will need to know how to join with other groups to go to the courts and legislative chambers to design new programs or salvage old ones. But you will also have to learn how to present your arguments in a clear way, marshaling accurate evidence of need, proposing creative strategies, and documenting the potential for success of your programs.

To make this text more accessible to the beginning student, we have organized the chapters into three sections. In the first, we present the context of human service work, answering the major questions students are probably asking: What is a human service agency, what do human service workers do, and what are the barriers that keep people from using human services? Then we describe how human service work has changed through the years, discuss different intervention strategies, and explore the attitudes, values, skills, and knowledge that bind together all workers, regardless of their problem area or credentials. After that, we discuss the conflicts and dilemmas that are likely to occur as we try to incorporate the values of our field into our daily practice. Finally, we pose and then try to answer questions about the social welfare system. We discuss the major social welfare programs and how we can keep ourselves up to date so we can guide our clients through this ever-changing maze of rules and regulations.

After exploring the foundations of human service work, in the second section we examine in detail the ways in which human service workers implement each of the interventions. This section begins with a chapter on working with diversity. Subsequent chapters describe the skills involved in interviewing, counseling and case management, working with groups, planning programs, and organizing for systems change. We have divided the chapter on social welfare into two chapters, one devoted primarily to the issues of poverty.

In the final and shortest section, we present information that human service workers need to know about the legal issues that cut across all the interventions. Fittingly, the final chapter offers words of wisdom about keeping your spark alive and avoiding burnout. This is an especially important chapter because in the next several years, all of us will be challenged to work harder and more creatively until the current wave of slash-and-burn budget cutting has abated.

This field is filled with "alphabet" agencies and jargon, so when new terms are introduced they are highlighted and defined within the text and again in the glossary at the back of the book. Finally, each chapter ends with a summary so you can review the information presented. These summaries can also be read before beginning the chapter, which can be helpful to the student who likes to study a road map in advance of a journey. Questions for discussion and web sites for further information on the topics just discussed close each chapter.

Interviews with human service workers and quotes from case records, newspaper clippings, and novels are included to keep the text lively and help readers feel greater empathy for problems that might be distant from their own life experiences.

We hope that the charts, checklists, and samples of interventions will continue to be useful as you venture out to a volunteer job or an internship. All the examples have been drawn from the authors' combined total of more than fifty-five years of work in social service agencies. Between us, we have had experience in a family service agency, a neighborhood poverty program, and a program for youth at risk, a large recreation center, and a research bureau. We have taught for many years in college human service programs. Both on campus and in community agencies, we have led training groups and done research on adoption, special needs, and the social welfare system. Both of us have raised children and have struggled through our own developmental milestones, both giving help and receiving support from others.

Returning to the seesaw analogy, we must confess that the current state of affairs in our own country and in the world is quite perilous; it is hard not to feel down-hearted. But both authors have lived through several periods in the past when prospects for the future of our field seemed bleak and they have experienced the upswings after the periods of downswings. We hope our readers will keep informed and keep involved in bringing the upswing about.

We would like to thank the reviewers of the previous editions for their thoughtful and valuable feedback: Donna Blake, Genesee Community College; Patricia A. Dolan, Northern Kentucky University; Karole Kinsey Fuller, Kirkwood Community College; Sharon K. Hall, University of Houston, Clear Lake; Sandra Haynes, Metropolitan State College of Denver; Carabelle McNeill, Touro College; Larry Sheffield, La Sierra University; and Cate Solomon, Lasell College, as well as David Birnbach, who reviewed the section on managed care.

We would also like to thank the reviewers of this edition: Susan E. Claxton, Floyd College, and Pamela Kiser, Elon University.

We have tried to infuse this book with some humor. Although human service work can be intensely draining, we think there is as much need in this field for a good laugh as there is for an empathetic tear or a flash of rage at injustice. We are passionate about our work and hope we communicate that.

B.R.M. & B.S.

What Are Human Services? What Do Human Service Workers Do?

HUMAN SERVICE NETWORKS

What are human services? What do human service workers do? These are logical questions for a beginning student to ask and for an introductory text to answer. But the answers are not as straightforward as you might expect. A professor of human services described the challenge of answering these seemingly obvious questions.

> While I was in college, my friends and family kept asking me, in a challenging way, exactly what is a human services major? They wondered what a big guy like me was doing studying for that kind of a field. I'd try to give them a short, clear answer. They never seemed completely satisfied.
>
> That was irritating enough when I was in college, but even after I graduated with a bachelor's degree in human services, my friends and relatives kept right on asking me what I was really going to do to earn my living. If I fell back on my stock answer, about how I was in the business of helping people to help themselves, I always sounded hopelessly muddled.
>
> How do you explain all the things you are *really* doing when it looks as if you are just "hanging out" on a street corner with a gang of teenagers? As a young outreach worker hired by my town, "hanging out" was a large part of my job description. Sometimes I'd be playing pool or shooting baskets with the kids in the local recreation center. Later on in the day I might spend a few hours drinking coffee with a family around their kitchen table. I took kids on camping trips. I held their hands when they ended up in the hospital with an overdose of drugs or a broken leg from a gang fight or football game. I'd chew the fat with the clerks at juvenile court and visit with my kids going in or coming out of the courtroom.
>
> I was a sounding board for the parents, the kids, the local merchants, and the police. Of course I can't point to an adult and say it's because of my work that he made it up and out of trouble. But I think that what I did made a difference in some of the kids' futures.
>
> Twenty years later, one of my students complained to me that she had the same problem. How could she justify the usefulness of spending three hours sitting in front of a television set with five mentally challenged adults? How could she explain what she was doing when she was eating a hamburger in a luncheonette or throwing a Frisbee around the park with her clients? She'd get frustrated when one of her friends would say, "You get paid for doing that? You have to go to college to learn how to do that? Now, my major—engineering, business, computers, etc.—that's real work!"

Helping is such a natural part of our everyday lives that it is hard to think of it as a specialized activity for which people must be trained. Think back over the past few weeks. Chances are that someone—a coworker, friend, or relative—has asked you for help. Perhaps a friend was having trouble with a love relationship and needed to talk about it. If you listened with empathy and tried to understand her view of the problem, you were giving a human service.

An attentive listener and a strong shoulder to cry on might have been all your friend needed. However, if the same type of problem continues to occur, she might need more than a warm, accepting friend. She might need to talk with an experienced counselor who has helped other young adults juggle the conflicting needs of intimacy and independence.

Professional counselors work in private practices, at family service agencies, in hospital outpatient clinics, in mental health centers, in women's advocacy programs, and in the guidance offices of high schools or colleges.

All of us, at some time in our lives, will be on both sides of the helping process, giving or asking for support. Problems are part of living, and no one—regardless of education, income, or profession—is immune. A college president might have a disintegrating marriage, a business tycoon might give birth to a severely retarded child, and a famous sports star might contract HIV. When the economy dips or a hurricane hits the coast, thousands of people from all walks of life lose their jobs, their homes, and their sense of security. If we live long enough, we will have to cope with the death and illness of many people we care about. And throughout the life span, we will face our own critical junctures, transitions, and changing capacities.

People can follow many different routes to find help within the human service network. The route chosen is likely to be influenced by:

- The nature of the problem
- Someone's hunch about the causes of the problem
- The resources available in the local community
- The cost and the person's ability to pay
- The climate of the times that creates fads about "the right thing to do when you have problem X, Y, or Z"
- The history of the circumstances that person is confronting
- Luck or chance (e.g., an aunt mentions that she knows a counselor who has helped her; the topic is discussed in advice columns such as Dear Abby or Ask Beth)

Research indicates that most referrals are made by word of mouth. When people are in pain, they are likely to ask the advice of someone they trust. A member of the clergy, doctor, bartender, or hairdresser can often inspire the courage to walk into a social service agency. Currently, many of us **google search** the web for information about our problems and for suggestions of places to go for help. The opinions of people who have used different services are, of course, very varied. A potential client must sort though a maze of conflicting thoughts and feelings. Too much information can be just as debilitating as too little, but that is a common problem of our cyber culture. Human service workers spend a great amount of time, energy, and creativity getting accurate messages out to the public.

Throughout the pages of this book and in your own work in the field, you will quickly discover that there is no simple path to finding help. Because people are complex, human service problems are multifaceted. So we have had to create a variety of social services. Programs that cluster around one particular problem area are called **human service networks** or **delivery systems**.

A paper written by Kathy Holbrook, a first-year student at Westwood Community College, paints a vivid picture of the variety and complexity of one of these networks. The assignment was called "The Helpee Paper." Kathy's instructor asked the students to think back to a time in their lives when they had faced a painful personal crisis. They were asked to describe that situation and then evaluate the help they received from professionals, volunteers, family, or friends.

In the many years the instructor has assigned this paper, he has never had a student who was unable to remember a painful episode. Students have written about homesickness at camp; the death of a pet; problems with drugs, alcohol, and eating disorders; the divorce of parents; and conflicts around the choice of a college or career. Because the students select their topics, they decide how much personal material they want to reveal.

Google search
Clicking onto a web search engine owned by Google Inc., which is the most-used search engine on the web, receiving millions of queries and postings each day.

human service networks (or delivery systems)
Programs and entitlements that offer help in dealing with different but complementary parts of an overall problem.

Some students choose to share their papers with the class. While listening to these stories, class members feel the intensity of the emotions that conflict engenders. They also learn about the complex barriers that surround the acts of asking for and receiving help. In addition, the students receive a true-to-life picture of the patchwork quilt of agencies and worker roles that make up each of the human service networks.

After reading about Kathy's attempts to tread her way through the human service network of alcohol abuse, you will read about two other paths Kathy might have followed if her problems had developed differently. As you read these three accounts, try to identify all the human service agencies and workers Kathy encountered.

My Experience Receiving Help

by Kathy Holbrook

When I read the assignment for this paper I had mixed feelings. On the one hand, it opens up a lot of wounds. On the other hand, I know that if I want to be a human service worker I have to learn from my own experiences. And every time I talk about the problems my family had with my dad's alcoholism, it can help someone else. That's the main lesson I learned from the Alcoholics Anonymous (AA) meetings I've attended. Well, I guess I've started this paper already.

I can't pinpoint when the problem began. As I look back, I realize the problem was always with us but I didn't have a name for it. I thought the way we lived was just the way things were in everyone's family.

We had a big house in Westwood. My father worked for years for the same stock brokerage firm. He could make or lose thousands of dollars a day of other people's money. It was high pressure all the time.

When I was little we didn't see much of Dad. He had to work very hard to keep up with the rest of the community. People where we live keep moving: a bigger house, a pool, a summer place on the lake, a boat, ivy-league colleges for their kids. Mom was the "typical" housewife. She did all the chauffeuring to Scouts and swim team and came to all our plays alone when Dad was in the city. The first ten years it seemed like we were mostly like everyone else. I knew Mom and Dad always kept liquor around because they did a lot of entertaining.

But in my first year of high school everything got worse. Sometimes I'd get up in the morning and Dad would be asleep on the sofa with his clothes on. Sometimes he wouldn't get up for breakfast. I'd hear Mom phoning his boss, saying he was sick or that he couldn't get the car started. I began to notice that she often didn't tell the truth about Dad.

Then he started coming home during the day. He'd drink until he'd pass out, sometimes right in the living room. I'd ask Mom if I could have friends over and she'd say I couldn't. After a while no one was invited to our house for dinner parties anymore. I felt as if we were living in a cave with a locked door across it. Mom even kept the window blinds down in the afternoon. I think she didn't want the neighbors to see Dad at home, especially when he hadn't shaved or changed his clothes.

I tried to talk to my brothers about it, but they would blow me off. My brother Dennis and Dad got into such a bad fight that Dennis moved into his girlfriend's room at college. Chuck, my oldest brother, has always been a bookworm. He'd just crawl into his room and read or listen to music all the time. Even at dinner we were never together anymore. If we were all there, Mom was nervous or Dad would get up and leave in the middle. She'd cook a big meal and he wouldn't come home or he'd say the food was no good and he'd yell. He never hit her, but he would slam his glass down so it would break or knock over his chair when he left the table.

I was still his special little girl, though. He'd always ask me to stay around the house and he'd give me dollar bills for being so good. Sometimes I'd take off his shoes when he was asleep on the sofa. A couple of times I got up at night and covered him when he was lying on the couch.

My mom started to go to church a lot. The priest came to our house to talk to my dad. Finally, I came home from school one day and Mom said we were leaving. We would stay at my aunt's house until Dad packed his things and left. Then we could come back. That's when she told me that he was an alcoholic. He was sick and it wasn't his fault, but he had to make himself well if we were going to be a family again.

We stayed at my aunt's house for two weeks. Mom finally went to court and got a restraining order. The marshal made Dad leave the house, and he wasn't even supposed to visit us. The only time we got together was at the meetings with our psychologist, Dr. Hightower. I hated those sessions. My brother Dennis would shout insults and Dad looked like he was going to cry. Chuck wouldn't say anything.

Mom and I started going to Al-Anon meetings together. That's a support group like AA but it's for families and friends of people who drink too much. I had one teacher at school whom I really liked, so one day I broke down and told her about Dad. She took me by the hand to see the guidance counselor. He was the one who got me to go to my first Alateen group. I went a few times during activities block. I liked talking to him alone in his office, but I wasn't comfortable in the group. There were kids in it I didn't trust. I was sure they would spread it around about my family being such a mess.

Dad went away to a hospital for alcoholics. His company wanted him back so badly that they sent someone to our home from the personnel department to convince him to go into a program. They were willing to pay for his treatment through his health insurance. We had family meetings with him at the hospital. My mom would see the same social worker because she was pretty depressed by now. I think she took medication for her nerves. He stayed there for three months. Then he went to the state rehabilitation office and got vocational counseling because he knew he couldn't go back to the tension of wheeling and dealing in the stock market. It was too stressful a place for him and most of the people in his company drank too much at business lunches and dinners.

After ten months Dad moved back home. He started a small landscape company. A retired man who used to run a business in town helped him get it

all together and they became buddies. My mom works now as a nurse's aide.

Last January the whole family celebrated the seventh anniversary of Dad's sobriety. We went to his AA group. It was a terrific family reunion. Father Brian was there, too, because he had so much to do with helping my family get straightened out. The only dark spot is Dennis. He came to the party, but he is still very angry. He holds Dad responsible for all the bad times. Actually I think Dennis is drinking now, too. He is very bitter.

I'm not glad that I had to go through this mess, but some good things came out of it. Dad is a really laid-back guy now. He sort of takes things as they come. He and Mom are closer than ever.

Through this I got interested in the field of alcohol counseling. I have paid my dues. I'd like to work in schools teaching kids about alcohol and drug abuse. I've been a member of Students Against Drunk Driving (SADD) and have become very self-confident. I can speak before groups now and I don't feel like I have to please everyone anymore. I speak my mind.

Alternative Scenario 1

Finally I came home from school one day and Mom said we were leaving. We would stay at my aunt's house until Dad packed his things and left. Then we could come back. That's when she told me that he was an alcoholic. He was sick and it wasn't his fault, but he had to make himself well if we were going to be a family again.

Until then Dad had never lifted a hand to anyone in the family, but now he was so angry at Mom he tried to strangle her. He followed us to my Aunt Catherine's house and kept banging on the door. Mom kept calling the police, but he kept coming back. My aunt has two little kids and we were messing up her family. Even though my Dad was in bad shape, he managed to get to the bank and withdraw all their money. My Mom had to call my brother Dennis and ask him for enough cash to get us through the next couple of days. She got a restraining order from the court forbidding Dad to come near us.

Finally, Mom phoned Renewal House and they sent a van to pick us up. Chuck stayed on with my aunt. Renewal is a shelter for battered women. Would you believe we heard about it from my aunt's cleaning woman? She had a sister who was being beaten by her boyfriend and she lived there for a couple of months. They won't give out their address over the phone in case there is someone looking for you who might hunt you down and hurt you. They have to be secretive.

The whole thing was really humiliating and scary. I didn't like the neighborhood; there were a lot of empty lots and rundown houses. But when we walked in, it was quite a surprise. The shelter was old but clean and very homey. They had travel posters on all the walls and lots of plants. The center director was our lifeline. She told Mom about everything she needed to do.

A volunteer drove me back and forth to school. Mom went to the Welfare Department and eventually she got us AFDC (Aid to Families with Dependent Children). * It wasn't nearly as much money as we were used to, but it was enough to contribute for the room and board at Renewal House. She got a Medicaid card so I could go to the hospital for my allergy shots.

Mom started getting very short-tempered. I couldn't blame her, but it was awful for me. I didn't like living there and not being able to go to my friends' houses or to after-school clubs. All I did was go to school and come home. I went to a social worker at the Westwood Mental Health Clinic, but I didn't like him.

After two years my folks got divorced. I have seen very little of my father and it hurts that he doesn't call. He is remarried. Mom went back to school, so she was never around and I hated where we lived. Dennis and Chuck have just gone their own ways.

By the time I began my sophomore year I was very depressed by the whole situation. One night I thought about killing myself and how I would do it. I called the Samaritans, a hot line for people who are thinking about suicide. The woman on the phone talked to me for a few nights and then suggested I go to Alateen at the Mt. Auburn Hospital. I stuck with that group and made a lot of friends there.

Now I am a member of ACOA, Adult Children of Alcoholics. Groups have been really important for me. There are other people out there like me and we are tough survivors. I'm also active in SADD, Students Against Drunk Driving. I think when I finish my

degree I'd like to become an organizer. The women from MADD, Mothers Against Drunk Driving, are really dynamite people. I'd like to try to change the laws that make alcohol so available.

I finally got my act together enough to finish high school and get into college. I see Ms. Applehorn at the counseling center here. She has a way of making me feel I am worth something. She reminds me how far I have come. I guess I got the help I needed, but my Dad never did. He went to AA and to a place called Emerge for men who use violence. But he hasn't changed much.

Alternative Scenario 2

Finally I came home from school one day and Mom said we were leaving. We would stay at my aunt's house until Dad packed his things and left. Then we could come back. That's when she told me that he was an alcoholic. He was sick and it wasn't his fault, but he had to make himself well if we were going to be a family again.

We stayed with my aunt and uncle for four or five months. I began to notice that Mom was changing. She had always had one or two drinks to keep my Dad company, but I never saw her as a drinker. She started not getting up to give me and Chuck breakfast. Some days she didn't even get dressed. My uncle had a bad temper and I know he wasn't happy we had moved in. I spent a lot of time with my brother Dennis and his girlfriend, but they were both working and going to school. Chuck got an apartment with another guy and moved out.

I started not coming home so as to avoid the whole scene. I did a lot of stealing things from local stores. I always had a pocket full of change. I even tried drinking beer with the high school kids, but luckily it just made me fall asleep. I know that with both my parents being alcoholics, I could easily become addicted also. I won't even take a social drink now.

The youth patrol officer would pick me up, give me a lecture, and send me home. The only things that still mattered to me were Scouts and my brothers. My Scout leader was more like a mother than Mom was. She took me to a child-guidance clinic and the worker

---

*The title and regulations of this income support program were changed by the Welfare Reform Bill of 1996. This will be discussed in Chapter 6, "The Social Welfare System."

there tried to get my Mom to come in and talk. When she wouldn't do it, they filed a complaint with the Department of Social Services. They accused her of neglecting me and took me out of my aunt's house. I was very angry, but the worker found me a foster home. I didn't have a choice, so I went. Ms. Braun is an older, single lady whose kids have grown up. She was what I needed, strict but very loving.

Mom died two years later. She'd had a heart condition for a long time, and with all the trouble with Dad and her drinking she didn't give herself proper care. My two brothers weren't settled down enough to take care of me. My foster mother asked me if I wanted to be her daughter permanently.

The people in the Department of Social Services who supervise adoptions felt she was too old. They wanted to put me with a younger couple. Ms. Braun got a lawyer from legal services and she fought for me. The judge finally gave me to her. In some ways social services was right about her being too old. She doesn't always understand about this generation. At times I resent her. I was in a group for teenagers who have been adopted. It was good

to talk it over with the leader and the other kids. I found out I had it really good. The leader signed me up to get a "big sister" from Catholic Charities. I could really talk to her. She was attending Westwood Community College. Dolores is the one who convinced me I could go to college and maybe study for the same degree.

For a while I saw a psychiatrist and I was on antidepressant medication. I don't feel I need to use it now that I am getting on with my life.

Ms. Braun and my Scout leader and my two brothers are my family. When I graduated from high school, they all gave me a surprise party.

I sometimes think about what would have happened to me if I hadn't had Dolores, my Scout leader, and my foster mother. They were able to see that even when I was acting up, I really did not want to be in trouble. Even the youth patrol officer gave me positive support. He had the right combination of toughness and caring.

Though I'm in human services now, I want a job in a business firm. I want to dress up, buy a decent car, and get away from all of these problems.**

**To read an in-depth autobiographical portrait of the impact of alcohol abuse on family life, see Suzanne Somers's *Keeping Secrets*, 1988. For a new approach to treating alcoholism, see Jay and Jay (2000). For excellent descriptions of the tasks involved in treating adult children of alcoholics, see Ruben (2001) and Middleton-Moz & Dwinell (2010).

Helpers Have Varied Backgrounds and Job Titles

In the three scenarios described in the previous section, Kathy, a young woman who could have been sitting next to you in a college class, encountered twenty-five different helpers at various agencies. Although each had a different job title and performed somewhat different tasks, they all offered human services. How many of these did you identify?

1. Priest
2. Psychologist
3. Family therapist
4. High school guidance counselor
5. Teacher
6. Vocational counselor
7. Self-help group leaders (AA, Al-Anon, Alateen)
8. Personnel department counselor
9. Rehabilitation specialist
10. Drug counselor
11. Social worker (at drug clinic)
12. Shelter director
13. Shelter volunteers
14. Hot-line worker

15. Organizer for a social action group (e.g., SADD, MADD)
16. Transitional assistance counselor
17. Therapist (in college counseling center)
18. Scout leader
19. Youth patrol officer
20. Child-protective-services worker
21. Foster parent
22. Adoption caseworker
23. Lawyer (at public legal services)
24. Psychiatrist
25. Volunteer Big Sister

Each of these twenty-five people brought to his or her work a different mixture of education, training, and life experience. For example, the teacher and guidance counselor performed their human service tasks as only one part of their overall jobs. Each probably graduated from college with a bachelor's or master's degree in education. It is likely that they have some formal certification or license from their cities or states that permits them to call themselves *teacher* or *guidance counselor*. Along with their formal training in education methods, they had some psychology and sociology courses as undergraduates. The guidance counselor probably took a few additional courses that involved working with people and their problems.

In Kathy's high school there might have been a school adjustment counselor, school social worker, or school psychologist. Any one of them might have started Kathy on the path of finding services. All of them have been certified by their school boards and have advanced degrees.

The family therapist, the counselors, the rehabilitation and vocational workers, and the shelter staff director are likely to have graduated from college with two- or four-year degrees. Some might have studied beyond college, earning specialized degrees in clinical psychology, counseling, social work, rehabilitation, health education, or perhaps one of the newer fields, such as family systems therapy, drug and alcohol counseling, or human sexuality.

Most states have boards or professional associations that certify psychologists, social workers, and psychiatrists, but there are few uniform standards. There are no standard criteria for licensing of counselors on the national level. Each state can decide what combination of degrees and years of experience it will require for the counselors it certifies. Selection of staff for a particular agency might be governed by the biases of the board of trustees or director, who are convinced that only workers trained in one specific therapeutic model should be hired. Thus, we cannot predict the scope or depth of a particular counselor's expertise simply by knowing his or her job title.

The term *social worker* has in the past been used loosely, but this is beginning to change as more and more states are establishing firm standards for the persons wishing to practice. Officially, the term *social worker* should be applied only to a professional who has earned an undergraduate bachelor in social work degree (BSW) or a graduate master of social work degree (MSW). More and more states are also requiring that in addition to the MSW or BSW the worker has passed further certifying exams.

Human service worker can often be an umbrella term. It identifies workers—such as a youth patrol officer, an organizer of a SADD chapter, or a director of a shelter—who, regardless of qualifications, fill the role of helper.

Several of the workers Kathy encountered had little or no formal education in the helping professions. Hot-line workers, self-help leaders, and foster parents often have education and training totally unrelated to the helping professions. For some of these individuals, providing human services is their central career, but for most of them, it is something they do on a part-time, interim, or volunteer basis.

In the past, these part-time or volunteer workers were not always viewed as an important part of the human service network. In recent years, however, that attitude has begun to change. Now these workers are being offered on-the-job training through workshops and seminars. Often they can earn academic credits that enable them to obtain college degrees and grow in knowledge, self-confidence, and public respect.

Helpers Have Different Agency Affiliations and Orientations

Human service workers are found in a wide variety of settings, ranging from a storefront center to the carpeted offices of the personnel department in a high-tech firm. Some human services, especially for the middle and upper classes, are provided in the homes or offices of private practitioners. But the majority of professional human service workers are financed by the public and are found in social service departments, community mental health centers, hospitals and health clinics, college counseling centers, and ministers' or rabbis' offices. Many private nonprofit groups, such as the Family Service Association, the Jewish Family Service, Catholic Charities, the Protestant Federation, and the Salvation Army, conduct large numbers of direct-care and social change programs. Although most human services are provided on an outpatient basis, some are given in **residential treatment centers** or **community residences**.

Many valuable social services are offered by citizen groups, which conduct programs that advocate for the rights of tenants, immigrants, veterans, homeless families, or some other special population. Citizen groups often hire human service workers to educate and mobilize the public. They work toward changing behaviors such as substance abuse, violence, or destruction of the environment. Often they lobby public officials or the courts to change the way social programs are funded and laws are enforced.

Although there is no way to collect accurate statistics on the number of people in this country who conduct or attend self-help groups, it is possible that these groups are now the single largest source of human services. These groups, usually patterned on the model developed by **Alcoholics Anonymous (AA)**, tackle every conceivable emotional, social, and physical problem that affects some subgroup in the community (White & Madera, web version; Wuthnow, 1994).

Most human service agencies are entirely or partially funded through grants from the local, state, or federal government. Many others are private nonprofit groups, often sponsored by religious denominations that raise money from fees, public appeals, and philanthropic foundations.

A smaller but fast-growing type of agency is the private, profit-making one. Some of these operate on the model pioneered by the fast-food restaurant chains. Entrepreneurs develop a model for a preschool child care center or for the treatment of head-injured people. If it is successful in one location, they open branches of the program in other towns. Perhaps they franchise the model, selling the agency name and method of operation to another entrepreneur. These agencies make their profit entirely from the fees paid by consumers and insurance companies or in performing under a contract with a public agency. Opinions are many and mixed about the emergence of for-profit social services. This is a controversial topic that you will likely debate in your classes and internships. This movement is often called the "privatization of social services."

residential treatment center A facility providing mental and physical services for a specific problem population, which requires that the person being treated stay within its walls for a specified period of time.

community residences Small living units, houses, or apartments located in communities that serve people who have disabilities or other special situations that render them unable to live on their own. (Also known as halfway houses, group homes.)

Alcoholics Anonymous (AA) A self-help organization that uses a specific twelve-step program for recovery from addiction to alcohol.

Raising the public's awareness to the devastating impact of drug and alcohol addiction is a never-ending task to which many workers devote their careers.

twelve-step program A program of healing activities designed by the founders of Alcoholics Anonymous.

co-dependency A mutually destructive relationship between a person who is addicted and his or her significant other who helps to continue, rather than break, the addiction.

Most staff members earn a salary, but agency volunteers work just for the gratification they receive. And there are differences in the hours that workers are on duty. A family worker in a day care center has to work evening hours to telephone or meet with working parents; a counselor for a group of special-needs adults might live in a community residence, working a few days a week around the clock.

Some agencies expect their workers, volunteer or paid, to operate within a particular treatment model or theoretical orientation. Their approach to the clients may be built on the theories of Sigmund Freud, Erik Erikson, or B. F. Skinner. You will read the work of these pioneer scholars in introductory psychology or human development classes. Other theories, such as those of Carl Rogers, Jean Baker Miller, or William Glasser, you are likely to read about in counseling courses or hear spoken of in your fieldwork (Hackney & Cormier, 1996; Okun, 1991; Seligman, 1996). The **twelve-step** and **co-dependency** models, on which many addiction support groups are based, are currently much in vogue.

In addition, some agencies adhere to a specific set of religious or ethical principles. A staff member in a social service department of a Catholic hospital, for example, would be expected to suggest to clients only those options that are acceptable to the overarching principles of that religion. These agencies are currently being referred to as "faith-based social services." The extent to which public monies should support their services has been hotly contested in Congress and the media (Kaminer, 1997, 2001).

There is no overall approach that everyone in the human service field agrees is the most effective. A classic research study by Carkhuff and Berenson (1968) indicates that the variations among counselors' styles are so great that it is impossible to compare their methods and outcomes. With no clear evidence that one theorist has found the best method for creating mental health or social change, most counselors evolve a method created out of bits and pieces of many theories. This eclectic approach is further refined through years of experience. Finally, styles are filtered through the individual personalities of workers and the demands of the population they work with. With the widespread movement to **managed health care** programs, for example, much of a counselor's action plan is dictated by how long the client's health care provider will pay for mental health services.

Differences in social welfare laws from state to state add more diversity to the field. As you read about the history of social welfare in the United States, you will learn about the tug of war that has been going on between the federal government and the states in responding to social needs. Diversity and uniformity of social programs exist side by side. On the one hand, you could travel from California to Maine and find reasonably similar **Head Start** preschool programs in each state. On the other hand, if you visited foster care agencies in each state as you went from west to east, you would find fifty different sets of rules and regulations. Head Start is a federal program, so the rules that govern it are made in Washington, D.C., and disseminated to each state. But foster care and adoption laws are made on the state level, so we find wide variations in these programs. These discrepancies underscore our assertion that human service workers cannot assume that they know what social services exist, even in their hometown. In order to practice their profession, they must know how to construct a currently accurate profile of the services available in each specific community.

managed health care A health care system in which an individual must choose among the doctors included in a particular plan, such as a health maintenance organization. It generally stresses preventive health care but is often used as a cost-cutting measure.

Head Start A federally funded preschool program that aims to increase the readiness for public school of children from low-income families. It was begun by the War on Poverty in the 1960s.

FINDING THE APPROPRIATE HUMAN SERVICES PROGRAM

The local town hall is usually the first place to begin the search for an appropriate social service agency. There you will find the local health, recreation, and education departments; juvenile and elder services; and the like. The workers in these departments can describe the social services they fund, monitor, or license. They might have listings of services in each area.

The next source we turn to in exploring the human service network is the directories of social services published in hard copy or on the Internet by various private agencies. One type of directory is comprehensive; it lists a broad range of social problems and the agencies that deal with them. This sort of directory is generally compiled and distributed by the group that coordinates and raises funds for social services in a particular town. Such groups include the United Way, Community Chest, Community Council, Social Service Coalition, and Red Feather Agency.

In larger cities where the task is a major undertaking, the work of compiling resources might devolve on a private publishing firm. In Massachusetts, for example, a book titled *The Human Services Referral Directory of Massachusetts* (2002) is larger than the phone books of many towns in our country. A well-thumbed copy of that directory is likely to adorn the desk of almost every human service worker in the state.*

*The *Human Services Referral Directory* is now also published in New York (2002) and by other publishers under slightly different titles in many other states.

In recent years there has been a big push to get people out of what many deemed a "failed" welfare system. However, too often, the buck has simply been passed from federal government to state and local governments with insufficient job opportunities and job training, leaving families without the money for food, shelter, and health care.

The table of contents of a comprehensive directory affords a vivid display of the diversity of problems and agencies. The index of a human services directory might start off like this:

a	b	c
abortion	battered women	child care centers
abuse, physical	bereavement support	children's services
addiction	birth control	consumer protection
adoption	block associations	correctional institutions
aging	bulimia	counseling
AIDS		

The other types of directories are problem specific; they focus on one particular service area. Thus, individual booklets might list services for the developmentally delayed, addiction support groups, or early-childhood centers. Some directories are published by national organizations, which have chapters across the country; others are just for local services. A booklet listing services for senior citizens, for example, is likely to include some of the resources shown in the boxed text.

Some directories list only the objective information about an agency: location, activities, costs, and eligibility requirements. The subjective directories provide a more in-depth picture by describing agency services and then evaluating their quality of service. An excellent example of the more subjective type of directory was compiled by a group of students studying health care issues at the State University of New York at Stony Brook (Lefferts, 1982). In the process of this research, students learned an amazing amount about the quantity and quality of services in their town. An evaluative directory empowers both the consumer and human service worker, who can thereby make informed decisions when they choose an agency. Subjective directories are much more difficult to compile than factual listings. Each agency must be visited, all its materials must be read, and data must be found that offer feedback on the care that clients have received. And they must then be updated regularly.

Some agencies maintain hot-line phone services. One can call them, for example, to get information on sexually transmitted diseases, learn about various forms of cancer, or find a service agency for stepfamilies. Recently, we read that a new phone service, modeled on the 911 emergency phone system, has been put into place in many cities and states across the country (Griffin, 2007); it is called Dial 211. Recognizing that an aging population as well as the growing number of young people moving from one city to another face a host of perplexing life issues with no one to turn to for advice, this service will connect callers to agencies whose job it is to help people facing crises that might not be life threatening but are still serious. Perhaps the weather is cold, and there is no heat in the house, or perhaps a single mother cannot leave for her job because the babysitter has not shown up, or maybe there is no food in the house, and a paycheck or disability check will not arrive for days; now these people can call 211 on the phone and, hopefully, find assistance. Try dialing 211 in your town and see if the number is in service. If it isn't, that would be an issue to bring to the attention of a local legislator who might advocate for its inception.

Newspapers also contain information about new agencies that are opening or about the special projects and problems of agencies. The calendar page of the newspaper often lists workshops, seminars, and meetings of support groups. Often notices are placed by social agencies seeking volunteers or donations. Computer bulletin boards and chat rooms on the Internet can also be rich sources of information on virtually every social problem and program.

The classified section of a local newspaper as well as listings on web sites can provide clues to the social service networks in a town. Figure 1.1 shows a selection of want ads clipped from several cities.

American Association of Retired Persons (AARP)	Meals on Wheels
Congregate-living programs	Nursing homes
Council on Aging	Recreation centers
Day-activity programs	Residences
Elderhostel educational programs	Retired and Senior Volunteer Program (RSVP)
Elderly legal services	Shuttle-bus service
Exercise programs	Social action or issue groups
Homemaker/home health aides	Visiting nurses

CASE MANAGEMENT SUPERVISOR

Starting approximately August. BA degree with 6 years experience or MA degree with 3 years experience. Salary competitive. Submit resume to: P.O. Box 462, Little Rock, AR 72217

PART-TIME EXPERIENCED TRAINER

to supervise volunteers, organize & conduct workshops on alcohol & drugs, communication skills, building self-esteem. Send resumé to Box 911, Maryland, AR 72204

FULL & PART-TIME POSITIONS

open for single applicants. Work with emotionally disturbed teens in residential treatment setting. Experience preferred. Box 976

COORDINATOR

Colorado Community Improvement Program. Plan and implement Community Improvement Program including recruitment of entrants, technical assistance during program year, provide communities, neighborhoods, and organizations with information relating to community problems. Meet with city officials, chambers of commerce, civic leaders in public meetings. Related degree and experience preferred. Salary negotiable. Apply and send resumé to: C. Brill, ETO, Inc., 1470 S. Vermont St., Aurora, CO 80012

COORDINATOR/JOB PLACEMENT

Fulltime. Develops and coordinates vocational services for adult psychiatric population. B.A. + 1 year relevant exp. and 6 mo. exp. in industrial setting. Exp. may be substituted for part of education. Apply through July 10,

at Mental Health Center of Denver Co. Inc. 1333 Iris, Affirmative Action M/F, EOE.

CITIZEN ACTION

Progressive social change organization seeks individuals with political motivation for community outreach. Travel opportunities. 617-291-6090 before 1 p.m.

PSYCHIATRIC YOUTH WORKER

St. Agnes Home for Boys has immediate opening for experienced person to work closely with emotionally disturbed adolescent boys in our intensive treatment unit. Qualified applicant must be at least 21, have driver's license and car, have min. 2 years college with courses in the behavioral sciences, plus psychiatric work experience with disturbed children. Excellent benefits. Call 739-2362 Monday through Friday between 10 a.m. & 3 p.m.

DIRECTOR

Mondale halfway house for alcoholics. Position requires BA or BS degree, related area preferred & 2 yrs experience in treatment of alcoholism. May be a recovered alcoholic with at least 2 yrs of sobriety. Contact Human Services Center, P.O. Box 14, Mendenhall, MS 39114. An equal opportunity employer.

RELIEF houseparents/child care worker, 12:30 p.m. to 8:30 a.m., 5 day work week, 2 yrs. college or 1 yr. exp., to work at Boys Ranch. Call Mr. Yate, 726-9012.

COMMUNITY CASE WORKER

Duties include: recruiting Indian foster homes for public or private, assisting Indian families w/state courts concerning children.

Perform these services for the Indian People in Tucson. Call after 9:00 a.m., 712-9000.

ADOLESCENT CHEMICAL DEPENDENCY PROGRAM

Stoughton Medical Center, LaCrosse, Wis., is pleased to announce the start of a newly organized Adolescent Chemical Dependency Program. Program will consist of a 16 bed unit within an accredited medical center. We are seeking:

- Director—Full time, master degree level.
- Family Therapist—Full time, master degree level.
- Alcoholism Counselor II—2 full time positions, bachelor degree level.
- Counselor I—2 full time and 2 part time positions, knowledge of chemical dependency required.
- Recreation Therapist—full time, bachelor degree level.
Excellent salary and fringe benefits. Send resume to :

Stoughton Medical Center Personnel Dept., 1 Timm Ave. LaCrosse, WI 54601

CARE Givers—for pre-school, N.W. Detroit, min. 2 yrs. of child development courses required, call 812-9602.

EXECUTIVE DIRECTOR

For newly formed Homemaker-Home Health Aid Agency. Private, non-profit voluntary agency. Experience in health related field. Education required: B.S. degree, experience in fields of social work and public health. Submit resumé including references to:

Circle-Homemaker-Health Care, Box 26, Granville, OH 43023

FIGURE 1.1 Classified advertisements for human service jobs that have appeared in newspapers from different parts of the country

Source: Denver Post, Denver, Colorado; *Kansas City Times,* Kansas City, Missouri; *New Orleans Times-Picayune/States Item,* New Orleans, Louisiana; *Arizona Daily Star,* Tucson, Arizona; *Star Tribune,* Minneapolis, Minnesota; *Detroit News,* Detroit, Michigan; *Columbus Dispatch,* Columbus, Ohio; *Arkansas Gazette,* Little Rock, Arkansas.

BARRIERS THAT PREVENT PEOPLE FROM GETTING HELP

Despite the problems caused by her father's alcohol addiction, Kathy was quite fortunate in some ways. Her town had a variety of social services, and she was able to find and use them. For many people, things do not work out as well. Perhaps they resist seeking help or have difficulty locating, choosing, paying for, or using it.

Many barriers are encountered on the pathway to seeking help. When they are insurmountable, small problems balloon into large, often tragic ones. Because barriers interfere with our ability to serve prospective clients, we need to develop skills to recognize them and then negate or surmount them.

Some barriers, such as feelings of indecision and ambivalence, are inevitable. How could Kathy's father be certain that he had crossed the line that separates a social drinker from an alcoholic? How could he be certain that he needed professional help? How could he be sure that the hospital or group he ultimately chose was the right one for him? These kinds of feelings we call **internal barriers** to receiving help.

Other, more tangible barriers can stand in the way. Often there are no beds available in a detoxification unit when the client is ready. Frequently there is not enough money to train or pay staff to learn about a new treatment modality. The red tape of bureaucrats in government and in the insurance industry often interferes with a well-thought-out service plan. We call these **external barriers**.

We cannot always remove or mitigate the impact of internal and external barriers, but we must be aware of them. Both client and worker interact within the constraints these barriers impose and are challenged to work creatively around them, using all the intervention strategies we will describe in Chapter 3.

Following is a list of barriers to finding and using human services. The first six are primarily internal barriers that will need to be dealt with in the worker–client counseling relationship. The last five are more external to the client and are most appropriately dealt with by using the strategies of organizing and advocacy. But here, as with most categories, lines do blur.

Each of the first ten barriers is followed by some inner thoughts or questions that reflect them. We will discuss the last one in more detail.

internal barriers
Emotions or attitudes within a person that make it difficult for him or her to seek help.

external barriers
Barriers in the environment that make it difficult for a person to receive help.

1. The Difficulty of Evaluating the Seriousness of a Problem
   - Does my child have a learning disability that needs special help, or is he or she just developing a little bit more slowly than the other kids in the class?
   - Is it normal to be so furious at my parents? Are other teenagers as depressed as I am?
   - Is this kid in my class just mischievous, or is there some other more serious problem? Does he just have a high energy level, or is he biologically hyperactive?

2. The Tendency to Deny the Gravity of a Problem
   - I'm just a social drinker who sometimes has a bit too much. I can stop anytime I decide to. Can I really?
   - Well, I know he hits me once in a while. But don't all marriages go through rough spots?
   - There is no discrimination in this company; we just can't seem to find any qualified women (or disabled or Latino) supervisors. No one can say I didn't try, can they?

3. The Fear of Being Judged, Labeled, or Punished
   - If I get tested for AIDS and it turns out I'm positive, will I lose my job and my medical insurance? Will my family stick with me?
   - If I ask for an evaluation of my child's learning problems, will he or she be labeled retarded or be stuck in a low track for the rest of his or her schooling?
   - I know I don't have enough food in the house, but if I apply for food stamps, will my neighbors begin referring to me as the old lady who's a "welfare cheat"?

4. The Suspicion or Distrust of Human Service Workers and Agencies
   - I know they assure you that complaints of child abuse are anonymous, but how do I know they won't give out my name? Maybe my neighbor will come after me.
   - If I admit how mad I get at my child, will they try to take him or her away from me?
   - If I agree to a voluntary commitment to the hospital for an evaluation, will they decide I'm crazy and throw away the key?

5. The Shame of Not Being Able to Solve One's Own Problems
   - I don't see any other men bursting into tears when they get turned down for a job. Why can't I act like a "real" man?
   - I was always taught that you don't air your dirty linen in public; so, although I know the landlord is not giving me enough heat, won't I look like a crybaby if I complain to the rent board?
   - How can I ask for help paying my medical bills? My family has always taken care of its own.

6. Fear of the Unknown
   - If we start marital counseling and I say what I really think, will we end up in divorce court?
   - Maybe this school isn't as good as it should be, but if the parents start making decisions, won't it get worse? What do they know about education?
   - Living at home might be lonely for our son, who's developmentally delayed, but maybe when he's older we'll think about his moving into a community residence. How can we be sure he won't be hurt if he moves out into the world?

7. The Difficulties of Choosing the Appropriate Program and Helper
   - I've heard about three special programs for autistic children; how do I know which one is best?
   - Our committee has interviewed six candidates for the job of hot-line director, and they are all different. What kind of person (race, gender, age, degree) would make the best director?
   - My family has been going to this clinic for three years, and we don't seem to be getting along any better. Whom can I talk with to see if maybe we should try another approach?

8. The Inadequacy of Services
   - Will there be anyone in that program who understands my culture and speaks my language? Will any of the other staff be disabled the way I am? (Sue, Ivey, & Pederson, 1996)
   - We worry that the steep stairs will be hard to maneuver for many of the senior citizens, but what can we do? It is the only building we could afford.

- No one wants to have this prison (halfway house for addicts, drop-in center for teenagers) in the neighborhood; should we locate it on the edge of town, even though it can't be reached by public transportation.

9. The High Cost of Services
   - We don't have enough money for our day camp, so we have to save the spaces for those most in need. But how do you decide whom to reject?
   - I know that your mom needs this nursing home, but Medicaid doesn't pay the full cost, and we never get those payments on time anyway.
   - We could try to run a reform candidate for the school board who is in favor of racial integration, but can we pay the advertising costs to get enough publicity?

10. Past History, Reputation, or Public Image of a Program
    - First it was the antipoverty program, then Model Cities, and now it's privatization. I've seen them all come and go. Our neighborhood never seems to get any better. Why should I participate in this new program?
    - With all the taxes I pay, why do the schools still turn out kids who can't read?
    - As a legislator, I'm convinced that this town does not need another shelter for the homeless. Do you think the social workers complain about problems so they can keep their jobs?

11. Myths and Lack of Information about the Human Services

Because the field is so broad and the barriers to finding and using help so pervasive, the public is understandably confused. This lack of clarity can lead to hostility. Much of what people think they know about the role of the human service worker is, in fact, either incomplete or just plain wrong.

The public sees many other professionals—fire fighters, doctors, secretaries—doing their jobs; this is not the case with human service workers. We don't wear uniforms or have any observable symbols or tools of our trade. People usually visualize the human service professional primarily in the role of therapist, counselor, or welfare investigator, working one-on-one to solve individual problems or ferret out wrongdoing. Although these are important roles, they do not show the full dimensions of human service work.

Instead of working in a one-on-one counseling relationship with Kathy, for example, some human service workers tackled the problem of alcohol abuse by trying to change the social system that supports it:

- They made speeches about the need for funding alcohol education programs.
- They designed training programs for schools and private industry.
- They met with legislators to change the laws governing the advertising and sale of addictive substances.
- They conducted research to find out what kind of prevention programs work best.
- They published newsletters, books, and journal articles that disseminated the wisdom they have gleaned about alcohol intervention.
- They designed computer programs so that information about addiction could be easily retrieved.

These social change activities are just as important as the therapy or counseling interventions that the public identifies as the province of human service workers. Yet, the media does little to help the public get a well-rounded picture of the varied work of the field. Television programs show the exploits of doctors, emergency medical technicians, lawyers, detectives, newspaper reporters, and an occasional schoolteacher but rarely those of a human service worker.

Only one major network show—*Eastside, Westside*—featured a human service worker as its "hero." Each episode showed him interacting with people who were struggling to overcome difficult situations. The program dealt with racial prejudice, prostitution, alcoholism, marital discord, labor strikes, and runaway children. Most of the dramas were real-life situations, filled with suspense, emotion, conflicting values, and expectations. Because the program tried to hold a mirror up to life, many of the problems could not be resolved in neatly packaged, hour-long segments. Sadly—but accurately—the black family depicted on the show was not welcomed with open arms by their neighbors in an all-white suburb, the divorcing couples and runaway kids were not always reunited, and alcoholics often drifted back to the bottle. Although the critics liked it, *Eastside, Westside* ran for only one season. The uniqueness of the program lay not only in its portrayal of the excitement and frustration of human service work but also in its depiction of the wide-ranging activities of the human service worker.

Worse than the paucity of information about the field are the myths and misinformation projected by the popular media using human service workers as the objects of ridicule: "Hello," says the client. "Hmmm, now what do you really mean by that?" asks the counselor.

On the rare occasions that the theater or Hollywood movies depict us at all, they often portray us as narrow, rigid, inept snoopers. The social worker in Herb Gardner's

Encouraging responsible behavior and reducing the self-defeating cycle of alcohol and drug abuse require creative approaches. This wrecked car raises frightening questions about the fate of its once-carefree driver. Change in drinking patterns is painstakingly slow, yet we believe that change is always possible.

often-performed comedy *A Thousand Clowns* (1962) is a classic portrayal of this stereo-type. In it, a child-protective-services worker (with hair pulled back, glasses halfway down her nose, flat shoes, and a man-tailored suit) is sent to investigate charges that a man is corrupting his young nephew. He is romping with him through New York's parks and neighborhoods instead of sending him to school, where the boy could be taught to take life seriously. The uncle and nephew are portrayed as witty, energetic, loving people, while the young female social worker and her stuffy male supervisor represent the bore-dom of society, full of rigid rules and unfeeling bureaucracy.

The definitive parody of human service workers was written by Stephen Sondheim (1957) for *West Side Story*. Set in an urban ghetto, this musical drama is an updated ver-sion of the tragedy of Romeo and Juliet. In this saga of poverty, prejudice, and conflicting emotions, a group of teenage gang members tell a police officer about their misadven-tures with the human service workers they have been sent to. Each "helper" disagrees with the others and comes to a ridiculous, simplistic conclusion about the teenagers' delinquency. A judge says they are misunderstood neurotics, so he sends them to a thera-pist. The therapist says that delinquency is a social disease, so he sends them to a social worker to get a "good honest job." The social worker says they're not antisocial, they're only "antiwork" and could use a year in jail. And so they are sent back to court, right where they started!

A PARADOX

When we consider the barriers strewn along the path to getting help, we should think about them in their current context. When placed in perspective, these barriers reveal a frustrat-ing paradox.

At no time in the history of the social services has there been such a wide array of pro-gram approaches for solving social problems as there is today, although many programs are struggling to stay solvent. Thirty years ago, Kathy's father would probably have been fired from his job when his alcohol addiction began interfering with his performance. Back then, few companies hired trained mental health counselors for their personnel departments, and most workers could not afford the luxury of an inpatient facility to "dry out" and regroup. But Kathy's dad overcame barriers with the help of a professional **employee assis-tance program (EAP)** counselor at his firm. His health insurance plan paid for his stay at the rehabilitation center. He was lucky!

And certainly, attitudes toward addicts have improved. Thirty years ago, if a police offi-cer had encountered Kathy's Dad sleeping off his binge in a public park, he probably would have arrested him, and a judge might have charged him with disorderly conduct, public drunkenness, and the like. But by the time Kathy wrote this paper, most police officers had learned to define alcohol addiction as an illness.

So the barriers of inaccessibility and stigma, for example, should be toppling down for families facing the kinds of problems Kathy described. Right? Wrong! Strangely enough, this isn't happening. In actuality, in this new millennium, most health care plans, which at their inception were fairly generous with mental health benefits, are drastically cutting back on these treatments.

employee assis-tance program (EAP) Supportive services dealing with mental health or financial or legal issues that are offered directly to employees by their company or agency. Their goal is to reduce worker turnover and raise productivity.

At the same time, in public forums in the mass media and in the halls of Congress, the following demands are being shouted with louder and louder voices:

- Give the public tax cuts instead of social services.
- Allow each of the fifty states to make its own decisions about whether to fund specific social services.
- Bring to a halt the days of massive public support for social services.
- Admit that social services hinder rather than help troubled individuals.

In later chapters, we will return to these themes to see how they play out as human service workers try to ameliorate social problems in an ever-more-complex world in which priorities are moving away from dealing with social problems through governmental intervention.

CHOOSING OUR WORK ROLE

From one perspective, the wide range (some might call it a hodgepodge) of human service agencies can seem overwhelming. It is especially confusing to the student just starting a human service career. On the flip side of the coin, however, this incredible diversity offers each worker a chance to find the particular combination of worker roles, agencies, clients, populations, and problems that fits his or her unique talents.

As you read about Kathy's experiences, reflect on your own, and glance through directories and want ads, you will probably be attracted to some human service roles and repelled by others. These are natural reactions. While one person thrives working with youngsters with cerebral palsy, another might drown in feelings of frustration or hopelessness. That same worker who cannot cope with a physically disabled child might be able to coolly trade put-downs with the angriest streetwise teenager. One worker who can listen patiently and nonjudgmentally all day long to folks like Kathy's Dad would be tongue-tied trying to convince the zoning board to let her agency purchase a building when the neighbors have organized to block the sale.

We need to tune in to our instinctive feelings of attraction or repulsion to different human service tasks and roles. But we also need to keep our options open. We often surprise ourselves by discovering that we can do work that we thought we could never tolerate. We can also find ourselves unstimulated by a work role that we always thought we wanted.

Currently many students are being trained to be human service generalists. A **generalist** is knowledgeable about a wide range of resources, strategies, and subgroups and can operate comfortably in many agency roles. He or she does not necessarily identify with one human service subspecialty but works with a small number of clients, helping them confront and solve the gamut of life's problems. The generalist is often a team member or an assistant whose daily tasks grow out of a job assignment that complements the role of other helping professionals.

Some students take the reverse path, specializing in a specific role from the start of their careers. Trained to work as alcohol and drug abuse counselors or as mental health

generalist A worker who is knowledgeable about a wide range of resources and subgroups and who can use a variety of helping interventions.

technicians, they develop depth rather than breadth. Later on they might need to expand their skills as priorities shift or as they move up the career ladder. Whichever direction students take at the start of their career, they will probably continue to do a significant amount of growing as they search for the academic degrees and experience that suit them best.

Whether returning to school for advanced training or switching jobs, workers need to make choices about (1) the specific problems or populations they want to deal with, (2) the type of agency setting they enjoy, and (3) the strategies of intervention they are best at. These choices will be determined by personal attributes, lifestyles, and ideologies and by the accessibility of certain occupational roles.

Our Attributes

Most of us have been taught since childhood that talking about our good points is bragging or showing off, but in the human services, we must develop insight into precisely what we do best and least well. We need to estimate what our chances of growth or change will be in a specific job.

Although the same values and attitudes are basic to all types of human service work, there are differences in the kinds of people who can do intensive, one-to-one counseling and those who fare best in the rough-and-tumble atmosphere of community organization. Some of us are outgoing and articulate; others are more introspective and quiet. Some are comfortable filling a niche in a traditional structure; others like to be in charge or work alone. Each time we try a new field experience, meet clients and workers at different agencies, or read about human service work, we should try to visualize ourselves as full-time workers in that role. We need to figure out how its demands fit our personality and how much we are willing to change.

Our Lifestyles

Even as we start our human service education, we should think about the elements in an environment that bring out the best in us. Some of us, for example, are night people, so working a 2:00 P.M. to 10:00 P.M. shift in a teen residence or running evening parents' groups would be possible. Others are nine-to-fivers; perhaps they will choose to work in a school or on the day shift at a hospital or mental health clinic. All jobs require some mix of time, location, and structure, dictated by the sorts of populations the agency serves.

Some people feel strongly about dressing in a certain fashion; however, that desire might not fit a particular setting or subgroup. Others insist on having privacy or a place of their own. Obviously, a live-in job in a residence might not suit them.

Although we need to compromise on certain issues, others are vital and legitimate personal needs. As our lives change, the kind of work that makes sense for us also changes. The choice of a specific role need not be lifelong. Optimally, it should support the other parts of our lives as family members and citizens. The broadness of the human service field offers a unique chance to shift gears as circumstances require.

As our lives evolve through marriage, raising children, caring for elderly parents, facing an empty nest, or perhaps moving to a new area, our work life needs to accommodate those changes.

Our Personal Ideologies

Each of us comes to human service work with a unique set of philosophies, drawn from our religion or a general ethical framework. These beliefs must be compatible with the work we do. If a person has strong religious convictions about war, contraception, suicide, special types of food, or days of rest, these must be taken into account in choosing a place to work. We must not be self-conscious about acknowledging the primacy of these issues in our lives. Usually, we can find jobs that allow their expression. Although our values will come under constant scrutiny in the course of learning about the field and though many values might change, they should never be suppressed. If we try to deny them, they may subtly affect our work.

Likewise, many of us have political beliefs about how society should be organized—our personal visions of utopia. We choose the human service work that seems to be moving the community in that direction. As long as our politics or visions do not engulf our work, they add dimension and intensity to it. Some jobs might make demands that we cannot in conscience fulfill. We need to acknowledge these problems openly. Needless to say, having our own beliefs never means that we insist our clients agree with us. If we have too many rigid beliefs, it may turn out that human services is not the right field for us.

Agencies in the Local Community

Throughout this book, we underscore the changing nature of human service work. For example, priorities are not the same in a rural setting as in an urban center. Priorities change

Chapter 1   What Are Human Services? What Do Human Service Workers Do?

23

as the population shifts in age or ethnicity, inventions affect people's lifestyles—and election results redirect the national agenda. When the country is at war, having an economic recession, or embarking on a new crusade against mental illness, disability, or domestic violence, some agencies become obsolete and others expand. Funding patterns change dramatically in short periods. Sometimes the human services help to shape the political climate in the country; more often they are shaped by it.

You might, for example, read about shelters for young mothers who have AIDS. You might decide to work in one, only to discover that your state does not appropriate money for such shelters. This does not necessarily mean you won't ever work in one. Perhaps you will first have to join with others and use your organizational skills to create a public outcry for such programs. Once successful, you can retool, using your social change skills less and using your counseling skills more.

To get a visceral feeling for the highs, lows, and realities of human service work, let's meet Stephanie Lake, a worker whom Kathy might have encountered on her college campus.

INTERVIEW

Stephanie Lake, Program Coordinator, Drug and Alcohol Education Project

My work on the Drug and Alcohol Education Project began while I was a human services student. I met the director of the project, Margie Crooks, when she came to my class as a guest speaker. She was new on campus and looking for students to help get the program off the ground.

My college is hard to get to know. We are a work-study school. The students are on campus for several months and then leave for their job placements for the same amount of time before they return again. We are smack in the middle of a poor-to-working-class urban area. About half the students commute. A lot of our students have limited incomes and have to work part time. They have the usual problems of college kids—separation from family; roommate problems for the dorm students; and the tensions of traffic, parking, and home problems for the commuters. Then there are problems of studying, career choice, and all the baggage around social relationships and sexual identity. As on most campuses, there can be social pressures to drink too much and to experiment with marijuana. A lot of the kids come out of high school with these habits, or they come to college and think it is a chance to bust loose.

Although we have a Department of Student Counseling and a half-time counselor who specializes in drugs and alcohol, the administration decided to put more energy into education about, and the prevention of, substance abuse. That way, they don't just sit around waiting for the problems to come to them.

They made a really good choice in hiring Margie, because although she is youngish, she has a great background. She worked for several regional drug prevention centers. I volunteered to help her recruit students for a peer-counseling program called Peers Reaching Out, or PRO. We started with nine students. The first thing we did was a survey of attitudes and behavior. We walked around the student lounge for days with our clipboards. Because they knew their answers were anonymous, kids really opened up to us. We found out a lot about the services they used and what they might want. We also recruited a few peer counselors that way.

The next thing we did was form a committee. This was made up of university staff from different programs and student leaders. They became a brain trust to come up with ideas about the rules that needed to be changed and make suggestions for programs. I became the secretary to the group and still am.

They suggested that we needed more awareness on campus of the problem and the new program. The president declared a DRUG-AHOL Awareness Week. Faculty members agreed to invite speakers into their classes, and the resident assistants organized discussions in the dorms. We set up a table in the quad and took turns sitting at it every day for a week. We gave out literature on different aspects of the problem and had a drug board that showed the paraphernalia and effects of drugs and alcohol. We also had drug wheels that you use to figure out how much alcohol it would take to make you legally drunk.

The idea I was proudest of was the display of a totally wrecked car donated by a junkyard. We had it towed right into the center of the quad. The students could see in gruesome detail what can happen when you drive drunk. They stopped and asked a lot of questions. We also had a video going constantly in the main lobby about the crash involving that car.

After I volunteered for two quarters, Marge was able to hire me as a work-study student. I was put in charge of DRUG-AHOL Awareness Week, and each one has gotten better since then.

At first I was afraid to speak in front of student clubs, but I eventually got over that. I wrote articles for the student newspaper and was interviewed on the student radio station. I also used all my own contacts and was able to recruit a solid group of forty-five students. Some of them were in recovery themselves and some of them, like me, had alcohol abuse in their families. I organized the weekly training sessions, set up speakers, got videos, and stayed in touch with the peers between training sessions.

Margie taught me a lot about writing grants. I assisted her in gathering background information and in making presentations to foundations. One of them funded us for two years. As soon as I graduated, I was able to come on full time. Since then I have planned, organized, and implemented a twenty-four-hour DRUG-AHOL telephone hot line. This way, we can give out information and make referrals, and the students don't have to identify themselves if they don't want to.

I think I've also been especially pleased with the development of the campus task force. I've gone from being a student member to being one of the professional staff to whom people turn for suggestions. We had a major problem with our senior "bash." For years it's been a tradition for the seniors to bring champagne onto the quad the last day of classes and just get totally drunk. They would destroy the grass, break the bottles, and have a series of nasty accidents. We needed to stop it and yet, we recognized the seniors' need to celebrate. Our committee proposed that the university take over the celebration, providing the champagne, soft drinks, and plenty of food. That way, the seniors could have their party and we could help them drink in a responsible way. They grumbled the first year, but we pulled it off.

But this year the university decided we couldn't repeat it. The president felt we couldn't take the ethical or moral risk of providing liquor to students who would later drive home. So they gave them a beautiful, fancy, nonalcoholic party. Of course, the students went to the local bars right after it, but there is only so much you can do.

The other project I work on is a program called INSTEAD. From the student court, we get referrals of residents who have caused damage while drunk or who have been caught with liquor in the dorms. The university used to expel them from the dorms. Now we recognize they have a problem. They have to attend a six-session training course and do community service. I think this has helped a lot of them turn around. Some of the INSTEAD members go on to join AA. Some even stay with their volunteer work with neighborhood kids.

I have learned so much about administration and planning in this job. It is ending within the next month because the grant is over. This gives me a chance to explore going back to school for my advanced degree. I think maybe it's time to leave, but it's been great to grow with a program that has so much meaning for students and faculty. I am very pleased I chose to major in human services; it is the gateway education for so many different fields. Wherever I go I will take with me the insights I have gained through course and field work.

SUMMARY

1. Three possible routes for a young woman looking for help with her father's alcohol abuse were described. By following these paths, we encountered twenty-five different human service roles.

2. A picture of the human service programs in any one particular town can be discovered by calling the town hall or an umbrella funding agency, searching out directories of services, calling hot lines, and reading local newspapers.

3. Although services might be available, clients frequently have difficulty finding and using them. Barriers generated by internal and external pressures clutter the paths. We looked at a variety of these barriers by listening in on the nagging doubts and questions that reflect them.

4. The public often accepts stereotypes about who we are and what we do. People often lack accurate information about the full range of human service work.

5. The complexity inherent in human service problems leads to a proliferation of agencies and professional roles. This diversity can offer much choice to those seeking appropriate services or roles. People choose their work roles in the field by considering their own personal attributes, lifestyle, philosophy or ideology, and available programs.

6. The description of the daily work of a program coordinator for a drug and alcohol abuse education and prevention project reveals many important roles in the human service network.

7. Although treading the maze of the human service system is complex and frustrating, it is never routine and is often exhilarating.

DISCUSSION QUESTIONS

1. Some people believe that alcohol or drug abuse is a crime best left to the criminal justice system. Others believe that addiction is a moral failing and thus should be cured by the family and the church. Others assert that it is a problem that should be dealt with by the medical establishment and the social service networks. What do you think of each of these positions?

2. What is the situation with drug and alcohol use and abuse on your campus? What approaches does the

administration appear to be using if there seems to be a problem, and how effective do you think those approaches are?

3. If you were assigned to write a helpee paper the way Kathy was, would you be willing to write about a personal problem? Would you be willing to share your paper with your classmates after you wrote it (if you decided to fulfill the assignment)? To what extent do you think that asking students in a human services class to share personal

information with the instructor or with other students is an appropriate learning device? To what extent does it feel like an unjustified invasion of your privacy?

4. What human service workers have you personally met? Which ones do you know about in your community or on your campus? Which of their jobs seems like a set of tasks you might like to try out? Which would you prefer to avoid?

WEB RESOURCES FOR FURTHER STUDY

Occupational Outlook Handbook, U. S. Department of Labor
www.bls.gov/oco/

For hundreds of different types of jobs the *Occupational Outlook Handbook* tells you the training and education needed, earnings, expected job prospects, what workers do on the job, and working conditions.

In addition, the *Handbook* gives you job search tips, links to information about the job market in each state, and more.

U. S. Department of Health and Human Services
www.hhs.gov

For information about a governmental human service program, click on their Information and Resources Directory. It is an invaluable resource to keep human service workers up-to-date.

Prevline
http://free.ed.gov/resource.cfm?resource_id=532

Prevline is a national clearinghouse by the Department of Health and Human Services for alcohol and drug information. It offers fact sheets, video and audio files, news, research briefs, conference calendars, funding opportunities, and a kids section.

Hazelden Addiction Treatment Center
www.hazelden.org

Hazelden is a commercial publisher that publishes information about addiction and addiction treatment.

The National Mental Health Consumers Self-Help Clearinghouse
http://mhselfhelp.org

The National Mental Health Consumers' Self-Help Clearinghouse has played a major role in the development of the mental health consumer movement. The consumer movement strives for dignity, respect, and opportunity for those with mental illnesses. Consumers—those who receive or have received mental health services—continue to reject the label of "those who cannot help themselves."

Chapter 2

The Changing Nature of the Helping Process

A woman who is active in a welfare rights group called EMPOWER in Rochester, New York, describes how the group helped her change from feeling worthless and powerless to feeling in control of her life:

> I felt worthless and ashamed receiving a welfare check. I didn't even go to the bank on welfare-check day. I didn't want people to see me with that manila envelope—the one welfare checks come in. . . .
>
> The image that I would use for the way I felt about myself would be a social leper. I felt like I had a dreaded, contagious disease. . . . It took the beauty from my eyes, causing me to feel ugly; it took the hope from my heart, causing me to feel discouraged; it took the ideas from my mind, causing me to feel useless. . . .
>
> These feelings started to change when I met the founder of EMPOWER . . . Mr. Ingram treated us like respectable human beings. . . . My sense of worth was enhanced when church members treated me with courtesy and respect. . . . (Ingram, 1992, p. 95)
>
> As I began to feel good about myself, I began to entertain the notion that, as a person with worth, I was entitled to fair and legal treatment by the welfare establishment. . . . EMPOWER gives people the opportunity to take charge of their lives. Those who choose to do so then encourage others to do the same. . . . Together, using a collective voice, welfare recipients are growing in their ability to address with dignity a system that has too long failed to recognize their individual worth and value. (Maxwell, 1988, p. 13)

Welfare rights groups such as EMPOWER that help TANF (Transitional Assistance to Needy Families) recipients overcome welfare stigma stand firm as the ocean of anti-welfare sentiment threatens to engulf the country. Resentment against welfare recipients is not new, but its intensity has vastly increased since the early 1980s.

The poor have not always been treated with such suspicion and mistrust. In feudal times, people believed that God decreed their economic status, and the poor were not blamed for their condition. Each historical period creates conditions that shape people's attitudes about helping people. In this chapter, we trace some of those historical changes.

SOCIETY SHAPES HELPING BEHAVIOR

Human beings are social animals who have always helped each other (and, of course, also hurt each other). The kind of relationships that a society expects from its citizens and the way it organizes its important institutions—the family, the system of governance and control—can either nurture or stunt people's impulses to give help to relatives, friends, and needy strangers.

Anthropologists have shown that behavior varies widely among cultures. It is shaped by the food supply, the kinship system, the system of production, and relationships with other societies. It is easier to be loving and helpful in some societies than in others. Yet, if a modern society is to stay intact, it must encourage some form of mutual help. This is what the anthropologist Claude Levi-Strauss (1974) called the **principle of reciprocity**, which he considered the basic glue that holds together a society. That principle points to people's mutual obligations toward each other, based on caring and a sense of justice.

HELPING IN WESTERN CULTURE

Not only do different cultures vary in their helping behaviors, but our government, churches, and even private groups have always reacted differently to those in need of help. By exploring a small part of the history of a few institutions that are supposed to provide help, we see this evolution in concrete form. "But," you might ask, "why must I bother studying the past in order to do my job as a mental health aide (or probation officer) in the twenty-first century?" Each new view of the way people should be helped, or not helped, has left behind its skeletons. Buildings constructed during one era are still standing many years later; people trained under outmoded theories continue to practice. Lingering myths and misconceptions about crime, mental illness, and poverty are almost impossible to stamp out, even in the face of overwhelming scientific evidence proving them wrong.

principle of reciprocity   The principle that social relationships are based to some extent on an analysis of trade-offs that determines what each person must give to the relationship in order to get back certain benefits.

Social attitudes about behavior go through cycles. Sometimes they reverse themselves from one era to another. These immigrants to the United States, landing at Ellis Island early in the twentieth century, faced adversity, but their labor was welcomed. Now, many of their descendants vote to restrict the entry and social benefits of new waves of hopeful immigrants.

Change as a Cyclical Path

Change is not an upward, linear progression. Rather, changes in social attitudes and treatment methods tend to be cyclical. Yet, although the next spin in the cycle may look familiar, it doesn't come out exactly like the previous one. The philosopher Hegel called change a **dialectical** process. First there is the idea or action (a thesis), which inspires its opposite idea or action (antithesis). Out of the struggle of these two opposites comes a new synthesis. Then the process begins all over again. As you will see in the examples that follow, these cycles are strongly influenced by warring political ideologies, often seesawing between conservative ideas and more liberal ones.

We find ourselves periodically returning to the same debates about the legitimacy and effectiveness of such issues as:

- Birth control
- Capital punishment
- Educational methods
- Mental health treatment
- Rehabilitation of prisoners
- Women's rights

To understand the hodgepodge of rules, regulations, and social attitudes that surround our daily work in a hospital ward, a prison, or an old-age home, we need to know the possibilities, limits, and trade-offs of the many methods used in the past. Some of those may be, with variations, the methods of the future.

Tracing the overall history of helping in the United States as well as in western Europe reveals a tortured path, starting from the times when people in need were viewed as the responsibility of their families alone and perhaps were also given a little help from the church or a benevolent feudal lord, owner, or other master. With the decline of feudalism and the rise of mercantilism and industrialism, the responsibility for those people who could not help themselves began to shift more and more to town governments. Official overseers of the poor gradually replaced the church and almsgivers as the primary sources of help outside the family. Eventually, this task of providing help became a profession for volunteers or trained professionals.

Some governments have been reluctant to take on the full responsibility. The United States, for example, has been called a "reluctant welfare state" in comparison with most other industrialized nations. Today we watch as our government dismantles services that it once offered citizens. When George H. W. Bush was president, he wanted volunteers to take the place of government services and called for "a thousand points of light." When his son, George W. Bush, became president in 2001, he continued his father's efforts to increase dependency on voluntary organizations in social services. His "faith-based" approach proposed giving religious organizations more money to deliver social services and more freedom from government restrictions. This strategy is reminiscent of the nineteenth century, with volunteers and private philanthropies. Some officials have even suggested that we return to the practices of feudal days, when the church gave whatever help was available. Churches protest that they are not equipped to handle the job, and the Catholic bishops have called for more government help for the poor and oppressed (National Conference of Catholic Bishops, 1986).

Except for a generous outpouring of giving to the victims of the attacks on the World Trade Center and the Pentagon, many charities nationwide have experienced sharp drops in contributions since September 11, 2001. Even before September 11, people were reacting to the economic pinch by cutting back on their giving.

> **dialectical**   Refers to the principle that an idea or event (thesis) generates its opposite (antithesis), leading to a reconciliation of opposites (synthesis) and a continuation of the dialectical process.

Along with the shifts between private and public responsibility for helping has come a slowly changing set of social perspectives on people who need help. In feudal times, people were pretty much locked into their social status, and the rulers of society, buttressed by theologians such as St. Augustine, spread the word that the poor were poor because God willed it. If God willed it, the rulers argued, then it would be sacrilegious to change their status. The rich, however, could assure their own entrance into heaven by giving to the poor.

Sixteenth-century theologian John Calvin helped wed Protestant theology with the ideology needed for the rise of capitalism. He extolled the virtues of thrift, industry, sobriety, and responsibility as essential to the achievement of the reign of God on earth. The Puritan moralists of New England used his ideas to reinforce the work ethic needed for the newly emerging industrialism of the United States. The moral imperative to make money made it a stigma to be poor and ensured that programs which give money to the poor would be linked to efforts to get them to work for wages. (Mothers have always worked as caregivers, but without wages.)

A powerful influence on the treatment of the poor during the late nineteenth century was the adaptation of the ideas of Charles Darwin on evolution to the realm of sociology. Although Darwin did not draw any sociological conclusions from his work, Herbert Spencer, an English philosopher and one of the first sociologists, used Darwin's work to coin the phrase *survival of the fittest*. According to Spencer's interpretation, the fittest people in society were those who were able to make money. Poor people were declared unfit and accorded the same treatment doled out to common criminals. This philosophy is called **Social Darwinism**. Even before Spencer, this attitude had currency:

> Christian charity . . . enjoins a personal interest in the lower orders; visiting them in their cottages, even though they may seem "little better than savages and barbarians, with whom any familiar intercourse would be degrading . . . if not dangerous," might nurture in the poor a sense of gratitude to their superiors. (Trimmer, 1801, p. 11)

Darwin actually said that we are programmed to be cooperative and caring, according to one psychologist, Dacher Keltner, director of the Berkeley Social Interaction Laboratory. He wrote the book *Born to Be Good: The Science of a Meaningful Life* (Keltner, 2009), in which he says, "Our mammalian and hominid evolution have crafted a species—us—with remarkable tendencies toward kindness, play, generosity, reverence and self-sacrifice, which are vital to the classic tasks of evolution-survival, gene replication and smooth functioning groups." The beginnings of the industrial age ushered in the view that people with problems were morally depraved, almost as if they had a self-inflicted contagious disease. It was thought that they deserved punishment or removal from society. William Ryan calls that point of view **victim blaming** (Ryan, 1976). It is a point of view that has sunk roots deep into our society.

An equally radical but opposing point of view—and one that is generally less popular—has been battling the blaming-the-victim ideology ever since the sixteenth century. It defines human problems as a result of interacting personal and social forces, often beyond the control of the individual. It looks at individuals as embedded in families and communities and in economic and political systems that exert a powerful pull on personality development, social status, and life chances.

This alternative point of view, which looks at social systems, asserts that life situations are an inevitable part of the human condition in an industrialized society. Most old people

Social Darwinism
The application of Charles Darwin's theories of evolution to the human sphere by sociologist Herbert Spencer. The concept of "survival of the fittest" was used to justify accumulation of wealth and disregard of the needs of the poor.

victim blaming
Blaming a person for his or her own misfortune rather than considering the social forces that contributed to the problem.

deserving versus undeserving The discriminatory classification of people into higher and lower categories, considering some people to be more worthy of receiving benefits and services than others.

means-tested programs Programs that are available only to the poor, whose assets fall below a certain set eligibility level.

residual philosophy of social welfare A philosophy that believes the problem that requires help is not a "normal" social need but arises because of special circumstances brought about by individual deficiency.

institutional philosophy of social welfare A philosophy that looks at people as being embedded in a social system and as having predictable developmental needs.

universal programs Programs that provide income supports and social services to both the affluent and the poor.

retire from work; working parents need help with child care; everyone gets sick at some time; wage earners who support a family sometimes die or become disabled; women get pregnant and need prenatal care; everyone needs education in order to be a contributing member of society; many workers are injured; some babies are born with crippling diseases or develop them later in life. In an economic system that doesn't guarantee employment, some people lose their jobs. Life stresses take their toll on everyone, on some people more than others.

These opposing philosophies have resulted in very different approaches to giving help. The blaming-the-victim ideology always sees character defects in individuals. At best, it results in remedial programs to "cure" those defects. At its worst, it punishes people for what it construes as perverse or immoral conduct. Entire groups of people are blamed for their behavior. The poor, for example, are assumed to be poor because they lack initiative and the work ethic. The homeless are thought to have brought their condition on themselves through personality defects or lack of careful planning.

Means-Tested versus Universal Programs

Victim blamers feel superior to the victims. They assume that they could never be in the shape the victim is in. They separate people into "them" and "us." They are likely to give help sparingly and to separate people into **deserving versus undeserving**. They prefer **means-tested programs** for the most desperate people, and they investigate people's financial situations with a fine-toothed comb. They create demeaning and unattractive welfare programs so that people will be reluctant to accept the help.

The means-tested approach is often called the **residual philosophy of social welfare**. Proponents of means-tested programs are more likely to believe that the problem that requires help is not a "normal" social need but arises because of special circumstances due to individual deficiency. Help is often given on a temporary basis until the person is "rehabilitated"—educated, retrained, or otherwise made self-sufficient. Because recipients of these programs are assumed to have some deficiency, they are often regarded with suspicion, suspected of fraud, and subjected to various efforts to change their character. Applicants must prove that they have so little money and so few assets that they meet the criteria of poverty that the agency sets for eligibility. Temporary Assistance to Needy Families (TANF), the federal name for the program formerly called Aid to Families with Dependent Children (AFDC), is an example of a means-tested program.

Those who look at people as being embedded in a social system, and thus having predictable developmental needs, are more likely to regard social supports as a universal right. That philosophy of social welfare is called the **institutional**, or **developmental philosophy** of social welfare. Programs subscribing to this philosophy are called **universal programs**. Their adherents know that problems are bound to occur, so they provide for people in need in a way that respects the dignity of the individual. The programs they create—unemployment insurance; workers' compensation; family and children's allowances; old-age, survivors', and disabled persons' pensions, Medicare—are given as **entitlements**, which do not distinguish between "deserving" and "undeserving." Universal income supports and social services include both the affluent and the poor. Wealthy people who receive such aid will pay some of the cost through **progressive taxes**, whereby the rich are taxed at a higher rate than the less affluent.

Some social welfare programs are more politically protected than others. Because the middle class feels entitled to programs such as Social Security, it uses its political clout to protect those programs. Congress is cautious about cutting back Social Security but felt no need to put on the brakes in cutting back AFDC (now TANF).

Universal programs are much more widely used in European countries than in the United States. For example, most industrialized countries except the United States have what they call a *family allowance*, which gives a certain amount of money to families for each child they have. France has universal day care for working mothers. Most industrialized countries have a national health insurance system, paid by the government.

Liberals tend to prefer universal programs, which they believe create more solidarity between social classes, show more respect to claimants, and are easier to defend politically. Conservatives tend to prefer means-tested programs (programs in which people must prove great need). The words used to describe people who get these benefits reflect attitudes toward the programs. *People who receive benefits under universal programs are called* claimants; *people who receive means-tested benefits are called* recipients. *Claimants are claiming their rights; recipients are receiving whatever someone chooses to give them.*

Programs to Provide Money

From the seventeenth to nineteenth centuries, local officials gave meager amounts of cash to the poor in their homes or put them in almshouses or workhouses. The almshouses or workhouses were created to discourage people from asking for help. The fear of having to go to the poorhouse served to deter people from even admitting their hunger. "Outdoor relief" (assistance given to people in their homes) was preferred by the poor but viewed with suspicion by officials.

Eventually welfare programs were taken over by states, and the federal government later ran some. In the 1930s, the turmoil and massive unemployment that resulted from the Great Depression gave rise to the first large-scale federal involvement in income supports. The Social Security Act of 1935 established two categories of programs: universal and means-tested. This implicitly separated beneficiaries into the "deserving" and the "undeserving" poor. People who received the universal programs (Old-Age, Survivors', and Disability Insurance, popularly called Social Security) are automatically considered "deserving." People who received AFDC, the means-tested program (now called TANF), are contemptuously viewed as "undeserving."

During the civil rights era of the 1960s (as in the period of labor union organization in the 1930s), many people redefined poverty as the result of an unjust social system that blocked people's opportunity. Those who subscribed to this **opportunity theory** of poverty viewed the poor as men and women who shared the same qualities and aspirations as everyone else but were kept from realizing their potential by barriers of social class, ethnicity, sex, disability, age, or a combination of these factors (Cloward & Ohlin, 1964; Ryan, 1976).

entitlements
Benefits and services that people have a legal right to, as compared to those that are given at the discretion of officials.

progressive taxes Taxes that tax the rich at a higher rate than those who are less affluent.

opportunity theory
The theory that people are prevented from getting out of poverty because of their lack of social opportunities rather than because of their individual defects.

The War on Poverty

The last major expansion in the welfare state was the federal government's War on Poverty, which began in 1964 with the passage of the Economic Opportunity Act. Despite the name of the act, most programs of the War on Poverty did not follow the tenets of the opportunity theory. This theory (sometimes called *structuralism*) requires major structural changes in society, including the creation of more jobs and housing by the government and businesses. Secretary of Labor Willard Wirtz proposed a large-scale public jobs program that would have attacked poverty by transforming local labor markets (Glenn, 2001a). However, neither President Johnson, nor Congress, nor businesses were willing to do this, preferring instead to cut taxes, which they claimed would stimulate business to create jobs. "By default, the War on Poverty in the 1960s adopted the culture of poverty theory" (Ryan, 1976, p. 94) and aimed to change the social characteristics and potential of the poor rather than redistribute society's resources. One of the ways it did this was through educational programs—the Head Start program for early childhood education and the Job Corps for adolescents. It was also instrumental in securing the passage of the Elementary and Secondary Education Act of 1965.

The other major strategy of the War on Poverty—community action—had some prospect of changing social systems. It encouraged residents to participate actively in creating community change and challenging existing institutions. Bypassing structures of state and local governments, the federal government sent money directly to citizen groups. This stressed the value of citizen participation, a belief that grew out of the settlement house tradition.

For a few years, the exciting folks in the community action programs challenged business as usual in school systems and in welfare offices. It upset local officials to see one level of government and party financing the harassment of another level of government and party. Eventually those same officials muted the program's militancy. Present-day community action programs are generally content to run Head Start day care centers and fuel subsidy, surplus food, and weatherization programs to conserve heat in houses. Hardly a challenge to anyone!

The War on Poverty did, however, raise the consciousness of the nation to the plight of the poor. Although poverty was not abolished, it was greatly reduced during the 1960s, due to both an expanding economy and expanded social welfare benefits.

The Welfare Rights Movement

One of the most notable accomplishments of the community action program was the welfare rights movement. In 1966, Frances Fox Piven and Richard Cloward saw the movement as a strategy to end poverty (1966). They argued that the welfare rolls should be expanded to include everybody who was eligible (only half of all eligible people received AFDC), and this explosion in the rolls would create a political crisis for the Democratic party that would lead them to construct a more adequate system, such as a guaranteed annual income.*

*In 2010, the conservative David Horowitz and right-wing talk show hosts, including Glen Beck, claimed that the "Cloward and Piven strategy" was a vast left-wing conspiracy to destroy capitalism and the free market, and to establish a socialist state. This was of course absurd, as the Cloward and Piven strategy was meant to apply only to welfare, and the strategy failed to end poverty.

Although the government did federalize the programs for the aged, disabled, and blind under the Supplemental Security Income program, by the time the National Welfare Rights Organization had ended in 1975, AFDC was still stigmatized and left recipients in poverty.

Nevertheless, the movement won important victories. The Legal Services Corporation, funded by the poverty program, provided poor people with lawyers to fight for their rights. Going all the way to the Supreme Court to strike down welfare residency requirements and "man in the house" rules that had created welfare "fraud squads," which were used to search for men in mothers' homes during unannounced raids, the corporation won the right to appeal unfavorable welfare decisions.

The poverty movement also got more money for many poor people and created a fundamental change in consciousness about their rights. Women on welfare declared that their job as mothers is *work* and deserves society's respect and recompense. Their demands foreshadowed the later feminist demands for wages for housework and caregiving. The most important demand of the National Welfare Rights Organization was for a guaranteed annual income to provide an income floor beneath which no one could fall.

At the same time, or perhaps in reaction to these more radical explanations of poverty, victim-blaming theories resurfaced in the 1960s and have become stronger up to the present time. These theories have a stranglehold on the country and a powerful hold on people's thinking about the poor. Because they are helping to shape the destiny of the nation, it is important to trace their development.

Culture of Poverty versus Opportunity Theory

The backlash against the gains of the 1960s began with a movement of conservatives headed by Barry Goldwater, who ran for president in 1964. A concerted attack on welfare resulted in the Personal Responsibility and Work Opportunity Reconciliation Act of 1996. It was implicitly an attack on minorities and on women.

In the 1960s, some social planners and theorists revived long-dormant theories that place the onus for poverty on inferior heredity (it was called *bad blood* in our grandparents' time) (Eysenck, 1971; Herrnstein, 1971). They were especially eager to apply this theory to African Americans and other people of color.

Other social scientists asserted that the poor had a culture of poverty, a system of self-defeating beliefs passed on from parent to child. According to this theory, some groups of people stay mired in poverty because they lack basic psychological discipline. They cannot control their desires to own a TV, buy a bottle of whiskey, or have unprotected sex long enough to save sufficient money, study hard, or plan for their futures (Banfield, 1974).

Anthropologist Oscar Lewis first coined the phrase *culture of poverty* as he studied poor people in Mexico and Puerto Rico (1961, 1966). He believed, however, that people could fight their way out of this culture through political activism. Conservative social scientists who lacked this faith in the empowering potential of political action believed that the culture of poverty was unchangeable. Sociologist Edward Banfield (1974) argued that none of the programs of the War on Poverty in the 1960s had done any good. He believed that only authoritarian policies such as institutional care, separation of children from parents, or preventive detention based on the statistical probability of criminal behavior could even begin to eradicate it. Because these policies would be politically unacceptable, he advised the government to do nothing, since its growing bureaucracy of programs had no effect on the problem.

"Benign neglect" gained favor in the cynical and anxious 1980s and 1990s. In their study of what has gone wrong in the United States, Don Barlett and James Steele (1992) conclude that the "social contract" was canceled in the 1980s. *People had stopped believing that society had a responsibility to care for all its citizens.*

Victim-blaming theories captured the allegiance of many citizens in the 1980s. Earlier these people had been grudgingly willing to allow some expansion in the welfare state, but in the 1980s, they worried about their own downward mobility and their children's future. So they "returned to an older psychology of scarcity" (Katz, 1989, p. 138). Rather than look at the larger economic picture, especially the growing inequality of wealth, people often blamed welfare for *causing* their problems. Conservative critics capitalizing on those anxieties argued that welfare was not good for people or for business. Their prescription, called "welfare reform," was to cut benefits. The criticism of welfare was lumped together with a call for a return to traditional puritanical or family values.

One of the critics of welfare, George Gilder, wrote a book called *Wealth and Poverty* (1981), described by one reviewer as "the Bible of the Reagan administration" (Silk, 1981, p. 44). Gilder's advice to the poor was to work harder than the classes above them and to stay in monogamous families. According to him, men need to marry in order to channel their aggression, and the rise in female-headed families "unleashes the primitive impulses in men." Men in their natural states are "naked apes" in need of taming by women (Katz, 1989, p. 145). When the state provides for their children, men are "cuckolded by the compassionate state" (Gilder, 1981, p. 153). Gilder believed that inequality is good for society because it raises everyone's living standards, including those of the poor. The welfare system demoralizes the poor; it "erodes work and family and thus keeps poor people poor" (p. 82).

The Goldwater Old Right, which was focused on anticommunism, associated the War on Poverty with communism. In the 1970s, the New Right shifted its focus to social issues and developed the stereotype of the welfare queen, a stereotype that President Reagan skillfully used to political advantage (Williams, 1997). The welfare queen was presented

as a socially deviant woman of color (unwed teen parent, non-wage worker, drug user, long-term recipient). With shrewd use of dissembling imagery, exaggeration, and stereotyping, the New Right played to fears of the welfare recipient as "other" (Williams, 1997).

President Reagan's budget director, David Stockman, asserted that "there are no entitlements—period" (Katz, 1989, p. 151). In his book *Losing Ground* (1984), Charles Murray argued that illegitimacy, crime, and family deterioration are caused by AFDC payments and rules, and he recommended the elimination of virtually all social benefits except Social Security (Katz, 1989). Ten years later, in his book *The Bell Curve* (Murray & Herrnstein, 1994), Murray's racism was blatant. He argued that welfare should be abolished not simply because of the economic incentive it creates but because it encourages dysgenesis, the outbreeding of intelligent whites by genetically inferior blacks, Hispanics, and poor European Americans (Williams, 1997).

In response to the conservative alarm about welfare dependence, advocates for the poor countered that the problem was an undependable state. The Catholic bishops, in their pastoral letter on the U.S. economy, claimed that poverty violated a sense of community, deprived people of citizenship, and left them powerless. It "assaults not only one's pocket-book but also one's fundamental human dignity" (National Conference of Catholic Bishops, 1986, p. 93).

The bishops trumpeted their outrage like biblical prophets: "That so many people are poor in a nation as rich as ours," they wrote, "is a social and moral scandal that we cannot ignore" (p. 101). And in response to the call to "put those welfare mothers to work," the bishops took an increasingly unpopular stand in favor of giving mothers (or fathers) the right to stay home to care for their children and to be supported in this important work by welfare grants.

By the mid-1980s, the buzzword in poverty discourse was *underclass*. No one could define it precisely, and it sometimes seemed to have grown out of a vague, undefined fear of inner-city violence and drug use, teenage sexuality, minority teenage mothers and jobless youth, and single-parent families.

Underclass became another name for the "undeserving poor," and much of the focus was on teenage mothers and jobless youth. Once more, policymakers paid less attention to the structural causes of poverty—such as inadequate education, lack of jobs, or low salaries—than they paid to behavior that was largely caused by lack of opportunity. Instead of providing training and employment for black and Hispanic males, the policy response was to put more of them in jail. As wages have declined, more married women have had to enter the workforce to help meet their families' needs. This has helped to fuel hostility toward TANF recipients who stay home to care for their families. Politicians have found that anti-welfare programs win them votes.

By the time Bill Clinton was elected president in 1992, welfare bashing seemed to have become a national sport, right along with baseball. Although welfare bashing has always been popular, the flood of anti-welfare sentiment reached tidal wave proportions by the 1990s. Both the Democrats and the Republicans railed against what they termed the "dependency" of welfare mothers and vowed to get them off the rolls and make them "self-sufficient." President Clinton promised to "end welfare as we know it." The Republican-controlled House of Representatives, led by Speaker of the House Newt Gingrich, promised in 1994 to roll back the gains in the welfare state that began with the New Deal of the 1930s, and it set forth a proposal called the Contract with America. Opponents dubbed it the Contract on America. It proposed to eliminate many federal social welfare programs, including AFDC, turning such programs over to the states with federal block grants, and ending federal oversight. In August 1996, Congress passed and President Clinton signed the Personal Responsibility and Work Opportunity Reconciliation Act, ending sixty years of federal entitlement to cash assistance for poor families and forcing poor mothers to get waged work, a policy entitled "workfare."

Charles Murray said that illegitimacy was the "single most important social problem of our time" (1994, p. 20), despite the fact that teen pregnancy rates had actually dropped to the lowest rate in sixty years (CNN.com/U.S. News, 2000). Murray wanted to eliminate welfare for teenage parents, believing that when teenagers realize that there are no benefits that come to them when they become unmarried parents, they will stop having children. Not only would he deprive these individuals of AFDC grants, he would also deprive their children of child support from the father of the child. Children should receive support from the father only when the mother is married to him.

Of course Murray's idea that cutting off AFDC benefits will prevent pregnancy is absurd. Instead, it will help to restigmatize having babies without getting married, which is what the right wing quite clearly says it wants to do. Title I of the Personal Responsibility Act, titled "Reducing Illegitimacy," declared that "marriage is the foundation of a successful society" and went on to give a laundry list of so-called facts about illegitimacy that featured teenage mothers and linked criminality with absent black fathers. States have joined in this warfare against teen parents, passing laws restricting welfare and giving them rewards (dubbed "Bridefare" or "Wedfare" programs) if they marry any man, not necessarily the father of their child.

The Personal Responsibility Act was particularly tough on teen parents, requiring unmarried parents under the age of 18 to live with an adult and stay in school in order to receive benefits. About two-thirds of unmarried teen parents do live with their parents, but the ones who don't may be required to live in a group home or institution sponsored by the state. This law has resulted in many teenagers being dropped from the welfare rolls.

A rise in pregnancy rates does not necessarily mean a rise in sexual promiscuity. Most sexually active adolescents are involved in stable, intense relationships with only one partner (U.S. Department of Commerce, 1995). TV sitcoms and soap operas leave no doubt that society has become much more permissive about sex in the past three decades, and birth control has become much more available. Yet one cannot assume that a rise in sexual activity automatically translates into a rise in pregnancies. Research has shown that the most powerful factor in the decision to delay pregnancy until later in life is an adolescent's commitment to education and a future career apart from motherhood. Those who go on to higher education or fulfilling careers are not as likely to have babies as those who drop out of high school. Teens who have high educational expectations and school success are more likely to use contraception effectively. In discussing population control, President Clinton acknowledged that the best approach to birth control in developing countries is to educate the women, but he didn't apply that insight to teenagers in the United States. Instead, he blamed the AFDC program for encouraging teen pregnancy.

Sex education and easily available contraception reduce the likelihood of getting pregnant, but in the United States, communities hold pitched battles over introducing sex education into the schools. It is a rare high school that makes condoms available. Even when a school does offer a sex education course, it may be introduced too late and be too superficial to really help prevent teen pregnancies.

TANF does not encourage family breakup and out-of-wedlock births. Single-parent households are on the rise, but this is not due to TANF. The increase in childbearing by unmarried women cuts across class, educational attainment, and age lines and is happening worldwide. Most of this increase is in births to adult unmarried women, not adolescents. Unmarried mothers gave birth to 4 out of every 10 babies born in the United States in 2007, a share that is increasing rapidly both here and abroad. Much of the increase in unmarried births has occurred among parents who are living together but are not married (Harris, G., 2009). While the value of the TANF benefit has fallen during the past twenty years, the number of mother-only households has risen. The size of a welfare grant has no correlation with the number of pregnancies. Mississippi, which has the lowest TANF grant, has the highest rate of teenage pregnancies, whereas Vermont, with the highest TANF grant, has the lowest rate.

It is ludicrous to think that welfare causes poverty or teenage pregnancy. Suppose you studied accidents. Those who had to be carried away on a stretcher died more frequently than those who walked away from the accident. That doesn't mean that stretchers cause death. Welfare is like that stretcher. It does not cause poverty, although the meager welfare grants ensure that recipients will remain poor.

Welfare Reform and Racism

When Aid to Dependent Children was begun as part of the Social Security Act in 1935, the program was mainly for white widows, and it excluded most people of color. In the early years of the program, African American women were often excluded by rules that states imposed, such as "suitable home"* and "man-in-the-house"** rules, which were struck down by the Supreme Court in the 1960s. This was particularly true in the South. One southern field supervisor summed up the prevailing attitude toward African American women in the 1940s and 1950s by saying that the staff and board of the welfare department had a "unanimous feeling" that Negro women should continue to do their "usually sketchy seasonal labor or indefinite domestic service" rather than receive public assistance. They said that Negro women "have always gotten along," and "all they'll do is have more children" (Bell, 1965, pp. 34–35).

In the 1960s, the civil rights and welfare rights movements resulted in the inclusion of many who had been excluded from the original AFDC program. Legal service lawyers challenged exclusionary rules and won many victories. As a result, the number of African American women in the program increased by about 15 percent between 1965 and 1971. "The evolution of a right-wing critique of welfare in the early 1960s coincided with this shift in the racial composition of the AFDC population" (Williams, 1997, p. 1). Public officials, aided by the media, made people believe that AFDC was largely a program for African Americans, even though, until recently, the highest percentage of people on AFDC were European Americans.

President Reagan's image of the "welfare queen" going to the welfare office in a Cadillac instilled a vision of black women defrauding the welfare system. In fact, most welfare fraud is done by vendors—pharmacies, doctors, dentists, nursing homes, hospitals, and sellers of medical equipment. The government recovered $2.5 billion in overpayments for Medicare in 2009 as the Obama administration focused attention on fraud enforcement efforts in the health industry (*Boston Globe*, 2010). A study in Massachusetts showed that more than 93 percent of the money recovered from welfare fraud came from vendors. In 2008, the Attorney General of Massachusetts recovered $26.7 million in settlements and judgments in Medicaid fraud cases, the highest amount in three decades (*Boston Globe*, 2008). Two of the largest fraud cases in the nation were against for-profit hospitals for defrauding government health insurance programs. Three executives of the nation's biggest hospital chain, Columbia/HCA, were indicted in 1997 for conspiring to defraud government health insurance programs. The U.S. Attorney's office fined TAP Pharmaceutical Products of Illinois $875 million in September 2001 for price manipulation, the largest settlement ever in health care fraud (Dembner, 2001).

---

*"Suitable home" rules excluded a woman from AFDC if officials decided that her home was not suitable in some way. These rules were most often used against mothers who were not married.

**"Man-in-the-house" rules stated that women were forbidden to have a man in the house. Welfare workers often conducted midnight raids to try to find a man in the house.

However, as the welfare rolls continued to plunge, white recipients left the system faster than black and Hispanic recipients. In fiscal year 2008 there were 1,629,345 families receiving TANF, 31.5 percent of whom were white, 34.2 percent African-American, and 28 percent Hispanic (Administration for Children & Families, 2008). Minority welfare recipients were significantly more disadvantaged than their white counterparts. They face discrimination from prospective employers and landlords, and Hispanic recipients face the problem of learning English when there are not enough English as a Second Language (ESL) programs. The time limits imposed at the federal level and in many states are especially hard on African American and Hispanic recipients.

A study in Wisconsin found that despite having higher education levels and higher job training completion rates, black welfare recipients did not fare any better than Caucasians in terms of employment. Black welfare recipients were more likely to be required to take preemployment and Alcohol and Other Drug Abuses (AODA) tests than were whites (Bonds, 2006).

The assumption that AFDC was primarily for black Americans led to racially based policies based on stereotypes. Conservative views about the proper place of women being in the home might still apply to white women, but black women have always been expected to work outside the home, predominantly as domestic and agricultural workers. The 1967 amendments to the Social Security Act placed mandatory work requirements on AFDC recipients for the first time, and subsequent laws such as the Talmadge Amendment of 1971 and the Family Support Act of 1988 stiffened the requirements, culminating in the current draconian work requirements of the Personal Responsibility Act.

The restrictions placed on teen parents were also directed against minority teenagers, who are disproportionately represented in the teen parent population. Among many people, "teenage parents" has become a code word for minority women, and the attack on welfare has become an attack on them.

The War against Women

Welfare is one of the battlegrounds of the war on women. The National Organization for Women says that not only does the Personal Responsibility Act inflict suffering on poor women and their children, it also heralds a broader effort to pressure all women into a repressive sexuality, limited reproductive choices, and conventional family arrangements. The radical right wing understands the connection between a safety net and women's autonomy. By withdrawing federal assistance for women without male support (and also by attacking affirmative action, Title IX, and college financing), by branding welfare mothers with demeaning racial stereotypes, and by pauperizing them and questioning their fitness as mothers, the right is forcing every woman to depend economically on a man within a traditional marriage whether or not she wants to and whether or not the man is dependable. The economic alternative is made so harsh that women may find themselves unable to provide for their families and may have to give up their children to foster care or adoption.

Conservatives are worried about the decline of two-parent families. The 2000 census showed that the number of families headed by women who have children, which are typically poorer than two-parent families, grew nearly five times faster in the 1990s than the number of married couples with children. For the first time, nuclear families accounted for less than 25 percent of all households in the United States (Schmitt, 2001a).

The Personal Responsibility Act provides for an "anti-illegitimacy" bonus that gives extra federal money to states that lower their nonmarital birth and abortion rates. States have enacted a variety of programs to get this bonus. In Virginia, for example, cities conducted Marriage Before the Carriage contests, in which youth ages 12 to 21 could enter a drawing for a new car if they hadn't fathered or conceived a child in the past year. Mississippi established an abstinence unit of the state government, even though numerous studies have shown that abstinence education alone is unsuccessful in lowering birthrates. States have a financial incentive to promote abstinence to the exclusion of other family planning education through federal "abstinence only" money available under the federal welfare bill. More draconian measures have so far been voted down, as was Arizona's unsuccessful proposal to automatically make children of unmarried teen parents wards of the state and put the infants in the custody of the state's protective service system. A private group in California offered $200 cash rewards to vulnerable low-income or drug- or alcohol-addicted women who agree to have a Norplant implant or undergo sterilization (Davis, 1998).

Everyone knows that if women are to enter the waged labor market, they will need child care. The right wing has always resisted public provision of day care on the grounds that a woman's "natural place" is in the home; George Gilder (1981) said that a woman finds dignity and security beneath the authority of her husband. President Nixon vetoed a bill providing for universal day care. One of his aides said that it would "Sovietize child care." On the other hand, conservatives agree that a single-mother welfare recipient should be in waged work. The double standard for middle-class mothers and welfare mothers was revealed when Congress—soon after it passed the Personal Responsibility Act—passed a law in 1998 giving tax deductions to middle-class women who choose to stay home to care for their children.

All these policies limit the choices of poor women and further deepen the rift between poor women who have no choices and affluent women who do. These reproductive issues affect only poor women now, but they are related to the drive to limit reproductive choice for all women. The conservative talk about putting poor children into orphanages is not really about orphanages but about women: It is about reinforcing the sexual double standard.

Yet all the talk about taking their children away and putting them in orphanages serves to terrorize welfare recipients still further. The Latin root of *proletariat* means "people who have no other wealth but their children." That took on a poignant meaning when Charles Murray proposed a policy of cutting off AFDC payments to teenage mothers and using the money saved to provide orphanages for their children. Shortly before Christmas 1994, Speaker of the House Newt Gingrich championed a bill that would have let states use federal welfare money for orphanages. Critics invoked Charles Dickens and Scrooge; Gingrich countered with nostalgic images of Boys Town and Spencer Tracy. By the time President Clinton denounced the plan as "dead wrong," Mr. Gingrich was protesting that he had been misunderstood (Bernstein, 1996a).

CYCLES OF HELPING

To illustrate the dialectical nature of human service issues, we shall discuss four issues on the front burner of public attention: welfare, mental illness, juvenile justice, and criminal justice.

Cycles in Welfare Reform

We are using the term *welfare* in the way that the public generally understands it—Temporary Aid to Needy Families (TANF).[*] If we called all government financial transfer programs "welfare," then financial-aid grants to college students and veterans' benefits would come under that category. Although the amount paid to the AFDC/TANF program has been relatively small—less than 1 percent of federal government spending and about

---

[*]States have given different names to TANF. In Massachusetts, for example, the program is called Transitional Assistance to Families with Dependent Children (TAFDC).

3 percent of state spending—it garners a huge amount of public scorn. Much larger welfare grants go to the middle class and rich.

Welfare provides a good example of the cycles of reform. Frances Fox Piven and Richard Cloward (1971), two of the leading proponents of the opportunity theory, believe that welfare expands and contracts in response to changes in the economy and the political climate. The leading architects of the welfare rights movement, they believe passionately in political activism as a way to empower the poor.

Piven and Cloward argue that government officials expand welfare (public assistance) in times of civil turmoil. When the turmoil dies down, they cut back on welfare and use it to enforce work norms. They document the following cycles of expansion and contraction in welfare:

- Beginning of large-scale federal relief programs during the Great Depression as a response to civil turmoil.

- Cutbacks during the 1940s and 1950s after the turmoil of the 1930s subsided. Welfare was often withheld from people in order to force them into low-paid agricultural and factory work.

- Expansion during the 1960s as a response to civil turmoil (and as an attempt to build a new urban base for the Democratic party).

- Cutbacks from the 1970s to the present, after the turmoil of the 1960s subsided. During this period, welfare has been withheld to force women into the low-wage labor market.

As welfare and other safety net programs were cut back, the criminal justice system expanded. The United States has the highest incarceration rate on the planet—five times the world's average. The United States has 5 percent of the world's population, but 25 percent of the world's prison population. By 2010, there were about 2.4 million people incarcerated in federal, state, and county prisons, or on parole or probation. Senator Jim Webb introduced the National Criminal Justice Act in 2010 to study the criminal justice system and make recommendations for reform. There has been no in-depth or comprehensive study of the entire criminal justice system since The President's Commission on Law Enforcement and Administration of Justice, established in 1965 (Fisher, W., 2010).

THE DOWNWARD SLIDE

The upward climb of social welfare expenditures reversed in 1975. Expenditures then took a downward turn for the first time in three decades, beginning with the Ford and Carter administrations, moving down and even picking up roller-coaster speed during the 1980s. Congress and the Reagan administration conducted a massive assault on all entitlement programs for the poor and near-poor. Programs for the middle class suffered also.

Some states replaced the lost federal funds with state funds, but during the recession of the late 1980s and early 1990s, states raced to cut social welfare and implement punitive measures. Across the nation, state legislators and governors slashed benefits for low-income people more drastically than they had done since the 1980s. Fourteen of the thirty states with supplemental welfare programs, known as General Assistance, cut those budgets, affecting nearly half a million people.

principle of less eligibility The principle that the amount of welfare given to people should be less than the lowest wage so that people will not be tempted to take welfare rather than get a wage-earning job.

At the same time that corporations were being restructured, social welfare programs were also being restructured. As wages went down, so did welfare payments—no coincidence. According to a principle known in welfare circles as the **principle of less eligibility**, welfare payments in the United States are almost always kept below the lowest wages in order to encourage people to take any low-wage job rather than go on welfare. Many people assumed that the welfare state would expand forever. But, as Abramovitz (1992) points out,

> As long as investment in social reproduction meshed with the needs of profitable production and political control, social welfare programs remained intact and grew. But in the mid-1970s, changing economic and political conditions rendered the postwar social policies less conducive to the needs of business and the state, which then began to turn them around. (p. 33)

Twenty-five years ago, the consumer advocate Ralph Nader warned that the Republicans were engaged in a campaign to undermine people's trust in government so they could dismantle it because government sometimes prevented the worst depredations of capitalism. Now we see how farsighted Nader was. When people can be stopped from thinking that the government owes them anything, the safety net of the welfare state, never very strong, can be shredded entirely. Then there is no buffer to protect people from having to take any low-wage job, or to protect women from having to stay in a bad marriage, or even to protect people from homelessness. It seems that we have returned full cycle to the nineteenth century in welfare reform.

Welfare is like society's lightning rod, attracting people's anxieties and ambivalence about dependence and self-reliance—about work, about race, about sex, about mothers living without husbands, about our responsibilities toward one another, and about the nature of a just society. It has been more of a politically hot issue in the United States than in any other industrialized country. Some Europeans say that following the welfare scene of the United States is like reading the musty historical pages of the development of European welfare.

Cycles of Treatment of Mental Illness

If you have ever gone to a nursing home, you have probably seen a person who was acting so strangely that you thought he or she might be mentally ill. Did you wonder why that person was in a nursing home? Why wasn't he or she in a hospital, a group home, or an apartment with supportive services? The answer to these questions reveals one of the many twists and turns that treatment of the mentally ill has taken throughout history.

Again, we see the eerie similarity of present conditions to earlier times. In 1985, the president of the American Psychiatric Association, John A. Talbott, said

> In trying to reform the mental health system, we've gone from atrocious to awful. In colonial times, hordes of mentally ill people wandered from town to town. They lacked food, shelter, and care. That's exactly the situation today: we've come full circle. (Nickerson, 1985, p. 18)

One of the problems in discussing mental illness is that the very concept is like quicksand. Cancer or heart disease is diagnosed using laboratory tests. The diagnosis tells where the problem is located and what it looks like and offers clues as to how to treat it. Not so with mental illness.

The imprecision of the diagnosis of schizophrenia, for example, is illustrated by a study done by thirteen psychology researchers. They presented themselves at the doors of various mental hospitals, telling the admitting officers that they heard voices saying "empty," "hollow," and "thud." Otherwise, they told the truth about themselves. All of them were diagnosed as schizophrenic and admitted to the hospitals. After stays of varying lengths, some lasting as long as six months, each was discharged with a diagnosis of "schizophrenic on remission." Interestingly, their fellow patients were inclined to think they didn't belong in the hospital, while the staff was convinced they did. One nurse, commenting on the note-taking activities of one of the researchers, wrote on his chart, "Patient engages in compulsive note-taking activity" (Rosenhan, 1973, p. 253).

Mark Vonnegut (son of novelist Kurt Vonnegut) was diagnosed as schizophrenic and hospitalized for mental illness. However, when he recovered and wrote a book about his experience, most members of the psychiatric profession concluded that he had been misdiagnosed and was in fact simply depressed. "Mark's first response to news of this rediagnosis was to say, 'What a wonderful diagnostic tool. We now know if a patient gets well, he or she definitely did not have schizophrenia' " (Vonnegut, 1991, p. 33).

Except in the case of organic conditions such as brain tumors, mental illness can be diagnosed only by observing behavior. This has led some psychiatrists, such as Thomas Szasz, to say that it is inappropriate to label behaviors as diseases when, as far as anyone knows, they have no organic cause. Rather, Szasz says these are behaviors that are intolerable to the patients' family and friends and so are diagnosed as mental illness. Once labeled, the offending patient can then be removed from his or her family and put in a hospital (Szasz, 1961). Szasz does not deny that people who were labeled as mentally ill might be experiencing intense emotional anguish, but he argues that this is not a disease in the same sense as a physical disease, and he argues against forcing patients to accept treatment if they do not want it. This theory is, of course, very controversial. Many people who study the brain and treat mentally ill people believe that physiological malfunction can be demonstrated and treated.

There are a disproportionate number of people of color in mental hospitals. This is partly because of racial discrimination and partly because disproportionate numbers of them are poor. As Chesler (1972) points out, "Women of all classes and races constitute the majority of the psychiatrically involved population in America, Britain, Sweden, and Canada," (p. 333) "and most 'patients' over sixty-five, in asylums or in old-age homes, are, of course, women. Our society does not overly like old age or women" (p. xxii).

Political philosopher Michel Foucault (1987) points out that certain behaviors are regarded differently in different cultures and at different historical periods. For example, the holy man of the Zulus, the shaman, might be diagnosed as a hypochondriac or a hysteric by Europeans. In earlier times in some societies, the village idiot and the epileptic were thought to have special wisdom. Society, he says, locks up or excludes the mental patient because it does not want to recognize itself in the ill individual. "As it diagnoses the illness, it excludes the patient" (p. 63).

Foucault says that, up to about 1650, "madness was allowed free reign" (1987, p. 67). Society neither exalted it nor tried to control it; in fact, in France in the early seventeenth century, there were famous madmen who were a great source of entertainment for the public. But "about the middle of the seventeenth century, a sudden change took place; the world of madness was to become the world of exclusion" (1987, p. 67). Throughout Europe, institutions were built to house many different categories of people:

> The poor and disabled, the elderly poor, beggars, the work-shy, those with venereal diseases, libertines of all kinds, people whose families or the royal power wished to spare public punishment, spendthrift fathers, defrocked priests; in short, all those who, in relation to the order of reason, morality, and society, showed signs of "derangement." (Foucault, 1987, p. 67)

What all these groups had in common, Foucault says, was their *inability to work.* Whereas in the Middle Ages the cardinal sins were pride and greed, in the seventeenth century, sloth became the cardinal sin. Institutions imposed severe discipline, rules of silence, lockstep routines, strict spiritual guidance, and solitary reflection. Mentally ill people were stigmatized and made to feel guilty. That stigma is still powerful.

In about the middle of the eighteenth century, Europeans began to protest the widespread internment of people. A goal of the French Revolution of 1789 was to abolish internment as a symbol of ancient oppression, particularly for the poor. But this liberation did not apply to the mentally ill, who were considered dangerous. "Hence the need to contain them and the penal sanction inflicted on those who allow 'madmen and dangerous animals' to roam freely" (Foucault, 1987, p. 70). Thus, the mentally ill were left behind in the old houses of internment.

Internment of the mentally ill then became more medical (Foucault, 1987). Treatment freed the patients from some of the physical punishment but substituted "moral chains that transformed the asylum into a sort of perpetual court of law." Threats, punishment, deprivation of food, and humiliation were used to "both infantilize the madman and make him feel guilty" (p. 71).

In the nineteenth century, madness was thought to be contagious. Because it was thought unfair to criminals to expose them to the mentally ill, mentally ill people were separately confined in asylums. The doctor was not the servant of the patient but of the society. Foucault believes that the psychologization of madness that occurred in the nineteenth century was "part of the punitive system in which the madman, reduced to the status of a minor, was treated in every way as a child, and in which madness was associated with guilt and wrongdoing. . . . None of this psychology would exist without the moralizing sadism in which nineteenth-century 'philanthropy' enclosed it, under the hypocritical appearances of 'liberation'" (1987, p. 73).

Foucault did not see the disciplines of psychology or any of the other behavioral sciences as liberating. Rather, he saw them as a means of disciplining people for the economic needs of modern industrial society. Clearly this is a radically controversial point of view. We present it here not because we agree with all of Foucault's views but because it is being hotly debated in some academic circles and is forcing a reexamination of traditional views.

Unfortunately, when our society embarks on a positive social reform, the effort is often underfunded or incomplete, leading to new types of problems.

THE PROGRESSIVES AND THE REFORMERS

During the early twentieth century in the United States, social activists known as **Progressives** were shocked by the oppressiveness of the overcrowded prisons and mental hospitals that helped so few people. They did not, however, want to abolish them; rather, they thought that each inmate or patient would be cured if professionals could tailor a case-by-case treatment plan.

On the surface, the policy of treating prisoners or mental patients as individuals, collecting each one's life history, and making personalized treatment plans seems kinder and more scientific than predetermined prescriptions that ignore these people's backgrounds. However, what often happened in practice was that the professionals who planned or delivered such individualized treatments—judges, doctors, therapists, and wardens—were given an extraordinary amount of authority that was often abused (Rothman, 1971).

Modern reformers are closing the mental hospitals and returning the inmates to their communities, the very same places they were kept during colonial times. Indeed, treatment of the mentally ill has come full circle, but now the rationale behind it is different. The colonists of early America believed in the inevitability of problems; modern reformers believe that hospitals institutionalize people but do not heal them. The latter argue for the healing power of kin, community ties, and normal, everyday routines.

In the 1970s, the mental patients' and prisoners' rights movements joined in the fight for more humane, community-based treatment.

Progressives Members of the Progressive party in the early twentieth century who favored social reforms such as abolition of child labor, juvenile courts, and more individualized treatment of the mentally ill.

INTERVIEW

Judy Chamberlin, Mental Patients' Liberation Front

Judi Chamberlin was one of the founders of the mental patients' liberation movement. She called herself a "psychiatric survivor" of the mental health system. She not only survived but also went on to write a book about her experiences with mental illness and psychiatric hospitals. She also started an alternative service for discharged mental patients and was one of the leaders of the **Mental Patients' Liberation Front (MPLF)**. In May 1992, she received a Distinguished Service Award from the President's Commission on Employment of People with Disabilities for "promoting the dignity, equality, independence, and employment of people with disabilities." When people told Judi that she was not the "typical" ex-mental patient, she said, "My experiences aren't atypical. I'm typical. I went looking for help, and the state oppressed me."

Mental Patients' Liberation Front (MPLF) An organization of people who are or have been patients in psychiatric hospitals and who oppose many established psychiatric practices. MPLF has established support groups and alternative institutions.

Our first interview with Judi was in 1993. Our second interview was in June 2009,* when Judi was receiving hospice care in her own home. She died a few months after our interview. The following is a composite of the two interviews.

In 1988, Judi wrote *On Our Own*, a book about her own experience with depression forty-three years ago, when she was hospitalized against her will. That book became a kind of bible for the mental patients' liberation movement. In 2009, the sixty-four-year-old activist was dying of chronic obstructive pulmonary disease, an incurable lung disorder. She stopped hospitalizations and instead opted for home hospice care. An article in the *Boston Globe* (Lazar, K., 2009) talked about Judi's fight with her insurance company because they had discontinued coverage for hospice care. The article said that her insurance company recently told her that she had "used up" her hospice coverage, which was limited to $5,000. They told her that she could file an appeal, which she did. She said, "It seems so counterintuitive when you think about what the insurance company paid for me in 2008. They paid thousands of dollars for me to be in the hospital all the time. Hospice care will cost my insurance company much less." The representative from the insurance company, United Healthcare, offered to help her with the paperwork for an appeal. He said, "I wish there was a clearer process. Benefits do get used up."**

Her hospice (Visiting Nurse Association) assured her that they won't abandon her, but she worried that her daughter and her partner may be saddled with thousands of dollars in unreimbursed hospice bills when she is gone. She said, "My mother had a gruesome hospital death" from breast cancer. She described her mother's struggle to breathe, miserable and surrounded by machines as specialists hovered over her, suctioning fluid from her lungs in the last hours of life. That experience persuaded her father to choose home hospice care six years ago as he rapidly declined from congestive heart failure. "He wanted to die in his bed. He was relaxed and at peace."

Judi said that in choosing to follow her father's footsteps, she never envisioned that her hospice path would include such a battle. Neither did her primary care provider.

*The interview was published in *New Politics*, Winter 2010.

**Later, the appeal was successful.

The administrator at her physician's office, Arlington Family Practice, helped her with her appeal. She said, "I have never had an insurance company call me and say a patient has exhausted her hospice. I was devastated when they called me about her case. You mean this woman can't have hospice because she didn't die fast enough?"

Although I apparently haven't died fast enough, I wrote in the "reason for request" section of the appeal, "I do have a terminal illness and will need some method of care." And she added, "Since I become eligible for Medicare in October 2009, the plan's obligations would end then (providing I am still alive)."

Judi has spoken at conferences all over the nation and the world. She said the best conferences have been those to which users of the mental health system are invited. A 1988 conference in England, for example, called "Common Concerns," was attended by an equal number of workers and users. In the United States, the National Institute of Mental Health sponsored a pioneering set of dialogues in Florida. Users and service providers explored issues together. The National Conference on Mental Health Statistics contacted me and asked me to participate in the first conference involving users as well as researchers. This surprised me, because people don't usually seek out the opinions of mental patients. They think, "If you're mentally ill, what do you know?" Whatever a person has to say is suspect.

When students learn about the mental health system, they only hear the views of the professionals. They seldom empathize with the mentally ill or try to understand how it feels to be on the receiving end. If they want to have an honest dialogue with the mentally ill and ex-patients, service providers have to be prepared to face their anger and mistrust. People who use services have been treated in paternalistic and controlling ways, and this understandably has made them angry.

The attitudes of service providers have caused a split between the Alliance for the Mentally Ill (AMI), a support group for relatives and friends of mentally ill people, and the Mental Patients' Liberation Front (MPLF). Parents in the AMI argue, "We love our sons and daughters and want them to get help. We may trick them if we have to, whether they say they want it or not." The patient may not want to take drugs, but relatives often think they should and complain that patients don't take their medications. (Research has shown that a high percentage of all drugs, not just psychotropics, is not taken according to the doctor's prescription.)

Judi tried to promote dialogue between AMI and MPLF. Ex-patients and families have one thing in common: They didn't choose to be in the system. Professionals choose to be there. It is important to recognize that families have a valid perspective.

Judi said, "Some people accuse the MPLF of being totally opposed to drugs, but I believe in choice." Patients need to have all the facts, which are often kept from them. The professionals sometimes feel that if they give patients information, they only scare them. I tried drugs but didn't find one that helped me. For me, drugs didn't work, but I wouldn't tell anyone else what to do.

Research on phenothiazines shows what happens when patients don't have all the information. Although it is now well known that phenothiazines cause tardive dyskinesia (involuntary tics), not until recently did it come to light that they also cause tardive dementia, a loss of brain function. Patients can deteriorate mentally when they take the drugs. Professionals had not realized this earlier because they assumed that mental patients were deteriorating because of their illness.

The average doctor knows very little about drugs, often only what the advertisers say. Journals are filled with drug ads, and at medical conferences drug salespeople are all over the place. The field is controlled by profitable pharmaceutical companies. For example, there are two identical drugs for a heart condition, one generic and one with a trade name. The trade drug is six times as expensive as the generic, and that is the one that doctors prescribe most. A tranquilizer called clozapine used to cost $9,000 a year but has come down in price because of so many complaints. It doesn't cause tardive dyskinesia, as do all of the phenothiazines, but it can kill users if not correctly monitored.

Almost everyone in the psychiatric field has gone into diagnosing and drugs. Most of the professionals doing talking therapy are psychologists and social workers. There is very little clinical psychological training for doctors anymore, except for long, arduous psychoanalytic training. The conventional psychiatric wisdom is that you can't talk with psychotics. Most psychiatrists, and the AMI, believe that mental illness is primarily biological and can be controlled or cured only with drugs. The Alliance quotes statistics by the World Health Organization, which indicate that schizophrenia affects 1 percent of the human population worldwide. The AMI denies that stress or trauma causes mental illness, yet there is a good deal of research that challenges this belief. Researchers have tracked unemployment and mental hospital admissions, showing that mental illness rises with unemployment. Research about women in mental hospitals indicates that as many as 50 to 80 percent have been sexually abused.

Interestingly, the rate of recovery of mental patients is higher in third-world countries. I believe that is because they have stronger family and community ties. Also, traditional healers, who would be used more in third-world countries, sit with the patient, sometimes for days. In Africa, for example, a native healer spends several days observing the patient. That presence sets up a powerful therapeutic alliance. The healer does not think that it is important to ask questions but that it is important just to be there.

A few psychiatrists still believe in talk therapy and are cautious about using drugs. One of the best is Peter Breggin, who wrote an excellent book called *Toxic Psychiatry* (1991). Another important book is *Community Mental Health: Principles and Practice*, by Loren Mosher and Lorenzo Berti (1989), which proposes a blueprint for a comprehensive community mental health system. The authors maintain that before taking drugs, people should have a chance to get real community support. Once people start on drugs, they are likely to stay on them and have a hard time getting off. Mosher and Berti believe that a society can run mental health systems without hospitalizing anyone.

Drugs are used extensively all over the world. Most of the alternative mental health programs of the 1960s and 1970s have died, although a few proposals have been made for new ones. Although there has been a lot of talk about the innovative programs in Italy, where there are no long-term institutions, Italian practitioners still rely on drugs. Some community cooperatives have been set up there (not sheltered workshops, but co-ops actually owned and run by ex-patients).

This is what Judi said about hospice care:

They are on call 24/7 by phone. They provide my medication. A nurse visits twice a week, and a social worker visits. There are two volunteers who visit regularly. Hospice aims to help a person make the last part of life as good as possible. The hospital treats symptoms, and is not concerned with the quality of life. I pay for acupuncture, Reiki, and massage at home myself. The hospice organization that I had before included Reiki. It is very relaxing and helps me sleep.

I'm not religious, but a chaplain visits and she and I have good conversations. Lots of thoughts go through my head about dying. There are practical things to take care of, as well as philosophical thoughts. A lot of people don't want to talk about death and dying. A lot of people don't go into hospice until the last week of life. That is better than not going, but it would be better to go in earlier to work on issues of closure. A lot of families need to come to closure.

People's relatives and friends often have a memorial service after a person dies. I have thought about that a lot, and think I would rather have the memorial service before I die so I can enjoy it. That's one big project that I am planning. We will need to get a large hall because about 100 people will come. I will call it a "celebration of life." If I die before it takes place, people can still have it.*

The stigma of mental illness has lessened somewhat, but it is still very strong. It's not politically correct to make jokes about blacks or gays, but it still considered o.k. to joke about the mentally ill. People still assume that the mentally ill are violent.

However, there is more recognition that ex-patients have a role to play and some expertise. There are a lot of different support groups. Younger people are doing a lot of organizing on the Internet. One group is www.mindfreedom.org. David Oaks is the executive director. He is based in Eugene, Oregon. He is working with the World Health Organization and the World Psychiatric Association. Another is the National Empowerment Center, www.power2u. org. There are a lot of other in-person and on-line support groups. People are reaching out and finding people who have had similar experiences. So many people say, "I'm so alone." They feel cast out of the human race. It's a very scary feeling. When you link up with other people with similar problems and find out you're not alone, it is very reassuring.

The mental health establishment believes in medication. Professionals say, "You have to take your medication." For us, it's about what works. We believe that people should have the opportunity to lead ordinary lives, with needed supports. The issue is not whether you take medication or not. The issue is whether you're leading the kind of life you want. The journalist Robert Whitaker wrote the book *Mad in America*. He investigated the statistics of mental illness and found that the number of people diagnosed with mental illness keeps going up and the number of people on disability keeps going up, despite all the claims that drug companies make about medication. A typical antipsychotic drug causes severe obesity—100 pounds or more—and diabetes. But it is very profitable for drug companies. The power of drug companies keeps growing. Lots of doctors are getting huge amounts of money from drug companies, and lying about it. They get hundreds of thousands of dollars. Drug companies and doctors have everyone convinced that the problem is biochemical, but we see it as psychosocial. Poverty is a factor. Life on SSI (Supplemental Security Income) is pretty miserable because the grant is so low. There is a "Ticket to Work" option to encourage people to try working, and to enable them to return to SSI if it doesn't work out. But people are wary of trying that because

*The memorial service was held in August, 2009 at Boston University, with over 100 people in attendance. Judi died on January 26, 2010.

they know how hard it is to get on SSI, and they fear that they would be left with nothing if they were denied SSI.

A lot of people are scared, especially about health care. There have been deep cuts on programs that help people stay in the community. Mentally ill people are being sent to jail, and to emergency rooms. This country is spending billions to bail out banks and corporations. It is spending money for welfare for the rich, not for supports for the poor.

There are new problems surfacing with teenagers and kids. A new generation of kids has been on some drug since grade school. Their issues are medication at home and at school. They are very angry. They are often diagnosed as bipolar. Psychiatrists are even prescribing anti-psychotics for little children, as young as two years old. A little girl who was taking anti-psychotics died under still-undetermined circumstances, but it is clear drugs played a role.

Ours is a strength-based model. It is important to teach people skills, and train people to be advocates and mentors. That changes how people think about themselves. Instead of making sickness his identity and saying, "I'm Joe, I'm schizophrenic," he can see himself as somebody with something to give others. We aim to put people in positions of power over their own lives. When people feel powerless, they are overwhelmed. When everyone is making decisions for them, it is not surprising that they don't have good outcomes.

We no longer have many long-staying facilities. We have a lot of group homes, which are little institutions. There is a lot of homelessness among the mentally ill. People need their own homes, rather than an institution. We are looking at what kinds of supports people need. One support that people need is housing. There is no way to stabilize your life if you don't have a place to live. The Housing First program seems promising. The philosophy is to find an apartment for people first, and then offer social service supports that they need to stay in the home, on a voluntary basis.

Psychiatrists' PR efforts during the 1970s and 1980s misled the government, the public, and the media into believing that shock therapy was safe, and if it caused memory loss at all, the loss was short-term. Yet there is a lot of evidence that memory loss is sometimes massive, and memory may not return. Linda Andre has written a book, *Doctors of Deception*, a history of electroshock in the U.S. She says that electroshock treatment caused massive memory loss and ruined her life. Marilyn Rice told of how after a series of shock treatments, she returned to her professional job and when she went to the office to resume her job, she couldn't remember a thing about what to do. She became a crusader against shock treatment, and Linda Andre has succeeded her in this mission.

Women are more likely to be diagnosed with depression. Men are more likely to be diagnosed with schizophrenia or rage kinds of disorders, and are more likely to end up in the criminal justice system. The country's military culture encourages macho aggression, and discourages men from talking about their problems. Women are more socialized to talk about their problems. We have enormous numbers of soldiers returning from war with PTSD who are reluctant to ask for help. Since there is no draft in this war, poor people are taking the burden. Middle-class veterans had the GI bill after WWII, but that worked only for white people.

RECENT DEVELOPMENTS IN TREATING MENTAL ILLNESS

Beginning in about 1955, the state mental hospitals began to undergo **deinstitutionalization**. Ultimately, most of the patients were "reinstitutionalized" into shelters for the homeless, nursing homes, rest homes, and prisons. David Wagner (2005) studied this process of "reinstitutionalization" and compared the poorhouses and workhouses to present-day shelters for the homeless. He said, "These shelters have in many cases produced worse conditions than were the case in the poorhouses, poor farms, and city and county homes." Ironically, the reforms of the early nineteenth century that led to a massive growth of poorhouses were liberal, as was the deinstitutionalization movement (p. 18).

Public mental hospitals have been reduced or downsized from 560,000 resident patients in 1955 to fewer than 50,000 clients in 1998. Most acute in-patient care is now available in general hospitals. Average length of stay has fallen steadily to fewer than ten days (Mechanic, McAlpine, & Olfson, 1999). Managed care in private hospitals has resulted in large savings of 30 to 40 percent by some large corporate purchasers, with most of the savings being achieved by large reductions in length of stay (Feldman, 1998; Mechanic & McAlpine, 1999).

Some of the patients went home to their families and some went to halfway houses, foster care, or jail. Some were discharged to the streets or to shelters for the homeless. The rest went to nursing homes. Officially, patients who left the hospitals were supposed to be mainstreamed into the community, where they would receive supports. The Mental Retardation Facilities and Community Mental Health Centers Construction Act, signed into law by President Kennedy in 1963, was supposed to fund 2,000 mental health centers by 1980, but only 789 were eventually funded (Blau, 1992). Even those did not serve the chronically mentally ill in the way that was originally intended. Mental health professionals found the chronically mentally ill less rewarding to work with than the acutely ill or the neurotic. "Hence, a mere ten years after passage of the act, chronic mental patients had too few places to go, and even in those places, they were not exactly welcome" (p. 82).

A Justice Department study found that 56 percent of jail inmates in state prisons and 64 percent of inmates across the country reported mental health problems in 2006 (Harcourt, 2007). There were an estimated 350,000 men and women prisoners with serious mental disorders—four times the number in mental health hospitals (Fisher, W., 2010). Dorothea Dix, who campaigned in the nineteenth century to get mentally ill people out of jails and into mental hospitals, would be sad to see that her work was undone in the twentieth century.

Community mental health clinics aimed to consider the entire community as their field of service and to study the effects of social conditions and the environment on mental health. Socioeconomic status is strongly associated with the prevalence of mental disorders, and clinic staff looked at the relationship of class, culture, and gender to mental problems. Some clinic staff engaged in social action to change conditions that were contributing to problems. One example is the psychiatrist Matt Dumont. He practiced in a community mental health clinic in Chelsea, Massachusetts, where many low-income people lived. Many of the children had lead paint poisoning, which created severe neurological and behavioral problems. Dr. Dumont discovered that the paint on a bridge in Chelsea contained lead, and he engaged in social action to force the city to remove the paint (Dumont, 1992).

deinstitutionalization A large-scale reform movement that took people out of institutions and hospitals and returned them to their community with special services to aid their reintegration.

That kind of treatment is rare these days. The psychiatric profession now focuses on biological aspects of mental illness and prefers managed care for medication treatments over psychotherapy, counseling, or other modalities. Social workers and psychologists do the majority of talk therapy.

Peer support groups have become increasingly popular and are even accepted by mental health officials as being as effective as professional help, and sometimes more so. Medicaid reimburses peer support therapy in thirty states, and private insurers cover it in some states. Massachusetts has created a new job category—certified peer specialist—meant to formalize this kind of therapy (Goldberg, 2007b).

THE FAILURE OF DEINSTITUTIONALIZATION

Most psychiatrists assert that deinstitutionalization was made possible by the discovery of antipsychotic drugs, which allow patients to live a stable life outside the hospital. Although it is true that these medications have helped some people return to mainstream life, Blau (1992) points out that psychiatrists have often relied too heavily on drugs in their eagerness to empty the hospitals. An overreliance on drugs can prolong social dependency and produce neurological damage.

Pharmaceutical companies are spending large sums to get doctors to use their medicines by giving the doctors various perks. Some psychiatrists are lured by this largess to prescribe medications that they might not otherwise prescribe. One psychiatrist spoke out against this practice, which he himself had been doing. He said, "There's really no nice way to say it. If you're being paid to offer an opinion you're not all that confident that you believe, you're corrupt" (Goldberg, 2007a).

unintended consequences of reform Events that occur as a result of reform measures that were not planned or anticipated by the reformers.

The failure of deinstitutionalization to live up to its promise is an illustration of a principle that sociologists call the **unintended consequences of reform**. Sometimes a reform can become so perverted in the way it is carried out that its advocates, who held such high hopes for it, feel betrayed.

Mentally ill people are less likely to be considered unemployable when there is a labor shortage. In the United States during World War II, people who would later be labeled as unemployable were employed. "Virtually none of the disabled workers in the San Francisco Bay area was unemployed in 1942–1943" (McGowan & Porter, 1967). It is interesting to see how differently people are viewed when they are urgently needed. All adults were needed during World War II. That is when middle-class women worked outside the home in large numbers. After the war, they were told to go back home and raise their children.

THE PRIVATIZATION OF CARE

Medicaid stimulated the growth of private nursing homes and was paid for partly by the federal government. This encouraged states to shift much of the financial burden to the government by discharging patients to private nursing and boarding homes. Patients were federally subsidized by Social Security Disability Insurance (SSDI) and Supplemental Security Income (SSI). Yet money to develop community facilities was simply not allocated (Warner, 1989).

Patients' rights advocates won significant victories in the 1960s and 1970s, establishing the right to treatment in the least restrictive setting. In 1971, a precedent-setting Florida case, *O'Connor v. Donaldson*, determined that people could not be committed involuntarily to a mental hospital unless they were dangerous to themselves or others. Other states followed suit. However, we may now be witnessing a return to involuntary commitments. There is some public sentiment, sparked by a few well-publicized cases, that mentally ill people, and particularly those who are homeless, should be forced to go to hospitals for their own or the public's protection. Several states have revised their laws to allow involuntary commitment.

Cycles in Juvenile Justice

Closely following the adult prisons and insane asylums of the late nineteenth and early twentieth centuries came the establishment of reformatories or training schools for juvenile delinquents. This **child-saving movement**, as it is often called, was also spearheaded by the Progressives. Ironically, although the Progressives were appalled at the brutality of the asylums and prisons of the 1830s, they created new asylums of their own—for children who had gotten into trouble with the law or who had no parents able to care for them.

Criminal justice reforms during the Progressive era were aimed at professionalizing the police and other agencies of social control, diversifying their methods of operation, and extending the coercive functions of the state into new areas of working-class life. The Progressives were critical of the police and prisons because they often "aggravated conflict through corruption, brutality and general incompetence," consequently undermining the "legitimacy of the capitalist system itself" (Platt, 1977, pp. xxvi–xxvii).

Sociologist Anthony Platt (1977) believes that both compulsory education and the institutions of the child-saving movement (reformatories, orphanages, foster care homes, juvenile courts) were devised by certain segments of the middle and upper classes as new forms of social control and occupational tracking. Industrialists wanted to preserve social stability, and the juvenile courts and reform schools helped to do this. Furthermore, affluent women wanted careers, and social service was a respectable career for them. Of course, there are other scholars who disagree with this interpretation, believing that the creation of juvenile courts and reformatories was motivated by primarily humanitarian concerns to protect society and rehabilitate youngsters. And there are many, including the present authors, who believe that both points of view have some validity.

The juvenile court system was based on the belief that children who break the law should not be punished as if they were adults. Children's cases were reviewed informally by judges. Lawyers generally did not handle juvenile cases, as juvenile court is not based on an adversary model. Court-based probation officers investigated the backgrounds of the youthful offenders and reported to the judges. No jury sat in judgment, and no lawyer and prosecutor debated.

Juvenile reformatories were supposed to protect youngsters humanely from the corrupting influences of adult criminals. Although this sounds rational, in actual practice it meant that a youth found guilty was assigned to a reformatory *without trial and with a minimum of legal protection.* Legal due process was assumed to be unnecessary because reformatories were intended to reform, not punish. The judge and probation officer were assumed to be enlightened, free of self-interest, incorruptible, and always working in the best interest of the youth. Reformatories were built in the country, far from the residents' homes. Inmates were "protected from idleness, indulgence, and luxuries through military

child-saving movement A term used to describe the efforts of reformers in the late nineteenth and early twentieth centuries to rescue children from "unwholesome influences." The movement led to the development of children's institutions, foster care, and the juvenile court.

drill, physical exercise, and constant supervision" (Platt, 1977, p. 54). They were required to work at industrial and agricultural jobs but were given no more than an elementary education so that they did not "rise beyond their station in life." The reformatories were supposed to teach "the value of sobriety, thrift, industry, prudence, 'realistic' ambition, and adjustment" (p. 55).

CHANGE IN THE SYSTEM

Fifteen-year-old Gerald Gault challenged the fairness of the entire juvenile court procedure. He declared that he had not been treated in a humane way. In 1964 he was sentenced to a state industrial school in Arizona for six years for making an obscene telephone call. This misdemeanor carried a maximum sentence of two months in jail and a fine of $5 to $50 for adults. Gault brought suit against the state of Arizona, and in 1967 the U.S. Supreme Court declared that the juvenile court had indeed ignored the legal due process that is required by the U.S. Constitution. Speaking for the majority in the *Gault* case, Justice Fortas said:

> However euphemistic the title, a "receiving home" or an "industrial school" for juveniles is an institution of confinement in which the child is incarcerated. . . . Under our Constitution, the condition of being a boy does not justify a kangaroo court. (Platt, 1977, pp. 27–28)

This decision finally gave juveniles certain due-process rights. Now they have a right to know the charges against them, the right to have their own lawyer, and the right to confront and cross-examine their accusers and witnesses. They must be warned about self-incrimination and their right to remain silent. (Juveniles still do not have the right to a jury trial unless they are bound over to an adult court.)

So, once again reform had soured. The court the Progressives had hailed as a great reform in the nineteenth century was called a "kangaroo court" in the twentieth century!

Soon after the *Gault* decision, a reform-minded commissioner of the Massachusetts Department of Youth Services, Jerome Miller, shut down every state training school and reformatory in the state. He condemned them as unworkable and unreformable. Miller was brought in to reform the system after a series of scandals—including stories of beatings, isolation, and rape—had rocked the state's prison-like reform schools. His decision to shift state policy from warehousing juveniles in institutions to counseling and educating them in community-based group homes set off a debate that is still raging.

Critics charged Miller with being soft on crime and have continually called for more locked facilities, especially for repeat offenders. The 1991 "get tough on crime" climate prompted Governor William Weld of Massachusetts to file legislation calling for the prosecution of violent teenagers in adult criminal court, saying, "For too long, the response to violent crime in our cities has been to treat juvenile offenders like victims" (McNamara, 1991, p. 24). Weld was about to recommend the death penalty for juveniles who kill until Amnesty International suggested that Massachusetts would be altering its criminal code to conform to Iraq's.

Despite the calls for getting tough on juveniles,

> Miller's small-scale detention centers devoted to treating and educating delinquent youth was hailed by the National Council on Crime and Delinquency as a model. Yet

Miller's story about the Massachusetts experiment (Miller, 1991) almost didn't reach the public. One book editor rejected the manuscript because it might be "too compassionate for the times." (McNamara, 1991, p. 24)

Governor Weld's call to get tough on juvenile crime was echoed throughout the nation. Many juveniles have been bound over to adult courts and put in adult prisons. Boot camps grew substantially in the 1980s and 1990s. Thousands of juveniles have been put in them and often been treated harshly in them. There are no national regulations for these boot camps, and states are lax in their supervision. At least thirty-one teenagers in eleven states died at these camps between 1980 and 2001. A fourteen-year-old boy named Tony Haynes died in July 2001 at an Arizona desert boot camp. Investigators said they were told that before he died, counselors physically abused him and forced him to eat dirt (Janofsky, 2001).

A thirteen-member panel of experts, convened by the National Institutes of Health, reviewed scientific evidence to look for consensus on causes of youth violence and ways to prevent it. The panel concluded that scare tactics don't work; programs that seek to prevent violence through fear and tough treatment do not work. The trouble with boot camps, detention centers, and other "get tough" programs is that they bring together young people inclined toward violence who teach each other how to commit more crime. Further, laws transferring juveniles into the adult court system lead these teens to commit more violence, while there is no proof that they deter others from committing crime. The panel also found that programs that consist largely of adults lecturing, such as DARE, are not effective. Programs that offer intensive counseling for families and young people at risk, however, are more promising (Meckler, 2004).

States are now scaling back on boot camps or shutting them entirely. Commenting on the rise of boot camps, the Northeastern University criminologist James Alan Fox said there was very little evidence that boot camps would work. "But once a couple of boot camps opened, and they showed them on '60 Minutes' and '20/20,' filming these kids being screamed at . . . it was suddenly terrific. That's all Americans and political leaders really needed to invest in boot camps in a wholesale way" (Latour, 2002).

During the 1980s, American cities, with the support of the federal Department of Justice, established databanks that catalog teenagers believed to be real or potential delinquents. Loïc Wacquant, a sociologist at the University of California, Berkeley, describes this as "a convenient pretext for placing segregated neighborhoods and their residents under reinforced and penal surveillance" (Wacqant, 2009, p. 136). Wacquant gives a detailed discussion of the rise and fall of juvenile crime, emphasizing the lack of secure wage work. The fight against street delinquency became a moral spectacle that enabled political leaders to "reaffirm the authority of the state at the very moment they declare its impotence on the economic and social front" (Wacquant, 2009, p. 273). In a 2008 letter to the *Boston Globe*, Jerome Miller said that managerialism has become the prevailing ideology of DYS. Words like *care, help,* or *concern* have been replaced by terms such as *alternative punishments, setting limits,* and *structured environments*—usually code words for rationalizing isolation, neglect, and occasional staff violence (Miller, J., 2008).

Thousands of juveniles have been sentenced to life imprisonment. In 2010, the Supreme Court ruled that teenagers may not be locked up for life without chance of parole if they haven't killed anyone. However, more than 2,000 other juveniles will have no chance for parole because they killed someone (The StandDown Texas Project, 2010).

Cycles in Criminal Justice

In the 1960s, the goal for prisoners was rehabilitation. But now the goal is being tough on crime, and tough on prisoners. Wacquant believes that welfare reform and massive incarceration were two parts of the same policy of enforcing conformity to an unstable job market of temporary, part-time, low-paid, and flexible employment. Wacquant says that the government's policy for poor people is now "prisonfare and workfare" (Wacquant, 2009). In addition to enforcing low-wage work, politicians use "tough on crime" rhetoric to win elections, and cash-strapped rural communities build prisons to provide employment—sometimes the only employment available in the community.

The United States is the world's leader in incarceration with 2.3 million people in the nation's prisons or jails in 2010—a 500 percent increase over the past thirty years. These trends have resulted in prison overcrowding and state governments being overwhelmed by the burden of funding a rapidly expanding penal system, despite evidence that large-scale incarceration is not the most effective means of achieving public safety. Although most of the prisoners are men, the number of mothers in America's state prisons has reached a record high, yet many states have inadequate policies for dealing with the large portion of them who have children or are pregnant. Prenatal care is inadequate, pregnant women are often shackled during childbirth, and there are few community-based alternatives to incarceration enabling mothers to be with their children. Increasing numbers of juveniles are being tried in adult courts and are given life sentences. More than 60 percent of the people in prison are racial and ethnic minorities. For black males in their twenties, one in every eight is in prison or jail on any given day. These trends have been intensified by the disproportionate impact of the "war on drugs," in which three-fourths of all persons in prison for drug offenses are people of color (Sentencing Project, 2010).

More women—two-thirds of whom are mothers—are behind bars today than at any other point in U.S. history as a result of mandatory sentencing for drug offenses. The National Women's Law Center has published a report, "Mothers Behind Bars," that discusses how federal and state correctional laws can better meet the needs of pregnant and parenting women behind bars (National Women's Law Center, 2010b). Many of the mothers who have been sentenced to prison had previously received TANF. There is a close correlation between government's policy regarding welfare, incarceration, and child welfare. "Tough on crime" policies ran parallel to "tough on welfare" policy, and child welfare policy of terminating parental rights.* African-Americans are disproportionately represented in all of those populations. The sociologist Wacquant believes that between 1973 and 1996 a neoliberal revolution occurred in the wake of the progressive movements of the 1960s.

> This "post-Keynesian era of insecure employment" creates a "deficit of legitimacy" which the state handles by using the penal apparatus to hold as a club over those members of the working class who resist the discipline of the new fragmented service wage-labor by increasing the cost of exit strategies into the informal economy of the street. Those who are disruptive or who have been "rendered wholly superfluous" are neutralized of warehoused (Wacquant, L., 2009, p. 8).

---

*In her book *Shattered Bonds*, Dorothy Roberts documents the effect of terminating parental rights on parents, children, and the black community (Roberts, D., 2002).

At the same time, welfare was turned into "workfare" by the Personal Responsibility and Work Opportunity Act of 1996. The war on poverty has turned into a war on poor people, in what Wacquant describes as the current government policy on poverty—prisonfare and workfare. Both the men in the penal system and the women in the welfare system are considered morally deficient unless they periodically provide visible proof to the contrary. Their behavior must be supervised and regulated (Wacquant, 2009, pp. 115–116).

The increased reach of the prison system was achieved by implementing four major penal planks: (1) "Determinate sentencing," which drastically reduced judicial and correctional discretion; (2) "Mandatory minimums," which established irreducible sanctions without regard for the injuriousness of the crime; (3) "Truth in sentencing," which requires every convict to serve a minimum portion of his or her sentence before he or she becomes eligible for parole; (4) "Three strikes and you're out," inflexible sanctions imposed on recidivists and the implementation of life sentences—or twenty-five to life when the accused has committed three specially designated felonies.

Another reason for the increase in incarceration has been the imprisonment of undocumented immigrants. By the end of 2009, the U.S. government admitted over 380,000 a year in immigration custody in approximately 350 facilities at an annual cost of more than $1.7 billion (Detention Watch Network, 2009).

Some states are reevaluating their detention policy as they face budget deficits. A 2009 study by the Boston Foundation in Massachusetts found that spending on corrections agencies has exploded in the past decade despite only a modest increase in the number of people incarcerated, and accounts for a bigger chunk of the state budget than each of the budgets that oversee higher education, social services, and public health (boston.com, 2009). In February 2009, a federal three-judge panel in California ordered the prison system to reduce overcrowding by as many as 55,000 inmates. New York is putting more discretion in the hands of judges and more treatment options in the hands of offenders. Michigan has repealed most of its mandatory minimum drug sentences.

Prisoners have to put their lives on hold while they are in prison. There are few job training or rehabilitation programs in prisons. Government support for college programs in prison has ended. The Bard College Prison Program is one of the few programs left, and the college supports that. The government does not want either prisoners or welfare recipients to expand their opportunities by going to college.

After prisoners get out of prison, they cannot vote in many states. When they have a "Rap Sheet" (the FBNI Identification Record called the Criminal History Record Information—CHRI), they are often unable to find housing or get a job. They may lose their children to state foster care. Individuals wanted in connection with a felony, or violating terms of their parole or probation (called "fugitive felons" or "fleeing felons"), are prohibited from receiving SSI or TANF benefits. They were at first prohibited from receiving food stamps, but this has changed. Since 1998, they have been unable to receive federal financial aid for postsecondary education. Since 2001, veterans accused of being "fleeing felons" cannot receive veteran's benefits in health care, Vocational Rehabilitation and Education Service, Insurance, and Loan Guaranty service.

The definition of *fleeing felon* is confusing and imprecise. Databases are often inaccurate and are not kept current. A Bureau of Justice report said that in the view of most experts, inadequacy in the accuracy and completeness of criminal history records is the single most serious deficiency affecting the nation's criminal history record information system. CHRIs face the same problems of inaccuracies.

Some human service workers work with people who are on probation and parole or in rehabilitation programs. They can help ex-prisoners check their crime records to make sure the records do not contain inaccuracies. If human service workers work with prisoners, they can help children visit their parents to prevent termination of parental rights if the prisoners' children are in foster care. They can help released prisoners find jobs, get into education and job training programs, and find housing. They can work to change the system by lobbying for a more humane correctional system. Many states have social action groups working on reforming the corrections system. In Massachusetts, a group lobbied to get the law about criminal records (called CORI—Criminal Offender Record Information—in that state) amended so that employers cannot look at a person's CORI until after they have ascertained that a person is suitable for a job.

BEHAVIOR DEFINED AS A SOCIAL PROBLEM

When does a particular kind of personal or social behavior become defined as a "social problem"? Why did social-problems textbooks of the pre-1970s rarely mention such issues as sexism, wife abuse, incest, sexual harassment, rape, and discrimination against the disabled, whereas post-1970s textbooks prominently discuss these as social problems?

Behaviors become social problems when some people and organizations force those issues to the top of the public agenda. Wife abuse and rape were widespread before 1970, but they weren't defined as social problems until the feminist movement challenged traditional assumptions about women's place in society (Best, 1989).

More than most other countries in the world, the United States has clung to an individualistic philosophy, believing the Horatio Alger rags-to-riches myth that anyone can make it if he or she works hard enough. Sociologist C. Wright Mills (1959) distinguished between "private troubles" and "public issues." Troubles happen to individuals and to the relationships between individuals. Troubles are private and threaten private values. Issues, on the other hand, transcend one individual's inner life and are widespread within the community. Mills gives the following example:

> When, in a city of 100,000, only one man is unemployed, that is his personal trouble, and for its relief we properly look to the character of the man, his skills, and his immediate opportunities. But when in a nation of 50 million employees, 15 million men are unemployed, that is an issue, and we may not hope to find its solution within the range of opportunities open to any one individual. The very structure of opportunities has collapsed. Both the correct statement of the problem and the range of possible solutions require us to consider the economic and political institutions of the society, and not merely the personal situation and character of a scatter of individuals. (p. 9)

We know that as unemployment rises, so do alcoholism and drug use, homelessness, child abuse, divorce, domestic violence, crime and delinquency, mental illness, and so forth. The human service worker who treats each case as a personal trouble is doing a disservice to clients, society, and the profession. As novelist Kurt Vonnegut said, "Workers in the field of mental health at various times in different parts of the world must find them-selves asked to make people happier in cultures and societies which have gone insane" (Vonnegut, 1991, p. 32). Troubles call for personal struggle; social issues demand wide-scale social change.

DEFINING PROBLEMS

The Drug Scare

The process of defining problems and treating those problems is often more political than scientific. Both the definitions and the treatments go through cycles that depend more on the political and economic climate than on objective analysis. For example, two sociolo-gists, Craig Reinarman and Harry Levine (1989), studied the crack-cocaine "epidemic" and concluded that *crack use was no greater than it had been in previous years.* Rather, it was being called an epidemic as a dramatic ploy to sell newspapers, increase TV program rat-ings, and get votes for politicians. The drug scare led an overwhelming majority of both houses of Congress to vote for new antidrug laws with long mandatory prison terms, the death sentence, and massive funding for drug enforcement. Reinarman and Levine point out that during drug scares, all kinds of social problems are blamed on drugs, and certain groups are scapegoated, most often people of color and youth of all races.

In support of their argument, Reinarman and Levine examined nationwide surveys of drug use and showed that the percentage of eighteen- to twenty-five-year-old young adults who had ever tried cocaine peaked in 1982, four years before the current epidemic was announced, and it has *declined* since then. The issue became prominent before the 1984 presidential election and dropped sharply in both political speeches and media coverage after the election, only to return during the 1988 election year. As a *New York Times* story put it, the drug scares filled an issue vacuum because "there were no domestic or foreign policy crises looming on which the two parties could easily differentiate themselves" (Reinerman & Levine, 1989, p. 129). In evaluating the "epidemic" of drugs as compared to other substances, the sociologists point out that "for every one cocaine-related death in the U.S. in 1987 there were approximately 300 tobacco-related deaths and 100 alcohol-related deaths. Seen in this light, cocaine's impact is somewhat less dramatic than media and polit-ical accounts suggest" (p. 120).

The media have embedded in the public's mind the image of drugs running rampant in the ghettos. But studies have shown that a higher percentage of whites than blacks have used cocaine; whites are more able to conceal their drug deals and can hire lawyers when they are arrested. A study in 1999 showed that tobacco use was higher among white youths 12 and older (27 percent) than among black youths (22.5 percent) or Hispanic youths (22.6 per-cent), and that binge alcohol drinking was lower for blacks (16.5 percent) than for all other races (20 to 21 percent).

Despite these statistics, much stiffer prison sentences were given for the possession of a small amount of crack than for a larger amount of cocaine. Poor people are more likely to use crack because it is cheaper, and people of color are disproportionately poor, so a dispropor-tionate number of people of color are jailed for drug use ("All Things Considered," 1992).

However, in December 2007 the Supreme Court ruled that a federal district judge can reduce a sentence for crack cocaine and that the cocaine guidelines are advisory only, not mandatory. While they were defunding social programs, the Reagan administration ignored social problems such as unemployment and poverty and "social control replaced social welfare as the organizing principle of state policy" (Reinarman & Levine, 1989, p. 127).

The programs that get government funds are the ones that have been defined by officials as important. Methods of treatment are shaped by official philosophy. The largest proportion of antidrug money has been spent on law enforcement and jails rather than on drug treatment programs and supportive services for addicts. And, despite the seeming concern for "crack babies," there are fewer treatment resources for pregnant mothers than for any other population.

How the Media Demonize People

People get much of their information from the media, and when the media distort facts, people are more likely to have distorted views. We will examine how the media dealt with AIDS and with welfare to illustrate how the media can demonize a group of people.

AIDS

In his study of the way magazines dealt with AIDS, Edward Albert (1989) shows that national magazines were slow to pay attention to AIDS. When they first printed news about it in 1982, they focused on the homosexual lifestyle, sometimes in a sensationalized manner. This encouraged readers to conclude that AIDS was something that happened to "them," not "heterosexual readers" because "we" don't do those things. This raised the question of whether homosexuality, and AIDS, was a moral or a medical issue.

Because the public assumed that AIDS happened to "them," a socially devalued and powerless group, they did not insist that officials pay more attention to the disease. Newspaper coverage increased in 1983, when stories appeared about children being at risk, but decreased when the Centers for Disease Control indicated that there was no change in the at-risk populations. Media coverage increased in 1985, with the disclosure that the actor Rock Hudson had AIDS and it was implied that he was gay.

In 1985, the press began to suggest that AIDS was a threat to heterosexuals. "Beginning around the time of the death of Rock Hudson, a climate of fear emerged, quite different from that created when the press first typified AIDS as a disease of deviance" (Albert, 1989, p. 47). The press began to claim that the disease was spreading throughout the population. This climate of fear led to bitter debates about how to respond to the threat. Some people called for mandatory widespread testing; some advocated quarantine of those with the illness. William F. Buckley, Jr., even suggested in an April 25, 1986, editorial in the *National Review* that those with AIDS be given a tattoo so the rest of us could avoid them.

When the media finally presented AIDS as a disease that could affect anyone, AIDS began to be seen as a disease of the normal rather than just of the deviant. Increasingly, celebrities, homosexuals and heterosexuals alike, admitted to having AIDS. Arthur Ashe, a champion tennis player, got AIDS from a blood transfusion, and basketball star Magic Johnson got HIV from heterosexual contact. In the 1990s, the media became more sympathetic, speaking out against the stigmatization of AIDS victims, which was created in part by their early inadequate coverage of AIDS (Albert, 1989). By 2000, most U.S. adults were relatively well informed about the causes of AIDS ("HIV-Related Knowledge and Stigma," 2001).

The AIDS epidemic has increased people's homophobia about gays and lesbians. Although AIDS is caused by a virus, the fact that in the United States it first began and spread the fastest among male homosexuals propelled the belief that the disease was *caused* by being gay. Although 75 percent of people with the HIV virus across the world are heterosexuals, gay men have been hit the hardest in the United States. However, their contagion rate is leveling off, and the fastest-growing categories of victims of AIDS are minority women and their children.

Much of the change in public perception and official response to AIDS was created by organized groups of AIDS activists working tirelessly to educate the public and to force officials to act.

While new drug therapies and prevention education have made it possible to control the AIDS epidemic in the developed world, AIDS has reached epidemic proportions in the developing world, particularly in Africa and in many Asian countries. The same process of denial that took place in the United States is taking place with regard to AIDS in the developing world. After three years of frustrated lobbying to get permission to study the burgeoning growth of AIDS worldwide, two intelligence officers from the U.S. Central Intelligence Agency finally got permission in 1990 to do the study. Their study, "The Global AIDS Disaster," projected 45 million infections by 2000—inexorably fatal, the great majority in Africa. "The number beggared comparison. There were not that many combatants killed in World War I, World War II, Korea and Vietnam combined" (Gellman, 2000, p. 1). The author of the report, Kenneth Brown, said that the official reaction to the report was indifference.

Although many leaders were aware of the coming catastrophe for a decade, "Individually and collectively, most of those with power decided not to act" (Gellman, 2000, p. 1). James Sherry, director of program development for the Joint United Nations Program on HIV/AIDS, speaks bitterly of the crisis: "I can't think of the coming of any event which was more heralded, to less effect," he said. "The bottom line is, the people who are dying from AIDS don't matter in this world" (Gellman, 2000, p. 1). Racism was a big factor in this denial. One of Mr. Brown's colleagues at the National Intelligence Council said, "Oh, it will be good, because Africa is overpopulated anyway" (Gellman, p. 1).

In 2003, the World Health Organization adopted a plan called "3 × 5," setting a target of getting 3 million poor people on antiretroviral drugs by the end of 2005. At the AIDS conference in Bangkok in July 2004, WHO officials said their 3 × 5 program was "just short" of the July goal of 500,000 in treatment, but Laurie Garrett, a senior fellow for global health at the Council on Foreign Relations, criticized the lack of progress, saying, "We are 18 months away from WHO's self-appointed deadline, and the pool of new HIV infections grows at the rate of 8,000 a day (Garrett, 2004).

Most individuals living with HIV in the United States have access to treatment. "As a result of better health outcomes, individuals living with HIV are returning to employment, some working specifically within the field of HIV/AIDS, especially in peer-based services to clients" (*Journal of HIV/AIDS & Social Services,* 2006). However, not all groups have benefited equally from HIV treatment. "People of color, particularly African Americans, drug users, and other underserved populations lag behind on progress in survival rates. Moreover, after years of decline, AIDS deaths have been on the rise again since 2001" (*Journal of HIV/AIDS & Social Services*, 2006). Federal and state budget cuts on support services have had an impact on clients and the agencies that serve them. Besides medical treatment, clients need income supports, housing, food, and transportation. They also need informal support from family and friends.

Nothing for Years

Nothing for Years,
life continues as if
something hideous wasn't
coiled within
then the sudden purple lump,
death's calling card,
a warrant to strip-mine flesh.
At the end, each ounce
of muscle razed,
only wasted bones left,
yet the eyes grown
huge with knowing
they did
nothing for years.

—Chris Mandell

Welfare

Conservative policymakers have successfully dismantled the safety net for poor people, often using the media to turn the public and government officials against the poor, particularly welfare recipients. They created think tanks such as the Heritage Foundation, the Manhattan Institute, and the American Enterprise Institute that put out a stream of books and magazines and flooded the press with news releases.[*]

Fairness and Accuracy in Reporting (FAIR), an organization that analyzes press coverage, conducted a three-month study of the media's coverage of welfare issues from December 1, 1994, to February 24, 1995, in the period leading up to the Welfare Reform Bill (Flanders, Jackson, & Shadoan, 1997). Most of the people interviewed by the media were males, most were politicians and government officials, and most gave the official line that

---

[*]For a valuable analysis of the right's assault on welfare, see Lucy Williams' booklet *Decades of Distortion* (1997).

spending on the poor ought to be restricted. State and local officials most often interviewed were Republican governors who ran punitive programs, such as Tommy Thompson of Wisconsin and John Engler of Michigan. Few of those reports included any dissenters from the get-tough approach.

Welfare recipients were seldom interviewed, and when they were, they were given limited roles, and at worst they were attacked. In one vivid example, multimillion-dollar earner Diane Sawyer of ABC devoted a segment of *Prime Time* to grilling a group of teenage mothers receiving AFDC (*Prime Time*, 1995). Explaining that "to many people these girls are public enemy No. 1," Sawyer harangued them on behalf of "taxpayers" who were "mad as hell." "Answer their question," she demanded: "Why should they pay for your mistake?"

Sixteen-year-old Lisa Wright, one of *Prime Time's* interviewees, tried to point out that when it comes to taxpayer dollars, AFDC is "such a small percentage now, you know, of the amount of money taxpayers send in. Most of the money is going for defense." But Sawyer was having none of it: She dragged the discussion right back to female "irresponsibility" (Flanders et al., 1997, pp. 30–31).

Jonathan Alter (1994) linked "lascivious teenagers" to "every threat to the fabric of this country." Alter harped on the theme of shame for poor young women, comparing them to drunk drivers (p. 41). When they attacked teenagers on welfare, neither Sawyer nor Alter pointed out that 70 percent of so-called teen pregnancies are the result of sex with men over 20. A study by sociologist Mike Males suggests that 50,000 teen pregnancies a year are caused by rape, and two-thirds of teen mothers have histories of sexual abuse by a perpetrator averaging 27 years of age (Flanders et al., 1997, pp. 33–34).

The welfare recipients that the media selected to be interviewed often reinforced stereotypes. In a *U.S. News & World Report* cover story, "six of the seven pictures were of women of color, mostly African Americans. The only white woman pictured was described as clinically depressed, as if poverty only affects white people who are in some way handicapped" (Flanders et al., 1997, p. 34). Recipients shown in the media often had several children, even though families on welfare have an average of 1.9 children, slightly lower than the national average.

Reminiscent of much reporting on the AIDS crisis, stories on welfare drew a stark distinction between poverty's innocent and guilty victims. The acceptably innocent were children; the guilty were their moms. Although poor children certainly need defenders, poor children come from poor families. In the media, however, "innocent children" were often ominously separated from their guilty moms (just as "AIDS babies" were often described as more or less self-conceived) (Flanders et al., 1997).

Research and advocacy groups made up only 9 percent of media sources during the period that FAIR studied. After participating in two hours of a *Firing Line* debate on welfare, Frances Fox Piven commented to the *St. Petersburg Times,* "I am struck by how little evidence matters in talk about welfare" (Flanders et al., 1997, p. 37).

Yet the stereotypes that conservatives had created returned to haunt them when they wanted to persuade businesses to hire welfare mothers. How could you ask a CEO to hire people whom you had previously described as lazy, undependable, and oversexed? A year after the Personal Responsibility Act had been passed, a *New York Times* article reported that "welfare recipients, last year's political pariahs, are shedding their outcast status" (DeParle, 1997).

The NBC affiliate in Montgomery, Alabama, WSFA, had a weekly feature portraying a welfare family in favorable terms. On St. Louis radio, an advertising campaign praised those with the "guts to get off welfare." In Charlotte, North Carolina, there were billboards—paid for by the county and posted by the Chamber of Commerce—urging employers to give recipients a chance.

The effort to erase the stigma of welfare was coordinated by the Welfare to Work Partnership, which was established in 1997 with President Clinton's encouragement. It included corporate executives and aimed to persuade business leaders to hire welfare recipients. It conducted an advertising campaign with the slogans "Welfare mothers make responsible employees" and "Welfare to work is a program that creates independence" (DeParle, 1997). Politicians and corporate executives, with the help of the media, were rehabilitating the welfare recipients that conservatives had demonized.

Preventive Health Care

If we all ate tofu, carrots, green vegetables, and brown rice and gave up smoking, dieted, and got plenty of exercise, would we all be healthy? Filled with advice from nutritionists and doctors, the Living and Health pages of newspapers give that message. They cite studies showing the beneficial effects of exercise and a healthy diet.

How can these healthy habits help the poor? Poverty is bad for your health. A British commission, named for its chairman, Dr. Black, studied the health of people in several countries, including Great Britain. It found that health policy directed to individual health (regarding smoking, diet, and exercise) improved the health of middle-income and rich people but not the poor. The poor are exposed to such deleterious conditions by their work, housing, and low income that individual behaviors often cannot overcome these disadvantages. The death rate of a blue-collar worker is 2.6 times higher than that of a doctor or lawyer. The Royal Commission called for a return to the **public-health approach**, which asserts that life span is more influenced by improvements in housing, living standards, and sanitation than by improvements in medical intervention, surgery, and acute care (Townsend, 1992).

During the 1970s in England, despite countrywide improvement in living standards, the gap in health between the rich and the poor widened. The Royal Commission, after studying scientific evidence, said that gap could be closed only by (1) providing better housing and adequate income to the poor, (2) increasing wages, and (3) increasing government payments to the aged, single parents, the disabled, and the unemployed.

Food programs, vaccination, and fluoridation are three examples of the success of preventive public-health measures. The WIC (Women, Infants, and Children) food program in the United States for low-income mothers and children has proved that providing healthy food to children and pregnant women has prevented health problems such as infant mortality, low birth weight, and low resistance to disease. Fluoridation of the water has prevented millions of cavities. Today, immunology is such an accepted practice in Western culture that it receives little public attention. Only when there is a breakdown in controls and specific disease rates rise does the general public become aware of the existence of the public-health prevention approach (Friedlander & Apte, 1980, pp. 368–369).

public-health approach   A preventive approach to social problems as opposed to a remedial approach. It implements large-scale programs to meet people's basic health and nutritional needs in order to prevent illness.

MEDICATION   INCARCERATION

A judge must decide the fate of a person who is accused of committing a crime but who also might be mentally ill or stressed out by homelessness. Should special courts be set up to diagnose and mandate treatment? Can therapy or medication be useful when it is coerced?

Public health is concerned with preventive health care, and that is a concern of human service workers. Where an illness is a large-scale problem—as are black lung disease among coal miners; brown lung disease among textile workers; hypertension among black people; cancer among asbestos workers and people living near hazardous wastes; and stroke, cancer, and heart disease among the general population—human service workers deal with the problem on three levels:

1. They work to prevent the causes of illness when they are known.
2. They work to develop appropriate and adequate services.
3. They work with the victims of these public-health problems in giving health-related services.

THE HISTORY OF HUMAN SERVICE WORK

Human service is a broad umbrella category that includes many different kinds of work. Among the first human service workers were doctors and nurses, teachers, lawyers, and the clergy. During the nineteenth century, the people whom we generally call human service workers today began to define their work and organize themselves into professions. They have taken a variety of routes to define their work as they responded to changing definitions of problems, technological innovations, and political and economic realities. Some of the professions under the human-service umbrella today are:

- Claims workers in government benefit programs—e.g., welfare, unemployment, Social Security, Medicaid, food stamps
- Cooperative extension workers (often called *extension agents* or *county agents*)
- Counselors (school, employment, rehabilitation, and career planning and placement counselors)
- Music therapists, art therapists, and dance therapists
- Residential-care workers with children, the disabled, the aged, people with drug or alcohol problems, parolees, and delinquents
- Psychologists
- Social workers and social service aides
- Speech pathologists and audiologists
- Therapy and rehabilitation workers (occupational, recreational, and physical therapists)

We shall briefly trace the history of the profession of social work as it evolved from nineteenth-century forms to the present, and the history of the newer human service profession.

The COS and the Settlement House Movement

Charity Organization Societies (COSs) The earliest professional social work agencies, organized first in England and later in the United States; they claimed to deliver "scientific charity" through case-by-case work of "friendly visitors."

The roots of social work were nurtured by two major wellsprings: the **Charity Organization Societies (COS)**, from which casework and counseling grew, and the settlement house movement, which pioneered group work, community and social change, and advocacy.

The COS first began in England, expanding later to large cities in the United States. They tried to be orderly in their distribution of relief funds through what they termed *scientific charity*. Their "friendly visitors" sought to separate the "deserving" from the "undeserving" poor through case-by-case investigation of their life situations. The COS thought that poverty was perpetuated by indiscriminate relief giving, which made people lazy, or by defects in character. The present-day Family Service Societies grew out of these COS, and people who worked in them organized most of the schools of social work in the United States. The kind of thinking that dominated the COS certainly exerted an influence on the entire social work profession. The Columbia University School of Social Work (originally the New York School of Philanthropy), the first university school to award a degree in social work, opened in 1898 under the auspices of the New York Charity Organization Society.

settlement house movement A movement of the late nineteenth and early twentieth centuries that established agencies in city slums of England and the United States, where professionals gave group services and engaged in social action on behalf of the slum dwellers.

Social work also derived from the **settlement house movement** of the late nineteenth century. Although the early settlement house workers did not call themselves social workers, social work graduate schools began in the 1940s to include group work and community organizing in their curriculums.

The settlement house movement was exemplified by the work of Jane Addams at Hull House in Chicago. A young woman from a rich family who was profoundly shocked by the poverty and exploitation of immigrant families in the urban slums of Chicago, she established a community center to help immigrants solve their social, educational, recreational, and survival problems. Hull House attracted a dedicated core of privileged yet concerned young staff, mostly volunteers, who "settled" (lived) in the house (thus the name "settlement house"). These volunteers helped the newly arrived families to care for their young children and conducted classes in English, citizenship, and the like. Addams imprinted on the field the values of respect for cultural differences and reaching out to clients where one finds them—on the stoops of their houses, at the corner bar, in the factory, and on assembly lines. She also promulgated the belief that society needs to work in a variety of ways to conquer social and personal problems. She loved the city and understood the power of groups to give support to their own members and to apply pressure for needed changes in the laws and customs of their communities. Four labor unions were organized at Hull House. Chambers (1980) records the history of the settlement house movement. He describes how settlement leaders supported the organizing efforts of working women, walked picket lines to demonstrate labor solidarity, testified before civic groups about the needs and rights of working women, and helped raise strike funds.

The settlement workers wanted to bring together the privileged and the underprivileged to share some of the finer things of life. Music, drama, art, and dancing clubs and classes were opened to the immigrant neighbors. Workers, college students, and alumni could live for a time in the settlements, playing basketball, chatting on stoops, and participating in the life of poor neighborhoods.

Jane Addams drew a sharp distinction between her kind of work and the work of the "friendly visitors" of the COS. She did not think they were "friendly" at all in the moralistic way they drew distinctions between the "deserving" and the "undeserving" poor. She wrote about the

> difference between the emotional kindness with which relief is given by one poor neighbor to another poor neighbor, and the guarded care with which relief is given by a charity visitor to a charity recipient. The neighborhood mind is at once confronted not only by the difference of method; but by an absolute clashing of two ethical standards. (Addams, 1902, pp. 19–20)

Mary Richmond, one of the leading lights of the COS and author of the first major theoretical work on social casework, *Social Diagnosis* (1917), reciprocated Jane Addams's contempt, accusing the settlements of doing harm by their misguided charity.

Like the organizers of the COS, most of the settlement house workers came from a religious tradition and viewed their human service work as an expression of their beliefs. However, the settlement house workers had a somewhat different vision of the causes and the remedies of poverty. Although not usually radical in their political views (anarchists, communists, and socialists would not have claimed them as their own), they were more inclined than the organizers of the COS to put some of the blame for poverty on greedy businesspeople, landlords, and corrupt politicians.

Many of the settlement house workers were Progressives who struggled to expand the role of the state in social welfare. They sponsored reforms such as the juvenile court movement and the establishment of kindergartens. As we have seen, in their trust of the state, they ignored the state's potential for violations of human rights. At their lowest, they sought to force the immigrants' rich kaleidoscope of lifestyles and values into a more docile, homogenized U.S. style. At their best, they had a vision of a more just society and believed that their reforms could create it. That thread of reform resurfaced in the New Deal of the 1930s, the New Frontier of the Kennedy era, and the Great Society of the Johnson era. Not until the liberation struggles of the late 1950s and 1960s was the view of the state as benign parent challenged and the "rights revolution" begun.

Bertha Reynolds, an outspoken advocate of social change, summed up the difference between the settlements and the COS. She commented that although the COS and settlements were interested in the same reforms, the settlements organized neighborhoods to act for themselves, whereas the charities helped families in need. A settlement worker told her:

> You caseworkers see people only when they are in trouble and at their worst. We live with them in good times or bad, and see them at their best. It makes our attitude different. We encourage them to take social action and help them to do it effectively. We abhor charity. (Reynolds, 1963, p. 30)

As the Progressive reform movement died, so too did much of the reform thrust of the settlement houses. Workers no longer live in the houses and often do not even live in the same neighborhood. Many settlement houses are now primarily social and recreational centers. The sounds of square dance music and then of rap and heavy metal replaced the angry arguments of union organizers exhorting crowds of garment workers to fight for their rights. Some settlement houses, however, continued to be involved in social action in their communities, particularly during the War on Poverty. Chicago settlement houses helped to shape Chicago's War on Poverty, brought about major changes in the city's police department, and reformed the child welfare system in Illinois (Seever, 1987).

Social Work Schools

From two groups attempting in their own fashion to aid the troubled and poor emerged a profession with noble aims but built on a shaky alliance. When schools of social work developed their curriculums, the COS wielded the most influence. As social work developed its education during the next fifty years, the casework model of the COS became the major skill in the field. Social workers counseled families, worked in child-protective agencies, arranged foster care and adoption for children, helped the families of sick people plan for release and rehabilitation, and worked on mental health teams with psychiatrists and psychologists.

Jane Addams drew on sociological rather than psychological theory. She was well connected with the world-renowned sociology department of the University of Chicago. But at that time, clinical psychology had not yet been developed, and sociology "offered little in respect to managing face-to-face interaction with clients; and that is where psychiatry could be applied" (Specht, 1990, p. 348). The individualistic philosophy of the COS laid the foundation for social work's almost wholesale acceptance of psychiatric theory, beginning in the 1920s. The most popular of these theories were the psychoanalytically oriented theories of Sigmund Freud.

Beginning in the 1950s, social workers were increasingly influenced by the humanistically oriented psychologies of Carl Rogers (1951), Abraham Maslow, and others, and some later incorporated what Specht (1990) calls popular and New Age psychologies—"transcendental meditation, rolfing, hypnosis, and the scores of other therapies now available" (p. 19).

Although there was no return to the theory of moral depravity that held sway in the nineteenth century, the adoption of psychology as the almost exclusive theory of social work education slowly moved professionals away from the neighborhood and group work of Jane Addams. The adoption of behaviorist theory by many schools of social work, beginning in the 1960s, did little to change the individualistic focus of the profession. The introduction of social systems theory in the 1970s (Pincus & Minahan, 1973) emphasized the interaction of the person with the environment; but although systems theory is widely discussed in social work schools, the overwhelming majority of social workers are trained to work one-on-one. Group work and community organizing expanded to meet the social ferment of the 1960s and early 1970s but contracted when the ferment subsided.

Current Trends in Social Work

As social services are becoming increasingly privatized, so is social work. The fastest-growing sector of social work is private practice (Barker, 1995). As states passed licensing laws, workers became eligible to receive **third-party payment** for therapy through the clients' insurance.

Social workers' reasons for preferring private practice over agency practice vary. Earning more money is certainly one of the major reasons; another is that many workers are dissatisfied with the bureaucracy and restrictions of agency practice and yearn to control their working conditions and choose the types of clients they will serve (Abramovitz, 1986). There is intense debate within the profession, and there have been pitched battles among the National Association of Social Workers (NASW), the National Institute for Clinical Social Work Advancement, and the American Board of Examiners (Battle, 1990). Those who oppose the trend believe that the rise in private practice amounts to turning our back on the poor, who cannot afford to pay $70 to $150 per hour for therapy and cannot get insurance coverage for it. Those who favor it argue that social workers are as qualified to do therapy as are psychologists and should have that choice.

As more social workers with MSW degrees go into private practice, the public social services are increasingly staffed by those without MSW degrees. College graduates with degrees in social work, psychology, sociology, or human services fill those jobs. They provide care for the elderly, neglected and abused children, the disabled, and the mentally ill, a large proportion of whom are poor and minorities.

Undergraduate social work programs were established in state colleges, mostly in sociology departments, during the Depression, to staff the new public welfare agencies created by the Social Security Act. The bachelor of social work (BSW) credential was accepted by the Council on Social Work Education (CSWE) in 1966, but it was not until 1970 that NASW admitted BSW workers as members. The CSWE allows graduate schools to admit BSW members with advanced standing if they choose. Thus BSW graduates can often finish an MSW degree in one year rather than the two years usually required.

third-party payment   A payment made by an insurance company or a government program for medical expenses incurred by an individual.

Loan Forgiveness

The NASW is promoting loan forgiveness for social workers. It supports proposals to provide loan forgiveness for social workers in child welfare and schools, as well as other practice areas. You can find out if you are eligible for these programs by contacting the U.S.

Department of Education Federal Student Aid Information Center at 1-800-433-3243 or you can go to www.federalstudentaid.ed.gov. You can also take a look at two bills that offer loan forgiveness for social workers and other human service workers, and they are: (1) Higher Education Act and (2) College Cost Reduction Act of 2007.

Another federal program that helps social workers is the National Health Service Corps Loan Repayment Program. In exchange for two years serving in a community-based approved site that has a shortage of health professional or Health Professional Shortage Area, this program offers fully trained and licensed clinical social workers $50,000 to repay their outstanding student loans (Student Loan Blog, 2010).

The Roots of the Human Service Field

The field of human services was born in the 1950s and since then has expanded in fits and starts. The term *human service*, as opposed to *welfare*, was given the official stamp of approval when the federal Department of Health, Education, and Welfare (HEW) changed its name to the Department of Health and Human Services (HHS) in 1980.

Having declared MSW social workers as nonessential and too expensive, the federal government set out to create a new profession of human service workers. Although saving money may have been one reason for this, there were also other factors at work. Some liberal federal bureaucrats saw social work as too traditional and rigid to deliver adequate services to the poor. The civil rights movement created pressure to open up service professions to minorities who had previously been excluded. Then too, there was money available for social services, and many professions wanted a piece of this action. Government expenditures on social welfare rose dramatically, nearly tripling between 1960 and 1970, and another infusion of funds came with the passage of Title XX legislation in 1975, which funded social services. College educators from a variety of disciplines—counseling, education, special education, psychology, social work, and others—scrambled for Title XX funds.

The new human service workers included the indigenous neighborhood people ("new professionals") recruited during the War on Poverty by social agencies, schools, and hospitals; community college graduates with an associate degree and a major in human services or a related field; and graduates of four-year human service programs. The following influences have helped the human service profession to grow:

1. *The civil rights and liberation struggles.* During the civil rights and liberation struggles of the 1960s, people of color, feminists, gays, and youth declared that mainstream social work was irrelevant. It was too white, too middle class, and too patriarchal. They created their own alternative self-controlled agencies: the Black Panther breakfast program, feminist health collectives, parent co-op day care centers, shelters for battered women, gay and lesbian counseling centers, and shelters and drug counseling centers for alienated and runaway youth. Most of these were not staffed by professional social workers, although an occasional social worker sympathetic to the agency's ideology might work with it.

2. *The OEO War on Poverty.* In its War on Poverty, the Office of Economic Opportunity (OEO) challenged the COS mentality of established social work. The OEO set up new agencies to do battle with the social work gatekeepers to get more benefits and services for

clients. Actually, because most workers in departments of welfare are not BSW or MSW social workers, OEO's war with welfare was not in a strict sense a war with the social work profession but instead with government bureaucracy. However, OEO officials tended to view the profession of social work as the enemy of change.

Many establishment agencies eagerly accepted OEO money, and some highly professionalized agencies, such as Family Service Societies, for the first time hired "indigenous workers" from the communities they served in order to forge links between the agency and the service users. Many professional child welfare social workers were challenged, for the first time in their careers, by poverty lawyers defending parents of foster children. Poverty lawyers entered areas that had in the past been the domain of social workers.

3. *The New Careers for the Poor movement.* The **New Careers movement**, conceived of and best articulated by Arthur Pearl and Frank Riessman (1965), was begun as part of the War on Poverty to create human service careers for poor people. Finding that they were blocked in their quest for upward mobility by lack of credentials, one of the movement's leaders, Audrey Cohen, started the College of Human Services in New York City. She announced her intention to "change the whole pattern of credentialing as it now exists" (Houston & Cohen, 1972, p. 22).

The **career ladder** concept, in which a worker with incomplete training could move up through on-the-job experience and training, was built into some antipoverty legislation. Many agencies and colleges drew upon antipoverty funds to set up training courses and programs.

4. *The growth of community colleges.* The burgeoning growth of community colleges in the late 1960s and the 1970s spurred the growth of human service programs—more than 500 by 1996 (di Giovanni, 1996). This gave the New Careers students another way to gain a credential and, aided by antipoverty money and grants, many associate's degree graduates found jobs in agencies and schools. President Obama's administration has increased funding for community colleges.

5. *Deinstitutionalization and contracting out.* Deinstitutionalization created a demand for workers in community residences, prerelease centers, mental health clinics, and other community settings. This, along with the increase in contracting out of services to private agencies, created new agencies that were not part of the MSW or BSW tradition. Workers came from many disciplines. Contracting out not only took some turf away from social work but also weakened public-service unions, bringing down the wage scale in both the public and private sectors.

Some people consider Dr. Harold McPheeters the founder of the human services field. In the 1960s, Dr. McPheeters of the Southern Regional Education Board (SREB) applied for and received a grant from the National Institute of Mental Health (NIMH) for the development of mental-health programs at community colleges in the Southern region of the country. This was the beginning of the associate-level human service degree in the United States (Woodside, M. and McClam, T., 1990).

The National Organization for Human Service Education (NOHSE) was founded in 1975 at the Fifth Annual Faculty Development Conference of the Southern Regional Education Board. It unites educators, students, practitioners, and clients in a conversation about preparation of effective human service workers. In 1976, the NIMH gave funds to the

New Careers for the Poor movement A movement that began in the 1960s to train workers who do not have extensive formal credentials for human service jobs.

career ladder A specific path of jobs that relates accomplishment and tenure to upward mobility.

SREB to create national standards for training and reviewing human service programs (Brawley, 1980). Out of this project came the Council for Standards of Human Service Education (CSHSE), formed in February 1979. In 1982, the National Commission for Human Service Workers was incorporated to provide a national system for voluntary registration and certification of human service workers (National Commission for Human Service Workers, 1982).

NOHSE is now called the National Organization for Human Service (NOHS), and SREB is now called the Southern Organization of Human Service (SOHS). There has been an increase in both four-year human service programs and two-year programs in community colleges, and there are now PhD programs. Judy Slater, the president of NOHS, says that the NOHS is revising the Code of Ethics so that more programs will have a way to identify if they are meeting the standards of the Council. They have developed a practice-based examination for certification. The exam is based on case scenarios. A board-certified practitioner will be designated a Human Service—Board Certified Practitioner (HS-BCP). To be eligible to apply for the HS-BCP national credential, an applicant must have a degree from a regionally accredited college or university, or a state-approved community or junior college at the technical certificate level or above. Applicants must also have completed the required postdegree experience. The number of years or hours is outlined in the HS-BCP application packet. To apply, download the 2010 HS-BCP packet at: www.cce-global.org/extras/cce-global/pdfhs/hs-bcp_application-standard.pdf.

New Disciplines

Among the first professionals to retool for the human service field were elementary and high school teachers who were faced with layoffs because of declining student enrollment. A 1979 survey "revealed that more than 300 schools, colleges or departments of education had human services programs" (Vogel, 1979). One of the authors of this book, Barbara Schram, started a human service program in one of them. The American Association of Colleges for Teacher Education recommended relieving the oversupply of teachers by diversifying to produce a new kind of teacher, a human service educator.

Although psychologists have always been in the human services, a branch of psychology called *professional psychology* is more oriented toward counseling than toward research. The first school of professional psychology, accredited by the American Psychological Association in 1974, seems especially oriented toward health services, the field that accounts for a large proportion of the growth in social welfare spending since the 1960s.

In sociology, a specialty called *clinical sociology* has developed, whose practitioners, particularly family sociologists, do therapy with individuals, groups, and families. Their counseling theories include a sociological perspective that examines the difference between private troubles and public issues.

Finally, in the field of child abuse and neglect, which for decades was the almost exclusive province of social work, doctors and lawyers gained prominence. Advances in radiology in the 1960s made it easier to diagnose abuse, and the term *battered-child syndrome* was coined. Since then, many child abuse units have been located in hospitals rather than in social agencies. Lawyers also became involved in defining abuse and neglect and in representing parents, children, and states in court cases.

Declassification and Deprofessionalization

Many states have moved to declassify civil service jobs, removing them from the exclusive province of social work and broadening the qualifications. The NASW and the CSWE countered the move to declassify social work jobs by lobbying for state licensing legislation. State NASW chapters were urged to make licensing a high priority on their agenda. NASW also countered declassification moves by seeking to prove the worth of the BSW and MSW credentials to state civil service and merit system boards. Ironically, social workers, many of whom had never wanted to be in the public welfare agencies in the first place, fought declassification efforts to keep them out.

Breaking Down Boundaries

Much of the human services literature, particularly the New Careers literature, displays the missionary zeal of a movement. To the extent that human service workers are struggling on the side of the poor and the dispossessed, as in the New Careers movement, we applaud their efforts. They enabled thousands of poor people, especially poor women, to get jobs they would never have had otherwise and provided a vital missing link between the poor and their communities. We also agree enthusiastically with the pleas of human service workers to break down the artificial boundaries between disciplines and open up the field to anyone who can enrich it. The New Careers people from the communities served by social agencies have a gut-level knowledge of their neighbors' lives that a social worker commuting from an affluent white suburb cannot hope to match.

Many people are made tense by the introduction of a staff member with different credentials. In highly stratified organizations such as hospitals, much effort can be wasted and tempers strained as the traditional helpers try to find ways to fit the newly arrived worker into the pecking order. Some new workers or students in field placements have walked into the middle of such power struggles and inherited long-smoldering conflicts. Tensions are often greater where staff morale is low, communication is poor, and there is a lack of adequate orientation before a new role is inserted into an existing system. Thus, if a residential treatment center hires, for the first time, a human service worker, everyone involved in that system needs to do some serious thinking about the new person's job description. Often, if other workers are given a voice in shaping it, they are less resistant to change when the eager generalist appears on the scene. If newcomers are left to carve out their own job description or are given superimposed ones, toes are bound to be stepped on.

There are no easy ways to avoid turf battles in institutions, but forewarned is forearmed. Professions tend to solidify their boundaries, and most workers have understandable concern about their responsibilities and privileges. Good humor and a nonthreatening attitude, coupled with an individual's sense of his or her potential contribution, can go a long way in dealing with boundary disputes.

Many of the conflicts within a profession and between professions center on social class, race, and gender differences. Sometimes the fight may seem to be about credentials, but it is really about white people, middle-class people, heterosexuals, or nonhandicapped workers wanting to preserve their exclusive status.

Whether we are called human service workers or social workers, we give the best service possible. There is room for many flowers to bloom in the social service field, and each of those flowers must prove its competence and its dedication.

SUMMARY

1. People have always helped, as well as hurt, each other. The nature of a society shapes people's helping impulses. One anthropologist believes that the principle of reciprocity is the basic glue that holds a society together.

2. A review of the history of helping gives perspective on how changes in society shape the methods of helping. To understand the present, we need to know the past.

3. At the beginning of industrialization, people who needed help were regarded as morally depraved. That attitude shifted somewhat to the view that problems are often beyond the control of the individual.

4. Universal programs, such as Social Security, cover people of all social classes. Means-tested programs, such as TANF, cover only the poor and are usually stigmatized.

5. Welfare gradually shifted from local, to state, and then to federal responsibility. In recent years, it has drifted back to the responsibility of state and local governments.

6. During the rise of Protestantism, especially Calvinism, the poor were regarded as people who had been denied the grace of God and were treated as criminals. They were placed in debtors' prisons and workhouses. This attitude pervaded American society until well into the twentieth century.

7. During the civil rights era of the 1960s, many people redefined poverty as a result of an unjust social system. This gave rise to an opportunity theory of poverty, as opposed to a victim-blaming theory.

8. Political ideologies often define personal and social problems. Such influence characterizes, for example, the following issues: the drug "epidemic," the response to welfare, an individual versus a systems approach to health care, and the roles and privileges of men and women.

9. The forms of helping go through cycles. For example, welfare reform, the care of the mentally ill, and the treatment of delinquents and adult prisoners have all run cyclical courses.

10. The Progressives attempted to individualize the treatment of prisoners and mental patients. However, given unchecked authority, professionals often violated clients' rights.

11. The contemporary response to mental illness is deinstitutionalization, which places clients in more normal settings in the community, although there are not enough community facilities.

12. Judi Chamberlin, one of the founders of the mental patients' liberation movement, talks about the treatment of mental illness. She also discusses the hospice program she participated in before her death.

13. The Progressives instituted the child-saving movement, creating juvenile courts, foster care, compulsory education, and orphanages. Some regard these institutions as new forms of social control and occupational tracking of the poor.

14. Ostensibly, the juvenile court system was more humane for children, but its failure to provide the due process of adult courts resulted in many injustices. The Supreme Court's 1967 *Gault* decision gave juveniles some due-process rights.

15. The United States is the world's leader in incarceration. A disproportionate number of prisoners are black or Hispanic, partly because of the war on drugs, which criminalized possession of small amounts of drugs.

16. The media often distorts facts about people's problems, including its coverage of AIDS and welfare.

17. The public-health approach, stressing preventive care, has saved more lives than medical intervention, surgery, and acute care.

18. The first professionals to do social welfare work with the poor were social workers. The two early strands of the profession were the COS and the settlement house movement.

19. The human service field began in the 1950s and since then has grown with the impact of deinstitutionalization, the War on Poverty program, the New Careers movement, and the proliferation of community colleges.

20. New federal programs help college students to repay loans.

DISCUSSION QUESTIONS

1. The federal minimum wage in 2010 was $7.25 per hour. Why do you think Congress and the president have been unwilling to raise that wage to an amount that would support a family? What amount do you think the minimum wage should be?

2. The government of Finland gives each new mother a complete layette for the baby, or 150 Euros (about $210 in 2004). A parent who gets on a bus in Helsinki with a baby in a carriage or stroller does not have to pay the bus fare because people think the parent should not be distracted from caring for the baby. Single mothers not only suffer no stigma in Finland, they are considered to be doing valuable work for the country by raising children. These attitudes are quite different from attitudes toward mothers in the United States who receive welfare. Why do you think there is such a difference?

3. Why do you think welfare has become a political issue in the United States?

WEB RESOURCES FOR FURTHER STUDY

National Organization for Human Services (NOHS)

www.humanservices.org

The mission of NOHS is to strengthen the community of human services by:

- Expanding professional development opportunities
- Promoting professional and organizational identity through certification
- Enhancing internal and external communications
- Advocating and implementing a social policy and agenda
- Nurturing the financial sustainability and growth of the organization

National Association of Social Workers (NASW)

www.socialworkers.org

The National Association of Social Workers (NASW) is the largest membership organization of professional social workers in the world, with 145,000 members in 2010. NASW works to enhance the professional growth and development of its members, to create and maintain professional standards, and to advance sound social policies.

Social Welfare Action Alliance (SWAA)

www.socialwelfareactionalliance.org

The SWAA is a national organization of progressive workers in human services. Founded in 1985, the SWAA is based on key principles that reflect a concern for peace and social justice and coalition building with progressive social movements. These principles articulate a need by social service workers for a practice and theory that responds to progressive concerns. The SWAA holds a national conference every year.

The National Empowerment Center

www.power2u.org

The mission of the National Empowerment Center, Inc., is to carry a message of recovery, empowerment, hope, and healing to people who have been diagnosed with mental illness: "We carry that message with authority because we are a consumer/survivors/expatient-run organization and each of us is living a personal journey of recovery and empowerment. We are convinced that recovery and empowerment are not the privilege of a few exceptional leaders, but rather are possible for each person who has been diagnosed with mental illness."

National Network of Abortion Funds (NNAF) Access and Equality Contingent

www.nnaf.org

The NNAF raises funds to help low-income women get abortions when necessary. It lobbies to increase access to choice, which includes the choice to have children and to have the resources to care for them. The Access and Equality Contingent seeks to broaden the feminist agenda to be more inclusive of issues that affect low-income women such as welfare and poverty. It lobbies against the Family Cap provision and marriage promotion programs in welfare law and against the Hyde Amendment, which prohibits federal funding for abortion.

National Organization for Women (NOW)

www.now.org

NOW is the largest organization of feminist activists in the United States. Since its founding in 1966, NOW's goal has been to take action to bring about equality for all women. NOW works to eliminate discrimination and harassment in the workplace, schools, the justice system, and all other sectors of society; secure abortion, birth control, and reproductive rights for all women; end all forms of violence against women; eradicate racism, sexism, and homophobia; and promote equality and justice in our society.

Community Voices Heard
www.cvhaction.org

Community Voices Heard is a member organization of low-income people, predominantly women with experience on welfare, building power in New York City and State to improve the lives of our families and communities.

National Alliance on Mental Illness (NAMI)
www.nami.org

NAMI is the nation's largest grassroots mental health organization dedicated to improve the lives of persons living with serious mental illness and their families. Founded in 1979, NAMI has more than 1,100 local communities across the country that join together to meet the NAMI mission through advocacy, research, support, and education.

Gray Panthers
www.graypanthers.org

Members of the Gray Panthers lobby to protect and expand health and welfare benefits for older Americans and organize for peace. Their assertive strategies fly in the face of stereotypes that depict the elderly as passive grandparents glued to their rocking chairs.

Older Women's League (OWL)
www.owl-national.org

Founded in 1980 as the Older Women's League, OWL is the only national grassroots membership organization to focus solely on issues unique to women as they age. OWL strives to improve the status and quality of life for midlife and older women. OWL is a nonprofit, nonpartisan organization that accomplishes its work through research, education, and advocacy activities conducted through a chapter network.

Chapter 3

Intervention Strategies

A human services student intern in a human resource department of a high-tech corporation wrote this entry in her fieldwork journal:

> While I was covering the reception desk yesterday, a woman who works in the employee cafeteria came into the office. She is convinced that her boss is sexually harassing her. I described to her all the possible places she could go to get some action on her complaints. Then I told her my honest opinion of the trade-offs of each pathway. After a few sentences she interrupted me, saying, "Okay, enough, just tell me what is the best thing to do!" I gave her one of our usual yes-but-then-again answers.
>
> "Damn it!" she shouted, "How come you middle-class professionals never give a simple answer to a simple question?"

This student knew that with personnel problems, just as with all other human service problems, there are no easy, one-size-fits-all solutions. Action plans cannot be designed the way a chemist combines elements—two parts of hydrogen mixed with one part of oxygen produce water. In our field, we never can predict exactly what the outcome of our words or actions will be. Because that reality is often forgotten, people become frustrated by the endless duplication, contradictions, and lack of clarity they find when dealing with human service problems. For every problem a person faces there are several possible ways to try to alleviate it. These ways are called "intervention strategies" and every one of them has a set of trade-offs.

Irritating as this situation may be, it is inevitable. Three basic forces create this seemingly endless diversity of approaches and consequences.

1. Value conflicts in a pluralistic society
2. Historical changes in theories and resources
3. The concept of multicausality

We will briefly introduce the first two factors, but in this chapter, we will focus primarily on the impact of the concept of multicausality on the design and implementation of intervention strategies.

Value Conflicts: As you read the chapters on value conflicts and working with diversity, you will find that there is very little agreement in our society on issues as basic as the nature of human nature and the legitimate functions of government. The definitions of what constitutes proper parental discipline, the appropriate role of males and females, attitudes toward sexuality, consumerism, and even the legitimacy of social protest vary according to our race, religion, ethnic heritage, educational level, and the extent of our assimilation into U.S. society. Our socioeconomic class, sex, region of the country, ideology, age, and stage in life also exert an impact on our opinions and actions.

Historical Changes: The attitude of society toward social problems, and the helping process, undergo constant shifts. New theories on the causes of and cures for social problems keep emerging. Programs established in one era reflect the state of theory at that time. But agencies rarely change as fast as the dominant views. People trained at one time, when certain theories held sway, continue to operate under those theories long after they have been discarded or revised by others. Sometimes, if people keep on working in their old-fashioned way, old theories are likely to come back into fashion, just like clothes stored in the attic. The results of local and national elections as well as landmark legal cases often change the dominant ideology of the role of government or the private sector.

THE CONCEPT OF MULTICAUSALITY

When a person sets out to solve a problem, the most logical first step is to try to find out what has caused it. When the cause has been identified, a rational plan to solve the problem can then be designed. But as we try to neatly match solutions to problems, six principles of **multicausality** complicate the process.

1. *In dealing with social problems, we can never establish causality with any solid degree of certainty.* Even though we may have collected all the data we could about a person, we still end up with a best guess, an informed hunch, or a hypothesis to explain the causes of his or her problem. For example, it is easy to make the assumption that if infants are picked up every time they cry, they will become spoiled. But it is equally possible that if infants are allowed to cry for long periods of time, they will become frustrated. As we watch a child who constantly seeks attention from a teacher, we cannot tell if the child's behavior is caused by too much or too little parental supervision at home. We also cannot tell if it is because of a genuine inability to understand the work and the child needs more instruction, or if it is because the work is too easy and the child is bored and ready to move on.

If we were to read all the books on the shelf of a library under the heading "Child-Raising Manuals," we would find many different views among the experts. Whether children should be spanked, breast-fed, sent to day care or kept at home, taught the alphabet early, and so forth are questions with many different answers (Breitbart & Schram, 1978). Dr. Benjamin Spock, author of a best-selling manual on raising a healthy child, did a major revision of his book (Spock, 1946, 1976). If you tried to follow his parenting advice in 1946, you would have raised your little boy or girl very differently than if you read his revised book thirty years later. Spock looked back at his first book and was shocked by his own sex-role stereotyping. In his later books, he confessed that his thinking had undergone a dramatic change (Spock & Morgan, 1989).

When we read about the lives of famous people, we find every possible kind of parenting. Some have excelled in life presumably because of supportive home environments, but others have excelled despite their negative home environments. Some of these people were orphans, some were the only child in the family, and some had many siblings. In landmark

multicausality
The view that personal or social problems are caused by many interacting factors, often too complex to allow a precise assessment of causality.

autobiographies, such as *Manchild in the Promised Land* (Brown, 1965), authors struggle to understand the impact of their early experiences on their adult personality and life choices and rarely can they come up with answers. Jerome Kagan (1989), an eminent Harvard University child development specialist, has found that the more he studies, the less he is convinced that there are very many linkages between a person's early childhood characteristics and his or her personality as an adult.

2. *There is rarely one simple cause of a problem*. When we observe negative behavior, either in a social system or in an individual, we can be absolutely sure that more than one factor is responsible. Beware of popular wisdom and tabloid newspapers that will try to sell you simple reasons for a complex phenomenon. Headlines shout:

POLITICIAN DECLARES LACK OF DISCIPLINE IN HOME
IS MAJOR CAUSE OF RISE IN JUVENILE DELINQUENCY

or

SCHOOL AUTHORITIES SAY INADEQUATE CRIMINAL
JUSTICE SYSTEM IS CAUSE OF CRIME INCREASE

or

SOCIAL REFORMERS DEMAND INCREASE IN JOBS
TO STEM YOUTH CRIME

or

LACK OF RECREATIONAL FACILITIES CITED AS
CAUSE OF JUVENILE DELINQUENCY

And as newspapers search for reasons that can be crammed into eye-catching headlines, supermarket magazines offer articles titled:

THE SECRET OF A HAPPY MARRIAGE

or

HOW YOUR BIRTH ORDER DETERMINES YOUR PERSONALITY

posttraumatic stress disorder (PTSD)
A common anxiety disorder that develops after exposure to a terrifying event or ordeal in which grave physical harm occurred or was threatened. Family members of victims also can develop the disorder. PTSD can occur in people of any age, including children and adolescents.

Pop culture encourages people to blame their problems on a single event in their lives—the "one cataclysmic event" theory of social causation. In television dramas, the kindly therapist helps the distraught woman remember the horrible experience that led, twenty years later, to her mental breakdown; released from the prison of her repressed memory, she walks out of his office into the waiting arms of husband and children, made whole again. Veterans, refugees, and victims of violent assaults often suffer **posttraumatic stress disorder (PTSD)** from the devastating things they have seen and felt. But neither the development of their problems nor the solutions to these problems are ever that simple.

3. *Human service problems are the result of many intertwined personal pressures and social forces*. The problem of delinquency among young men and women involves so many

Young men & women
delinquency

different developmental stresses, such as family, peer, and school pressures, that it would not be possible to overcome delinquency by changing only one aspect of a teenager's life.

If we look at another of the headlines, we will find that there are no compelling research data proving that when fewer women worked outside the home, youth crime was substantially lower. Historically, poor and working-class women have always had to work outside their homes to feed their families. And given both the current economy and the realities of many women's desire for jobs and careers, it is hardly practical to expect all mothers to stay at home, even if that would solve the problem.

It is also unlikely that just increasing the length of prison sentences would stop the crime epidemic. Who gets caught, the bail set, and the kind of punishment given are more often connected to the socioeconomic status and race of the alleged perpetrators than to guilt or innocence. And the debate on capital punishment waxes and wanes, with no compelling evidence that it reduces the incidence of major crimes.

Although a severe lack of jobs, especially for young people, undoubtedly does encourage youngsters to resort to criminal behavior, jobs alone do not stop crime. Youth need to be trained adequately for rewarding jobs, and the jobs offered must hold the promise of a future. In addition, if simply having a job assured honesty, we would not have the widespread white-collar fraud that has led to the downfall of many banks and stock companies.

THE NEW SEXUAL REVOLUTION

Each major social change, such as the sexual revolution, brings with it a host of both negative and positive consequences. This leads to the further proliferation of social programs to deal with them.

Too much leisure time with nothing to do surely encourages some juvenile crime, especially vandalism, but recreation centers alone would not account for a large reduction in crime statistics. Video arcades, movie theaters, and even sports teams do not necessarily create mentally healthy people.

Rising delinquency rates probably do result from inadequacies in the family, the courts, the economy, the schools, and recreational facilities. Delinquency may be encouraged by lack of opportunity due to discrimination. It is also propelled by social attitudes that place an inordinate stress on consumerism. And it may also be encouraged by a general breakdown of social supports, such as religious institutions and extended family networks.

Finally, there is the individual enmeshed in all these systems. Individuals bring with them their own strengths and weaknesses, some inborn and some learned, as well as their unique combination of luck and chance.

Another human service problem that is the result of many complex personal and social events is child abuse. Many people believe that child abuse is caused by poverty or that parents who were beaten as children will become abusive parents. But these two reasons account for only some unknown percentage of abuse. All victims of child abuse do not come from poor families, and many adults who were abused as children do not become abusers.

To understand the full dimension of any social problem, we must systematically analyze all the contributory causes. To do this type of multicausality analysis, we drew a circle to represent the whole problem (see Figure 3.1). Then we divided it into several pie-shaped pieces. Each piece contributes to the whole problem.

When we work for social change, rarely do we expect to be the target of police action. But Cheri Honkala, a member of the Chippewa tribe, discovered what it felt like to be treated like a criminal when she joined a protest against the lack of affordable housing.

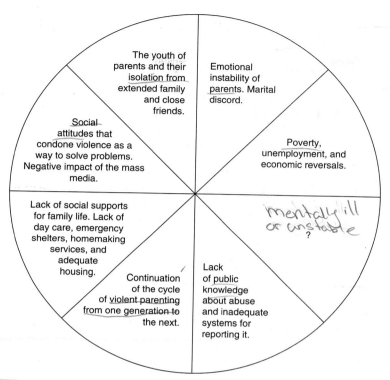

The youth of parents and their isolation from extended family and close friends.

Emotional instability of parents. Marital discord.

Social attitudes that condone violence as a way to solve problems. Negative impact of the mass media.

Poverty, unemployment, and economic reversals.

Lack of social supports for family life. Lack of day care, emergency shelters, homemaking services, and adequate housing.

mentally ill or unstable?

Continuation of the cycle of violent parenting from one generation to the next.

Lack of public knowledge about abuse and inadequate systems for reporting it.

FIGURE 3.1   Possible causes of child abuse

As you study Figure 3.1, remember that many of the theories of causation are tentative. Some reasons have yet to be found, and we are not sure of the relative importance of each of the wedges to the total problem. Research in the field of child abuse reveals much contradictory data (Gary, 1991; Kadushin, 1980). After a few more years of study, we will probably omit one wedge or diminish its size. For example, we used to think that poverty and harsh working-class-style discipline were the major contributors to abuse. Then, as our reporting systems improved, we became aware of many middle- and upper-class families involved in child abuse. These families might have avoided detection earlier because they used private doctors who were less likely than those in public hospitals to diagnose a bruise as being the result of parental abuse or neglect. And in suburban schools, as opposed to inner-city schools, teachers rarely considered the possibility that a child's injury had been inflicted by his or her parents.

We have also realized that there are different forms of abuse and neglect. When sexual and emotional abuse are included in the definition, there is little doubt that this problem does not respect boundaries of socioeconomic class.

As you study the pie chart, you will notice that the several reasons for child abuse described are generated from different sources. The inner psychological pressures that drive adults to hurt children are intertwined with the exterior pressures exerted by social institutions and world events.

4. *Some causes of social problems are deeply rooted, and others are secondary causes or symptoms of a deeper problem.* After we look at the many causes that lie behind a human service problem, we must try to rank them in some order of priority. Then we focus our efforts for change on the causes that might have the most powerful impact. These are called the **root causes**—the reasons behind the reasons. Usually the root causes are the most deeply buried and the most intractable. Visualize a large tree you want to remove from your garden. It is held in place by a series of roots, some close to the surface and others firmly embedded. The surface ones may be the easiest to remove, but they do the least to dislodge the whole tree.

We know, for example, that during periods of economic recession, there seems to be a rise in family violence. Yet we can do little to stop job layoffs in the automobile factories or recapture the market from foreign competitors. However, by recognizing the social costs of unemployment, we can work to establish more job-retraining programs. We can also lobby the federal government for extended unemployment benefits and organize support groups that help families deal with the upheaval in their lives without taking it out on their children and one another. And we can work for political candidates who share our values.

Exploring root causes, like everything else connected with causality, is a matter of action and reflection, trial and error. For example, a woman enters counseling convinced that her constant depression is a result of her husband's infidelity. Her husband complains that she is no longer willing to go out with him or entertain their friends as they used to. He feels rejected by her and has sought companionship in a series of brief affairs. After meeting with the couple together and separately, the counselor suggests that she visit yet one more physician. Although her family doctor had given her a clean bill of health, the specialist diagnoses her constant lack of energy as chronic fatigue syndrome. Unfortunately, there is no quick cure for this biological condition. Perhaps the couple's situation will remain the same for a while, but the definition of the root causes of their problem is now very different. They might still need supportive therapy. He might still be unhappy with her inactivity, but he is likely to feel less rejected. Now, perhaps, he can be more understanding. If he is less angry, her mood is likely to improve. And if the basic commitment to each other is still strong, perhaps they can find new, more sedentary ways to enjoy being together.

5. *Although many people appear to have the same problem, they may have it for a different set of reasons.* If one were to visit a meeting of Alcoholics Anonymous (AA), it would be easy to assume that the participants were all there for the same major reasons. True, they all have problems with alcohol. But what constellation of causes has led them to become alcoholics? There are many subgroups within this seemingly homogeneous assembly:

- Subgroup A includes people who were raised in an alcoholic family.
- Subgroup B includes people who are in a relationship with an alcoholic lover or spouse.
- Subgroup C includes people who have an undiagnosed and untreated biological condition such as **anxiety disorder** or **attention deficit/hyperactivity (ADHD)** disorder.
- Subgroup D includes people who are in a profession that requires a great deal of social drinking.
- Subgroup E includes people who have recently experienced a major life trauma, such as death, divorce, job loss, or diminished physical capacity.

root causes
The critical causes of a particular problem that seem to have contributed most significantly to its emergence.

anxiety disorder
A biological condition in which feelings of extreme fear, tension, and dread often overwhelm the person, even when there is no apparent threat to their well-being.

attention deficit/ hyperactivity disorder (ADHD)
A biological condition with early onset and often long duration that interferes with a person's capacity to focus and sustain interest, especially when the agenda is set by an outside authority, as in a school or work setting.

Likewise, if one were to observe a group of eighteen third-grade students in a tow wide tutoring program, it would be easy to assume that they all have the same proble Even though they are all labeled learning disabled and their scores on a standardized r ing test place them two years behind their peers, we may discover after getting to kno.. them that:

- Three need eyeglasses and one needs a hearing aid.
- Two are very bright but have short attention spans.
- Three have a specific learning disorder, such as dyslexia.
- Five are attending a school that has large classes, inexperienced teachers, and high staff turnover.
- Two have serious problems at home that divert their energy.
- One frequently comes to school hungry, cold, or physically ill.
- For two, we can find no reasons at all. (Maybe they are just late bloomers.)

Of course, each of the causal factors just described is filtered through the screen of the child's unique personality and habitual way of coping. Just as there are no two identical faces in the world (except for identical twins), there are no two identical psychological profiles.

Figure 3.2 shows a multilayered maze that illustrates the many forces shaping our attitudes and actions. These forces begin to influence us from the moment our genetic makeup is determined by the combining of a sperm with an egg. The impact that sex, race, and physical abilities and disabilities will have on a specific child's future life will be mediated by his or her family, culture, neighborhood, and other significant events and groups.

6. *Even when people encounter similar experiences, they do not necessarily react in similar ways.* In a very personal account of his internment in a Nazi concentration camp during World War II, the late psychologist Bruno Bettelheim (1950) wrote about being both victim and professional observer. He described the ways inmates adjusted to life under intolerable circumstances. Many died resisting the guards, others acquiesced almost humbly, some escaped, some collaborated, some took leadership roles for the first time in their lives. Differences among the prisoners seemed to be based on their life experiences before their internment and their personal characteristics, occupations, and skills, as well as on large doses of luck and chance.

It was impossible to predict in advance how concentration camp survivors would fare in the future. Some, like Bettelheim, gained strength from adversity and went on to have outstanding careers. Some became bitter, withdrawn, and distrustful. Still others became profoundly more appreciative of the basic pleasures of family and friends. Likewise, children who are too bright or creative for the class they are placed in do not all act alike. One simply grins and bears it, another withdraws into daydreams, another becomes the class clown, and another becomes the star pupil.

The concept of multicausality also helps to explain why siblings are often so different. Even though they grow up with the same set of parents, go to the same school, live in the same neighborhood, perhaps even have the same type of physical disability, we can never predict precisely how each one of them will think or act. Surprisingly, the reverse is also true. Scientists have identified cases in which identical twins, reared apart from birth, displayed remarkable similarities in adulthood. Although their environments were very

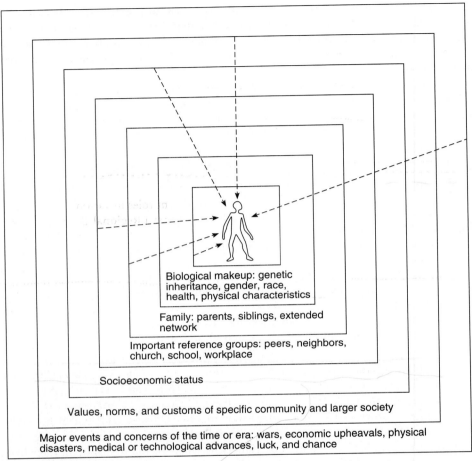

Biological makeup: genetic inheritance, gender, race, health, physical characteristics

Family: parents, siblings, extended network

Important reference groups: peers, neighbors, church, school, workplace

Socioeconomic status

Values, norms, and customs of specific community and larger society

Major events and concerns of the time or era: wars, economic upheavals, physical disasters, medical or technological advances, luck, and chance

FIGURE 3.2   Six sets of forces that shape our actions and attitudes

dissimilar, their DNA—their genes—exerted a remarkable impact on their abilities and personalities.

Learning about the concept of multicausality helps us to understand why so many different strategies are needed to alleviate personal and social problems. It also helps us understand why so much experimentation accompanies any effort to intervene in a social problem. As our understanding of a problem deepens and the world changes, our strategies expand and change.

For example, those who believed that the availability of alcohol was the root cause of alcohol abuse lobbied long and hard to get it outlawed. They succeeded in passing the Eighteenth Amendment to the U.S. Constitution. The Prohibition Act banned the sale of alcoholic beverages all across the United States. Although it appeared to be a logical strategy of intervention, the act was a disaster. Criminals quickly took the place of the alcohol producers, and we had a situation that looked very much like the drug wars that are being fought in the streets of many U.S. towns today. The Prohibition Act was repealed in 1933, and liquor again became widely available. And, once again, it wreaks havoc on family life. Should we try to decriminalize drugs in the same way? What are the pros and cons of doing that? The debate rages on.

Some people are working to make alcohol less available by banning alcohol advertisements, raising the minimum drinking age, and banishing alcohol from campus events. Can you think of five other strategies that might be used in the battle against alcohol abuse?

THE STRATEGIES OF INTERVENTION DEFINED

Although workers use many strategies and assume different roles in various settings, their actions are neither random nor idiosyncratic. The Southern Regional Education Board (1969) surveyed a large number of human service workers in the field. It identified thirteen of the most consistently used worker roles or strategies of intervention. Those roles and strategies have stayed the same from that time to the present, even though many of the problem areas have changed. We added one more, and in Table 3.1 we divided them into three categories: **direct-service strategies**, which deliver services directly to those in need;

direct-service strategies Worker actions that deliver services directly to clients.

An excellent way to increase one's understanding of the world, both as a worker and as a citizen, is to volunteer for a Sister City Project. Members of families in a poor village in Nicaragua work side by side with visitors from the United States to build low-cost, sturdy houses.

TABLE 3.1 Strategies of Intervention

Direct-Service	Both Direct-Service and Systems-Change	Systems-Change
Caregiving	Group facilitating	Planning
Case managing/counseling	Outreaching	Administering
Teaching/training/coaching	Mobilizing	Data collecting and managing
Behavior changing	Advocating	Evaluating/researching
	Consulting	
	Assisting a specialist	

Source: Categories derived from Southern Regional Education Board, 1969.

systems-change strategies Acts aimed at helping clients by creating or improving the organizations that are supposed to deliver services to them.

Disabilities Resource Center (DRC) An office that coordinates the academic support services that enable students with physical, mental, or educational disabilities to pursue their class work.

systems-change strategies, which create, maintain, or change the institutions and groups in which services are delivered; and a middle category of strategies that combines elements of direct-service work and elements of systems-change work. See also Ginsberg (1998) on careers in social work.

The boundary lines that separate one intervention from another and those that divide the direct-service from the systems-change strategies are fluid. A worker might shift from one intervention strategy to another over the course of a week or in the course of an hour. We warn the student that these worker strategies are not brand names like products on a supermarket shelf. Agencies may use them interchangeably or in ways that differ from the way we are defining them. But categories, although imprecise, are useful insofar as they help us visualize the two overarching goals of all human service interventions:

- Helping individuals change their lives
- Helping to improve the environments in which people function

The following interview with the coordinator of the **Disabilities Resource Center (DRC)** at a large university shows Ruth Bork using virtually every one of the direct-service and systems-change strategies. After you have read the descriptions of the strategies that appear after the interview, go back and see if you can identify how she employs each of them in her daily work.

INTERVIEW

Ruth Bork, Administrator, Disabilities Resource Center

It is hard to believe that I've been in this job for over thirty years. I was the first staff member hired, so I had the rare opportunity of starting an agency from the bare walls. My job has grown and changed so much. I work on a variety of levels, from the individual students all the way up to the president's office. Since the passage of the **Americans with Disabilities Act (ADA)**, my job has expanded even more.

My primary task is meeting the special needs for supportive services and accommodations for any student at the university who has a documented disability. This includes students who have significant visual or hearing impairments, problems with mobility, learning disabilities, or psychiatric conditions. Some of the students are permanently disabled from birth or through accident or illness. Some are temporarily disabled.

As my staff has grown, I've delegated more and more of my direct-service work. Now I do a great deal of supervision and administration. I keep one day each week to catch up on all my administrative paperwork but try to keep my contact with the students ongoing. I get much of my job satisfaction from meeting young people and watching them grow in self-esteem and confidence.

Counseling begins from the moment students are accepted. They need help in finding the package of resources that can get them through the class work and social life of a large university. For example, if a student has a mobility impairment, I review his or her program to make sure that the classes needed for his or her major are held in accessible buildings. If they aren't, I get the class moved. I also have to make sure that a student in a wheelchair can get from one part of the campus to another in the class break time. Nothing is worse for the student's morale than to have the class start without him or her or to keep everyone waiting.

Sometimes I advocate with a department chairperson for changes in the student's academic program because a learning disability makes mastering certain subject matter almost impossible. Perhaps a major is very prescribed, requiring certain courses in sequence, but the student can handle only a limited number of courses at one time. The university will have to make an exception. If there is fieldwork, we may have to arrange transportation; if there is a conference with an instructor, the student might need a sign language interpreter.

The DRC hires, trains, and schedules note takers, who sit in on classes and provide the student with a coherent set of notes. We have one staff member whose whole job it is to schedule sign language interpreters and note takers for students with a variety of limitations.

I'll arrange for books to be delivered if the student has a condition such as arthritis and has a hard time standing in a two-hour line at the bookstore. We make sure that the university library has the latest Braille writers and that the dorms are equipped with alarm systems and telephones for the visually and hearing impaired. Our students have a right to anything that gives them a level playing field with the able-bodied students. Equal opportunity means many different things.

Training and teaching the faculty and staff take up a lot of my time. They need to be aware of the needs as well as the feelings of the different segments of the disabled population. I run workshops and conferences. I am available to consult with faculty on individual students in their classes.

The fastest-growing segment of the population we serve is the learning-disabled (LD) students. Their disabling condition is invisible. It requires a lot of consciousness raising to help professors realize that being late or incomplete on an assignment can be part of a biological disability. Many of the LD students take untimed tests in our office, where there are few distractions. Faculty members have to change their mindset from "lazy and unmotivated" to "student who needs organizational support services."

Americans with Disabilities Act (ADA) A congressional mandate that guarantees many rights to people with physical and mental disabilities, especially in the fields of employment and architectural access.

I encourage the students to tell the faculty what their abilities and disabilities are and what it is they need in order to get the most from school. Labels don't tell us much because every student, whatever his or her disability, has a different set of circumstances and personality.

I serve as the adviser to the DSO, the Disabled Students Organization. This is a social group, but more importantly, it is a voice for the students. One voice isn't very loud, but when several are raised all at once, the university pays attention. Sometimes the students win their demands and sometimes they have to compromise, but I still encourage them to make decisions and take action. Now the DSO is protesting because the administration plans to move our office. The new space is larger, but it will be in the subbasement. Some students see that as an insult. They have felt swept under the rug in their own communities, so they want a central location. I don't think they will win this battle, but I think it is worth voicing their opinions.

We also run support groups. These are led by the disabled students, counseling interns, and occasionally a faculty member. These groups help the students to realize that they aren't alone, and the more experienced students can pass on wisdom about the system. Instead of me deciding and telling others what needs to be changed, I can get varied opinions through the groups. They have been catalysts for improvements.

We've been working for many years to make the buildings on campus more accessible. Federal laws require that physical barriers be removed. For example, we now have chair lifts installed in the buildings, so wheelchair riders can go from one level to another. We also have published special maps of the campus so that a new student who uses a wheelchair can quickly learn how to get around. We take the barriers one at a time, and we work on a specific architectural modification. In the older buildings, that is very hard to do.

When I was a student here, the elevator in the main building had heavy doors that had to be opened by hand. This was impossible for a person in a wheelchair or for anyone with a back problem. That elevator has finally been replaced. Ramps have been built, and bathrooms have been modified in all the buildings. Elevators now have Braille numbers on the floor selector panels. Each of these improvements was carefully thought out and took months to accomplish.

I thought that the study of architectural modifications was completed in 1990, but additions to the ADA required us to reassess the campus for barriers. We reconvened a committee to do that. I also serve on several other committees representing the interests of our students. I am on the orientation committee, the student retention committee, and the group that advises the counseling center.

I don't have a disabling condition myself but several of the staff do. They help me to stay sensitive. I also try to keep up with my reading. I've just finished a book on counseling students with learning disabilities (Baumberger & Harper, 2007). It always amazes me how much more there is to learn. Our library is here for any students on campus who want to use it for their research.

I'd like to tell you what a typical day is like, but there is no such thing. A student may come in with a problem concerning a class or an internship. I may get a call from an administrator who wants information on the cost of a chair lift. Lately the university attorney has been struggling with some lawsuits that have been brought by staff members who have disabilities and don't feel they have been treated fairly. As people with psychiatric conditions move into the mainstream, there are more students and staff on campus who present challenges to faculty and administrators. I act as a consultant on those cases.

The problems I deal with range from A to Z—from administrative problems to zero sensitivity. For example, I might advocate on behalf of someone who's living in a building that needs to be made accessible and the landlord wants him or her out of there. So my work isn't contained just within the school. I deal with all the facets of our students' lives if they ask me to.

Networking and referral and resource collecting are important aspects of my work. If a student is having trouble with financial aid, the athletic department, or a roommate, that can be his or her most pressing concern. It needs to be addressed.

Resources for my students are everywhere. For example, I was working with a student who had a head injury from a car crash. She wanted to get involved with other young people like herself. I called around and found a Head Injury Foundation group in the suburbs. There wasn't one in this area, but she collected names of others who were interested. They met and I helped them start a group. I strive to empower people to help themselves and others.

I also have to keep sharpening my administrative skills as the job gets more complex. I have learned how to propose and keep a budget, do annual reports, write memos and action plans, do research, chair meetings, and speak up on behalf of the disabled-student population.

As the civil rights of people with disabilities expand, my office and my job also expand.

DIRECT-SERVICE STRATEGIES

Caregiving

When using a caregiving strategy, the bulk of a worker's time and effort is spent meeting the client's immediate needs. In jobs such as home health aide for the elderly, provider of **respite care** for the family of the physically handicapped child, or counselor in a residence or family planning clinic, the worker gives emotional support and physical care and helps in obtaining additional services. Ruth's office recruits part-time personal care attendants, workers who give direct care by helping a disabled student get ready in the morning, by note taking, or by reading to a student who is blind. They perform caregiving tasks in almost every one of the interventions. Many entry-level jobs in human service require that a large percentage of worker time be spent on caregiving tasks.

respite care
Care in which a paid worker relieves a person who is a primary caretaker so that the caretaker can pursue outside tasks or have some free time.

Case Managing/Counseling

Case-managing and counseling interventions aim at making sure that individuals locate and obtain the services for which they qualify. Vocational rehabilitation agencies, welfare departments, family agencies, hospitals, school systems, children's protective agencies, and large institutions such as city governments or universities employ workers who use these strategies.

Sometimes the worker is referred to as an *ombudsperson*, a Scandinavian word for a professional go-between, a red-tape cutter who carries a person's complaints to the highest authority. Workers who do counseling or case management are assigned a number of clients—a caseload. These workers stay in touch with these people to make sure that services are reaching them. Because entitlements are often buried in many different laws, programs, or agencies, few people can find their way through the maze alone. Human service workers often organize hot lines and special resource centers so that connections can be made between the public and the programs they need.

Although human service workers provide emotional support and assist clients in finding and using services, generally they do not perform the type of insight counseling or therapy done by a more highly trained psychologist or clinical social worker.

Teaching/Training/Coaching and Behavior Changing

In recent years, more and more human service workers have been using teaching/training/coaching and behavior-changing interventions. They prepare clients of institutions or hospitals for an eventual move into a community residence and from there to live on their own. Through role-playing, guided field experiences, modeling, and reward systems, they teach survival skills to people who are physically or mentally disabled. These skills, which include finding and keeping a job, managing money, using public transportation, and enjoying recreational outlets, are called "the skills of daily living."

Such intervention strategies are also employed by public school staff workers as they try to mainstream (integrate) children with special needs into regular classrooms. A special-education worker may go into the home of a family to show parents techniques that will help their developmentally delayed preschooler do routine tasks and prepare for school. The use of an **early intervention program** is increasing in importance with every age group. The government agencies that fund programs have realized that money invested in solving problems early on saves a great deal of money down the line.

Human service workers often train peer leaders or mentors to help in the running of drug and alcohol awareness programs. Ruth uses these interventions when she orients new note takers and tutors or models techniques for faculty members to use when they have a student who is hearing impaired.

early intervention program A program that attempts to deal with a person's (often a child's) problem at the first sign of difficulty.

DIRECT-SERVICE AND SYSTEMS-CHANGE STRATEGIES

Group Facilitating

Traditionally, YMCAs and YWCAs, Scouts, 4-H clubs, Junior Achievement groups, settlement houses, and recreation centers have used group facilitating strategies. Group workers help members develop their leadership qualities, build confidence, and expand their skills and cultural awareness.

In recent years, the use of group techniques has grown beyond the recreational setting. The deinstitutionalization of the mentally ill and physically handicapped has led to the creation of many small, community-based programs. There are social clubs for ex-mental patients, prerelease centers for people completing jail sentences, and group homes for juvenile offenders. Day care programs for preschool children as well as for elderly and disabled adults also use group interventions.

Support groups bring together divorced parents, adult survivors of battering, persons caring for a person with AIDS, compulsive gamblers, overweight individuals, or older women entering the workforce for the first time. Human service workers may facilitate such a group. When an able peer leader emerges, they often withdraw, providing consultation as needed.

Many agencies use groups to orient new clients and volunteers. Some adoption and foster care agencies ask experienced parents to orient prospective ones, just as Ruth asks a junior or a senior to lead a support group for first-year students who share his or her disability.

Outreaching

Because she has learned that she can never simply sit in her office and wait for clients, Ruth has developed many creative outreach strategies. Through meetings, phone calls, and extensive networking, she spreads the message about the DRC's services to members of the university community. She invites them to visit the office and get to know her staff.

Mental and physical health agencies, recreation centers, and both private and government youth-serving agencies often employ outreach workers. They work with youth gang members to reduce inner-city violence. During the summer months, many suburban towns employ college students to monitor the town parks. They mingle with the neighborhood teenagers and try to head off the problems that often develop when teenagers with too much time and money hang out together. After they become accepted by the teens, they can plan recreational programs with these teens.

Outreach workers at day care centers and other early-childhood programs might visit churches and clinics to obtain referrals. They also spend their time sitting in living rooms and around kitchen tables answering questions about their program or sharing educational techniques. Departments of social service use outreach workers—sometimes called "home finders"—to locate and monitor appropriate foster homes for children, teens, and the elderly.

Prevention programs rely a great deal on outreach strategies. Some of you may have encountered a human service worker visiting your high school or Scout troop. Perhaps he or she showed a film and gave a talk to raise awareness about alcoholism, drug abuse, safe sex, or domestic violence. Perhaps the worker was there to recruit volunteers.

Mobilizing and Advocating

There has probably never been a day in the years she has worked at the DRC that Ruth has not heard at least one complaint from a student, a faculty member, or a staff member. Complaints are warning signs that something is not going as well as it should and needs to be improved. Working in a large university, she has often had to mobilize a great deal of clout to smooth out the rough spots. Perhaps a faculty member refused to let a student use a tape recorder even after the student explained why it was necessary. Ruth might have had to go up to the next level of authority, exerting pressure through the department chair, the dean of the college, or the academic provost.

Perhaps parents are futilely demanding that the city park department clean up a rubble-strewn lot so it can be used as a safe play space. They may turn to a human service worker to learn how to mobilize enough citizen pressure to get action.

On a more sophisticated level, perhaps a citizens' task force with a human service staff person is mobilizing public sentiment to exert pressure for the reorganization of an unresponsive school board or police department. Human service workers mobilize the power that brings about change at board meetings, at public forums, in the courts, and occasionally on picket lines.

Consulting and Assisting a Specialist

Some human service workers share their special knowledge and skills with clients, the public, and other professionals. Since July 1992, when the ADA was supposed to be fully implemented, Ruth has been serving on a task force that monitors how well the university is complying with it. If there are problems with an employee who is deaf, she calls on her staff member who specializes in hearing impairments. If there are issues she does not know enough about, the university seeks another consultant.

Professionals from other fields tap the special knowledge of human service workers by organizing interdisciplinary teams. In an adolescent psychiatric unit of a hospital, for example, each patient is assigned a team composed of a doctor, a nurse, and a human service worker. The human service worker generally interviews or visits the family and represents their needs when the team meets to evaluate each patient's progress.

When employed by a government licensing or monitoring board such as the Office of Elder Affairs, human service workers visit nursing homes, for example, to make sure they are providing adequate care. If there are inadequacies, they share their expertise in programming, budgeting, or staff relations.

Some lawyers, doctors, and therapists employ human service workers to act as their eyes and ears with community groups or other mental health professionals. In this role, human service workers are likely to employ any one, or all, of the strategies discussed so far.

SYSTEMS-CHANGE STRATEGIES

Planning

Of course, planning is an integral part of all interventions. But some human service workers develop special expertise in this role. They spend most of their time researching, designing, organizing, monitoring, and evaluating a new or expanded program to fill a gap in the human service network. You are likely to find a planner hard at work in a library, at a computer terminal, or in the offices of foundations and government bureaucracies.

In small agencies such as community residences, all the staff use planning interventions to organize fund-raisers, outings, social events, and volunteer orientations. Ruth started out using mostly counseling interventions, working one on one with each student. But now, as her staff has grown and her expertise has expanded, she has become so adept at planning that she could move into any setting and put together a program proposal to start a new service.

Administering

Although traditional human service agencies and government bureaucracies are most likely to be administered by an experienced staff person with an advanced degree in psychology, medicine, social work, or public administration, newer, small-scale institutions assign staff with human service degrees to administrative roles. Even a recent graduate may be given the job of directing a small program for mothers with AIDS or a shelter for women who have been battered. Although the center may accommodate only five or six women at a time, it requires the same range of skills needed to run a large hospital or school. Money must be raised and accounted for, the facility must be furnished and maintained, forms must be submitted, staff must be recruited and trained, and mailing lists and other clerical details must be completed.

Collecting and Managing Data

If a student at Ruth's university who has broken a leg on a ski trip cannot find out about the services available at the DRC, then the services are worth very little. The mushrooming of human service programs and entitlements on college campuses and in the larger community has led to new methods for finding, assessing, and utilizing resources. Compiling specialized resource booklets and designing web sites that are attractive and accessible require vital human service skills. Keeping a computer updated with information on programs for eating disorders or narcotic addiction enables a counselor at the DRC to make a useful referral.

Laws are constantly changing. They are also written in legal language and are difficult to understand. Human service workers write pamphlets that translate complex legal jargon into standard English. With this information, a mother with a sick child and no money can find out how to apply for Medicaid or file an appeal if she is denied fuel assistance or food stamps.

Evaluating/Researching

Although human service workers are likely to turn to a variety of experts to find statistics and research data, they too must be prepared to carry out a small-scale survey or a web search for up-to-date information on a particular disability or medication.

As community-based programs have become more decentralized, their funding sources have had to work harder to keep track of them. Human service workers need to learn to help design and implement evaluation plans. They collect statistics, interview clients, and write reports of program events. The funding or renewal of a program often depends on how well social workers have assessed client attitudes and needs and kept their services responsive to the population they serve.

At the end of each fiscal year, Ruth submits a budget request for the DRC for the upcoming year. She has been able to document the need for expanded budget and services through her systematic research. In addition, an outside evaluator visits the program each year, and Ruth assigns two staff members to help the evaluator assess student satisfaction with the services of the DRC.

ACTIVITIES AND TASKS USED TO IMPLEMENT EACH STRATEGY

The interview with Ruth Bork showed her using all of the strategies of intervention. What you could not see, however, is the way she goes about implementing them. Whether she is counseling a head-injured student, drafting a plan to remove an architectural barrier in a dormitory, or organizing an orientation meeting for faculty, she proceeds in an orderly way, using the same activities for each intervention.

Seven tasks must be performed in order to implement each strategy of intervention:

1. Gathering data
2. Storing and sharing information
3. Negotiating contracts and assessing problems
4. Building a trusting relationship
5. Designing an action plan
6. Implementing the action plan
7. Monitoring and evaluating the work

A worker always begins by gathering data and ends by evaluating his or her work. Although we have listed these activities and tasks by number, we do not mean to imply that one must be completed before proceeding to the next. In actual practice, several may be done simultaneously. But the message we wish to impress on the reader is that our work is never random. There is an underlying pattern of tasks needed to implement each strategy. If we skip one of the following tasks, we risk a failed intervention.

Gathering Data

Ruth needs to paint the fullest picture possible of each student's problem situation. Yet it is much harder for her to collect relevant information than it would be if she were a biologist or physicist. Many of the data she collects and acts on are at best incomplete and variable. We cannot take a temperature or do a blood test to find accurate information. Sometimes a person's words may be cheerful, but the tone of voice reveals pain. To more fully understand the emotions behind words and to grasp the complexity of each student's situation, Ruth uses many data-gathering techniques. She collects data through conducting interviews, reading, doing research, and attending conferences and workshops. Only after the data have been gathered can she begin to plan how to help each student.

INTERVIEWING

Interviewing underlies all of Ruth's work. The quality of information she gathers before making a plan depends on how skillfully she conducts an interview. The first part of the interviewing process is asking appropriate questions. Through role-playing in a class or a training situation, students develop skill in phrasing questions in a way that avoids steering the listener into a preconceived path or into a verbal trap. Ruth has learned when to ask open-ended questions that provoke maximum expression. She uses focused questions to elicit accurate information about dates, times, and places. She often asks for clarification.

When asking questions and listening to a client's or colleague's thoughts, she uses her active-listening skills. Active listening is distinguished from the more passive kind of social listening by its total concentration. She remembers precisely what has been said and reflects back ideas and feelings to make sure she understands.

Active observing is also part of interviewing. Ruth tries to grasp the full significance of what is being said by assessing the emotional tone of the words as well as by observing facial expressions, hand movements, posture, and gestures—in other words, *body language.*

READING, RESEARCHING, AND ATTENDING CONFERENCES AND WORKSHOPS

Usually some historical records can be gathered before starting an intervention. The counselors at the DRC have access to their clients' test scores and high school grades as well as statements from guidance counselors and doctors. When a new worker is assigned to the Learning Disabled Students' Support Group, notes from past meetings that were compiled by previous group leaders can be useful. Human service workers read whatever background data they can find. But all information has limitations. Records are written by people who have brought their own biases to the recording or testing process.

Much data gathering goes on at case conferences or committee meetings. Sometimes workers do their data gathering at libraries or on the web. In the professional journals, they learn about a research or demonstration project on a particular problem. They go to workshops where clients, coworkers, or professionals from allied fields gather to share information.

An integral part of data gathering is focused visiting and observation. In some programs, this involves visiting the homes, classrooms, or workplaces of clients to gain some firsthand insights into their strengths and weaknesses as they interact with the system. Visiting another program can be a refreshing treat for workers who have been locked into the routine of their own agency.

Storing and Sharing Information

One of Ruth's crucial responsibilities is keeping records. Information is never randomly jotted down. Recording has a purpose, and the DRC workers practice the skills of focused note taking. Professional recordings or minutes separate a worker's personal evaluation or judgment from the observable or verifiable data.

Careful collection and sharing of information is a direct expression of respect for clients and coworkers. It also protects workers from accusations of mismanagement. Ruth needs to document how money has been spent by her staff, and she must keep track of her clients' unmet needs.

Negotiating Contracts and Assessing Problems

Nothing defeats the helping process as much as lack of direction. For each new intervention, Ruth negotiates a working contract, which articulates mutual expectations and the rules of the road with clients, faculty, and colleagues. A contract might be written or verbal, but it must be clear. And it often changes over time as reality shapes goals.

Building Relationships

Ruth begins building a relationship with a student (or faculty member or administrator) from the first moment of contact. She continues to nurture the relationship throughout the helping process. The primary tool all workers must have is their ability to communicate warmth, concern, empathy, and knowledge.

If Ruth cannot gain the trust of students or colleagues, she will be ineffective, no matter what else she is able to do. In each of the strategies, relationship building is critically important. The case manager/counselor must be able to energize and empower people just as much as the agency administrator or researcher.

Designing and Implementing Action Plans

Many social agencies, especially those that receive public funds, require that a formal action plan be written and accepted by client and worker before any services begin. These plans commit to paper the problems, the goals, and the specific ways they will be worked on within a set period of time. Formal written plans are used extensively with special-education services in public schools. By law the school staff, the human service workers, the client (if old enough or competent enough), and the family must all sign a statement that they have been part of the process of deliberation and agree to implement the Individualized Education Plan (IEP).

In programs that employ behavior modification approaches or in which basic survival skills are being taught, Individualized Service Plans (ISPs) help both worker and client be clear about the small tasks that must be worked on from day to day. In Ruth's office, there is a written plan in each student's file. Both the student and the case manager sign the plan and review it periodically.

For a first-year student who has both receptive and expressive language problems, Ruth suggested the following items for her action plan:

1. For the first semester, she will take a reduced load of two courses.
2. A note taker will accompany her to class.
3. Three times a week, she will attend the DRC for skill building with a tutor and three other students.
4. She will continue seeing an occupational therapist twice a month to help her with eye–hand coordination.
5. She will attend two workshops on study skills offered by the counseling and testing center.
6. She will arrange to take some vocational preference tests at the counseling center to help her decide on a major.
7. She will check back in with Ruth three times during the quarter for fifteen-minute sessions to evaluate each of the preceding activities.

To make sure each part of the plan is implemented, Ruth will write a memo to the staff member who schedules tutors, write a letter to the department chair explaining the need for the reduced course load, and send a referral form for testing. During the fifteen-minute check-in sessions, she will offer an attentive ear and a lot of encouragement.

Monitoring and Evaluating the Work

Because individuals, environments, and social interactions are in perpetual motion, human service workers become skilled at critically looking at and reshaping their contracts, relationships, action plans, and methods of implementation. A worker who is in tune with the dynamic state of the problem-solving process is always asking questions: How are we doing? What seems to be getting in the way of X, Y, and Z? Have I fully understood how the client feels about this?

In order to answer these questions, the worker needs to learn how to use a variety of evaluative feedback techniques. Obviously, the client is the primary source of feedback. Workers also use supervision or consultation from more experienced colleagues to check on how their work is progressing.

Sometimes workers administer small survey questionnaires. Case records, statistical data on meetings, referrals, visits, and other daily activities form the basis of evaluation reports or summaries. These reports can then compare one period of time with another, one client group with another, and one intervention strategy with another.

PUTTING TOGETHER THE INTERVENTIONS AND THE ACTIVITIES

Now that we have described the human service interventions and the activities that are used to implement them, the pattern underlying all of Ruth's work should become clear.

Figure 3.3 is a page from Ruth's calendar book that lists the notations that she made about three appointments. On this particular day, she will be using a planning intervention for a meeting with the architects, using a group-facilitating intervention with new faculty members, and using a counseling intervention with a student in crisis.

Figure 3.4 shows the three interventions from the appointment book listed down the left-hand side of the chart. The seven activities Ruth will use to implement each intervention

---

Schedule for Tuesday, September 10th

10:00 A.M.:	Meet with Larry Colring, an architect, to review plans for new fire alarm system for disabled students in Croner Hall.
	(*A PLANNING INTERVENTION*)
12:00–2:00 P.M.:	Lunch meeting—Lead a discussion on teaching students who have documented disabilities. Orientation of new faculty members.
	(*A GROUP-FACILITATING INTERVENTION*)
3:00–4:00 P.M.:	Meet with Margaret Clinton; she has severe asthma and is thinking of dropping out.
	(*A COUNSELING INTERVENTION*)

FIGURE 3.3 Sample calendar

ACTIVITIES NEEDED TO IMPLEMENT THE INTERVENTIONS								
		Gather Data	Store and Share Information	Negotiate Contract	Build Relationships	Design Action Plan	Implement Plan	Monitor and Evaluate
THE INTERVENTIONS	Drafting the plan for the dormitory	Read manuals and visit a college dorm						
	Organizing orientation meeting for faculty	Review results of survey of students attitudes toward faculty behavior in class						
	Counseling a new student	Review admission file; speak to dorm counselor; interview student						

FIGURE 3.4 A model of the activities a worker engages in for each intervention employed. We have filled in the first column. On the left side of this chart, we list three interventions that a worker would likely carry out during the day. Across the top of the chart, we list each of the activities the worker would perform to carry out the interventions. We filled in the activities for gathering data; can you fill in the rest?

are listed across the top. As you can see, she has already begun each of these interventions by gathering data. Of course, what Ruth needs to find out and where she will go to get that information will be different for each intervention.

To collect data for her meeting with Larry Colvin, an architect, Ruth read two manuals on modifications of alarms for the hearing impaired and the blind and visited a college with a building similar to the one they will be discussing.

Before she speaks to the new faculty members about teaching students who are handicapped, she will review the results of a recent attitude survey. Each of the students served by the DRC was asked to describe specific faculty behaviors that encouraged his or her learning and those that hindered it. The faculty members need to hear these statements "from the horse's mouth."

Before she interviews Margaret, she will gather data by looking at the student's admissions file, speaking to the nurse at the health service, and interviewing the dorm counselor who knows her best. She will also tap into her many years of experience to assess the degree of crisis in Margaret's situation.

After she collects the necessary information, Ruth will store it in the form of notes, memos, or other written communication. She will need to file it carefully so it is at her fingertips when she needs it again. Then she will think about the contract she has negotiated with the architect, the faculty group, and the student. What can she do for them? What does each of them expect of her? And so it will continue through each of the activities, until she completes the intervention and evaluates how it has gone and how it might go better next time.

The next time you are assigned a new task in your fieldwork, before you panic, take a deep breath and visualize this chart. Begin to make a list of the background information

Often several human service strategies are combined in one event. These students planned and are now conducting a Valentine's Day flower and cake sale. With the money raised, they will purchase books to use when they volunteer as tutors for women at a local prison.

you will need. The more systematically you proceed in collecting data, the more confident you will be when you negotiate contracts, build relationships, and design and implement your action plans.

The chapters in Section 2 of this book describe the strategies and activities we have just introduced in this whirlwind tour of a human service worker at work.

SUMMARY

1. Solutions to social problems should flow from a diagnosis of the possible causes of the problems.

2. The uniqueness of people and their problems calls for diverse, tailor-made interventions.

3. Strategies of intervention are overall approaches to the helping process that have been identified by studying the tasks that workers do in their daily practice.

4. All of the intervention strategies are necessary and equally important. They are used at different times by the generalist worker. Some workers specialize in a few of the strategies.

5. The fourteen strategies can be divided into those that directly assist the person with the problem and those that maintain or change the systems within which the person interacts and services are delivered.

6. The direct-service strategies are caregiving, case managing/counseling, teaching/training/coaching, and behavior changing. The mixed direct-service and systems-change strategies are group facilitating, outreaching, mobilizing, advocating, consulting, and assisting a specialist. The systems-change strategies are planning, administering, data collecting and managing, and evaluating/researching.

7. The seven worker activities used for each intervention are gathering data, storing and sharing information, negotiating contracts and assessing problems, building a trusting relationship, designing an action plan, implementing an action plan, and monitoring and evaluating an action plan.

8. By looking closely at three strategies of intervention used in Ruth's work as coordinator of the DRC, we can see how she follows a similar pattern, always starting with data gathering and progressing through the other activities that end with monitoring and evaluating the work that has just been done.

DISCUSSION QUESTIONS

1. In the discussion of multicausality, we assert that just as there are no two identical faces in the world (except for same-egg twins), there are no two identical psychological profiles. What might account for the often enormous differences in the personalities and interests of two siblings raised in the same family? For example, one might be an honor student and school council leader, while the other lives for sports and is content to be at the bottom of her class.

2. Ruth Bork provides many services for special-needs students, the largest segment of which is the learning disabled. How fair do you think it is for the "mainstream students" when their LD classmates are given extra time for tests or can have a person take notes for them in class? Discuss the differences between "equal treatment" of students and "equitable treatment" of students.

3. How might you explain to an engineering major the reasons why organizing a bake sale to raise money for a tutoring program is a valid educational experience for a human service class?

WEB RESOURCES FOR FURTHER STUDY

Strategies

When you want further information on any of the strategies discussed in this chapter, you can Google the specific skill or theory you are interested in (e.g. multicausality, interviewing, group work, community organizing). There is a wealth of published material. If you want to know more about a specific field and what is required in the job, the *Occupational Outlook Handbook* of the Department of Labor is a useful source. Here are some specific web sites from that source:

Social workers: www.bls.gov/oco/ocos060.htm

Social and Human Service Assistants: www.bls.gov/oco/ocos059.htm

Probation Officers and Correctional Treatment Specialists: www.bls.gov/oco/ocos265.htm

Disabilities

www.makoa.org

This site is a directory of many kinds of disability resources and links leading to accurate, informative sources. Each disability has several of its own web sites.

Chapter 4

Attitudes/Values, Skills, and Knowledge

If we were to go on an around-the-clock tour of the human service agencies in Urban Center, U.S.A., we might find:

1. A young college student and a middle-aged homemaker hunched over telephones in a church basement, listening with great care to the words of the people on the other end of the lines. One of the callers is a recently widowed elderly man talking about ending his life. The other caller is a frightened teenager pouring out an anguished account of date rape.

2. In a union hall on the other side of town, an articulate, angry woman is holding the rapt attention of her neighbors at the weekly strategy meeting of the Citizens United for Economic Justice. Though she had to quit school after the sixth grade, she is organizing a campaign to raise welfare benefits for the poor people in this community, who have been suffering from a recent upsurge in unemployment. The next speaker has a degree in political science. He is an outreach worker for a legal services program. He explains the intricacies of lobbying at the state house in support of subsidized, affordable health care.

3. In an old but brightly painted two-story house, a young man, a rehabilitation counselor, is teaching a cooking class to four adults. Though totally blind, they are preparing themselves for the day when they will leave this community residence to move into their own apartments.

As we continue our tour, we will meet workers who have a dizzying array of titles, qualities, styles, backgrounds, and motivations. Most typically, they will be working as parts of teams or coalitions that combine laypeople and professionals. They are working as staff members or are serving on committees and boards, sharing their expertise and uniqueness. At times, this mixture of people from different backgrounds is cooperative and supportive; sometimes it is abrasive or adversarial. Often laypeople and professionals work in different ways toward similar goals.

So far we have seen incredible diversity in the roles, titles, agencies, and interventions of the profession. Without a doubt, it is infinitely easier to describe the training of a doctor, a lawyer, a printer, a chemist, or an elementary school teacher. Each draws on a specific body of knowledge and skill. Each works in a limited number of institutions or roles. Usually there are great differences between the abilities of these professionally trained workers and the ordinary "man in the street." We wouldn't feel very safe having our tonsils taken out by a garage mechanic who did a little surgery in his spare time.

This is not true in the human services. The highly trained professional, the person with a recent degree from a community college, a hot-line volunteer counselor who makes his or her living as an insurance broker, and a fellow sufferer in a support group all can play pivotal helping roles.

The fact that many types of people are helpers—caregivers, counselors, organizers, group leaders, and activists—does not make our profession any less dignified or prestigious. In fact, this inclusiveness is its strength.

So, what is it that binds all human service workers together? We think it is the common core of attitudes and values, skills, and knowledge of the helping relationship. Although formal training in college is likely to increase the competence of a human service worker, many people from all walks of life can share some common attributes. Effective helping is both an art and a science. The artistic qualities are definable, but we cannot always teach them in a classroom. Creativity, compassion, and warmth, for example, are attributes a person needs to have before entering a training program.

Let's look first at the helping relationship and its common attributes.

THE PROFESSIONAL HELPING RELATIONSHIP

A key element shared by all human service workers is the **professional helping relationship** they build with their clients. It differs in both structure and content from the purely social relationship.

In our personal lives, we might accompany a friend to a nursing home to lend moral support as he or she visits a dying grandmother. We might take care of a child while his or her parents go out to vote or attend an open-school night. In our professional role, we might talk about a baseball game with the members of a foster parent group before their meeting begins. However much these interactions might seem similar, our friendships and our professional helping relationships are uniquely different, and a competent helper is always aware of this.

> **professional helping relationship**
> A relationship between a worker and client(s) that follows a pattern determined by the goals and ethics of the human service field.

The Structure of the Professional Helping Relationship

Five qualities distinguish the professional relationship from the purely social one.

1. *The professional helping relationship exists for a limited time, whereas friendships might last for many years.* In a professional helping relationship, a time schedule may be agreed on at its inception. For example, a worker and a group of teenagers who are physically handicapped might agree to spend six sessions discussing issues of sexuality. Or a worker in a rehabilitation agency might say: "We shall work together until my client has found a job and seems to have settled into it."

Whatever the duration of the relationship, we commit ourselves to ending the relationship just as soon as the client no longer needs it. We strike a subtle balance between setting someone adrift too soon and hanging on so long that we encourage dependency.*

Saul Alinsky (1969, 1971), a pioneering community activist, always stressed that the human service worker who built a strong neighborhood action group should expect eventually to be thrown out by the indigenous leadership. Once the group members develop skill and self-confidence, they are likely to view the outside professional as excess baggage. Strange as it sounds, the aim of all human service workers is to work themselves out of the professional helping relationship and maybe even out of a job!

2. *The professional helping relationship has a clear focus, whereas friendships have many purposes—some superficial, others profound—most of them vague.* Though the focus of a professional helping relationship may change as it progresses, both client and worker need to agree on an initial set of tasks, stated in action outcomes:

"I am going to this vocational counselor because I want to find a job so I can leave the residential treatment center and be on my own."

or

"I came to Renewal House because I need a safe shelter from my husband, who has been beating me. As soon as I find an apartment, get some legal help, and sort out my finances, I will move out."

or

"I work for the Children's Protective Services and have been asked by your son's teacher to visit you to see if you can use any of our services for families."

negotiate a contract To forge an agreement between a helper and a helpee about what will be included in their work together.

The helper and helpee **negotiate a contract** in which tasks and goals are spelled out. Some of these initial goals are likely to change. Sometimes the contract is a grudging one. Perhaps the client has been forced to see the worker in order to earn extra privileges on the locked ward of a mental hospital or to gain early release from prison. (The concept and skills involved in contracting are discussed more fully in Pincus and Minahan, 1973; Shulman, 2008; Zayas and Katch, 1989.)

3. *The professional helping relationship depends on a division of labor.* Although friends often complement each other in many ways, the division of roles and responsibilities in a social relationship is random. The professional helping relationship is a collaboration, but each of the parties has specified tasks. The person being helped shares expertise about the problem—basic facts as well as fears, hopes, and expectations. The helper shares knowledge of resources, alternative strategies, obstacles, and the prospects of different courses of action. Each has the right to make certain decisions. Whenever possible, most of the decisions should be made by the client, who must live with the decisions.

---

*Unfortunately, in an age of managed care and cost cutting, forces outside our own reasoned judgment may decide when the professional helping relationship must terminate. This will be discussed further in Chapter 9.

4. *The professional helping relationship is disciplined, whereas in a friendship each person is relatively free to act on impulse.* Of course, friends learn what to do and what to avoid if they want their relationship to last. In the professional helping relationship, much of the informal trial and error is replaced by a set of operating principles.

Even when the human service worker appears to be horsing around in the locker room with the basketball team member or drinking coffee with his or her parents, he or she is behaving in a conscious manner. Workers can relax, but they cannot lose track of the tasks that need to be done. The role of the worker is not to solve the clients' problems but to be a catalyst in the problem-solving process.

Even in informal settings, everything the client says must be kept confidential. Throughout the book, we will discuss the realistic difficulties in maintaining absolute **confidentiality**. But as a general principle, workers accept this basic tenet of the helping relationship.

Although a recreation leader might have a splitting headache or a devastating family problem, on the job his or her personal issues take a back seat. Disciplined workers can, to an amazing degree, ignore their own illness or personal troubles when working. Afterward, in the privacy of their own homes, these irritants might resurface, as annoying as ever.

5. *The professional helping relationship is built on acceptance.* A friendship without some degree of mutual attraction is likely to end as soon as a more appealing companion comes along. A professional helping relationship, however, is not built primarily on mutual attraction. Without judging (or perhaps even liking) a client, the worker tries to understand the person's problem, accepting feelings without necessarily condoning specific acts. Of course, if a worker cannot emotionally connect on any level with the essential humanness of a client's predicament, the client should probably be reassigned to someone else (Keith-Lucas, 1972).

From the helpee's point of view, physical or intellectual attraction may make a counseling relationship more pleasant, but the ultimate success of the relationship will be gauged by how much help was received in overcoming the helpee's problems.

confidentiality
Secrecy of information that a client reveals to a worker.

The Content of the Professional Helping Relationship

Although the structure of the professional helping relationship sets the stage for competent human service intervention, its content—words and actions—is, of course, most important. Figure 4.1 illustrates the three components of this content.

These three components are the threads that bind all human service workers into a profession, whatever their title, label, or academic certification. *Attitudes* are feelings or thoughts about people or things; *values* are the worth we place on them. A person might be described as warm and outgoing; these traits are expressions of attitude. How important others think these qualities are depends on how high or low a value they place on such personality traits.

It is not always easy to separate attitudes and values from skills and knowledge. All are inextricably interwoven in our work. We will separate them into categories only because it is easier to describe them that way.

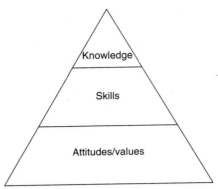

FIGURE 4.1   The pyramid model of the components of the helping relationship

THE PYRAMID MODEL

Professionals in every field require a combination of attitudes and values, skills, and knowledge, a constellation that has been dubbed the "ASK" concept (Schulman, 2008, Sue). In Figure 4.1, we represent the three components in the form of a pyramid. Any professional who lacks one of these components will be less than satisfactory. For example, a doctor who is a brilliant diagnostician (skills and knowledge) but also is cold and brusque (attitude) and lacks a comforting bedside manner might slow down the patient's recovery. The race-track driver who has the bravado to compete (attitude) but has not carefully studied the engine in his new car (knowledge) is likely to lose the race or have an accident.

Of course, the constellation of specific attitudes and values, skills, and knowledge varies from one profession to another. Those of the engineer, for example, are very different from those of the typical human service worker. Vocational preference tests are constructed on the assumption that by studying the attitudes and values of members of occupations, a profile of the typical worker can be constructed. As students answer questions about their attraction or repulsion to different ideas or activities, they move closer to the norms of one occupation and further away from others.

Not only do the attitudes and values, skills, and knowledge areas vary from one occupation to another, but so too does the relative importance of each dimension. For example, in the training of doctors, knowledge and skill are stressed the most. That annoying doctor who lacks an empathetic bedside manner (attitude) can still be elected to high office in a medical society for his or her brilliance as a diagnostician. He or she's even likely to be sought out by anxious patients willing to put up with gruffness as the price of being cured.

With human service workers, however, all three dimensions have equal weight. Their work is very holistic, perhaps more so than any other profession. But each component of their work must be built on the base of appropriate attitudes and values.

For example, it is possible for a guidance counselor to be knowledgeable but be of no help to a student. Perhaps you have met Mr. Schroder. He knows all about college requirements and the Scholastic Aptitude Tests (SATs). But if he does not have the warmth to relax that shy, inarticulate student sitting before him, he may never find out what Eric really wants to do after graduation. Lacking empathy and insight (attitudes and values), he doesn't sense Eric's ambivalence about going to college. He rambles on. Eric barely hears him and will soon forget what he has been told. Mr. Schroder never notices that although Eric has ostensibly come for college counseling, he wants to take time off from school but is worried about hurting his parents.

Or consider Ms. Jorgensen, who announces to Alice at the start of their interview that her record indicates that she "isn't college material" or that "girls shouldn't go into airplane mechanics because it is a man's field." All Ms. Jorgensen's well-meaning advice about the advantages of secretarial school will fall on deaf ears. Alice withdraws, feeling labeled and pigeonholed. Perhaps she does need to think more carefully about her choices, but the abrupt judgment thrust on her by the guidance counselor is a setback to the vocational exploration that needs to get done.

These two workers giving vocational counseling do not show a grasp of key attitudes and values. They have not analyzed their stereotypes about the ideal college student or the proper occupational roles for women. They have not spent time getting to know the unique person who sits across from them. By not being self-aware and sensitive, they are likely to continue to discourage other students. Perhaps a young woman yearns to be a doctor or carpenter or a young man has an intense but self-conscious interest in nursing or early childhood education. How might they react to judgment-laden advice from counselors who are unaware of their own biases?

Attitudes and Values Form the Base of the Pyramid

Human service education and work must always start from a solid base of appropriate attitudes and values. On that base, knowledge and skill can then be added. Some people argue that human service work is based much more on profound faith than it is on theory and skills. The late Paul Halmos (1966), a British sociologist, carefully analyzed the literature of the field of counseling and concluded that:

> The literature of counseling is an inspired literature as much as it is a scientific one, and even in their ascetic disowning of inspiration the counselors testify to an inspired dedication. . . . They use a language of reverence, and even a theological language and imagery, as if they could not do their job effectively without their evocative power. . . . The counselor applies himself in a way which suggests a set of convictions, a powerful mood, a moral stance, a faith. (pp. 6–7)

Halmos went on to assert that counselors seemed rather ashamed of subscribing so outspokenly to humanistic values and relying so heavily on them. They feared that this might make their theory seem less scientific. He urged them not to feel shame but to be proud to be the bearers of those values.

Although attitudes form the base of the pyramid, they are not in themselves sufficient to help the person who must take the next steps in solving the problem. The worker at the local mental health agency who is filled with empathy (attitude) for the family of a recently blinded child might be able to give appropriate emotional support, but if she does not know how to find the best resources for the education, recreation, and rehabilitation of children who are blind (skills and knowledge), she won't be of much assistance.

Bruno Bettelheim, an eminent psychologist, underscored this point in the title of his landmark book on working with disturbed children: *Love Is Not Enough* (1950). He asserted that human service work, like effective parenting, involves love coupled with wisdom and the skills to communicate both.

The pyramid concept is especially important to understand as you begin your training. Most human service educators visualize the pyramid in their minds even if they do not draw this diagram for their students. Their teaching style assumes that the starting point is attitudes and values. They often use first names, encourage students to share their backgrounds, sit in a circle, and stimulate discussion to elicit students' ideas on controversial topics. Although they are using a method of interaction aimed at helping class members sharpen their self-awareness and self-confidence, students sometimes worry that the class is not academic enough. One faculty member expressed her surprise at the students' hesitant reactions to her teaching style.

At each class session, I would come into the classroom hoping to find the students buzzing to each other about their fieldwork or the controversial speaker we'd heard the day before. Instead, they'd be sitting seats apart from each other in the vastness of the lecture hall. They waited for me to start, as if nothing could happen among them until I arrived. Every day I'd insist they get up, push the tables to the side, and form the chairs into a circle. Although they were much more animated when sitting in a circle, they still seemed to view the furniture moving as a pointless waste of energy. They resisted, and I got frustrated. I felt that they did not believe that listening to each other's ideas and experiences was an important part of their education.

After that disappointing semester, I got the idea of starting off my first class with a discussion of the attitudes/values, skills, and knowledge pyramid. Once the students understood that we were exploring the attitudes and values at the base of the triangle—as we played name games or argued about capital punishment—they stopped worrying about memorizing my words to repeat for the final exam. They even stopped resenting the work involved in moving chairs into a circle.

These students realized, as we hope you do, that without a firm, broad base, a pyramid will topple over!

ATTITUDES/VALUES, SKILLS, AND KNOWLEDGE: AN OVERVIEW

Table 4.1 lists the attitudes and values, skills, and knowledge areas that are of vital importance to the professional helper. We have already warned you that the categories are bound to overlap. In addition, our list is neither definitive nor exhaustive. Your course instructor or field supervisor is likely to say of us, "They have missed this vital concept or given too much importance to that one."

It is easy to understand differences in emphasis. If you compare the catalogue description of the program you are enrolled in with a similar one at another college, you will probably find much variation in the courses offered and the competencies stressed. Because human service programs are relative newcomers on most campuses, they have grown out

TABLE 4.1   The Content of the Helping Relationship

Attitudes/Values	Skills	Knowledge

Patience	Data gathering
	    Interviewing—active looking,
	    listening, and question asking
	    Observing
	    Researching
	    Attending conferences
	    Visiting
		Human growth and development

Empathy		Abnormal growth and development
Self-awareness		The impact of society and culture on behavior
Capacity to deal with ambiguity and take risks		The dynamics of groups and organizations

Willingness to ask for help and offer feedback	Storing and sharing information
	    Keeping records
	    Writing reports
		The social and political forces that affect helping

Belief in people's and systems' capacity to change	Building relationships	Social problems, special populations, and resources
Open-mindedness, skepticism, and rejection of stereotypes	Negotiating contracts	Issues of research and evaluation
	Forming action plans	

Humor and a light touch	Implementing action plans
	    Intervening
	    Referring	

	Monitoring and evaluating
	    Giving and receiving feedback
	    Constructing evaluations	

of, or remain under the wing of, more established behavioral fields. They take their coloration from the particular academic department that gave them life. If the program is under the wing of the Psychology Department, the course content stresses counseling and interpersonal skills, whereas course work emphasizing social, cultural, and institutional elements of mental health and treatment might take a backseat.

The reverse is true of the programs that the authors of this book have taught in. Our academic backgrounds are more sociological. We stressed social change, social welfare policy, and group and community interventions.

Whatever their predominant focus, most human service programs incorporate many dimensions of human behavior and use methods that provoke active learning of concepts and skills.

Before reading the descriptions of human service attitudes and values, skills, and knowledge, rest assured that no human service worker ever masters all of them. Each of us understands, accepts, or integrates some areas better than others. As challenges occur, such as a new job or an unusual situation, we stretch ourselves to learn more, sharpen our skills, and explore the impact of our attitudes and values on our current tasks.

Most of us are likely to change direction several times in our careers. Sometimes the change is a response to political upheaval; sometimes it is a move to renew ourselves and avoid burning out as work becomes too draining. We may have counseled individual clients for many years and then discovered that we enjoy managing or planning an agency. Some workers start their careers by doing recreation with children who have disabilities and then later engage in advocacy with the elderly or with troubled families.

Our beliefs about the value of people of differing classes, ethnic groups, ages, and genders begin early. These nursery school children are learning to respect varying lifestyles by taking trips around the city and being exposed to differences and similarities in the families and cultural backgrounds of their classmates.

In order to make the components of the model less theoretical, let's look at the work of John Torrente, a counselor at Sanctuary House. As you read about his work, see how many elements of attitudes and values, skills, and knowledge you can identify.

INTERVIEW

John Torrente, Outreach Counselor at Sanctuary House, a Shelter for Teenagers

Sanctuary is just what its name implies. It is a safe haven. Many of the teenagers have run away from their parents' homes. Maybe there was some abuse or they felt no one wanted them around. A few are running from the consequences of some of their own antisocial actions. Some have left—with or without permission—from foster families, institutions, or community residences. There are as many stories as there are kids. You learn early on that you can't judge in advance why they left and how justified it was.

A few of them have had jobs and places to live, but something went wrong. Maybe they broke up with their lovers or their roommates, or the rent got raised and they had to leave. They come from all income brackets, races, and religions.

I am one of six outreach counselors at Sanctuary. This is my second year on the full-time staff. I go to college part time during the day. I've been working on and off at the house for four years. I began as a volunteer when I was in high school as part of a community service club. I used to go one evening a week with some of my classmates, and we would help to cook dinner. In our high school, we put on dances to raise money and ran raffles and things like that.

Because of my excitement about the house, my father got involved, too. He is now on the board of directors. He's an accountant, so he helps a lot. My mom and my girlfriend also volunteer here. My mother works in the thrift shop, and my girlfriend comes with me when she is home from college.

It's easy to get hooked on this place. The woman who runs it is a sister from a Catholic religious order. She doesn't fit any of the stereotypes of a nun, though. She is one tough cookie and she has seen it all; nothing shocks her. She is a human dynamo who manages to rev us all back up again when everything looks particularly hopeless. She is a genius at wheedling money and donations out of people. It's mostly because of her that the house has grown so phenomenally. It started in a small storefront in Highland Heights, then moved to a big private house. Now we are located right in the middle of the downtown section in what was once a fancy hotel.

Starting out with three cots in 1983, we now can sleep about seventy teenagers, mostly in two-bedded rooms. In the middle of February, when it gets incredibly cold on the streets, we usually put up about twenty more young people in a dorm-style arrangement in what was once the ballroom of the hotel.

To do my kind of work, you have to be a night person. I start at about 8:30 or 9:00 P.M. three nights a week and work straight through until maybe 6:00 in the morning. Then I'm on a day shift one day over the weekend. The staff goes out in pairs, a male and a female, looking for kids who need shelter. Two teams cover the train station, the bus depot, and once in a while the airport.

We know the sections of town where the kids gather. They go in and out of the bars and fast-food places in what we fondly call "the combat zone." That's the district for cheap hotels, dirty book stores, and X-rated movie houses. We're always looking for the new kids. These are the ones who have recently left their homes. They are trying to hook up with somebody for a bed and a meal. We spot them in the Greyhound bus terminal. They are hanging around the fringes of the groups of kids who congregate there to socialize. They usually don't have much luggage, no one meets them, and they seem hesitant. We try to make a quick assessment and then start talking to them. If we've guessed right and they have some kind of problem, we try to get them to come back to the house with us. Noreen, the nun I mentioned, welcomes them, gives them a meal, and tries to find out what's going on.

Noreen never pressures the kids. If they don't want to talk, that's okay. They don't even have to tell us their names. Noreen and the other counselors let them know that what matters to us is that they are safe. When and if they are ready to trust us enough to tell us what pressured them to leave home, then we'll see what can be done. Sometimes kids open up the first night, and it will all come pouring out. They'll call their folks or the place they ran away from, and we'll put them on a bus home. There is a national program run by one of the bus companies that guarantees passage back home to any runaway kid if an agency verifies his or her story.

We try to assess the situation they came out of. If they tell us there was physical or sexual abuse, we let them know that they have options. They can stay for a while at Sanctuary House or find a shelter back in their own communities. No kid, no matter what he or she might have done, deserves to be hurt so badly that he or she has to run away. Sometimes we'll call an agency for them in their hometown and a counselor will meet the kid's bus and start working with the kid and family. Often the counselor calls a priest, rabbi, or a friend who'll meet the kid's bus when they get home. When kids first run away, they often think there is no other solution. Maybe we can help them see that there are people in their own communities who can help them. Maybe then they can slowly move back home.

It's possible, though, that what they were running away from isn't much safer than roaming the streets after dark in this town. A lot of the parents seem like very troubled people themselves. Of course, some seem like ordinary folks who are going out of their minds with worry and facing marital or employment problems of their own. We never meet most of the parents, and we very rarely hear how things worked out, so all of this is guesswork.

If it seems kids are deep into alcohol or drugs, we'll invite them to stay for the night and then link them up with a rehabilitation program the next day. We can't handle teens with active substance abuse problems at Sanctuary. It seems like a contradiction to say we are there for the kids and then reject some of them, but Sister Noreen learned early on that if the house was filled with drugs, then no one was safe.

The streetwise kids can often describe some sobering realities to the newcomers, but the reverse can also be true. Sometimes kids who have been out on the streets teach the new kids survival techniques we wish they wouldn't learn. We run groups every night in which we encourage the more mature teenagers to help the newcomers find safer solutions. Sometimes they'll take advice more readily from another kid than from an adult. Facilitating the group sessions is a tricky job, but when they work well, they are very effective interventions.

We tap into a broad network of services. If kids are determined to make it on their own, we can refer them to programs where they can complete their high school education. We also have counselors who try to find foster homes for them in their home city if that seems appropriate. We try everything we can to keep them from making a life on the streets.

Sometimes, though, life on the streets seems exciting and romantic to them, especially at first. You can make a quick buck and there are no adults around to tell you what to do. Once they are out there a while, they often change their minds. After a while, though, it's hard for them to leave. We have a saying around here that after two or three months on the street, "you can't go home again." In even that short time, the kids have seen so much human degradation and done so many things just to survive that they are not kids anymore. They feel like they wouldn't fit in with their friends back at their high school. They are often too embarrassed to face their relatives.

If a kid has already been on the streets for a while, sometimes he or she develops serious health problems. We have a clinic at Sanctuary and contacts with local doctors who volunteer to see our kids. Sometimes a young woman thinks she is pregnant. Often that's the case. Many of the kids pick up sexually transmitted diseases. They even have dental problems that have grown outrageously from being neglected.

The constant problem for us is that there are plenty of other people around the terminals and on the streets who have things to offer the kids. The pimps are doing some of the same things we are. They're also trying to spot the greenhorns. But they offer them a hot meal and a bed along with a line of cocaine. Their offers come with plenty of strings attached. They will be just so generous to the kids until they have the kids in their debt, and then they show the kids how to "repay." Usually it's by turning tricks, a young woman or young man having sex with a "john." The kids have to give the pimps a large part of the money they earn through prostitution. A recent article about teen runaways in the *New York Times* (Urbina, 9/27/09) cited the research that indicated that nearly a third of the children who flee or are kicked out of their homes each year engage in sex for food, drugs, or a place to stay. The problem of prostituted children just keeps growing, especially as the Internet has made finding clients easier.

Other people are offering the kids a chance to pick up money delivering drugs and running illegal betting slips. It's hard for us to compete with the kind of money these kids can make. At first, money means independence, not having to go back to a home that they hated or to grown-ups who order them around. But in the end, they trade one kind of confinement for a worse one.

Sometimes I go out with the Sanctuary van. It's a soup kitchen, infirmary, and office. Most nights we have a volunteer nurse. We park in a location where a lot of street kids congregate. There is an area down by the docks that is used as a pickup spot by men who want to buy teenage boys for sex. They come driving in from the suburbs. They have their suits and ties on like they just came from work. Sometimes they arrive in their work trucks. You wonder what is going on with their families while they are down here. They look over the line-up and invite a kid into their car, go off for an hour, and then bring the kid back to the dock.

We offer the kids coffee, medical help, and conversation. If they want to go back to the center for the night, we drive them there. You have to be careful not to pressure them or they just avoid you. If they think you will call the cops every time you see something illegal, they won't tell you anything.

Of course, we have limits as to what we can ignore. If we think they have a weapon, it's always a judgment call. Can you get them to give it to you? Do you call the police? If you do, will the word get out and then will all the other kids stay away from the van? It's never easy. You need to be a good listener, try not to judge them, and take it one step at a time.

One night a week I spend at the house just playing around with the kids who are living there. When they are there for a while, we try to get them into a job or further education. We have link-ups with programs that train young people in computers. One kid is going to a community college. We have a terrific volunteer who teaches kids to lay carpets. He has gotten four of them decent-paying jobs.

The night I spend at the house I lead a rap group. We have a women's group to talk about special issues that concern them. We have a group for kids who have been sexually abused and a young parents club that some kids continue to attend even after they've left the house. I also work with the house council. We try to get the guests to take responsibility for running parts of the house.

I love the work, but I can see signs that I'm beginning to burn out. You have to focus on small successes. You can't think in absolute terms, like this kid went home and everything worked out fine. Life isn't that simple. The thing that keeps me going, in addition to Noreen, is the rest of the staff. We do a lot of social things together and rally around each other when there is a crisis. We are always celebrating someone's birthday or graduation or thirty days of sobriety.

I finish my courses next May. I think I want to get a master's degree in counseling. I'd like to get more skill working with groups of kids. I think maybe I will work in a high school. If adults could help teenagers talk about their problems before they get so serious, we could prevent runaways, the date rapes, and depression, as well as teen suicides and the outbreak of violence.

I'm doing my senior seminar paper on teenage kids who are in crisis—runaways, suicides, addicts, etc. I'm looking at what it is that causes such serious problems and what teachers, counselors, and parents can do to try to head it off before kids hurt themselves or others. I've just finished two books that really impressed me. The one about boys and what society often does to help mess them up is entitled *Raising Cain: Protecting the Emotional Life of Boys* (Kindlon & Thompson, 2000),* and the one about the pressures that girls experience is called *Reviving Ophelia: Saving the Lives of Adolescent Girls* (Pipher, 1998). Those recent school shootings were horrifying, but frankly, they didn't come as a surprise to many of us who work with troubled kids. We see those isolated, unhappy kids every day.

*See also Canada (1998); Evans, Fitzgerald, and Frantz (2000); Guetzloe (1999); Jenson and Howard (1999); Sheldrick (1999); Sourander, Heltstela, Helenrus, and Pina (2000); and Szyndrowski (1999).

ATTITUDES AND VALUES OF THE HUMAN SERVICE WORKER

Patience

The worker who thrives in this field understands and accepts how slow, painful, and awesome change is. John Torrente sometimes feels annoyed when kids refuse the services he offers them. Sometimes he'll spend three or four nights without any of the kids on the docks coming back to the house. He's faced disappointment many times when a kid has dropped out of a job program or has broken his sobriety. But usually he manages to control his impatience. He sets small, achievable goals, taking comfort in any signs of progress.

When the frustration with two steps forward and one step backward becomes too overwhelming, he heads for a gym and works out. He spends time talking with his supervisor, and sometimes he asks to change his job assignment for a while. When he is really feeling burned out, he finds that raising funds for the house, instead of doing direct work, can renew his energy.

No matter how slow or discouraging the change effort, the effective worker deflects feelings of impatience away from the clients. They can't be punished for the worker's often justifiable sense of frustration.

We also need to be patient with ourselves. Our skills seem so inadequate when we watch young people nightly put themselves and others in danger and we cannot stop their downward slide. Rarely do we know all the facts; seldom can we control the many forces buffeting our clients. We have no magic solutions.

John has had to divest himself of the rescue fantasies he had when he came to Sanctuary. But as he learns to accept his own and his clients' limitations, he must also guard against drifting into callousness or complacency. He has seen kids and parents change, and he knows that his agency can make a difference.

Human service workers walk a tightrope between *what is* and *what might be* and between the reality of the moment and a vision of change for the better.

Everyone can find a way to contribute his or her energy to improve the lives of his or her fellow citizens. These middle school young people are helping to clean up a local park as one of the many volunteer projects their club takes on.

Empathy

John tries hard to understand the difference between *sympathy,* feeling sorry for another person, and **empathy**, putting oneself in the shoes of another. Needless to say, no worker can ever really know precisely what it is like to occupy someone else's skin. It is especially hard when that other person is of a different race, gender, or age or has a different set of abilities (see Rivera & Erlich, 1995; Schram, 1971, Sue, 2005). But he tries hard to see the world as it might look through a set of eyes very different from his own. Empathy is a path we walk, not a destination we can ever be sure we have reached.

Empathy requires a finely tuned, intuitive sensitivity to other people, the kind that one finds in good fiction or poetry. Sometimes as we read a novel, hear a song, or look intently at a great painting, we have an amazing moment of recognition. We see our own thoughts reflected and are surprised that someone can touch us so deeply. It is this profound understanding of the human condition, with its complex and ambivalent emotions, that explains why the plays of William Shakespeare, written in the late 1500s and early 1600s, can still bring tears to our eyes today.

Small empathetic moments occur in the simplest of situations. On the playground, a group leader instinctively feels the momentary distress of a little boy who dropped his lollipop in the mud. He had licked it until it fit precisely into the roof of his mouth. Understanding the seemingly minor but significant disappointments of childhood, the

empathy
An attempt to put oneself in the shoes of another person, to feel or think of a problem from another perspective.

worker does not rush in to offer a new lollipop, nor does he dismiss the tears as overreacting. He simply puts his arm around the child's shoulders and says, "What a shame that it fell!" Then perhaps they can try to find another treat.

To sharpen empathetic understanding, John taps the well of his own experiences. He hasn't been an alcoholic, but when he's counseling a compulsive drinker, he remembers how it felt when he tried to stop overeating, quit smoking, or disengage from an unhealthy love affair. Although he has never been discriminated against because of his race or religion, he can recapture the feelings of impotence he felt as a young child being unfairly scolded by his parents or teachers. He is not severely physically disabled but can remember a time when a broken arm or sprained ankle kept him from joining the gang for bike riding or playing ball.

All of us have distant memories of shoplifting, skipping school, lying, or disappointing our parents through fear, ignorance, or peer pressure. These memories can help us avoid rushing in to judge harshly a person with whom we are working.

The famous therapist Carl Rogers listed empathy as one of the three vital counselor attributes that can lead to positive change. The other two are nonpossessive warmth and genuineness (Rogers, 1951). These three attitudes are important in all major counseling theories. In fact, there is accumulating evidence that therapy is effective only when these attitudes are present at high levels, no matter what the particular school of psychology or counseling method used (Davis, 1994; Okun, Fried, & Okun, 1999; Nystul 2010, Truax & Carkhuff, 1967; Truax & Mitchell, 1971).

> The empathetic counselor must see beyond conventional facades, refrain from imposing personal interpretations and judgments, and be willing to risk understanding another person's private logic and feelings, which in superficial daily contacts the counselor might view as weak, foolish, or undesirable. (Hammond, Hepworth, & Smith, 1977, p. 3)

This kind of "unconditional positive regard" that flows from empathy may seem impossible:

> It may seem that we are requiring of the helping person a kind of "freeing love" which is a high spiritual quality unlikely to be possessed by a normally fallible human being.

Empathy, rather than judgment, is a key human service attitude. These college students learned that prisons offer few educational opportunities that might improve the prospects of inmates when released. They decided to collect used books, read request letters from prisoners, and send them packages of donated books.

In one sense this is true. It is only this kind of concern and the empathy which springs from it which brings the apparently impossible command to love one's enemies within the realm of practicability. It is only by transcending like and dislike that one could possibly "love" those one "dislikes." (Keith-Lucas, 1972, p. 107)

To test the strength of this value in yourself, consider how you would be able to work with a man who had murdered his own child. On most people's scale of values, that crime may be the most reprehensible. Could you work with such a man without being repelled by him?

A French filmmaker in the 1950s considered this question in a film called *We Are All Murderers*. At the time the film was made, France had the death penalty and executed people by using the guillotine. A man was charged with murdering his own baby and confessed to the crime. Unemployed, he lived with his wife and baby in a tiny, cramped apartment. The baby cried constantly. The man was profoundly depressed by not being able to care for his family. He cracked under the stress and hit his baby. He did not intend to kill the child, but he did. He was convicted of murder and sentenced to death. The film raised the issue of individual guilt as opposed to the guilt that society must share in the provocation of such a crime.

Many times John has wondered how he would act if he had been the child or parent in one of the many hair-raising stories he has heard at Sanctuary House. Sometimes he even wonders what he would do if he found himself sexually attracted to young boys. Would he sneak down to the pier to buy sex in the dead of night? How would he feel on the drive back to his suburban home? Often he finds himself saying, "There, but for luck and chance, go I!"

Self-Awareness

John is genuinely fascinated by his reactions to the things he sees around him. He constantly wonders about the complex forces that have shaped these feelings. He has had to be willing to reexamine all of his attitudes and values. How does he feel about money, work, marriage, war, sex, homosexuality, and abortion? Each of his opinions has been challenged by things he has seen and heard. He has been provoked to explore whether the attitudes and values transmitted by his family are still valid for him.

John has had to find the courage to talk openly about emotion-laden topics such as rape and suicide. He believes that each woman should have a right to choose what to do about her body, so he supports legal abortion. Sister Noreen opposes it on religious and ethical grounds. They have agreed to disagree with each other on that topic. Both positions are defensible, but they must be openly acknowledged. If they are kept underground, they can direct or constrict the clients' own exploration of possible courses of action.

Effective human service workers need to be clear about where their own and their clients' problems overlap. Many young workers, for example, are still separating from their parents. When working with teenagers, these workers have to be alert to keep their own anger or ambivalence about dependence from influencing the way their clients feel or react toward their families.

The most important part of self-awareness is being able to sketch an increasingly accurate portrait of one's own strengths and weaknesses, likes and dislikes. John has been learning how to say, "I can do that task very well, but I don't feel competent in doing some other task. I need help."

Some of us can work with exquisite patience with a multidisabled person; others enjoy the liveliness of healthy children in a recreation center. Some workers cannot tolerate the slowness of the elderly infirm; others thrive on working with that population. The ability to live with other people's emotions and express our own is not something most of us can do automatically. We may need to undertake some personal-development work in this area. Nichols and Jenkinson (2006), in discussing the preparation of support-group leaders, help workers assess their readiness. They suggest that you think about these questions:

- Do you think that you are aware of and open to the flow of feelings in your daily life? Do others confirm this to be so?
- Are you able to say that you value your own feelings and allow their expression rather than strive to mask them?
- Are you able to share your feelings with a trusted companion without being defensive?
- Are you able to receive and experience the painful feelings of others in a relaxed, accepting manner without wanting immediately to placate, soothe, or distract them from expressing those emotions?
- Do you believe that if a person expresses or acts out feelings in a group, you will be able to allow this to unfold without needing to take control and return the discussion to more matter-of-fact issues?

Finally, John tries to set limits on himself by learning his warning signals of fatigue and frustration so he can keep from burning out. Because they care profoundly, many of the staff members at Sanctuary House pay no attention to all the extra hours they work. But they cannot afford to neglect their own support network of friends and family. Ultimately, they serve the teenagers best if they nurture themselves.

Capacity to Deal with Ambiguity and Take Risks

None of us is comfortable with ambiguity. Uncertainty creates tension. Yet John has come to understand that when working with people, one is never sure of what has gone on in the past or will happen in the future.

The young people he works with are so complex that there can be no guarantees that a "correct" action will produce the "right" results. The expression "the operation was a success but the patient died" is often true in the human services.

When working with the general public, there are many unknowns. Last month John organized a community meeting for prospective volunteers. He took enormous care with all the details. He double-checked the invitations for accuracy and clarity, made sure the meeting place was conveniently located, brought refreshments, arranged for child care, got a good speaker on the topic of runaway youth, and then waited expectantly for the crowd that never came. There were probably twenty different reasons so few people showed up. One person had a household emergency, another got tickets to a World Series game. Everyone had a reason for not attending that seemed legitimate to them. So John swallowed his disappointment and did the best job he could with the few volunteers-to-be who attended the meeting. Next month he will try again.

Often John must close the book on a child's problem without being able to read the last chapter. How can he know if the addicted teenagers he worked so hard with for so long will stay off drugs for six months, one year, or a lifetime? Usually the staff loses track of the young people after they leave the program. When a young person returns to her family in a distant city, John often wonders if she was able to talk out the disagreement that made her run away. But he will probably never find out.

John has to act with very little and very inaccurate background information. Sister Noreen has been around homeless youth a long time and has sharpened her ability to distinguish the drug abuser from the occasional user. But even she cannot be sure if a teenager is telling her the truth about where his or her money went. Was it really lost, or did he or she spend it on cocaine?

When Noreen was a protective service worker, she often had to decide whether to leave a child over the weekend with a family that had been accused of abuse. If she removed the child, there was no guarantee that the foster family she placed the child in would be much better than the family he or she had just left. She learned early in her career that the human service worker has to be a risk taker.

Just last week John had to decide at 6:00 A.M. whether to cancel the buses he had leased for Sanctuary's annual family outing. At 6:00 A.M., the sky was overcast and the forecast was for rain. If it didn't rain and he cancelled, a lot of disappointed folks would be angry at him. If they went and it poured all day, the long-awaited event would be a disaster. He decided to risk it. They went, the sky was overcast and dropped a few sprinkles, but no major problems spoiled the day's activities. Was it good judgment or good luck? A little of each, perhaps!

If young children are in a supportive environment, they will be comfortable encountering differences in skin color, language, or physical abilities. In the words of a song from the musical *South Pacific* . . . you've got to be taught to hate . . . before you are 6 or 7 or 8 . . . you've got to be carefully taught.*

South Pacific is a play, with music by Richard Rodgers, lyrics by Oscar Hammerstein II and book by both Hammerstein and Joshua Logan.

The outreach counselors live with ambiguity because their job tasks are necessarily ill-defined. They are required to make moment-to-moment decisions:

- Which park should they visit?
- What youngster should they talk to?
- At what point should they call the police when they witness a drug deal or a fight?

Each decision is a judgment call made in a split second. Phoning the police too frequently might make it impossible to build relationships with these volatile and troubled young people. Waiting too long to respond might result in another teenager or staff member getting hurt or even killed!

Capacity to Ask for Help and Offer Feedback

To increase his effectiveness while struggling with ambiguity, John has developed a positive attitude about asking for help. When he couldn't decide whether to cancel the trip, he woke up two other staff workers and got them to help him. A burden is always lighter if someone else can carry it with you.

As he has matured and become more able to acknowledge his weaknesses, John is able to say, "I don't know that, but if you give me an hour, I'll find out," or, "I've tried to do that, but I wasn't able to; can you help me?"

Knowing when to ask for assistance or for an honest appraisal of his or her work is the mark of a self-confident human service worker. A less-secure worker needs to bluff, pretending false expertise. But the field is so vast and ever-changing that no one could ever know everything. Social welfare legislation, laws, and entitlements are evolving daily. New programs are added, old ones cut back. No matter how many years Sister Noreen has worked with homeless youth, if she were to shift to another problem area, perhaps working with the educationally or physically disabled, she would be a novice.

Sanctuary offers an orientation program for new staff and volunteers and in-service training for everyone. Even staff members who have been in the field for a long time need to keep learning about the ins and outs of this particular program, population, and community.

Just as important as asking for help is the willingness to give honest feedback to others. In our personal lives, much of our social interaction is superficial. We often give stock answers to standard questions: "How are you today?" provokes the anticipated neutral answers. We are hardly going to share our inner problems with all the neighbors or tradespeople we meet during the day. But at Sanctuary when someone asks, "How did I do?" or "How could I have done it better?" they have a right to expect a thoughtful and honest reply. Sometimes a less than positive evaluation is momentarily painful, but if the person learns from it, then it is a gift.

Belief in the Capacity to Change

At the risk of stating the obvious, John has to be a person with a powerful belief in the capacity all of us have to grow and change. His clients need a lot of help, but most of them are not permanently stuck in destructive patterns. He knows they often resist change; they fear the unknown consequences that change may bring, no matter how painful their current reality.

As he tries to assess realistically how much growth is possible or how fast it can happen, John has to struggle to maintain his own delicate balance. On the one hand, John has energy and optimism; on the other hand, he sometimes feels rage and frustration. All the workers at Sanctuary juggle feelings of pessimism and optimism. The discouraging reality of the life they see on the streets exists side by side with their hopes for the futures of the young people. No worker ever has enough time or resources or skill.

Although our minds and bodies cannot tolerate perpetual rage, we should be intolerant of injustice wherever we encounter it. We need to hold firm to our convictions about equal opportunity and the potential of equal access (Pantoja & Perry, 1992). A veteran human service worker once said that she was an optimist in her heart and a pessimist in her head. What does that mean to you?

No matter how discouraged he gets, John still appreciates the astounding plasticity, flexibility, and resilience of people. Human behavior has an almost infinite range of possibilities. The brutality of the street pimps and child pornographers contrasts sharply with the altruism and decency of all the volunteers who give up their evenings to help out.

Because he realizes that each of us is capable of acts of cruelty as well as altruism, John rejects glib generalizations about human nature, such as:

"People are no damn good!"

"People are only out for themselves!"

"Nowadays parents don't care about their kids!"

When things are falling apart, John looks to see what forces in the environment might be inhibiting human potential. He struggles to understand the obstacles in people's paths rather than retreat into fatalistic conclusions about their inferior heredity, moral lassitude, or psychological deviance.

John also has to stop himself from feelings of hopelessness when he sees city workers who seem so overwhelmed with their caseloads that they appear to throw up their hands in defeat.

Open-Mindedness, Skepticism, and Rejection of Stereotypes

John has learned that being open-minded is a requirement of his job. Open-mindedness is often derided. A comedian once described the open-minded person as one whose head is so porous that the wind whistles through it. Others describe the open-minded person as someone whose two feet are firmly planted in midair.

Of course John has opinions, but by keeping his mind open to new information, he protects himself from casting his first impressions in concrete. He meets someone, forms a preliminary estimate of his or her situation, and then continues to change that impression as he learns more.

John must keep from generalizing about a whole group from the behavior of one person. Even though, for example, he sees many men who are homosexuals abusing young boys, he knows that most homosexuals, just like most heterosexuals, would never do that.

Though he hears many horror stories of family indifference, he also knows that many parents have struggled long and hard to do the "right thing" against insurmountable odds. We live in a culture that encourages aggressive behavior and competition. Often peer pressure and the media have more power than the values of the parents.

Human service workers need to see beyond the simplistic bigotry of common stereotypes that declare that:

- The Irish drink too much and beat their wives on Saturday night.
- The Scots are thrifty to a fault.
- The Poles are stupid.
- The Jews are acquisitive.
- Women are passive, emotional creatures who yearn to be dominated.
- Men are like beasts when aroused and can't control themselves.

Each of these facile stereotypes must be questioned. Although the differences in behavior or attitudes among cultures or groups should be acknowledged—sometimes celebrated and sometimes regretted—shortcuts to understanding these variations should be rejected.

Ethnic background, race, class, and gender play significant roles in the socialization of every child. Still, no two people, even those from the same background, are ever identical. The teenagers want the staff to understand their lifestyles and stresses, but they would resent being labeled as "suburban, middle-class, Christian white teenage underachievers with domineering divorced parents." Although that kind of labeling sounds like a caricature, John has heard a surprisingly large number of workers referring to the teenagers at Sanctuary with shorthand labels that deny the humanness and uniqueness of the runaways. But categories and labels can be important in qualifying a client for a particular service or benefit. They must be used, but used with care and only when needed and accurate.

Humor and a Light Touch

John, like many of the young people he works with, finds that laughing, sometimes even at himself, is a great way to get rid of tension. A belly laugh, like a good cry, cleanses the system, putting a difficult situation back into perspective. One of John's favorite teenagers is a streetwise eighteen-year-old whom the kids have nicknamed "Flash." He is in perpetual, often impulsive motion. He is likely to say or do almost anything. John told him one day that he was going to get him a sweatshirt with his motto printed on it. In big, bold letters it would read:

READY! FIRE! AIM?

It took Flash a few minutes to understand the joke, but once he got it, he repeated it with obvious relish. And perhaps it slowed him down a little the next time he was quick to anger or become defensive.

Because working with these very troubled kids can be fraught with so much pain, humor might seem out of place. But John has discovered that many times a serious message can be effectively communicated through good-natured teasing. He uses tact and timing to moderate his wit. By picking up signals that he is being insensitive when he teases, makes a pun, or giggles at the absurdity of life on the streets, he can quickly back off or apologize.

Human service workers, especially in group or community settings, often socialize with their clients and coworkers at potluck suppers, holiday celebrations, and open houses and in the after hours of weekend workshops or retreats. They need to learn how to organize these occasions so they are not too threatening. Touchy issues will always surface when we cross the fragile boundary line between client and worker or worker and supervisor.

Traditional mental health practitioners such as doctors, psychologists, and psychiatrists often rigidly cling to boundary lines. Human service workers don't. When they work and when they relax, John, Noreen, and the other staff confront ambiguity, take risks, and individualize every situation.

SKILLS OF THE HUMAN SERVICE WORKER

Gathering Data

Every day John is asked dozens of questions that he doesn't know how to answer:

"Do you think Larry is telling the truth about where he got that money he has been flashing around?"

"If we send her home on that bus, who will meet her at the other end?"

"Where did Gloria go? I haven't seen her in a week, but I heard she was badly beaten up. Is it a rumor?"

"Where can we get money to purchase a van?"

"Where can we find a volunteer to teach an Introduction to Computers class?"

"What do other centers do when guests are caught in each other's rooms in compromising positions?"

"What is herpes? Is it catching? Is it terminal?"

John often responds, "That's a good question; I really don't know." Then, because he is a conscientious worker, he goes on to say, "But I'll find out what I can and call you back on Tuesday [or in an hour]."

The process of finding out as much as possible about a topic is called *data gathering*. John has been trained to use a variety of methods. In some ways, he is rather like a detective on the trail of insight and information. These are some of the data-gathering skills he uses:

- Asking questions of clients, coworkers, and his supervisor
- Listening to answers and remembering what he has learned
- Systematically observing
- Going to the library to read newspapers and journals or surfing the Internet
- Attending workshops, conferences, and seminars
- Visiting homes, other agencies, and the like

INTERVIEWING

Throughout the time you work in human services, you will keep increasing your skill in phrasing questions that help people to think more clearly. You will learn a great deal about how to establish an atmosphere that helps the interviewee relax and become engaged in the process of information sharing. The counselors at Sanctuary must learn how and when to ask questions while preserving a young person's dignity and right to privacy.

When John conducts an interview with a young runaway's parents, he is trying to find out as much as he can about the family's situation and assess its potential resources. Each person needs the space to tell his or her own version of the crisis that precipitated the family breakup. He will listen to each family member and try to tune in to the emotions that might be surrounding the words. The counselor discovers that everyone has his or her own story to tell, and everyone has stories that never get told (Cottle, 1974). If John is lucky, he will have several interviews he can use to fill in the background.

Often John must act quickly in a crisis situation, condensing all his data collecting into a few hectic moments. A fight erupts on the docks and he must quickly decide how serious it is. Should he call the police or try to break it up himself? He reviews all he knows about these young men. He has a brief exchange with one of the leaders to see how seriously he is taking it. Based on his past experience, John makes an educated guess as to whether they are likely to have weapons and if they are likely to use them. To an outsider, it might look as though the fight will turn violent. But after a few minutes of this process, John is able to distinguish "dissing," a street game of trading insults, from the kind of genuine anger that will leave one of the participants dead or injured.

Whether talking to a public official over the phone or at a meeting, conferring with a parent or teacher, or sharing information with a coworker about a referral, John uses the following skills.

ACTIVE LISTENING

After asking questions, John uses his skills of active listening. Each guest at Sanctuary has a unique style of communication. He has to remember and file away for future reference precisely what has been said. He has to be able to rephrase the ideas and feelings of the speaker to make sure he has understood correctly. He counts on such data so that he can point out connections between what is said at one time and at another.

When actively listening, John also "hears" the emotion that surrounds words. He listens to the sounds of silence: words left unsaid, hesitations, pauses, small sighs. By checking back with the interviewee, he avoids the pitfalls of overanalyzing or overinterpreting (Wolvin & Coakley, 1992).

ACTIVE LOOKING

From his study of psychodynamics, John has learned about the theory of the unconscious mind. He knows that people do not always do and say exactly what they mean. It is not easy to put one's feelings into words. Careful scrutiny can often tell us more than any words can convey.

The workers at Sanctuary also use active looking to better understand their group or community. By absorbing the many small details of a neighborhood, for example, John can make educated guesses about the stresses and the quality of life of its residents. He can walk into the game room and notice the small signs that signal trouble is brewing.

READING, RESEARCHING, AND ASSESSING

Because John encounters his clients in random, often unpredictable ways, he usually starts out by knowing almost nothing about them. In most other agencies, workers have access to a variety of background information. Reading through a client's file is a form of research. A file might include:

- Notes from previous professionals
- Employment records
- Test scores
- Medical records
- Records of monetary grants
- The results of some type of investigation or a court case

Reviewing published material and web sites is also a form of research. When, for example, he is writing a proposal for a grant, John wades through the books in the library that list philanthropic foundations and searches the databases of funding sources. Then he collects evidence of the agency's need for a new or expanded service. For example, he read an article in the *New York Times* about a recreation center that conducted an all-night gym program in a high-crime neighborhood, believing that it played a role in the reduction of townwide crime statistics. He'll clip that article and attach it to his proposal to lend support to his assertion that recreation can have a positive impact on vandalism.

John has become adept at using directories of community resources so that he can make referrals to job training, housing, and medical services for his clients. He always wondered why he had to take subjects such as statistics and research in college; they seemed so far removed from the human service field. Now he realizes how much he depends on his skills of finding information. Recently he needed to find the most accurate material on AIDS for a client. Before that, he had to find out how an adopted child goes about seeking out his biological parents. He has to learn to wade through the endless amount of material his search engine produces, screening the material for accuracy and relevance.

ATTENDING CONFERENCES AND WORKSHOPS

At least three times a week John participates in a case conference. It might be held at Sanctuary, the local courthouse, the mental health clinic, or the Department of Social Services. At these meetings, the teenagers, their families, and a variety of mental health workers pool their perspectives about a young person's problem. Learning how to gather and present information at a case conference is an important set of skills.

Occasionally John has been able to attend professional conferences and workshops. He recently went to one organized by the Coalition for Homeless Youth. He networked with other workers and came back newly energized.

MAKING HOME OR AGENCY VISITS

John finds that visiting a young person's home or another social agency provides him with in-depth knowledge. Observing for himself helps him gain insights into the strengths and weaknesses in an environment. When he visits a local health center, shelter, or school, he reads the graffiti on the walls and the notices on the bulletin boards. He can evaluate the atmosphere on first entering the front door or sitting in the waiting area. He forms initial impressions of the kind of service the agency might give his clients by the messages it projects to him.

Storing and Sharing Information

Once gathered, information about a particular client, problem, or program must be put into a useful format. John resists writing records and is often reminded by Noreen how important this skill is. At Sanctuary the workers enter a description of their daily activities in a computerized log book. This is used for continuity from one shift of staff to the next or from one period of time to the next. If good records have been kept, a young person won't be asked to summarize in a few sentences his or her complex set of problems when a new worker comes on staff.

At the end of any major event—a camping trip, parent workshop, or community fair—John writes an evaluation. He describes how the money was spent, what equipment was used, and what pitfalls he encountered. If he takes the time to sit down at the computer and write a full description, the next worker who repeats that activity can build on his successes and try to avoid his failures. To start again each time from scratch would be a misuse of everyone's scarce time and energy.

At Sanctuary the staff rotate taking notes on the decisions made at meetings. The meeting records help keep absent members in the mainstream of the group. Minutes act as reminders of significant deadlines, changes in laws or regulations, and other vital data. Behind every error—a name omitted from a list or a person who does not receive a meeting notice—lies a lost opportunity.

An entire program can rise or fall on the quality of its administrative detail. When a budget is reviewed, the bits and pieces of paper—bills, invoices, moneys taken out and brought in—can determine whether a program will be continued or terminated (Kettner, Moroney, & Martin, 2003; Lewis, Lewis, Packard, & Souflee, 2001; Schram, 1997).

Building Relationships

If John cannot build a relationship with a runaway child, he will never be able to help him or her. Gaining the trust of teenagers is especially hard. Even an adult as young as John still represents the adult world that these young people are busy rebelling against (Zayas & Katch, 1989).

John has found that there are no formulas for building a relationship. Stock empathetic phrases such as "I can understand just how you feel," or reassurances such as, "I'm sure everything will work out fine!" are perceived by the teenagers as being patronizing and hollow. And they are!

Sometimes, with all his skills, John just doesn't connect with a particular teenager. The elusive element of "cohesion," the bond that develops between people, just isn't there. There are workers who cannot connect with certain clients and clients who find it impossible to trust anyone. John has had to honestly admit when he is having difficulty relating to a particular young person. If he can, he adjusts his approach. No one on the staff considers it a failure if a relationship does not gel. Of course, if John found that he couldn't build a relationship with most of the young people he worked with, he would obviously be in the wrong job.

Negotiating Contracts and Assessing Problems

The process of sorting out mutual goals, roles, and tasks is called *negotiating the contract*. At Sanctuary the contract between clients and workers is not actually written. Instead, it is discussed during the initial stages, when a client first begins working with a staff member.

A contract begins by stating mutual expectations. Global statements such as, "I am here to help you," "We are meeting to change the way the police act toward street kids," or "I want you to make my son behave" are only starting points. The counselors break down large goals into small, do-able steps that can build, one on top of the other. The discussion of mutual expectations and consequences includes a description of who will do what in the change effort and which consequences will follow which actions. At Sanctuary the young people are not allowed to use drugs in the house. They need to know what will happen if a worker finds them shooting up in the bathroom. They also need to review the rules of confidentiality. Will their parents be called? If they have a weapon, will it be taken away? Under what circumstances will the police intervene?

Some parents or young people expect John to solve their problems by giving advice or orders; others think he will sit back and remain mute, like the psychiatrists they have seen in movies. Of course, he does a little of both.

Constructing Action Plans

In most agencies, Individualized Service Plans (ISPs) spell out the goals that will be worked on and the tasks that can accomplish them. At Sanctuary there are no formal, written action plans. The staff sets short-term goals with and for each resident. John tries to keep those goals in mind. They shape the choices he makes about how to spend his time.

Because so many of the teenagers have no ability to see beyond their next meal and warm bed, the staff tries to teach them how to chart a course and stick to it in a variety of ways. When planning a house dance or trip to a beach, John tries to help the residents make lists of the jobs that need to be done, when they must be completed, and who is responsible for doing them. If they don't keep careful track of their plans, the kids often backtrack over each other's trails, leaving important pieces of work undone or rushing to do a month's worth of work in a few hours. Lack of clarity creates conflict.

By teaching them how to use an action plan, counselors seek to enable their clients to accomplish two goals: organize a successful event and, more importantly, practice a method of systematic problem solving. Translating goals into concrete actions can help clients avoid emotional overload. All these youngsters have had crises in their lives and have reacted by withdrawing or striking out. John tries to bring some order into their chaotic lives.

Implementing Action Plans

To translate plans into reality, John meets with a youngster who is looking for a job. He offers encouragement and shows him how to use the job listings or locate an employment agency. Another of his clients has just moved into an apartment. He refers her to a day care center for her two-year-old son and helps her apply for financial assistance. Another resident has a court appearance; John briefs her on her rights and offers to go with her. Helping clients make decisions, release emotions, and locate and use services are ways he assists them as they implement their action plans.

Although John might spend most of his time doing individual casework, he also has had to learn to run a group. Because Sanctuary is short of staff, he teaches a small class in word processing and coaches an occasional baseball game. All these activities help implement Sanctuary's overall goal of helping each teenager survive the transition into adulthood. Like John, most human service workers are willing to do a little bit of everything.

Monitoring and Evaluating

John has learned how to use many techniques to elicit feedback. It is not easy to be objective about one's own work. He asks his clients and coworkers how he is doing but knows that most people have a hard time being constructively critical. The board of directors of Sanctuary has hired a professor from a local college to conduct a yearly evaluation. She interviews the staff and residents, summarizes the agency's progress, and then helps the board and staff set goals for the next year.

BASIC KNOWLEDGE OF THE HUMAN SERVICE WORKER

Human Growth and Development

All college human service curriculums are likely to include courses called Self and Society, The Person in the Environment, or, simply, Introduction to Psychology or Human Growth and Development.

These courses describe the major milestones and developmental tasks that a newborn infant faces as he or she grows through childhood, adolescence, young adulthood, adulthood, and old age and finally faces death. They discuss the basic needs shared by all human beings, regardless of their particular culture or the era in which they live. Students are challenged to think about how human beings meet their needs for association and acceptance, for work, play, sexuality, and spirituality.

Many of the major theorists disagree with each other about what causes people to think or act as they do. But the struggle to understand and synthesize their varying perspectives sharpens the intellect. It has provoked John to take a second look at many of his facile assumptions about the nature of human nature.

Abnormal Growth and Development

After studying "normal" or "typical" behaviors at different stages, most students learn about the forces that stunt development. They explore the ways in which biology, genetics, and family and social relationships contribute to mental breakdown, stress, family disorganization, and various forms of physical and mental disabilities. Through the study of nontypical or deviant behavior, they begin to understand the complex, intertwined issues of causality. Understanding how psychological problems develop has helped John to seek out the multiple resources needed to cope with or overcome them.

Sanctuary House does not base its work on one particular psychological theory. At John's internship in a community residence for developmentally delayed adults, the staff was expected to act in accordance with a rigid program of behavior modification. John is more comfortable working in an agency in which staff have the latitude to pick and choose from a variety of approaches.

Impact of Society and Culture on Behavior

While he was studying some of the psychological, genetic, biological, nutritional, and inter-personal forces that shape human behavior, John also had to understand their social context. While the family is an important influence on personality formation, so too are the many groups within which individuals interact.

The study of socioeconomic class, social role and status, ethnicity, peer group, family, religious institutions, school, and community—with their norms, myths, pressures, and subtle messages—has helped John to further understand why people act as they do. Realizing how cultures place expectations on behavior and mete out punishments for non-conformity, John begins to see order in the confusing crosscurrents of our pluralistic, het-erogeneous society.

The Dynamics of Groups and Organizations

Once he recognized the ways in which groups influence attitudes and behavior, John was curious about how they form and maintain themselves. In studying small groups such as the nuclear family, the gang, or the clique, he discovered that they have much in common with larger, more diffuse organizations such as workplaces, schools, and social agencies. Groups develop patterns of predictable behavior, rules, regulations, and rituals. These eventually determine how well the members will accomplish the goals of the group.

Learning how bureaucracies form and how they can be changed has helped the staff of Sanctuary secure services and resources for clients from a panoply of often unresponsive city agencies. It has also helped them look critically at the house itself to figure out how it could be improved.

Social and Political Forces That Affect Helping

Although no human service worker can possibly absorb all the political, economic, and sociological data about society, he or she needs a basic understanding of how communities are organized and how they are changed.

In anthropology and sociology courses, John has learned about variations in beliefs from one culture to another. He has learned that there are different definitions of how men and women should treat each other, how children should be socialized, and how the aged and the young should relate to each other.

These insights drawn from history and cross-cultural analysis prepare the human service worker to suspend quick judgments about what is right and wrong. They warn us that there are no carved-in-stone ways to run a world, a community, or an individual life.

Study in this area might also include knowledge about how laws are introduced, implemented, and amended. John still does not know enough about how the legislative and judicial systems affect the delivery of social services to homeless youth. He has some clear ideas about what he would like to see happen. He will need to keep on learning.

Social Problems, Populations, and Resources

John's human service courses and his internships introduced him to many social problems and special-population groups. He has learned a little about the problems of crime and corrections; mental and physical disabilities; hospitalized, neglected, and abused children; family relations; alcohol and drug abuse; death; suicide; survival in the rural or urban community; poverty; and discrimination. He has learned about discrimination based on social class, age, ethnic or religious status, and the tensions surrounding sexual identity. All are issues he sees played out in his work every day.

Although he has not learned in depth about all these issues, John has begun to understand how social problems are identified, how new problems rise to prominence on the social agenda, and how new services to deal with them come into being. He has learned that mental illness, alcoholism, aging, childhood, and male–female relations, among other issues, have changed in dramatic ways in the past several decades. Mental illness was once considered a moral depravity, later it was treated as a wholly psychological disturbance, and now it is viewed as an illness with both psychological and biological roots. Definitions have shaped interventions.

John knows a bit about the general shape of the social welfare system. Now that he is a committed newspaper reader, he attempts to keep up with the ever-changing legislation in the field.

Research and Evaluation

Although John is probably never going to have full responsibility for conducting formal research projects, he needs to understand the language of research. He has helped out in the formulation of projects and tries to read them as an alert consumer.

Research in the human services is particularly complex, controversial, and problematic. Human beings are infinitely unique and are perpetually bombarded with conflicting demands and environmental stressors. It is always hard to pinpoint the exact causality of any social problem or its solution. There are probably as many reasons for a youngster to leave home as there are residents at Sanctuary House.

Despite the limitations, research and evaluation studies need to be conducted in the social services. Results are sometimes used for increasing our knowledge base. More often, studies are used to decide whether funding of a particular program should be sustained, increased, or terminated. See York (2009) for an excellent review of the issues.

SUMMARY

1. It is difficult to draw a boundary line between the lay helper and the professional helper.

2. The boundary lines between professional specialties in the human services are often unclear. Work roles overlap.

3. Regardless of formal credentials or titles, competent helpers share a commitment to the content and structure of the professional helping relationship.

4. The structure of the professional helping relationship differs from the purely social one. The professional relationship:

    Exists for a limited time
    Has a clear, agreed-on focus
    Has a division of labor
    Is disciplined
    Is built on acceptance rather than attraction or affection.

5. The helping relationship is composed of three components:

    Attitudes and values
    Skills
    Knowledge

6. The three components of the helping relationship build on each other like a pyramid, with attitudes and values at the base.

7. Though all the components are of equal importance, the training of human service workers begins with attitudes and values.

8. The key attitudes and values are
    Patience

    Empathy
    Self-awareness
    Capacity to deal with ambiguity and take risks
    Capacity to ask for help and offer feedback
    Belief in people's and systems' capacity to change
    Open-mindedness, skepticism, and rejection of stereotypes
    Humor and a light touch

9. The basic skills are
    Gathering data, interviewing, and researching
    Storing and sharing information
    Building relationships
    Negotiating contracts and assessing problems
    Constructing action plans
    Implementing action plans
    Monitoring and evaluating

10. The basic knowledge areas are
    Human growth and development
    Abnormal growth and development
    The impact of society and culture on behavior
    The dynamics of groups and organizations
    The social and political forces that affect helping
    Social problems, special populations, and resources
    Research and evaluation

11. No worker embodies or masters all the attitudes and values, skills, and knowledge described. They form a model that helps set goals for professional development.

DISCUSSION QUESTIONS

1. What do you think is meant by the statement "empathy is a path we walk, not a destination we can ever reach"? How might you prepare yourself to try to empathize with one of your classmates who comes from a different ethnic or religious background than you do, or is of the opposite sex, or has a different sexual orientation, or perhaps has a different set of abilities or disabilities than you do?

2. To what extent do you think you could work with homeless youth who often might appear angry at adults or might be sexually provocative or manipulative? How do you think you would react to having to deal with the "johns" or pimps that often prey on the youngsters? How might you react to the parents from whom they have run away—sometimes with good reasons?

WEB RESOURCES FOR FURTHER STUDY

Homeless and Runaway Tens
www.standupforkids.org
wwwmockingbirdsociety.org
www.hhs.gov/homeless

For more information on the problems and program strategies of working with homeless and runaway teenagers, these web sites should be very helpful. The second site is especially concerned with teenagers who become homeless after "aging out" of the foster care system. The third site is the official Health and Human Services site, and it has a section on homeless and runaway youth.

Attitudes and values of the human service worker
For further description of the qualities needed for human service work.

National Organization for Human services
www.nationalhumanservices.org

Bureau of Labor Statistics
http/www.bls.gov/ocos/oco060.htm

Chapter 5

Values and Ethical Dilemmas

Betty is advising a welfare recipient on how to deal with a welfare worker. The worker is required by law to ask the client where her former husband is and to give his Social Security number. Then the worker will turn over this information to the Department of Revenue, which will pursue the man aggressively for support. The welfare recipient knows where her former husband is, but is afraid to tell the worker because her husband had beaten her and she fears he would be abusive to her again. The woman asked what she should do. Betty knows it is wrong to lie to the worker, yet she also knows that it would be in the woman's best interest to tell the worker that she doesn't know where her former husband is. What should Betty tell the woman? What would you do?

Linda is a case worker in the child welfare department. The school guidance counselor has reported a mother for neglect of her child. The child is malnourished and listless. She cannot apply herself to her studies. Linda talked with the mother and found out that she formerly had received money from Transitional Assistance to Needy Families (TANF), but had reached that state's two-year time limit and had been cut off from TANF. She tried to feed her child and often went hungry herself, but even with food stamps, she did not have enough money to feed the child adequately.

Linda's supervisor advised her to place the child in foster care, but Linda knew that the agency did not have enough good foster parents and was having trouble recruiting them because so many women were working, and the agency did not pay enough to foster parents to make it worth their while to be foster parents. She could place the child in a foster home where there were already more children than the agency usually allowed, but would the child be any better off than in her own home? It would be traumatic for the child to be taken from her mother whom she loved. Yet she would probably get enough to eat in this foster home, even though the foster mother would not be able to give her the attention that she needs. What should Linda do?

Every attitude and value carries with it the seeds of conflict and insoluble dilemmas. Debates about the **ethics of helping** are not just mental gymnastics best left to university scholars or cloistered philosophers. Human service workers face dilemmas or value conflicts of one sort or another every day, no matter what their role in an agency.

Sometimes there are conflicts between what we have been taught is correct behavior and what our clients do. For example, perhaps our parents, church, and school taught us that it is wrong for a woman to get an abortion; yet we may work with many people who do not share this value. Or perhaps, because everyone we knew said so, we might believe that most welfare recipients are lazy people avoiding work. Yet we find that assumption false when we read research on the subject. Which path do we follow when we must choose between our vision of life and our client's, between a long-held belief and research findings?

Value conflicts are often caused by the realities of our work. We know that our ethics dictate a certain path, but the efficiency needs of the bureaucracy that employs us or provides funds and the pressure of public opinion—especially in an election year—demand actions counter to our convictions. Human service workers know that whoever pays the piper calls the tune!

CAN WORKERS BE COMPLETELY UNBIASED?

Our social class, ethnic group, or gender has shaped many of the values we hold. These values may be very different from those of people from another group. This difference can create problems in the helping relationship.

Some theoreticians urge workers to be objective and "value free," which means being careful not to impose their own values on their clients. Yet in practice this is simply impossible. Even if one only grunts and says "uh-huh," the timing of the noises can reflect a value judgment about which of the client's statements warrant attention; inflections of the voice can give a sense of approval or displeasure. Inevitably there will be some differences between the client and the worker in attitudes toward politics, religion, sexuality, culture, social class, time orientation, or the environment, or in beliefs about human nature. Some of those **value conflicts** may not be very important. A Democrat can help a Republican, or vice versa, without needing to agree on the respective party platforms. But if the worker honestly believes that abortion is murder and the client wants help in terminating a pregnancy, that can create such a serious problem in their working relationship that special effort is required to soften or eliminate the conflict.

In the following pages, we will look at some of the areas that can lead to **value dilemmas** and conflicts, either within us as workers or within society as a whole. Often the dilemmas or conflicts occur simply because human situations are by nature unclear and complex. The choices open to our clients are all imperfect, and each carries unknown consequences. "The horns of a dilemma" is an apt phrase. The very definition of a dilemma implies that it is an impossible situation with no solution. We shall give some case examples and ask you to think through the values and ethics involved in each example, using the questions in Figure 5.1.

ethics of helping
An ethical commitment to help others rather than engage in dog-eat-dog competition.

value conflicts
Disagreement brought about by differences in values between people.

value dilemmas
A situation in which competing values make it difficult, if not impossible, to determine the correct choice.

DILEMMAS SURROUNDING THE VALUE OF SELF-DETERMINATION

What happens when one person's right to control his or her own behavior clashes with another set of rights? **Self-determination** is a value held in such high esteem in the social work profession that the National Association of Social Workers (NASW) code of ethics puts it at the top of its list of professional values: "The social worker should make every effort to foster maximum self-determination on the part of clients."

self-determination
A person's right to determine his or her own life plan without interference.

Questions to Guide Decision Making

1. What values are promoted by the action?

2. What values are violated by the action?

3. Is the client competent to decide? If not, how should a decision be made? Who should make it? How should we define *competence*?

4. How does the social worker's position/power affect our evaluation of the action? How does the institutional setting affect our evaluation?

5. What alternative actions are possible? (Evaluate each in terms of questions 1 through 4.)

6. How do your own values affect the way you evaluate the action? Would your client or agency make a different evaluation?

In evaluating each course of action, consider the client's right to self-determination; such values as privacy, trust, honesty, and respect; the good or harm of the action for the well-being of the client/others/community.

FIGURE 5.1 Human service dilemmas

Source: Rhodes (1989).

Lynn Atkinson, a social work professor who believes that social workers should not force their services on clients, defines self-determination as follows:

> In working with people, social workers must respect the right of individuals to choose their own life paths. Although a social worker may disagree with the choices or the values of a particular person, the social worker must respect that individual's right to believe and do as he or she wishes and honor that right by not forcing the person to do something that is against that person's will. (Atkinson & Kunkel, 1992, pp. 159–160)

In a rejoinder to Professor Atkinson, another professor of social work, O. Dale Kunkel, points out that subsections of the code of ethics on self-determination "quickly hedge by characterizing the legal conditions under which client self-determination is not primary" (Atkinson & Kunkel, 1992). Kunkel argues that social workers often must work with clients who do not come to them of their own free will because they know they have a problem and want to solve it. Social workers must investigate complaints of child abuse and neglect with or without the client's consent; they counsel alcoholics and drug abusers who have been court ordered into treatment; they work with juvenile delinquents and adult criminals who are incarcerated or who are on probation or parole; they treat mentally ill people who have been involuntarily committed to hospitals. Many of these people could assert that their self-determination is being abridged.

What happens to the value of self-determination when someone has or might be hurting himself or herself or others? Consider the following case reported in a local newspaper. If the judge asked you to give your professional opinion of what should be done, what would you say?

Social and Moral Issues in the Case of a 96-Year-Old Woman

KENNEBUNK, ME —It would be a cruel euphemism, a gross understatement, to say that Nellie Teach lives in squalor.

Neither words nor pictures can adequately capture the wretchedness in which this feisty and fiercely independent 96-year-old woman makes her home.

The kitchen resembles a dung heap. She sleeps and lives in this room; all others are barricaded by rubbish. The stench made at least one social worker ill. The three burners on her gas stove are fully ablaze to heat the room; cardboard containers sit precariously close to the flames. The floor beneath her bare feet is rotted away.

This is home to Nellie Teach, a home she has lived in for decades and which she adamantly refuses to abandon. The faded white two-story house is owned by a disabled, elderly nephew who cannot make repairs to it. "I don't want a nice apartment," she said last week. "I don't want something that belongs to someone else. I don't want people interfering with me."

People who look in on Nellie Teach—neighbors, nurses and doctors, state social workers—fear for her life. They want to clean her house or find her new quarters. But Ms. Teach will not clean up, and she will not go. Doctors say she is mentally competent, so she cannot be removed against her will. The town, as a last resort, went to court last month. They have asked for the authority to "cleanse, disinfect and fumigate" her home.

The conflict between a community that wants to help and a woman who refuses help has opened a panoply of social, moral, and legal questions that are neither unique to Nellie Teach's situation nor easy to answer. Officials in Kennebunk say there are other people in town just like her. Advocates for the elderly say every community in Maine has its Nellie Teaches.

Compassion seems to have dictated the actions of those who have tried to help Nellie Teach. Yet many people say the state and the town should leave her alone, that they are trying to evict a poor, hapless woman. Others say too little is being done to help her. "We're either blamed for being intrusive or not doing enough," says A. Ricker Hamilton, regional program manager for the Maine Department of Human Services.

"How do you intervene and still respect the rights of the individual?" asks Lee Tallion, community care director for Southern Maine Senior Citizens, Inc. "Nellie Teach has a right to do what she wants until legally she endangers herself or someone else."

Nellie Teach is a staunchly independent woman who reached adulthood long before welfare became commonplace. The state is an institution that is feared by the Nellie Teaches of New England. It engenders distrust, even contempt.

Some people question the town's suit, wondering whether a serious health hazard does exist. After all, her living conditions have been horrendous for years, according to neighbors and social workers. Nellie Teach is 96 and in excellent health, given her age, according to doctors who have seen her recently.

People wonder what will happen to Nellie Teach if the town should win its suit. "This lady," says her physician, "has always found the cracks in the system to prevent anybody she doesn't want from coming into her house and changing the status quo. I think a person's independence is to be cherished. But there's a line somewhere that must be drawn." (Adapted from Berney, 1984.)

This case is a vivid illustration of the complexity involved in making ethical decisions—individual rights versus the rights of the community. When they conflict, human service workers have to decide which takes precedence. Yet in Nellie Teach's case, officials disagreed about the danger she posed to herself or society.

On the surface, this case involved an issue of public health, but some of the unspoken issues may have involved deeper levels of anxiety about cleanliness and neatness and the moral implications of dirtiness and disorder. "Cleanliness is next to godliness" is an old saying from our Puritan heritage. Many of our ethical dilemmas come from conflicting moral standards. Sometimes the conflict is framed in terms of bureaucracy versus the individual. Bureaucrats who are removed from the life of the local community are often more likely to see issues in abstract, impersonal terms and in terms of the demands of their job. Nellie Teach's neighbor who took her food saw no problem, whereas the director of the public health department saw a public health problem that he had to do something about.

Human service workers employed in public welfare are confronted daily with ethical dilemmas. An especially painful one was posed during the 1950s and early 1960s when, in some cities, workers were ordered to make night raids on single-parent welfare recipients to see if an unauthorized male was living in their homes (in which case the males would be responsible for their financial support). Knowing that the Supreme Court had declared this practice unconstitutional, a social worker who lived by the values of the profession was faced with the choices of quitting the job, fighting the ruling powers, or violating the ethics of the profession.

One worker who sued the department of welfare for violating the rights of clients to privacy was, in fact, fired for insubordination, but that worker's courage eventually helped put an end to the practice.

Self-Determination and Child Abuse

Now consider a case that deals with the widespread conflict between a client's style of parenting and an agency's concept of what is appropriate child rearing. This case is summarized from a newspaper article.

CASE EXAMPLE

Falsely Accused, a Mother Fights Back

SCITUATE, MA—The call that brought terror into Brenda Frank's life came on September 17, 1986. A social worker with the Department of Social Services informed Frank that an anonymous complaint of sexual abuse and neglect of her two young daughters had been filed against her.

"I was frozen. Shocked. It was beyond my comprehension," said Frank, during a recent interview in the living room of her modest two-bedroom apartment in this seaside town. "The allegations included the fact that my 4-year-old, Emily, was still being breast-fed occasionally and that both girls (Emily and Rebecca, or Becky, then 6) slept in my bed with me."

Where did such allegations come from? Did she have an unknown enemy out there somewhere?

"I felt so vulnerable," said Frank. "Everything you do is put under a microscope by DSS and you have to defend your every move. I stopped letting the girls sleep with me. I wouldn't let them go outdoors to play in case they fell and got hurt. It was all so very isolating. But I didn't know who to trust. I didn't want anyone to see me, the lady accused of abusing her kids, riding my bike around town or walking down the street."

When Frank received the phone call from DSS, she had been separated from her husband for five years and was a stay-at-home mother living on welfare. Although finances were always an issue, Frank said she was grateful to have two healthy children, a roof over her head in a town with good schools, nearby stores that she could reach by bicycle, new friends, and like-minded young mothers she met through La Leche League (a group advocating breast-feeding until a child naturally weans herself).

Frank describes what happened when the worker from DSS came to her home:

"I was very nervous and frightened and had my mother, a nurse, come for support," said Frank, who had read dozens of books on nutrition, childbirth, and parenting during her two pregnancies. "But I felt sure that all I had to do was explain the La Leche philosophy of child-led weaning and give her some of their literature. I thought I would show her their literature and the stuff I've been reading about the concept of mother and child sharing a bed. I had a book by Tine Thevenin called *The Family Bed: An Age-Old Concept in Child Rearing.*

"I told the worker that I didn't agree with the fact that in our country children are expected to sleep alone at night in their own rooms behind closed doors. I told her my girls slept with me because I wanted them to feel safe at night."

Several days later she got a letter from DSS telling her that the allegations against her had been substantiated. It said:

"You have neglected to guide your children in age-appropriate individuation development and have exposed your children to sexual stimulation with your belief in the concept of the 'family bed.'"

"In other words," said Frank, "I was found guilty of the way I had chosen to parent."

Frank believes the person who anonymously reported her to DSS worked at her complex and might have been angered by Frank's advocacy against the use of pesticides on the grounds and for the ability of elderly residents to have pets.

Frank turned to a lawyer for help. They appealed to the commissioner of DSS for a review of her case. It was under this review that the allegations against her were dropped. But it would be 1989—two years later—before her name was finally taken off DSS's central list as an alleged perpetrator.

Frank may have won her own battle, but she has not remained silent. She continues to testify before state legislatures, to pore over books in law libraries, and to counsel others. (Doten, 1991)

Although Frank won her case, the politics at the Department of Social Services (DSS) did not change until a well-publicized case of a child being peremptorily removed from a foster home in September 1992 created a public furor. The governor ordered the creation of a special commission to investigate DSS policies and procedures. Several bills were introduced in the legislature to create an appeals process for removing children from biological or foster parents due to Frank's advocacy. Now there is an automatic review process in place. (Doten, 1991, p. 31)

Child-welfare agencies across the nation are under fire from groups of all ideological points of view. Many states have had lawsuits brought against them:

- From conservatives objecting to the agency invading the sanctity of the family;
- From advocacy groups claiming that the agency fails to protect children because it is understaffed and underfunded and does not adequately train workers;
- From parents claiming that their rights have been abused by intrusive social workers;
- From parents claiming that the agency doesn't give them the services their children need;
- From foster parents claiming that the agency does not treat them like co-professionals and does not give them enough help.

In May 1992, about 200 aggrieved people held a rally in the parking lot of the Division for Children and Youth Services (DCYS) in Concord, New Hampshire. They were supporting Stephen and Joan DeCosta, both born-again Christians whose four children were placed in foster care during a highly publicized dispute with the division in 1989. The DeCostas were accused of child abuse when the children's grandmother reported that one of the DeCosta children had been spanked until he bled. The DeCostas are part of a group of parents who claim they have a right to decide how to discipline their children, while DCYS maintains it has an obligation to draw the line. "A district court judge found the DeCostas guilty of abuse, but the case was resolved by a consent decree between the family and the division. The family was reunited, which the division insists is always its ultimate goal" (Doten, 1991, p. 31).

The Frank and DeCosta cases represent very different child-rearing philosophies. The DeCostas subscribe to the biblical injunction "Spare the rod and spoil the child." Most parents in the United States probably spank their children, but child-welfare agencies seem to be moving in the direction of regarding spanking, especially severe spanking, as child abuse. They are concerned about the rise of violence in our society, and perhaps spanking sends the wrong message to a young child. Most shelters for battered women do not allow the parents to spank their children while they live in the shelter.

Child protection workers have little guidance from state laws about what constitutes abuse. Parents in all fifty states are allowed to hit their children. There are limits to what is allowed, but out of reluctance to legislate parental conduct, state lawmakers have shied away from getting too specific about those limits, instead letting courts consider the matter case by case. A Legal Aid Society's training guide for its lawyers who work in New York's Family courts cites the following cases:

In one case, inflicting cuts and bruises on a child was deemed "excessive corporal punishment," amounting to neglect, the most basic and frequently charged form of child mistreatment. But in another case, shaking a child and causing her to hit her head on the pavement was ruled allowable.

Hitting a 9-year-old with the buckle end of a purse strap for leaving his 2-year-old sister alone in a room was acceptable. Hitting a child with a belt for lying on the floor, kicking a table and peeling paint off a wall were not.

Leaving red marks on the face of a 13-month-old constituted neglect. Dragging an 11-year-old out of a car by the collar, scraping his neck, and throwing on the ground, scraping his knee, did not.

In a case where a father was charged with abuse, a more severe infraction than neglect, judges held that biting a girl on the face and arm, leaving severe bruises, did not cross the line. In this context, the threshold for abuse was intentionally causing or risking a physical injury that involved disfigurement of "protracted impairment of physical of emotional health."

In 2008, Cesar Rodriguez was accused of murder for killing his seven-year-old stepdaughter Nixzmary. He admitted that he routinely beat Nixzmary with a belt, hit her with his hands using "all my force," threw her on the floor, and held her head under cold water the night she died in January 2006. He admitted duct-taping her emaciated thirty-seven-pound frame to a chair and binding her with bungee cords. Mr. Rodriguez's lawyer Jeffrey T. Schwartz argued that Mr. Rodriguez gave Nixzmary the same kind of discipline that Mr. Rodriguez's father had given him, including hitting him a lot and holding his head under cold water. This corrected

Mr. Rodriguez/s waywardness and helped him grow up to be a decent father. Mr. Schwartz said, "It was done to him, and it didn't kill him."

The City Council of Oakland, California, introduced a resolution in 1999 to make Oakland the nation's first official No Spanking Zone (Gorov, 1999). They planned to place stop signs with that message in libraries and other public buildings. "We want people to know it's not a good idea to hit kids. And when the government takes a stand against it, it helps them realize they're not supposed to do it," said Dr. Irwin Hyman, a psychologist who runs the National Center for the Study of Corporal Punishment and Alternatives at Philadelphia's Temple University (Gorov, 1999).

Opponents of the purely symbolic resolution countered that local government has no business telling parents how to discipline their children, and that laws already exist to protect youngsters from child abuse. (The resolution did not pass.)

Twenty-three countries have passed bans on parental corporal punishment, including Sweden, Norway, Finland, Chile, the Netherlands, New Zealand, Spain, and Venezuela.

GENUINE CHILD ABUSE VERSUS FALSE CHARGES

Parents of children in day care centers have been divided into warring camps over the issue of what constitutes child abuse. Day care centers have set up strict guidelines for touching children, making teachers cautious about physical contact. Parents have become more cautious about putting their children in day care centers. Ann Withorn, a professor of human services at the University of Massachusetts, believes that conservative officials consciously manipulate people's sexual anxieties in order to discourage parents from using day care centers, thus taking the pressure off the government to provide funding for them (Withorn, 1994).

This conspiracy theory is, of course, quite controversial. False memories and false accusations occur, but so do actual cases of child abuse. Clearly, abuse must be treated as an outrageous and impermissible assault on children. At the same time, there is a great deal of hysteria about sexual abuse, and some innocent people, such as Brenda Frank, have been victimized by this hysteria.

This issue presents human service workers with the complex problem of differentiating between genuine sexual abuse and false charges. In Frank's case, her consulting psychiatrists judged that breast-feeding children to a late age and allowing children to sleep with her did not constitute sexual abuse. When experts disagree on the issues involving parenting styles and lifestyles, there are no easy answers for human service workers.

Self-Determination When Treatment Is Mandated

To regain custody of their children, some mothers have been ordered to undergo treatment for their substance abuse and counseling for their personal problems. Under these conditions, it is very possible that a client will go through the motions of **mandated treatment** simply to gain the promised benefits or avoid punishment. But can people change if they are forced to accept help? Consider the following case, in which a mother did what she had to get her children back but never liked what she had to do. This is an actual case, described by Robert Ingram (1992), a social work therapist and one of the founders of Empower, a welfare rights group.

mandated treatment   Treatment that is legally required by the courts or by government officials.

CASE EXAMPLE

Alice

"I was working in a nursing home as a nursing assistant. I didn't want to ask welfare for anything. It felt good. I worked from 7 to 3. My 12-year-old daughter was supposed to take my 6-year-old son to nursery school and then go to school herself. They were mad because I was working so the kids didn't go to school. They fooled around and they set the house on fire.

"They [social service department] took the kids. I was missing work, and I lost the job. They said the kids were emotionally upset. Any kid would be if he was taken out of his home. They wouldn't let me see the kids. They told me that if I go to therapy, I'd get my kids back. They didn't say anything about how long I'd be in therapy. They told me it would be up to the therapist to say when the kids could come home. The therapist was like a judge. [I] went to the therapist.

"All he wanted to do was talk about the past. What the . . . does the past have to do with it? The therapist said it was up to the judge when I'd get the kids back. The judge said it was up to the protective worker, and the worker said it was up to the therapist. It took me a year and a half to convince the therapist that I was well enough to have the kids at home. I was calmer because I had a job and had something to do with my time."

Ingram asked her if the therapist said anything to her or gave her medicine that helped her to be calm, and she said, "No." She went to the therapist once a month at first. Ingram asked her if it wouldn't have been better to go more often to learn or do whatever it was to get the kids back.

[Alice said], "I don't know. That's the way it was set up. I used to tell him, 'I'm doing good.' There was nothing to talk about. It got to be boring. I told him, 'I'm not trying to be rude, but I have better places to be.' He'd sit there and shake his head yes. He had no suggestions at all. After a year and a half, the therapist sent a letter to the judge, suggesting that [my] younger child should be returned home and that the therapy should continue. Then I had to go twice a month, with my son. It was a pain. I had to get him out of school early. It was messing up his school work. [My] employer was concerned that I was taking time off work to go to therapy. The therapist told me I didn't have to work but he wouldn't help me get SSI [Supplemental Security Income]. . . ."

[Ingram] asked her how she finally stopped seeing the therapist. She said that he resigned from his job. He tried to persuade her to continue with another therapist but he let her go when she insisted that she did not need to continue in treatment.

Ingram treats mandated clients, leaving the decision about whether to submit to the therapy up to the client, and recommends developing a contract with the client in the beginning. The contract certifies that the client is in treatment if he or she at least shows up regularly for interviews. "Once the therapist demonstrates his or her trustworthiness by adhering to the contract, the client may begin to work on the issues that attracted the attention of the mandating agency" (Ingram, 1992, p. 96).

Sometimes treatment is not mandated by an agency but is forced on a client by his or her family or friends. One drug treatment program, for example, occasionally kidnaps addicted adolescents at the parents' request and physically forces them to remain in treatment. Some of these adolescents later thank their parents for doing it, believing that they would not have kicked the life-destroying addiction on their own. Others are still angry at their parents for violating their autonomy.

Parents of mentally ill children are often eager for their children to be hospitalized and to take psychotropic medication, even while the children resist both hospitalization and medication. In our interview with Judi Chamberlin in Chapter 2, Judi talks about how parents in the Alliance for the Mentally Ill often push for hospitalization and medication against the wishes of their children. The Mental Patients' Liberation Front believes in complete freedom of choice. Its members develop self-help support groups and alternative treatment methods and hope they can win voluntary membership.

Some therapists advocate the use of **aversive behavioral treatments** that employ harsh methods of discipline as a training technique for clients who have been given up as hopeless by other agencies. A residential treatment institution for autistic children in Rhode Island came under fire in 1991 for such a treatment. The Massachusetts Office for Children filed suit against the institution, charging that it treated children cruelly with "white noise" and physical punishment. Many of the parents supported the institution, saying that the treatment helped their children control their behavior. In the course of the debate, some psychologists came forward with testimony claiming that there are more advanced and humane methods of treatment that are just as effective. However, the Office for Children lost the suit, and the institution continued this form of problematic behavior management.

> **aversive behavioral treatment** A form of behavior modification based primarily on punishment rather than reward.

Self-Determination Is Undermined When Clients Are Manipulated

Although it is not easy to know how to handle the ethical dilemmas of mandated treatment, at least both client and worker openly acknowledge that there is coercion in the relationship. But there is another kind of coercion that undermines self-determination. **Manipulation** by the worker is subtle and harder for a client to detect and to defend against. For example, before the 1960s, social workers were so convinced that unmarried mothers should give their babies up for adoption that they often subtly manipulated the clients into accepting that choice. By presenting no other options and services, unmarried mothers were geared to giving babies up for adoption. Homes for unwed mothers offered no opportunities to learn parenting skills, and no day care was provided. Unable to visualize any other path, young women, whether they had worked through the issues or not, simply agreed to give up their children even before their children were born. Often that might have been the best course of action, but manipulation violates the tenet of self-determination.

> **manipulation** Attempts to influence someone's behavior or thoughts by covert, unstated methods rather than open, explicit methods.

In discussing the philosophical implications of manipulation, Rhodes argues that manipulation should usually be avoided and needs always to be carefully monitored. If the worker believes that coercion is necessary, it should generally be undertaken *with the client's knowledge*. Otherwise, social workers may be able covertly to force actions on clients that society and clients would not allow if these actions were made explicit (Rhodes, 1989).

Rhodes argues that, because it is impossible to be ethically neutral in human service work, workers should be open with clients about their ethical commitments so that clients can make an **informed choice**. "How much a therapist reveals must depend upon the relationship and the client's ability to process such information" (Rhodes, 1989, p. 120).

> **informed choice** A choice that is made after a person has been given all the relevant information about the issue.

SOME CURRENT ETHICAL CONFLICTS

Conflicts Surrounding AIDS

The issues that surround AIDS are fiercely debated. Some children with AIDS have been excluded from nursery schools and public schools because of parents' anxieties about contagion. Other school directors, principals, and parents have welcomed those children into their schools, convinced that such children are not a danger to the other children and that the youngsters need to live as normal a life as possible, despite having such a traumatic illness.

AIDS has also raised debate about whether medical personnel should be routinely tested, whether prostitutes or other prisoners with AIDS should be held in prisons for periods longer than their sentences to protect the public, whether condoms or clean hypodermic needles should be distributed, and even whether AIDS victims should be quarantined.

Many of those debates contain more heat than light. It is important for human service workers to base their thinking about AIDS on the most up-to-date medical information, which is willingly provided by local public-health agencies or AIDS action groups.

It is easy to fall into the trap of accepting simple stereotypes, such as assuming that all business corporations have the single-minded goal of making money. These folks, sorting grocery items at a free food bank, are employees of a large corporation, which encourages its workers to help their fellow citizens, on company time.

Conflicts Surrounding the Right to Die

Some conflicts between the individual and the community spring from conflicting interpretations of morality. For example, does an individual have a right to choose to die, or does the state have the right to forbid that choice? If a terminally ill person wants to die, should a doctor help her or him do so? Do parents have the right to decide on **euthanasia** (also called mercy killing) for their terminally ill child?

The following case was reported by the Hastings Center, an organization founded in 1969 to study issues raised by the advances in medicine, the natural sciences, and the social and behavioral sciences. The Hastings Center studies "organ transplants, human experimentation, prenatal diagnosis of genetic disease, life-extending technologies, recombinant DNA research, health policy, and control of human behavior" (Hastings Center, 1979, p. 1).

euthanasia Active intervention in hastening death, usually made by a doctor with the permission of the dying person or his or her family.

CASE EXAMPLE

Andrea

Andrea was a 9-year-old girl who had been diagnosed as having cystic fibrosis at the age of 13 months. Since then she had been hospitalized twelve times, eight times during the last year.

When admitted for the last time, she was already receiving an experimental antibiotic, which was being administered in an attempt to control a resistant pneumonia superimposed on severely damaged lungs, a result of her underlying disease. She was at that time a severely ill, emaciated child with moderately labored breathing. She seemed to have no interest in her environment and refused to communicate with anyone but her mother.

The parents indicated that in the event of a cardiac or respiratory arrest, they did not want their child to be resuscitated, and the appropriate medical order was written. The child was not involved in these conversations or subsequent decision making.

As this child's condition continued to decline, the parents asked the doctor how much longer she would live and how she would die. At one point the father said: "Watching your own child die is worse than dying yourself." This comment led to a discussion of active euthanasia utilizing intravenous potassium chloride or a similar drug. The physicians pointed out that no matter how hopeless a situation or how much suffering the patient and family were enduring, the law prohibits the active taking of a patient's life. They refused to consider this option. The following day, Andrea's heart began to fail. Her condition became progressively worse, and she died approximately forty-eight hours later. During these last two days, her parents were in great despair because of her steadily deteriorating condition. They felt helpless and impotent to alleviate their daughter's distress. Medical treatment was continued to the end, and no measures were taken to hasten Andrea's death.

Approximately two months after her death, the mother was asked if she would still have given permission for active euthanasia if she had been offered that option. She replied, "Yes."

Should active euthanasia be permitted to spare the patient and family from suffering when death is inevitable? Does it make a difference if you are deciding about a child, a young adult, or an elderly person? Do you think you would think the same way if it were your relative? What if the doctors were wrong, what if a new medication were about to be discovered that could have saved Andrea's life a few months later? How can we be sure?

In his commentary on this case, James Rachels (1979), a philosophy professor, points out that the American Medical Association (AMA) says that active euthanasia is not only illegal but immoral as well. The AMA condemns mercy killing as "contrary to the most fundamental measures of human value and worth." However, the AMA statement goes on to say that allowing patients to die by ceasing treatment is in some circumstances all right. Rachels argued that the doctors should have given a lethal injection to end Andrea's suffering. The doctors chose not to prolong Andrea's life by aggressive treatment, so evidently they felt that prolonging Andrea's life was pointless. "If it was pointless for her to endure, say, a four-day period of dying, why should we choose a course that requires her to endure a two-day period of dying?" (Rachels, 1979, p. 19).

Another philosophy professor, Philippa Foot (1979), disagreed with Rachels. She thought that active euthanasia was risky in this case because of Andrea's inability to decide for herself. She believes that "we are apt to think about [active euthanasia] in a confused and superficial way. This is one reason why there is so much danger in supporting any kind of active euthanasia, never mind its extension to children and noncompetent adults" (Foot, 1979, p. 20).

Since the Nazi death camps, decisions about euthanasia have taken on an ominous cast. No one can afford to be casual about taking human life for any reason or under any circumstances. Dangers lurk behind what seems to be an otherwise logical and compassionate policy. We don't honestly know how we would decide the case of Andrea, but we can understand the reasoning of all the people involved.*

Conflicts Surrounding Reproductive Choice

Fierce battles have raged over the issue of abortion for nearly four decades. In this deeply personal and intimate area, most people have firm opinions. Because social science is never value free, we should state our biases on this hotly contested issue. Along with most other feminists, we believe that women should have the right to choose whether to have a baby, a right that the Supreme Court affirmed in its 1973 *Roe v. Wade* decision.

This decision protects a woman's right to privacy regarding what she does with her own body through the second trimester of pregnancy. Both the decision and the right have been contested ever since. The pro-choice faction fights to retain the right to an abortion for all women. The anti-abortion faction works to make it illegal in the same way that murder is outlawed.

The *Roe v. Wade* decision was modified in July 1992 in the case *Planned Parenthood v. Casey*. This case involved a Pennsylvania law that required physicians to give counseling that encouraged childbirth to women seeking abortions. After the counseling, women

---

*The commentaries on the case of Andrea and others in the *Hastings Center Report* are more complex than our brief summary indicates. We suggest that it would be worthwhile for students to read some of this material at length, as the discussions give an excellent frame of reference for thinking through ethical issues. The address of the *Hastings Center Report* is 21 Malcolm Gordon Road, Garrison, NY 10524-4125. E-mail: mail@thehastingscenter.org.

DUNAGIN'S PEOPLE

"DON'T WORRY. WHEN SEX EDUCATION IS PRESENTED IN A CLASSROOM SETTING, IT WILL BECOME AS FOREIGN TO THE STUDENTS AS MATH AND SCIENCE."

There is a fierce debate today about sex education, with the government advocating "abstinence only" programs and others arguing that young people should be told about all the options. This cartoon suggests that any sex education program given in school will not be relevant to students' actual life experiences.

would be required to wait twenty-four hours before undergoing an abortion. The law also required that the woman's spouse be notified, as well as the parents of a minor teenager.

The Supreme Court upheld all the Pennsylvania requirements except spousal notification. A narrow five-judge majority held spousal notification to be unconstitutional because it was "unduly burdensome," particularly to women in abusive or otherwise dysfunctional marriages. It did not, however, consider a twenty-four-hour wait to be unduly burdensome to poor women. Many women cannot afford the extra travel, lodging, and child care costs they would need for an abortion. For these women, such extra costs can turn a burden into a veritable ban on access to abortion. The Hyde Amendment passed by Congress in 1976, which banned using publicly funded Medicaid money for abortion unless a woman's life was in danger, had already limited access to abortion for poor women. Many states stopped funding "medically unnecessary" abortions. Poor women could not afford abortions. In October 1977 Rosie Jiminez, a Texas woman, died from an illegal abortion in Mexico after Texas stopped funding Medicaid abortions.

Other Supreme Court decisions have weakened the *Roe v. Wade* decision. Several states have passed laws restricting abortion in various ways. Restrictions include requiring waiting periods, informed consent, and parental notification and allowing abortion only in cases of rape, incest, and risk to a woman's health. Many of these restrictions are now being contested in the courts. In March 1993, the Supreme Court upheld a lower-court decision that prohibited Louisiana from virtually outlawing abortions. This affirmed that states have no constitutional right to outlaw abortions. A Colorado law that prohibited Medicaid funding for abortions in cases of rape or incest was struck down by the Supreme Court in 1995, leaving intact a federal law that forces states to provide Medicaid funding of abortions for victims of rape or incest.

Anti-abortion activists have succeeded in intimidating doctors and clinics through the use of militant, often frightening demonstrations. Doctors and other clinic workers have been murdered. Most doctors now do not want to risk doing abortions. In 2010, there was no known abortion provider in 87 percent of the counties in the United States, where a third of women live (Bazelon, E., 2010).

In 1973, hospitals made up 80 percent of abortion facilities. After the *Roe v. Wade* decision, mainstream medicine backed away from abortions because of anti-abortion agitation. Feminist activists stepped in to set up stand-alone clinics to provide abortions. Fifteen years later, 90 percent of abortions were performed in such clinics (Bazelon, 2010). At the same time, medical schools increasingly refused to make abortion training part of their curriculum (*Our Bodies Ourselves*, 2010). However, an abortion-rights campaign, led by physicians themselves, has resulted in more medical schools training doctors to perform abortions. Jody Steinauer, an OB-GYN professor at the University of California at San Francisco, began the campaign in 1992. She organized the group Medical Students for Choice, which now has 10,000 members. The Accreditation Council for Graduate Medical Education—which represents the medical establishment—decided, for the first time, to make abortion training a requirement for all OB-GYN residency programs seeking its accreditation. This was opposed by anti-abortion advocates and, the following year, Congress passed the Coats Amendment, which declared that any residency program that failed to obey the Accreditation Council's mandate could still be deemed accredited by the federal government. Today, about half of the more than 200 OB-GYN residency programs integrate abortion into their residents' regular rotations. Another 40 percent of them offer only elective training.

People who oppose abortion made a further assault on the right to abortion through their efforts to ban what they called *partial-birth abortion*, a term that doctors considered medically meaningless. This ban, passed by Congress and signed into law by George W. Bush in 2003, was declared unconstitutional by Federal District Court Judge Phyllis J. Hamilton in 2004. Judge Hamilton said that the act creates a risk of criminal liability during virtually all abortions performed after the first trimester.

Writing for the National Organization for Women, Michele Keller said:

> Judge Hamilton noted that the Bush Administration passed extreme legislation with complete disregard for women's health and the law. The law would have barred safe abortions as early as 13 weeks by prohibiting a medical procedure regarded as the most effective in preserving a woman's health and future fertility. (Keller, 2005)

Another hotly contested issue in the abortion fight was mifepristone (formerly known as RU 486), the drug regimen that terminates pregnancy within the first five weeks, which can be taken by women at home. Anti-abortion forces tried to prohibit it; pro-abortion forces fought to have it legalized. After much research, the Food and Drug Administration (FDA) finally approved it in 2000. During his 2000 campaign, George W. Bush pledged to sign any legislation that restricts mifepristone. In August 2002, anti-abortion groups petitioned the FDA to ban mifepristone. However, it continues to be sold legally.

The "morning-after pill," called "Plan B," has also been a hotly contested issue, even though pro-abortion forces insist that it is not an abortion because it prevents the fertilized egg from being implanted in the wall of the uterus. In August 2006 the FDA ruled that it could be sold over the counter to women 18 and older. Plan B lowers the risk of pregnancy when started within 120 hours of unprotected intercourse.

Whether or not abortions are legal, women will continue to get them. One researcher says that the real public policy question is not whether we will have abortions but what kind of abortions we will have (Miller, 1992).

The kind of abortions performed while they were illegal was often very dangerous. In his 1955 survey of female sexual behavior, Kinsey, A., Pomeroy, W., and Martin, C. (1948) reported that 22 percent of his married respondents said they had had at least one abortion. Kinsey claimed that illegal abortion in the 1960s was estimated to be the third largest moneymaker for organized crime, exceeded only by narcotics and gambling, and he pointed out that most large public hospitals had septic abortion wards to treat the large number of life-threatening infections from abortions performed under nonsterile conditions.

Anti-abortionists won another victory in 2010 when the Obama administration denied abortion coverage for women whose pre-existing conditions will place them in "high risk pools" that were established through the recent health care reform legislation. Cecile Richards, president of the Planned Parenthood Federation of America, stated:

The very women who need to purchase private health insurance in the new high-risk pools are likely to be more vulnerable to medically complicated pregnancies. It is truly harmful to these women that the administration may impose limits on how they use their own private dollars, limiting their health care options at a time when they need them most. This decision has no basis in the law and flies in the face of the intent of high-risk pools that were meant to meet the medical needs of some of the most vulnerable women in this country. (*Our Bodies Ourselves*, 2010)

THE FETAL PROTECTION MOVEMENT

A recent tactic of the anti-abortion movement has been the campaign to protect the fetus from harm. Anti-abortion activists claim to care only about the health of the fetus, but as columnist Bob Herbert (1998) pointed out, they have a hidden agenda, to define the fetus as a person. If a fetus were defined as a person, abortion would logically become, under the law, murder (p. 17).

In 1998 Governor Tommy Thompson of Wisconsin signed into law a bill that permits the state to take into custody pregnant women who exhibit a serious and habitual "lack of self-control" in the use of alcohol or drugs. The bill defines *unborn child* as a human being from the time of fertilization to the time of birth and gives the state the right to appoint a legal guardian to represent the interests of the fetus.

The fetal protection movement has not made any serious effort to provide women with the treatment they need for alcohol and drug abuse—or even adequate prenatal care. That is not part of its agenda. "When South Carolina began locking up pregnant addicts for criminal child abuse, there was no residential treatment for pregnant addicts in the entire state. Wisconsin still has long waiting lists of pregnant women seeking addiction services" (Herbert, 1998, p. 17).

Anti-abortionists succeeded in getting a law passed declaring it a crime to harm a fetus, called The Unborn Victims of Violence Act. It was passed by Congress and signed into law by George W. Bush in 2004. This law gives a fetus the same rights as the pregnant woman. Kim Gandy made the following observations on the law:

The sponsors of this cynical bill have devised a strategy to redefine the Fourteenth Amendment, which guarantees equal protection of the law to "persons," which has never been defined to include fetuses. The inventive language of this bill covers "a member of the species *homo sapiens* at any stage of development." Such a definition of "person" could entitle fertilized eggs, embryos and fetuses to legal rights—ultimately setting the stage to legally reverse *Roe v. Wade.* (National Organization for Women, 2004a)

CRACK BABIES

It is hard to be clear about our values when we are bombarded by the agendas of so many different individuals, organizations, and the media. Newspapers want to sell papers, and TV shows want to get a large audience, and they often sensationalize stories in order to do this. The crack baby story is a good example.

The development of crack significantly reduced the price of cocaine and increased the availability of the drug, expanding its use from the middle and upper classes to urban minorities. Once cocaine abuse became crack abuse, the problem became sociopolitical rather than strictly medical (Musto, 1988). The rate of substance abuse among black women and among white women was about the same, according to a study of pregnant women in Pinellas County, Florida, although black women used cocaine more often than white women. However, despite similar rates of substance abuse, black women were ten times more likely to be reported to the authorities (Chasnoff, 1989). For the media, the

The issue of decriminalization of marijuana, especially for medical purposes, is very controversial. Advocates and opponents of making the growing, sale, and possession of "pot" legal, give strong arguments to support their positions.

demonization of drug-abusing parturient women made better copy than did detailed elaborations of the complexity of the germane issues (Lyons & Rittner, 1998).

It is true that using substances such as crack, alcohol, cigarettes, and amphetamines can be harmful to a developing fetus. Yet the media seized on the issue of crack babies and created an atmosphere of hysteria with news about a problem of "epidemic" proportions. It exaggerated the numbers involved.

It is difficult to assess the causes of damage to a newborn. If the mother used any cocaine, the assumption is often made that all the damage to the child was due to cocaine when in fact there may have been multiple causes, including malnutrition. Most of the mothers are poor, and some are homeless. One researcher asks, "What would be the public implications if . . . we learned that what we thought were drug effects were actually due to poverty and not to drugs per se?" (Lester & Tronick, 1994, p. 118).

The media created the impression that any baby whose mother had used crack was ruined for life. Yet research suggests that the damage done to the newborn may not necessarily be permanent. Many babies can recover from the effects of crack-cocaine *if given adequate treatment and support.* The permanent damage some of them suffer may be the result of the family's *poverty and lack of adequate health care, housing, and other social supports.*

Some of the findings of this research have begun to find their way into the popular media, but the earlier scare stories had a profound effect on politicians and officials. Record numbers of single mothers are in prison for first-time drug offenses. A 2005 report by the American Civil Liberties Union (ACLU) said:

The rate of imprisonment of women for drug crimes has far outpaced that of men, particularly women of color and low-income women. Women of color use drugs at a rate equal to or lower than white women, yet are far more likely to be affected by current drug laws and policies. Selective testing of pregnant women of color for dug use as well as heightened surveillance of poor mothers of color in the context of policing child abuse and neglect exacerbate these racial disparities. (American Civil Liberties Union, 2005)

Women who are mothers find treatment difficult to access because many residential treatment programs make no provision for the children. Pregnant or parenting women are penalized for the alleged risk to their fetuses or children posed by their drug use or addiction, rather than being given the support necessary to appropriately address their situation. In the absence of viable drug treatment options, women's drug use and addiction are more likely to be treated as criminal justice issues than the health problems they truly are. (p. 2)

Sexual violence at the hands of correctional officers as well as the severe inadequacy of medical care are but two of the conditions faced by women on the inside. A mother's prolonged incarceration often leads to the destruction of relationships with her family, financial hardship to the caretakers of the children left behind and, all to often, placement of children in an already overburdened and problematic foster care system, which can result in termination of her parental rights. Elders are left without caregivers, and communities without workers (p. 3).

As a result of the so-called war on drugs and promotion of "fetal rights," women's reproductible rights have been attacked through the criminal prosecution of pregnant women who use drugs. An estimated 200 women in more than thirty states have been prosecuted in charges of "drug delivery, "drug possession," or "fetal/child abuse" based on evidence of drug use during pregnancy (ACLU, p. 15).

As we sort out our values, we need to be careful not to be swept up in popular hysteria about a problem, and we need to distill the true facts from all the myths and stereotypes.

ATTITUDES TOWARD ABORTION ARE DEEPLY ROOTED BELIEFS

When does life begin? This is an abstract philosophical question, which most of us probably answer according to our value system and not by scientific evidence. Catholic theology holds that life begins at conception, although some believe that the Catholic hierarchy does not represent the views of most American Catholics on this issue nor the practice of Catholic women who have abortions at the same rate as the national average for all women. Some orthodox Jews believe that life begins with the sperm, even before it meets the egg. Other religious groups, such as the Mormons and fundamentalist Christians, oppose abortion on religious grounds.

Many of the most militant anti-abortion demonstrators have come from the ranks of fundamentalist Christians with conservative politics. Although they sponsor a few social service agencies geared to help women keep their babies, as a group they pay little attention to the policies that make it easier for poor women to raise children—adequate TANF grants, affordable housing, good wages, child care, and so forth. One of the authors of this text (Mandell) circulated a petition to raise AFDC grants at an anti-abortion demonstration. No anti-abortion protestors signed it, and some expressed their opposition to or ignorance of welfare. Many pro-choice counter-demonstrators, on the other hand, eagerly signed the petition.

Despite our own pro-choice stance, we have great respect for those who oppose abortion because of their deep commitment to preserve life and who express that commitment after the children are born by working for a more equal distribution of tax money and an end to war. The Catholic Workers are one such group of dedicated pacifists and social activists who oppose abortion.

Human service workers need to inform themselves thoroughly about the issues, be as clear as possible about where they stand, and make their position known to clients so that their biases do not subtly influence clients to make choices they may later regret.

STEM CELL RESEARCH

If a fetus deserves the same protection as an existing child, does a stem cell also deserve that protection? Is using embryonic stem cells for research equivalent to an abortion? This is the subject of fierce debate between pro-abortion and anti-abortion forces.

Embryonic stem cells, harvested from five-day-old fertilized eggs, may offer the best hope for curing some serious diseases, such as Alzheimer's, Parkinson's, type 1 diabetes, and arthritis. Scientists believe that embryonic stem cells can be regenerated into customized replacement organs that resist rejection. Research suggests that these cells can become insulin-producing cells that would ease the burden of diabetes (Rosen, 2001).

Federal research guidelines allow only the use of excess embryos stored at fertility clinics, a by-product of the widely accepted practice of in vitro fertilization, and then only with permission of the parents who produced the embryos (Rosen, 2001). Although the issue has been framed as an abortion issue, even the opponents of abortion are split on this. Senator Orrin Hatch, an anti-abortion stalwart, was open to the possibility of stem cell research, defending his position by arguing that people who are pro-life are also pro-life for existing life.

President George W. Bush, who had received a good deal of support from opponents of abortion, agonized over the decision, and in the summer of 2001, he compromised by allowing research on what he described as sixty self-sustaining colonies of embryonic stem cells that existed in the United States and abroad. Researchers objected that there were far fewer than sixty but seemed to accept President Bush's decision as better than nothing. However, researchers expressed doubts about the usefulness of the existing colonies, which used material from mouse cells and bovine serum. Critics of Bush's policy say this contaminates the colonies. This is a good illustration of how ideological positions can affect the direction of scientific research.

In September 2009, President Obama issued an executive order that expanded embryonic stem cell research. However, a federal district judge blocked the executive order, saying it violated a ban on federal money being used to destroy embryos. The ruling came as a shock to scientists at the National Institute of Health and at universities across the country, which had viewed the Obama administration's new policy and the grants provided under it as settled law (Harris, 2010).

SEX OFFENDERS

How do you prevent sex offenders from molesting children? Pass a law to prevent them from getting near children? After the murder of seven-year-old Megan Kanka by a released sex offender living on her street, public outcry created a call for programs to provide the public with information regarding released sex offenders. Congress passed a law in 1996 called "Megan's Law," which requires all states to conduct community notification but does not set out specific forms and methods, other than requiring the creation of Internet sites containing state sex-offender information. Beyond that requirement, states are given broad discretion in creating their own policies. The law was an amendment to a previous law passed in 1994, which required convicted sex offenders to register their addresses with local law enforcement (National Center for Missing & Exploited Children, 2007).

At least thirty states and thousands of municipalities nationwide have passed residency restrictions for sex offenders (Ward, 2008) and have designated areas where sex offenders are not allowed to live—near schools, playgrounds, day care centers, and other places where children congregate—in the hope of preventing repeat offenses. Does it work? There is increasing evidence that it doesn't. Studies have shown that family members or acquaintances perpetrate most sexual molestation of children, that many sex crimes are never reported, and that sex offenders often molest beyond the areas where they live. Some scholars believe that the measures could put children in greater danger, not less—because the sex offenders go underground, because therapy works to prevent re-offense, and because limited resources are wasted enforcing the laws. No one who has professional experience in the management of sex offenders thinks these laws make much sense.

Many people ignore or minimize the issue of the civil liberties of the sex offender, believing that he poses such a great danger that his civil liberties are not important. However, the residency laws pose serious civil liberties concerns. These measures apply to convicts after they have been punished and released and served their parole. In many cases, homeowners are exempt while renters may be required to move. And this type of post-release regulation doesn't exist for other criminal classes. For example, arsonists are not prohibited from living near gas stations. In some cases, the strict residency restrictions have caused more issues than they have solved. Many sex offenders cannot find housing in urban areas and often are forced into homelessness (Dunlap, 2010).

One of the nation's most aggressive attempts to limit the mobility of sex offenders was struck down in Georgia in 2007 by the Georgia Supreme Court, which declared the state law unconstitutional. The Georgia Supreme Court ruled that, by forcing a sex-offender from his home, the law violated his Fifth Amendment right to be safe from the government "taking" his property. The ruling said, "It is apparent that there is no place in Georgia where a registered sex offender can live without continually being at risk of being ejected" (Whoriskey, 2007). (We discuss this case more fully in Chapter 14.)

CONFLICTING VIEWS ON THE NATURE OF HUMAN NATURE

The Declaration of Independence states that people have an inalienable right to life, liberty, and the pursuit of happiness. But in daily life, no one is guaranteed a job, and no one is guaranteed an income or a home or food. No matter how compassionate a worker in a welfare department is, he or she is forced to convey the message to clients that society does not place them in high enough esteem for even a poverty-level income.

Although welfare recipients' taxes have already paid for some of the money they receive, taxes probably do not cover all of the money received. Money must come from the haves to help the have-nots. This is also true of Social Security. Most people get back a good deal more than they paid into the fund. *Yet the crucial question is not whether people should get back only as much as they paid but whether society as a whole has a responsibility to care for its members when they are having a hard time.*

Your values about the kind of society you want to live in are partially shaped by your beliefs about human nature. Each of us has a mental picture of the "normal" child or adult,

There are arguments for and against the New York City health department's campaign to distribute more than 1 million free condoms. Advocates argue that using condoms will reduce the spread of AIDS. Opponents assert that easy availability of condoms could increase sexual promiscuity, increasing transmission of the virus. What do you think?

even if we have never articulated it. If we are program planners, administrators, or food stamp clerks, our basic view of people will be expressed in many direct and subtle ways as we plan or implement social programs.

These are some of the most common views of the nature of human nature. Which ones come closest to yours? In what ways do your views differ from your parents', your peers', or your neighbors'?

The Belief That People Need to Be Civilized

Some people believe that human beings are born basically evil—born in sin. Although they may be redeemed by the grace of God, they must be kept under control by the rules and regulations of society and civilization.

For **Thomas Hobbes**, a seventeenth-century English philosopher, the human condition was characterized by both desire and rationality. If everyone pursued desire fulfillment, that, according to Hobbes, might lead to conflict with others and to lives that are "nasty, brutish, and short." But every rational person wants to live and to live in peace. Thus he or she accepts authority to regulate, and perhaps curb, desire. Considering the times in which he lived, a period of constant war, Hobbes's conclusions are understandable.

Some people have interpreted William Golding's widely read novel *Lord of the Flies* (1959) as a Hobbesian allegory. In this story, a group of English schoolboys, stranded by an airplane crash on a desert island, create a social order that looks very much like the Hobbesian scenario of dog-eat-dog survival, with restraints of authority removed. (Others point out that the boys were simply duplicating the authoritarian society of the supposedly civilized English private school from which they came.)

People who subscribe to a view of human nature similar to Hobbes's are likely to advocate a strong authority and favor "law and order" approaches to human problems. Clearly, Hobbes doesn't believe in self-regulation. A social worker sharing Hobbes's distrust of self-regulation might give clients vouchers rather than cash, keep careful watch over their behavior, and invoke strong punishment for deviations.

The Belief That People Are Basically Rational

While Hobbes was propounding his theories, **John Locke**, another English philosopher and scientist, had a different view. He believed that if people followed their own self-interest, a rational, just society would result. Locke rejected the traditional view that babies were born with fixed selfish ideas or brutish characteristics. He believed instead that a child came into the world with a *tabula rasa* (blank tablet) on which the world could inscribe itself through the experience of the five senses. People in the helping professions who follow a philosophy similar to Locke's would be likely to subscribe to a more environmentally oriented psychology such as that of the **behaviorist** B. F. Skinner (1974). The assumption in his work is that with the appropriate stimuli, correctly administered, human social behavior can be positively shaped and changed.

Hobbes, Thomas A seventeenth-century philosopher who believed that people need a strong authority in order to regulate their desires.

Locke, John A seventeenth-century English philosopher and scientist who believed that if people followed their own self-interest, a rational, just society would result.

behaviorist A theorist who believes that behavior can be shaped or changed by the systematic application of rewards for behavioral compliance with the demands of the caregiver or therapist.

The Belief That People Are Corrupted by Society

Rousseau, Jean-Jacques   An eighteenth-century Swiss-French philosopher who believed that people were good by nature but corrupted by civilization.

Jean-Jacques Rousseau, an eighteenth-century Swiss-French philosopher, put forth the idea that people were good by nature but corrupted by civilization: "Man is born free, but is everywhere in chains." He believed that education should draw out the knowledge that people are born with, in contrast to the "banking" theory of education, which holds that knowledge should be deposited in people's empty heads. Education, according to Rousseau, should allow the free development of human potential. Paolo Freire (1970), a Brazilian adult educator, subscribed to a theory of education called "conscientization," which is similar to Rousseau's theory. According to Freire, poor people's education should begin by raising questions about their life situation, why they are so poor, and why they have been kept from getting the education they need.

The Belief That People Need to Be Connected to Each Other

Several nontraditional and feminist psychologists suggest that, in contrast to the individualistic and competitive orientation commonly found in men, women are socialized to place value on nurturing, cooperation, and nonviolence. Carol Gilligan (1982) asserts that women choose their actions when faced with a moral dilemma according to what effect their choice will have on the others who are involved rather than by referring to abstract concepts of justice. Caring and responsibility for others are central to their moral concerns.

Psychologist Jean Baker Miller (1976) says that these "feminine" traits that have been traditionally regarded as weaknesses are, in fact, strengths. They take us beyond the "macho" succeed-at-any-cost attitude. She suggests that men as well as women need to strengthen their ability to empower each other without needing to dominate or control.

Not everyone agrees that women are naturally more caring than men. We all probably know selfish women who don't care about other people's feelings, and men who are very caring. As many feminists warn, we should avoid "essentialist" thinking, which believes that women and men have essentially different and unchanging characteristics.

CONFLICTS CAUSED BY BUREAUCRATIC DEMANDS

Most human service workers, unless they are in private practice or a small independent agency, are employed by bureaucracies that have organizational needs that may be contrary to the needs of workers and clients. In fact, they often pit workers against clients. A welfare worker, for example, may be convinced that a TANF claimant needs more money than the grant allows but is unable to help the client because of state and federal regulations.

According to Max Weber (Gerth & Mills, 1958), a nineteenth-century sociologist, bureaucracy is supposed to make work more efficient, to substitute dependable rules for arbitrary decisions, to treat people more fairly, and to judge workers on merit rather than favoritism. But bureaucracies also depersonalize and objectify people. They divide work into specialized components so that no one has the satisfaction of seeing a job through to completion. They set up hierarchies of authority that take away the autonomy of workers.

One of the most pervasive problems of modern society is **bureaucratization** of work and of relationships. In human service work, this is especially serious because our work requires warm and genuine relationships between people.

The occupational hazard for workers in a bureaucracy is the tendency to "go along to get along." Most workers want to keep their jobs and do what is required, even when it is not in the best interest of clients. Social psychologists have studied the tendency to go along willingly with authority. One of the most famous of these studies is the Milgram experiment on blind obedience, which explored the conditions under which people would refuse to obey immoral commands (Milgram, 1974). Milgram asked people to "shock" subjects with varying amounts of "electricity" each time they made an error on a task. (Subjects were not actually shocked but were trained actors who simulated being shocked.) Far more people obeyed the commands than either Milgram or others predicted. Milgram concluded that a person's conscience is diminished in a hierarchical system and that in authority systems, people are more likely to see themselves as agents who carry out other people's wishes rather than as autonomous decision makers.

Another classic study that revealed people's willingness to go along with authority was the prison experiment that Zimbardo, Haney, Banks, and Jaffe (1982) conducted with healthy college students. Half of the students were instructed to be "prisoners," the other half "guards." In a very short time, the students were adopting the behavior they had been assigned. The experiment had to be discontinued because of the sadism of some of the "guards" and because some participants, especially the "prisoners," were breaking down emotionally.

bureaucratization
Increased organizational centralization, hierarchical control, larger workplaces, and decreased autonomy for workers.

Guidelines for Dealing with Conflicts in a Bureaucracy

The task of debureaucratizing society is an enormous one that requires the best creative thoughts and efforts of all of us. We need to accept responsibility for the ethical and political dimensions of our work. Rhodes (1989) suggests that workers can do that by:

- Speaking out about their beliefs, showing the politics behind alternative courses of action, and pointing out inconsistencies in the way the agency does its work. Speaking out is a skill that requires as much planning and thought as the most carefully planned case presentation.
- Forming alliances with other workers and with clients to organize social action on policy issues.
- Questioning the rationale behind rules and regulations rather than docilely implementing policies with which the workers disagree.
- Offering expertise on legislative committees, pushing for legislative action, and educating the public about human service issues (pp. 154, 156).

The Client as Our Employer

The concept that the client is our employer is closely related to the value of self-determination—the belief that only clients can decide what is best for themselves. Even when the client does not pay a fee for our service, we subscribe to the belief that the service should be responsive primarily to his or her needs, not to the workers' or agency's needs. Yet clients are rarely asked to evaluate our services, make suggestions for improvement, serve on boards, or attend case conferences. Overworked agencies are under pressure to "process" people through the system in as short a time as possible.

Some workers who have undergone long and arduous training in the profession may not understand why their clients' opinions about what they need should be valued. This is especially true when their clients are poor, incarcerated, or mentally unstable. Nevertheless, just as in a relationship with an architect, a real estate agent, or a lawyer, the client has the right to decide which problems are most pressing and which treatment methods are most acceptable.

Professionalization creates built-in conflicts about how to behave with clients. Social work comes out of a nineteenth-century paternalistic tradition. Gratitude was expected from "deserving" clients. Help was refused to the "undeserving." Although twentieth-century professionals no longer hold such expectations, old attitudes linger. When money or services are defined as everybody's right, as with Social Security, beneficiaries feel entitled to the benefit and do not feel any obligation to be grateful or behave in a certain way. However, when a service is not presented as an automatic entitlement, there are ambiguous behavioral expectations. Both the giver and the recipient resent a relationship in which one person does all the giving and the other does all the taking. Self-help groups derive much of their attraction from the fact that power is shared equally among the members. *The relationship of a human service worker to a client is inherently unequal because of the power differential. The worker is in a position to give or withhold benefits.*

In the chapter on diversity, we suggest that some cultural groups expect a very personalized helping relationship, and therefore it is important to structure the relationship to meet their expectations. A classic study of helping relationships in child abuse and neglect (Berkeley Planning Associates, 1978) concluded that two of the most important factors in helping parents were a more friendly, personalized relationship and the down-to-earth assistance given by parent aides. This was true for a wide variety of cultural groups. Rhodes (1989) concluded, after reviewing four studies of client satisfaction, that

> Client satisfaction and client change depended to some extent on clients' perceptions of their workers as "friends." And such friendship had the following qualities: empathy, caring, flexibility, patience, suggestions rather than advice, reciprocity in the form of sharing aspects of one's personal life, and immediate concrete help in the mode requested. In addition, many small social activities were viewed as important to befriending: "calling in for a cup of tea, accepting an invitation to a party, sending cards while on holiday, extending a home-visit to play with the children. . . ." (p. 164)

These clients did not seem to make a sharp distinction between "friend" and "professional" when they liked their worker. If a worker was only a professional and not a friend, the worker was usually viewed with hostility or at least distrust (Rhodes, 1989).*

Studies of clients' opinion of human service workers are rare, and the few that Rhodes cited are not necessarily the last word on professional practice. Some of the findings, such as the importance of "many small social activities," are contrary to much of the advice that the professional literature gives caseworkers.

---

*Studies that Rhodes reviewed included Mayer and Timms (1970), Sainsbury (1974), Rees (1979), and Keefe and Maypole (1983).

We would understand much more about client satisfaction if every agency regularly asked for feedback. The fact that this is done so rarely suggests that professionals have not yet fully accepted clients as their employers, whom they are obliged to satisfy.

Social Class Differences between Workers and Clients

Human service workers are often of a different social class than their clients. A large proportion of agency clientele are poor, and the social class of workers generally ranges from lower to upper middle class. Sometimes workers impose their class-based values on their poorer clients. This was evident in one study of adoption workers. It showed that middle-class workers selected adoptive parents who were "shockingly similar" to themselves (Maas & Engler, 1959, p. 374). The typical husband and wife were white and Protestant, had strong inner controls and little personal flexibility, placed a heavy emphasis on education and ambition, were task oriented, lived in a single-family home, earned much more than the average income, and had at least a high school degree. Yet there are surely other kinds of people who can be excellent parents.

In the 1960s, some research showed that caseworkers believed that people should not rely too heavily on their relatives for help (Leichter & Mitchell, 1967). Caseworkers at that time were mostly white, upwardly mobile, and middle class. They tended to discourage dependence on extended-kin networks. Their attitude has changed somewhat because later research showed that networks play a major role in the lives of poor and working-class families. In fact, we have come to realize that these networks constitute a source of strength for all families. Yet, despite agencies' professed goal of strengthening the family, the bulk of state child-welfare money is spent on foster care rather than on homemaker service, respite care, parent aides, and day care for hard-pressed families. All of these could strengthen a crumbling family, so that the child would not have to be placed in a foster home with strangers.

CONFLICTS DUE TO THE VARIATION IN NATIONAL VALUES IN THE UNITED STATES

Although it is as hard to generalize about national values as about individual or ethnic-group values, some dominant themes stand out in each nation. At times these themes conflict with one another. In the United States, the democratic and humanitarian values expressed in our Constitution stand side by side with the Protestant ethic, which says that all people who work hard enough can "pull themselves up by their own bootstraps." Social Darwinism maintains that in society, as in the jungle, only the most fit can and should survive.

These contradictions help us understand the mixture of progressive and surprisingly punitive legislation that makes up our social welfare system. The values implicit in the punitive legislation often strongly influence public opinion and misconceptions about welfare assistance. In the United States, people in need of financial assistance often receive less help and are more stigmatized than they are in several European countries.

It is interesting to see how these values of competition, individualism, and a belief that people are in control of their own destiny affect the view of people in the United States toward the mentally ill. Anthropological studies of cultural attitudes toward mental illness show that many other cultures are more tolerant of mental illness than the United States and other Western societies. Schizophrenics actually seem more likely to recover in less-developed countries, such as Mexico or India (Bass, 1992).

Anthropologist Janis Jenkins found that Mexican and Indian families are more likely to believe there are forces *outside* each person's control that influence their ability to ward off disease. They are, therefore, much more likely to believe that the person suffering from mental illness deserves sympathy, support, and special treatment. Latinos are also more likely than European Americans to believe that even severe mental illness is curable. When people *believe* that they will be cured, they are more likely to be cured. In the United States, on the other hand, we are more likely to stigmatize mentally ill people because of the dominant belief that people are autonomous and in control of their own destiny (Bass, 1992).

Jenkins (1981) found that Latino families seem to be more tolerant of unusual behavior, such as hearing voices or having delusions of grandeur, because of the way Hispanic cultures view religion. Jenkins speculated that in the Latino culture, people often talk to Jesus and the saints and feel close to spirits, so family members are not as concerned about a patient hearing voices as they are by disruptive or disrespectful behavior (Jenkins, 1981).

In contrast to the greater tolerance of Latino cultures toward mental illness, European American adults are more likely to see mental illness as a personal weakness.

Age and Aging

ageism The practice of discriminating against people because they are old; attitudes associated with the practice.

Increasing awareness of race and sex discrimination has been followed by an increased awareness of age discrimination. Robert Butler (1975), former director of the National Institute of Aging, coined the term **ageism**. In a culture that values youth, attractiveness, productivity, and activity, older people are often devalued. Professionals who work with them sometimes share society's dominant attitudes. Many professional psychiatrists feel inadequate treating older people (Cyrus-Lutz & Gaitz, 1972). Some human service workers have misconceptions about the inevitability of the degenerative process. Although there is no evidence suggesting there must always be a decline in the mental activity, responsibility, and even sexual prowess of the elderly, it is difficult not to be influenced by these widely held misconceptions.

Sexual Orientation

homophobia An unreasoning fear or loathing of people who have intimate sexual relationships with people of the same sex.

The lesbian folk singer Betsy Rose sings a song about a lesbian telling her mother for the first time that she is a lesbian. In contrast to the shock and consternation that most mothers would express, Betsy Rose's imaginary mother in the song is delighted and says, "Darlin', I'm glad you're gay!" The song is presented humorously, and the audience laughs because it is so contrary to what happens in real life.

Homophobia (the irrational fear and stigmatization of homosexuality) is deeply ingrained in society, and human service workers are not immune to it. It was not until 1973 that the American Psychiatric Association declared that homosexuality was not a mental illness and removed it from its list of psychiatric disorders. Two years later, the American Psychological Association followed suit.

Despite the lack of scientific evidence for regarding homosexuality as an aberrant or degenerative disease, homosexuals have been a stigmatized minority in many societies. They were one of the first groups the Nazis forced into concentration camps in Poland and Germany. They were required to wear a pink triangle as an identifying symbol, in the same way that the Jews had to wear a yellow star. It is important to remember that the mentally ill and retarded were also locked up in the concentration camps, as were Gypsies, Masons, Seventh-Day Adventists, and others whom the Nazis viewed as less than human. When we define any-one as being less human than we are, we have taken a step toward the death camps.

Because they are stigmatized, gays and lesbians often stay in the "closet"—that is, they pretend to be heterosexual. It is often traumatic for them to publicly acknowledge their sex-ual orientation. It may be especially hard for older people, because the stigma was even more severe in their youth.

As early as 1948, the Kinsey study reported that among men between the ages of 16 and 55, 13 percent were homosexuals for at least three years, 25 percent had more than incidental homosexual experience for at least three years, and 37 percent had at least some overt homosexual experience to the point of orgasm (Kinsey, Pomeroy, & Martin, 1948).

It is a safe bet that, whether you know it or not, you work with, learn with, or are taught by a gay person, whether or not they identify themselves as such. The homeless mother in a battered women's shelter, the undocumented immigrant from El Salvador in an English as a Second Language program, the man in a nursing home with Alzheimer's disease, the runaway teenager on the street, your supervisor—any of them could be gay. They are not likely to tell you until they trust you. It is important not to make any a priori assumptions about a person's sexual orientation. If, for example, you are a hospital social worker and are called to help a man who was brought to the hospital because of a bicycle accident and someone needs to be notified, you might ask him, "Could you tell me the name of someone who is close to you who could come to help you?" rather than asking, "Do you have a wife I should phone?"

As of 2010, same-sex marriage had been legalized in five states—Connecticut, Iowa, Massachusetts, New Hampshire, and Vermont—and Washington, D.C. When even long-term gay couples cannot legally marry, they do not have the same rights as married hetero-sexuals. Gay companions are not automatically consulted about their mates' welfare, as are husbands and wives. Occasionally one reads in the newspaper about a gay or lesbian who has had an accident and is seriously disabled. Although the lover has on a day-to-day basis acted as a legal spouse and would logically be the one to care for his or her mate, the parents of the disabled person insist on gaining custody, and the wishes of the accident victim are ignored.

At some point, you might be asked to make a recommendation to a judge in a custody case. As a human service worker, you are more likely to be concerned with the capacity of parents to nurture their child than with that parent's sexual orientation. Several stereotypes exist about gays and lesbians as parents:

- They will sexually abuse children in their care
- The children will grow up to be gay
- Children will be psychologically harmed by being raised by two parents of the same sex
- Children will be harmed by the social stigma

Research has not shown that any of these stereotypes are supported by the facts. Heterosexual men do most sexual abuse of children. Children of gay parents are no more likely to grow up gay than are children of heterosexual parents. (Remember, heterosexual parents raised the vast majority of homosexuals.) Studies that compare children of lesbians and gays with children raised by heterosexuals show that gay men and lesbian parents do not differ in child-rearing practices or lifestyle from other parents. Apparently their children have no more adjustment problems than do other children. "In fact, there is some evidence that children of lesbians have a greater appreciation for diversity of all kinds and value tolerance more highly than others, having seen first-hand the toll that prejudice like homophobia can take" (Appleby & Anastas, 1992, p. 360). For example, the lesbian singers Betsy Rose and Holly Near show appreciation for diversity by signing their concerts for the benefit of deaf people. As for stigma, there is no clinical evidence of stigma or unusual emotional problems in these children (Kirkpatrick & Hitchens, 1985).

New reproductive technologies, especially artificial insemination, have opened up the possibilities for childbearing for younger lesbians. Some gays and lesbians also want to become foster or adoptive parents. "Social workers in medical and child-welfare settings increasingly find themselves dealing with lesbian clients as they give birth, and with gay and lesbian clients seeking adoptive or foster children or who come for help with the vicissitudes of parenting" (Appleby & Anastas, 1992, p. 359).

KEEPING VALUES STRAIGHT IN A TIME OF WAR

The 9/11 attack on the United States and the subsequent war on Iraq and Afghanistan have created value dilemmas for everyone in the country. Human service workers share in the world's grief and bewilderment as we try to sort out the issues. How do our core values shape our reactions to this crisis? Does our profession have anything special to offer the world?

Frederic Reamer, a social work professor, looks to the core values of social work as guidance for these times, and his advice is appropriate for all human service workers (Reamer, 2001). One of the core values is respect for the dignity and worth of the person. Social workers (and all other human service workers) have a strong belief in human dignity and worth. But what about our response to the terrorists? Should we also be expected to respect their dignity and worth? "As an analogy, must social workers who help rape victims respect the dignity and worth of rapists? Must social workers who help abused children respect the dignity and worth of the abusers? What, if any, are the limits of social workers' long-standing commitment to being non-judgmental? In an abstract sense, some social workers argue, practitioners can feel angry toward the rapist or child abuser and still respect that individual's basic human worth and dignity and right to assistance. It is this respect that gives these social workers the strength, stamina, and fortitude to work with offenders and help them achieve the insights and behavior change that can prevent future misconduct and harm" (p. 23).

Social workers are also called upon to respect individual difference and cultural and ethnic diversity. At the same time, social workers sometimes struggle to distinguish the ethical from the unethical. "At what point does a culturally accepted child rearing practice, such as physical beatings, become an ethically unacceptable form of child abuse? . . . By extension, at what point does the Taliban government's treatment of its citizens—especially its women—become ethically intolerable? Cultural relativism and tolerance have their

In 2003 the state of Massachusetts legalized marriage between two persons of the same gender. In response to this break with tradition, some legislators attempted to amend the U.S. Constitution to make such unions illegal.

place in social work, but they also have their limits. There is a bottom line in social work ethics. The challenge, of course, is deciding where to draw that bottom line" (p. 23).

Reamer concludes with important advice to all of us: "Social work's core values can ground us during these frightening times as we seek to regain our balance and equilibrium. If we're not careful, our understandable outrage, fear, and anguish can lead us to view the enemy as a dehumanized demon that must be annihilated no matter the cost to our own soul. As much as possible, we must resist the temptation to retaliate in a way that compromises our fundamental values and principles" (p. 23).

In addition to examining our individual values, it is important to study the politics of the country's wars. Spending on war means less money for safety net programs and social services.

FINDING YOUR WAY THROUGH THE MAZE OF ETHICAL CONFLICTS

How do we find our way through the thicket of ethical dilemmas and ambiguity? The first thing we need to do is learn to tolerate ambiguity. Rhodes (1989) says that resolving ethical dilemmas is not a hopeless undertaking. First, we need to separate them into those that can be solved and those that demand action but can't be solved. Human service workers are under pressure to believe that all problems are solvable, yet they are called on to work with problems that nobody has yet been able to solve—poverty, alcoholism, and drug addiction, as well as problems that are an inevitable part of life—old age, disabilities, and death. Rhodes cautions us to "recognize the immensity of the task we are expected to do and the inevitable failures that must result" (1989, p. 9).

Rhodes recommends that we set aside time to focus on the ethical dilemmas we face every day. If we avoid the issues, we will "muddle through," assuming that we are helping others when we may not be. Agencies could help workers with this by setting aside time for workers to discuss ethical issues. Rhodes says,

> *Dialogue is central to ethics. Only through sustained and open dialogue can we develop ethical positions.*

This assumes that:

1. We can communicate across different views;
2. We can be open to each other; and
3. We need other views in order to fully reexamine our own. (1989, p. 19)

SUMMARY

1. No one is value free. Our values are shaped by many influences: families, friends, school, church, the workplace, and our social class, ethnicity, and gender.

2. The value of self-determination is important in the human service professions.

3. Despite its importance, self-determination is difficult to follow in practice, especially in work with involuntary clients.

4. Decisions about self-determination must weigh the good of the individual against the good of the community.

5. Child-welfare agencies are under fire across the nation. Complaints come from biological parents, foster parents, and advocacy groups.

6. Human service workers disagree about treating clients who are ordered to receive treatment. Some refuse, believing that the client's right of self-determination is an overriding value. Others believe that they can often overcome resistance and their help will be accepted.

7. Self-determination can be violated by manipulation as well as by overtly coercive methods. Manipulation should be avoided.

8. Some current ethical dilemmas center on the treatment of AIDS patients, the right to die, and reproductive choice.

9. One's view of human nature shapes the service one gives. Three views of human nature were proposed by Thomas Hobbes, John Locke, and Jean-Jacques Rousseau.

10. Bureaucracies often conflict with meeting the needs of clients and workers.

11. Workers need to take responsibility for their own beliefs and speak out about them.

12. Conflicts about national values affect policy and practice. A mixture of progressive and punitive values shapes welfare policies.

13. Clients are our employers, though they are seldom asked their opinion about our services. Feedback from clients improves practice.

14. Social class and other differences between workers and clients often interfere with giving and taking help.

15. There are misconceptions about the process of aging.

16. Conflicts about sexual orientation affect human service policy and practice.

17. Dialogue is central to dealing with ambiguity. Only through dialogue can we carve out the most ethical positions.

18. It is hard to keep our values clear in a time of war. We offer some guidelines.

DISCUSSION QUESTIONS

1. Although self-determination is an important value in human service work, it is often hard to follow in certain kinds of work. In what ways could self-determination be maximized in the following situations if you were the human service worker?
   a. A parent has been reported as being abusive to a child.
   b. A person who was driving while drunk has been mandated to get treatment.
   c. A delinquent is on probation.

2. A woman says she would rather die than go through the debilitating processes that are inevitable with her illness. She is fifty years old and has early-onset Alzheimer's disease. What are your thoughts on this?

3. You are given the job of leading a discussion between pro-choice and pro-life people. How do you structure this discussion?

4. In some open adoption arrangements, the biological parent and the adoptive parents continue to have contact with each other after the adoption, and the biological parent is allowed to have frequent contact with the child. What are the possible advantages and disadvantages of this arrangement? Do the same issues that apply to open adoption also apply to artificial insemination, when the child who is born as a result of the insemination is allowed to contact his or her father?

5. Why do you think that few social agencies have institutionalized a process to get regular feedback from clients?

WEB RESOURCES FOR FURTHER STUDY

The Hastings Center
www.thehastingscenter.org

The Hastings Center is an independent, nonpartisan, and nonprofit bioethics research institute founded in 1969 to explore fundamental and emerging questions in health care, biotechnology, and the environment.

National Association of Social Workers (NASW)
www.socialworkers.org

The NASW code of ethics is intended to serve as a guide to the everyday professional conduct of social workers.

National Organization for Human Services
www.nationalhumanservices.org

Ethical Standards for Human Service Professionals are on this NOHS web site.

Self-determination theory
Deci, E., & Ryan, R. (2004) *Handbook of self-determination research*. Rochester, N.Y.,: University of Rochester Press.

Chapter 6

The Social Welfare System

Sandra remembers standing in line at food pantries last year thinking, "I'm working and here I am in a food line. It's hard." Those were the worst times for Sandra and her three children. She was driving a van for elderly and handicapped people, but not making enough to pay her rent and buy food. "We had a meal every day but it wasn't enough. I didn't eat," she says. "Joey [then 11] was always hungry" (Project Bread/The Walk for Hunger, 1991).

It is a warm July evening. Through the windows, a mother and her two children listen to the sounds of a carnival in town. They walk up the street. Standing on a small hill, they watch the Ferris wheel go around and spot the glow from the new rocket ride. The mother and the children walk slowly back home. The children look over their shoulders at the lights from the rides. Their mother does not have the money for the entrance fees. (Schein, 1995)

What can a human service worker do for these two families? To answer this question, we must look not only at the social welfare programs that might help them but also at the kind of society they live in and whom that society chooses to help. We describe the major social welfare programs in the United States and the social context of those programs.

We have found that students in human service and social work programs often regard social policy as a boring course. Students may not immediately see the relevance of these programs to their lives, yet some benefit programs and social services may help them. For example, if they have worked, even as work-study students, the Earned Income Tax Program could give them some money. If they are low-income, they may be able to get food stamps. If they get a low-paying job after they graduate, they may be eligible for food stamps. (Many Walmart employees get food stamps.) When students practice in the human service field, it is essential for them to know which programs could help their clients. And when they vote, they need to know which politicians plan to cut benefits and services and which want to expand these benefits and services. Your vote may help to save your job.

SOCIAL WELFARE PROGRAMS AND POLICIES

Social welfare programs encompass those goods and services that a society believes to be a collective responsibility. They include Social Security, public assistance, food stamps and food vouchers, medical care, housing and housing subsidies, child care, unemployment and workers' compensations, veterans' benefits, and personal social services.

The major health and welfare systems in the United States are patchy, uneven, and scanty. The term *social welfare system* implies a sense of order, comprehensiveness, and rational planning. But that is not the way things are. In fact, the social welfare system is more like a patchwork quilt. Bits and pieces of theories, interventions, and funding are patched together to form programs and helping agencies.

Of course, this system differs from a quilt. A quilt comes together as a whole piece to keep someone warm in bed on a cold night. The system does not serve everyone's needs equally. It is always in the process of being pieced together and is also increasingly being ripped apart. Despite its status as what has been called a "reluctant welfare state," the U.S. programs of assistance have raised millions of people out of poverty, given medical care to the poor and the aged, provided compensatory education, and provided food, housing, and cash assistance to the poor, the elderly, and the disabled. We discuss some of these programs here.

Temporary Assistance to Needy Families (TANF)

Politicians score points by being "tough on welfare" and "tough on crime." Sometimes they link the two issues, as if being on welfare were a crime. Temporary Assistance to Needy Families (TANF) has drawn fierce fire in the anti-welfare war. It is a program that provides income to families with dependent children, generally headed by a single parent but also available on a limited basis to two-parent families. About 95 percent of the single parents are women.

Cash assistance to needy families was part of the Social Security Act of 1935. The program was first called ADC (Aid to Dependent Children) because parents were not included. Mothers were not included until 1950, and unemployed fathers were not included until 1965, when the name of the program was changed to Aid to Families with Dependent Children (AFDC). Until 1996 the federal government set guidelines and shared program costs with the states; the states set benefit levels. Everyone who was eligible was entitled to assistance. That is no longer true. The Personal Responsibility and Work Opportunity Reconciliation Act (PRWORA) of 1996 ended federal control over AFDC and gave the states block grants to run their own programs. By ending the entitlement status of AFDC, the federal government, for the first time in sixty years, no longer guaranteed that it would help families in need. Conservatives in Congress proclaimed a victory; liberal senator Edward Kennedy, who voted against the bill, proclaimed it "legislative child abuse" (Edelman, 1997). Journalist Bob Herbert called it "officially sanctioned brutality" (Herbert, 1996).

The state programs that were held up as models for other states to copy were the more punitive ones. The most outspoken advocate of dismantling welfare was Governor Tommy Thompson of Wisconsin, who was appointed director of the federal Department of Health and Human Services (HHS) by President George W. Bush in 2001 (and resigned in 2003). He implemented the "W-2" program in Wisconsin, which called for replacing welfare with work. In this program, women were required to work when their children reach 12 weeks of age and there was a two-year time limit for supported work or community service (Miranne & Young, 1998). The program was more successful at kicking people off the rolls than helping families. During the recession, 40 percent of Wisconsin's children received food stamps.

In April 2008, Wisconsin scaled back its workfare program and began a pilot program called Real Work for Real Pay, where participants in real jobs earned a pay check and were trained to develop job skills (Crisp, & Fletcher, 2008).

The Wisconsin TANF program was sued in 2010 by Legal Action of Wisconsin, Inc., the American Civil Liberties of Wisconsin, and the Milwaukee branch of the NAACP, on the grounds of discrimination on the basis of race and disability in the administration of the W-2 program. A study found that there were significant racial disparities in sanction rates for alleged failures to comply with program requirements. Both Latino and African-American program participants were sanctioned at a higher rate than white program participants. The settlement of the lawsuit required administrators of the W-2 program to ensure that qualified individuals with disabilities receive reasonable accommodations, which may include job training and supports for a longer time period than what is typically afforded, sign language interpreters, or in-depth services from the Wisconsin Division of Vocational Rehabilitation (U.S. Department of Health and Human Services, 2010).

TIME LIMITS

There was no time limit on AFDC, but the Personal Responsibility Act set a lifetime time limit of five years in which people could receive assistance. Some states set shorter time limits than the federal limit. States are free to set no time limit at all if they want to pay for the program out of state funds after the federal time limit is up, and Maine did that. The law does not require that assistance be in the form of cash. It can be in the form of vouchers. Some states even turned over the program to counties (Edelman, 1997).

WORKFARE

After two months of being on welfare, recipients are required to find a community service job if they have not found paid employment. Community service work is usually menial work, such as raking leaves, picking up garbage, or washing dishes in a school cafeteria. In some cities, workfare workers have replaced regular workers. Although the law prohibits the direct substitution of welfare recipients for currently paid workers, some localities have circumvented this requirement by not renewing expired employment contracts with paid workers. In many localities, low-wage workers were displaced by workfare "trainees" working off their welfare benefits at less than the minimum wage—sometimes as little as $1.50 an hour (Cooper, 1997). In mid-1997 in Baltimore, 1,000 workers had lost jobs to welfare trainees, despite the fact that city workers had only two years before won a city ordinance guaranteeing a living wage to anyone employed under contracts with the city (Cooper, 1997).

The largest workfare scheme in the United States was the Work Experience Program (WEP) in New York City. Only 5 percent of WEP participants found jobs (Crisp, & Fletcher, 2008). Thousands of New York City workfare participants did the work once done by higher-paid city workers (Greenhouse, 1997). They were exposed to hazardous working conditions, including limited or no access to protective clothing, toilets, and drinking water. They sued the city and in August 1997, a state Supreme Court justice ruled that the city was obligated to provide these necessities (Greenhouse, 1997). In July 2001, the federal government sued the Giuliani administration in New York City, charging it with doing too little to protect women in workfare jobs from sexual and racial harassment by their supervisors. The Giuliani administration said that welfare recipients in the city's workfare program were not employees and had no legal right to protection from sexual discrimination or sexual harassment in the workplace (Greenhouse, 2001). Unions fought this discrimination, and workers won some rights given to regular employees.

Four *New York Times* reporters looked at the Work Experience Program (workfare) in New York City and found the following: Workfare didn't lead to full-time jobs (Finder, 1998), many participants took the place of full-time workers (Greenhouse, 1998), mothers faced acute lack of day care (Swarns, 1998), and tough workfare rules were used as a way to cut welfare rolls (Toy, 1998).

A study of workfare programs in the United States, Canada, and Australia, found that "there is little evidence that workfare increases the likelihood of finding work. It can even increase unemployment by limiting the time available for job search and by failing to provide the skills and experience valued by employers. Workfare is least effective in getting people into jobs in weak labour markets where unemployment is high" (Crisp, & Fletcher, 2008).

EDUCATION AND TRAINING

Prior to the 1996 legislation, states were able to allow activities that helped prepare people for work, such as job training, education, or rehabilitation in substance abuse programs or disabilities. However, the 1996 legislation has a much narrower definition of what constitutes work-related activities. Only a year of education and training is allowed, and it must be directly related to a specific job that does not require a bachelor's or an advanced degree. States could allow more education if they paid for it out of state funds. Maine used state funds in its "Parents as Scholars" program to support some TANF recipients in four-year college programs.*

No more than 30 percent of a state's recipients can be in education and training. Outside this 30 percent, mothers could still undertake training, but only if they first worked or looked for work at least 20 hours a week.

During the 1996 welfare reform debate, the majority of policymakers treated work and education as if they were entirely different concepts. Senator Phil Gramm of Texas put it this way:

> Work does not mean sitting a classroom. Work means work. Any farm kid who rises before dawn for the daily chores can tell you that. Ask any of my brothers and sisters what "work" meant on our family's dairy farm. It didn't mean sitting on a stool in the barn, reading a book about how to milk a cow. "Work" meant milking cows. (Congressional Record, 1995)

*The Patsy Takemoto Mink Fellowship each year gives scholarships of $2,000 to assist low-income women to achieve an educational objective. The fellowship is named for the woman who represented her native Hawaii in the U.S. Congress. She fought against welfare reform in Congress. Her daughter Gwendolyn Mink, author of *Welfare's End*, established the fellowship, along with Patsy Mink's husband, to honor her deceased mother.

Gwendolyn Mink believes that welfare should go beyond helping low-income mothers care for their children. It should also open opportunities to education at all levels, and provide child care as well as assistance in overcoming personal barriers to employment. Mink explained that the Fellowship is a small nonprofit and reaches only a handful of women a year. The Foundation can be reached at http://www.patsyminkfoundation.org/.

Senator William Armstrong of Colorado expressed the same sentiments a decade earlier, asserting:

> People on welfare ought to work, work, work . . . because it is good for the soul, because it is fair to the taxpayers, because it rankles people who are paying taxes to support these programs to see people who are recipients not get out and work. (Davis, M., 2010)

Senator Gramm's comments indicate that he believes that work is hard, messy, maybe painful and involuntary; education, on the other hand, is pleasurable and self-directed. Congress and the executive branch "have continued to draw a tight line between work activities and educational pursuits. . . in part to show that they are tough on welfare and welfare recipients and that welfare is not simply a 'college scholarship' program that allows low-income people to leapfrog over the struggling middle class" (Davis, 2010). In 2010, the conservative political scientist Lawrence Mead echoed Senator Gramm's sentiments when he testified before the U.S. House of Representatives that "the main thing the American people want out of welfare reform is for more adult recipients to go to work and stay there. They would oppose any policy change that allowed more recipients to go to school in place of work, especially when ordinary taxpayers not on aid lack the same opportunity. . . Advocates have to be reminded that the main point of the work test is not to help out the recipients. It is to discharge a debt to the society" (Mead, 2010).

It is an artificial division to draw a sharp distinction between work and education. Cooperative education combines the two by providing practical work experience with study. Community colleges, with their flexibility and responsiveness to local communities, embody the idea that work and education are intimately related. The influential educational theorist John Dewey subscribed to this approach to learning.

Only former recipients with at least a two-year postsecondary or vocational degree are likely to escape poverty by earnings alone. Since the Personal Responsibility Act was passed, there has been a precipitous drop in college enrollment among welfare recipients. This massive exodus of recipients from college does not bode well for their future ability to climb out of poverty. People with college degrees have less than a one in fifty chance of being poor compared to one in five for those without.

Very few TANF recipients have access to education and training. A 2010 study found that nationally less than 8 percent of "work-eligible" adult TANF recipients were engaged in education or training activities (U.S. House of Representatives Committee, 2010). The training that recipients did get was largely very short-term training, often lasting three months or less. When Kentucky had more than 30 percent of recipients enrolled in vocational education, it faced penalties from the federal government. The Deficit Reduction Act of 2005 that reauthorized TANF increased their work participation rate targets for states and imposed a new and demanding requirement that all hours of participation be extensively verified and documented. The attendance and documentation requirements have proven so burdensome that TANF case managers are less likely to refer clients to education activities in general and college in particular (King-Simms, 2010).

CASE EXAMPLE

I started going to school to get my GED two years ago, then started college classes. My case manager said that a degree in culinary arts wasn't acceptable, so I switched to an AA degree, working part time and going to school full time. My case manager said I could only get childcare for the time I was working, not in school, and that I would lose my TANF. I said that wasn't a possibility and we could not live off of food stamps and medical benefits. I had to be really persistent and very vocal to get the benefits my family needs.

I work 19 hours a week, but the requirement is 20, so I have to do one hour of community service. Here is my typical day. I get up at 5 A.M. and get my daughter ready and we are on the bus by 6 A.M. It takes 3 buses and 2 hours to get us to the daycare, then me to college. I work from 8 to 10 at the college, and then to class from 10 to 12. Instead of a lunch break I go to the work source office for an hour of community service and then back to school. If it's Tuesday or Thursday I go to class from 1:15 to 3:05; if it's Monday, Wednesday, or Friday I go back to work from 1:30 to 3:30. The buses home take 3 hours, because of the afternoon schedule, so my daughter and I get home at 6:30, unless we have to stop at the store for groceries, then it's 7:30. We have dinner, bath time, and my daughter is in bed by 8. I stay up until 11:30 or 12:30 doing homework, then get up at 5 A.M. to start it all over again.

It's hard because I don't have support. Being a full-time student and working 20 hours a week is hard on me and not fair to my daughter. Single parents have the hardest time because we don't get the chances others have. Please remove the barriers to education so I can finish school and build a better life for my family. (Young, 2010)

The changing structure of the economy over the last twenty years has placed a growing premium on education and training beyond high school. Those who have at least a two- or four-year college degree have seen their earnings hold steady (and for women, rise) while the earnings of those with only a high school diploma have dropped substantially—for men, by about a third. High school dropouts are the worst off—their earnings have fallen almost by half (College Board 2005). A 2007 study found that 41.5 percent of adult TANF recipients have less than a high school degree, and more than half have exactly a high school degree. Less than 5 percent have any post-secondary education (McSwain, & Davis, 2007).

CASE STUDY

It's Not Because We Made Bad Choices

I work as a home health aide and have to get up at 4:45 in the morning to be to work by 6:30, three days a week. I'm also trying to finish a program to get my associate's degree in nursing and am looking for an apartment so I can get out of the homeless shelter where I live. I'm looking for a place, but it's hard to find anything. I only make $200 a week, and most two-bedrooms are $700 a month. I tried to find a studio, but most landlords don't want kids in a studio. I also need to buy a car to be able to get back and forth to school (I've been borrowing a friend's car but can't for much longer) and welfare keeps giving me a hard time—telling me I don't need a car and I should be saving money. But I live in Lowell and go to school in Lawrence, and I have a 4-year-old! Do you know how hard that would be to get back and forth without a car and still do the housing search and all the other things we have to do at the shelter?

We have to turn in forms that list where we looked for housing each week, and we have to have twelve—no matter what. If the landlord doesn't return your call, it doesn't count. Even if there are only six listings in the paper, they tell you that's not enough—that you have to try harder. It's so degrading. You know, besides being homeless, we have other issues, and we should be treated with respect. I have low self-esteem, and it's really hard to keep myself going, but they just keep piling more things on us. There are all these mandatory meetings that you have to go to even if they don't have anything to do with you. Like going to these employment sessions on how to get a job. I already have a job! But I still have to go because it's mandatory. You know, anybody could end up in this predicament—it's not because we made bad choices. That's the way life is. Some people are lucky, and some are not. And a pat on the back would be so much better than constantly putting us down. (Massachusetts Coalition for the Homeless, 2000)

CHILD SUPPORT—"DEADBEAT DADS"

The Personal Responsibility Act required states to impose harsh sanctions on families where a parent does not "cooperate fully" in collecting child support and establishing paternity. The definition of "cooperating fully" is subject to various interpretations. For a time, Massachusetts was dropping families from the rolls if the mother was unable to provide such information as the father's Social Security number, his whereabouts, and place of employment, even when the mother did not have this information. A class action suit brought by legal services stopped the practice (Mandell, B., 1997).

The *"cooperate fully" requirement may be life-threatening for women who are fleeing from battering husbands or boyfriends.* They may be in great danger if they give information about their batterer to the welfare department because there is no guarantee that the welfare worker will not inform him of a woman's whereabouts.

It is certainly reasonable to expect children's fathers to support them, but it is not reasonable to expect to recoup large amounts of money from men who have little or no money. In 1989, the average *annual* child support award for poor mothers was only $1,889 (Bassuk, Browne, & Buckner, 1996).

A high proportion of mothers on welfare have been subjected to domestic violence. In the general population, about 22 percent of women experience domestic violence at some point in their adult lives, while most studies estimate that 50 to 60 percent of welfare recipients experience violence in their lives (Lawrence, 2002). Children are also likely to be abused when their mothers are abused.

Men who batter women often prevent them from working or attending education and training programs, as illustrated by the following story:

When Bernice Haynes tried to get off welfare by enrolling in a job training program, her boyfriend tossed her textbooks in the trash. He refused to watch their two children while she was in class. And he would pick fights with her when she tried to study.

"Before the final exam, we fought all weekend from Friday to Monday morning," says Haynes, 31, who lives on Chicago's West Side. Haynes never got the chance to open her books over the weekend. "When I went in that Monday, I was exhausted—from the constant verbal abuse, the putdowns, from trying to keep myself alive—that test wasn't on my mind." She flunked. Haynes, who had been attending classes for a year and was trying to become a licensed nurse, was kicked out of the program—just twelve weeks before graduation. (Gonnerman, 1997, p. 21)

People disagree on the child support issue. Many people, including some middle-class feminists, believe that the state should force all fathers to pay support, regardless of the mother's wishes. They assume that this would help reduce the need for welfare. Others believe that the choice of whether to enforce a support decree should be left up to the mother. Many mothers have begged the state to collect child support and have given all necessary identifying information, but the state has done nothing. In Sweden and Finland mothers have no anxiety about getting child support from their husbands because the government pays child support advance payments when the absent parent cannot or does not pay child support (Mandell, B., 2004a).

Public opp·ng [handwritten marginal note]

Voicing her opposition to mandatory paternity establishment and child support provisions, Gwendolyn Mink (1998) says,

They mark poor single mothers as a separate caste, subject to a separate system of law. The system of law under which they live penalizes their moral choices, prescribes intimate associations that may be unwanted, and infringes rights guarded as fundamental to the personhood of all other citizens. (p. 73)

Many believe that in their zeal to make fathers pay, Congress and the president subjected all fathers whose children are on welfare to police state tactics. "They are subject to liens, withholding of wages, credit investigations, and exposure to employers, among other sanctions. They further indenture poor fathers (as well as irresponsible ones) in work programs ordered by courts and state agencies" (Mink, 1998, p. 91). Depending on what state he lives in, a delinquent father may lose his driver's, occupational, and recreational licenses (Valentine, 1997). If he owes more than $5,000, he may lose his passport.

BEHAVIORAL REQUIREMENTS

Welfare reform not only aims to get people to work but also to enforce certain behaviors. These rules reveal a profound distrust of the parenting abilities and sexual behavior of the poor. The Family Cap policy prohibits cash assistance to a child born while the family receives TANF. "Learnfare" reduces the grant if a child truants from school, and "Shotfare" reduces the grant if parents do not get their children immunized. Wisconsin was the first state to institute Learnfare. Yet, despite a study of the program that showed that the program "had no detectable effect on school participation" (Johnson, 1996), Wisconsin continued the Learnfare program.

In a misguided effort to control substance abuse, the federal law stipulated that people convicted of drug felonies are prohibited from receiving a TANF block grant or food stamps *for life.* Congress removed that restriction for food stamps in 2009.

Policymakers and legislators believed that the Family Cap policy would reduce the birth rate of TANF recipients, but there is no evidence that it accomplished this. Instead, it led to children's malnourishment and higher rates of hospitalization of infants and toddlers. Dr. Deborah Frank, a pediatrician who studied the nutritional status of patients at a

Boston City Hospital clinic, found that 14 percent of her malnourished patients were children from families that had been capped. "If there was a medicine that gave 10 percent of children failure to thrive, it sure wouldn't be approved by the FDA," said Frank, referring to the U.S. Food and Drug Administration.

Nearly half of states have a Family Cap policy. However, in view of the fact that the Family Cap failed to reduce additional births and in response to criticisms of the policy, some states have done away with the policy.

State officials seem so doggedly determined to defend these restrictive policies that they ignore research showing that they accomplish little. There is little evidence that marriage will pull substantial numbers of people out of poverty. A national study of unmarried parents "highlights the fact that for unmarried mothers living in poverty, economic stability is seen as a prerequisite to marriage. Helping single parents succeed requires policies aimed at boosting their educational and economic prospects. Once economic stability has been achieved, marriage may become a more attractive option" (Children's Defense Fund, 2004a, p. 5).

As for the illegitimacy bonus given to states, three of the five states that received the bonus didn't even have policies or programs to achieve these goals. In effect, they received a bonus for demographic changes that they had nothing to do with. And "abstinence only" programs were found to be ineffective in changing sexual behavior (Mandell, B., 2004b).

In 2002, the Bush administration decided that the federal government needed to promote heterosexual marriage and proposed a new federal program—the Healthy Marriage Initiative—dedicated to that purpose. In 2005, the Republican-controlled Congress authorized the program and appropriated $500 million for it over five years. A rigorous evaluation of the program, published in 2010, showed that the program was a failure. The researchers found that the program had no effect on the likelihood of couples staying together or getting married, and no effect on relationship quality (Fremstad, 2010).

Charitable Choice

The PRWORA contains a "Charitable Choice" provision that requires states, if they contract with nonprofit organizations to provide social services, to include religious organizations as eligible contractees. Charitable Choice has been a hot political issue. President

Bush wanted religious organizations to be exempt from antidiscrimination laws in hiring. The opponents of Charitable Choice fear that it will lead to religious proselytizing, discrimination in hiring, a lowering of professional standards, a loss of tax money, and further erosion of public social welfare provisions. They fear that it will undermine the strong U.S. tradition of separation of church and state. Its proponents claim that faith-based social services are more effective, but there is no research evidence to support this claim. Mark Chaves, a sociologist at the University of Arizona who has conducted numerous national surveys of church-based social programs, says, "It can't be said strongly enough how little we know about whether religion makes a difference in the effectiveness of delivering services" (Press, 2001, p. 20).

The Charitable Choice bill exempts faith-based programs from the state education and training requirements applied to all secular providers. Many people fear this will create a dangerous two-tiered system. The former director of the National Association of Alcoholism and Drug Abuse Counselors expressed his concern about this. He said, "Because this is a disease, and it is in the proper domain of public health, and if you are out there promoting what you are doing as treating addiction, you should be properly licensed" (Press, 2001, p. 24).

Although Congress has mandated that there must be a nonreligious alternative offered to recipients of services who don't want faith-based services, states need not inform beneficiaries of their right to seek an alternative. Some areas may not have any alternatives. There have been lawsuits that raise constitutional questions. One of these was a case involving state funding for a Bible class in Texas. Another involved a Christian twelve-step course for addicted fathers in Wisconsin (Press, 2001, p. 25). When Alan Yorker, a Jewish man, applied for a job as a psychologist at the United Methodist Home in Decatur, Georgia, in 2004, he was told, "We don't hire people of your faith." Mr. Yorker was angry enough to file a lawsuit (McClellan, 2004).

The Anti-Defamation League (ADL), a Jewish organization, spoke out against Charitable Choice, arguing that faith-based social services endanger religious freedom and are unconstitutional. In 2008, the ADL sponsored a bill in the Colorado legislature which would have forbidden discrimination in hiring by religious agencies. A coalition of faith-based agencies opposed the bill, and it did not pass (Nussbaum, 2008).

On the national level, conservatives have largely backed Charitable Choice and liberals and progressives have expressed deep concern about the provision. At the grassroots level, however, there is a confusing set of alliances. One study of more than 1,200 churches shows that congregations that are already engaged in social outreach programs seem more likely to apply for government funds, while those that keep to themselves are less likely to apply. Overall, politically conservative congregations are much less likely to apply for government funds than are middle-of-the-road or liberal congregations.

In addition, race and class affect which congregations are most interested in applying for government funding. Predominantly minority congregations are substantially more likely to be willing to apply for government funds than are white congregations. "It is no surprise that African American and Latino churches, which have historically served their own community in an effort to augment limited government services, would be more comfortable taking on broader social service responsibilities" (Baker, 2001, p. 8). However, because their resources are limited, they are not likely to extend themselves to serve a broad range of people. Minority congregations are likely to be poor and poor congregations have a far more limited access to money, volunteers, and social capital. They are unable to help welfare recipients to find employment because few of their members are in a position to hire anyone or know anyone who does.

IMMIGRANTS AND LINGUISTIC MINORITIES

The current anti-immigrant sentiment has resulted in repressive immigration laws and severe cutbacks in funding for welfare. The PRA was most severe toward legal immigrants, cutting off their access to any benefits except emergency health care. They were denied SSI, food stamps, and Medicaid. (Illegal immigrants never had access to those benefits.) Several states pay for immigrant benefits out of state funds, but state benefits are usually lower than federal benefits. In July 1997, Congress voted to change the law to restore some of the benefits to people who entered the country before the law was passed in August 1996, but it did not restore food stamps or Supplemental Security Income (SSI) to most immigrants, and legal immigrants have to wait five years after they enter the country in order to receive free medical care.

This law has resulted in severe hardship for immigrants, forcing them to forgo medical care and even food. Despite working full time, immigrant families cannot take part in programs that were created for working poor families.

Immigrants who are applying for a green card (a permit to work and reside in the United States) must document a constant work history during their stay in the United States, making it all the more imperative that they find work. Many are in a bind because they couldn't get authorization to work due to the multiple-year backlog at the Immigration and Naturalization Service, and the recent recession has also contributed.

Many welfare offices and other social service and health agencies do not provide translators. Human service staff of community-based organizations often have to accompany clients to appointments at the welfare office, where waits are long and language barriers high. Workers often do not refer people to ESL classes. One community service worker said, "We have a lot of clients who don't know English so that they're not able to complete forms and attend training and things so they're not really at a level where they're even able to take advantage of the few things welfare is offering" (Cahill, 2000, p. 38).

The Effects of Welfare Reform

The main message of TANF was to downsize the rolls, and states downsized dramatically. Officials who supported the Personal Responsibility Act point to how well it has been working because it has drastically reduced the welfare rolls. In 1994, there were 14.2 million recipients; in 2007, there were 4 million (Edelman & Ehrenreich, 2010).

Peter Edelman was an assistant for planning and evaluation at the HHS in the Clinton administration, resigned in protest when Clinton signed the PRWROA. This is how he described the implementation of the Act:

> These are the techniques of radical reduction: shut the front door almost completely, staff the back door with the equivalent of a tough nightclub bouncer; and, in between, hassle applicants to the point where they just give up and go away.

Cuts in state budgets affect every citizen. These students need state subsidized tuition in order to finish their degrees (and learn to phrase their protest signs in proper English grammar).

At the front door many states just say no, evoking memories of the pre-1960s period, when unbridled discretion rules. Some cloak the turndown with the euphemism of "diversion," which means, "You look able-bodied. Go out and look for a job."

At the back door there is sanctioning—kicking people off the rolls because they were late to a work assignment (no excuses for sick children, late buses, or car breakdowns) or didn't show up for an appointment at the welfare office (no excuses for failure to receive notice of an appointment or inability to understand English). In some states multiple infractions of this sort can result, legally, in lifetime disqualification.

In between there are requirements to bring an entire dossier of documents in order to navigate the application maze, intrusive questions about the applicant's private life, assignments to demeaning work programs that sometimes ask people to work without necessary protective equipment, regular and irregular summonses to come in for redetermination of eligibility, and much more. Many needy people refuse to undergo the indignities associated with asking for help. (Edelman, 2009)

The goal of the law was not to reduce poverty. In fact, it increased poverty dramatically. During the expansive economy of the 1990s, many former recipients found jobs, although about half the jobs paid less than the poverty level. And two out of five former recipients ended up with neither jobs nor welfare. During the recession of 2008, only 22 percent of poor children were in families receiving cash assistance, down from more than 60 percent in the mid-1990s. And six states had caseloads of 10 percent or less of poor families with children (Edelman & Ehrenreich, 2010, p. 17).

Since the start of the recession in 2007, the number of Americans receiving TANF has increased less than 10 percent, even though unemployment has nearly doubled and the number of people receiving food stamps has grown more than 50 percent. Carmen R. Nazarlo, the assistant secretary of HHS in charge of welfare policy, said that some states with some of the worst economic conditions are not seeing significant caseload increases. The Government Accountability Office, an investigative arm of Congress, said, "We found no clear association between the change in the number of families receiving cash assistance in a state and its unemployment rate" (Pear, 2010).

As people lost their TANF benefits, those whose children were disabled often turned to SSI for help, which pays more than TANF. The number of children's mental disability SSI cases rose from 809,500 in 2000 to 1.20 million in 2009 (Wen, 2010).

A large-scale study of kindergarten children who had received TANF showed that they lagged behind non-TANF children in reading, math, and general knowledge. The gap lessened but persisted in later years. The researchers recommended increased funding of early childhood education and school-based social services (Moon & Hegar, 2006). But instead of increased funding, child care subsidies were cut back during the recession, making it even harder for low-income parents to work. States faced budget crises, and child care was one of the casualties when they made cutbacks (Goodman, 2010).

Child abuse and neglect have increased. Between 1995 and 2001, there were steady increases in the number of children with substantiated reports of abuse and neglect and in the number of children referred to foster care services. An increasing proportion of children remained in foster care for more than one year. Family income is related to the speed with which children return home; children whose mothers had higher incomes went home more quickly than did children whose mothers had lower incomes (United Press International, 2004).

When she was asked how welfare mothers manage when they are cut off welfare, Sharon Hayes, author of *Flat Broke with Children: Women in the Age of Welfare Reform*, said:

> They get by in the same way the poor of New Orleans and Haiti are getting by, by cobbling together every available source of aid and support, and then trying to learn how to adjust to constant suffering and insecurity. Increasing rates of domestic violence are just one hidden story here (Pollitt, 2010)

Some people claim that mothers who have jobs provide good role models for their children. However, that depends on the stability of their work and the amount of wages they receive. A study by the Upjohn Institute for Employment Research found that when work is stable and well paid or leading to higher income and brings about regularity of life, it provides a good role model for children. However, low-wage work available to lower-skilled individuals coming out of welfare does not usually fit such a bill. Children whose mothers experienced greater job instability, particularly due to being laid off or fired, have consistently worse behavior problems and poor academic progress. Fluctuating work hours and full-time employment in jobs with little wage potential are strongly associated with the probability that the child will repeat a grade. The researchers conclude that "a child's behavior at a given point is determined by the quality and quantity of time a mother spends with her child up to that point" (Morales, 2010).

Welfare recipients have always been in and out of the workforce, often because of their child care responsibilities. They have traditionally used AFDC as a substitute for unemployment insurance, for which they are usually ineligible because much of their work is temporary or part time. Unemployment insurance is popularly thought to be for "deserving" workers who are out of work for no fault of their own. Some people believe that if unemployment insurance were expanded to include those low-wage workers who are not now eligible for it, it could provide a more dignified income supplement to women who would otherwise have to go on welfare (Handler & White, 1999). Some states have put programs on the agenda to extend either temporary disability insurance or unemployment benefits to workers with caregiving needs (Gornick, 2001).

NOT ENOUGH CHILD CARE

The law does not provide enough money for child care for working parents, and most states do not add enough of their own money to provide the necessary child care. Under the TANF program, there is no entitlement to child care, even though it is an absolute necessity if parents are to enter and stay in waged work. The cost of child care is a major drain on a working parent's income. Patching together safe, reliable, and child-positive care is a job in itself.

Many of the jobs the mothers get require part-time, before-school, after-school, evening, swing-shift, and weekend schedules. Mothers often have to make many arrangements, combining formal care with family neighbors and sibling care. These arrangements often break down. Children are often left in the home alone. Many of the older girls in families are pressed into service to care for the younger children while their mother works, which of course impedes their own schooling and development.

Quality of child care is another problem. Parents who are unable to find or afford good quality child care are often forced to make do with inadequate arrangements. A study done by the Families and Work Institute of children cared for in about 225 homes of relatives and nonrelatives in Los Angeles, Dallas, and Charlotte, North Carolina, rated only 9 percent of the home-based care as high quality. More than half, or 56 percent, of the care was rated as merely custodial and 35 percent was judged harmful to the children's social and educational development ("Workfare's Missing Link," 1996).

NOT ENOUGH TRANSPORTATION

Under the Family Support Act of 1988, anyone in education and training was provided with transportation costs. This is not required under PRWORA, and lack of transportation is a major barrier to getting a job. The majority of recipients do not have cars, and those who do have unreliable ones.

Two-thirds of all new jobs are in the suburbs, but three-fourths of welfare recipients live in rural areas or central cities. A study of transit service from a point in Boston in which a high population of welfare recipients lived to the high-growth areas for entry-level employment found that more than 66 percent of existing jobs could not be reached within two hours—even though most of the city's welfare recipients live within one-half mile of public transit

(Lacombe, 1997). Furthermore, public transportation services offer inadequate hours of operation and infrequent service. And transportation is expensive.

The problem with transportation in rural areas is also severe. In many parts of Maine, for example, there are no buses. One woman regularly hitchhikes nine miles to a training program.

> Poor women . . . find themselves stranded, unable to scrape up enough money to buy or maintain cars. Pressed by welfare deadlines to seek employment outside their home, they are relying on bicycles, or squandering their money on taxicabs, or walking for miles in the dead of winter, or missing their appointments. (Barry, 2000, p. A26)

WELFARE AND HEALTH

Both the mothers on welfare and their children have a high rate of disability. This interferes with the mothers' ability to get a paid job, both because of their own health problems and because they need to stay home to care for disabled children.

About half of TANF recipients have a disability themselves or have a family member with a disability. Food Stamp recipients have similar prevalence of disability as TANF recipients. Low-income single mothers generally have disability rates that are higher than all adults, but lower than TANF and Food Stamp recipients (Lopresi, & Maag, 2009). Some states exempt disabled parents and parents caring for a disabled child from the work requirement, but there are stiff requirements for proving disability. Emotional and cognitive disabilities are especially hard to prove.

Most of the parents have disabilities that do not qualify them for SSI but still restrict their ability to work. If the TANF program used the definition of disability included in the Americans with Disabilities Act, many more women would qualify for assistance. The federal welfare law expressly provides that the ADA applies to all activities funded with TANF funds, and these standards are the ones that states should use. The definition of disability under ADA rules is a physical or mental impairment that substantially limits one or more major life activities of the person, while SSI is for severe disabilities that are expected to last at least twelve months or result in death and which prevent substantial gainful activity.

The most common mental health problems are depression, posttraumatic stress disorder, and general anxiety disorder. According to one study, about 42 percent of heads of households receiving TANF meet the criteria for clinical depression—more than three times the national average (Solomon, 2001). What appears to many people as "laziness" is actually depression.

Many parents have learning disabilities, up to one-half of recipients in the state of Washington. In many cases, women are not aware of their learning disabilities and in most states there are few attempts to diagnose and help women to overcome their disabilities.

THE FUTURE OF TANF

The Personal Responsibility Act expired on October 1, 2002. By then—five years after states were required to have new welfare policies in place—Congress was supposed to decide whether to reauthorize the existing law or replace it. Congress had extended the law several times, but "the reauthorization effort became trapped in a political tug of war between

When the funding of safety net programs is reduced or eliminated, the people who are turned may often end up exchanging prison time for that unavailable rehabilitation.

Republicans (who wanted tougher work requirements added to the law) and Democrats (who wanted increased federal money for child care)" (Besharov, 2004). Grassroots welfare activists were in the odd position of fighting to keep the existing law, which they don't like, because they feared that a new law would be worse. TANF was extended until April 2005 without changes. It was reauthorized in that year as the Deficit Reduction Act of 2005, which contained stricter work requirements. The law was due to be reauthorized again by October 2010, but Congress deferred full reauthorization until September 30, 2011.

The TANF Contingency Fund was created in welfare reform to help states respond to increased needs during hard economic times, but legislation was passed in 2010 that will essentially end funding for the Contingency Fund for fiscal year 2011. The American Recovery and Reinvestment Act of 2009 (also called the stimulus bill) allocated $5 billion to a new Emergency Fund under the TANF block grant, which provided 80 percent reimbursement for increases in TANF-related expenditures in three specified areas, including subsidized employment. States used these funds to support a range of subsidized jobs programs, including transitional jobs, summer jobs, programs for youth in low-income families, and supported work models for individuals with disabilities in low-income families. These programs were not limited to workers in families receiving TANF (CLASP, 2010). If the state didn't make the necessary spending, it didn't get the money. Some state legislatures said they didn't have the money to pay the 20 percent matching funds (Harris, 2009). This fund was not renewed in 2010.

When the TANF Emergency Fund expired on September 30, 2010, tens of thousands of people lost subsidized jobs supported by the fund (Schott, & Pavetti, 2010).

Organizing for Change

Advocates are organizing to try to get a more humane law when it is reauthorized. The U.S. House of Representatives Committee on Ways and Means held a hearing on education and training in TANF on April 22, 2010. Several organizations and individuals testified.* Everyone except Lawrence Mead argued for expanding education and training opportunities. Gwendolyn Mink made the most far-reaching proposals for change in TANF. Her proposals are as follows:

- Get rid of time limits.
- Broaden the definition of work. Guarantee academic and vocational freedom to all recipients who engage in work-related activities. Recipients should not be tracked into certain majors/training programs of prohibited from others based on the government's view of what field of study/training is appropriate.
- Broaden the definition of work to include (a) education; (b) caregiving for one's own children; (c) substance abuse and mental health treatment activities; (d) overcoming barriers and time constraints imposed by efforts to escape domestic violence.
- End mandatory cooperation with paternity establishment and child support enforcement for all custodial mothers—take it out of TANF altogether.
- Guarantee immediate access to TANF income assistance to those who are fleeing domestic violence.
- End immigrant exclusion.
- Restore and improve the child care guarantee for recipients who are engaged in labor market work activities (including preparation for the labor market).
- Increase TANF benefit levels to 150 percent of the federal poverty line and provide a transportation subsidy to any TANF participant who must travel more than five miles to a job. Continue TANF as a wage supplement for those who work part time.
- Get rid of all surveillance of recipients. Fix/end barriers to participation in TANF, including diversion programs, discretionary application denials, arbitrary case closings, all sanctions.
- End marriage/fatherhood promotion with TANF.

Organizers agree that the first step toward getting a more humane law is to change attitudes toward the poor. Peter Edelman (1997) says,

> We have been reduced to the politics of the waitress mom. She says, all too legitimately, "I bust my tail. I don't have decent child care. I don't have health coverage. Why should

---

*Some of the organizations that testified are CLASP, Center for Economic and Policy Research, Institute for Women's Policy Research, and Legal Momentum.

'these people' get what I don't have?" (p. 57) Advocates say to this waitress, "You are right. You deserve to have a job that pays enough to support a family, and you deserve good child care and health coverage. Join us in working for these things for everybody."

As Gwendolyn Mink says, we do indeed need to end welfare—"but as poor mothers experience it, not as middle class moralizers imagine it" (Mink, 1998, p. 134). The means-tested AFDC/TANF program has always been stingy and punitive. The late British social welfare scholar Richard Titmuss said that programs for the poor are poor programs. Whatever programs we work for should be universal ones, inclusive of all people; otherwise they take on the stigma that is always directed at poor people. Examples of such universal programs are:

- A family allowance granted to every family with children;
- A guaranteed annual income for all citizens;
- Refundable tax credits for children;
- Individual Development Accounts for families and children, in which individuals save money in an account which is matched and can be used to accomplish life goals such as getting an education, buying a house, or starting a business. This program exists on a limited basis in a few localities.

We need to create a real safety net, including restoring entitlement to financial assistance, establishing a minimum level of cash assistance that is high enough to meet basic needs, and providing all benefits to immigrants, including undocumented immigrants.

We also need to work on improvements for all workers—an increase in the minimum wage, paid family leave, guaranteed child care, comparable worth policies, decent unemployment compensation, universal public health care, a full employment policy, investment in education and vocational training, and aggressive enforcement of anti-discrimination laws. "This end to welfare will take us down many paths, all leading to gender justice" (Mink, 1998, p. 139).

Most Americans would not feel that welfare reform has been a success if people were still in poverty after leaving the welfare rolls. The public might be ready to support stronger job supports and removal of time limits that are forcing large numbers of people into poverty if they are better informed about the effects of welfare reform (Sen, 2000).

Universal welfare programs such as Social Security have powerful constituencies who fight to retain their benefits and have won major victories against government cutbacks. Means-tested programs such as TANF have little political support and must join with powerful allies. The National Welfare Rights Organization achieved significant victories in the 1960s and early 1970s because they were allied with the Civil Rights and anti-war movements. The women's movement would seem to be a logical ally for welfare recipients today, since the majority of welfare recipients are women. Countries where women have strong political power, such as Sweden and France, have strong women-friendly services such as universal day care and generous family leave provisions. The leadership of NOW has been exemplary in their resistance to welfare reform, but they have been unable to bring along large numbers of their constituency. Some feminists, preoccupied as they are with getting ahead in the work world, think there is nothing wrong with requiring welfare recipients to work, even if the work is flipping burgers for the minimum wage.

Labor is another potential ally for welfare recipients who have entered the paid workforce. (We purposely specify "paid" workforce because mothers are working for no wages when they care for their children.) Now that there is a five-year lifetime limit to welfare benefits, they will have no other source of subsistence but paid work, and workplace organizing will be crucial. Resistance to welfare retrenchment needs to focus on full employment as well as on the welfare programs themselves. Living-wage campaigns in the United States are an important part of the struggle, as are union struggles to keep jobs, wages, and benefits.

Unions have occasionally become involved in welfare issues, as in New York City, where workfare took away jobs from unionized workers. Many unions have won family-friendly benefits for their members. Service Employees International Union (SEIU) organized 604 former welfare recipients in Milwaukee, Wisconsin, who care for their parents, employed by the nonprofit agency New Health Services (NHS). These workers were paid at the rate of $7.10 an hour, with no benefits of any kind. After their union was certified, they went on to negotiate a contract for higher wages, improved training, health insurance, and pension benefits (Glenn, 2001a).

Churches, especially the Catholic Church, Unitarian Universalists, the American Friends Service Committee, and the United Church of Christ, have given strong support to the welfare struggle.

Many welfare recipients and their allies have fought to liberalize welfare rules on both the state and national levels. Lawyers have brought many lawsuits against repressive and discriminatory practices. They have used Title VI, which prohibits federally funded programs from discriminating on the basis of race, color, or national origin, to file administrative complaints. Grassroots activists and legal advocates have also used Title VI to bring about meaningful access to public benefits and related services for individuals with limited English proficiency (Hallums & Lewis, 2003).

Our strongest ally may eventually be the middle class. Many middle-class people are only one paycheck away from welfare. When enough of them realize that they, too, are deserving of a safety net, we will have a powerful constituency to struggle with us for a more humane welfare state. There is much debate these days about the "mommy track" in careers. Women who stay home to care for their children may not be able to advance their careers. Women who work have to juggle work and child care. Joan Blades, who, with her husband Wes Boyd, founded the liberal Internet site MoveOn.org, founded an Internet site called MomsRising.org. The group made a documentary called *The Motherhood Manifesto* about the obstacles facing working mothers. The group is organizing to get universal child care, paid maternity and paternity leave, and to end workplace discrimination against mothers (Jesella, 2007).

Social Security

If you ever had a job, you no doubt noticed that money was taken out of your paycheck for FICA (Federal Insurance Contributions Act). That is your contribution to Social Security (officially called Old Age, Survivors, and Disability Insurance [OASDI]). The program is funded by employee and employer taxes. In 2010, employees paid 6.2 percent of their wages for Social Security and 1.45 percent for Medicare, and employers paid the same.

In August 2010, there were 53,398,000 retired workers and their families, 6,390,000 survivors of deceased workers, and 9,958,000 disabled workers and their family members on OASDI. On June 30, 2010, retired workers received an average of $1,158 per month in benefits; retired workers with spouses received an average of $1,900 per month. There were 4,306,000 children who received Social Security payments in 2010 (Social Security Online, 2010b). These children and their widowed or retired parents receive little or no media attention, in contrast to the enormous amount of media attention paid to families who receive TANF assistance. Most people would be surprised to learn that fewer children received TANF assistance in 2008—a total of 2,992,340—than received Social Security in 2008 (more than 3.2 million) (Social Security Administration, 2010).

Social Security Disability Insurance (SSDI) is the part of Social Security (OASDI) that pays benefits to disabled workers (under full retirement age) and their dependents. In 2010, there were 9,958,000 disabled workers and their family members who received an average monthly benefit of $1,803 (Social Security Administration, 2010).

Social Security has been a hugely successful antipoverty program. In 1959, more than 35 percent of people age 65 and over lived in poverty. With the expansion of Social Security, poverty in 2008 was 7.9 percent for all people age 65 and over. Women made up about two-thirds of the elderly poor. In 2008, 21 percent of elderly blacks were poor, even though blacks made up about 9 percent of that population (Cawthorne, 2008).

Despite the success of the program, however, there are efforts to dismantle it as a public program. For the past decade, conservatives have sought to privatize the program by having people invest some or all of their savings in the stock market. They raised the alarm that the system will go broke as the aging population increases and the number of younger working people decreases. They proposed various ways to cut back the program such as raising the retirement age and taxing benefits. The one thing they didn't propose was to raise the cap on the amount of money that is taxed. In 2010, only $106,800 of an individual's wages was subject to taxes for Social Security, although there is no cap on Medicare. In other words, all income earned over $106,800 is not taxed by Social Security, so Bill Gates pays the same amount of Social Security tax as someone earning $106,800 (Social Security Online, 2010). If the salary cap was removed and all wages were subject to a payroll tax, there would be more than enough money to keep Social Security solvent. And if the newly hired state and local government workers were brought into the system, the two measures together would easily solve the long-term financing problems (Mandell, M., 1997).

In her book *Pitied but Not Entitled*, Linda Gordon (1994) argues that the deserving/undeserving, universal/means-tested split was built into the Social Security law at its inception because of the differing philosophies of the men who developed the universal parts of the act and the women who developed the means-tested ADC. The women were social workers who directed the Children's Bureau. Although they had been heavily influenced by the suffrage movement and helped to create many programs for mothers and children, they shared the elitism and racism of many in the Progressive movement of the early twentieth century. They felt morally superior to immigrants and blacks, and as social workers they felt it their duty to supervise these people on an individual, case-by-case basis. They envisioned a small program with "deserving" women, mostly widows and their children. They thought of it as a temporary program, presumably until women got married again. They ignored the large numbers of single mothers who could not—or would not—rely on a husband for support.

The people who built the social insurance program, on the other hand, wanted a program that workers were entitled to. They were not interested in people's character flaws. They developed the unemployment compensation system, workers' compensation, and old-age insurance. But they shaped a program that responded to the needs of working men and to the elite of the working class, those with steady jobs with major employers and professionals. It left out single mothers, the working poor who had low wages, and workers who were not wage earners, such as farmers, sharecroppers, and small-business owners. African Americans were not included initially because they worked at jobs that were not covered, such as domestic and agricultural work. Only much later were those people included. Female homemakers were never included in their own right, only as dependents of their husbands. Wives were expected to stay home and depend on their husbands' wages. Men were expected to earn a "family wage" to care for their families.

Because it is a universal program and therefore politically protected by middle-class voters, Social Security has so far been relatively protected from large cutbacks, although there have been cutbacks for college students, the disabled, and the very poor. Its administrative costs are remarkably small—only 0.5 percent of total benefits paid out.

Although there have not been large publicly visible cutbacks in Social Security, there have been less-visible cutbacks through denying disability claims, delays in approving applications, and in appeals hearings for those who have been denied SSDI.

CASE EXAMPLE

Patrick Garbiras, a homeless man, was unable to work because a seizure disorder and three operations over 14 months, including an open-heart surgery, have left him feeble. Social Security records show that Mr. Garbiras worked and paid federal taxes all but three years between 1973 and 2004, and if deemed disabled, he would be eligible for monthly payments of $1,247 per month. However, the day after Mr. Garbiras's open-heart surgery, the federal agency denied his claim, citing insufficient medical evidence. With that denial, Mr. Garbiras joined the ranks of the 1.6 million Americans—65 percent of all applicants—whose claims for Social Security or Supplemental Security Income disability benefits were rejected last year. Mr. Garbiras lived in Brooklyn, where the average wait for an appeal hearing in the past two years was 503 days. (Gill, 2007)

Supplemental Security Income

Supplemental Security Income (SSI) is a federal means-tested program for the aged, disabled, and blind, including children. It was created as part of the Social Security Act in 1974, consolidating two former programs called Old Age Assistance (OAA) and Aid to the Permanently and Totally Disabled (APTD). OAA and APTD were structured in a way similar to AFDC in that states provided matching funds, but SSI federalized these programs.

In August 2010, there were 7,892,141 SSI recipients. Federal monthly payments in 2010, without state supplements, were $498.90 for an individual (Social Security Online, 2010). Several states supplement the federal SSI payment. Some states provide a cost-of-living allowance for SSI, but some do not.

Members of the Gray Panthers lobby to protect Social Security for older Americans. Their assertive strategies fly in the face of stereotypes that depict the elderly as passive grandparents glued to their rocking chairs.

CUTBACKS IN SSI AND SSDI BENEFITS

Because it is a means-tested program for poor people, SSI is more politically vulnerable to cutbacks than is Social Security. Disabled people faced severe cutbacks in their benefits in 1980 when President Ronald Reagan and Congress pushed 491,000 people off the rolls of SSI and SSDI, arguing that some people were taking advantage of the system and could go to work. As a result of protests by beneficiaries and their advocates, laws were passed that required medical proof of improvement in the condition of beneficiaries before they could be terminated from SSI. Half of the people who fought back, about 200,000, were put back on the rolls (Blau, 1992).

The second large-scale onslaught on SSI came with the Personal Responsibility Act of 1996, which cut off all legal immigrants from SSI. Some have since been reinstated.

The definition of SSI eligibility for disabled children was also narrowed, which resulted in removal from the rolls of 100,000 to 200,000 of the 965,000 children who received SSI (Edelman, 1997).

The law also cut off benefits for about 40,000 people with drug or alcohol addictions. Conservatives argued that SSI checks were fueling addictions. George McGovern, one-time Democratic presidential candidate and father of Terry McGovern, who died of alcoholism, said, "It means that members of Congress who voted for that legislation still don't understand that alcoholism is a disease, and a fatal disease if it's not treated. I regard it as the number-one health problem in this country" (Conklin, 1997, p. 25).

In 2010, the Social Security Administration ended cash assistance for more than 3,800 indigent refugees who are severely disabled or older than 64. All of the refugees fled persecution or torture. Many are too old or infirm to work and are not yet eligible to become U.S. citizens.

Federal law sets a seven-year limit on payments to refugees. In 2008, Congress provided a two-year extension of benefits for elderly and disabled refugees, asylum seekers, and certain other humanitarian immigrants including victims of sex trafficking. The extra eligibility period ended in 2010, and Congress did not extend it (*International Herald Tribune*, 2010).

Cutbacks in eligibility are not the only way to reduce the rolls. They are also kept low by bureaucratic barriers. Applying for SSI is a very difficult process. Some people have waited up to two years to have their application accepted. Advocates advise applicants to appeal denials. By the third appeal, many applications are accepted.

General Assistance

General assistance (or general relief) programs give cash grants to people who do not qualify for TANF, SSI, or Social Security. Such a program is funded entirely with state or local money, without any federal matching funds. Benefits are very low, and these programs are generally the first to be cut when states cut welfare programs. Not all states have a general assistance program. In those that do not, if able-bodied people have used up their unemployment insurance or if they were in a job that was not covered, there is no cash assistance at all for them. They would probably still be eligible for food stamps.

Eligibility varies among states, but in general the program is for single individuals or childless couples, including individuals who are disabled for less than a year or who are awaiting a determination of whether they are sufficiently disabled to qualify for SSI. Elderly people who do not qualify for SSI or Social Security are generally eligible. Some states give general assistance to people who have exhausted their unemployment insurance, but others don't. Some families who are not eligible for TANF receive general assistance.

During the 1991–1992 recession, Michigan abolished its General Relief program, ending benefits for about 82,000 recipients. Follow-up studies in Michigan and Ohio, which ended benefits after six months, showed that relatively few former general assistance recipients became employed after their benefits were ended, and those who did were in low-wage and often temporary jobs. In Michigan there was a 50 percent increase in homelessness. In Ohio the ranks of the homeless increased substantially (Nichols & Porter, 1995).

Food Stamps (Supplemental Nutrition Assistance Program, SNAP)

Food stamps aren't really food stamps any more. Electronic benefit transfer (EBT) cards replaced coupons for food stamps across the nation in 2004. The official name has been changed to Supplemental Nutrition Assistance Program (SNAP), but people still generally call the program food stamps.

The food stamp program is paid for by the U.S. Department of Agriculture. Administered by state welfare departments, its purpose is not only to feed low-income people but also to provide subsidies to farmers. Stores and banks also receive money for participating in the program. People can buy most foods with the cards, but they cannot use the cards for non-food items such as paper goods, diapers, toiletries, and cigarettes.

Legal immigrants who have lived in the United States at least five years and all those under 18 became eligible for food stamps in 2003.

Cutbacks in the food stamp program began in 1981, when the Reagan administration and Congress cut funds used to advertise the program for outreach. Then, between 1982 and 1986 they cut $6.8 billion from the budget, eliminating 1 million hungry people and reducing benefits for the remaining 20 million (U.S. Department of Commerce, 1997).

The next major onslaught against the food stamp program came with the Personal Responsibility Act of 1996. The Republicans had hoped to eliminate entitlement to food stamps, but the agribusiness lobby stopped that. Yet Congress made deep cuts, including making legal immigrants ineligible, and cutting the amount of benefits. Before 2009, the food stamp program limited food stamps to three months out of every three years for unemployed adults under age 50 who were not raising children. The Obama administration eliminated that restriction.

During the recent recession, people who were previously middle class joined people who were already poor to apply for food stamps. In 2010, 6 million Americans had no other income than food stamps, and food stamps provide help at a level that is just 37 percent of the poverty line, which was $18,310 for a family of three in 2010. Philadelphia had more than 427,000 residents—a quarter of the city—receiving food stamps in 2010, but more than 150,000 people who were eligible were not receiving them (*New York Times*, 2010b).

The American Recovery and Reinvestment Act of 2009 (the stimulus bill) gave $20 billion to the food stamp program (United States Department of Agriculture, 2009). All recipients will see a boost in their benefits, from 13.6 percent for those at the maximum benefit, and larger percentage increases for others. The additional amount will be $63 for a family of three in the lower forty-eight states and the District of Columbia (Food Research Action Center, 2010b).

There is a little-noticed clause in the federal food stamp law that could allow more low-income college students to qualify for food stamp/SNAP benefits. State agencies have the discretion to broadly define the scope of what constitutes a "state and local government employment and training program" and, in doing so, exempt more postsecondary students from the longstanding federal ban on food stamp/SNAP benefits for students. Massachusetts has taken advantage of that discretion, and now community college students in the state who are enrolled in any certificate or degree program that is considered a "Perkins eligible" career and technical education program (or that the college otherwise determines will lead to employment) will qualify for SNAP. The student is not required to meet the other qualifying student exemptions such as caring for a young child, receiving a work study grant, working twenty hours a week, and so on (Baker, 2010).

The Social Security Administration has a web site to help people compute the amount of food stamps they may be eligible for: www.foodstamps-step1.usda.gov.

Special Supplemental Food Program for Women, Infants, and Children (WIC)

The WIC (Women, Infants, and Children) program is sponsored by the U.S. Department of Agriculture. It provides vouchers to purchase specific foods, such as baby formula, milk, eggs, and fruit juice. It also gives nutrition screening and nutrition counseling to pregnant and postpartum women, infants, and children under five years of age.

An estimated 9.3 million people received WIC benefits in 2009 (U.S. Department of Agriculture, 2009a). WIC is not an entitlement program. Federal funding is determined annually by Congress. Some states supplement the WIC program. Although most eligible infants are covered, about 20 percent of eligible women and children are not covered.

WIC has proven its value by reducing low birth rates, reducing the number of infants who die, and reducing the number born with developmental disabilities. WIC has encouraged greater use of prenatal and pediatric care. It saves Medicaid money because fewer low birth weight infants require hospitalization after birth.

WIC is more popular than TANF with legislators, even though both programs feed children. When the WIC program was started, planners made the decision to bill it as a nutrition program, rather than a welfare program, and to have it administered by health clinics in order to avoid the stigma of welfare. Some states have expanded their WIC program even as they cut back on TANF. Yet even this popular program has not been immune to cutbacks on both the state and the federal levels.

Human service workers who work with pregnant women or parents of young children can make sure that their clients know about WIC. Even illegal immigrants are eligible for the program.

School Breakfast and Lunch Programs

School breakfast and lunch programs are sponsored by the U.S. Department of Agriculture, which provides states cash to administer the programs and supplies 20 percent of the food. Children from families with incomes at or below 130 percent of the poverty level are eligible for free meals. Those with incomes between 130 percent and 185 percent of the poverty level are eligible for reduced-price meals.*

During the 2008–2009 school year, more than 31.3 million children got their lunch through the National School Lunch program (U.S. Department of Agriculture, 2009b). More than 7.5 million children participated in the school breakfast program. Nationwide, more than 81 percent of schools in the lunch program were also in the breakfast program. The federal government doesn't require schools to serve breakfast.

For low-income children, these meals are often a lifeline. School lunches provide one-third or more of the key vitamins and minerals children need; school breakfasts provide one-fourth or more. School lunches and breakfasts help improve children's achievement and behavior in school, make them healthier, and help prevent them from getting overweight.

*See Chapter 7 for an explanation of the poverty line.

One of the keys to breaking the cycle of poverty in families is through the educational achievement of their children. After-school programs and small-group tutoring help to compensate for overcrowded classrooms in poor communities.

There has been some criticism of the nutritional value of the food served in these meals. Studies show that school lunches are higher in fat and sodium content than the government's recommended guidelines.

As the nation becomes increasingly concerned about childhood obesity, there has also been a great deal of criticism of foods offered at schools through vending machines, school stores, or snack bars. These include carbonated sodas, fruit drinks with low percentages of juice, salty snacks, and high-fat baked goods. School cafeteria "a la carte" lines most commonly sell desserts, ice cream, chips, and fruit drinks. Major beverage companies have exclusive contracts with half of all school districts. These high-calorie foods, low in nutritional value, are contributing to high obesity rates among children and adolescents.

As poverty and hunger increase, school lunch and breakfast programs are more important than ever. One study found that only about one-half of the children who needed the school breakfast program received it, and fewer than one-half of the states' schools offered it. Children often do not want to take the meals because they feel ashamed. Federal regulations prohibit any separation of the free-lunch students from all the others, but schools still do it, fueling the children's understandable resistance to being stigmatized. Some school systems avoid this stigmatization by offering "universal" school breakfast programs, programs that serve breakfast at no charge to all students. These include New York City, Cleveland, and Kansas City, Missouri.

Medical Aid Programs

MEDICARE

Medicare is a federal universal program; Medicaid is a means-tested program. Everyone on Social Security, whether rich or poor, is eligible for Medicare, but only low-income people can receive Medicaid. In 2009, there were over 45 million enrollees age 65 or older on Medicare, as well as younger people with permanent disabilities, among them patients afflicted with End Stage Renal Disease (*New York Times*, 2009).

Medicare helps pay the hospital and medical costs for people ages 65 or older, as well as for disabled Social Security recipients. Under certain limited conditions, Medicare pays some nursing home costs for Medicare beneficiaries who require skilled nursing or rehabilitation services, if the nursing home is Medicare certified. The Program of All-inclusive Care for the Elderly (PACE) provides help to people who need a nursing home level of care but would prefer to remain in their own home with the help of their family and friends, community services, and professional care agencies.

If medical expenses exceed what Medicare pays for, some elders pay private insurance to cover the balance, or they might seek Medicaid.

In 1983, the Reagan administration and Congress, in an effort to limit Medicare expenses, created a program called diagnosis-related groups (DRGs). Under this program, a hospital is paid a set fee for each particular diagnosis. Many people were concerned that hospitals were releasing patients sooner than was medically advisable. Some people have complained that their managed care plans refuse to pay for treatments ordered by doctors, and two patients sued. The suit went to the Supreme Court, which ruled in June 2004 that patients cannot sue in state courts when their managed care plans refuse to pay for treatments ordered by doctors. Patients can still sue in federal courts, but they can seek only reimbursement for the benefits they were denied, not compensation or punitive damages for any additional costs or harm stemming from such denials (*New York Times*, 2004).

Medicare did not cover prescriptions until 2003, when Congress passed a Medicare bill that pays part of the costs of some prescriptions. George W. Bush took credit for it and thought it would help him get votes from seniors, but the bill received intense criticism. Some people thought that because it relied on private insurance companies, it was a "first step on the way to destroying Medicare as a benefit for all senior Americans" (Lieberman, 2006).

With Medicare Parts A and B, which cover hospital services and doctor visits, the government pays providers directly. Under Part D, the government pays some 260 private insurers—including pharmacy benefit managers, HMOs, and pharmacies—to provide the coverage. If seniors want the benefit, they must buy it from one of those private carriers. To force them to sign up, Congress imposed a financial penalty (growing more onerous over time) for those who didn't get on board by May 15, 2006.

Seniors became confused when they tried to sort out which plan was best. There are seventy-three different types of cards available. These cards offer different discounts, based on what types of medicines are purchased and where they are purchased. Millions of seniors called special hot lines set up by the Centers for Medicare & Medicaid Services, which administers those programs, but they were subject to long waits and often couldn't get the information they needed. In 2007, Medicare provided funding to all fifty states for health insurance counseling.

The new law prohibits Medicare from negotiating for lower drug costs, as the Veterans Administration is able to do for veterans. Drug companies lobbied hard against allowing Medicare to negotiate lower prices. Representative Sherrod Brown, an Ohio Democrat who voted against the bill, said that seniors he has talked to have "an intuitive understanding that this bill was written by the drug and insurance industries" (Washington, 2004, p. A1). The new drug benefit is the biggest expansion of Medicare since the creation of the program in 1965, but patients will still face substantial costs.

There is no limit placed on what pharmaceutical companies can charge for prescription drugs in the United States, as there is in Canada. As a result, drugs in the United States cost two to three times more than they do in Canada. Some people are getting prescription drugs from Canada, and pharmaceutical companies have lobbied to make that practice illegal. In Amherst, Massachusetts, seniors are teaching each other how to order cheap prescription drugs from Canada on the Internet, a practice that federal officials say is both against the law and dangerous. Rosemary Morgan, who, at age 66, ordered her breast cancer drug from Canada Rx for $44—a 90 percent discount from U.S. prices—said, "My understanding is it's legal, but if it's not, you can chain me to a fence with all the other bald-headed ladies" (Kowalczyn, 2001).

MEDICAID

Congress enacted Medicaid in 1965. In 2010, the program covered 46.9 million people (Sack, & Pear, 2010). About 70 percent of the benefit spending goes to the aged and disabled. Children, their parents, and pregnant women comprise about three-fourths of Medicaid enrollment, but only about 30 percent of the benefit spending goes to these groups. Medicaid pays for about 40 percent of all births in the United States and about one-third of all children's health care. It covers about one-third of people whose incomes fall below the poverty line. It finances about two-thirds of all nursing home stays. Many people who are eligible for Medicaid do not enroll in the program.

Medicaid is the largest source of federal grants to states. Because it is means tested, it is more vulnerable to cutbacks than is Medicare. Although the program started as mostly a welfare program for the poor, during the boom years of the 1990s many states took advantage of rising revenues to cover the near-poor and working poor and added benefits. However, when the economy slowed and states faced fiscal crises, many states reduced payments to hospitals and nursing homes, eliminated many services, or found ways to discourage enrollment. The most severe cutbacks were in Mississippi, which ended Medicaid eligibility for some 65,000 low-income senior citizens and people with severe disabilities in 2004 (Herbert, 2004).

President Bush proposed to turn Medicaid over to the states in the form of block grants, but Congress did not act on that proposal. Medicaid has a more powerful political constituency than does TANF because large numbers of middle-income people have elderly parents in nursing homes whose bills are paid by Medicaid. It is the Medicaid program, not Medicare, that pays for the bulk of nursing-home care. In addition, hospitals and physicians receive Medicaid payments, and they all have substantial political clout.

Officials sometimes label Medicaid a "budget buster" because as medical costs have skyrocketed they have taken a large chunk of state budgets. Many cost-cutting measures target the elderly and disabled, who have exhausted most of their life savings in paying nursing-home bills. The following story is similar to thousands recounted in the nation today.

Nursing Home—An Agonizing Decision

In the mythical American family, Grandma never soils the bed sheets. Or wanders into traffic. Or slips her nightgown over her dress at bedtime.

She lives in her own home. She cooks Sunday dinner for a table full of children and grandchildren. When her health fails, she moves in with a daughter, who cares for her without any disruption to the younger woman's work or family life. When she dies, she goes peacefully in her sleep.

It is hard to pinpoint the exact moment when the myth began to unravel for Judy Keane. It might have been the year her sister died of cancer and her brother-in-law of a brain seizure, leaving Judy—a widow herself—to care for her mother, Mary, just as

Mary had cared for them when Judy's father died young.

It might have been the winter morning Judy slipped out of work to check on Mary, only to find her outside—barefoot, in night clothes—while the home health aide lounged in front of the TV.

It might have been the night an ambulance carried Judy away from Mary's relentless needs on a stretcher, her heart racing with anxiety.

Or it might have been the tearful afternoon when she and her mother finally said the words "nursing home" out loud.

"Unless you have experienced it, you can't understand it," Judy said after her regular visit with her 88-year-old mother at Marian Manor in South Boston. "You wonder how many of his mother's diapers Newt Gingrich has changed." (McNamara, 1995)

Medicaid is paid for by both state and federal tax revenue. The federal government specifies the minimum services that must be offered, which states can broaden but not narrow. If people on Medicaid need false teeth or eyeglasses and are lucky enough to live in a state in which the Medicaid program pays for these items, they will be able to chew food and read. If, however, people who need dental care or eye care have the bad luck to live in a state without this Medicaid coverage, they will have to eat strained food and stop reading. Hard as this may be, those Medicaid recipients without dental or eye care coverage are still better off than an unemployed fifty-six-year-old who is in a general assistance program in a state that provides little medical care for the unemployed. Many poor people are ineligible. Most poor childless adults do not qualify for the program.

A national survey conducted in 2007 by the health research division of Public Citizen, a consumer advocacy organization, described the Medicaid program as "severely challenged." The survey pointed out that states vary widely in their eligibility criteria, the scope and quality of their care, and the amount they reimburse physicians providing it. The top five states, in order of rank, were in Massachusetts, Nebraska, Vermont, Alaska, and Wisconsin. The bottom five, with lowest-ranked last, were South Dakota, Oklahoma, Texas, Idaho, and Mississippi. The researchers concluded, "Most of the states are failing in one or more areas, and some of them are failing in most areas" (Brown, 2007).

The recession that began in 2007 put even more stress on the Medicaid program. Facing relentless fiscal pressure and exploding demand for government health care, virtually every state made or considered substantial cuts in Medicaid, even as Democrats pushed to add 15 million people to the rolls. A survey by the Kaiser Family Foundation found a record one-year increase in Medicaid enrollment of 3.3 million from June 2008 to June 2009, a period when the unemployment rate rose by 4 percent. The Medicaid program pays doctors and hospitals at levels well below those of Medicare and private insurance, and often below actual costs. Large numbers of doctors, therefore, do not accept Medicaid patients (Sack, & Pear, 2010).

Health Insurance

CHILDREN'S HEALTH INSURANCE PROGRAM (CHIP)

Congress started a State Children's Health Insurance Program (CHIP) in 1997, which extended coverage to more low-income children. In 2008 there were 7.4 million children in the plan, plus 334,616 adults (CMS, 2009). In 2009, Congress passed and President Obama signed a bill to expand coverage to include about 4 million more children, including children of legal immigrants with no waiting period. (Children of legal immigrants previously had to wait five years before getting coverage.) The program relies on a mixture of state and federal funds, combined with premiums paid by families on a sliding scale depending on income.

Democrats want to expand the children's health program as a first step to universal coverage, a goal endorsed by all the party's major candidates for president. The Bush administration opposed this. Michael Leavitt, the secretary of HHS, said the program "should not be the vehicle by which we insure every adult and every child in America." Representative John Dingell, Democrat, of Michigan, who led House efforts to expand the program, countered by saying, "It's a great investment. One of my problems with this administration is there are people who know the cost of everything and the value of nothing" (Pear, 2007). (President George W. Bush twice vetoed bills that would have expanded the program to cover more children.)

The United States passed a national health reform bill in 2010 that did not contain a public option, but did provide insurance to nearly 32 million Americans who are currently uninsured. However, over 18 million were left uninsured. Some of its features included:

- Health insurers cannot deny children health insurance because of preexisting conditions. A ban on the discrimination in adults will take effect in 2014.

- Seniors will get a rebate to fill the so-called donut hole in Medicare drug coverage, which severely limits prescription medication coverage expenditures over $2,700.

- Insurance companies can no longer cut someone off when he or she gets sick.

- Any new plan must implement an appeals process for coverage determinations and claims.

- Medicare payment protections will be extended to small rural hospitals and other health care facilities that have a small number of Medicare patients.

- Chain restaurants will be required to provide a "nutrient content disclosure statement" alongside their items.

- The cut-off age for young adults to continue to be covered by their parents' health insurance rises to age 26.

- Lifetime caps on the amount of insurance an individual can have will be banned. Annual caps will be limited, and banned in 2014.

- The program expands eligibility for Medicaid to include all non-elderly Americans with income below 133 percent of the federal poverty level.

- The program amends the Higher Education Act to include mandatory funding for the Pell Grant and increases the amount of the Pell Grant.

- The program increases mandatory funding for community health centers to $11 billion over five years.

- In 2014, everyone must purchase health insurance or face a $695 annual fine. There are some exceptions for low-income people.

- Employers with more than fifty employees must provide health insurance or pay a fine of $2,000 per worker each year if any worker receives federal subsidies to purchase health insurance (*Huffington Post*, 2010).

Fuel Assistance

The fuel assistance program, officially called the Low Income Home Energy Assistance Program (LIHEAP), is a federal program that provides eligible households with help in paying a portion of winter heating bills, as well as help in weatherizing their apartments and homes. It is a means-tested program. Eligibility is based on household size and the gross annual income of every household member, eighteen years of age or older. In 2009, household income could not exceed 150 percent of the federal poverty guidelines or 75 percent of the state median income (Administration for Children & Families, 2009). Households must apply for the program each year at the Fuel Assistance Agency.

There is never enough money to meet the need. State and local officials in cold-weather states often plead with Congress to release funds for the program. The funds are often supplemented by state funds and private charities such as the Salvation Army and churches. Some oil is provided by Venezuela through CITGO, a Venezuelan oil company. The president of Venezuela, Hugo Chavez, who sees President Bush as the embodiment of greedy and oppressive capitalism, has made a political statement by giving some free oil to the poor in the United States. The CITGO/Venezuela Heating Oil Program was initiated in 2005 following Hurricane Katrina. The natural disaster prompted CITGO to provide millions of gallons of discounted fuel to low-income communities around the United States, including Native American tribes. In 2006, CITGO made extra efforts to include Indian country. Of the 163 tribes participating, 151 are in Alaska. A few tribes declined to participate in the program as a protest against President Hugo Chavez calling President Bush "the devil" (Indian Country, 2006).

The fuel assistance program does not have strong political support in Congress from either Republicans or Democrats. However, there is less support from warm-weather states that don't need fuel assistance. The Sunbelt is represented both by more members of Congress and by more fiscal conservatives.

Unemployment Insurance

The U.S. Employment and Training Administration and each state's employment security agency provide unemployment benefits to eligible workers who are unemployed through no fault of their own (as determined under state law) and meet other eligibility requirements of state law. In general, benefits are based on a percentage of an individual's earnings over a recent fifty-two-week period—up to a state maximum amount. Benefits can be paid for a maximum of twenty-six weeks. Additional weeks of benefits may be available during times of high unemployment (U.S. Department of Labor, 2007). There is an extended benefit program (authorized through the Social Security Acts) that may be triggered by state economic conditions. Congress has often passed temporary programs to extend benefits during economic recessions. In July 2010, legislation that provided an extension of federal extended unemployment benefits through November 2010 was signed by the president. The extension restored unemployment benefits to the 2.3 million unemployed Americans who had run out of basic unemployment benefits (Open Congress, 2010).

Unemployment insurance (UI) is funded by a federal unemployment tax levied on the state and federal taxable payrolls of most employers. Three states also require minimal employee contributions. The amount of benefits varies widely between states, with some states giving over twice as much as others. Some states supplement the basic benefit with allowances for dependents.

Because unemployment insurance in the United States typically does not replace even 50 percent of the income the unemployed received on the job, and because it is limited in time, the unemployed often end up using welfare programs such as food stamps or accumulating debt and sometimes becoming homeless.

As unemployment has increased and unemployment benefits have been cut back, millions of workers have used up their unemployment benefits without finding work.

Unemployment insurance does not help many low-wage single mothers when they become unemployed:

> With welfare benefits no longer an entitlement, and the large majority of welfare recipients who are in the workforce, unemployment insurance is now the primary safety net to protect children living in low-income households from the havoc that an unexpected job loss can cause. (National Employment Law Project, 2004)

However, most welfare recipients work in the low-paid wage service sector, which is less likely to provide these benefits, and workers are less likely to have a union to help them with the UI claim.

In their efforts to cut costs, businesses have pressured the states to cut unemployment insurance. The value of the benefits has also dropped, as states tightened their benefits to reduce the unemployment tax on employers and to make states more attractive for executives looking for places to open businesses.

People whose jobs are permanently displaced end up accepting jobs that initially pay about 16 percent less than they earned before. For manufacturing workers, the average wage cut is 20 percent. A program called "wage insurance" has been introduced in Congress to stabilize incomes of people who lose their jobs because of an economic jolt and take lower-paying jobs. The program would pay as much as 50 percent of the difference between a person's old and new wage—with a maximum benefit of $10,000 per year—for as long as two years. Most Republicans favor it, and Democrats are divided on it. The most vocal opposition comes from labor unions and groups aligned with organized labor. Labor leaders assert that wage insurance would effectively subsidize downward mobility by providing money to employers offering the lowest wages possible.

"It's basically about getting workers to take bad jobs quickly," said Thea Lee, policy director at the AFL-CIO. "This seems to be giving up on the possibility of trying to get workers into better-paying jobs" (Economist's View, 2007). Many fear that Congress is likely to pay for it by cutting back on traditional unemployment insurance and on Trade Adjustment Assistance, a benefit and training program for people who lose their jobs as a result of foreign competition.

Earned Income Tax Credit

The Earned Income Tax Credit (EITC) is a federal income tax refund intended to offset the loss of income from payroll taxes owed by working-poor families and individuals. Some states provide an additional EITC, refunding a percentage of the federal EITC.

Single or married people who worked full time or part time at some point in 2010 can qualify for the EIC, depending on their income.

- Workers who were raising one child in their home and had income of less than $35,535 (or $40,545 for married workers) in 2010 can get an EIC of up to $3,050.

- Workers who were raising two children in their home and had income of less than $40,363 (or $45,373 for married workers) in 2010 can get an EIC of up to $5,036.

- Workers who were raising three or more children in their home and had income of less than $43,352 (or $48,362 for married workers) in 2010 can get an EIC of up to $5,666.

- Workers who were not raising children in their home, were between ages 25 and 64 on December 31, 2010, and had income below $13,460 (or $18,470 for married workers) can get an EIC up to $457. (Center on Budget and Policy Priorities, 2010a)

Most increases in social welfare in the United States since the 1970s have been done through the tax system. EITC now spends more federal money than was budgeted for AFDC in the late 1990s or than its successor. It raised more children out of poverty in 1996 than all other government programs combined, although it provides less money to the very poor and nothing to those without money. Employers like this program because it subsidizes wages and may reduce the incentive of workers to fight for higher wages. It has functioned more to offset the decline in wages than to better workers' conditions. However, in 2003 the government began an attempt to cut back the EITC through stricter eligibility requirements and investigation of claimants.

Millions of eligible workers do not receive the EITC because they do not know they qualify, how to claim the credits, or where to find free tax filing assistance. The Internal Revenue Service (IRS) sponsors a Volunteer Income Tax Assistance (VITA) program to help low-income workers file their tax forms. Human service workers can perform a valuable service by directing their clients to one of these programs. Some cities have established a VITA site. Some communities may have several VITA sites. Others, such as rural communities, may lack the VITA sites they need.

Human service workers can advise their clients that they can save a substantial amount of money by using a free VITA site rather than a commercial tax preparer.

The Child Tax Credit (CTC)

The CTC is a federal tax credit, like the EITC, that in 2010 provided parents a deduction of up to $1,000 for children less than seventeen years old. To be eligible, one must have taxable earned income above $3,000 and have either a Social Security number or an Individual Taxpayer Identification Number. Immigrant workers with either type of number may be able to claim the CTC refund. Thousands of low-income taxpayers with children do not claim the CTC (Center on Budget and Policy Priorities, 2010b). Human service workers can do a great service to working people by telling them about the CTC.

Child Care Tax Credit (CCTC)

The CCTC is a federal tax credit that allows working parents to deduct a percentage of their child care costs from the federal income taxes they owe, if they pay someone to care for a child, spouse, or dependent. Unlike the EITC, the federal CCTC is not a "refundable" tax credit. A family may receive the CCTC only as a credit against federal income taxes owed.

Personal Social Services

Government programs that spend the most money are those for education, health, income maintenance, housing, and employment. Expenditures for other personal social services account for only 6 percent of total expenditures. Even though they account for a small percentage of total expenditures, they are very important to both human service workers and recipients. In fact, many graduates of human service programs will work in these programs, which include such services as

- Day care for children of working parents
- Homemaker service and home health care for children, the disabled, and the elderly
- Respite care, to provide a breathing spell for overburdened parents, foster parents, or caretakers of people with disabilities
- Child welfare work
- Community residences for mentally ill, mentally retarded, and delinquent individuals
- Shelters for battered women, homeless people, and runaway teenagers
- Community mental health centers
- Children's institutions
- Community services for the aged
- Recreational programs
- Family planning counseling
- Correctional and penal programs

- Care of disabled, frail, and retarded individuals
- Veterans' programs
- Services to the military
- Drug and alcohol programs
- Disaster relief
- Legal assistance
- Counseling in various settings for various kinds of problems
- Information and referral services

The personal social services make up a diverse collection of programs that grew rather haphazardly in response to various social needs. They can be crucial to a person who needs help. Here are some examples:

- George Silva has a severe mental illness and cannot work. He needs counseling and perhaps medication supervised by a psychiatrist or psychopharmacologist in order to function again.
- Laurie De Simas needs help finding day care for her child so she can take a job outside the home.
- Mary and George Smith are unable to bear children. They need the help of an adoption agency to get a child.
- Mr. Longo is frail but may be able to stay out of a nursing home if he has a homemaker and a home health aide to look after his needs.
- Cheryl Rezendez was totally disabled by a stroke. She will need nursing care or intensive home care.
- Ann Rice works 9 to 5, and her school-age children need a community center to care for them after school.

These are important services used by the middle class as well as the poor. Most of us will need some social services in the course of our lifetime.

INTERVIEW

Interview with Rashaad BenSalem, Red Cross Volunteer Disaster Worker

I began volunteering for the Red Cross when I was in high school as part of a service club. I helped out at their blood drives. When I started doing some clerical work at the chapter headquarters, I met a lot of very experienced Red Cross folks, both volunteer and paid staff. The more I heard stories of what they did for and with people in times of crisis, the more I came to respect the incredible job they are doing. A lot of people don't really know quite what the Red Cross is. It isn't an official part of the United States government but it has the authority—as well as the obligation—to perform all kinds of disaster services, as well as working with the military to give family services for the military, such as investigating requests for hardship discharges. It began in 1900, when it was chartered by Congress.

After the overwhelming disaster at the World Trade Center in 2001, and then with Hurricane Katrina a few years later, a lot more people have begun to pay attention to what they do for their fellow men and women, not just in the United States but all around the world, like with the tsunami in Indonesia. But Red Cross people are sensitive about being identified just with those kinds of dramatic events. They are quick to point out that although those catastrophes got a lot of public attention, the ongoing work of the disaster units is just as necessary but much less in the public eye. In my Red Cross chapter in Louisiana, we respond to disasters ranging from a single-family house fire to floods, tornadoes, hurricanes, you name it—any natural or people-made destructive event. Sometimes we go to other parts of our state or even to another state, when there is sudden trouble and not enough local trained people to deal with it. We work to fill the immediate needs of the people who are affected as well as of the responders themselves, like the fire fighters, police officers, social workers, and construction or demolition crews. Everyone is deeply involved in a disaster—victims, workers, often the whole community.

A disaster the size of Hurricane Katrina destroys much more than houses. It uproots an entire social system and does untold damage, for years to come, to the people who lived in those homes.

Although many volunteer workers continue to go to the Gulf Coast to participate in the rebuilding effort, the federal government's provision of money and expertise has been woefully inadequate for a disaster of this magnitude.

When I turned 18 and was in community college, I took an introductory course in disaster relief at the chapter, and later on I signed up for a four-day intensive training. After I got my associate's degree, I became a full volunteer member of a DAT (Disaster Action Team). I got so involved with the work of my team that I decided to take a job in my Dad's grocery store for the year so I could take time off when I was needed. To be a member of a team you have to be flexible and able to go anywhere in the United States, with little or no advanced warning, and you have to be able to stay for a minimum of three weeks if you are needed. You also need to be able to live under adverse conditions and work long daily hours for extended time. Luckily I have always been an exercise nut, so I am in good health and have a lot of physical capacity.

But not everyone needs to be physically strong; emotional strength and resilience are just as important in disaster work because you are doing some very stressful stuff. You deal with people who might have lost their homes, their life savings, their family mementos, their furniture and clothing, their pets, their neighbors, and their friends. Mostly what disaster victims have lost is that basic sense of security that we all walk around with and also that feeling that they are able to protect their families, especially their kids and their older relatives. All of a sudden, often in a matter of minutes, it is all gone. Just last week in this county, thunderstorms with heavy rainfall hit Quachita Parish. Several homes had water in them due to flash floods, and there were numerous house fires due to lightning strikes. Chapter caseworkers worked with two very upset ladies who had flooding in their home. Neither of them had any insurance to cover their losses. Our chapter was able to provide referrals for financial assistance as well as cleanup workers and kits. An elderly couple lost everything to a fire caused by the lightning. They needed lodging, food, clothing, a walker, eyeglasses, and critical medications. The quick replacement of their medications prevented further trauma in their lives.

Later in the afternoon, our caseworkers met with two individuals whose house burned to the ground. That led to three very serious injuries and maybe to the death of a relative. These people spent a few hours in our office, talking with counselors. The warmth and skills of our mental health specialist got them to take the first necessary steps to deal with what will be a long-time recovery process. Their names and contact information were passed on to our local mental health agency so that staff there can follow up. Most important, you have to let people know that they aren't alone and that we want to hear them tell us what they need. A lot of people in these situations aren't used to asking for help or feeling so powerless, so we need to give a lot of emotional support and reassurance that what they are feeling is very natural.

So, what is it that we actually do when we swing into action? Well of course it varies from one event to the next and also in terms of who is on the team and what the leader assigns to us. But generally we assist in the conversion of high school gyms, warehouses, and open spaces, turning them into temporary shelters as needed, providing beds, towels, toilet articles, phones, toys for the kids, etc. Some of us do damage assessments and write up assessment reports for the construction crews and other responders as well as for our central office. We provide food for the victims and for all those who are helping to cope with the event. Often we are involved in helping people reconnect with loved ones, with pets, with neighbors, and with coworkers. When the dust settles a little, we help the victims file papers for insurance or for benefits that might be available to them from the federal or local relief agencies or from private nonprofit groups. We take folks to the hospitals and sometimes just sit with someone who is too upset to begin to take the next step. We need to be especially sensitive to the styles of different ethnic groups and to the special needs of folks with alcohol or drug problems as well as to those people, who are so isolated or poor that they have almost no resources or support network.

Vital-Service Delivery Programs

SERVICES FOR THE AGED

Kris Bentley recently graduated from college with a degree in psychology. She is a case manager in a home care corporation—an agency that works with older people. She visits people in their homes, when they cannot get to the home care office, and helps them figure out what services they need and how to get those services. She can arrange for meals on wheels, homemaker service, home health service, and chore service, as well as recreation. If her agency cannot provide a service, she refers her clients to agencies that can. The part of the job that Kris likes best is listening to people's stories about their lives. She also likes counseling people about the problems they are facing.

THE OLDER AMERICANS ACT

The Older Americans Act of 1965 created a new federal agency, the Administration on Aging, within the former Department of Health, Education, and Welfare. It established or encouraged many new services for elderly people:

- Nutrition programs
- Housing and transportation assistance
- Homemaker and home health care
- Legal services
- Chore services
- Senior citizen centers
- Day care centers
- Telephone reassurance
- Job training and placement

These services are delivered through area agencies on aging. But the funding is insufficient, and many old people are not receiving the services they need, either to remain at home or, for the 5 percent of the people who need it, to secure appropriate institutional care.

Housing for the elderly is often built by local sponsors, with financial help from the federal Department of Housing and Urban Development. The War on Poverty also created some service programs for the elderly, including:

- Retired and Senior Volunteer Program (RSVP), which seeks to match work and service opportunities with elderly volunteers
- Foster Grandparent Program, which pays the elderly for part-time work as mentors, tutors, and caregivers for at-risk children and youth with special needs
- Service Corps of Retired Executives (SCORE), which provides consulting services to small businesses

FAMILY CARE

You may have heard people say that families do not care for their elderly as they did in the "good old days." Studies show that this is not true. Almost one-quarter of U.S. households provide home-based care to friends or relatives age 50 or older. Nearly three-quarters of these caregivers are women. They provide an average of 50 percent more hours per week of informal care than men (Young, 2002).

Since colonial times, women have done most of the caregiving, both paid and unpaid. They care for their own children, and they care for other people's children. They are the primary caregiver's of aged and disabled relatives, both their own and their husband's relatives. And they are the primary caretakers of other people's aged and disabled relatives. Ninety-three percent of caregivers in long-term care facilities for the aged are women.

When most workers take time off from work for caregiving responsibilities, they feel the pinch. Three-quarters of caregivers for older people work full or part time, and half of those who work are making some sort of work-related adjustments such as going to work late, leaving early, or taking time off from work. Some give up work entirely. These work adjustments take a large financial toll.

A substantial number of adults who provide care to a parent, age 65 or older, report symptoms of depression. Two out of three informal caregivers are in ill health. Routine caregiver tasks can cause acute and chronic physical strain, particularly when caregivers lack appropriate training. Although most caregiving is short term, prolonged responsibilities take a toll on the emotional and physical health of caregivers. Caregivers worry about not having enough time to spend with their spouse, partner, or children, or by themselves (Young, 2002). These people need supportive services such as respite care.

FOSTER CARE AND ADOPTION

Kathleen is a caseworker in a child welfare agency, where she is responsible for foster care and adoption placements. She investigates reports of child neglect and abuse and determines whether foster care placement is indicated or whether she can help a family stay together. This is very rewarding work, but it is sometimes stressful. Kathleen sometimes feels that she needs the wisdom of Solomon to make the decisions that will change children's lives. She works in a well-funded and supportive private agency, where she has help with these decisions and with her work from her supervisor, colleagues, a psychologist, and a psychiatrist. Most child welfare workers are in state agencies, where they are overwhelmed by high caseloads.

Like all other caring professions dominated by women, foster care is both undervalued and underpaid. Most social work staff are female, except for the executives, who are mostly male. Many foster parents are married couples, but the foster mother does most of the day-to-day care of the children. Social workers are often unionized, especially in public agencies, but foster parents are not, although there is a national organization of foster parents, with state chapters. The money that foster parents receive from agencies is usually called "board payments" rather than "wages." This carries the message that foster parents are not considered to be professionals, but are doing the work out of their love of children. Foster parents often complain that they spend more on the children than they receive.

In 2008, there were about 463,000 children in foster care (U.S. Census Bureau, 2010b). One of the most recent changes in the child welfare system has been the major growth in the number of children in state custody who are living with their relatives. About one-fourth of all children in foster care are living with relatives, mostly grandparents (U.S. Department of Health and Human Services, 2010b).

From the 1950s to the present, black children have been disproportionately represented in out-of-home care nationally. Although blacks comprised 12.9 percent of the U.S. population in 2009, 30 percent of foster children were black, while 40 percent were white (U.S. Department of Health and Human Services, 2010b). Black children are at greater risk for being reported as abused or neglected. Black children are less likely to be placed in adoptive homes and are likely to remain two-and-one-half times longer than white children who also waited for permanent homes. A study by the Center for the Study of Social Policy showed that black children are more likely to be steered into foster care at disproportionate rates than whites, and are often "negatively characterized and labeled" by child welfare workers (National Public Radio, 2009). In her book *Shattered Bonds*, Dorothy Roberts documents the racism embedded in the child welfare system. Commenting on the Adoption and Safe Families Act, she says, "When Congress stated that its aim was 'to make sure that every child has the opportunity to live in a safe, stable, loving and permanent home,' it had in mind terminating the rights of Black parents, not reducing poverty or building stronger supports for families" (Roberts, 2002). The bulk of funding for foster care goes into taking children from their parents and placing them in foster homes, not in family preservation programs that would strengthen families.

Children are often removed from their homes or schools without warning; subjected to intrusive interrogations, medical examinations, and/or strip searches; and placed in foster homes or group residences while the legal system sorts out their future. This can be a terrifying experience for children and families. The number of emergency removals has increased in the past two decades.

Approximately 2 percent of all U.S. children are adopted. As of 2007, 25 percent were adopted from other countries; 37 percent were adopted from foster care; and 38 percent were adopted privately (Child Trends Databank, 2007). Many human service workers arrange adoptions at public child welfare agencies, and some work in private adoption agencies.

In 1997, President Clinton signed into law the Adoption and Safe Families Act. The law was intended to promote adoption or other permanent arrangements for foster children who are unable to return home, and to make general improvements in the nation's child welfare system. The law was a response to a concern that children were remaining in foster care too long without a permanent plan. It resulted in terminating parental rights sooner, but it also has resulted in depriving many parents of their parental rights. Advocacy groups say that "there have been heartbreaking consequences for some mothers who deserve to keep their children" (Crary, 2003). The act directs state governments to start termination proceedings once the parent of a child in foster care has been in prison at least fifteen months. It is an inflexible time limit and once parental rights are terminated, it is usually impossible for a mother to reverse that judgment. " 'Even if women have relatively short sentences for nonviolent offenses—if they don't have family members to step in, they lose their kids,' said Joanne Archibald of Chicago Legal Advocacy for Incarcerated Mothers" (Crary, 2003).

Federal investigators have found widespread problems in child welfare programs. Some states, including New Jersey and Florida, received national attention because of scandals in their child welfare programs. But no state was found to fully comply with standards established by the federal government to assess performance in protecting children and finding safe, permanent homes for those who have suffered abuse or neglect. Some of the charges included: significant numbers of children suffered abuse or neglect in foster homes; caseworkers did not visit children often enough to assess their needs; and children were not provided promised medical and mental health services. A report on child welfare in Texas was even more negative than the federal report. The comptroller of Texas, Carole Keeton Strayhorn, said, "Some of these children are no better off in the care of the state than they were in the hands of abusive and negligent parents. . . . Some children have been moved among 30 or 40 temporary homes. Some have been sexually, physically and emotionally abused while in the system. A few have even died at the hands of those entrusted with their care" (Pear, 2004).

Mental Health Services

Fred is a psychologist in a community mental health center. He is a member of a clinical team that includes social workers, psychologists, psychiatrists, and mental health nurses.

Before 1981, the clinic got its funds directly from the federal government, but after the passage of the Omnibus Budget Reconciliation Act of 1981, it had to compete for its share of the block grants that the federal government gave the states.

Fred has a varied caseload. He counsels people who have been recently discharged from a mental hospital. Some live at home, some in a community residence. Most are comfortable with their living arrangements, but one has consulted a lawyer about suing the state for placing her in a group home rather than in a private apartment. The lawyer believes that because the ADA protects people with disabilities from discriminatory treatment, a person who is placed in a group home is being treated differently than a person who can choose to live in his or her own apartment.

Fred's clinic is getting more and more patients who have been "dumped" by private hospitals on to financially strapped public hospitals and community services. A study showed that hospitals with managed care plans are particularly likely to reject uninsured patients and discharge patients when their insurance runs out, whether they are better or not (Kilborn, 1997). Fred's clinic is in a state that has privatized its mental health care. Public hospitals used to take everyone, but private hospitals eager to make a profit are less likely to accept seriously ill or uninsured patients.

Most of the long-term patients are receiving medication for mental illness, supervised by the clinic psychiatrists. Some check their patients often to see how they are responding; others seem casual about checking. Part of Fred's job is to alert the psychiatrist about any unusual symptoms he observes. Fred took a course on drugs in graduate school and keeps up-to-date on the literature. He has mixed feelings about drugs, feeling that they do some good but are overused. He prefers to emphasize talk therapy. Not all psychiatrists agree with him, and they have most of the power in the clinic. Because Fred does not have a medical degree, he is not authorized to dispense drugs or to give any official advice about them.

Some of Fred's clients suffer from what some psychiatrists call free-floating anxiety. They are able to function fairly well at their work and with their families but need Fred's support to help them function. Fred also does family therapy. Fred knows, almost by memory, the American Psychiatric Associations' *Diagnostic and Statistical Manual of Mental Disorders IV* (1995) because every patient has to have a diagnosis in order for the clinic to get reimbursed by private insurance, Medicaid, or Medicare. He wishes that he did not have to label everyone, and he does not agree with all the labels, but he knows that is the way the clinic gets paid.

Fred is aware of the power of self-help groups. He often refers his clients to a local group for manic depressive and depressive patients, a widow-to-widow group, the Alliance for the Mentally Ill, or the Mental Patients' Liberation Front. Fred feels that the state Department of Mental Health has not vigorously recruited minority staff or trained the present staff in cultural sensitivity. He takes courses and reads a lot about different cultures. He also tries to get to know people from different cultures. Not all the staff are as concerned as he is. He has winced at episodes of cultural insensitivity. It does not surprise him that some people of color do not return to the clinic after their first visit.

Medical Social Work

Dorothy is a medical social worker in a hospital. Medicare legislation in 1966 stipulated that if a hospital sets up a social work program, it should be under the direction of an MSW. That same legislation expanded the number of hospital social workers. More were hired after the 1978 amendments to the Social Security Act, which provided expanded benefits for patients with end-stage renal disease. To qualify for that funding, hospitals had to hire MSW social workers to treat those patients (Rossen, 1987).

Dorothy works with a multidisciplinary team of doctors and nurses, psychologists, nurse clinicians, physical therapists, occupational therapists, and patient advocates. She helps make living arrangements for patients after they leave the hospital. This is called *discharge planning*. In child-welfare agencies, social workers are almost always in charge, but a social worker in a hospital is sometimes the low woman or man on the hierarchical totem pole, unless the hospital administration establishes clear role divisions. Dorothy also helps victims of domestic violence, including victims of rape, child abuse, spouse abuse, and elder abuse. She was trained in crisis intervention and continues to receive in-service training. She has friends who work in other medical settings, such as

- Home health care
- Hospice services
- Nursing homes
- Employee assistance programs (working with the employees of a corporation or organization)
- Health maintenance organizations (HMOs)
- Visiting-nurse associations
- AIDS clinics
- Health education
- Private practice

All states and the District of Columbia have some form of legal regulation for social work practice. Because insurance companies grant third-party payments to licensed social workers, programs are eager to hire licensed workers.

Services for the Disabled

Disabled people won a landmark victory in 1990, with the passage of the ADA, which outlaws discrimination against people with disabilities. The ramps you see on buildings, the leveled sidewalks for wheelchair access, the signer for the deaf at an event are all efforts at complying with the ADA. Here are two examples of the ADA's victories:

- Jackie Okin is now in law school studying to be a civil rights attorney, because the ADA forced the Educational Testing Service and College Entrance Exam to schedule more dates in 1994 for people with disabilities to take the new SAT. Previously people without disabilities were given several dates to take the exam, while more than 20,000 people with disabilities were given only one date. Jackie said that the ADA gave her an equal chance to take the SAT, and it has made a huge difference in her life.

- Kevin Holmes served successfully for ten years as a police officer in Aurora, Illinois. But because he had diabetes, he was excluded from the state's pension fund. He would not receive the retirement pension available to other officers, and if he was impaired in the line of duty, he would not receive any disability benefits. In response to a suit filed by the Department of Justice, Illinois enacted legislation to eliminate discriminatory provisions in its police and fire pension code (U.S. Department of Justice, 2001).

John Hockenberry, an award-winning television commentator and radio host, became a paraplegic in an auto accident when he was 19. He comments on the advances that have been made since the passage of the ADA:

Almost two decades into this landmark civil rights law, people determined to share their distinct talents have begun to take their places in the American mainstream. The signs of their presence go far beyond handicapped parking spaces and wheel-chair ramps. Thanks to their persistence, today you are as likely to see a person with a disability on the ski slopes as you are in your workplace. And the momentum is picking up. (Hockenberry, 2005)

The United States leads the world in protecting the rights of its citizens with disabilities. Other countries, including Japan and China, have used the ADA as a model in developing their own laws. Yet there remain daunting challenges in health care, technology, and especially jobs. The jobless rate for disabled people in the United States was officially 14.3 percent in 2010. Since this figure counts only those looking for jobs, the real unemployment rate for the disabled, experts say, probably exceeds 50 percent (Hunt, 2010).

There are other laws, in addition to the ADA, that cover the developmentally disabled. The term most commonly used for mental retardation since 1975 has been *developmental disability*, which describes the level of functioning that makes people eligible for federally funded programs. The Developmental Disabilities and Bill of Rights Act of 1975 and an amendment of 1978 have defined *developmental disability* as a severe, chronic disability of a person that results from mental and/or physical impairment; begins before age 22; is likely to continue indefinitely; results in substantial limitations in functioning in self-care, language, learning, mobility, self-direction, and economic self-sufficiency; and results in the need for individually planned and coordinated services of lifelong or extended duration (Golden, 1990).

Because the law covers only severe disabilities, many mildly disabled people are not eligible for these services. The legal limitation affects the poor disproportionately because there is a high correlation between poverty and disability, yet often poor families have the fewest services made available to them.

The diagnosis of mental retardation used to be determined solely by scores on intelligence tests, such as the Wechsler or the Stanford-Binet. In the 1980s, the American

Association of Mental Deficiency decided that adaptive-behavior tests, which showed how a person actually performed, should become a part of the diagnostic criteria for mental retardation (Grossman, 1984).

Later changes to The Developmental Disabilities Act have encouraged independence, productivity, and community integration for adults. They have encouraged the phasing out of sheltered workshops, which segregated the mentally retarded into low-paying work, and have encouraged the placing of people into regular jobs. They have also included people with the diagnosis of cerebral palsy, epilepsy, and autism.

The work of one human service worker exemplifies these bills:

> Tricia Doherty works in a community residence for four retarded men. She teaches them the skills they will need to function in life. In fact, it took her three years to teach them to walk around the block without kicking stones, bothering strangers, or wandering off the route. She needed three more years to train the three most advanced residents to go to a nearby supermarket by themselves. She showed them how to observe traffic lights and look both ways at intersections. . . . Today the three men shop by themselves and have jobs that pay almost as much as Doherty's. (Golden, 1990, p. 50)

These men achieved success through this painstaking process because they were able to learn from one staff member over a long period of time. Unfortunately, there is a high rate of staff turnover in community residences. "Few workers are willing to stay more than a year or two in a draining job that pays just above the poverty line" (Golden, 1990, p. 50).

Community residences throughout the nation vary. Even in the same state, there are vast differences among them. The lack of start-up capital keeps many patients who could live in the community languishing in hospitals. Because of exclusionary zoning practices, it is usually difficult to open a residence in the pleasant tree-lined streets of affluent communities. Many must be located in poor neighborhoods and in run-down buildings. The NIMBY syndrome—Not in My Back Yard—is the perennial complaint of people concerned that bringing in people whom they consider "undesirable" will lower the value of their property.

Disabled people won a victory when the U.S. Supreme Court in 1999 made a landmark decision in *Olmstead v. L. C.*, holding that unjustified isolation in an institutional setting was discriminatory under the 1990 ADA. Many disabled people have been confined in nursing homes because the current Medicaid reimbursement system allocates more money to institutional service providers rather than community-based programs. This Supreme Court decision forced states to provide care and treatment in "the most integrated setting" possible. The Court noted in its decision that the ADA includes language which states, "historically, society has tended to isolate and segregate individuals with disabilities" and "discrimination against individuals with disabilities persists in such critical areas as . . . institutionalization" ("Equal Choice for the Disabled and Seniors," 2001, p. 12).

Services to the Military

The wars in Iraq and Afghanistan have focused the nation's attention on enlisted men and women and veterans and the kinds of services they are receiving. In 2007, the issue made headlines when the *Washington Post* reported that soldiers were receiving inferior medical attention at Walter Reed hospital, long considered the best hospital in the nation for veterans (Priest & Hull, 2007).

Most medical services in the VA are still very good, but there are serious problems in the system. The war strained the financial resources of the nation. There have not only been cutbacks in services for soldiers in the Iraq and Afghanistan wars, but even soldiers who were stationed in other areas have been threatened with pay reductions. Guardsmen stationed in Kosovo since the fall of 2006, helping to keep the peace in a volatile area, received an extra $225 per month in tax-free combat pay. The Pentagon considered "whether that duty, largely overshadowed by the Iraq war, no longer qualified for 'imminent danger pay' and should be reclassified midway through the soldiers' deployment" (MacQuarrie, 2007, p. B1).

Due to funding cuts, some 263,257 veterans were denied enrollment for VA health coverage in 2005. To cut costs, enrollment was suspended for those deemed not to have service-related injuries or illnesses. One of the reasons for the inferior care at Walter Reed was privatization. Walter Reed had given a five-year $120 million contract to a private company run by an ex-Halliburton executive, who fired many support personnel (Burger, 2007).

One study by *Army Times* found that the Army systematically shortchanged wounded soldiers by keeping their disability ratings low. According to the General Accounting Office, the number of soldiers approved for full disability benefits fell from 642 in 2001 to 209 in 2005, in spite of a huge influx of wounded and disabled from the Iraq war. If soldiers are rated 30 percent or more disabled, they are entitled to disability retirement pay, medical benefits, and commissary privileges where prices for goods are significantly lower than in the civilian market. A rating below 30 percent means they get severance pay and no benefits (Hallinan, 2007).

A *Newsweek* investigation revealed a grim portrait of the application process for disability benefits. It showed an overloaded bureaucracy cluttered with red tape; veterans having to wait weeks or months for mental health care and other appointments; families sliding into debt as VA case managers study disability claims over many months, and the seriously wounded requiring help from outside experts just to understand the VA's arcane system of rights and benefits. (Ephron & Childress, 2007 p. 32)

Daniel Cooper, the VA's undersecretary for benefits, told *Newsweek* reporters in March 2007 that the VA had a backlog of 400,000 applications and appeals. As more servicemen and women return from Iraq, the backlog was likely to increase. Cooper said the average waiting time for a benefit claim was about six months, but *Newsweek* found many veterans who had waited much longer. Veterans' advocacy groups such as Veterans for America have helped many veterans win their claims (p. 33).

The long-term cost of caring for veterans from Iraq and Afghanistan will be enormous. A study cited by *Newsweek* projects that at least 700,000 veterans from the global war on terror will flood the system in the coming years.

Many more wounded soldiers are being kept alive in the Iraq war than was the case in previous wars. In Vietnam and Korea, about three Americans were wounded for every one who died. In Iraq, sixteen soldiers are wounded or get sick for every one who dies. Better body armor and helmets are shielding more soldiers from fatal wounds. And advanced emergency care is keeping more of the wounded alive. But that means an increased burden on the VA's health care system (Ephron & Childress, 2007).

Veterans in rural areas were particularly disadvantaged. Specialized care is concentrated in urban areas, while 6 million of the veterans live in rural areas.

There is a shortage of mental health workers at many of the VA's hospitals and clinics across the country. According to a senior VA manager, "The system doesn't treat mental health with the same urgency it treats general health care" (p. 35).

One study found that more than three out of ten returning soldiers from Iraq and Afghanistan have a "mental disorder," but there are not enough psychologists to meet the need, and the psychological staff on the job is overwhelmed. Many of them are burned out.

The war has put a strain on marriages. One wife of a National Guard soldier, Carmen Artaega, who separated from her husband, Dustin Jolly, "blamed their marital fracture on the lonesome strains of military life. He was away too much. She was too far from family and friends. 'I was so young,' said Carman, 23, 'totally out of my element.'" She reconciled with her husband when he returned from Iraq, but he was suffering from PTSD and was hard to live with. "With Carmen, Dustin could be short-tempered. He seemed always on alert. Loud noises frightened him. His leg seemed in perpetual motion, bouncing up and down like it had a life of its own. Sometimes at night, he urinated in the sink. Frequently, he awoke with a start, his face dripping with perspiration" (Farragher, 2006).

Some families have joined an anti-war group, Military Families Speak Out. One member of this group, Stacy Bannerman, wrote about her husband coming home with PTSD and said, "It was hard to reconnect after more than a year apart, and the open wound of untreated PTSD made it virtually impossible . . . we just couldn't find our way back together after the war came home" (Bannerman, 2007).

Over the past fifteen years, the military has made great strides to retain married service members by improving schools, health programs, and child care. But the military has been especially challenged by the ever-growing ranks of the bereaved.

Of the 3,350 Americans who died in Iraq and Afghanistan through January 2007, 1,586 of them—47.3 percent—were married. There were more than 2,000 children left behind. Fort Hood, Texas, established the first-of-its-kind support center for women and children whose husbands and fathers have died in Iraq and Afghanistan.

"It's our sanctuary," said Ursula Pirtle, whose daughter frequents a playroom at the center. Three-year-old Katie never met her father, Heath. He was killed in Iraq in 2003. (Crary, 2007)

The support center was established as a result of activism by spouses and their allies who have been vocal on bases and at congressional hearings in pressing for more compassionate, effective support, including counseling programs for spouses and children.

Susan Kinsella, a professor who teaches students from a nearby military base, tells us that there is a vast array of social services in all branches of the military—more services, in fact, for the enlisted people than for the general population (Kinsella, 2007). Social workers with an MSW degree are the preferred hiring choice, although people with other degrees are hired as well. The Army has a family advocacy program that does both individual and group work. It provides family life consultants and training for parents. It teaches how to deal with stress and does a lot of work on how to reintegrate soldiers into family life. The Office of Public Affairs helps determine whether soldiers are eligible for an extra supplement for food stamps. Soldiers at lower pay grades are often eligible for food stamps.

New programs are cropping up all the time, based on the needs of the soldiers. So a human service worker in this environment has to be flexible, fast, and ready for changes. The pay and benefits for military social workers are good. You can be a civilian and work in the social service military programs in the states, but social workers in mental health and in hospital settings (usually with an MSW degree) are deployed as well. They go where the military goes. The family advocacy program people stay on the posts.

Rapid deployments over the past several years have been difficult for military families. Assistance with PTSD is at the forefront of services. The military wants to prevent PTSD and catch it early upon return. (At the base where Kinsella teaches, soldiers are on their third rotation.) The Sexual Assault Prevention and Response program is new on this base (Kinsella, 2007).

The Sexual Assault Prevention and Response program is now a mandated program, and all branches of the military have it. It was established as a result of complaints of women soldiers and subsequent media coverage, particularly an article in the *New York Times Sunday Magazine* (Corbett, 2007). A study by the Department of Defense (DOD) in 2003 found that one-third of a nationwide sample of female veterans seeking health care through the VA said they experienced rape or attempted rape during their service. Of that group, 37 percent said they were raped multiple times, and 14 percent reported that they were gang-raped. A change in DOD policy in 2005 allowing sexual assaults to be reported confidentially led to the number of reported assaults across the military to rise by 40 percent.

A study of women VA outpatients found that woman who had been sexually assaulted had symptoms of current depression three times higher and symptoms of current alcohol abuse two times higher than other women (Hankin et al., 1999).

Since the Tailhook episode in 1991, which involved sexual violence against women at a naval party, the Pentagon has become more concerned about sexual assaults. "There are far more women in areas of combat now as well. Over 160,000 women had seen active duty in Iraq and Afghanistan by April 2007" (Nader, 2007).

Human service workers need to become aware of services available to soldiers and veterans. In addition to services on military bases, the VA has Vet Centers that welcome veterans home by providing readjustment services and assisting them and their family members in making a successful postwar adjustment. In addition, TRICARE is the DOD's regionally managed health care program for active duty and retired members of the uniformed services. TRICARE covers the health, dental, and mental health needs of soldiers and their dependents. And Veterans' Outreach Centers are nonprofit agencies that receive state funds to support veterans and their families. They give financial assistance based on need (Women Veterans' Network, 2007). Army Emergency Relief gives financial assistance and scholarship help to soldiers and their families. The Red Cross also gives some financial assistance and provides other services.

it will be a great day
when
our schools
get all the money
they need
and the air force
has to hold
a bake sale
to buy a
bomber

WHERE THE MONEY COMES FROM

If you work in a human service agency, you will want to know who pays your salary and how secure it is. If, for example, you were working in the JOBS program, placing welfare recipients in jobs, when the federal government abolished that program, you would join your clients in the ranks of the unemployed.

Funding comes from different levels of government—county, city, state, and federal—and from private sources. In theory, some agencies are public, and others are private (voluntary, nonprofit), but in practice, there is a complicated mix of public and private agencies. Some agencies that call themselves "private" get most of their funds from the government, and public agencies sometimes hire personnel from "private" agencies to do some of their work. Sometimes when agencies are privatized, workers find themselves making less money for doing the same job they did when they were state workers.

Most private, nonprofit agencies were historically organized under religious auspices and were a major source of charity. Now most of them are more public than private, sometimes getting as much as 90 percent of their funds from public sources. Even programs that decide not to take government funds get a subsidy in the form of a tax exemption.

Private Enterprise and Social Welfare Programs

Since the 1960s, state and local governments have been hiring more and more private corporations to do some of the work that state bureaucracies used to do themselves. This is called **contracting out**. Corporations want to make profits on human service. Public officials and corporations want to reduce the growing power of public-employee unions, and they weaken unions by contracting services to private corporations.

Corporations have continued to enter the social welfare field, particularly since the inception of Medicare and Medicaid in 1965, when the government began paying large sums to doctors and hospitals. This **privatization** has occurred on a large scale in health care, especially in hospitals, nursing homes, and group medical care. Hospital chains such as Hospital Corporation of America and Humana sprang up in the 1970s and are making large profits. Nursing homes had become a $25-billion-a-year industry by the early 1980s, when 70 percent of them were under proprietary, for-profit management (Stoesz & Karger, 1991). By the 1980s, human service corporations had established themselves in child care, ambulatory health care, substance abuse care, psychiatric care, home care, assisted living facilities, and continuing care. Even some prisons have been privatized.

Unable to break their dependency on government funds, corporations are crying for profits from the 1996 welfare law. Small corporations were already in the welfare business before the 1996 welfare law was passed. Curtis & Associates "supplements its successful welfare-to-work jobs clubs with accessories like 'motivational fortune cookies' at $3.99 a dozen. A sample message is, 'The way to control your future is to work hard today' " (Bernstein, 1996b, p. 1). Maximus, Inc., a consulting company in McLean, Virginia, made $100 million in business in 1996, including $7 million in welfare-to-work programs in Boston, two California counties, and Fairfax, Virginia (Bernstein, 1996b).

Lockheed Martin, the $30 billion giant of the weapons industry, began in 1995 to sell its Texas Integrated Enrollment System as a newer, better, privatized public assistance program. The defense giant's proposal promised to save the state up to 40 percent on its welfare program. The designers included a veritable roll-call of former state and congressional officials. It took a massive fight in Texas by the Texas State Employees Union and others to stop it at the state level, but Lockheed didn't give up. Congressional leaders immediately proposed a "welfare flexibility bill" that would allow Texas to privatize its entire welfare system. A national battle ensued in Congress, with leadership from Service Employees International Union (SEIU) and other unions only narrowly defeating the "Lockheed Martin" legislation (Bill of Wrath, 1998).

A survey of privatized programs by the SEIU showed that the for-profits' current management of human service programs reveals fraud, embezzlement, massive cost overruns, extremely high error rates, technical incompetence, improper benefit denials, and "revolving door" hiring (Service Employees International Union, 1997). In Wisconsin, the two largest work-to-welfare agencies in Milwaukee were found to have misspent welfare funds. Maximus admitted to inappropriately billing the state for $411,000, and the Legislative Joint Audit found an additional $1.6 million that wasn't well documented. Maximus spent the money on disallowed meals, parties, and attending conferences (Gowans, 2000).

The corporations also have used welfare reform to get into the child welfare business. Lobbyists managed to persuade legislators to delete the word *nonprofit* from an old section of child welfare law. Before the law was changed, only foster families or nonprofit institutions

contracting out   A system whereby a government agency contracts with a private agency to do some specified work for pay.

privatization Changing the funding and administration of social welfare programs from the public to the private sector.

could get child welfare money to care for children who are removed from homes judged unfit. Children can no longer count on government help to stay in their own families, but if they are placed in an institution or a foster home, an open-ended stream of federal revenue covers up to 75 percent of the cost of placement (Bernstein, 1996b).

OUR VISION

Most of us have a vision of the kind of society we would like, and this vision varies from one person to another. Some people say that from the 1980s to the present is "the mean season." Visions are meaner now than they were in the 1960s. During the 1960s, many people envisioned a compassionate society that would assure people that they would not have to fear unemployment, hunger, homelessness, or going without health care or child care. People made proposals for full employment, for national health insurance, for a guaranteed annual income, for a children's allowance. But they did not get any of those proposals, and some people even stopped dreaming about them.

We believe that it is important to keep the vision, to keep on talking about our vision of the good society, and to keep working to realize it. Knowing what we want helps us to recognize windows of opportunity when they arise and to put our weight on the side of forces that may do some good.

SUMMARY

1. The United States has been called a "reluctant welfare state," but its social welfare programs have helped millions of people.

2. The federal Personal Responsibility and Work Opportunity Act of 1996 created the Temporary Assistance to Needy Families (TANF) program, which ended the entitlement of case assistance to needy families and gave block grants to states to administer the program and set their own guidelines, within federal constraints.

3. TANF set a federal time limit of five years for people to receive assistance. Some states set shorter time limits.

4. TANF set strict behavioral requirements.

5. TANF limited the amount and kind of higher education that recipients could receive.

6. The "Charitable Choice" provision of TANF requires states to include religious organizations as contractors of services.

7. TANF cut off access to any benefits except emergency health care to legal immigrants. This was later modified to make some immigrants eligible for benefits.

8. The main goal of TANF was to downsize the rolls, which states accomplished by restrictive practices.

9. Information about the following social welfare programs is updated: Temporary Assistance to Needy Families; General Assistance; Social Security; Supplemental Security Income; Emergency Assistance; Medicaid; Medicare; the Women, Infants, and Children food program; Supplemental Nutrition Assistance Program (food stamps); Unemployment Insurance; Earned Income Tax Credit; Child Tax Credit; Child Care Tax Credit.

10. Some social services use a small proportion of government spending for social welfare and are important to rich and poor alike.

11. Some of the fields of service described include services for the aged, foster care and adoption, mental health services, medical social work, services for the disabled, and services for the military.

12. The wars in Iraq and Afghanistan have put stresses on service men and women and their families.

13. The Veterans' Administration has a large backlog of disability claims and appeals, which they have not processed.

14. Funding for social services comes from local, state, and federal governments, as well as from private sources.

15. Social services are becoming increasingly privatized. Corporations are taking over services that were once run by the state.

16. Our vision of a future society includes a guarantee of adequate income, housing, health care, child care, and full employment.

DISCUSSION QUESTIONS

1. If you were put in charge of developing an ideal system of social supports, what would your system look like?

2. Discuss the attitudes toward welfare recipients that you have encountered in your family, school, and community. How were these attitudes developed? Does your attitude differ from other attitudes you have encountered?

3. Legislators in Congress voted to restrict payments for prescriptions for the aged on the grounds that people overuse the medical system when they don't have to pay for it. What do you think of this reasoning? Do you think you would overuse medical care if you got it free?

WEB RESOURCES FOR FURTHER STUDY

Children's Defense Fund (CDF)
www.childrensdefense.org

CDF provides a strong, effective voice for all the children of America who cannot vote, lobby, or speak for themselves. It pays particular attention to the needs of poor and minority children and those with disabilities. CDF educates the nation about the needs of children and encourages preventive investment before they get sick or into trouble, drop out of school, or suffer family breakdown.

Child Welfare League of America (CWLA)
www.cwla.org

CWLA is the nation's oldest and largest organization devoted entirely to the well-being of America's vulnerable children and their families. The site provides information about CWLA advocacy tips, action alerts, and child welfare statistics.

Food Research and Action Center (FRAC)
www.frac.org

FRAC is a leading national organization that works to improve public policies to eradicate hunger and undernutrition in the United States. FRAC is a nonprofit and nonpartisan research and public policy center that serves as the hub of an anti-hunger network of thousands of individuals and agencies across the country.

Center on Budget and Policy Priorities
www.cbpp.org

The Center on Budget and Policy Priorities is one of the nation's premier policy organizations working at the federal and state levels on fiscal policy and public programs that affect low- and moderate-income families and individuals. The center conducts research and analysis to help shape public debates over proposed budget and tax policies and to help ensure that policymakers consider the needs of low-income families and individuals in these debates. It also develops policy options to alleviate poverty.

National Women's Law Center
http://www.nwlc.org

A staff of nearly sixty advances the issues that cut to the core of women's lives in education, employment, family and economic security, and health and reproductive rights—with special attention given to the needs of low-income women and their families.

Legal Momentum
www.legalmomentum.org

Legal Momentum is the nation's oldest legal defense and education fund dedicated to advancing the rights of all women and girls. Over the past forty years, Legal Momentum has made historic contributions through litigation and public policy advocacy to advance economic and personal security for women.

Center for Law and Social Policy (CLASP)

www.clasp.org

CLASP seeks to improve the lives of low-income people. It develops and advocates for federal, state, and local policies to strengthen families and create pathways to education and work. Through careful research and analysis and effective advocacy, CLASP develops and promotes new ideas, mobilizes others, and directly assists governments and advocates to put in place successful strategies that deliver results that matter to people across America.

Coalition on Human Needs (CHN)

www.chn.org

The Coalition on Human Needs is an alliance of national organizations working together to promote public policies that address the needs of low-income and other vulnerable populations. The Coalition's members include civil rights, religious, labor, and professional organizations and those concerned with the well-being of children, women, the elderly, and people with disabilities.

Chapter 7

Poverty

There was a time in our history when average middle-class or upper-class citizens rarely encountered a poor person. If they stayed out of certain poor neighborhoods, often derisively referred to as "the other side of the tracks," they could pretty much avoid encountering too many poor people as they went about their daily lives. The poor were virtually invisible to many of their fellow citizens. Today, the poor are still invisible to many of us, but in a different way—although we encounter them in every facet of our daily lives. The person who does your paperwork at the car rental desk when you are going on vacation—a well-dressed and well-spoken gentleman—is poor. His company has downsized its staff (outsourcing the work he used to do), and he has lost his job. He hasn't been able to find another one on his level. The mortgage on his house has been foreclosed, and he is facing bankruptcy. The person who bags your groceries, although of a "certain age," discovered after thirty years of loyalty to his employer that his pension funds mysteriously disappeared, along with his health care and his secure old age. Now, living on a scant Social Security check, he has come to work as a bagger in the supermarket to pay his rent and his wife's medical bills.

The home health aide, upon whom his wife depends, since she is rapidly descending into Alzheimer's disease, is a poor person. Though she works as much as fourteen hours a day, she does not make even the minimum wage, and of course she gets no overtime pay or vacation or sick leave when her children need her to stay home with them. The person who serves you a hamburger and fries, cuts your hair, pumps your gas, and answers the phone at the cable company often has a family to support and lives in a town with high rent, gas, and electric bills.

All of these people and many more you see every day have "McJobs" (ABC online, 2007) which the *Oxford English Dictionary* describes as "unstimulating, low-paid with few prospects" and, we might add, with few benefits.

Most of the people you will be working with will be poor or near poor. We all need to examine our own attitudes about the poor in order to avoid adopting a widespread view of poor people as generally inadequate and incompetent and in need of reform. That view shapes many service programs for the poor. For example, shelters for homeless families have many rules to discipline the residents in ways that shelter administrators and/or welfare departments believe to be necessary. A researcher who studied homeless shelters objected to this approach:

> By making many aspects of their programs mandatory . . . shelters give the impression that homeless people will not take the initiative on their own to look for work or housing, enroll their children in school, or keep their

living spaces clean. They must be forced to do so. By mandating budgeting classes, shelters suggest that people become homeless in part because they are irresponsible with their money. It is in a sense a symbiotic relationship: shelter programs influence the ways housed people think about homelessness, the views of the housed public—whether ordinary citizens or policymakers—affect the formation of shelter programs and how such programs treat homeless people. (Williams, 2003)

In foster care programs, human service workers sometimes fall into the trap of confusing poverty with neglect, which can lead to taking children away from their parents rather than helping parents to get out of poverty. In adoption programs, adoption workers sometimes assume that a rich adoptive family is better than a poor one simply because it is richer. When this prejudice against the poor is combined with racial prejudice, it can lead to preferring a middle-class, white adoptive family to a poor black family, even when the black family has closer emotional ties to the child. Here is an example:

> A 10-year-old African American girl was living with warm, stable African American foster parents who wanted to adopt her. The girl's relatives lived close by and frequently visited her. Even though the girl wanted to stay, the child-welfare agency tried to place her for adoption with strangers, a white couple from an affluent suburb. The relatives feared they would lose contact with her because none owned a car. They felt this move was motivated by the social agency's elitism—"money equals a more loving family." The aunt said, "A child belongs to people who love it, even if they are not rich." (Matchan, 1992, p. 1)

Prejudice against the poor has permeated social policy since the country began. It leads to creating categories of who is "deserving" and who is "undeserving." Poor single men and women have been regarded as less deserving of help because it is assumed that they should be working. Poor mothers have been regarded as more deserving but are still the objects of suspicion that they may be cheating the welfare system or may be immoral. Poor children are regarded as "innocent" and more deserving of help. But they are, after all, children of poor parents, so the distrust of their parents sometimes leads to harming the children by denying aid to their parents.

DEFINING POVERTY

How much money do you think a family needs to escape poverty? A "self-sufficiency" standard developed by researchers at Crittenton Women's Union found that in 2010 a family with one adult, one preschooler, and one school-age child living in the Bronx in New York City needed to earn $60,934 a year, while in South Manhattan it required $91,552 a year to be self-sufficient (Pearce, 2010). This standard took into account the costs of child care, housing, health care, and transportation, in addition to food, now estimated to consume about 10 percent of a family's budget, but it did not allow for any luxuries.

But what does *poverty* mean? The federal poverty line is based on a formula arrived at in 1963, which set the poverty line at three times the annual cost of food under a "low-cost budget," without considering housing, fuel costs, or child care costs, all of which have escalated substantially in the past forty-five years. The poverty line is the same for all the states except for Alaska and Hawaii, which are higher. The 2010 poverty guidelines for the forty-eight Contiguous States and the District of Columbia were: $10,830 for one person; $14,570 for two people; $18,310 for three people; and $22,050 for four people. The federal poverty line is an outmoded measure that grossly misleads the public into thinking that only a small percentage of the U.S. population is poor (Rosenthal, 2007). In 2009, 43.56 million people lived below the poverty line, 14.3 percent of the population (Casey, 2010).

Wider Opportunities for Women (WOW) has estimated the actual costs of meeting a family's basic needs. The standard is not luxurious or even comfortable but not so low that it fails to adequately provide for a family. The cost of living varies between states and localities within states, so it is customized for different localities. WOW has also computed the wages required to meet the standard. Even in the states with the lowest wages required to meet the self-sufficiency standard, the wages were far above the national minimum wage, which in 2011 was $7.25 per hour.*

For example, in Erie County Pennsylvania in 2010 a family consisting of one adult, one preschooler, and one school age child needed $46,676 to be self-sufficient. The poverty line for a family of three was $18,310. The cash value of the basic public assistance package, including TANF, SNAP (food stamps), and WIC, amounted to $11,661 per year for three-person families in Pennsylvania. This was just 24 percent of the self-sufficiency standard and is 64 percent of the federal poverty level.

If you used the self-sufficiency standard's yearly wage as the official poverty line, rather than the government's level, the number of poor people in the United States would be millions more than the estimated overall poverty in 2009 of 47.8 million people (Fox News, 2011).

The poverty line is used in determining eligibility for some government benefits. Some benefits, such as fuel assistance and Medicaid, use a higher percentage of the poverty line than 100 percent. TANF payments are below the poverty line in all states, far below in southern states. Setting the percentage often becomes a struggle between advocates and legislators. In Massachusetts, for example, the eligibility level for shelter for homeless families in 2010 was 130 percent of the poverty line. Legislators tried to cut that back to 100 percent of the poverty line. Whichever the level, if clients earn even a dollar more, they remain homeless.

Even the U.S. government recognizes that the poverty line is not a realistic measure. The U.S. Census taken in 2010 did some revised poverty calculations with the census data it collected. However, that was not used to revise the federal poverty line, which is codified by law.

The income gap is one way to measure poverty, but the wealth gap is also crucial, and racial disparities are drastically greater in terms of wealth than in terms of income. "The median wealth for single white women in their prime working years, age 36–49, is 61 percent of the wealth of their male counterparts, who own $70,030. The corresponding ratio between women and men of color is nearly off the charts, at just 0.05 percent—$550

---

*Some states (California, Connecticut, Illinois, Massachusetts, and Washington) have a higher minimum wage.

versus $11,000. Almost half of single black and Hispanic women have zero or negative wealth. Single black women have a median wealth of $100 and Hispanic women of $120—dramatically lower than white men ($43,800), white women ($41,500) or black men ($7,900)" (Hollar, 2010).

Wealth is particularly important in an economic crisis. It influences your ability to retire or support yourself in old age. Women of color have had the highest foreclosure rates of any group during the current recession—both as a result of their lack of wealth and their being targeted for subprime mortgages, regardless of their income level. "Wealth also helps people get ahead. Home equity can be borrowed against to send children to college, for example, and wealth can be passed down through the generations to provide them with more stability, access and options. Family wealth is the biggest predictor of the future economic status of a child, giving lie to the old American 'bootstraps' mythology" (Hollar, 2010).

INCOME INSTABILITY

The poverty level measured at one point in time tells only part of the story. Incomes have become increasingly unstable and unpredictable. Jacob Hacker, a Yale professor, says, "Over the past generation the economic *instability* of American families has actually risen much faster than economic *inequality*" (Hacker, 2006, p. 2). Economic insecurity isn't just a problem of the poor and uneducated. With families needing two earners to maintain a middle-class standard of living, they are facing the loss of benefits they once had on the job such as pensions and health insurance. The job market has grown more uncertain and unstable. Families are making investments in buying a home, gaining new skills, and raising well-educated children, but are paying the price when those investments fail. Hacker calls this the Great Risk Shift, a shift from providing guaranteed collective benefits to shifting responsibility to individuals.

Raising the Minimum Wage

When the Democrats won a majority in Congress, one of their first actions was to submit a bill to raise the federal minimum wage from $5.15 to $7.25 over a two-year span. Still, the minimum wage isn't enough to meet a family's needs. The national campaign to raise the minimum wage has succeeded in raising wages for many workers and raising the minimum wage in states. High school and college students have been active in campaigns to get higher wages for employees at their schools and cities and higher minimum wages in their states. The activist organization ACORN won living wage or minimum wage ordinances in fourteen cities (Living Wage Resource Center, 2007). Unfortunately, ACORN has sharply reduced its organizing because it lost its government funding. A right-wing organization, seeking to destroy ACORN, publicized a video it took of a couple posing as a pimp and a prostitute seeking advice about how to advance their business, and the video gave the impression that an ACORN staff member gave them this advice. It later developed that the video was doctored to look worse than what actually happened, but before this information could be publicized, the U.S. Congress voted to withdraw funds the government had given it for housing organizing (ACORN, 2010).

Nevertheless, organizing for a living wage continues. In May 2010, activists representing low-income communities in New York City rallied behind legislation that would raise the minimum pay to $10 an hour for workers at development sites that benefit from city financial support (Chen, 2010).

Of course, the best solution for providing a living wage is to raise the federal minimum wage to a level that would guarantee all workers a living wage. This is the goal of an organization called Universal Living Wage, which is campaigning to raise the federal minimum wage by indexing it to the local cost of housing throughout the United States. Of the 3.5 million people who experienced homelessness in 2010, 42 percent of them worked at some point during the week, according to the federal government. "These folks come from our 10.1 million minimum wage workers. Clearly, the work ethic is there, but the wage to afford basic housing is not" (Universal Living Wage, 2010).

Barbara Ehrenreich, author of *Nickel and Dimed: On (Not) Getting By in America*, decided to find out how anyone could live on the $6 or $7 an hour that will be earned by the roughly 4 million women about to be pushed into the labor market because of welfare reform. She worked undercover—as a maid in Maine; a waitress in Key West, Florida; and a Walmart clerk in Minneapolis—to get material for her book. Although she took the same kind of jobs and lived in the same kind of housing as welfare mothers, she was better off than they were because she had no children to support, and she had a car. Ehrenreich found that she couldn't afford even basic needs, such as housing or food, on her pay. She was surprised and distressed to learn about people's dire poverty, such as the maid in Maine who eats hot dog buns for lunch. She commented, "I was shamed by that. There are all kinds of levels of ignorance. I've talked to people who thought everyone was getting $15 an hour because that's what they pay their housekeeper" (Dougherty, 2001, p. D4).

Ehrenreich says that we shouldn't use the word *unskilled*. She says, "Every job requires a lot of concentration, memorization, quick thinking. Those things take intelligence and skill" (Dougherty, 2001, p. D4). A common misperception is that low-wage earners are stupid and that if they were smart enough, they'd be able to better their situation. Ehrenreich does not believe this. She says,

> The implication is that they have some terrible problem, or made awful mistakes to get into that weird position. But about 30 percent of the workforce is in this position. It has increased since the mid-80s with the elimination of high-paying union jobs that a high school graduate could get. More and more people who might have been in manufacturing 20 years ago are driving a forklift or something like this, so it's not that the person is stupid. (Dougherty, 2001, p. D4)

Changes in the Economy

In "Allentown," Billy Joel's lament for lost jobs in Pennsylvania's coal country, disillusioned workers wait in vain to realize "the promises our teachers made/if we worked hard, if we behaved." Written in 1982 after massive layoffs at nearby Bethlehem Steel, Joel's song presaged the wrenching changes in the U.S. economy that have kept so many unskilled industrial workers from achieving the modest prosperity their fathers enjoyed ("Every Worker's Dream," 2005).

Automation of factory work, outsourcing of jobs overseas, global competition, and the decline of union strength contribute to the loss of well-paying blue-collar jobs. Many of those laid off workers will end up employed in the service industry with few benefits or prospects.

The state of the economy has a powerful influence on what kind of social welfare system a society provides. Since the 1970s, there have been vast changes in the U.S. economy and in the global economy. A process of **deindustrialization** has taken place, in which manufacturing work has declined—especially in heavy industries such as auto, steel, and aircraft—and both high technology and service work have increased. Corporations have downsized, manufacturing jobs have been automated, and jobs have moved overseas. Industries that once paid decent wages have been **deregulated** and have fought unions, with the help of the government. Fewer than 8 percent of private-sector workers are in unions today, in contrast to 30 percent after World War II (Kuttner, 2007).

Transnational corporations are increasingly dominating national as well as international economies. Corporate leaders influence legislators to cut back on funds for social welfare because they are eager for funds to expand their corporations and are eager to slash the safety net in order to lower wages. When there is no safety net, people are forced to take any job at any wage rather than starve. At the same time, a massive corporate restructuring creates growing impoverishment of both the working class and the middle class. Workers without a college education have been particularly hurt by the decline of manufacturing jobs. Also, since men have historically held the vast majority of manufacturing jobs, deindustrialization has caused their earnings to decline. Most men can no

deindustrialization A shift in the economy in which manufacturing work has declined and both high technology and service work have increased.

deregulation The process of removing government regulations of corporations, usually resulting in fighting unions and lowering wages, with the help of the government.

longer support an entire family on their paychecks. Working in an auto plant in Detroit used to pay good wages. Flipping hamburgers at McDonald's will not support a family.

Detroit, once a thriving center for automobile manufacturing, illustrates the effects of deindustrialization:

> Detroit, a city of less than a million people, over 80 percent of whom are African American, in a metropolitan area of over 4.5 million, has become something like the epicenter of the crisis of deindustrialization adversely affecting black communities around the country. (In February 2007,) DaimlerChrysler announced it will cut 13,000 jobs in North America. . . . Much of the effect would be in southeastern Michigan, where 5,300 people will lose their jobs over the next two years. . . . An additional 1,000 Michigan jobs will go, as Chrysler explores selling support businesses not involved in its core car-building, and 1,000 will be lost because of "productivity improvements." (Boice, 2007a)

The Recession

During the last decade, there was rank speculation on Wall Street, similar to what happened in the 1920s before the Great Depression. More money was invested in the financial market than in production. Instead of producing goods, the country was "producing" bets. Wall Street had become a giant casino. The housing market crashed, leading to many foreclosures and bank crises. With the banks in trouble, businesses could not borrow and although the Federal Reserve lowered the interest rates to almost nothing, this still did not stimulate the economy. The result was more foreclosures, high unemployment, and business failures.

The economist Paul Krugman fears that we are in the early stages of a third depression. The austerity results from Republicans and conservative Democrats refusing to authorize additional aid to state governments, which is resulting in budget cuts at the state and local levels. Krugman says that because policymakers haven't yet done enough to promote recovery, there has been a stunning resurgence of hard-money and balanced-budget orthodoxy, which will result in tens of millions of unemployed workers, "many of whom will go jobless for years, and some of whom will never work again" (Krugman, 2010).

Unemployment

In 2010, the official unemployment rate was 9.8 percent and was expected to remain roughly at or near this level for the foreseeable future. The *New York Times* columnist Bob Herbert described the unemployment situation in June 2010:

> Unemployment is crushing families and stifling the prospects of young people. More than 15 million Americans are out of work, and more than 44 percent have been jobless for six months or longer. Nearly a quarter of the 15 million unemployed have been jobless for a year or more. New college graduates are having a terrible time finding work, and many are taking jobs that require only a high school education. Teachers are facing the worst employment market since the Depression. Entire communities are going under. Some inner-city neighborhoods, where joblessness is off the charts, are becoming islands of despair. Rural communities and rust belt cities and town are experiencing their own economic nightmares. (Herbert, 2010)

ELGIN, IL—When Daniel Taylor met Illinois U.S. Sen. Dick Durbin, the Elgin man shared his experience as he struggled to keep his home and talked of his effort to obtain a home mortgage modification that could help him avoid going into foreclosure. After losing his job, Daniel Taylor tried for a loan modification to keep his home from heading into foreclosure. He is still waiting a finial decision on his application.

Months later, Taylor is still waiting to hear whether he will qualify for a permanent modification under the Home Affordable Modification Program (HAMP), a federal program that reduces a homeowner's mortgage up to 31 percent.

His life remains in limbo. "I have no idea what's going on," he said.

It has been the same story for months. He is exhausting his savings trying to keep his Mariner Drive home. Initially, Taylor was told he didn't qualify for the program because he had money in a savings account, which he said is for emergencies. He later received a letter indicating he had received a temporary modification. Still, he's not sure what's happening with the mortgage. The mortgage is up to date, although late fees are being added every month because he's not paying the full amount, he said. He gets differing information from bank officials about whether the temporary modification will become permanent.

"It's up in the air," Taylor said. "I'm paying what I am supposed to pay, but they have me sitting in limbo."

Taylor is the new face of those caught up in the mortgage crisis, which is entering into a new phase that likely will affect thousands more homeowners. While President Barack Obama's administration unveiled the HAMP program a year ago, homeowners caught in this latest wave may find themselves without much help—meaning the crisis will continue to evolve and affect families and neighborhoods into the foreseeable future.

Taylor's home is not one of those McMansions that were the fad a few years ago. The house is comfortable, of average size and in an average neighborhood. He bought the home seven years ago following a divorce. Taylor has joint custody of his 12-year-old daughter.

Lately, Taylor has noticed more and more vacant houses on his block. He's counted three or four within a block, including one just around the bend from his home. Taylor is hoping to avoid the same fate. He finds himself surprised to be in this situation. He never missed a mortgage payment, and he even paid a month ahead. He has excellent credit and has managed his debt. But a year ago, he lost his job as a salesman with a St. Charles car dealership when General Motors closed down dozens of dealerships.

For a while, Taylor paid his mortgage with his savings, but now, he needs that cash for everyday living expense and emergencies, Taylor said. He's been trying to find a job but needs to find one that pays close to what he used to earn—more than $30 an hour. Given the continuing high rate of unemployment in the area, it won't be an easy task. So far, he has had no luck finding a job.

Taylor's mortgage is "under water," meaning the house is worth less than the mortgage balance—by about $16,000. Selling the house is not a financially sound option, which is why he applied for a HAMP. A mortgage modification would mean he could take a lower-paying job and still pay the mortgage. But he is becoming more frustrated about the process of applying for the HAMP program. Taylor has a friend who tried three times before receiving a modification.

"The banks aren't willing to work with anybody," Taylor said. "It's like someone's got a noose around your neck and you're just waiting for someone to kick the chair. Everyone says you can live the American dream." The banks, however, "take the American dream away from you," he said. The American dream is turning into a nightmare for homeowners trying to save their homes. (Carr, 2010)

Foreclosures involving subprime rates were the first wave, which hit in late 2008, said Johnny Placeres, executive director of Neighborhood Housing Services of the Fox Valley. "I think we saw more than 50 percent were subprime loans," Placeres said. "I'd say the majority of the subprime lenders went belly up . . (they) were not doing" home loan modifications to keep delinquent homeowners from foreclosure.

Placeres recalls the real estate boom of just five years ago. Back then, banks would give anyone a loan, even a "no doc" (no documentation) loan. "Those loans—prospective homeowners didn't even have to show proof of employment—were the norm," he said.

"Homeowners caught up in the first wave had no help," Placeres said. "Some of the banks were doing loan modifications on their own, but the banks would only help people who were on the verge of losing their homes," he said. HAMP was created in early 2009 to assist homeowners in reducing their mortgage payments and stave off foreclosure.

These are the people behind the double-digit unemployment rate announced every month. They are considered middle to upper class—people who've been able to hold off foreclosures until now. HAMP is "a good program, but because the second wave of foreclosures has a lot to do with job loss, people who are unemployed are not going to be eligible," Placeres said. "If you have no income, they can't work with you. However, we do see if one spouse is unemployed and the other one is working, the unemployment income will be considered. Right now, there's no help for those people other than time is on their side," Placeres said (Carr, 2010).

In 2010, the unemployment rate for young people between the ages of 18 and 29 was 14 percent, approaching the levels of that group in the Great Depression. And 23 percent of that age group is not even seeking jobs, according to data from the U.S. Bureau of Labor Statistics. The total, 37 percent, is the highest in more than three decades and a rate

reminiscent of the 1930s. Many young people who can't find a job are moving in with their parents. In 2008, the first year of the recession, the percentage of the population living in households in which at least two generations were present rose nearly a percentage point, to 16 percent. The high point, 24.7 percent, came in 1940, as the Depression ended, and the low point, 12 percent, in 1980 (Uchitelle, 2010).

Unemployment insurance is generally extended beyond the usual twenty-six weeks in times of persistent joblessness. It was extended twice during the recession, but in May 2010, the Senate went home for a holiday weekend without extending benefits. In July 2010, Congress finally acted on a resolution to extend unemployment benefits. The measure extended jobless benefits beyond the traditional twenty-six weeks to somewhere from sixty to ninety-nine weeks, depending on a state's unemployment rate. But many jobless people exceeded those limits. Those who have been unemployed for more than ninety-nine weeks are called "the 99ers." They are adjusting to a harsh reality with no income (Luo, 2010). In December 2010, Congress extended unemployment benefits for thirteen weeks, as part of a tax bill that continued tax cuts for both the rich and the middle class. This did not help the "99ers."

The official unemployment rate does not give the whole picture. It does not count those who have given up looking for work or those who are in government "retraining" programs. It does not count those who have taken early retirement to avoid being laid off but would prefer to be working. It also does not count the "underemployed"—those with part time or seasonal jobs who would rather have full-time jobs.

Who Is Poor?

Before the recession, middle-class people with stable jobs felt economically secure, but when they lost their jobs, many middle-class people became poor, and many lost their homes when they weren't able to pay their mortgage. People who were already poor before the recession were forced into deeper poverty and many became homeless. As the middle class fell into the lower class, there was a widening gap between the rich and the poor, and the ranks of poor people swelled.

CASE EXAMPLE

Coleen McEneany used to be a private investigator (PI). Her husband worked for Circuit City as an information technology specialist. But the PI work dried up in the recession, and Circuit City closed. With their daughter, they moved into the Fremont home of her mother, a retired sixth-grade teacher. While the home has a swimming pool in back and well-tended garden, the family resources were stretched so thin that they now depend on food and help from Tri-CityVolunteers. Ironically, she knew about the food pantry because she and her husband were both donors to the program back when they were working. Nevertheless, with a degree in criminal justice, Coleen has hopes that she'll somehow find a job. In the meantime, she is taking course for a degree in early childhood education. (Bacon, & Edwards, 2010)

Belinda Schell worked at the Diamond Glass Company plant in Royersford, Pennsylvania, from 1984 to 1990, earning more than $10 an hour. In 1990, she and 500 coworkers lost their jobs because the plant closed. The Diamond Glass Company plant was one of the thousands of corporations in the United States that were involved in the corporate takeover craze of the 1980s. In those leveraged buyouts, managers and investors bought companies with money borrowed from the company's future earnings, and to pay off their debts, they laid off workers and often closed plants. In her new job as a nursing-home aide, Belinda earns considerably less than she earned at Diamond Glass. "It is an occupation that the federal government touts as a growth industry that will provide many jobs, mostly low paying, as the aged population continues to grow." (Barlett & Steele, 1992, p. 15)

Some groups, including women, minorities, and children, are poorer than others.

The U.S. Census poverty data for 2009 showed the largest number of poor people in the fifty-one years since poverty has been measured, 43.56 millions. It also showed the highest poverty rate for single-mother families, 38.5 percent, since 1998; a 13.9 percent poverty rate for adult women compared to the 10.5 percent for adult men; a 20.7 percent poverty rate for children; a 25.3 percent poverty rate for Hispanics; and a 25. 9 percent poverty rate for blacks compared to a 9.4 percent for non-Hispanic whites (Casey, 2010).

WOMEN

Women, on average, are poorer than men because they earn less than men. The wage gap is larger for older women. In 2010, women under age 35 who worked full time earned around 90 percent of what their male counterparts earned. But women over age 35 earned only about 75 percent as much as their respective male counterparts (Rampell, 2010). The wage gap is much larger for African-American and Latina women, with African-American women making only 61 cents, and Latinas only 52 cents, for every dollar earned by white, non-Hispanic men. For the 9.9 million families that are headed by single mothers and who rely almost exclusively on a woman's wage, lowered earnings have a serious impact on their economic security. Female-headed households—which make up to 85 percent of single-parent families—have been particularly hard-hit, with an unemployment rate of 11.3 percent" (National Women's Law Center, 2010).

Single mothers face not just financial poverty but poverty of time as well. All working mothers are under pressure to juggle child care with work, but single mothers must do it alone. Affluent people can buy many of the services a wife used to do at home. But routine household tasks take even more time for poor families. A well-off family buys new clothes, sometimes from catalogs or online (which saves time but is often more expensive); buys food at the most convenient market or eats out; does laundry at home with its own washer and dryer or takes it to a dry cleaner; and drives one of its new, well-maintained cars. A financially pinched family, on the other hand, combs through second-hand clothes and mends clothes, searches for food bargains or stands in line at a food pantry, takes clothes to a laundromat, relies on public transport, nurses a clunker car, or arranges a ride. The well-off family has enough savings to "splurge with the urge," using a checking account, credit card, or ATM to pay bills conveniently. The financially pinched family struggles to figure out how to make the money last through the week (or month), robs Peter to pay Paul, pays bills in person, and purchases money orders (Albelda & Tilly, 1997).

Older women are highly vulnerable to poverty. On average, they are likely to live several years longer than their male partners. And they are more likely than men to run out of resources in late life. If they are divorced, they may not get their husband's assets unless they get a favorable legal settlement. A woman who either took time off to raise the children or never entered the labor force could find herself with neither assets nor job skills needed to keep her out of poverty. "In the United States, the share of elderly women living in poverty is highest among divorced or separated women (37 percent), followed by widowed women (28 percent), never-married women (22 percent,) and married women (10 percent)" (Yin, 2008).

Women are more likely than men to work in part-time and temporary jobs that don't pay benefits or pensions. Because their wages are lower, their future Social Security pensions will be lower. They get no pay, private pension, or Social Security if they stayed home to care for their children.

Older women are less likely than elderly men to have significant family income from private pensions. "In 2006, only 23 percent of unmarried women aged 65 or older were receiving their own private pensions (either as a retired worker or survivor), compared to 30 percent of unmarried men. In 2008, the average annual Social Security income received by women 65 years and older was $11,377, compared to $14,822 for men" (Social Security Online, 2010).

CASE EXAMPLE

The Service Employees International Union has been organizing low-paid workers, including janitors and home care workers. Here is the story of Aurora Villareal, a woman who works two part-time jobs in Houston:

> With only part-time jobs available, I have to work two jobs. One of them is at the 100 Louisiana building, where my job is to clean bathrooms on seven floors in four hours. I am paid $5.25 an hour. Completing each bathroom consists of cleaning the mirrors and walls, taking out the trash, mopping the floors, refilling toilet paper

and cleaning the doors. To finish in time, you have to rush. And I have to rush because I have to be on time to my second job.

> My second job is as a janitor in the Toyota Center. I take a short bus ride from my first job to the next. The bus costs $7 a week, which costs me more than an hour's work. Working part-time is hard. It is hard on my family. I don't get to see my husband some days because I do not come home until he has left. Working part-time causes stress because I worry about how to make ends meet. (Service Employees International Union, 2006)

MINORITIES

While white people are facing a recession, people of color endure a severe and durable enough recession that it amounts to an economic depression (Huezo, et al., 2009). People of color face a disproportionate impact of the economic downturn because of preexisting structural and institutional racial inequities. People of color are concentrated in occupations that are more vulnerable to the economic downturn. They are more likely than whites to be

Many of the "working poor" are only a step away (or a paycheck away) from joining those people who have had to seek out homeless shelters or find spots to occupy on the streets.

laid off and are more likely to be unemployed and underemployed. Equal pay for equal work has never been a reality. Wages have always been lower for people of color than whites, making it much more difficult for people of color to save a financial cushion. Workers of color are subject to hiring discrimination and abuse ranging from wage theft to forced part-time work that renders them ineligible for benefits (Applied Research Center, 2009).

CASE EXAMPLE

Sandra Hines, a middle-aged Black woman, lost her family home to foreclosure. Like the great majority of American families, the family source of wealth in communities of color is in housing. The family moved into a rental house, but it, too, was hit by foreclosure. Her story, combined with the stories of millions of other people of color who have recently lost their homes and most of their assets—wealth that was allowed by government policies (or lack thereof) to transfer to corporate interests—represents the latest chapter in a long-standing and intensifying racial wealth divide.

Leo Shipman, a 24-year-old Black man with a goatee and short hair, dressed in a new, white t-shirt,

recently lost his job in Detroit. The unemployment rate in the city hit 22.2 percent in January. "My biggest worry is my son," he said about his 3-year-old. "You don't know how you're going to feed them. He doesn't know the bills are running up, but I do."

When Shipman is not taking buses and taxis to drop off resumes or running from one job interview to another, he waits at the Tried Stone Baptist Church in Detroit, where his mother works as a receptionist. The church sits on a block among shuttered houses in a part of Detroit that has struggled for decades. Porches are overgrown with bushes, and windows are covered by plywood planks. The streets were largely empty of cars and pedestrians when we arrived to meet Shipman.

"How many houses you see burnt down, how many people you see walking up and down the streets with no good shoes on their feet?" asked Shipman about his neighborhood. When we arrived to interview him, a pipe had just burst in the church's basement.

At 3:00 P.M., Shipman left to pick up his son. The boy spends his time between his parents, and Shipman puts a lot of pressure on himself to "make it on my own," to live independently and help support his son. His son's mother still has a job. Even when Shipman was working, he was barely able to scrape by, earning about $380 a week ($9.50/hour) as a thermal press operator at a small company that makes plastic truck-bed liners for Dodge and other auto companies.

At the end of November 2009, the company told all but three of its 30 workers that they were being let go because demand had evaporated with auto sales at their lowest since World War II. With only a high school education—he's been trying to enroll in a technical college—securing a living-wage job proves elusive if not impossible. Because he had been under-employed, Shipman had no unemployment check coming in at the time. He's not sure what he'll do. (Applied Research Center, 2009)

Black families have much less wealth than white families. In 2007, white families had a median value of $100,000 in financial instruments, such as retirement accounts, pension funds, stocks, bonds, and Certificate of Deposits (CDs). But the median value of African-American family financial holdings was only $5,000. The gap would fund full tuition at a four-year public university for two children, plus tuition at a public medical school (Jackson, 2010).

CHILDREN

UNICEF studied child well-being in twenty-one wealthy countries and published its findings in a 2007 "report card" (United Nations Children's Fund, 2007). If it had been a school report card, the United States would have received an "F." The report looked at six dimensions of child welfare, from infant mortality to whether children ate dinner with their parents or were bullied at school. The Netherlands, followed by Sweden, Denmark, and Finland, finished at the top of the rankings, while the United States was twentieth and Britain twenty-first. One of the study's researchers, Jonathan Bradshaw, said "children fared worse in the United States and Britain, despite high overall levels of national wealth, because of greater economic inequality and poor levels of public support for families. . . . They don't invest as much in children as continental European countries do," citing the lack of day care services in both countries, and poorer health coverage and preventive care for American children. The United States was rated last in the health and safety category, based on infant mortality, vaccinations for childhood diseases, deaths from injuries and accidents before age 19, and whether children reported fighting in the past year or being bullied in the previous two months (McHugh, 2007).

The United States had the highest child poverty rate of any of the countries, with 21.7 percent of children living in households with incomes less than 50 percent of the national median, and it has the highest infant mortality rate, with seven children dying out of every 1,000 born (United Nations Children's Fund, 2007).

Only 3 percent of eligible infants and young children (0–3) are enrolled in Early Head Start and only about half to two-thirds of children eligible for Head Start are enrolled. Studies reveal that those enrolled in high-quality early childhood education programs are subsequently more likely to complete higher levels of education, have higher earnings, and be in better health and be in stable relationships, and are less likely to commit a crime or be incarcerated (Children's Defense Fund, 2008).

"Poverty in early childhood poisons the brain" was the title of a 2008 article in the *Financial Times*, which summarized research that was presented at the American Association for the Advancement of Science. Neuroscientists have found that many children growing up in very poor families with low social status experience unhealthy levels of stress hormones, which impair their neural development. The effect is to impair language development and memory for the rest of the child's life (Krugman, 2008).

Poverty is very bad for a person's health, both physical and mental. Poor children are at increased risk for any number of health problems, including attention deficit disorder, asthma, dental disease, and injuries resulting from accidents or physical abuse and neglect. They score lower on developmental tests, and they have a higher mortality rate (Aber, Bennett, Conley, & Li, 1997). They also have higher levels of depression and antisocial behavior, particularly under conditions of persistent poverty. Low-income adults are also at greater risk for health problems.

Hunger

Since the recession began in December 2007, the number of people going hungry has increased dramatically. Approximately 49 million people, including 17 million children, experienced food insecurity in 2010, according to the U.S. Department of Agriculture, which defines food insecurity as the lack of resources required to sustain the nutritional needs of family members. Children are considered food insecure if, in the last year, they did not eat enough, did not eat for a day, skipped a meal or were hungry because their family could not afford adequate food. Food-insecure children are more at risk for being overweight and for having poor health, poor academic performance, and poor psychosocial functioning (Science Daily, 2010). Households with children experience more food hardship than other households. Nearly one in four such households suffered food hardship in 2009 (Food Research and Action Center, 2010).

Some people think that the obesity of poor people proves that they aren't really poor, as they must have enough money in order to eat too much. However, food insecurity is likely to contribute to obesity. Food-insecure individuals are more likely to consume large portions of food when food is available to compensate for times when food is scarce. In response to frequent periods of hunger, the body tends to store fat, which can lead to obesity:

> Households that have limited resources are more likely to sacrifice the quality and variety of food consumed in lieu of quantity. Foods that are higher in fat, calories and sugar often cost less and tend to have a longer shelf life than healthier alternatives such as fruits and vegetables. Fast food chains are concentrated in low-income urban neighborhoods and their low-cost "extra value meals" are laden with saturated fat. Parents use other techniques to stretch available food, including preparing low-cost dishes, amending rotten food, and diluting drinks, stews and casseroles. Unfortunately, this places their families' health at risk. (Children's Defense Fund, 2005a)

George Orwell, a British novelist who wrote about poverty in *The Road to Wigan Pier*, said this about poor people's diets:

> Would it not be better if they spent more money on wholesome things like oranges and whole meal bread or if . . . they saved on fuel and ate their carrots raw? Yes, it

would, but the point is that no ordinary human being is ever going to do such a thing. The ordinary human being would sooner starve than live on brown bread and raw carrots. And the peculiar evil is this, that the less money you have, the less inclined you feel to spend it on wholesome food. A millionaire may enjoy breakfasting off orange juice and Ryvita biscuits; an unemployed man doesn't. . . . When you are unemployed, which is to say when you are underfed, harassed, bored and miserable, you don't *want* to eat dull wholesome food. You want something a little bit "tasty." There is always some cheaply pleasant thing to tempt you. Let's have three pennyworth of chips! Run out and buy us a two-penny ice cream! Put the kettle on and we'll have a nice cup of tea! *That* is how your mind works when you are at the P.A.C. [welfare] level. . . . Unemployment is an endless misery that has got to be constantly palliated, and especially with tea, the Englishman's opium. (Orwell, 1961, pp. 88–89)

When people have lost their jobs, exhausted their unemployment benefits, and can't get cash supports, their only resource is food stamps, now called Supplemental Nutritional Assistance (SNAP). Their numbers were rising before the recession as tougher welfare laws made it harder for poor people to get cash aid, but they have soared by about 50 percent between 2008 and 2010. SNAP/food stamp participation in 2010 hit a new record of 39.4 million persons. One in eight Americans received SNAP/food stamps. In 2010, about one in fifty Americans lived in a household with a reported income that consisted of nothing but a food-stamp card. TANF, the main cash welfare program, has scarcely expanded during the recession; the rolls are down about 75 percent from their 1990s peak. Unemployment insurance has rapidly grown but still omits nearly half the unemployed. Food stamps, easier to get, have become the safety net of last resort. A *New York Times* survey found that about 6 million people live in households with no income. About 1.2 million are children. The general public is more supportive of food stamps than the cash assistance of TANF since they buy only food. And the federal government pays for the whole benefit, giving states reason to maximize enrollment since states share in the costs of TANF (DeParle, & Geberloff, 2010). Since the recession began in December 2007, caseloads have increased 48 percent in food stamps but just 12 percent in TANF. Even before the recession began, TANF was reaching only a minority of eligible families (Legal Momentum, 2009).

CASE EXAMPLE

A skinny fellow in saggy clothes who spent his childhood in foster care, Rex Britton, 22, hopped a bus from Syracuse two years ago for a job painting parking lots. Now, with unemployment at nearly 14 percent and paving work scarce, he receives $200 a month in food stamps and stays with a girlfriend who survives on a rent subsidy and a government check to help her care for her disabled toddler. "Without food stamps we'd probably be starving," Mr. Britton said.

A grandmother whose voice mail message urges callers to "have a blessed good day" Wanda Debnam,

53, once drove 18-wheelers and dreamed of selling real estate. But she lost her job at Starbucks this year and moved in with her son in nearby Lehigh Acres. Now she sleeps with her 8-year-old granddaughter under a poster of the Jonas Brothers and uses her food stamps to avoid her daughter-in-law's cooking. "I'm climbing the walls," Ms. Debnam said. (DeParle, & Geberloff, 2010)

In Lake Forest, Illinois, a wealthy Chicago suburb, a food pantry in an Episcopal church that used to attract people from less affluent towns nearby has lately been flooded with people who have lost jobs. In Greenwich,

Conn., a pantry organizer reported a "tremendous" increase in demand for food since December, with out-of-work landscapers and housekeepers as well as real estate professionals who have not made a sale in months filling the line. (Bosman, 2009)

The U.S. Conference of Mayors survey of twenty-seven cities in 2009 found that the need for emergency food assistance increased by 26 percent from 2008. Cities also reported an increase in food requests from middle-class households that used to donate to food pantries. The three main causes of hunger that people cited were unemployment, housing costs, and low wages (The U.S. Conference of Mayors, 2009). According to a 2010 survey, Feeding America was providing food to 37 million Americans, including 14 million children. This was a 46 percent increase over 2006. One in eight Americans relied on Feeding America for food and groceries. Food banks nationwide were feeding 1 million more Americans each week than they did in 2006. Thirty-six percent of the households they served had at least one person working. More than one-third of households reported having to choose between food and other basic necessities, such as rent, utilities, and medical care (Feeding America, 2010).

Homelessness

When the housing boom began to cool in 2006, an increasing number of homeowners began to fall into foreclosure. That rise in foreclosure blew up the house of cards Wall Street had built around mortgages, leading eventually to the near-collapse of the financial system,

Advocates for affordable housing stage a ceremony to commemorate the memory of men and women who died anonymously on the city streets. They hope this will call attention to the waste of so many lives.

the global recession, and a drop in property values not seen since the Great Depression. Four years later foreclosures continued to rise, despite several rounds of efforts by the federal government to break the cycle. In the first quarter of 2010, there were 930,000 foreclosure filings. Nearly 228,000 troubled loans qualified under President Obama's plan for long-term payment reductions; another 108,000 long-term modifications were pending. Some 6 million borrowers were more than six days delinquent (*New York Times*, 2010).

Renters were more adversely affected by foreclosures than owners. The National Low Income Housing Coalition estimated that 40 percent of families facing eviction due to foreclosure were renters, and 7 million households living on very low incomes were at risk of foreclosure. Rentals tend to serve younger Americans and those with lower incomes. There is a widening gap between the need for, and supply of, housing affordable to extremely low-income renters (those living on 0–30 percent of the area median income). For every 100 extremely low-income renter households, there are no more than 63 affordable homes in any state in the country. The most common causes of foreclosure were unemployment and health problems/health care costs. The most common post-foreclosure living situations were living with family and friends and emergency shelter (Foreclosure to Homelessness, 2009).

As housing costs have risen, wages have declined, more jobs pay low wages, and increasing numbers of people cannot afford housing (including the middle class). Hurricane Katrina made matters worse for poor people. Nearly five years after the hurricane, thousands of displaced residents in Mississippi and Louisiana are still living in trailers. According to a U.S. Census Bureau report, five years after the storm, 44,200 New Orleans homes remained too badly damaged to be lived in (About.com Guide, 2011). Many neighborhoods seem barely touched since the flooding. Much of the Lower Ninth Ward, with its concrete slabs and grassy lots, still looks like an oversize graveyard. According to the Greater New Orleans Community Data Center, New Orleans has roughly the same number of abandoned or vacant residences as recession-ravaged Detroit, a city more than twice as large as New Orleans (*New York Times*, 2009).

Immediately after the hurricane, the Federal Emergency Management Agency (FEMA) provided 134,000 temporary trailers and mobile homes to house people. After formaldehyde and toxics were found in the trailers, the federal government made it a priority to vacate the temporary trailers. In June 2009, FEMA and HUD (Housing and Urban Development) announced programs to help move residents from the trailers, including $50 million in housing vouchers. Four years since Hurricane Katrina, there were still nearly 3,000 mobile homes and trailers across the Gulf Coast housing victims of that disaster (*USA Today*, 2009).

Even with low wages, many poor people could afford housing if they had access to government-subsidized public housing. However, the federal government has been cutting back on building housing and providing subsidies for housing since the early 1980s. There is a ten-year waiting list for Section 8 vouchers in Massachusetts, and no more are being given out. The federal government chose to subsidize private housing for poor people through Section 8 vouchers rather than build housing because it did not want to interfere with private real estate interests. Real estate interests have decimated rent control in most cities, as rents continue to rise beyond the ability of people to pay them.

red-lining The practice of keeping blacks out of white neighborhoods.

The Western Regional Advocacy Project documents federal cutbacks in housing:

- Between 1983 and 2005, HUD built only 256,000 new public housing units, as compared to 755,000 new units between 1976 and 1982.

- In recent years, more than 200,000 private-sector rental units have been lost annually, and 1.2 million unsubsidized affordable housing units disappeared from 1993 to 2003. (Western Regional Advocacy Project, 2006, p. 1)

While the federal government has been cutting housing for the poor, it has increased housing subsidies for the affluent through tax benefits for home homeownership. Every year since 1981, tax benefits for homeownership have been greater than HUD's entire budget and have dwarfed direct expenditures for programs that benefit low-income renters (Western Regional Advocacy Project, 2006, p. iii).

As the federal government cut funds for housing, it increased military spending. "The U.S. government plans to spend more money on one destroyer than it spent on all 2005 capital expenses for public housing" (Western Regional Advocacy Project, 2006, p. 24). As long as the wars in Iraq and Afghanistan continue, there will be less money for human needs.

CASE EXAMPLE

On September 12, 2008 my husband's company sent everyone home. The company could no longer afford to pay their employees. We have had no money coming in since then and absolutely no prospects. Our savings are all gone . . . our home is being auctioned off. So much for the American Dream.

This should not be happening. We were the middle class and now we are poverty stricken. We had two cars, money in the bank and a reasonable mortgage. My husband is an electrician and simply cannot find a job anywhere. (Foreclosure to Homelessness, 2009)

Although there have always been some homeless people, their numbers increased dramatically during the Reagan administration, when the federal government cut back on building houses and subsidizing housing for low-income people and cut back on social assistance programs. Urban renewal and gentrification forced people out of low-rent housing, and wages declined with deindustrialization and outsourcing. **Red-lining** kept African Americans out of white neighborhoods. Cities used land use policies to help corporations and real estate interests squeezed out the poor (Wright, 1997).

Federal Housing Programs

As homelessness surged in the 1980s, organized groups of homeless peoples, advocates, service providers, charities, lawyers, health professionals, and churches brought the nation's attention to homelessness. In response to this, Congress passed the Stewart B. McKinney Homeless Assistance Act in 1987, the first and only major federal legislation devoted solely to addressing homelessness. "A small portion supported some transitional housing and mobile health care programs, [but] Federal funding of HUD's low-income affordable housing programs . . . continued to be cut." (Western Regional Advocacy Project, p. 17)

In the 1990s, the federal government funded "supported housing" programs, called Housing First, which focused on "chronic homelessness" of severely disabled people. It did not fund new housing. In the beginning, it leased hotel rooms, replaced current residents with homeless people, and installed a few caseworkers in the front office. However, in July 2010 a New York–based organization called Common Ground started a "100,000 Homes Campaign" with the goal of placing 100,000 chronically homeless people into permanent supportive housing by July 2013. They were joined by twenty organizations that focus on homelessness, veterans' affairs, mental illness, housing, and health care. As of December 2010, 6,816 people were housed. Several cities, including New York, Denver, Wichita, Kansas, and Norfolk, Virginia, have significantly reduced their street populations (Bornstein, 2010).

The federal government created a program in 1993 named HOPE VI, which involved destroying much existing public housing and replacing it with housing that encouraged middle-class people to live there, on the theory that contact with middle-class people would be good for poor people. The goal of HOPE VI was to get residents off welfare and into work. Here is the government's official version of the goals of the program:

> HOPE VI occurred in the context of welfare reform. The Personal Responsibility and Work Opportunity Reconciliation Act changed the old welfare system. Operating in this new environment, a central focus of HOPE VI projects is to help residents overcome obstacles to work, and placing residents in employment. (U.S. Department of Housing and Urban Development, p. 2)

Much of the public housing that was destroyed for the HOPE VI program was not actually "severely distressed." The HOPE VI program "resulted in the forced displacement of tens of thousands of families and the permanent loss of large amounts of guaranteed affordable housing" (National Housing Law Project, 2002).

The federal government has invited local communities to apply for McKinney funds to end chronic homelessness. Many communities are competing for a small pool of McKinney homeless assistance funding, but the funds cannot begin to end homelessness.

The American Recovery and Reinvestment Act of 2009 (also called the "stimulus bill") allocated $12.7 billion for housing. Among other things, it included $4 billion for repairing and modernizing public housing, $2 billion for Section 8 housing rental assistance, $1.5 billion for rental assistance and housing relocation (HUD.Gov.Recovery, 2009).

The Recovery Act's $1.5 billion *Homeless Prevention and Rapid Re-housing Program* was designed to "help communities move away from simply reacting to homelessness toward a strategy of preventing it from occurring the first place" (U.S. Conference of Mayors, 2009). The goal was to place people in housing rather than shelters, but there was never enough low-rent housing or Section 8 housing vouchers to accomplish that, so thousands of homeless people are still being placed in shelters.

COUNTING THE HOMELESS

It is hard to know how many people are homeless because in most cases, homelessness is a temporary circumstance. Counting the homeless at one point in time does not give a full count because many are "invisible"—living in cars, camps, parks, boxes, caves, or box cars, or doubling up with relatives and friends.

Counting the homeless has been described as a "high-stakes numbers game." Officials want the numbers to be low; advocates want them high, and there is continual debate about them in academic circles. A study in 2005, based on counts of homeless people from a sample of homeless service providers from across the country, found 744,313 people in the United States who were homeless in January (National Alliance to End Homelessness, 2005). This study counted how many people were homeless at a specific point in time, so it did not count how many were homeless during the year. The researchers extrapolated the number and estimated that between 2.3 and 3.5 million people are homeless in a given year—nearly 1 to 2 percent of the total population. The numbers are higher now since the foreclosure crisis. A 2008 survey of 159 service providers across the nation found that an average of 19 percent of their clients had become homeless due to foreclosure (Foreclosure to Homelessness, 2009). A fall 2008 survey of 1,716 school districts found that nearly all school districts reported increasing numbers of homeless students (Foreclosure to Homelessness, 2009).

*Homeless Shelters**

There are over 6,000 shelters in the United States but there are never enough shelters to house the homeless even temporarily. Many homeless individuals will not go to a homeless shelter because they are crowded and dangerous. If there is no place to store belongings, they often are stolen. Some of the residents have emotional problems which are exacerbated, or caused by, their homelessness. To avoid these dangerous conditions, some people sleep in the streets, in parks, in their cars, RVs, or in train or bus stations. Some live in tents in the woods or build temporary shelters in out-of-the-way spaces in the city, which are often torn down by the city. Some homeless people prefer the freedom and privacy they have in their own encampments to rigidly controlled shelters (Dordick, 1997; Wagner, 1993; Wright, 1977).

Shelters may ultimately be more expensive than permanent housing. Many people believe that in spite of that, cities rely on shelters because building houses would compete with the real estate industry and would establish government responsibility to provide housing for people. And there is money to be made in the shelter industry. "In the mid-1980s, one-third of New York City's welfare hotel business went to two separate business partnerships that together grossed $25 million in rents" (Blau, 1992, p. 159). New York City sold some welfare hotels that the city owned, and contracted with the owners to house the homeless, "paying them $1.2 million a year to house families in a hotel that it had owned outright just four years earlier"(Blau, 1992, pp. 159–160).

Shelters for families are generally subsidized by state and federal funds, which contract out the job of running them to charitable nonprofit agencies. Families generally stay until they have found permanent housing. When states use welfare funds to fund them, shelter residents have to conform to welfare regulations as well as shelter regulations. Some shelters are very strict and some are more flexible. Even the privately funded apartments in Massachusetts, called "scattered site shelters," have strict regulations. A man who lived in one of these apartments told me, "They can inspect your apartment any time they want, without prior notice. They are very fussy about housekeeping. If you don't have the corners of your sheets tight, they can sanction you. After three sanctions, you have to leave." He was

*Most of this material is taken from an article by Betty Reid Mandell, "Shelters for the Homeless: A Feeble Response to Homelessness," in *New Politics,* Summer 2007.

angry at the way he and his wife were treated, but he had to hold it in because there is no place else to go. He said, "They force you to save money in the shelter. When I was working I was earning $800 a month, and they tried to force me to save $500 a month, which was completely unreasonable."

During her outreach work at welfare offices in Massachusetts, a coauthor of this book [Mandell] heard a variety of opinions about shelters from the residents and ex-residents, ranging from "It's like a prison" to "It's pretty good." Here are some of the comments:

- A young woman was in a teen shelter and was sanctioned because she didn't attend school daily. She couldn't attend daily because she had various appointments to keep and because she was depressed. Being homeless made her more depressed. (A large proportion of shelter residents and welfare recipients are depressed.)

- A woman said that being in a shelter is like being in prison. They keep checking up on you, criticizing your housekeeping, the children's noise, and so on. They treat you like a child. She has had to move several times, and this isn't good for the children. Yesterday she was running around all day looking for furniture, getting documents, and so on, and she is exhausted. She is lucky in having a good support group, including good doctors, and relatives that help her out.

- A woman likes the director Lara, thinks she is on the side of the women and really wants to help them. But she doesn't like David. He tells her that she can't "just sit around doing nothing." The woman says this is one of the better shelters. She has her own room, comfortably furnished with a couch and a refrigerator. There is a common kitchen where the food is delivered and you can either eat there or take your food to your room. The food isn't all that great but is okay sometimes. Curfews are 9:30 on weeknights, 11 on Saturday. The woman has been here for three months. Some people stay a year. She longs to get her own apartment and dreams that she has one.

Blaming the Victim

Many people believe that the cause of homelessness can be found in people's individual deficiencies. This "blaming the victim" approach deflects attention from the real causes. Homelessness is caused by poverty, insufficient affordable housing and insufficient money to pay for housing, and a weak or nonexistent safety net of income maintenance and support services.

It is true that many homeless people are alcoholics or drug addicts, but they need a home while they are coping with their problems, and they need treatment programs, and both are in short supply. It is also true that many of the homeless have emotional problems. Who wouldn't have emotional problems if they were homeless? But they need a home while they are coping with their problems and they need support services. Both are in short supply. A disproportionate number of foster children who have "aged out" of the foster care system are homeless. A disproportionate number of veterans are homeless. It is the fault of the government that they are in this condition, but the government has deserted them. A large percentage of homeless women have been abused (McCourt & Nyden, 1990). While they may need a temporary refuge to escape the abuser and counseling to help them heal, they also need permanent housing, child care, a job that pays a living wage, and social supports.

The focus on individual problems leads to stereotyping of homeless people as deviant and degenerate, drunk or drugged, or crazy. When these stereotypes are embedded in people's minds, they view every beggar as a scammer. Stereotyping leads to criminalizing the homeless, allowing cities to sweep them from the streets (U.S. National Coalition for the Homeless, 2006). It gives implicit permission to delinquent thugs to beat them up. One man made a series of documentaries in which homeless men fight each other while being plied with liquor. Reality show producers took the homeless on shopping trips as a subject of amusement. On the Boston radio station WBCN-FM, deejays Opie and Anthony ran an event called the Homeless Shopping Spree, taking street people to a high-end shopping center, giving them liquor and money to shop, and ridiculing their purchases for the amusement of their listeners. Boston's Mayor Menino publicly expressed his outrage at the show.

THE HOMELESS

Some take shelter in silence,
huddling fetally,
their only home that one remembrance.
Some speak uncontainably,
having no walls to hold the words in.
Some rage at each other,
having no space to save rage for those
who are anyhow too sheltered
from their own hearts to care.

—Chris Mandell

RESISTANCE

Many individuals and organizations—including churches, college professors and students, lawyers, health professionals, social workers, and social agencies—are trying to solve the problem of homelessness. Community organizers have made a few courageous forays into confrontational strategies such as creating tent cities or taking over empty buildings. In the richest nation in the world, it is an outrage that millions of people have no home. It need not be.

France endorsed housing as a legal right in January 2007 after an organizing group calling itself "The Children of Don Quixote" (*les Enfants de Don Quichotte*) set up 100 red tents on the Canal Saint-Martin in Paris and moved into a vacant office block to draw attention to the homeless sleeping outside. Soon after this, France established a legal right to housing (Gehmlich, 2007). After Hurricane Katrina, the housing authority of New Orleans closed down all the housing developments, scattered the residents across the country, and barricaded their homes, which were then looted. Some residents of those housing developments have reoccupied their units, with the support of volunteers and friends. They sent out a nationwide appeal for help with installing solar panels and electricity. These brave people survived a disaster and resisted an indifferent government to reclaim their homes. Despite militant protests, however, in December 2007 the New Orleans City Council voted to demolish the housing and build mixed-income housing.

Lawyers across the nation have documented violations of the rights of homeless people and sued institutions, states, and cities for those violations (U.S. National Coalition for the Homeless, 2006). The National Law Center on Homelessness and Poverty has said that homelessness is a violation of the International Covenant on Civil and Political Rights, and it submitted a "shadow report" that documented these violations to the Human Rights Committee on May 31, 2006 (National Law Center on Homelessness and Poverty, 2006). It is a radical statement to say, as the Universal Declaration of Human Rights* does, that every human has a right to housing. If housing becomes a universal right, then poor people who need housing will not be stigmatized.

Sweden has been a pioneer in public programs to enable elderly people to live in their own homes as long as possible. Homelessness is rare, and substandard housing is virtually unknown in Sweden. Affordable housing has been assured through public ownership and financing of large portions of the housing stock and income-tested housing benefits for families and the elderly.

Finland does not have shelters for homeless families because the Finns believe that families should not be in shelters. Rather, they help families obtain public or subsidized housing. Single mothers are not stigmatized; in fact, they are considered to be doing valuable work by caring for children.

BANKRUPTCY AND FORECLOSURES

By early 2007, the collapse of the U.S. housing boom had brought with it widespread defaults on subprime mortgages—loans to home buyers who fail to meet the strictest lending standards. "Working people, disproportionately Latino, African American, and Asian, who were lured in the home ownership market by all sorts of exotic loan arrangements now face foreclosures in increasing numbers" (Boice, 2007a).

Bankruptcies have continued to rise during the past two decades. However, in 2005, Congress passed a law that made it harder to file bankruptcy. This was particularly hard on women, who outnumber men in bankruptcy filings. More than 1 million women found themselves in bankruptcy court in 2005, outnumbering men by about 150,000.

> Women with children . . . are more vulnerable than ever before. They're spending more on the basics, so they have less flexibility in their budgets if something goes wrong. Single women early in their career tend to have lower income and higher expenses.

---

*The Universal Declaration of Human Rights, which the United States voted to support when it was ratified by the United Nations in 1948, states that "everyone has the right to a standard of living adequate for the health and well-being of himself and his family, including food, clothing, housing and medical care and necessary social services, and the right to security in the event of unemployment, sickness, disability, widowhood, old age, or other lack of livelihood in circumstances beyond his control (United Nations, 1948).

That puts them at risk. Older women often have much less built up in retirement funds and are counting on home and cash assets that won't be protected in bankruptcy. Single mothers, who often work in low-wage jobs, are 50 percent more likely to file for bankruptcy than married parents, and three times more likely than childless couples. (Gardner, 2005)

Health Insurance

One of the reasons for bankruptcy and foreclosure is the lack of health insurance. There were more than 47 million U.S. citizens without health insurance in 2007, nearly 16 percent of the population. A study of bankruptcy filings found that about half of them were due to medical expenses (Himmelstein, Women, Thorne, & Woolhandler, 2005).

Even middle-class insured families often fall prey to financial catastrophe when they are sick. The benefits of American medicine are available only to those with access to the health care system. Uninsured Americans experience poorer medical outcomes than the insured:

- Uninsured Americans experience a generally higher mortality and, specifically, a higher in-hospital mortality.
- Uninsured Americans may be up to three times more likely than privately insured individuals to experience adverse health outcomes.
- Uninsured patients have been found to be up to four times as likely as insured patients to require both avoidable hospitalizations and emergency hospital care (American College of Physicians, 2007).

Canada has universal insurance, called a single-payer plan. The government insures all its citizens; there are no private insurance companies. People can choose their own doctor, and the doctor bills the government. A study that compared Canada's system with the U.S. system found that Canada spends about half as much on health care per person as does the United States, yet Canadians live two to three years longer. "Compared with Canadians, US residents are one third less likely to have a regular medical doctor, one fourth more likely to have unmet health care needs, and are more than twice as likely to forgo needed medicines. Problems accessing medical care are particularly dire for the US uninsured" (Lasser, Himmelstein, & Woolhandler, 2006).

A majority of U.S. citizens say that the federal government should guarantee health insurance to every American, especially children, and are willing to pay higher taxes to do it, according to a *New York Times/CBS News* poll in 2007. "While the war in Iraq remains the overarching issue in the early stages of the 2008 campaign, access to affordable health care is at the top of the public's domestic agenda, ranked far more important than immigration, cutting taxes or promoting traditional values" (Toner, Elder, Thee, & Connelly, 2007).

Despite fierce opposition from the Republicans in Congress, President Obama signed a health reform bill in 2010. It was not a single-payer plan, but relied on private insurance companies to administer health insurance. We discuss details of the plan in Chapter 6.

Behind President Obama, as he signs the Health Care Reform bill of 2010, hang the portraits of the past presidents who have tried, unsuccessfully, to provide health care for all Americans.

Income Inequality

Income inequality has been rising in the nation for decades, and it continues to rise. "The earnings gap is now the widest since 1928, with the richest 1 percent of Americans having captured most of the economy's 2005 growth, and the bottom 90 percent getting nothing" (Kuttner, 2007). In 2010, the top one-tenth of 1 percent of Americans earned as much as the bottom 120 million (Reich, 2010). Amazingly, the richest 1 percent of American households now has a higher net worth than the bottom 90 percent (Sachs, 2010). With traditional middle-class jobs vanishing along with factories, the nation's labor force is stratifying into a skilled, well-paid elite and a mass of lesser-skilled workers struggling to hold on to their standard of living.

Some economists and sociologists believe that income inequality is one of the causes of the recent financial crisis. Inequality puts too much power in the hands of Wall Street titans and enables them to promote polices—like deregulation—that could put the system in jeopardy and lead to another financial crisis. David A. Moss, a professor of economic and policy history at Harvard Business School, has looked at the data that show a correlation between income inequality in the Great Depression of the 1930s and in the current recession:

> In 1928, the top 10 percent of earners in the United States received 49.29 percent of total income. In 2007, the top 10 percent earned a strikingly similar percentage: 49.74 percent. In 1928, the top 1 percent received 23.94 percent of income. In 2007, those earners received 23.5 percent. (Story, 2010)

The income gap tells only part of the story. There is an even wider gap in wealth (the total resources of a household minus its debts). The gap between the very rich and the poor is reminiscent of the Gilded Age in the 1890s.

There is a growing backlash over extravagant pay packages for U.S. corporate executives. Labor unions, Democratic lawmakers, and shareholder activists are up in arms over multi-million-dollar payouts to chief executives, even those with mediocre records. The median pay of U.S. CEOs at publicly traded companies rose 16 percent in 2005, to 2.9 million. It was nearly $7 million for those in the Standard & Poor's 500. CEO pay in 2007 was 411 times that of an average worker in 2005, up from 107 times average pay in 1990 (Lever, 2007).

The vast majority of federal deductions and benefits to enhance upward mobility ended up in the hands of the wealthiest Americans. For instance, between 72 percent and 98 percent of deductions for retirement savings, health insurance, home mortgages, self-employed health insurance, and preferential rates on capital gains in 2006 went to the top 20 percent of income-earning Americans (Jackson, 2010).

The inequality gap has affected people's chances of upward mobility. The vast majority of U.S. college and university students attend public, not private, institutions, and tuitions at those institutions have been steadily rising. As wages have stagnated since the 1970s, most Americans are finding it ever more difficult to pay for public higher education. Students are graduating from college with increasing levels of debt. "The U.S. Department of Education says that in 2004–2005, two-thirds of students graduated from colleges and universities with debt averaging $15,500 at public universities and $20,00 at private schools" (Wolff, 2007).

One reason for the increase in income inequality is the growth of the prison population. It is not only the prisoners who are impoverished; their families are also impoverished when they lose the income of the person in prison. The people are imprisoned in their youth, the years when non-prisoners are increasing their earnings and job skills. They face discrimination when they get out of prison because employers are reluctant to hire ex-convicts.

The inability of felons to vote in some states has also contributed to the inequality in wealth. "By Election Day 2004, the number of disenfranchised felons had grown to 5.3 million, with another 600,000 effectively stripped of the vote because they were in jail awaiting trial. . . . If felons were allowed to vote, the United States would have a different president. Disproportionately poor and black, felons choose Democrats in overwhelming numbers. . . . Had they been allowed to vote in 2000, . . . Al Gore's margin in the popular vote would have doubled to a million" (DeParle, 2007).

Income inequality results in inequality of people's life span. "Asian women in Bergen County, New Jersey typically live at least 30 years longer than Native Americans in South Dakota" (Allen, 2006). Asians in the United States have a life span of 84.9 years, while blacks living in high-risk areas have a life span of 71.1 years (Allen, 2006). A review of about 200 academic papers on inequality found that societies with more equal distribution of income have better health outcomes than ones in which the gap between the richest and poorest in society is greater (Wilkinson, 2010).

In the summer of 2001, Congress and the Bush administration enacted a tax cut of $1.35 trillion and sent tax rebate checks to millions of people. President Bush and his allies argued that the money they sent to citizens would boost a slowing economy by increasing consumer purchasing power. They also believed that the tax cut would take much of a projected budget surplus off the table, therefore reducing the size of the government and making it impossible for the Democrats to spend money on social

MY MOM SAYS A TRICKLE DOWN ECONOMY IS WHERE THE RICH PEOPLE NEED MORE MONEY SO THEY CAN AFFORD TO TAKE VACATIONS FROM THE STRESS OF KEEPING PEOPLE UNDER EMPLOYED OR ON WELFARE AND THE POOR PEOPLE ARE USED TO THE STRESS SO THEY SHOULD GIVE MORE MONEY TO THE RICH AND PAY ALL THE TAXES AND LIVE IN THE STREETS AND THAT'S WHY WE'RE LIVING ON BOX MACARONI & CHEESE THIS WEEK...

programs. This tax cut left less money for child care, affordable health care, job training, and better schools. The tax cut benefited the rich more than the poor: The bottom 80 percent received less than one-third of the benefits; 40 percent of the benefits went to the richest 1 percent of taxpayers (Reich, 2001). A study by the Urban Institute found that the top 1 percent of households received tax cuts averaging $41,1077; the middle fifth received tax cuts averaging $760; while the bottom fifth received tax cuts averaging $29 (Sherman, & Stone, 2010).

Stimulus Spending versus Deficit Reduction

The American Recovery and Reinvestment Act of 2009 (the stimulus bill) was intended to create jobs and promote investment and consumer spending during the recession. No Republicans in the House and only three Republican senators voted for the bill.

The rationale for the stimulus comes out of the Keynesian economic tradition that argues that government spending should be used to cover the gap created by the drop in consumer spending during a recession. The bill allocated $787 billion for various purposes. It included federal tax cuts, expansion of unemployment benefits and other social welfare provision, and spending in education, health care, and infrastructure, including the energy sector. Some of the social welfare and education provisions included increases in Medicaid, Head Start, Adoption assistance and foster care, child care and development, community health centers, Veterans Health Administration, Pell Grants, education of homeless children, job training, and payments to Social Security recipients, people of Supplemental Security Income, and veterans receiving disability and pensions.

There are sharp differences of opinion among economists about Keynesian theory, which calls for spending to stimulate the economy, and deficit reduction theory, which advocates fiscal austerity in order to avoid increasing the deficit. The Keynesian economist Paul Krugman says, "While long-term fiscal responsibility is important, slashing spending in the midst of a depression, which deepens that depression and paves the way for deflation, is actually self-defeating. . . . We are now, I fear, in the early stages of a third depression. It will probably look more like the Long Depression (of 1873) than the much more severe Great Depression. But the cost—to the world economy and, above all, to the millions of lives blighted by the absence of jobs—will nonetheless be immense" (Krugman, 2010b).

THE IMPORTANCE OF SOCIAL SUPPORTS

A UNICEF report talks about the importance of social supports in relieving poverty and shows how poverty was reduced in countries with generous supports. Part of the reason for poverty in the United States is the weak level of those supports and the fact that many people eligible for those supports do not receive them. Investing in poverty-reducing programs has lifted millions of children and families out of poverty (UNICEF (2007).

It is up to the citizens of a country to work for the kind of compassion for people that the statement reflects. Many European countries do not view single mothers as a "problem." In Sweden and Finland, single mothers are often privileged in social programs such as subsidized child care programs, housing allowance, and child support advance payments (in which the state pays child support when the absent parent cannot or does not). Sweden's child care system is universally available. Parental leave for birth or adoption replaces wages for thirteen months. Two months of this leave are reserved exclusively for fathers, and men are increasingly taking more responsibility for child care (Bennhold, 2010). Parents can also take up to sixty days of leave per year for the care of a sick child under the age of 12, compensated at 80 percent of wages. Sweden has universal health insurance, and universal allowances for families with children, as well as a national pension.

Cutbacks in public funding for medical assistance programs and limitations imposed by private managed care companies have drastically altered the health care field. Hospital workers often resort to direct action to maintain their own working conditions and standards of patient care, as Suzanne Dennehy is doing here.

INTERVIEW

Suzanne Dennehy, Hospital Workers' Union Intern

At the union I've done every kind of thing, from attending eighteen sessions of contract negotiation between Cape Cod Hospital (CCH) and the hospital workers' union (Local 767, SEIU), to actually making the picket signs and marching, and so forth. Both sides of the table are stalling, waiting to see what Medicare changes are going to occur. At the midnight hour when the contract ran out last week, CCH finally took subcontracting off the table. It had, of course, threatened jobs. CCH will reopen the issue in one year, though.

About four weeks ago, CCH gave us all a presentation on the new health insurance they're trying to force on the workers, who are not happy about this. They've grown fond of their Blue Cross Health+ gold card and don't want to switch. This is the second and most important issue, after subcontracting. I thought, "We're all acting like it's normal to be here (talking about insurance benefits and plans), but if we had the right to national health coverage, none of us would be sitting here debating this issue.

I have no love for big business and insurance companies. I see how workers stay job-locked just to keep their health insurance. I see how the health care industry names the tune to which we all dance.

It feels natural out there on the picket lines and in the march, for me. I wonder what all this means later when I drive home alone. When I arrive home, I crank up Pete Seeger's "We Shall Overcome" on my new powerful stereo system that my son bought me. I stare at the miraculous march, at all those workers in the photograph . . . and get goose bumps. Yeah, we shall overcome. Justice as a theme to ponder.

Governmental Response to Poverty

Hurricane Katrina in August 2005 made people aware of the dire poverty in America. The governmental response to it on all levels was too little and too late. At least 1,836 people lost their lives, and Katrina was responsible for $81.2 billion in damage. The term *Katrinagate* was coined about the delayed response to the flooding of New Orleans, and the subsequent state of chaos. Residents were stranded for days without food, water, or shelter. People died from thirst, exhaustion, and violence days after the storm had passed. Some people believed that the government's delayed response was due to the fact that the majority of people affected were black. During a benefit concert for Hurricane Katrina relief on NBC, Kanye West was a featured speaker. He deviated from the prepared script at the end of his speech with the statement "George Bush doesn't care about black people."

Conservatives often complain about "throwing money at problems," but as the novelist Kurt Vonnegut said, "Why throw money at problems? That is what money is for" (Vonnegut, 1991). As poverty increases, the fight between conservatives who resist giving money to end poverty and those who believe "that is what money is for" intensifies.

Conclusion

Poverty causes or exacerbates most of the problems you will be working with. If we eliminate poverty, or even if we substantially reduce it, many problems would be solved. No one of us can eliminate poverty, but all of us can work on it in some way.

SUMMARY

1. A widespread view of poor people as generally inadequate and incompetent and in need of reform shapes many service programs for the poor.

2. Prejudice against the poor has permeated social policy since the country began. It leads to creating categories of who is "deserving" and who is "undeserving."

3. The federal poverty line is based on a formula arrived at in 1963, which is outdated. Wider Opportunities for Women has shown that the actual cost of living is much higher.

4. Many families need two earners to maintain a middle-class standard of living.

5. When the Democrats won a majority in Congress, one of their first actions was to submit a bill to raise the federal minimum wage from $5.15 to $7.25 over a two-year span.

6. Since the 1970s, there have been vast changes in the U.S. economy and in the global economy. A process of deindustrialization has taken place, in which manufacturing work has declined and both high technology and service work have increased. Deregulation has resulted in fewer protections to workers.

7. An economic recession was caused by rank speculation on Wall Street and a crash in the housing market. It resulted in massive housing foreclosures, bankruptcy, and job loss.

8. The official unemployment rate in 2010 was 9.8 percent. The actual unemployment rate was much higher.

9. U.S. Census data in 2009 showed the largest number of poor people in the fifty-one years since poverty has been measured.

10. Women receive lower wages than men. Single mothers, older women minorities, and children have a higher incidence of poverty than white men.

11. Hunger has increased dramatically since the recession began.

12. The number of people receiving food stamps has increased dramatically since the recession began.

13. Increased poverty has resulted in increased homelessness.

14. Many people believe that the cause of homelessness can be found in people's individual deficiencies. This "blaming the victim" approach deflects attention from the real causes.

15. There are never enough shelters to house the homeless.

16. The main reason for homelessness is lack of affordable housing. Apartments have been turned into expensive condominiums, single-room-occupancy hotels have disappeared, and government-subsidized housing has been slashed.

17. Most of the response to homelessness has treated surface problems by providing shelters and food rather than getting to the root of the housing problem.

18. UNICEF studied child well-being in twenty-one wealthy countries and published its findings in a 2007 "report card." If it had been a school report card, the United States would have received an "F."

19. Food insecurity is likely to contribute to obesity.

20. The UNICEF report talks about the importance of social supports in relieving poverty and shows how poverty was reduced in countries with generous supports.

21. Corporate leaders influence legislators to cut back on funds for social welfare because they are eager for funds to expand their corporations and are eager to slash the safety net in order to lower wages.

22. More than 47 million U.S. citizens did not have health insurance in 2007—nearly 16 percent of the population.

23. Income inequality has been rising in the United States for decades and continues to rise.

24. Hurricane Katrina in August 2005 made people aware of the dire poverty in the United States. The governmental response to it on all levels was too little and too late.

DISCUSSION QUESTIONS

1. Discuss the attitudes toward the homeless that you have encountered in your family, school, and community. How were these attitudes developed? Does your attitude differ from other attitudes you have encountered?

2. Some people think that poor people who are overweight are proof that they aren't really poor. What do you think of this?

3. Why do you think that the governmental response to Katrina was too little and too late?

4. How do you think globalization affects human service workers?

5. Why are children of color the hardest hit by poverty?

6. Why do you think there is prejudice against the poor?

7. J. P. Morgan recommended that the difference in pay between a chief corporate executive and the average worker in that corporation should be in a ratio of twenty to one. Today in the United States it is 700 to 1. Why has there been no public outcry about this?

WEB RESOURCES FOR FURTHER STUDY

National Coalition for the Homeless
www.nationalhomeless.org

The mission of the National Coalition for the Homeless is to end homelessness. It focuses its work in the following four areas: housing justice, economic justice, health care justice, and civil and voting rights. Its approaches are grassroots organization, public education, policy advocacy, technical assistance, and partnerships.

RESULTS: Ending Hunger and Poverty
www.results.org

RESULTS is a nonprofit grassroots citizens' lobby that identifies sustainable solutions to the problems of hunger and poverty, nationally and worldwide, and works to generate the resources necessary to make those solutions succeed. Its web site features information about the organization, action alerts, background on hunger and poverty issues, Capitol updates, articles about the organization, and links to other web sites.

Center on Budget and Policy Priorities
www.cbpp.org

The Center on Budget and Policy Priorities does thorough research on public policy, particularly policy affecting low-income people. Its areas of research include tax policy, food assistance, health policies, low-income immigrants, labor market policies, low-income housing, poverty, Social Security, fiscal policy, unemployment insurance, and welfare reform/TANF.

Measuring poverty
http://www.google.com/search?q=Measuring+Poverty+and+Economic+Inclusion

This is a December 2008 article by Shawn Fremstad, published by the Center for Economic and Policy Research, about measuring poverty and its effect on economic inclusion.

Improving the measurement of poverty
http://www.google.com/search?=improving+the+measuremet+of+poverty

This article is by Rebecca M. Blank and Mark H. Greenberg, published as The Hamilton Project for the Brookings Institute. It discusses how the present measure of poverty could be improved.

Chapter 8

Working with Diversity

The election of Barack Obama as the first black president of the United States was hailed by some as proof that we are in a postracial society where race doesn't matter. The Tea Party soon gave the lie to that belief by portraying Obama as an alien, not really a loyal American—a foreigner, a clown, a Hitler, a socialist—and by demanding vigilante action against dark-skinned people. Rand Paul, who received the support of the Tea Party when he ran for the Senate in Kentucky in 2010, said that he would probably not support the section of the Civil Rights Act that forbids discrimination by private businesses (e.g., the young people who staged sit-ins at lunch counters to protest discrimination during the civil rights movement).

The facts also give the lie to the belief that we are in a postracial society, as we point out in Chapters 2, 6, and 7.

Yet, the country *has* come a long way in overcoming racism. The comedian Chris Rock asked, "What does it say about America when the greatest golfer in the world [Tiger Woods] is black and the greatest rapper [Eminem] is white?" While much of Rock's comedy targets the racism that is directed against black people, in this statement he was celebrating the fact that in the United States today "no role or occupation (at least in sports and music) is now determined by skin color" (Gallagher, 2003, p. 31).

We celebrate the progress that the United States has made in combating racism. The civil rights movement of the 1960s ended legal segregation. White and black people now eat together in restaurants, sit together in public transportation, go to school together, play on the same sports teams, and marry one another. Advertisements show black models in yachting clothes. Tiger Woods sells sneakers; Michael Jordon sells underwear. But do these media pictures give the true picture of race relations in the United States? Have we finally ended discrimination against people of color?

Many people think so. National polls show that a majority of whites believe that discrimination against racial minorities no longer exists. They believe that blacks have as good a chance as whites to find a job and are as well off financially and educationally as whites. When people are asked to explain why so many blacks aren't doing well, "the most popular explanation is that of black people's lack of motivation or willpower to get ahead" (Schuman, 1997).

Most black people don't see it that way. Author bell hooks writes about her childhood as a black girl. She learned as a child that to be safe, it was important to recognize the power of whiteness, even to fear it, and to avoid encountering it. She remembers walking from her home to visit her grandmother:

> It was a movement away from the segregated blackness of our community into a poor white neighborhood. I remember the fear, being scared to walk to Baba's, our grandmother's house, because we would have to pass that terrifying whiteness—those white faces on the porches staring us down with hate. Even when empty or vacant those

porches seemed to say danger, you do not belong here, you are not safe.

Oh! that feeling of safety, of arrival, of homecoming when we finally reached the edges of her yard, when we could see the soot black face of our grandfather, Daddy Gus, sitting in his chair on the porch, smell his cigar, and rest on his lap. Such a contrast, that feeling of arrival, of homecoming—this sweetness and the bitterness of that journey, that constant reminder of white power and control. (hooks, 1997, p. 175)

Times have changed since black people had little intimate contact with whites, but bell hooks believes that the feeling of impending danger has never completely left black people, even when they have adopted the values, speech, and habits of white people. She says that even though it was a long time ago that she visited her grandmother, she still has associations of whiteness with terror. "All black people in the United States, irrespective of their class status or politics, live with the possibility that they will be terrorized by whiteness" (hooks, 1997, p. 175). She says that most white people don't understand this terror.

A look at some facts contradicts the belief that we have achieved equality between people of color and white people. In Chapter 7 we discuss the disparities in income and wealth. Other disparities include:

- *Home ownership and housing discrimination.* In 2009, 74.5 percent of white households owned their own homes compared to 46 percent of blacks and 48.4 percent of Hispanics (U.S. Census Bureau, 2009a). "Even when homeseekers contact housing providers by telephone, linguistic profiling (whereby the provider recognizes the race of the caller and provides less service to those with a recognizable black voice) results in African Americans experiencing discrimination in efforts to buy or rent a home even when they do not even meet the housing provider" (Squires, 2006). In 2010, the U.S. Department of Housing and Urban Development (HUD) estimated that more than 2 million instances of housing discrimination occur each year, but fewer than 1 percent are reported (Carlton, 2010).

  Dark-skinned Latinos face far more discrimination than do light-skinned Latinos.

  Blacks are the least favored neighbors by all other racial and ethnic groups. When asked to describe their neighborhood preferences, one-fifth of whites opted for a neighborhood that has no blacks, as did one-third of Hispanics and more than 40 percent of Asians (Squires, 2006).

  Black and Hispanics lost their homes to foreclosures proportionally more than did whites; 8 percent of both African Americans and Latinos, compared to 4.5 percent of whites, had their homes foreclosed. These disparities hold even after controlling for differences in income between the groups (Gruenstein, Li, & Ernst, 2010).

- *Health.* Whites have lower rates of diabetes, tuberculosis, pregnancy-related mortality, and sudden infant death syndrome (SIDS) and are more likely to have prenatal care in the first trimester than blacks, Latinos, or Asians. African Americans face a higher risk than any other racial group of dying from heart disease, diabetes, stroke, and hypertension. Affluent blacks suffer, on average, more health problems than the poorest whites (Drexler, 2007).

    Life expectancy for U.S. white males in 2006 was seventy-eight years compared with seventy years for black males and eighty-one years for white females compared with seventy-seven years for black females (National Center for Heath Statistics, 2008).

- *Health insurance.* Minorities are more likely to be uninsured than whites, even when accounting for work status. This results in lack of access to health care and more health problems. Nearly 70 percent of nonelderly whites receive employer-based insurance while only 40 percent of Hispanics, 48 percent of blacks, and 43 percent of Native Americans/Native Alaskans receive such coverage (American College of Physicians, 2010).

- *Professional advancement.* Blacks and Latinos are underrepresented as lawyers, physicians, professors, dentists, engineers, and registered nurses.

- *Racial profiling.* In California, since 1991 between 80 percent and 90 percent of all motorists arrested by law enforcement officials have been members of minority groups. In Maryland, although only 21 percent of drivers along a stretch of Interstate 95 are minorities, including blacks, Latinos, Asians, and others, 80 percent of those who are pulled over and searched are people of color. Racial profiling has come to be known as "driving while black (DWB)" (ACLU, 2007).

- *Job discrimination.* White job applicants with a felony conviction on their record were more likely to get a job than comparable black applicants with no criminal record. Applicants with white-sounding names are more likely to obtain employment than those with black-sounding names (Squires, 2006).

- *Political representation.* In 2007, the House of Representatives had forty blacks, only 9 percent of 435 members. The House had twenty-four Latinos, 5.5 percent of the membership. On the other hand, blacks and Latinos comprised over 12 percent of the population. The Senate had only one black, Barack Obama (out of 100 members), and three Latinos. There have been only six black Senators in the history of the United States, and there have been only six Latinos since 1928 (Congressional Black Caucus, 2007; LatinosVote.com, 2007). There is only one black governor, Deval Patrick of Massachusetts. There is only one Latino governor, Bill Richardson of New Mexico.

In 2007–2009, there were sixteen women in the Senate (16 percent of the total) and seventy in the House (16 percent of the total).

- *Voting rights.* Blacks who lived in Florida in the 2000 presidential election were four times as likely as whites to have their ballots invalidated (Parker & Eisler, 2001). Most convicted felons are prohibited from voting, and a disproportionate number of prisoners are people of color.

- *School segregation.* A 2010 study sponsored by Harvard School of Public Health found "gross levels of disparity" between schools that white and black children attend. Children of color "continue to attend very different schools than white children." In Chicago, the average black student goes to a public school that is 74 percent black while the average white student goes to a school that is 6 percent black. Forty-three percent of both Latino and African American students attend schools where the poverty rate is more than 80 percent. Only 4 percent of white students do. The study concluded that "issues of persistent high racial/ethnic segregation and high exposure of minority children to economic disadvantage at the school level remain largely unaddressed" (Jackson, 2010).

AN OVERVIEW OF THE STRUGGLE FOR EQUALITY

The founding fathers of the United States—all white and Christian—did not grant the vote to women or to black men. In fact, they gave the vote only to people who owned land. Those excluded from having a say in how the country was run have had to gain their equality through long, hard struggles. Frederick Douglass, an African American leader who literally fought his way out of slavery, said that power concedes nothing without a struggle. It never has and it never will.

A look at history shows this to be true. The Civil War freed the slaves, and the Fifteenth Amendment of 1870 gave blacks the vote. But they were kept from using it until the civil rights movement that began in the 1950s struck down segregation laws (called Jim Crow laws) in the South. Then the Civil Rights Act of 1964 prohibited racial and sexual discrimination, and the Voting Rights Act of 1965 banned practices that disenfranchised blacks.

The first wave of the women's movement in the late nineteenth and early twentieth centuries fought long and hard for the Nineteenth Amendment of 1920, which gave women the right to vote. The second wave of the women's movement, beginning in the 1960s and continuing to the present, renewed women's struggle for equality on many fronts. Gays and lesbians began to fight for equal treatment when they resisted police repression in 1969 at the Stonewall Club in New York City, and their struggle continues. The struggle reached a new level when Massachusetts legalized gay and lesbian marriages in 2004. Since then, four other states and Washington D.C. have legalized gay and lesbian marriage.

Many stigmatized groups began their struggles for equality and self-esteem in the 1960s, giving birth to advocacy groups such as the National Welfare Rights Organization, Mental Patients' Liberation Front, Disabled People's Movement, and others.

But power does not yield easily. The backlash against the liberation movements of the 1960s and early 1970s bubbled up in the mid-1970s, picked up steam in the 1980s, and led to a volcano of conservative repression with the Republican takeover of Congress in 1994 and their Contract with America, which essentially dismantled many of the social gains of the previous decades.

Conservatives oppose affirmative action programs that were established in the 1960s and 1970s. There are fierce fights against immigrants, bilingual education, multicultural curricula, sex education in schools, gay and lesbian rights, and abortion. In the past three decades, laws have been passed to deport illegal immigrants, cut off welfare benefits and food stamps for legal immigrants, end affirmative action for minorities, and end bilingual education. Women, on average, still earn only 77 percent as much as men with the same level of education.

Where does the human service worker fit into this political maelstrom? When the battle enters directly into the social service field, the worker has to make choices about implementing restrictive policies. For example:

- If you work in the welfare department in a state that has an English-only law and you don't know Spanish, how do you explain the regulations to a Spanish-speaking client? Policies won't be printed in Spanish, and the agency might not employ a Spanish-speaking worker.

- Massachusetts passed a law prohibiting the placement of foster children with homosexual foster parents, but after years of organizing work by homosexuals and their allies, it then passed a law forbidding discrimination against homosexuals. If you are a worker in a state child-welfare agency and the legislature passes a law saying you can't place foster children with homosexual foster parents, what will you do if you disagree? Do you obey the law, even against your convictions? If you do, how do you resolve the internal conflict this is likely to cause? Do you oppose the law, and if so, how? Do you work with the movement that is fighting against it by joining demonstrations, writing letters to the editor, lobbying your legislators? Do you simply place a child with a foster parent whom you know to be homosexual but tell the foster parent to keep his or her sexual orientation a secret?

- If you are a human service worker in a state that has passed a law denying services to legal immigrants, what will you do? In California, some workers could not in good conscience obey such a law, and they vowed to continue to give services. Many teachers in California refused to obey a law that eliminated bilingual education and continued to teach as they had done before the passage of the law.

Some legislation may not require you to make such agonizing choices but will nonetheless affect your work environment and agency practice. If affirmative action is ended, your agency may become less diverse. If you are white, you will have fewer opportunities to work with people of color. African American, Hispanic, Asian, and Native American clients will have less chance of getting a worker who shares their culture.

Regardless of what you do about the politics of diversity, you will always need to understand how the issues affect your clients, or you will be shortchanging your clients and shortchanging yourself as an effective worker. If you belong to a group that has been discriminated against, you probably have already had personal experience that will help you to identify with a client who has also faced discrimination. If, on the other hand, you have never experienced discrimination, it may be hard for you to identify with people's reactions to it.

Understanding Oppression and Privilege

Individuals can be dominated by other individuals for a variety of reasons. Siblings often oppress each other; parents sometimes oppress their children. In this discussion, however, we are talking about social forces that hold people down, hem them in, and block their ability to lead a good life. Oppression occurs because of structural inequalities in society.

Privilege is the other side of the coin of oppression. If Group A has something of value and keeps Group B from having it, Group A is privileged, and Group B is oppressed. Any individual, however, could be privileged in one respect but oppressed in another. One way to look at this was devised by Patricia Hill Collins (1990), who constructed a "Matrix of Domination" that integrates categories such as gender, race, class, sexuality, age, and ability. This matrix assumes that everyone is shaped by some combination of interacting social categories, and everyone experiences varying degrees of privilege and oppression depending upon his or her social location or place. In the African American community, for example, there are vast differences in lifestyle and outlook between affluent professionals and executives and the people on the bottom rung of the income and status ladder, yet the color of their skin ensures that both groups will face some discrimination. The lifestyle of Barack Obama, with his prestigious Harvard degree, is far different than the lifestyle of an unemployed black man.

In all ethnic groups, women have less power than men (although the patriarchal tradition is stronger in some cultures than others). But wealthy women have more power than poor women. A rich woman who is abused by her husband is unlikely to go to a shelter for battered women. She can afford to leave and rent an apartment or buy a house, provided that she has access to the checkbook or charge account and her psyche has not been battered to the point of helplessness.

Ethnicity is only one of the many factors that determine people's standing in society and feelings about themselves. Social class and gender are also powerful influences. Anthropologist Oscar Lewis (1966) maintained that social class was a more powerful determinant of behavior than ethnicity. He believed there was more similarity between poor people in the barrios of New York City and poor people in the favelas of Sao Paulo than between the poor Puerto Rican and the rich Puerto Rican. Although both the poor and the wealthy might share certain cultural beliefs and behaviors, their differing social class positions would result in different self-identities.

Psychologist Robert Coles (1977) studied many children in different groups, including children from wealthy families. He said that one of the most outstanding attitudes of rich children is their "sense of entitlement." They know they will inherit the country. Most poor people don't expect to inherit anything. All they can hope for is to win the lottery.

Since we are all participants in a society with a significant amount of sexism, racism, and homophobia, it is inevitable that we have internalized some of these cultural beliefs. We don't need to feel guilty about that, but we do need to examine our own position in society and our own attitudes. Battling discrimination is a lifelong process in which the authors of this book are also engaged.

A group of Harvard psychologists have devised a test to detect prejudice called the Implicit Association Test (IAT). The test attempts to measure "implicit prejudices"— subconscious attitudes, those that lie outside our awareness and may contradict our conscious ideas about equality and fairness. The researchers say that tests of thousands of people yield some striking results:

> Eighty percent of all respondents implicitly favor young over old, 75 percent of white respondents implicitly favor white over black, and more than 70 percent across the board favor straight people over gay people. (Berdik, 2004, p. K1)

If you would like to know how you score on the test, visit https://implicit.harvard.edu/implicit and take a sample test.

COLORBLIND PRIVILEGE

In the TV program *The Colbert Report*, the comedian Stephen Colbert says, "I don't see race. People tell me that I'm white and I believe them, but I don't see race." Colbert is spoofing the conservative talk show host Bill O'Reilly, who minimizes the influence of race and tends to deny racism. In fact, Colbert understands the importance of race in the United States. He knows that race is part of the self-definition of all of us. In a chapter about race in his book *I Am American (And So Can You)* he says, "We're all the same. Unfortunately, not everyone sees that. They get too hung up on little things like 'appearance' and 'history' and cultural identity'" (Colbert, 2007).

The African American comedian Chris Rock said that no white man would trade places with him, "And I'm rich."

Pretending race doesn't matter, doesn't fool anyone. Instead, experimental psychologists say, it pushes our responses down into our unconscious, where ideas we would actively eject reside. In tests of implicit association, researchers asked study participants to pair terms with faces. White people found it easier to link black faces with guns than with tools. White participants also found it harder to see black people as equally "American" with whites or Asian-Americans (Lehrman, 2008).

People's desire for money and influence helps to perpetuate some racism and sexism. In April 2007, Don Imus, a radio and TV "shock jock" talk show host, described the Rutgers University women's basketball players as "nappy-headed ho's." The majority of the players were African Americans, and they called a press conference to protest his statement. There were many demonstrations against Imus. A media watchdog group taped the incident and put it on YouTube. The national media featured the incident for several days, and it sparked a national discussion about race. MSNBC fired Imus but later hired him back.

Many influential people appeared on the Don Imus show because it gave them publicity and helped them sell their books. They were often uncomfortable with his racist and sexist remarks but chose to ignore them because they wanted to appear on the show. When some of them assessed their behavior later, they admitted that they should not have ignored the remarks. The deciding factor in canceling the show was the loss of money when large advertisers pulled their ads.

Some people argued that Imus's racism and sexism was no worse than that of some popular black rap singers, whose lyrics are laced with sexism and violence. Again, corporate money helped to perpetuate their behavior because they were making a lot of money. After the Imus incident, some corporations began to reassess their support for these singers.

Some groups are protesting this kind of music, including a black women's group at Spelman College.

The sociologist Charles A. Gallagher maintains that colorblindness "maintains white privilege by negating racial inequality" (2003). The belief that the United States is free of **racism** and discrimination and that people get ahead only on their merits allows whites to believe that being white or black or brown has no influence on their economic situation. It allows whites to believe that their material success was gained only by individual hard work, determination, thrift, and investments in education, and has nothing to do with institutional racism. It also allows whites to avoid feeling any guilt about institutional racism.

People who are reading this book are likely to be college students. It hasn't been easy for many of you to get to college and it might not be easy for you to stay in college until graduation. Many of you work part time, or even full time. Many of you are poor and are trying to work your way out of poverty. You may be in debt for college tuition. If you are white and someone suggests that you are privileged because of your white skin, you may think that is ridiculous. You don't feel privileged. You have worked hard to get where you are. Yet we suggest that you examine some of the things that made it possible for you to get where you are. You might discover that you did in fact have some privilege because of your white skin. One of the authors of this book (Mandell) did that examination of her own life and found that despite her growing up poor, she did indeed enjoy certain privileges that were denied to people of color. She began this exercise when she was doing outreach work at a welfare office to give people information about their rights. The following case study is the description of her self-examination.

racism Hatred or intolerance of another race or other races. Beliefs that one's own race is superior.

CASE STUDY

You've Been Well Cared For

I was sitting in the Homeless Unit of the Grove Hall Department of Transitional Assistance (DTA, welfare department) chatting with some women. One was living in a homeless shelter in Saugus, a town on the north shore of Massachusetts; the other was applying for shelter. They were ashamed to be here. They said that they had worked and held responsible jobs. Life had dealt them raw blows. One had to leave her job because of an injury to her spine, which seemed to require endless treatment, and she didn't know when she could return to work. The other had various medical problems. She was infuriated because the DTA worker was "jerking her around." She had an appointment for 9, and it was now 11, and they still hadn't seen her.

They cared deeply about their children. The woman who lived in Saugus was driving her daughter to Boston every day so the child would not have to switch schools. I told her that a recent federal law requires the home school district to provide transportation from the shelter to the child's home school. I pointed to the sign on the wall that told about this and urged her to call the number.

The woman who was being "jerked around" said in a resigned voice, "It's all down hill when you get old. I'm 45, and I don't think things will get any better." I protested, "Come on, I'm 78, and I'm not going down hill. I'm still here fighting." The women were amazed. "You're 78?" they said. "You've been well cared for. We've been battered around all our lives."

I've been thinking about that a lot. I think the women were implying that I had been treated better in life because I am white, while prejudice and discrimination against African Americans had given them harsher treatment than I had faced. Was that true?

As a child, I didn't feel privileged. My father was one of the last homesteaders to get free land from the government, but he got the worst land—dry land in the prairies of Colorado where it seldom rained and the dust storms were so fierce that you literally couldn't see your hand in front of your face if you were outside, while the wind whipped sand through the cracks of the windows and doors. On a freezing winter day the car broke down coming home from the school, which was seven miles away, and we froze our fingers and toes walking home for two miles.

My parents lived in constant dread of the bank foreclosing on the mortgage, and one day they held an auction to sell off cattle and machinery so they could pay the mortgage. We were eager to watch the auction, but my parents made us go to school so we would not witness their humiliation.

Still, we kept the farm, and somehow all four of us children went to a public college where the tuition was cheap. My sister and I raised and sold prize 4-H steers and saved the money for college. I pumped gas at a filling station during World War II, helped with bookkeeping at the gas station, typed letters for a local cattle rancher, and when I went to college, had a work-study job and a scholarship. I paid for my graduate school with part-time secretarial jobs and stints as a group work leader at the YMHA and Community Church in New York City. I didn't mind working, even enjoyed much of it, but I never felt that I had a privileged life.

Yet as I thought about it, I did get better breaks in life because of my white skin. When I read the history of the Homesteading Act, I learned that African Americans were discriminated against and didn't get even the poor land that my father got.

The Mexican American children whose family came to town to pick sugar beets attended my school, but they had to leave because their family moved on to other migratory work when the beets were pulled. My family were permanent residents, and I could stay in school.

When I went to Grange Hall dances, I noticed that the two sons of the only African American farmer in our neighborhood stood on the sidelines and never asked any of the white girls to dance. I would have been shocked if they had asked me to dance, but I think I would have been pleased, too, because they were handsome and I had secretly wanted to get to know them. An unwritten community prejudice had

kept us from getting to know one another. That was not privilege for me—that kept me from living as full a life as I could have.

At college I joined a sorority that I later discovered did not allow African Americans to become members. I tried to resign but was told that no one was allowed to resign. Their racism was mandatory!

The parents of one of my best friends in college were living in a Japanese American concentration camp, having been put there during World War II. I gave speeches against the injustice, and I knew that because my parents were white, they were never under suspicion of being spies.

I taught at a state college, and since I retired, I have lived on the state pension, as well as Social Security. Many African Americans weren't covered by Social Security because it did not cover domestic workers or agricultural workers for many years. Even when they were covered, they often received less money because the work had paid so little.

I have had health problems too, but the state health benefit, combined with Medicare, pays for almost all of my medical care and I can choose any health care provider I wish. I can afford to pay for massages, acupuncture, and weight training classes and to buy both prescription drugs and herbal medicine. I know that I am privileged in this compared to Medicaid recipients, who have a limited choice of doctors and cannot get all the services they need, and compared to people who work in low-wage jobs that don't provide health insurance.

So yes, I have been privileged. Those women in the DTA office asked why I came to the office and did this kind of work. I told them that I had been a social work professor at Bridgewater State College, and I believed in not only talking about my knowledge and beliefs but also acting on them. They commended me and said that it was good to stay active and involved. "It's sure better than sitting on the couch and clicking the remote."

I agreed. I am privileged to be able to use my knowledge to come to the DTA office and tell a homeless woman that she does not have to drive her child twenty miles to school and back every day and that the school system is breaking the law if they don't pick up the child. I am privileged to know enough to go into a fair hearing with a woman and point out to the worker and the hearing officer that they are breaking the law by cutting off the woman's welfare benefits. I am privileged to help a woman apply for food stamps. And I am privileged to know the brave mothers who come to the DTA and keep their spirits up for the sake of their children (Mandell, 2004b).

The late playwright August Wilson spoke about attitudes toward blackness:

When you go to the dictionary and you look up black, it gives you these definitions that say, "Affected by an undesirable condition." You start thinking something's wrong with black. When white people say, "I don't see color," what they're saying is, "You're affected by this undesirable condition, but I'll pretend I don't see that." And I go, "No, see my color. Look at me. I'm not ashamed of who I am and what I am." (Lahr, 2001, p. 52)

Overt racism is easy to spot, but covert racism is subtler. Counselors who relate to minority clients as though race is unimportant are disregarding the central importance of color to the client. They also disregard the influence of their whiteness upon the client.

Color consciousness is the opposite of color blindness. It is based on the premise that the client's problems stem essentially from being a person of color. A color-conscious counselor places too much weight on the color of the client and assumes that all problems are due to the client's ethnicity.

Impact of Prejudice on Self-Esteem

Positive self-esteem is at the core of mental health. In the following anecdotes, consider how prejudice and discrimination might negatively affect people's feelings about themselves:

- A seventy-year-old person recounted the following incident: "I was driving into a parking lot and a youngish woman was driving out. She evidently didn't like the way I was driving, because she screamed at me, 'Where do you think you're going, you old bat?' "

  The seventy-year-old woman had never considered being old as the most important part of her identity but here she encountered a woman who saw her age as the most important part of her identity and as a degraded status. The yelling woman combined her anger about a person's driving with her contempt of old people. Because the older woman was secure in her identity, and in her driving ability, she was able to pass this incident off with a shrug. But this example of ageism is representative of the mountain of insults that older people face, insults that can wear down a shaky self-confidence.

- A lesbian student is told by one of her teachers that she has no right to wear a necklace with a cross on it because lesbianism is against God's will. The teacher forces her to "come out of the closet" to the class about being a lesbian, and when she does, some class members turn on her angrily. The student is hurt and angry, feeling that she has been emotionally violated.

- Battered women are not only physically abused, they also face a barrage of emotional insults from their batterers, often to the point of agreeing with the batterers who tell them that they are worthless.

- Two social psychologists, Claude Steele and Joshua Aronson, tested the effects of expectations on students' performance. They gave graduating black high school students GRE exams. When they told the students that white students get better scores on those exams than black students do, the students' self-confidence went down and, true to the prediction, on average their scores were lower than those of white students. But when they were told that the exam was not being used to evaluate ability or qualification, their scores went up and were as good as the scores made by white students (Steele & Aronson, 1995). When their anxiety about performance was removed, black students worked up to their full potential, which is as great as that of white students. This study is one of the many that disprove the premise of the widely publicized book *The Bell Curve* (Herrnsteih & Murray, 1994), that the intelligence of black people is consistently lower than that of white people. Steele and Aronson also conducted a similar experiment with women, using math tests, and the results were the same.

How can a human service worker combat prejudice and discrimination? We need to work on three levels—with the larger community, with small groups, and with individuals. Working for community-wide social change involves social activism. Causes that might be embraced include the women's movement, gay and lesbian liberation, welfare rights, antiracism, immigration issues, ageism, disabled patients' liberation, mental patients' liberation, and body-image liberation.

The most effective change in social attitudes is brought about by large-scale movements. Liberation movements not only change public attitudes but can also raise the self-esteem and self-confidence of oppressed people. People often internalize their oppression and come to believe that they are like what the oppressor says they are. When they join with similarly oppressed people, the very fight to free themselves raises their self-esteem. "Say It Loud: I'm Black and I'm Proud" is a slogan to counter the demeaning belief that black people are inferior. Gay Pride marches help restore pride to gays and lesbians. The women's movement has had a profound effect on women's self-esteem, giving support to women's quest for equality with men. The welfare rights movement helped welfare recipients feel themselves to be worthy and productive people.

On an individual level, the most important job for human service workers is to understand the culture of their clients. We use the word *culture* broadly. In a sense, every individual you work with is from a different culture. But in this chapter, we focus particularly on groups that have been oppressed because of their ethnicity, social class, gender, sexual orientation, or physical or emotional status.

UNDERSTANDING ETHNICITY

The Definition of Culture

There is no one agreed-on definition of *culture*. We will use the term to connote a group of people who share history, language, traditions, and networks. They may also share a minority social status. More importantly, they see themselves and others see them in a special way, although their ethnic and cultural status may have slightly varied meanings for each individual (Lukes & Land, 1990).

During World War II the U.S. government forcibly interned thousands of U.S. citizens of Japanese ancestry. The official reason was that they might spy for Japan, our enemy. Yet the German Americans and Italian Americans, both of whose ancestral countries also opposed us, were not harassed. Why do you think Asian Americans were treated so much more harshly?

Theories about cultural identity have changed over time. The melting-pot theory, popular among the "establishment" of the 1960s, implicitly assumed that the white, Anglo-Saxon culture was the ideal that other cultures should aspire to. The theory proved to be inadequate. Ethnic groups never totally assimilate into the majority culture, and they have asserted their right to be unique.

During the War on Poverty, some sociologists proposed a cultural-deficit theory (Moynihan, 1965), which assumed that minority cultures were inferior to the mainstream. This theory called for socializing minorities into the mainstream culture. That was one of the guiding principles of the Head Start early-childhood program.

Through the organized efforts of those supposedly deficient cultural groups, the cultural-deficit theory yielded to a theory of cultural difference, which focused on the uniqueness of each minority culture but implied that each was separate from the dominant culture. However, that too was inadequate, as there is much overlap between the minority and dominant cultures.

A current theory is called **bicultural theory**. It states that, although people are socialized into their minority culture through family and ethnic community, they are also influenced by the dominant culture through social institutions and the mass media. No one is quite sure how people incorporate cultures. Each person goes through the process with varying degrees of success. A totally bicultural person moves easily between two cultures, feeling at home in each, to the extent that the dominant culture allows this (Lukes & Land, 1990).

bicultural theory
A theory asserting that although people are socialized into their minority culture through family and ethnic community, they are also influenced by the dominant culture through social institutions and the mass media.

Anthropologists say that a person's ethnicity is situational, asserting itself according to the situation (Green, 1982). An African American person might speak black English with other African Americans, but, when with white people, may speak the dominant form of English. It is important to know how people deal with ethnicity in cross-cultural interactions as well as within their culture. Here is what one black woman says about this:

> Learning formal English has left me, and many like me, at the crossroads between "Black is Beautiful" and "White Equals Wealth." The pressure, from both communities, to choose one direction is daunting. Being black is in no way synonymous with using slang, but we all want to stay true to who we are, and be proud of it. . . . The glares I encounter when talking on the train with friends, the stares I receive when I report that I am trilingual in that I speak English, Spanish and slang, the offended feeling I get when white people tell me how articulate I am, and the anger I feel when my friends tell me I am "acting white"—these are all different ways of asking me to choose a side. . . . When asked once by my college roommate about my newfound crush, I answered, "His swag is through the roof!" She, being unfamiliar with slang, did not understand. How could I let that slip? What I really meant was that I was utterly impressed by the way the young man carried himself. I liked his style. (Sturdivant, 2010)

It is absurd that the amount of melanin (pigment) in one's skin or the tightness of the curl of one's hair should cause another person to do anything more than casually notice these features as two of the many that distinguish one person from another. Yet the social meaning of these features in the United States has built up over three centuries, beginning with the arrival of the first slave ship from Africa. Since its arrival (and the thousands that came after), no one in this country has been casual about color. Ever since the arrival of those three fateful ships that Christopher Columbus led to the American continent in 1492, the rulers of this country have subjugated native populations and constricted them with minority status in their own lands.

Advances in genetics and biotechnology in the past few decades have caused a dramatic shift in thinking about race. Most anthropologists now agree that race is not a biological reality at all. It is nothing more than a social, cultural, and political invention (Chandler, 1997). But that is not how the general public sees it. A biological anthropologist at Yale University, Jonathan Marsh, said that changing most people's minds about race is "like convincing someone in the 17th century that the Earth goes around the sun and not vice versa. What you think is out there is different from what's really out there" (Chandler, 1997, p. A30).

The mapping of the human genome provided scientific proof that human beings are not divided into separate biological groups. J. Craig Venter, whose company, Celera Genomics, mapped the human genome, said, "It is disturbing to see reputable scientists and physicians even categorizing things in terms of race. There is no basis in the genetic code for race" (Stolberg, 2001, p. 1 wk).

While we agree that there is only one race, we go on to discuss race as a social construct because it is a concept deeply embedded in people's ideas about themselves and others.

The actress Lonette McKee, who played the role of Alice in the TV series *Queen*, has both African American and Finnish-Swedish ancestry. Her mother told her that she had the best of both worlds. But McKee does not agree. She said that the world doesn't tell you that when you look for a job or when you have a job and don't get paid what you are worth. She says, "It's a political, social reality—one drop of black blood, you're black. To look at yourself any other way is a lie. And we're involved in a system designed to weed us out, to keep us out of the mainstream" (Smith, 1993, p. 30).

Media Stereotypes

The media has a powerful influence in shaping our attitudes. A comparison of how the media presents black and white people shows that black people are likely to be shown in a more unfavorable light than white people. For example, consider the media treatment of six fatal schoolyard shootings over eight months by white youths in American small towns.

Kip Kinkel, 15, the boy who allegedly killed his parents and two classmates in a gun rampage in Oregon, was "skinny," "slight," "diminutive," or "freckle faced." A *Newsweek* story described him as having "an innocent look that is part Huck Finn and part Alfred E. Neumann—boyish and quintessentially American." A Roxbury judge, Milton Wright, said, "Quintessentially American? That always means white" (Dowdy, 1998, p. E1).

Luke Woodham, convicted in Mississippi of killing two students, was described as "the chubby, poor kid at Pearl High School who always seemed to get picked on," a "nerd," and "intelligent but isolated" (Dowdy, 1998, p. E1).

Michael Carneal, who allegedly killed three students in West Paducah, Kentucky, was "thin" and "a solid B student." Mitchell Johnson and Andrew Golden, who allegedly killed four girls and a teacher in Jonesboro, Arkansas, were "little boys." Andrew Wurst, who allegedly killed a teacher in Edinboro, Pennsylvania, was a "shy and quirky eighth-grader with an offbeat sense of humor" (Dowdy, 1998, p. E1).

Contrast these benign descriptions with the media treatment of young African American and Latino killers. They have been called "maggots," "animals," and "super predators." Julian Bond, chairman of the National Association for the Advancement of Colored People, comments, "If this were black kids doing this, you'd see op-ed pieces . . . talking about a pathology of violence loose in the community, about some dangerous elements being unleashed, about the breakdown of family values" (Dowdy, 1998).

News accounts of young black killers in court often describe them as "blank faced," "dazed," or "showing no emotion." "Unlike the more human terms given the white school killers, young black suspects often are not described physically at all. Often, the first description of them is whether the youth was in a gang" (Dowdy, 1998, p. E1).

Boston District Attorney Ralph Martin says that many young black suspects are "seemingly sweet of countenance, and lacking in obvious bravado" (Dowdy, 1998, p. E1), but he rarely sees black youth described that way in the newspapers.

Alvin Poussaint, a Harvard Medical School psychiatrist, notes that although there is wide media discussion of mood disorders and depression for the white teenage killers, "there is little of that for low-income African-American and Latino youth killers who suffer at higher levels of the kind of depression that precedes violence" (Dowdy, 1998, p. E1).

Julian Bond comments that it is time that the United States looked at factors behind youth violence that cut across race and class. He says, "It seems to me there's kind of a pathology out there, some kind of love of guns, a gun culture out there that's dangerous and insidious" (Dowdy, 1998, p. E1).

Ethnic Identity

It is risky to generalize about ethnic traits. There is much variety within each culture. For example, some of the literature on working with ethnicity points out that although the usual advice in interviewing technique is to look someone straight in the eye, that would be the wrong technique for some Asian, Latino, and Native American groups, who might interpret that as hostility. In her autobiographical novel *The Woman Warrior*, Maxine Hong Kingston (1977) shows that this advice would be wrong for an older woman, Moon Orchid, who was newly arrived from China, but right for her nieces, who were acculturated to the American tradition of looking people straight in the eye:

> "Good morning, Aunt," they said, turning to face her, staring directly into her face. Even the girls stared at her—like cat-headed birds. Moon Orchid jumped and squirmed when they did that. They looked directly into her eyes as if they were look- ing for lies. Rude. Accusing. They never lowered their gaze; they hardly blinked. . . . Sometimes when the girls were reading or watching television, she crept up behind them with a comb and tried to smooth their hair, but they shook their heads, and they turned and fixed her with those eyes. She wondered what they thought and what they saw when they looked at her like that. She liked coming upon them from the back to avoid being looked at. They were like animals the way they stared. (Kingston, 1977, p. 133)

Stereotypes can both demean and exalt a group. For example, Asian Americans are sometimes seen as the "model minority," a homogenous group of high achievers taking over the campuses of the nation's most selective colleges. A report by New York University, the College Board, and a commission of mostly Asian American educators and community leaders, pokes holes in stereotypes about Asian Americans and Pacific Islanders. It points out that the term *Asian American* is extraordinarily broad, embracing members of many ethnic groups. "Certainly there's a lot of Asians doing well, at the top of the curve, but there are just as many struggling at the bottom of the curve," said Robert T. Teranishi, the N.Y.U. education professor who wrote the report, 'Facts, not fiction: Setting the record straight' " (Lewin, 2008).

An important guideline for a human service worker is to seek to understand how each individual person is affected by his or her ethnicity. To do that, there is no substitute for asking the person. If you were working with many people from a culture different from yours, you would be wise to read as much as possible about that culture, including the liter- ature of the culture. That will enrich your life as well as help you in your work. If their lan- guage were different from yours, it would also help you to learn their language. We are the first to admit that this isn't easy. One of the authors of this book (Mandell) has been strug- gling to learn Spanish so she can talk with Latino people who come to the welfare office where she does outreach. She has been taking Spanish courses for many years, but she is still far from being fluent. Yet even her halting attempts to communicate with Latina women are appreciated, and the women help her with the language.

The Power of Names

Before we discuss ethnicity, we need to explain some terms. You may wonder sometimes what you should call a particular group of people. Do you call old people elderly, senior citizens, or simply old? How do you designate people who do not have all possible physical or mental functions? Are they handicapped, disabled, differently abled, physically challenged, developmentally disabled, or people with disabilities? Are American people of African descent called African Americans, black, or Negro? Are American people with Mexican ancestors called Mexican Americans or Chicanos (Chicanas)? Are people whose native language is Spanish called Hispanics or Latinos (Latinas)? Are indigenous people Indians, Native Americans, First Nations, or a specific tribal name?

The name that a group chooses to be known by is important because it reflects that group's self-identity. When a group is oppressed, the name it chooses becomes a political as well as a linguistic issue. For example, people with disabilities generally do not like to be called simply *disabled* rather than *people with disabilities* because the former term implies they are deficient in some way and not whole people.

In the course of their liberation struggles, American people of African descent said they no longer wanted to be called *colored*, because that term carried connotations of lower status, so they changed their designation to Negro. During the civil rights movement of the 1960s, they proudly declared that their skin color should be a source of pride rather than shame, so they called themselves blacks. Later on, as they proudly claimed their African heritage, politically active people used the term *African Americans*. Recently the trend seems to be to return to the term *black*, partly out of consideration for West Indians, who do not consider themselves African Americans, and partly because *black* is an easier term. The term *people of color* is often used to describe people of ethnic groups that are not considered white or Caucasian, but some people point out that these are not entirely accurate terms because Caucasians are not actually white, and many Latinos are white, even though they may be considered under the rubric of people of color. Similarly, some politically active people of Mexican descent changed the old term *Mexican American* to *Chicano* (for males) and *Chicana* (for females).

As these name changes take place, not everyone in the group adopts them, and often the old names linger on alongside the new ones. For example, the word *colored* is still part of the name of the National Association for the Advancement of Colored People (NAACP). Many people still call themselves Mexican Americans rather than Chicanos (Chicanas). Although many indigenous people prefer the term *Native American* to *Indian*, some activists are now saying that both terms are reminders of colonialism. They prefer the term *First Nations* or *First Americans*, or their tribal names. *American Indian* is also an accepted term. The Census Bureau calls all Spanish-speaking people Hispanics but makes it clear that "persons of Hispanic origin may be of any race."

Some names are acceptable to people of minority status if used by someone of their own ethnicity, but not if used by someone who is not of their ethnicity. For example, there has been a long-standing debate among African Americans about whether the term *nigger* is acceptable when used by black people. The comedian Dick Gregory vowed never to use it again after he had used it in a book, but some black people argue that it is a good-natured expression of solidarity.

As authors, we use the terms that we believe are in current usage by people who are in the forefront of their particular group's liberation struggles. When more than one term is in current usage, we use both. When you are in doubt about the term a particular person prefers, ask that person.

BROAD CATEGORIES DISGUISE LARGE DIFFERENCES

Many different nations are lumped under the categories "Asian American" and "Latin American," but these broad categories obscure enormous national differences. One could no more speak of a "typical Asian" than of a "typical European." Immigrants from Japan, China, Korea, Cambodia, Vietnam, Laos, and the Philippines all speak different languages and come from vastly different cultures. Immigrants from Colombia, El Salvador, Argentina, Guatemala, Mexico, and Puerto Rico all speak Spanish, but they too come from very different national cultures. Although Haiti and the Dominican Republic share the same Caribbean island, their people speak different languages and have different histories and cultures.

The Census Bureau has finally recognized the reality that many people are of more than one race and for the first time in 2000 allowed people to select more than one racial category. The Census Bureau records "race" and "Hispanic ethnicity" as separate questions. Thus, a Hispanic person can be of any race. Officially, the proportion of ethnic groups in the United States in 2008 was as follows: Non-Hispanic white 65.6 percent; Black or African American 12.8 percent; Hispanic origin 15.4 percent; Asian 4.5 percent; American Indian and Alaska Native 1 percent, Native Hawaiian and other Pacific Islander 0.2 percent; Two or more races 1.7 percent (U.S. Census Bureau, 2010).

The Hispanic population has surpassed the black population recently, and there is a trend toward an increasing Hispanic population.

Discrimination Hurts Everybody

The college students who scrawl JAP (Jewish American Princess) on a dorm door have been infected with a contagious, chronic virus. Having learned how to hate one group of people, they are likely to turn on others from backgrounds they do not understand or feel threatened by.

Prejudice and discrimination have economic, psychological, and political causes. In recent years, as the job market has contracted and wages have gone down, people's anxieties and fears about competition for jobs have increased. Many working people look for scapegoats, and we have seen a frightening increase in hate groups such as the Ku Klux Klan, American Nazi Party, Aryan Nation, and right-wing militias. The bombing of a federal building in Oklahoma City in 1995 was an example of these groups' potential for violence and the danger that hate inspires.

Prejudice is widespread and is directed against many kinds of people. The comedian Tom Lehrer satirized the pervasiveness of prejudice in his song "National Brotherhood Week." Following are some excerpts:

> Oh the white folks hate the black folks;
> And the black folks hate the white folks.
> To hate all but the right folks is an old established rule. . . .
> Oh the poor folks hate the rich folks,
> And the rich folks hate the poor folks.
> All of my folks hate all of your folks;

It's American as apple pie. . . .
Oh the Protestants hate the Catholics;
And the Catholics hate the Protestants.
The Hindus hate the Moslems,
And everybody hates the Jews.
During National Brotherhood Week, National Brotherhood week,
Its National-Everyone-Smile-at-One-Anotherhood Week.
Be nice to people who are inferior to you.
It's only for a week, so have no fear.
Be grateful that it doesn't last all year. (Lehrer, 1965)

In his classical study of prejudice, psychologist Gordon Allport described a racist as a person who is suspicious and distrustful of anyone perceived as "different" and who is a "super-patriot," believing that all newcomers or those who are different from the mainstream pose a threat to an idealized and more secure past (Allport, 1954). Allport's study discovered that bigoted people go through life feeling threatened. They are insecure, cannot live comfortably with themselves or others, and are burdened by guilt. They insist on a strict code of morality in order to try to control their own instinctive feelings, which they mistrust.

Prejudice generally leads to discrimination against the feared group. It is a way to shore up the prejudiced person's weak ego by feeling that he or she is better than other people. It is also a way to protect privileges, by keeping other people out of jobs, housing, or other benefits they need.

Sociologist Robin Williams says that "racial ideologies developed to rationalize the social, economic, and political domination initially developed to enhance the resources and privileges of white Europeans" (1966), a domination that persists to the present day. Discrimination harms all workers. Discrimination against people of color and women enables management to pay workers low wages and to rationalize cutbacks in social spending. Anti-Semitism enables the power elite to use Jews as scapegoats to deflect anger away from those in control. As long as they are fighting with each other, minority groups cannot unite to bring about equality and equity for everyone.

The closing off of equal opportunities to people of color has not only caused incredible hardship to them and to their communities, but it has also created social instability that threatens all of society. Rising unemployment in the black community has affected the structure of the black family. Sociologists have pointed out the relationship of black male unemployment to the rise in single-parent families. Although he does not claim that this is the only reason for the rise in female-headed families, sociologist Robert Staples says that "the percentage of black women heading families alone . . . corresponds closely to the percentage of black males not in the labor force. Men want to help support their families and lose self-esteem when they cannot find work" (1988, p. 321). The massive incarceration of black men and women is another reason for the instability of black families.

Until the problems of unemployment and low income are solved, none of the other problems of the African American community can be solved. Slavery, and the decades of racism that followed, created a workforce in which "blacks still predominate in those occupations that in a slave society would be reserved for slaves" (Ezorsky, 1991, p. 74).

There is also a correlation between the numbers of unemployed young men and the crime rate. The official response to crime has been to build more prisons, at great expense to the taxpayer, but as the director of the American Civil Liberties Union points out,

Crime rates correlate, not with how many prisons are built, but with the proportion of young people in the population and the percentage of those young people who are unemployed, uneducated and face a bleak future. Most violent crimes are committed by alienated young men, who have no reason to hope and nothing to lose—a dangerous mix. (Glasser, 1992, p. 16)

Institutional Racism

How does institutional racism or sexism differ from individual racism or sexism? Imagine a situation in which no worker in an agency holds strong racist (or sexist) views, yet the policies of the agency are constructed so that minorities don't receive fair treatment. Such a situation is an example of **institutional racism (sexism)**. It is larger, more powerful, and harder to change than one person's attitudes, because interconnected systems and policies perpetuate it. Even if a policy may appear fair and neutral on the surface, it can become racially discriminatory in the way it is practiced. Institutional racism is pervasive in all of society's institutions, including human services.

Research has shown that adoption workers favor affluent parents over low-income parents. When agency policy blindly gives preference to adoptive applicants because of a high salary, a home in the suburbs, and a professional occupation, these criteria will necessarily discriminate against minority applicants. Treated unequally by the society they live in, they are less likely to make a high salary, live in a well-serviced neighborhood, and have a stable work history in an occupation that requires long and costly training. *This adds up to institutional racism.*

Institutional racism can be attacked through changing social policy and legislation. One of the purposes of a practice called "subsidized adoption," which was given federal support in the Child Welfare and Adoption Act of 1980, was to make adoption financially possible for those prospective parents who had been denied access to the chance to earn the money that qualified them to adopt. Now, more people of color and of low income are able to share their lives with those children who need a home, many of whom because of unequal opportunities are themselves from low-income and/or minority groups.

Another example of institutional racism occurs in the criminal justice system. The hypothetical stories that follow are based on research that contradicts the widespread belief that drug use is primarily confined to the black ghetto. In actual fact, white youth sell and use drugs at higher rates than black youth. Institutional racism seems to be at work here:

William Greer, an African American youth, was picked up by the police while he was using crack on a ghetto street corner. He was unemployed and could not afford a lawyer to represent him in court. The legal aid lawyer appointed to defend him was overworked and could not spend much time with William; in fact, he talked with William for just a few minutes before court began. He advised William to plead guilty and plea bargain rather than ask for a jury trial. The judge, known to be "tough on drugs," sentenced him to a mandatory five-year prison sentence.

Jack Clifford, a white college student, was sniffing cocaine at a party. He had purchased the drug in the suburbs from another student who was known as someone who always had drugs for sale. The party got wild and a neighbor called the police. Jack had to appear in court on a drug charge. His parents hired a skilled lawyer. She asked the judge

---

institutional racism (sexism) Discrimination against a racial group (or gender) practiced by an organization or an institution, usually perpetuated by an interconnected system of policies and practices.

to allow Jack to get psychiatric treatment for his drug habit rather than go to jail. The judge agreed, knowing that the parents were successful professionals in the community.

Generally, the deviant behavior of poor urban people (minorities are overrepresented among the urban poor) is more likely to be defined as criminal and handled in the criminal justice system. Conversely, the deviant behavior of whites is more likely to be defined as a mental health problem and handled in the mental health system (Morales, 1978). To explain this difference, researchers look to the dynamics of institutional racism.

A Houston Law Review study found that black people are more likely than white people to get the death sentence. Defendants who kill whites are more likely to be sentenced to death than those who kill blacks. All else being equal, blacks are more likely to be sentenced to death than whites in more than three decades since the Supreme Court reinstated the death penalty in 1976 (Liptak, 2008).

Institutional racism is pervasive in the criminal justice system. Black and Latino youths are treated more severely than white teenagers charged with comparable crimes at every step of the juvenile justice system, according to a comprehensive report sponsored by the Justice Department and six of the nation's leading foundations (Butterfield, 2000). The report found that minority youths are more likely than white youths to be arrested, held in jail, sent to juvenile or adult court for trial, convicted, and given longer prison terms. At each additional step in the juvenile justice system, things get worse for minority youth than for white youth. Here are the shocking facts (Butterfield, 2000):

- Among young people who have not been sent to a juvenile prison before, blacks are more than six times as likely as whites to be sentenced by juvenile courts to prison.

- For those young people charged with a violent crime who have not been in juvenile prison before, black teenagers are nine times more likely than whites to be sentenced to juvenile prison.

- For those charged with drug offenses, black youths are forty-eight times more likely than whites to be sentenced to juvenile prison.

- White youths charged with violent offenses are incarcerated for an average of 198 days after trial, but blacks are incarcerated an average of 254 days and Latinos are incarcerated an average of 305 days.

Mark Soler, the president of Youth Law Center, said, "These disparities accumulate and they make it hard for members of the minority community to complete their education, get jobs and be good husbands and fathers" (Butterfield, 2000, p. 2).

A black boy born in 2001 has a 1 in 3 chance of going to prison in his lifetime; a Latino boy a 1 in 6 chance; and a white boy a 1 in 17 chance. A black girl born in 2001 has a 1 in 17 chance of going to prison in her lifetime; a Latino girl a 1 in 45 chance; and a white girl a 1 in 111 chance (Children's Defense Fund, 2009).

In the past, when studies have found racial disparities in the number of adult black or Latino prison inmates, critics have said that it was because members of minorities committed a disproportionate number of crimes. Soler said while that may be true, it does not account for the extreme disparities found in the report, nor for disparities at each stage of the juvenile justice process. He said, "When you look at this data, it is undeniable that race is a factor" (Butterfield, 2000, p. 2).

The nation's war on drugs unfairly targets African Americans, who are much more likely to be imprisoned for drug offenses than whites even though far more whites use illegal drugs than blacks:

> According to a 2006 report by the American Civil Liberties Union, African Americans make up an estimated 15 percent of drug users, but they account for 37 percent of those arrested on drug charges, 59 percent of those convicted and 74 percent of all drug offenders sentenced to prison. Or consider this: The U.S. has 260,000 people in state prisons on nonviolent drug charges; 183,200 [more than 70 percent] are black or Latino. (Huffington, 2007)

Overall, black men are sent to state prisons on drug charges at thirteen times the rate of white men. Drug transactions among blacks often are easier for police to target because they more often occur in public than do drug transactions among whites (Fletcher, 2000).

"We've spent a lot of money and we've wasted a lot of lives," said James Alan Fox, a criminologist who teaches at Northeastern University. "The war on drugs was a failed policy which resulted in the overincarceration of drug offenders, most of whom are not dangerous" (Rodriguez, 2001).

The United States has the highest incarceration rate on the planet—five times the world's average. A total of 2,380,000 people were in prison in 2010. The United States has 5 percent of the world's population but 25 percent of the world's prison population (Fisher, 2010). The Justice Department's Bureau of Justice Statistics attributes much of the increase to get-tough policies enacted during the 1980s and 1990s, such as mandatory drug sentences, "three strikes and you're out" laws for repeat offenders, and "truth in sentencing" laws that restrict early releases.

The "get-tough" sentencing laws adopted by the federal government and most states have forced judges to impose prison terms for certain crimes, including drunk driving and drug possession or selling. More than four in five of drug related arrests in 2008 were for possession of banned substances, rather than for their sale or manufacture. Four in ten of all drug arrests were for marijuana possession, according to FBI data (Eckholm, 2008).

These laws have resulted in a disproportionate number of arrests of blacks and Latinos. The possession of five grams of crack—the weight of five packets of sweetener—results in a five-year mandatory minimum jail sentence, whereas it takes 500 grams of powdered cocaine—the weight of 500 packets of sweetener—to get the same penalty. Ninety-five percent of those convicted of crack offenses are black and Latino, although almost two-thirds of crack users are white (Jackson, 2007). More than 81 percent of those convicted for crack offenses in 2007 were African American, although only about 25 percent of crack cocaine users are African American (Margasak, 2009). These harsh sentences for crack users do nothing to solve the problem of drug abuse. The recidivism rate for those who get treatment is much lower than for those who don't, but there are not enough drug treatment facilities. Although more blacks and Latinos than whites get prison sentences for drug use, proportionately more white people die from drugs.

The racial inequalities of the war on drugs also disproportionately affect pregnant women of color. "Despite similar or equal rates of illegal drug use during pregnancy, African American women are ten times more likely to be reported to child welfare agencies for prenatal drug use" (Drug Policy Alliance, 2003).

Fortunately, the Supreme Court ruled in December 2007 that the sentencing guidelines were merely advisory, not mandatory. Budget constraints are forcing states to reconsider the enormous amount of money they have spent on building prisons. State spending on prisons has grown from $12 billion in 1987 to $49 billion in 2007 (Jackson, 2008). State spending on corrections rose 127 percent since 1980, while higher education expenditures rose just 21 percent (Fisher, 2010). Crime is down, and voters are saying they are more concerned about issues like education than with street violence. A voter initiative in California provides for treatment rather than prison for many drug offenders.

In 2009, the Obama administration joined a federal judge in urging Congress to end a racial disparity by equalizing prison sentences for dealing and using crack versus powdered cocaine. Assistant Attorney General Lanny Breuer said the administration believes Congress's goal should be to completely eliminate the disparity between the two forms of cocaine. "A growing number of citizens view it as fundamentally unfair," Breuer said. Jurors have expressed an unwillingness to serve in crack cocaine cases because of the disparity. The Obama administration was also seeking to increase drug treatment, as well as rehabilitation programs for felons after release from prison. The Justice Department was working on recommendations for a new set of sentences for cocaine (Margasak, 2009). Senator Jim Webb, a Democrat from Virginia, submitted a bill to Congress in 2010 to establish a commission, the National Criminal Justice Commission, to study the criminal justice system and make recommendations for change. He said, "America's criminal justice system has deteriorated to the point that it is a national disgrace" (Fisher, 2010).

Discrimination against Arab Americans and Muslim Americans

Discrimination against Arab and Muslim Americans has been around for a long time, especially in the workplace, but since 9/11, it has risen at alarming rates and spread into many other areas of life.

CASE STUDY

What a Human Service Worker Needs to Know about Arab and Muslim Americans: Meet Luby Ismail

Lobua "Luby" Ismail awoke before dawn in her hotel room near Orlando, Florida, knelt on the floor, and bowed low in the direction of Mecca to say her morning prayers. She finished dressing, wrapped her Muslim headscarf, or hijab, snugly around her dark features and, after a light meal, headed off to lead a cultural training session at Walt Disney World Resort.

Ismail sat in silence in the front of the room while the trainees, all of them Disney World employees, arrived. She then scrawled a message on the blackboard: "The first part of this session will be nonverbal, okay?"

As the students nodded in agreement, she wrote another message, asking the trainees to share with their training partners, in writing, some assumptions that society—or the class members themselves—might make about a woman who looks and dresses like she does.

[To the student who is reading this book: *Put this book face down on the table and write down five words that come to your mind as you picture this Arab woman.* Now read the responses that Luby got and compare them with yours.]

The responses her trainees came up with ranged from *submissive* and *uneducated* to *foreign* and *someone who is not my friend.* Other responses she might have heard—especially if she had been accompanied by an Arab man—might have been *Ali Babi, Sinbad, The Thief of Baghdad, white slaver, abuser of women, slave owner, polygamist, sheik, oil millionaire*—images drawn from books and the media . . . and since 9/11, *religious fanatic and bomber.* Even Sesame Street, the children's educational TV program, has one character dressed in stereotypical Arab garb, and he always teaches negative words such as *danger.*

Ismail then broke the silence by proclaiming in perfect English that she is a born-and-bred American who was the pitcher for her ninth-grade softball team and student body president in high school and who today is a wife and business owner. She is one of many advocates engaged in a campaign to pierce the stereotypes about Islam and its followers, called Muslims. These advocates want to help employers make their workplaces more comfortable for the country's growing numbers of Muslims, who may be of any race or from any part of the world (Panaro, 2004).

The following basic facts will help you avoid simplistic assumptions (a.k.a. stereotypes) (Adams, 2002; Deen, 2003):

- Although some articles assert that Muslims are the second largest religious group in much of Europe and North America, it is very unclear exactly how many Muslims there are in the United States. Estimates of the number of Muslims range from a high of over 6 million to a low of 1.6 million. Why is there such a wide disparity and why does it matter? First of all, it is important to know that the Census does not ask people their religion.

  Groups that hold to the higher number include those who want to assert the growing importance and/or electoral impact of this religious group. This includes many Muslim American Associations, as well as fear-monger groups who decry the supposed threat they pose. Groups that espouse the significantly lower number might use that figure to minimize the relative importance and impact of the Muslim community in the overall society or quell the fears of the alarmists.

  Many people who are born into the Muslim faith do not necessarily attend a Mosque. On the other hand, there is some evidence that there is an increasing (but difficult to know how large) growth of homegrown converts to this religion. In any event, this is a cautionary note—be skeptical about numbers and always think about who is making the estimates, what data they are using, and what they might gain from the information they present.

- There are twenty-one separate primarily Arab nations.

  There is no simple definition of who an Arab is. That word refers to those who speak the Arabic language—but some of those twenty-one countries' version of Arabic are different from the others and several Arab countries have internal ethnic groups who speak a totally different form of Arabic or some non-Arabic language. There are also several countries with large Muslim populations who do not speak Arabic and consider themselves Arabs.

- There are two more terms that are often used to describe people like Luby (or her ancestors): Middle Easterners and Muslims (not Moslems). The first refers to geography and the second to religion. But not all persons who consider themselves Arabs or Muslims come from the Middle East (e.g., Indonesia, and some countries in Africa)—and not all Arabs are Muslims. Some are Christians, some are Hindus, and a few are atheists (they practice no religion). For many years (before the state of Israel) numbers of Jewish people lived in the predominately Muslim countries and felt themselves to be culturally Arabs. To complicate matters, there are three countries in the Middle East that are not Arab or wholly Muslim: Iran, Israel, and Turkey.

- While some Arab/Muslin Americans are very wealthy, many others are extremely poor, and there is a growing professional middle class. Arab/Muslim Americans as a whole are more highly educated than are many other ethnic groups.

- Arab/Muslim Americans are very family oriented and often come from large families. They tend to shun social service intervention in private affairs. While conversation is very important and articulate, many who hew closely to the Muslim faith do not accept public touching of the opposite sex.

- Religious discrimination is currently at an all-time high. Most Americans know very little about the Muslim faith and the importance of articles of clothing, such as head coverings, scarves, as well as beards. Often the wearing of these is prohibited in schools and workplaces, and practicing Muslims may not be given the time or space for the daily prayers that are fundamental to their religion. Yet these observances are protected under the U.S. Constitution and Section VII of the Civil Rights Act.

When surveyed, many Americans stated that Muslims face more discrimination inside the United States than any other religious group. In fact only gays and lesbians are seen as facing more discrimination. Results of a survey among 2,010 adults revealed that two-thirds of non-Muslims say that *Islam* (another term for the religion) is very different from their own faith although they are unsure what the Muslims do believe (Pew Research Centers Forum on Religion and Public Life, 2009).

But most importantly, a record number of Muslims in the United States are complaining of serious employment discrimination and harassment on the job. "There's a level of hatred and animosity that is shocking" says Mary Jo O'Neil a regional attorney at the Phoenix office of the EEOC (Equal Employment Opportunity Commission). "I've been doing this work for 31 years and I've never seen such antipathy toward Muslim workers" (Greenhouse, 2010). Although Muslims make up about 2 percent of the population, they accounted for about 25 percent of the complaints submitted to the EEOC. During the same period, complaints by other religious and racial groups declined.

AN IMPORTANT CURRENT CONTROVERSY

In 2009 a group of Muslim citizens purchased a building at 51 Park Place in New York located two blocks from the destroyed World Trade Center. They drew up plans for a thirteen-story Islamic Cultural Center, which would include a 500-seat auditorium, theater, performing arts center, fitness center, swimming pool, basketball courts, culinary school, bookstore, food court, child care center, a September 11 memorial, and a Muslim prayer space (not an official Mosque). The developers named the proposed building The Park

51 Center after its address, but most of the media refer to it incorrectly, as the "Ground Zero Mosque." The pattern for such a cultural center is similar to two major Jewish Centers in the city that are open to all people, as this center would be. Although the building would not be visible from the World Trade Center, opponents have argued that a mosque so close to the site of the tragedy would be offensive to the memory of the thousands who died in the conflagration and an affront to families and friends who mourn them since the pilots of the planes and the plotters behind the attack were Muslims.

Supporters of the project, including the mayor of New York City, asserted that in this time of great tension between Muslims and the general population, a center such as Park 51 could increase multicultural appreciation and demonstrate our tolerance and openness. Both prominent supporters and opponents of the project include the families of the 9/11 victims as well as the American public as a whole.

Unfortunately, the project was being hotly debated during the lead up to the extremely divisive 2010 congressional elections and it became a hot issue in many candidates' campaigns. The president and several Democratic office seekers voiced support of the center's location or stayed out of the debate, while many Republican candidates were vociferous in denouncing it.

George Salem, the Chairman of the Arab American Institute (AIA), who is a long-time Republican voter, tried to defuse the rancor he has encountered with an open letter to other Republican party members. He wrote:

> We need to reach the day when race-baiting against Arabs and Muslims ends in this country. The mosque issue is the most recent manifestation in American politics where politicians can target Arab and Muslim Americans with impunity. It is in our national interest to end this deplorable practice. Over a billion Muslims in the world watch this and paint Americans with a broad brush as people who hate Muslims. Our public diplomacy efforts in the Arab world are seriously undermined by this form of negative and hurtful politics and it must end. (Salem, 2010)

As we go to press, the Park 51 center is still a major controversy.

WHAT CAN A HUMAN SERVICE WORKER DO TO STOP DISCRIMINATION AGAINST MUSLIM AMERICANS?

1. Learn more about the religion and customs of Muslims and Arabs, and whenever you encounter misinformation, try to set the record straight.

2. Support your clients or fellow citizens who are being denied their rights to practice their religion (as long as such practice does not endanger others) in their school or work place by suggesting accommodations that administrators might make. When helpful suggestions fail to result in changes, encourage persons who feel their rights are being abridged to file complaints with the top level of administration or the town or state commissions against discrimination. It is always more effective if the complaints come from other members of the affected population and if coalitions are built with like-minded individuals outside of the ethnic group or religion.

3. Remember that while it is important to learn about groups other than the one you belong to, be aware that there are enormous differences both among various populations and within groups who share some characteristics. For example, some very observant Catholics oppose abortion rights and work to repeal *Roe v. Wade*, other co-religionists reject abortion for themselves but support the legal right to choose. Similarly, some Jewish people eat only kosher foods and wear special clothes, others eat what they wish and dress like the mainstream population, while still attending synagogue or special celebrations for Jewish holidays.

Anti-Semitism

There is a long history of discrimination against Jewish people. For hundreds of years in many countries of the world they have been persecuted and punished simply because they were born of Jewish parents and chose to follow their faith. In recent history, the Nazis efficiently exterminated 6 million Jews in death camps in the 1940s.

Since the end of WWII, discrimination against Jews has lessened a great deal in the United States but they are still arbitrarily excluded from some neighborhoods, job promotions, or social clubs, causing pain and damage to their self-esteem. American Nazi skinheads, the Ku Klux Klan, and militia groups still spread their virulently anti-Semitic messages. The Anti Defamation League, a Jewish support organization, publishes a yearly audit of anti-Semitic assaults, vandalism of synagogues and centers, and harassment. While the 2009 audit included over 1,200 specific incidents, they have found a decline of the more obvious assaults but point to a great increase in anti-Semitic websites, blogs, and other cyber bullying (ADL, 2009).

Jewish people constitute only about 2 percent of the entire U.S. population, and their numbers are diminishing because of low birthrates and marriage to non-Jews. American Jews now have an out-marriage rate of 54 percent.

In contrast to people of color, no physical characteristics distinguish a Jew from a non-Jew, because they have come here from every corner of the world. American Jews have no common language, other than English (although Hebrew is spoken in Israel and in orthodox religious practice and Yiddish was often spoken by an earlier generation of Eastern European Jewish immigrants). There is enormous variation in their involvement in Judaism and their identification with its practices and culture. Although always a small percentage of the population, Jews have been in this country since the 1700s with most coming from Eastern Europe in the 1900s.

Currently, most people of Jewish ancestry are clustered in urban areas, primarily in New York and New Jersey, and in white-collar professions, although this was not so in their early immigrant days. They are not, as a group, economically deprived. They are also represented in most professions.

Some Paradoxes of Prejudice against Jewish People

Prejudice against whole groups of people is a very difficult phenomenon to understand because it serves many psychological, economic, and political purposes for those who express negative attitudes. It is difficult to eradicate these negative attitudes because the stereotypes and misinformation upon which they are built are essentially not rational.

Those who hate others have some self-interest or some self-delusions in continuing to hate or act upon the hatred. The following paradoxes are issues to think about.

1. Despite the generally high level of economic security of Jews in the United States, their voting patterns have overwhelmingly supported candidates who place priority on the needs of the have-nots, women, and ethnic minorities over the demands of the haves and the industrial complex (Svonkin, 1998).

   In the unsuccessful bid for the presidency of Kerry in 2004, 76 percent of the Jewish community voted for him while in the successful campaign of Barack Obama in 2008, 78 percent of the Jewish community voted for Obama. Members of Congress from Jewish backgrounds are among the most supportive of civil rights in both the Senate and House of Representatives. During the era of agitation for the end of racial segregation in the l960s and 1970s, the Jewish community played a highly supportive role. Speaking at the historic march on Washington for racial equal in 1963, along with Martin Luther King, Jr., Joachim Prinz, president of the American Jewish Congress, said *"Our ancient history began with slavery and the yearning for freedom. During the Middle Ages my people lived for a thousand years in the ghettos of Europe. It is for these reasons that it is not merely sympathy and compassion for the black people of America that motivates us. It is, above all and beyond all such sympathies and emotions, a sense of complete identification and solidarity born of our own painful historic experience"* (Prinz, 1963).

   Despite this tradition of Jewish people siding with the underdog, survey data indicate that many residents of low-income communities, predominately in urban areas, when asked about their attitudes toward Jewish people, express many negative views. Residents of poor ghetto communities often perceive Jewish people as being the source of their exploitation in the person of landlords or employers. It is not an easy thing for people who find themselves left out of the American dream to find the source of their distress. Interestingly, minority group members with high levels of education (college and above) from the same ethnic groups hold less stereotyped opinions. With exposure to books and many different types of people, prejudice seems to lessen (Anti-Defamation League, 1998). Certainly it is clear to many people of color that Jews because of their white skin have had the opportunities to disappear into the mainstream in ways that people of color rarely have the luxury of doing.

2. With the escalating violence between the state of Israel and the Palestinian refugees and the cold war between Israel and many of the Arab nations, tensions between Muslims and Jews have grown alarmingly. At the same time, paradoxically, the prejudice against both Jews and Muslims has risen, exacerbated by the terrorist attacks on 9/11, the explosions in England and Spain in 2006, the wars in Afghanistan and Iraq, and the more diffuse war on terror.

Some Paradoxes of Prejudice against Arab Americans and Muslim Americans

An increasing number of U.S. citizens polled assume that many members of the Muslim community in the United States are potential terrorists or terrorist sympathizers, whether they are citizens of long-standing or recent immigrants. Currently, wearing a headscarf or having a noticeably Arabic-sounding surname or face can put a person in danger of rebuffs from neighbors, scrutiny from the authorities (the CIA, FBI, and local police) and, especially, the security screeners at airports.

In the most basic measure of negative attitudes, a 2006 poll (Ellis, 2006) found that 46 percent of Americans expressed generally unfavorable opinions of Islam. This is a new high and nearly double what it was in early 2003, In the same poll, 39 percent of the respondents said they felt at least some prejudice against Muslims and favored requiring Muslims, including U.S. citizens, to carry a special ID as a means of preventing terrorist attacks in the United States. (Editor's note: This practice would represent the same type of thinking that branded all Japanese Americans, regardless of how many years they lived in this country, as being potential spies or saboteurs, during World War II.) About 20 percent of those polled stated that they would not want a Muslim as a neighbor. At the same time, most of those polled admit to knowing almost nothing about this religion, and most did not personally know a Muslim person. Many of the respondents based their opinions on the activities of a small number of people they learned about from various media sources.

In addition, those who turn their negative thoughts into violent actions, such as committing hate crimes, often have not even known the actual ethnicity or religion of the victims they have targeted (Cohen, 2006; Ellis, 2006). Finally it is most paradoxical that, just as many Americans assume that a large portion of Muslims in America are sympathetic to Osama Bin Laden, both Muslims and non-Muslims often confuse people of the Jewish faith with citizens of the state of Israel and blame them for our conflicts with the Arab world. Though many American Jews might support the concept of a Jewish homeland, others are very critical of the way Israel deals with the displaced Palestinians and the encroachment of settlements in Palestinian territory. The important point is that American Jews, just like Muslim Americans, are most likely to put the interests of their own country above that of any other land.

Fighting Back against the Rising Tide of Prejudice

There are some positive developments in resisting the rising tide of prejudice:

1. *Across the United States, groups have organized special interfaith vigils and celebrations.* Many towns have enlarged or started human rights councils to protect the civil rights of citizens and to rally around those who have been harassed. Legal advocates have come forward to help when rights have been violated. Most importantly, conversations are taking place across religious lines.

2. *Many schools have begun or expanded their "teaching tolerance" curriculums.* The Southern Poverty Law Center of Montgomery, Alabama (SPLC, Teaching Tolerance), has expanded its twenty-year-old program that helps elementary and high school teachers promote tolerance in the classroom and learn how to respond to hate crimes. The classroom is one of the best places to counteract many of the misconceptions that lead children to adopt stereotypes and mistaken ideas about religious or racial groups.

3. Many colleges and adult education institutions have organized classes and seminars to teach the history of the Muslim and Arab countries, their contributions to world culture, and the shape and variations within the practice and beliefs of the adherents of the religion.

4. Advertisers and business owners who long ignored the substantial population of Muslim Americans are beginning to focus on ways to use the cultural aspects of the Muslim religion to help sell their products. An article in the *New York Times* (Story, 2007) reported that the chief marketing office of a large advertising agency plans to encourage clients such as Johnson & Johnson and Unilever to market to American Muslims by being sensitive to their special dietary needs, dress requirements, holidays, and so on. This kind of reaching out can say to a population, "We understand what your lives are like and we think you are an important part of this country" (while it makes more money for the companies). The *Times* article reports that a McDonald's in the Detroit area (which has a large Muslim population) now serves *halal* (meat prepared according to Muslim law) Chicken McNuggets, and Walgreens has added Arabic signs to its aisles. Ikea, which has recently opened a store in the area, has been touring local homes and talking to Muslims to figure out their needs. The store plans to sell decorations for Ramadan (just as it sells for Christmas, Easter, and Chanukah); it will include some catalog material in Arabic, and female Muslim employees will be given Ikea-branded hijab (a traditional part of Muslim dress) to wear over their heads, if they wish.

Advertisers that try to target their programs or ads to the Muslim community will face the same dilemmas they would face if selling to the Protestant, Catholic, or Jewish communities. Just what approach companies should take to reach Muslims is far from clear. The market is diverse, including African Americans, South Asians, Caucasians, and people from the Middle East, some very observant, others quite secular. Welcome to the wonderful world of diversity!

Affirmative Action

Affirmative action, a policy that gives some preference in admissions, hiring, or promotion to equally qualified members of underrepresented minority groups, is one of the mechanisms that attempts to redress the inequalities that minorities have historically encountered. African Americans have not only suffered from slavery, but also from many forms of discrimination since slavery. In housing, for example, the Federal Housing Administration, which underwrote one-third of all new housing construction from 1937 to 1972, required that all properties "continue to be occupied by the same social and racial classes" (Chappell, 2004). The Interstate Highway Act of 1956 directly displaced 330,000 poor families, mostly black. State laws and local zoning ordinances artificially concentrated both poverty and wealth and sharply segregated people on the basis of ethnicity and social class (Chappell, 2004).

Federal support for affirmative action has weakened since the 1980s and the policy continues to be under fierce attack. White people who feel they have been denied opportunities because of affirmative action have fought it in court on the grounds that it violates the equal protection clause of the Fourteenth Amendment. In a case brought against the University of Michigan, in 2003 the Supreme Court ruled that colleges could consider race in admissions but must also treat students as individuals and not accept or reject them solely on the basis of their skin color. Soon after this decision was handed down, Ward Connerly, a member of the University of California Board of Regents who led successful ballot initiatives in California and Washington states that ended racial preferences, contin-

ued his campaign in Michigan to put a similar measure on the ballot there. In Colorado the bill that would have banned affirmative action in the state was defeated by one vote in the Republican-controlled state senate. That one vote was cast by Senator Lew Entz, a Republican, who crossed party lines to deliver the deciding vote. Senator Entz had a large constituency of Latinos, who favored affirmative action (Klein, 2004).

A 2009 CBS News/New York Times poll found 50 percent of the population in favor of affirmative action, with 41 percent opposed. Six in ten Republicans opposed such programs, while 67 percent of Democrats favored them. However, there was broader support for programs that make special efforts to help people from low-income backgrounds get ahead, regardless of gender or ethnicity. Eight in ten favored this, with just 15 percent opposed (Dutton, 2009).

While affirmative action is often divisive and cannot by itself achieve racial equality, we believe it is still an essential device to counteract institutional barriers to minority advancement. Ezorsky reports, for example, that 80 percent of executives find their jobs through networking, and over 86 percent of available jobs do not appear in the classifieds:

> Historic patterns of discrimination and segregation which exclude blacks from white neighborhoods, business and social clubs have locked blacks out of a remarkably high percentage of job opportunities simply because they do not have the necessary white contacts to learn of the jobs or to be considered for them. (Forman, 1992, p. 172, reviewing Ezorsky, 1991)

Furthermore, some hiring criteria, such as diploma requirements or standardized tests, often work against minorities. Many tests are culturally biased, drawing material from the white middle-class world. This bias can be overcome either by constructing culturally sensitive tests or by giving training in test taking. For example, the highest pass rate on the National Teachers' Exam is by graduates of Grambling University, which has a primarily African American student body. That has been attributed to the fact that the university requires its students to take a test-taking course (Hacker, 1992).

Even when they are hired, blacks are discriminated against through seniority-based promotions, layoff plans, and the "glass ceiling" (an invisible but real barrier to advancement) of tradition. Because they are the last to be hired, they are the first to be fired and among the last to be promoted (if they ever are).

Many universities have admission practices that favor upper-class people. Critics say that a policy of "legacy admissions," which gives preference to children of alumni, amounts to affirmative action for upper-class whites. President George W. Bush was admitted to Yale through a legacy policy, as he himself has admitted that he was not accepted to Yale on the strength of his grades. The legacy policy at Texas A&M University helped more than 300 white students qualify for admission every year but only about 30 blacks and Hispanics. After Texas A&M did away with affirmative action for minorities, the school decided that it was inconsistent to keep a legacy policy that favored white students and did away with that policy. Georgia and California have also ended legacy policies in their state schools (Talk of the Nation, 2004a).

Affirmative action has become a lightning rod that attracts people's anxieties about race. It "dominates the nation's obsession with race relations" (Holmes, 1997, p. 1) and seems to have become magnified out of all proportion to its real significance in people's lives. When public opinion polls ask whites whether they ever lost a job or a promotion or were denied college admission as a result of affirmative action, few say yes.

Affirmative action costs little in comparison with social services. It hardly affects the majority of Americans. Most students who are eligible for college are accepted, regardless of affirmative action (Holmes, 1997).

We can get some idea of what will happen when affirmative action is eliminated by looking at what has already happened in California, where Proposition 209 spelled the end of affirmative action in that state in 1997. There has been a dramatic decline in minority applications to medical and law schools at the University of California. Most applicants who were accepted did not enroll because they felt unwelcome. Just one of the fifteen blacks accepted to Berkeley's Boalt Hall law school enrolled in the fall of 1997. Only fourteen of the forty-six Hispanics admitted enrolled. The two Native Americans who were accepted turned the school down (Gorov, 1997). Hashona Braun, a black student at the law school, said, "We really don't feel welcome here anymore, and the people who aren't here yet feel even more unwelcome" (Gorov, 1997, p. A1). Michael Rappaport, dean of admissions at UCLA's law school, said, "Another way of looking at it is that there are fewer blacks in Boalt than at the University of Alabama in the days of George Wallace. That's what's so frightening" (Gorov, 1997, p. A1).

One of the many programs that was ended because of Proposition 209 was a state-funded program called CAL-SOAP, or California Student Opportunity and Access Program. The program's math classes aimed to give minority students an edge in math when applying for college. CAL-SOAP recruited about 200 seventh-graders a year who scored at least a 2.4 grade point average and then worked with them until they went to college. It also mentored and trained college students to work intensively with the teenagers. The program had a 100 percent college attendance rate. Norma Lara, a former CAL-SOAP participant and a student at the University of California at Berkeley, was the first in her family to attend college. She now worries about her thirteen-year-old twin sisters. Lara says that Proposition 209

> says we're all one big happy family in California. We're all equal. Our education system is great. But it's obviously not true. We don't have a level playing field. In order for everyone to have the same opportunity, the education system has to be equal. They have to reform the school system before they can take that away. (Katz, 1997, p. L7)

Some people argue that economic diversity is as important as racial diversity, and we need to refocus on a new kind of affirmative action based on social class. Affirmative action helps middle class more than low-income minorities. Low-income white people as well as low-income minorities are also disadvantaged in college admissions. In the 146 most selective universities, low-income students make up only 3 percent of the student body. In two-year colleges generally, about two-thirds of those from the top economic quartile go on to a four-year college, while in the bottom economic quartile, only about one-fifth do (Talk of the Nation, 2004b). This economic stratification is getting worse as colleges increasingly grant scholarship money on the basis of merit rather than need. As college tuition becomes more expensive, low-income students are increasingly priced out of college.

On a day when many of us celebrate our Thanksgiving festival, two children from the Wampanoag Nipmucs look across at the Mayflower replica. Native Americans gathered together for a day to mourn over the plight of their people since the Pilgrims landed.

IMMIGRATION

As the United States celebrated the 500th anniversary of Columbus's "discovery" of the nation, people from the First Nations reminded us that they had already "discovered" this nation and had been living in it for a long time before Columbus appeared at their shores. The rest of us immigrated here from another country, and the African slaves were forcibly brought here. Some Mexican Americans came with the territory when the United States won the Mexican American War in 1848 and annexed Mexican land in the Southwest. The following are vignettes about three children who immigrated after the Vietnam War and what it was like for them.

A twelfth-grade Lao Mien boy who immigrated from Laos at age 14 told an interviewer:

The school was so big! There was no one who could speak Mien and explain to me. My uncle had told me if I needed any help to go to the Dean. My teacher asked me something and I didn't understand her. So I just said "Dean, Dean" because I needed help. That is how I got my American name. She was asking me "What is your name?" Now everybody calls me Dean. It is funny, but it is also sad. My name comes from not knowing what was going on.

A ninth-grade Filipino girl who immigrated with her parents declared:

Our parents don't come [to school functions] because they don't know any English. I don't even tell them when they are supposed to come. They dress so different and I don't want our parents to come because the others will laugh at them and tease us. We are ashamed.

A Cambodian boy who immigrated was reminded of his past:

In an elementary school in San Francisco, a teacher is playing "hangman" with her class as a spelling lesson. One "Limited-English-Proficient" (LEP) student, a Cambodian refugee, bursts into tears and becomes hysterical. Later, through an interpreter, the teacher learns that the student had witnessed the hanging of her father in Cambodia. (Portes & Rumbaut, 1990, pp. 180–181)

People immigrate because they need work or perhaps their own countries are at war or in crisis. Sometimes, as with the legacy of the war in Vietnam, our own country has helped to bring about the crisis conditions. Ultimately the problem of immigration would have to be solved by stabilizing countries' political situation and by ending world poverty. Yet instead of alleviating poverty, some national and international policies have increased poverty in underdeveloped nations:

The United States supported repressive military dictatorships in the Southern cone between 1964 and 1985 leading to waves of political refugees and exiles. The U.S.'s wars against nationalist and leftist movements and governments in Central America in the 1980s set millions of migrants in motion. Then in the 1990s the North American Free Trade Agreement (NAFTA) between Canada, Mexico and the United States, had a devastating impact on the Mexican economy, ruining poor farmers who also migrated to seek work in the United States. More generally, the Washington Consensus, the regime of neoliberal globalization imposed on Latin America by the United States, the International Monetary Fund and the World Bank resulted in a more or less continual crisis of their economies causing high unemployment and persistent poverty, which has driven more and more farmers and workers to seek work in the United States. (La Botz, 2007)

IMMIGRATION IN THE UNITED STATES

Some Background to the Current Situation

The United States has more immigrants in the country today than at any other time since 1910, the high tide of the great European immigration that began in the 1880s. Almost 12 percent of the U.S. population today is made up of foreign-born individuals—more than 33.5 million people. Over half come from Latin America, one-quarter from Asia, and most of the rest from Europe, with others from the rest of the world. Minorities now make up one-third of the U.S. population:

> The U.S., with a population of 300 million people in October 2006, accepts over one million legal immigrants every year, with the nations of Mexico, China, India, Philippines and Cuba providing 37 percent. However, in addition, an estimated 500,000 immigrants also enter the United States illegally each year, most coming from Latin America. The United States today has over 10 million undocumented immigrants, though nobody knows for sure how many. (Some estimate the number as 12 million.) Close to 60 percent come from Mexico, while almost a quarter come from Latin American countries. About 10 percent come from Asia." (La Botz, 2007)

Illegal immigrants often suffer sweatshop-like working conditions and low pay because they are afraid that if they complain they will be reported to immigration authorities and deported. Barbara Ehrenreich (2007) describes how some domestic workers who are undocumented immigrants are treated like slaves by rich Americans.

Fluctuations in Immigration Policy

The immigration policy of the United States has fluctuated between the country's need for labor and people's xenophobia and fear of losing their jobs to foreigners; it has also been influenced by foreign policy. When the country needed workers in the nineteenth and early twentieth centuries to build the railroads, work in the mines and the steel mills, and weave cloth, it especially welcomed European immigrants for these jobs. African slaves were brought in primarily to work on southern cotton plantations. Chinese immigrants were brought in to help build the railroads in the West, especially for menial work that white men refused to do.

After the railroads were built, the country no longer wanted Chinese people and passed restrictive legislation to keep them out. They didn't even allow the Chinese men who had built the railroad to be present when the golden spike was driven to mark the joining of the two railroads (Hsu, 1971). This was one example of the rising tide of racist fears that led to the United States excluding people of color. Some of the fears were fueled by competition for jobs. Organized labor feared that Chinese laborers would be used as strike breakers, which did sometimes happen.

Immigration policy in the United States has always made distinctions by race, ethnicity, and socioeconomic class. Japanese people were excluded in 1907, except in Hawaii where they were needed as agricultural workers. In 1924, the United States adopted a national-origins system that limited admissions from each European country to 3 percent of the foreign-born population here as of the 1910 census. That resulted in favoring northern Europeans over southern and eastern Europeans for nearly half a century. Most Asians were still excluded, but there were no limits on migrants from the Western Hemisphere (Schmitt, 2001b).

The eugenics-based racism that produced the restrictive 1924 immigration law increased the distance between white and black people. White immigrants bought homes in racially-restricted areas, resulting in all-white neighborhoods, and a kind of American apartheid.

The civil rights movement helped to achieve more fairness in immigration policy. The Immigration and Nationality Act of 1965 eliminated racial criteria and replaced country-by-country quotas with a system that awarded lawful permanent resident status* based largely on family or employer sponsorship.

The author Calvin Trillin, a connoisseur of ethnic food, is grateful for the Immigration Act of 1965 because it brought in a rich variety of ethnic food. He says, "I have to say that some serious eaters think of the Immigration Act of 1965 as their very own Emancipation Proclamation" (Trillin, 2001, p. 42). Immigration policy before 1965 "reflected not simply bigotry but the sort of bigotry that seems to equate desirable stock with blandness in cooking. The quota for the United Kingdom was so high that it was never filled. Asians were, in effect, excluded" (p. 42).

But the pendulum swung again in the 1980s. The Immigration Reform and Control Act, passed by Congress in 1986, was a response to increasing concern about illegal immigration, particularly across the Mexican border, but also from other war-ravaged Latin American countries. Now employers can be fined and sentenced to prison for hiring illegal aliens. That is why, if you start a part-time job at a restaurant or store, your employer will ask you to give proof of your citizenship.

The act has contributed to discrimination against both legal immigrants and illegal immigrants. Many employers hire and then exploit illegal immigrants, forcing them to accept substandard wages and working conditions because they fear deportation. Employers also sometimes assume that anyone who has a Spanish name or speaks English with an accent is an illegal immigrant, and so they refuse to hire immigrants who actually have valid work permits (Schaefer, 1989).

The Immigration Act of 1996 provides for "expedited removal" of immigrants and represents a major change in the country's treatment of immigrants. Columnist Robert

---

*Someone with Lawful Permanent Resident (LPR) status can work without limitation, travel in and out of the country, and petition for spouse and children. After five years as an LPR, he or she can apply for naturalization and become a U.S. citizen. If married to a U.S. citizen, the LPR can apply for citizenship after three years instead of five years.

Since the end of the Vietnam War, the United States has received many refugees from that country. A worker facing a client who has lived in that culture should try to learn about how this legacy will affect his or her attitudes and values.

Kuttner sees it as one aspect of a growing police state. Kuttner (1998) says that under the provisions of the act,

> legal permanent residents who make innocent technical mistakes face Kafkaesque nightmares. Hundreds of U.S. married couples have been separated for years because a foreign-born spouse neglected to fill out paperwork.
>
> People guilty of only technical lapses have been led off in handcuffs and jailed. Legitimate Canadian and Mexican business people, including corporate board members, have been barred from entering the United States and treated like common criminals because they lacked some immigration form.
>
> Other long time legal residents have been deported abruptly because of minor legal problems decades ago. The law disdains due process, makes judicial appeal almost impossible, and reinforces the thuggish tendencies of the Immigration and Naturalization service. (p. F7)

The 1996 law changed the rules for about 300,000 refugees from Nicaragua, El Salvador, and Guatemala who fled civil wars in the 1980s and were given temporary protection from deportation. The law made it more difficult to stay in the country ("Flaws in

Immigration Laws," 1997). The law made it harder for people to go back to the country and reenter this country. It also stipulates that legal immigrants who leave the country and then return—even after a brief vacation—may be subjected to harassment and imprisonment without due process if they have any criminal record. This includes the most minor infractions. Unauthorized use of cable television service, for example, can be treated as an "aggravated felony" under the new law, and the Immigration and Customs Enforcement (ICE, formerly a part of Immigration and Naturalization Service, INS) may detain legal immigrants and begin deportation proceedings against them for it (*The Progressive*, 1997).

The Justice Department's attempt to speed deportations of thousands of immigrants convicted of crimes in the United States was dealt a setback in 1999 when the Supreme Court let stand Court of Appeals decisions that gave those immigrants the right to judicial review of their cases (Vicini, 1999).

The Immigration Act of 1996 and the benefit-cutting effects of the Personal Responsibility Act created panic in the immigrant community. Immigrants and their advocates fought back through both legal and political means. Lawyers in California challenged the law's income requirement as unconstitutional and discriminatory (Lewis, 1997). The twenty members of the Hispanic Congressional Caucus mobilized their resources to fight both the immigration law and the cuts in benefits of the Personal Responsibility Act. Congress and the president decided that they had gone too far in attacking immigrants and in 1997 they eased some of the immigration curbs of the law.

The fierceness of the anti-immigration sentiment was beginning to abate before the 9/11 terrorist attacks. The AFL-CIO, in an 180-degree policy turn, shifted from denouncing illegal immigrants as a threat to American workers, to calling for a general amnesty for them all (meaning they could stay and join a union) (Pertman, 2001). Some states have granted drivers' licenses to illegal immigrants. Virtually no business owners worried at all about being fined for hiring illegal immigrants. Cecilia Munoz, vice president of policy for the National Council of La Raza, the largest Hispanic civil rights organization, says, "Frankly, they'll take anybody they can get and undocumented workers are often the only ones willing to accept such poor wages" (Pertman, 2001, p. D2). Much of the shift in attitude stemmed from the need for workers. Offering driver's licenses to illegal immigrants so they can get to work benefits not only the workers but also the employers who need them (Pertman, 2001).

After the attacks on the World Trade Center and the Pentagon, fears about terrorist attacks led the White House and Congress to move rapidly toward making immigration laws tighter. The reversal, which came just as the administration had considered loosening its policies, sent a chill through legal and illegal Latino immigrants. Maria Blanco, national senior counsel for the Mexican American Legal Defense and Educational Fund, said, "People are very disappointed that, so soon after the debate seemed to be moving forward on immigration, it has taken a few steps backwards. Latinos don't want to be tainted by this broad brush" (Sterngold, 2001, p. A20).

In 2008, Congress authorized the Secure Fence Act, a multi-billion dollar plan to build hundreds of miles of fencing along the southern border of the United States to stem the flow of undocumented immigrants from Mexico (NOW, 2008). The bill was controversial. An organization of mayors, county commissioners, and economists, named the Texas Border Coalition, filed a federal lawsuit opposing the wall and asking for the constructions to be halted. Two environmental groups, Sierra Club and Defenders of Wildlife, supported the suit. Many homeowners complained that the wall cut through the middle of their properties. The president of the University of Texas said she had not been consulted about plans to build the fence, and it would leave the campus's technology center and golf course on the Mexican side of the fence (Archibold & Preston, 2008).

Although Homeland Security didn't build the full 700 miles of fence originally planned, it did tighten up gaps in the fence where immigrants had found easy access. It became increasingly dangerous for immigrants to cross the border as they had to travel longer distances in the hot sun.

Border patrol agents are aggressive in catching and deporting immigrants, and sometimes killing them. On April 1, 2011, Arizona activists marched against the increasing use of excessive and sometimes lethal force against illegal immigrants, and even Hispanic citizens. Three teens have been shot and killed while trying to climb the border fence (Medrano, 2011).

Many immigrants have died while trying to cross the desert and some activists have gone into the desert to give them water and directions, and to rescue them. One of those is Lois Martin, a retired social work professor. Following is an interview with her.

Savior in the Desert: Interview with Lois Martin, Volunteer Worker for Three Undocumented Immigrant Support Groups on the Arizona/Mexico Border*

Barbara Schram

INTERVIEWER: I know that you are a retired faculty member from an undergraduate social work program and before that you were a counselor at the Veterans Administration, a teacher in Africa as well as at many other agencies in the human service field. Why did you decide to spend your retirement years volunteering in the Sonora Desert in Arizona?

LOIS MARTIN: For many years I have been concerned about the problems facing immigrants from Latin America. I read about the terrible number of deaths of Mexicans that occurred in the Sonora Desert. That area is the border between Tucson, Arizona and Nogales, Mexico. So, when I moved to Arizona, I began volunteering, with Humane Borders, which was started in 2000 by two local ministers. Volunteers regularly drive four-wheel trucks across the vast dry

expanses of the Sonora Desert to refill the water stations we have built and also to leave barrels of water along the paths that Mexicans trying to get into this country, might follow, Many migrants, unable to get legal entry visas for the United States, walk for days (actually mostly at night when the risk of being found by the U.S. border guards is lower) across this stretch of desert. It is one of the few areas on the border that does not have a fence yet and it is less patrolled by the U.S. border guards than other stretches of the border between New Mexico and California. But, it is a torturous journey with temperatures often in the 100-degree range and no sources of drinkable water. There are no houses or other landmarks, so many of these seekers lose their way and die from dehydration, Often they get separated from their families or the group they

*This interview was originally published in *New Politics*, Winter 2011.

are crossing with. They fail by the wayside due to weakness or illness and their fellow migrants often cannot wait for them. Sometimes they are abandoned to die by the so-called, coyotes, criminals who smuggle people across the border for cash and then dump them in the desert, stealing both their money and their lives.

INTERVIEWER: What are the other groups you work with?

LOIS MARTIN: I have gone out into the desert with volunteers from the Samaritans. They focus mainly on locating lost or sick migrants and administering emergency medical treatment, or in the most critical cases, transporting them to hospitals in Tucson. If they recover they will be sent back to Mexico. I have taken first responders training, so although I am not a doctor or nurse, I can do some basic first aid and know how to treat dehydration. The third group I volunteer for is the newest one, No More Deaths. It was started in 2004, primarily by a bunch of young people who were outraged at seeing more and more dead bodies in the desert. The Border Patrol, which keeps a count of the so-called illegals who have died during the crossing, estimates that there have been at least 250 deaths this past year. That number reflects only the bodies they have actually found! Rev John Fife, the co-founder of the other two migrant support groups, says that the number of dead is probably much higher. He also said that ten years ago there were almost no deaths recorded. He asserts that the U.S. government has created a gauntlet of death where only the strongest survive. He believes that the Border Patrol knows how life-threatening the desert crossing in this area is, but it thinks that the threat of death will keep others from trying to enter Arizona. So, the volunteers from No More Deaths have set up shelters in several places in the desert where the migrants can get some food, some rest in the shade, and even maps that might keep them from getting so lost.

INTERVIEWER.   Since it is so dangerous to try to enter the United States illegally (and many Americans believe it is also wrong to do so) why do so many Mexicans (and occasionally other nationalities) try to do this? Why don't they wait for legal visas like other prospective immigrants do?

LOIS MARTIN: First of all most of these people who undertake the journey are desperately poor. They are trying as best they can to simply put food on the table for their families. Many were farmers who lost their land or who came to the border areas to work in factories that have now closed their doors and moved to places where labor is even cheaper than in Mexico. Surprisingly, globalization, which should help a poor country, has made their lives more difficult. An enormous amount of cheap food (our surplus crops) floods into shops in Mexico. The small farm owners cannot compete with American agribusiness companies in price, and so they lose their farms and lay off their workers. Finally, the waiting list for visas to enter this country legally is very long. Applying for a visa costs much more money than these people can raise and frankly they don't stand much of a chance of being accepted, even if they get the money and are able to travel from their homes to Mexico City where there is an American Embassy. U.S. visas usually go to professionals who have the special skills we need or who are sponsored by employers in the United States. The paradox of all this is that there are plenty of farm owners in the United States who count on low priced labor to plant and harvest the crops. There are also contractors who count on Mexican laborers for their building projects. Once they slip across the border into this country most find jobs and family members to help them.

INTERVIEWER.   What happens to the folks who get caught without documents crossing the border or living in the states without the proper papers?

LOIS MARTIN: Well, that is another very upsetting part of the story and it varies a lot according to where they are apprehended. If the Border Patrol finds them in the American part of the Sonora Desert they put them in trucks and drive them across the border to Nogales, which is the nearest Mexican town. That is a whole other problem. Once brought there they rarely have any money left to buy food or pay the bus fare back to their home village. They are virtually stranded. Nogales is full of impoverished people trying to survive .... Of course that leads to drug dealing, gang formation and the like. The volunteer workers from No More Borders have set up some centers in Nogales and work with a branch of the Mexican government to try to help these folks make contact with family and find a way to get back home if that is what they want to do. If Mexicans are found to be illegally in other parts of the United States, they are frequently imprisoned, sometimes for long periods of time before they are repatriated. I have interviewed many of these folks and their stories are heartrending. One young man was brought to the states as a young child. His parents never had legal status so he did not have it either. At the age of 25 years, with a steady job and a family he was picked up on a minor traffic violation in an urban center. When it was discovered that he wasn't legal, he too was literally dumped in Nogales, without being able to notify his employer or his family. . . .

INTERVIEWER: What are your future plans with the support programs?

LOIS MARTIN: My new project is to create a network around the country of former volunteers who can help those folks who are being held in deportation centers in various cities. Sometimes the deportees need someone to help them obtain back salary that is owed to them by their former employers or they need legal representation. We also need to improve our ability to monitor the abuses of over zealous border guards and of course we need to lobby Congress for genuine immigration reform.

INTERVIEWER: How does the Border Patrol react to the support and advocacy work the volunteers do?

LOIS MARTIN: Well obviously, they don't approve of what we do. They see us as interfering with the performance of their jobs. Now that Border Patrol is under Homeland Security they have stepped up their activities. Sometimes they cite us for littering, when they see us leaving water jugs. We have to waste the time of volunteer lawyers defending against the citations they issue.

INTERVIEWER: This all sounds like very draining work. What keeps you going?

LOIS MARTIN: I would have to answer it is people who give me the courage to continue my work. I have met some of the most amazing strong decent people among those seeking entry into the country. A group of five men I interviewed in Nogales came across a woman in the desert who was dying. Even though it meant they would be caught and sent back to Mexico, they carried her for several days till they could get to the Arizona border where she would get medical help. Of course each of the volunteers experience moments of feeling overwhelmed with despair but, luckily, there is always another volunteer to buck you up. The young people who work with us are especially inspiring. It gives me hope for the future to see such dedication. This is the most satisfying work I have ever done. I hope to keep doing it as long as my strength holds out.

According to the 2010 Census, about 30,000 people who are not American citizens are held in immigration detention on any given day, including children. (Fox News, 2010). Of the 80,000 unaccompanied immigrant children seeking entrance to the United States each year, approximately 75,000 are deported upon arrival. These children confront U.S. state and immigration officials who tend to be "oppressive and terrifying rather than reassuring and protective." The few who are allowed to stay are transferred to the Office of Refugee Resettlement Division of Unaccompanied Children's Services, but some children are thrown into detention facilities where they must await the outcomes of their immigration cases behind bars (Alejandra, 2010).

For several months in 2006 and 2007, the ICE carried out immigration raids in factories, meatpacking plants, janitorial services, and other workplaces employing immigrants. ICE called the factories "crime scenes" because immigration law forbids employers to hire them. This made the public think of the workers as criminals, although immigration violations are civil violations, not criminal violations. Many of the workers were deported and some were separated from their children. However, the employers received only light reprimands and none went to jail. (Immigration courts are civil courts. That is why foreign nationals in deportation proceedings have no right to court-appointed counsel even though the proceedings "feel" criminal. They do have a right to due process; the Constitution protects all persons in the Unites States, not just citizens or LPRs.)

The Southern Poverty Law Center investigated guest worker programs that allow labor contractors to maintain blacklists of workers who work slowly or demand their rights. "Public interest lawyers spend years in court, trying just to get back wages for cheated immigrants. Meanwhile, the Department of Labor almost never decertifies contractors who abuse workers" (Bacon, 2007). After agents raided Swift & Co. meatpacking plants, Homeland Secretary Michael Chertoff told the media the deportations would show Congress the need for "stronger border security, effective interior enforcement and a temporary-worker program." Bush wants, he said, "a program that would allow businesses that need foreign workers, because they can't otherwise satisfy their labor needs, to be able to get those workers in a regulated program" (Bacon, 2007 p. 1).

According to Bacon (2007):

> **Guest worker programs** are low-wage schemes, intended to supply plentiful labor to corporate employers, at a price they want to pay. Companies don't recruit guest workers so they can pay them more, but to pay them less. (p. 2)

guest worker program   A program that contracts immigrants to work for a specified time in the United States for a particular job, but does not hold out any promise of citizenship.

The Current State of Immigration Reform

In 2007, a compromise immigration bill was co-sponsored by Senators Ted Kennedy (Dem.) and John McCain (Rep.). The bill proposed to gradually change a system based primarily on family ties, in place since 1965, into one that favors high-skilled and highly educated workers who want to become permanent residents. Low-skilled workers would largely be channeled to a vast new temporary program, where they would be allowed to work in the United States for three stints of two years each, broken up by one-year stays in their homeland. At the time, there was a backlog of 4 million people who had applied to come to the United States legally (Archibold, & Preston, 2007).

The bill was very controversial. Some conservatives called it an "amnesty" bill and opposed any effort to legalize undocumented immigrants. Pro-immigration advocacy groups lobbied lawmakers to reject the bill, saying it would place onerous restrictions on illegal workers who want to win legal status, hurt efforts to unify immigrant families, lead to more enforcement raids and greater militarization of the border, and erode basic due process rights. Among those who favored the bill was Microsoft Corporation CEO Steve Ballmer, who threatened to move more high-tech jobs out of the country if electronics corporations didn't get more contract migrant labor (Bacon, 2007).

The bill did not pass. Anti-immigration sentiment, already strong, became even stronger in 2010 when Arizona passed a law that directed police to check the immigration status of anyone they suspect is in the country illegally. The law also made it a state crime to be an illegal immigrant. The law inflamed the national debate over immigration and led to boycotts against the state. The Obama administration sued the state.

Emboldened by the passage of the nation's toughest law against illegal immigration, Russell Pearce, the Arizona senator who sponsored the measure, put forth a proposal to deny U.S. citizenship to children born in this country to undocumented parents. Legal scholars laughed at the proposal and warned that it would be blatantly unconstitutional, since the Fourteenth Amendment guarantees citizenship to anyone born in the United States (Price, M., 2010).

Immigrants and their advocates worked to provide an avenue of citizenship for the children of undocumented immigrants by sponsoring a bill called the "Dream Act" in Congress. It was first introduced in the U.S. Senate in 2001and re-introduced there and the House of Representatives in 2009.

The Dream Act would have provided a path to citizenship for children of undocumented immigrants who had come to the United States as children with their parents. If they have been in the country continuously for at least five years, the students would be given the opportunity to earn permanent residency while they complete at least two years of college or two years in the military within a six-year period. It would also allow them to pay the resident rate of college tuition, rather than the non-resident rate that they now pay.

One of President Obama's campaign promises was to get the Dream Act passed, but Congress failed to pass it in 2010. President Obama promised that he would get it passed in the next Congressional session.

CASE EXAMPLE

Despite a Supreme Court decision, those banished for minor crimes may not return

VINCENZO DONNOLI was 9 when his family immigrated legally to New York. He stayed there, attending high school, marrying and divorcing, running a landscaping business and having five children. But at 51, alone and jobless, he is back in Pomarico, the hill town in southern Italy where his father was a shepherd, as a deportee banned for life from returning to the United States.

His offense: two misdemeanor convictions for possessing small amounts of cocaine, in 1988 and 2006, both guilty pleas resolved without jail time.

Retroactively, the immigration authorities added them up to equal an "aggravated felony" that required Mr. Donnoli's automatic deportation in 2009 (Bernstein, 2010).

In June 2010, the Supreme Court ruled that legal U.S. residents with minor drug convictions are eligible to have an immigration judge weigh their offenses against other factors in their lives and decide whether to let them stay. But deportees who were denied such a hearing had no means to get one. The U.S. Board of Immigration Appeals said it had no jurisdiction over any case after deportation. Government regulations prohibit any motion to reopen the case of someone who has left the country. The Obama administration, which planned to deport a record 400,000 people in 2010, showed no eagerness to open the door.

Daniel Kanstroom a professor at Boston College Law School, said, "The Supreme Court has said in a series of cases that the government's theories of deportation have been wrong for years. And yet the legal system has not developed a mechanism to right the wrong for the thousands of people who have been wrongly deported." No one knows how many cases could be affected, but public defenders' associations estimate that there could be several thousand. More than 34,000 noncitizens were deported for drug-related offenses in 2008 (Bernstein, 2010).

KEY ELEMENTS IN THE IMMIGRATION DEBATE

Immigration is a very complex issue and many people are confused about it. It engenders fierce, and sometimes vitriolic, debate. The following are some arguments and issues to consider as you think about the fate of immigrants in the United States.

1. *Some people compare present immigrants unfavorably to past immigrants.* Much of the anti-immigration sentiment seems to reflect a belief that there are "good" immigrants and "bad" immigrants. People whose ancestors arrived in the late nineteenth and early twentieth centuries believe that this qualifies them as real Americans. The early immigrants are remembered as good, hardworking assimilators, while the new ones are "inferior, parasitic, and implacably foreign." (Walker, 1995, p. 62)

While watching a festive parade in a small Mexican village, we need to look past the colorful costumes and think about the onlookers. Many of them unable to find work will make the torturous trek across our borders.

2. *People who are anti-immigrant sometimes exaggerate the health problems that immigration creates.* For example, in 2005, Lou Dobbs (a popular TV commentator) claimed there had been 7,000 cases of leprosy in this country over the preceding three years and attributed it to immigration. He said, "The invasion of illegal aliens is threatening the health of many Americans." In 2007, Dobbs appeared on the *60 Minutes* TV show. Researchers for the show had checked his statement, and on the show, interviewer Leslie Stahl said there didn't seem to be much evidence for it. The official leprosy statistics do show about 7,000 diagnosed cases—but over the preceding thirty years, not the preceding three years. James L. Krahenbuh, the director of the National Hansen's Disease Program, said, "It is not a public health problem—that's the bottom line . . . the 137 reported cases last year were fewer than in any year from 1979 to 1996" (Leonhardt, D., 2007, p. 2).

3. *People who oppose immigration say that immigrants are costing taxpayers money and taking advantage of such programs as welfare, Medicaid, and food stamps.* Alabama politicians who believed this passed a bill called The Deficit Reduction Act, which required a birth certificate or other proof of citizenship from people before they could qualify to continue or begin receiving Medicaid. The bill resulted in more than 5,000 people losing their Medicaid coverage for failing to provide a birth certificate or other proof of citizenship. Children were the largest group affected, and black people were disproportionately affected.

Alabama's Medicaid Commissioner said that Alabama doesn't have a large problem with illegal immigrants trying to cheat the state out of Medicaid dollars. Most of the people who lost their Medicaid were not immigrants, but they were unable to provide the requested documentation. After Medicaid officials realized what was happening, people were put back on the rolls (Angus Reid Global Monitor, 2007).

A bill was filed in the Texas legislature in 2007 that would not only deny public services to undocumented immigrants but also strip their American-born children of benefits as well. The bill challenges the Fourteenth Amendment to the U.S. Constitution, ratified in 1868, which states that all persons born in the United States are citizens of the United States and of the state where they reside (Bustillo, 2007).

A look at the facts contradicts exaggerated fears about the cost of immigration. The largest cost is the border control and law enforcement measures, according to a study by the Congressional Budget Office. But this study concluded that legalization of immigrants would contribute tens of billions to the federal Treasury (Milligan, 2007).

Illegal foreign-born residents contribute in many ways, such as paying Social Security and Medicare taxes. In 2002, illegal immigrants paid $6.4 billion in Social Security taxes for benefits that they would never receive (Steinberg, 2005). Illegal immigrants are not eligible for need-based aid, except limited emergency medical care and children's health care, as well as elementary and secondary schooling. Legal immigrants must be in the United States lawfully for five years before being eligible for aid such as food stamps and welfare. The exceptions are refugees, including Cubans, who are immediately eligible for federal need-based aid. U.S.-born children of illegal immigrants are citizens and are also eligible for such assistance (Milligan, 2007).

Undocumented immigrants were guaranteed access to a free public education (Kindergarten through twelfth grade) by a 1982 Supreme Court decision, but the 1996 Immigration Act prohibits undocumented immigrants from accessing any postsecondary education benefit. As a result, many states have blocked access to in-state tuition for undocumented students. An estimated 60,000 undocumented students graduate from the nation's high schools each year, and most are unable to pay out-of-state tuition at their public college, except in the few states that allow them to pay in-state tuition (Lazarin, 2003).

4. *The people who benefit most economically from immigration, aside from the immigrants themselves, are businesses and the wealthy.* David Card, an economist who studies immigration, said that when he moved to San Francisco, he noticed some changes from his lifestyle in Princeton. "In California, a professor has at least a gardener and maybe two, someone who cleans his house, and two or three day-care workers," he said (Cassidy, 1997, pp. 41–42).

The rich, despite the law prohibiting that practice, hire many undocumented immigrants. Two prominent cases involved people who were nominated for federal attorney general—Zoe Baird and Kimba Wood. President Clinton withdrew their nominations because it became known that they had employed illegal immigrants as nannies.

Aside from the economic benefits, we all derive enormous social and cultural benefits from living in a country with a large and diverse immigrant population.

5. *Some pro-immigration advocates minimize problems with immigration, such as its effect on African Americans.* In his article "Immigration, African Americans, and Race Discourse," Stephen Steinberg points out that African Americans have been historically disadvantaged by immigration (2005). After the Civil War, the 4 million emancipated slaves could have filled the labor needs of the North. However, businesses preferred to import white immigrants from Europe:

> Here was a missed opportunity to integrate blacks into the industrial labor force during the critical early stages of industrialization, and the failure to do so, set the nation on a path of racial division and conflict that continues to this day. (Steinberg, 2005, p. 43)

Steinberg (2005) questions whether the influx of another 25 million immigrants since 1965, and the millions more of undocumented workers, has "again made the Negro 'superfluous,' undercutting black progress. Here was another missed opportunity to integrate blacks into the economic mainstream" (p. 44).

Steinberg makes it clear that he is not calling into question the rights of immigrants. He says, "I am the grandson of immigrants, and the new immigrants have as much right to be here as I do, and to claim all the rights of their adopted nationality" (p. 45). But, he says, the rights of immigrants should not override the rights of African Americans.

> Immigration should be part of a national manpower policy that protects the interests of immigrants and native workers alike. A laissez-faire policy that relegates millions of immigrants to the vagaries of the "free market" only throws low-wage workers in pitiless competition with each other, and closes off avenues of mobility into more desirable job sectors. As a result, current policy exacerbates existing inequalities along lines of race, ethnicity, gender and class. (p. 53)

Some people have used the argument that immigration hurts African Americans in order to oppose legalizing it. Bill Fletcher, a board member of *Black*

Commentary, argues against this, saying that immigration is not the main reason for the problems of black workers:

> The economic reorganization which many people call de-industrialization has had a devastating impact on the Black worker, disproportionately so. The elimination and/or shrinkage of manufacturing jobs in urban centers has had the effect of hollowing out entire communities, destabilizing Black America economically, socially and politically. . . . Black America has witnessed the disintegration of segments of its working class and professional/managerial class.
>
> This crisis began well before there was a significant influx of immigrants, and it is this crisis that has been haunting us. This crisis has been compounded by the right-wing political assault on the public sector, largely through anti-tax revolts and privatization, which has resulted in both a decline in services and a decline in employment with the latter also having a disproportionate impact on the Black worker. (Fletcher, 2007)

Fletcher points out that where immigrants are displacing African Americans, as in construction, that is happening because employers want lower-paid, non-union workers. The solution is not to oppose immigration, but to oppose the lowering of wages:

> The problem is the system. And, just as African American workers were used in certain industries as low-wage workers in the late 19th and early-to-mid 20th centuries, in order to undercut higher paid workers, this changed dramatically through a combination of unionization and the Black Freedom Movement. . . . Low-wage workers will not be competitors if they cease being low-wage workers, i.e., if they are unionized and gain power in their workplaces or jobs. (Fletcher, 2007)

Resistance to Cutbacks in Immigrant Rights

Immigrants and their advocates have mobilized to resist their discriminatory treatment. Inspired by the freedom riders of the civil rights movement, thousands of immigrants participated in an Immigrant Workers Freedom Ride in October 2003. With organizing support from the AFL-CIO and other groups, they marched and demonstrated in 116 cities across the country, including New York City, where over 76,000 rallied to publicize a host of immigrant rights issues from equal rights in the workplace to immigration reform (Northeast Action, 2004).

Demonstrations occurred between March and May of 2006 in Los Angeles, New York, Chicago, and dozens of other U.S. cities in the largest social and political demonstrations in U.S. history. "As the immigrants left work or school to join the marches, in some areas the protests, dominated by Latino workers, had the effect of a general strike, shutting down local businesses and blocking traffic in the centers of major cities. Many carried signs reading, 'We are workers, and not criminals' and 'No Human Being is Illegal'" (La Botz, 2007, p. 24).

The AFL-CIO opposes guest worker programs and says immigrants should be given permanent residence visas, so they have labor rights and can become normal members of the communities they live in. America's labor unions see immigration reform as essential both to organizing immigrants and revitalizing the labor movement and to winning greater political power. "Almost every major labor organization has now taken a position calling

CATA, a migrant farm-worker organization, was one of the many groups from across the nation rallying for comprehensive immigration reform in Washington D.C. on March 21, 2010. The photo was taken by Franklin Soults, a member of the Massachusetts Immigration Reform Advocacy Coalition (MIRA), a group that also attended the rally.

for "comprehensive immigration reform" meaning legalization and a path to citizenship for those now here and guest worker programs with legalization and citizenship provisions" (La Botz, 2007, p. 32).

Religious sanctuary, the practice of being protected from deportation by staying in a church, has been revived. It was invoked in the early 1980s to prevent thousands of Central American refugees from being deported. In 2006, an undocumented Mexican cleaning woman, Elvira Arellano, invoked the ancient right of sanctuary in a Chicago church in a desperate effort to avoid being separated from her seven-year-old son, Saul, a U.S. citizen. Arellano said, "I was desperate. I remembered how Joseph and Mary were given sanctuary. I asked my church for sanctuary, and they agreed" (Sahagun, 2007 p. A2).

Discussing the repressive Immigration Act of 1996, a *New York Times* editorial ("Hard Times for Immigrants," 1997) warns of the threat to all of us:

> This law won political passage by attacking an unpopular group. That, historically, is how more widespread deprivations of rights have started. The law is not just an assault on vulnerable people who deserve protection from abuse, but a threat to the liberties of all Americans. (p. 14)

THE CONTROVERSY OVER BILINGUAL EDUCATION IN THE SCHOOLS VERSUS ENGLISH IMMERSION

Ron Unz, a California multimillionaire software developer and former Republican candidate for governor, sponsored California's Proposition 227, a voter initiative called English Only, aimed at eliminating bilingual education across the country. He spearheaded the defeat of bilingual education in California, Arizona, and Massachusetts, but in Colorado it was voted down. While Unz has funded many anti-bilingual education ballot initiatives, the English Only movement is led principally by a multimillion-dollar conservative organization called U.S. English (DePass, 2003).

Unz scoffs at research that says it can take up to seven years for students to become fully fluent in academic English. He proposed that they be given just one school year—180 days—to learn the language intensively before being mainstreamed into all-English classes. This program, called "English immersion," has eliminated most bilingual education programs. Those programs help LEP children keep up with their required academic competencies, such as math, history, and science, while learning English through ESL (English as a Second Language) classes. Many LEP students learn to speak conversational English within the first two years, but research consistently shows that it takes four to seven years before most students are able to use English to learn academic subjects and perform on par with native English-speaking peers (Massachusetts English Plus Coalition, 2003).

Unz and his supporters argue that the offspring of earlier immigrant groups were forced to learn English, and doing so helped them to succeed. Opponents of English immersion have argued that the initiatives are too punitive because teachers could be personally sued for speaking Spanish in the classroom. The program would also eliminate dual-language programs and parent choice. Latino opponents argue that the attack on bilingual education is an attack on their cultural identity. Many African Americans joined the struggle to save bilingual education, remembering their own struggles to become literate, being able to vote, and having equal access to education.

Arizona implemented a program called Structured English Immersion (SEI). In this program, significant amounts of the school day are dedicated to the explicit teaching of the English language, and students are grouped for this instruction according to their level of English proficiency. The English language is the main content of SEI instruction. Academic content plays a supporting, but subordinate, role. English is the language of instruction; students and teachers are expected to speak, read, and write in English. Teachers use instructional methods that treat English as a foreign language. In Arizona, SEI is required of all schools in the state.

Opponents of SEI brought the case to the Supreme Court, arguing that the Arizona SEI model is not research based and "contradicts the large and credible body of research evidence on effective instruction and school practices that produce high levels of academic achievement for ESL." In 2009, the Supreme Court ruled in ***Horne v. Flores*** that research on bilingual education instruction showed that there is documented, academic support for the view that Structured English Immersion (SEI) is significantly more effective than bilingual education (Mora, J., 2010). The Arizona SEI program continues.

Guidelines for Ethnic-Sensitive Human Service Work

People who have been discriminated against because of their skin color have reason to be mistrustful of white-dominated organizations, including (and sometimes especially) human service agencies. Unfortunately, agencies have a poor track record in eliminating discrimination. After the Civil War, such agencies were almost always segregated and poorly funded. The Charity Organization Society served very few people of color. In her autobiography, *The Woman Warrior*, author Maxine Hong Kingston (1977) gives an example of the feeling of alienation created by discrimination:

> Lie to Americans. Tell them you were born during the San Francisco earthquake. Tell them your birth certificate and your parents were burned up in the fire. Don't report crimes; tell them we have no crimes and no poverty. Give a new name every time you get arrested; the ghosts* won't recognize you. Pay the new immigrants twenty-five cents an hour and say we have no unemployment. And, of course, tell them we're against Communism. Ghosts have no memory anyway and poor eyesight. (pp. 184–185)

The distrust that discrimination creates affects all of us. An individual white person may never have discriminated against anyone, but the climate of fear that prejudice has created in a society may make every white person seem like a potential enemy until he or she proves to be trustworthy.

Of course, people of color can also express prejudice against white people when they believe that all white people are alike. And some light-skinned black people are prejudiced toward dark-skinned black people.

GUIDELINES TO BUILD TRUST

1. *Learn the culture.* You can learn a lot about a person's culture by asking sensitive questions. No matter how much you have read about a group's culture, you won't know how it affects the specific person you are talking with until you ask.

   Here is an example of an incorrect assessment of a person based on a lack of understanding of the culture:

   > A young Southeast Asian woman was ordered by the court to attend therapy for repeatedly shoplifting merchandise from a neighborhood grocery store. The young woman had been in this country less than a year and spoke minimal English. She was assigned to a white therapist who after several failed attempts to get the young woman to communicate her reasons for shoplifting informed the court that the client was withdrawn, uncommunicative, and appeared depressed.
   >
   > A young Asian paralegal working in the office at the time read the case and was able to shed some light on the problem. The Asian paralegal related that the item, repeatedly stolen from the store, sanitary napkins, was not openly displayed, or sold in public markets in the country of the Southeast Asian woman. . . . In the woman's country, it was considered highly improper for women to publicly acknowledge

---

*In this story of Chinese people in San Francisco, the Chinese regarded all non-Chinese people as "ghosts" because they seemed as alien as ghosts. Interestingly, her protagonist saw black ghosts as more friendly than white ghosts.

their monthly menses. Purchasing the pads outright or explaining her reasons for taking this product would have caused this woman great embarrassment and public shame, not to mention a breach of her ethnic and cultural values on proper conduct. (Boyd, 1990, p. 160)

2. *Create a welcoming atmosphere.* As soon as they walk in the office, people should receive the message that they are welcome. If the agency's clientele includes people who speak a language other than English, posters on the wall and informational brochures should be written in that language. The magazine rack could include local African American and Hispanic newspapers. Gays and lesbians will be reassured to see their own newspapers or magazines.

3. *Acknowledge the validity of their suspicion of you.* Research has shown that people from minority groups are less likely to return to a human service agency after the first interview than are people from the dominant culture.

   Maxine Hong Kingston (1977) talks of the reticence about discussing intimate affairs within the traditional Chinese culture, but she indicates that it was a much more serious offense to share secrets with the ghosts:

   They came nosing at windows—Social Worker Ghosts; Public Health Nurse Ghosts; Factory Ghosts recruiting workers during the war (they promised free child care, which our mother turned down); two Jesus Ghosts who had formerly

The U.S. government continues to build fences and increase security patrols to stem the flow of illegal immigrants pouring across the border with Mexico. At the same time, we rely on these immigrants to fill jobs as farm workers, domestics, day laborers, and other low-paying but vital jobs.

worked in China. We hid directly under the windows, pressed against the base-board until the ghost, calling us in the ghost language so that we'd almost answer to stop its voice, gave up. (p. 98)

The person who suffers from discrimination feels a dreadful wound, a humiliating degradation, and if he or she is strong enough to feel it, tremendous rage. (Most tragically, the individual may turn the rage inward against him- or herself.) *The Autobiography of Malcolm X* (Malcolm X & Haley, 1966) presents a vivid literary description of these feelings. An outstanding leader of the American Muslims in the 1960s, Malcolm X was assassinated in 1965. He gives us a personalized account of his disillusionment as he writes bitterly about the state welfare workers who claimed to be "helping" him. In the course of his life, he encountered a good many helping agents of the state and found them wanting. When he was a young boy, his father was killed by whites, and his mother had to struggle to keep the family together, eking out a living by cleaning houses. She hated to accept welfare assistance, but when she finally gave in, she was harassed by welfare investigators. They termed her *crazy* for, among other behaviors, refusing to eat pork, even though she was a Seventh Day Adventist and it was against her religion to do so. They also opposed her seeing a male friend, even though this made her happier than she had ever been before. Malcolm X held them partially responsible for his mother having to go to a mental hospital, and he said they were as vicious as vultures (Malcolm X & Haley, 1966).

Malcolm was placed in a foster home, and this is what he thought about that:

Soon the state people were making plans to take over all of my mother's children. . . . [A] Judge McClellan in Lansing had authority over me and all of my brothers and sisters. We were "state children," court wards; he had the full say-so over us. A white man in charge of a black man's children! Nothing but legal, modern slavery however kindly intentioned. . . . I truly believe that if ever a state social agency destroyed a family, it destroyed ours. We wanted and tried to stay together. Our home didn't have to be destroyed. But the Welfare, the courts, and their doctor gave us the one-two-three punch. And ours was not the only case of this kind. (pp. 20–21)

When Malcolm was about to enter the third grade, an English teacher asked him what kind of career he wanted. Malcolm said that he wanted to be a lawyer, to which the teacher replied:

"You've got to be realistic about being a nigger. A lawyer—that's no realistic goal for a nigger. You need to think about something you can be. You're good with your hands—making things. Everybody admires your carpentry shop work. Why don't you plan on carpentry?" (p. 36)

By raising people's consciousness about discrimination and pressuring organizations to change, Malcolm X and other civil rights activists helped reshape social services as well as other institutions of society. Since the 1960s, many ethnic groups have developed their own agencies and professional organizations, creating changes in the policies and hiring practices of white-dominated agencies. The National Association of Black Social Workers was formed in 1968 to improve the provision of social services to blacks and to spur the recruitment of black social workers (McRoy, 1990).

4. *Emphasize strengths in individuals and communities.* This is especially true when working with people who have been treated as inferior because people have already focused so much on their weaknesses.

   Emphasizing people's strengths is equally important when working with communities as it is when working with individuals. John McKnight (1992) believes that some professionals who claim to help others actually harm them by focusing on their weaknesses. He has developed a questionnaire designed to discover people's talents and a map called the Neighborhood Assets map designed to highlight a community's strengths. It lists strengths—cultural organizations, individual capacities, religious organizations, citizens' associations, home-based enterprise, social service agencies, and so on. McKnight also designed a map called the Neighborhood Needs map, which lists pathologies—slum housing, crime, mental illness, teenage pregnancy, alcoholism and substance abuse, illiteracy, and so forth. The Neighborhood Needs map is the one that people use most often, but it ignores the strengths of a neighborhood.

   The liberation movements of oppressed people have revealed their enormous strength and courage. Thousands of people have literally put their lives on the line to win their freedom. And there is the quieter but enduring strength they show by protecting their families and communities in the face of constant oppression and discrimination.

5. *Find sources of power.* Lorraine Gutierrez (1990) recommends that the worker and client together engage in a "power analysis" of the client's situation to assess the structural barriers a client faces and the potential strengths available to the client:

   > Clients and workers should be encouraged to think creatively about sources of potential power, such as forgotten skills, personal qualities that could increase social influence, members of past social support networks, and organizations in their communities. (p. 152)

6. *Use the network of family and friends.* The first strength of any group is family and friends. Many minority groups rely heavily on this support. Some students of Native American culture say that it is hard for Native Americans to accumulate resources, not only because of their low-wage work and unemployment but also because of their ethic of sharing with other family members.

   African American communities have a long tradition of mutual help. Carol Stack (1974) showed that although many families in a poor black community in the Midwest were officially designated "single-parent" families, they were actually extended-kin networks, sharing in child care. This was more typical among the very poor. As families became upwardly mobile, they were less likely to share their resources. Urbanization and industrialization have weakened extended-family networks for all of us. But the African Americans who shared their resources despite their poverty were expressing a higher value of caring and compassion than more affluent people, who were more preoccupied with "getting ahead."

7. *Use the community networks.* The ethnic neighborhood itself is a support system in which people can share their language, religion, food, memories, and experiences. Networks include neighbors; churches; political, social, and service organizations; newspapers; stores; restaurants; and bars where people gather. The church is an especially important support network in the African American community. In Hispanic

communities, the spiritualist is an important support to many people, and many Native Americans turn to the tribal medicine man or woman for support and guidance. In her study of ethnicity in the social services, Shirley Jenkins (1981) found that, in general, minority people prefer going to services in their own community staffed by bilingual and bicultural workers.

8. *Understand patterns of informality and friendliness.* Pedro de Cunha, a Portuguese American social worker, tells of common complaints among Portuguese immigrants regarding social agencies: "The social workers are too cold, too distant. They are never there when we need them; They don't really help; They never found us a job or an apartment" (de Cunha, 1983, p. 15). One of the problems, says de Cunha, is that the Portuguese come from a country that has not developed specialized helping agencies; instead, people tend to turn to the priest for help. The priest has many roles. Not only does he minister the Word and the sacraments, "but he is also the financial adviser, the marriage counselor, the funeral director, the father, the judge, the social worker" (p. 15). The grocer not only sells groceries; he "would not sell any groceries if he did not listen to the problems of his patrons, if he did not extend credit to those who cannot pay immediately, if he did not read the illiterate their mail" (p. 15).

    People from an agrarian society are more likely to expect help to come in the context of a personal relationship. They expect helping roles to be diffuse rather than specific. De Cunha recommends that workers be trained to understand their clients' background and expectations and become more comfortable being less formal and friendlier.

9. *Be willing to share yourself.* Workers need to be willing to share something of their own lives with clients, to make the atmosphere of the agency warm and nurturing. Perhaps you could serve refreshments or coffee, be willing to accept small gifts, be flexible about time, be willing to make an occasional home visit, and have at least one worker for walk-in clients.

10. *Understand clients' lack of resources.* People's poverty affects how they use social services. They may not even have the carfare or gasoline to get to the agency. If they do have a car, it is probably in poor repair and often breaks down. Clients may not be able to keep appointments because they can't afford baby-sitters or fear losing their job if they take any more time off from work. They may not have a checking account, so cashing a check might be costly and time-consuming.

11. *Give concrete services and information.* Because of their lack of resources, poor people need concrete help. Whatever your agency's activities, your knowledge of benefit programs might be more important than any mental health counseling. One formerly homeless woman said that she was in homeless shelters for four years because the workers there did not tell her about housing vouchers or how to get welfare benefits. It was not until she discovered a welfare rights group that she learned about her rights from other welfare recipients.

12. *Learn how to empower.* Oppressed people are relatively powerless. Women, who have less power than men, head a large proportion of poor families. Women of color make up a large proportion of the clientele in human service agencies. They are more than twice as poor as white women. They are overrepresented in low-status occupations and have on average a low level of education. The stress of having poor housing or no

housing, insufficient food and clothing, and inadequate access to health services takes a toll on their physical and mental health. Human service workers need to deal with the psychological effects of their clients' powerlessness and provide concrete resources to better their lives (Gutierrez, 1990).

The literature on empowerment indicates that small-group work is the ideal method for empowerment. In these groups, members receive support, reduce self-blame, learn new skills, and provide a potential power base for action (Gutierrez, 1990).

WORKING WITH WOMEN

Many college women, even those who do not call themselves feminists, are benefiting from the gains won by the women's movement, even though they might not be aware of the struggles that other women went through to win them. Although women have many struggles to endure before they achieve equality with men, the gains of the women's movement have been enormous. The women's movement has touched every aspect of women's lives. Women have fought for equal pay and advancement and have often won. They have defined some lower-paying jobs as equal in worth to higher-paying men's jobs, even though the jobs may be different, and won some major **comparable worth** lawsuits. They have entered fields previously defined as men's work, and some have argued that housework and caretaking, traditionally defined as women's work, should be paid wages and shared equally by women and men.

comparable worth
A practice of describing and paying wages for jobs according to their inherent difficulty and worth in order to help equalize women's wages with men's.

The Women's Movement and New Social Services

Some of the most dramatic changes in the helping process were brought about by the women's movement. By 1994, shelters for victims of domestic violence had been established in more than two-thirds of the 3,200 counties in the United States (Carden, 1994). Women also created rape crisis centers; women's health centers; feminist mental health services; and services for displaced homemakers, women substance abusers, older women, single parents, and ethnic minority women (Gottlieb, 1980a, 1980b).

Feminists created new social services because they believed that traditional social agencies were not in tune with women's needs. Drawing on Freudian psychology, traditional workers said that a woman who is battered by her husband might have a sado-masochistic need to be beaten. But feminists would assert:

- The husband is committing a criminal act by beating his wife and must be legally restrained.

- No one has the right to beat her for any reason.

- She might be staying with him because she has:
    No place to go
    No money
    Children to care for
    No marketable work skills
    Shame because of the stigma of being abused

- She might need supportive therapy, but she also needs:
    A court order
    A shelter
    A support group
    A job or an adequate welfare grant
    Decent, affordable child care
    Help in finding an apartment

Feminists also redefined rape. Traditional common wisdom assumed that women inadvertently "asked for it" with their behavior. Feminists defined rape as an act of violence used to control women. They told women that they didn't ask for it or deserve it. They taught women how to struggle against it and how to do the healing grief work to recover from the assault. They told women that there is no "allowable" rape—forced sex by a date or by a husband is rape. They also lobbied to change the laws that made reporting of rape another form of assault on self-esteem. In fact, feminists looked at every aspect of services to women and suggested new ways to view old problems.

Feminists took a new look at depression, menopause, and premenstrual syndrome and critiqued the way the medical establishment deals with them. Depression, for example, is much more prevalent among women than among men. Feminists believe this is due to the socialization of women rather than to any inherent female characteristics. This socialization includes:

- A stress on self-effacement, which leads to low self-image
- A sense of powerlessness and of lack of control over one's life
- Difficulty in asserting oneself
- An inability to cope with stress (Gottlieb, 1980a, 1980b)

Women, socialized to be passive rather than assertive, have a much greater tendency to turn their aggression on themselves than do men. This is generally considered to be one of the dynamics of depression.

Understanding New Theories about Women

There has been a flowering of feminist theory since the late 1960s that has had a profound effect on the human services. Feminist psychologists challenged some of the traditional Freudian theory that claimed women were "naturally" masochistic, passive, and envious of men. These psychologists helped women to feel comfortable with the assertiveness they had been taught to repress since childhood.

Feminist research has helped women reclaim their sexuality by rejecting the Freudian assertion that the only "healthy" orgasm is a vaginal one (Koedt, 1971). Ann Koedt showed that the vagina has few nerve endings and that the clitoris is more sensitive to sexual stimulation than is the vagina. (Kinsey had also shown this in his research on sexuality in the 1940s, but it was not until feminists focused on female sexuality that these findings became more widely understood.)

"Women's intuition" and emotionality, which had been ridiculed as inferior to the male world of "hard facts," won a new respectability when feminist researchers, in comparing women's ways of learning about the world and relating to people with men's ways, concluded that women's ways were different but might make for a more peaceful world.

How Feminist Theory Influences Our Practice

Feminist therapy introduced a sociological and political perspective that had been lacking in most traditional therapy, helping women as well as men to realize that their problems were not just personal troubles but also social issues. The women's movement was built through consciousness-raising groups, a model that was adopted by other self-help groups.

Yet much of feminist theory and practice has been focused too narrowly on middle-class white women, neglecting issues of social class and ethnicity. Women of color have written a wealth of literature and contributed research about their lives, and some white feminists realize that the assault on poor women is an assault on all women, particularly at a time when the middle class is eroding. However, although the leadership of the National Organization for Women (NOW) has been militant in fighting against repressive welfare policies, most NOW members have not been involved in welfare rights struggles.

That may be changing. When more than 1 million people attended the March for Women's Lives in Washington D.C. on April 25, 2004, there was the largest representation of women of color and low-income women that has ever attended a women's march. Cheri Honkala, a welfare recipient and leader of the Kensington Welfare Rights Union in Philadelphia, gave a moving speech about welfare and emphasized that choice for women involves not only the right to have an abortion but also the right to choose to have children and the resources to care for them. Toni Bond, a low-income woman who had been helped to get an abortion by the National Network of Abortion Funds, spoke powerfully about the importance of financial help to women who can't afford an abortion. (There has been no federal funding for abortions since the Hyde Amendment was passed in 1974.)

Feminist scholars have analyzed social policies and social services, exposing institutional sexism. Abramovitz (1988) described how Social Security regulations discriminate against women. By giving larger pensions to those who earned more in their work, women,

This woman's strength shines through her face. If she came for help, a worker would need to recognize that strength and help the woman draw on it.

who almost always earn less than men, receive lower pensions. Thus gender inequality is perpetuated through the life cycle. Further, by not including caretaking work as wage earning, homemakers are unable to draw a pension of their own but must rely on their husband's record of earnings.

A Gender Analysis of Child Welfare

More than thirty advocates in New York City, employing a feminist perspective, challenged the way the child-welfare system treated battered women and their children in New York City (Coalition of Battered Women's Advocates, 1988). This group mobilized after the widely publicized death of a child, Lisa Steinberg, and the battering of her mother, Hedda Nussbaum, by the child's father, an affluent attorney.

The coalition pointed out that women are often afraid to cry out for protection to the police or social service agencies for fear that they will lose their children or that the batterers/child abusers will retaliate against them or that no one will believe them. Often, service providers remove battered children from the home where a man is abusing his wife rather than force the abusive husband to leave. This can result in children being victimized a second time by the trauma of foster placement (Coalition of Battered Women's Advocates, 1988). Many of these women and their children become homeless when they leave the batterer. Subsequently, many mothers are charged with neglect, and their children are taken from them and placed in foster homes.

The advocates demand that the police and judges take women's complaints seriously, removing the batterer from the house rather than the nonabusive mother and her children, and doing everything possible to prevent further harassment. They call on agencies to provide more safe, short-term emergency refuges for women and children and ask that funds used for foster home placement be used instead to provide violence-free homes for the children. Advocates also ask that service providers receive training in domestic violence, as few know even the basic facts about it.

The advocates lobby for more affordable housing, more community-based services such as day care, legal assistance, health care, substance abuse prevention, child abuse prevention, and job-training programs. They point out that undocumented abused women are especially at risk for fear of deportation, that lesbian mothers fear losing custody of their children if they ask for help, and that women of color face racist assumptions that their children are at a higher risk of abuse. Domestic violence affects women of every race and class, yet the poor, who are disproportionately non-English speaking and/or black, are most often victims of involuntary intervention by police and child protective workers (Coalition of Battered Women's Advocates, 1988).

WORKING WITH GAYS AND LESBIANS

In Chapter 5, we discussed the value judgments people make about gays and lesbians. Here we will put forward some guidelines for human service workers in their work with this particular population.

Betty Carter (1995), a feminist therapist and director of the Family Institute of Westchester, tells the story of how her awareness was raised about the needs of lesbians:

My awareness was . . . raised by a trainee . . . who was an out lesbian. At the end of the training, she told me what a wonderful experience she had because we had all been so open to her sexual orientation. "But can I tell you something?" she asked. I said, "Of course," knowing I didn't want to hear it. "You know, there is nothing that would let anyone like me know that I would be welcome here." I was totally startled because I had never thought about how stigmatized groups do need a sign that they are welcome. She pointed out that we had no featured course on gay or lesbian families. (p. 12)

Since then, Carter has instituted a training program on lesbian and gay family issues. She seeks the expertise of lesbians, who understand the complex issues of being marginalized because they experience it in their lives. After hearing the personal experiences of women in lesbian families, heterosexual workers who used to wonder why they needed to spend so much time and attention on lesbians and gays "had an awakening: 'Oh, I never thought of how heterosexism would have affected someone that way'" (Carter, 1995, p. 14).

Carter uses what she calls a "gay lens" to take special notice of the effects of stigma. She says, "Until you tell me otherwise, I will assume everyone in your family and work system takes a dim view of your not being straight" (p. 15). The gay lens helps to define the task of therapy, which is empowerment. Carter tries to help them deal nondefensively and strategically with the way in which they are pushed to the margins of society, and she helps them to recognize it as a product of ignorance and fear that has almost nothing personal to do with them.

The gay lens not only helps Carter and other therapists work with lesbians, but it also helps them work with heterosexuals. Every new way of viewing issues has far-reaching implications for human service work. Carter describes how she uses the gay lens:

The "gay lens" challenges the way roles in relationships have become gendered. For example, if you ask about the division of chores in a heterosexual couple, it becomes clear who is in charge of the emotional life of the relationship and who will fix the boiler when it breaks. When we therapists are working with couples in a heterosexual relationship, most of us have stopped even questioning the fact that it is 99.9 percent of the time the woman who is in charge of emotions and the man who is in charge of the boiler. But when we look at lesbian and gay couples, it becomes clear that this isn't inevitable, because here you have two people of the same sex who have ungendered these roles. The emotional life still gets taken care of; the boiler still gets fixed. So how do they decide who does what, if it's not based on gender?

. . . The gay lens gives you a way to look at how same-sex couples manage to work these things out, and you can apply it to straight clients. This is no small matter. A fair division of housework and parenting would make life much more harmonious for heterosexuals. Most of our clients come in with some irritation or larger complaints about these matters, and I know I had started to believe it was impossible to achieve equity between men and women around the house. But then I'll see a gay or lesbian couple and suddenly realize it's not impossible for people to be total partners. Or, just as I'm about to give up on men for being exasperatingly unemotional, I'll work with a gay couple and be amazed by how open and tender they can be in expressing their feelings. (p. 14)

After Vermont legalized same-sex civil unions in 2000, researchers surveyed nearly 1,000 couples, including same-sex couples and their heterosexual married siblings. The researchers found that same-sex relationships, whether between men or women, were far more egalitarian than heterosexual ones. In heterosexual couples, women did far more of the housework, men were more likely to have the financial responsibility; and men were more likely to initiate sex, while the women were more likely to refuse it or to start a conversation about problems in the relationship. Controlling and hostile emotional tactics, like belligerence and domineering were less common among gay couples (Parker-Pope, 2008).

Gays and lesbians won a major victory in 2004 when the Massachusetts Supreme Court declared that the equal protection clause of the Massachusetts Constitution called for full-fledged marriage rights—and nothing less—for same-sex couples. Massachusetts became the first state in the nation to legalize same-sex marriages. Since then, Washington DC and four other states—Iowa, New Hampshire, Vermont, and Connecticut—have legalized same-sex marriages.

Gays and lesbians won another victory for equality in 2010 when Congress struck down the "Don't Ask, Don't Tell" rule of the military that forbade servicemen and women from admitting they were gay or lesbian while they served in the military.

WORKING WITH PEOPLE WITH DISABILITIES

People with disabilities are an oppressed group because they have not been allowed equal access to society's benefits. They are a minority both in absolute numbers and in the political meaning of the term.

People with disabilities have an acronym for people who define themselves as nondisabled: They call them TABs—temporarily able bodied. This word vividly reminds us that being able-bodied is only a temporary condition. Any one of us could get hit by a car when crossing the street or get hurt when skiing or diving. The recognition of our own vulnerability helps to lower that psychological barrier between "them" and "us," which is the biggest handicap of all.

The liberation movement of the disabled population challenged the arbitrary distinctions people make on the basis of differences in physical or mental functioning. Members declare that the real disability lies in society's unwillingness to structure its architecture, public facilities and space, cultural offerings, and so forth to open up the entire society to everyone regardless of their level of functioning.

New Definition of Disability Influences Our Practice

psychosocial model of disability   A model that looks at the entire environment of the person, including social attitudes, attitudes of other individuals, and the society that the able bodied have created.

Traditional models of disability focused on labeling each "disease," defining what people can do in the job market, and what functions a person can and cannot perform. The new model is a **psychosocial model of disability**. It looks at the entire environment of the person, including social attitudes, attitudes of other individuals, and the society that the able bodied have created (Roth, 1987). The psychosocial model of disability was recognized in public policy by Section 504 of the Rehabilitation Act of 1973, the first civil rights act for disabled people, as well as by the Education for All Handicapped Children's Act of 1975. That law required disabled children to be mainstreamed with able-bodied children as much as possible. The most sweeping civil rights law for disabled people was the Americans with Disabilities Act of 1990.

At different times in history and in different places, certain disabilities could be or were viewed as somewhat of an asset, not as a liability. Dostoyevsky, who had epilepsy, describes the aura preceding an epileptic seizure as a route to cosmic clarity. Julius Caesar had epilepsy in Roman times, when it was considered to be a holy disease. During the nineteenth century in the Western world, people with tuberculosis were considered especially refined, sensitive, and wise. If a character in a nineteenth-century novel was described in Chapter 1 as refined, sensitive, and wise, it was sure to be revealed by Chapter 8 that the character was dying of tuberculosis, or "consumption."

Obtaining an accurate count of how many disabled people there are is especially tricky because the number depends on whom you define as disabled. Some deaf people do not consider their deafness a disability because they are totally immersed in the deaf culture and take great delight in it. They would consider it a handicap to be deprived of that culture. When the deaf students at Gallaudet College for the Deaf successfully rebelled against a hearing person being chosen as president of the college, some of them declared that their deafness should not be defined as a disability and that they were as "normal" as anyone else. Neurologist and author Oliver Sacks (1989), who described that rebellion so vividly, tells of a community on Martha's Vineyard in Massachusetts in which so many significant citizens were deaf that everyone learned sign language. With no communication barrier, life was the same for the hearing and the nonhearing.

In 2008 there were 36,169,200 people in the United States who reported a disability, 12.1 percent of the population (Cornell University, 2008). In March 2011, the percentage of people with disabilities in the labor force was 21.0. The percentage of persons with no disability in the labor force was 69.7. The unemployment rate for those with disabilities was 15.6 percent, compared with 8.9 percent for persons with no disability (U.S. Department of Labor, 2011). There are a disproportionate number of disabilities among older people, poor people, people of color, and blue-collar workers. Disabled people are more likely to be unemployed or underemployed, and if they are employed, are more likely to earn less than able-bodied workers. They face discrimination in the job market and often have to navigate buildings not designed for their needs.

Six disabled Tennessee residents achieved a victory in 2004 when the U.S. Supreme Court declared that states can be liable for not making courthouses accessible. One of the people who sued was a man who refused to crawl or be carried up to a second-floor courtroom in a county courthouse to answer a criminal traffic complaint. He sued after the state charged him with failing to appear for his hearing (Greenhouse, 2004).

Human service workers who work with people with disabilities need to be informed about the eligibility guidelines for both Social Security Disability Insurance (SSDI) and Supplemental Security Income (SSI), as well as for workers' compensation, to make sure their clients get the benefits they are entitled to. Legal service lawyers who specialize in disability law can help with this.

Because applying for these benefits requires people to see and define themselves as disabled and thus unable to work, many people do not apply. This is a dilemma for both the client and the worker. On the one hand, clients are refusing needed income; on the other hand, people's self-definition and self-esteem are critically important to their mental health. Some people will accept general assistance even when the grant is much lower than SSI because they regard general assistance as short-term temporary help until they get a job.

SUMMARY

1. The election of a black president marked an advance in racial equality in the United States, yet this country is still far from a postracial society.

2. Racial inequality exists in housing and home ownership, health and health insurance, professional advancement, arrests and imprisonment, jobs, political representation, voting rights, and school segregation.

3. There has been a long struggle for equality in the United States, and the struggle continues.

4. Human service workers are faced with issues of diversity in all of their practice.

5. People who claim to be colorblind are actually ignoring an important aspect of a person's identity. They maintain white privilege by negating racial inequality.

6. Prejudice and discrimination may negatively affect people's feelings about themselves.

7. In order to fully understand people, we must understand their cultures.

8. The current theory about culture is bicultural theory, which assumes that people are socialized into their own culture and influenced by the dominant culture.

9. Having limited access to power defines a "minority group."

10. The United States has been run predominantly by white, heterosexual, Anglo-Saxon, English-speaking, middle- and upper-class able-bodied men. Those who differ have often suffered discrimination.

11. Latinos face discrimination sometimes on the basis of skin color and often because of not speaking English or because of speaking with limited fluency and an accent.

12. Acculturation is stressful, causing conflict between the older and younger generations in families.

13. Ethnicity, social class, and gender must be considered together.

14. In order to understand any group, we must understand its history.

15. Because minorities have been discriminated against, they are likely to be distrustful of white-dominated organizations.

16. Institutional racism is harder to change than individual racism because it involves interconnected systems and policies that perpetuate it.

17. The media often perpetuates stereotypes.

18. There are large differences within ethnic groups.

19. The drug war is a failed policy that resulted in the overincarcertion of drug offenders, most of whom are not dangerous.

20. Black men are sent to prison at thirteen times the rate of white men.

21. Discrimination against Arab and Muslim Americans has risen at an alarming rate since 9/11.

22. Most Americans know very little about the Muslim faith.

23. Discrimination against Jews has lessened since WWII, but they are still discriminated against in some neighborhoods, jobs, or social clubs.

24. Affirmative action has become a lightning rod that attracts people's anxieties about race.

25. The immigration policy of the United States has fluctuated between the country's need for labor and people's xenophobia and fears of losing their jobs to foreigners.

26. The 1996 Immigration Act, which provides for "expedited removal" of immigrants, represents a major change in the country's treatment of immigrants.

27. A study by the Congressional Budget Office concluded that legalization of immigrants would contribute tens of billions to the federal Treasury.

28. The Personal Responsibility Act of 1996 denied federal help to legal immigrants in the SSI, food stamp, and Medicaid programs. In 1997, some SSI and food stamp benefits were restored.

29. The immigration bill that was debated in the U.S. Senate in 2007 proposed to gradually change a system based primarily on family ties, in place since 1965, into one that favors high-skilled and highly educated workers who want to become permanent residents. Low-skilled workers would largely be channeled to a vast new temporary program.

30. The elimination of bilingual education programs was an attack on immigrants.

31. It is important to emphasize people's strengths rather than their weaknesses.

32. Family and friends are the most important supports for people.

33. Most minority groups are poor and therefore need concrete supports from human service agencies. Telling people about the benefits to which they are entitled empowers them.

34. Workers need to be willing to share themselves, be informal, be flexible about time, and be willing to make home visits.

35. Feminists have created alternative social agencies and new theories.

36. Feminist practice strives to be egalitarian.

37. Understanding issues that affect gays and lesbians not only helps them but can also give new insights into heterosexual behavior.

38. Five states have legalized marriage for gays and lesbians.

39. The Don't Ask, Don't Tell law that forbade gays and lesbians in the military from being open about their sexuality was struck down by Congress in 2010.

40. The new definition of disability does not accept the medical model; rather, it sees the problem as the reluctance of society to accommodate the needs of the disabled population.

41. The Americans with Disabilities Act of 1990 requires sweeping changes in accommodations for people with disabilities.

DISCUSSION QUESTIONS

1. What do you think is a good immigration policy for a nation? What guidelines would you use in setting up such a policy? The National Catholic Social Justice lobby NETWORK calls for "just reform of immigration policy" and "a just U.S. foreign policy that fosters economic equity and alleviates global poverty." What do you think would be a just reform of immigration policy and a just U.S. Foreign Policy?

2. The Massachusetts Supreme Court ruled that there was no "constitutionally adequate reason" why same-sex couples should not enjoy the same legal rights as others. Opponents of that rule say that it will destroy traditional heterosexual marriage. On what do they base that argument? What do you think are the pros and cons of same-sex marriage?

3. Exercise: In group discussion, name several social identity groups that you think influence people's lives. This could include race, ethnicity, gender, sexual orientation, class, physical ability, religion, age, and any other. Identify where you fit in those groups in a notebook. During class discussion, share this information to the extent that you feel comfortable doing so. Discuss how (or whether) people are oppressed, or feel oppressed, because of their social identity. (No one should feel under any pressure to share personal information.)

4. Exercise: In group discussion, students share information on the neighborhoods you grew up in and organizations you belonged to. How diverse were these neighborhoods and organizations? Discuss the reasons for their diversity or lack of diversity.

5. France has passed a law saying that Muslim girls are not allowed to wear head scarves in school, as this violates the principle of the separation of church and state and erodes national identity. What do you think of this law?

WEB RESOURCES FOR FURTHER STUDY

Teaching Tolerance

www.splcenter.org/what-we-do/teaching-tolerance

Created by the Southern Poverty Law Center in 1991, Teaching Tolerance supports the efforts of K–12 teachers and other educators to promote respect for differences and an appreciation of diversity.

Facing History and Ourselves

www.facinghistory.org

Since 1976, Facing History has been engaging students of diverse backgrounds in an examination of racism, prejudice, and anti-Semitism in order to promote the development of a more humane and informed citizenry. By studying the historical development and lessons of the Holocaust and other examples of genocide, students make the essential connection between history and the choices they confront in their own lives.

National Council of La Raza

www.nclr.org

The National Council of La Raza (NCLR)—the largest national Hispanic civil rights and advocacy organization in the United States—works to improve opportunities for Hispanic Americans.

National Association for the Advancement of Colored People (NAACP)

www.naacp.org

The mission of NAACP is to ensure the political, educational, social, and economic equality of rights of all persons and to eliminate race-based discrimination.

National Organization for Women

www.now.org

The National Organization for Women is the largest organization of feminist activists in the United States.

LGBT social movements

en.wikipedia.org/wiki/LGBT_social_movements

A discussion of the social movements of lesbians, gays, bisexual, and transgendered people.

Beyond Prejudice

www.beyondprejudice.com

This site provides an extensive discussion of prejudice by Jim Cole, EdD, who conducts workshops and presentations on reducing prejudice. Includes information on how to conduct discussions and workshops about prejudice, exercises, and quizzes.

Betsy Leondar-Wright

www.classmatters.org

Betsy Leondar-Wright was formerly the Communications Director at United for a Fair Economy. Her book *Class Matters: Cross-Class Alliance Building for Middle-Class Activists* helps activists collaborate better across class lines to build stronger movements for social change. Her web site gives advice that she has gleaned from interviews with activists, resources, and information about class and how it intersects with other identities such as race, gender, disability, and sexual identity.

SisterSong: Women of Color Reproductive Health Collective

www.sistersong.net

The SisterSong Women of Color Reproductive Health Collective is made up of local, regional, and national grassroots organizations in the United States representing four primary ethnic populations/indigenous nations in the United States: Native American/Indigenous, black/African American, Latina/Puerto Rican, and Asian/Pacific Islander. SisterSong does community organizing, self-help, and human rights education on reproductive and sexual health and rights.

Abortion counseling or referrals

www.prochoice.com

This site counsels women on their options when they are pregnant and explains what is involved in whatever choice they make.

National Abortion Federation hot line (English/Spanish): 800-772-9100

National Network of Abortion Funds (NNAF)

www.nnaf.org

NNAF provides support and technical assistance to local abortion funds, aids in the creation of new abortion funds in areas where they do not exist, and provides visibility and voice for women facing financial barriers to abortion.

Chapter 9

Interviewing

The following are excerpts from an interview conducted by Karen (K), a first-year student in an MSW program. Fran W. (FW) is the client, a twenty-six-year-old white female, mother of six-year-old Ann (A) and girlfriend of George (G).

K: You look sad.

FW: I am. I am angry with myself because G and I did coke on Friday.

K: What happened?

FW: Well, he was upset and we were on our way home and we just did it. . . . I am so stupid. I can't believe that I did that. And I am having these dreams. I am in this slum with really sleazy people and I am looking for coke, but I never get any.

K: First of all, I think that you should not be so hard on yourself. You were sober for two weeks when you were using every single day. You should give yourself credit for that. This has been an issue with you for a long time. You are addicted. Obviously, you are not going

to be able to just stop and you may slip a few times. What do you think the dream means?

FW: Well, like I said, it is the frustration of wanting it and not getting it. Morning and around dinnertime are real hard. I go to bed and my leg starts shaking. . . .

FW: I get angry with A. When we are playing a game, I will snap at her. I love A. I would do anything for her. I love G too but I would not give up my life so that he could live.

K: Have you ever done coke in front of her?

FW: NO! I don't think she knows. . . . I close the door, but I don't know.

K: Children are very perceptive. When you get angry and you take it out on her, you may want to say that it is not her fault.

FW: Yeah, but she must get sick of hearing that I am not angry with her, I am just going through a hard time.

K: I think that it would be beneficial for her to hear that it is not because of her. If you said it a million times it would be fine. . . .

CHARACTERISTICS OF AN INTERVIEW

In the above interview, the counselor, Karen, is engaged in purposeful communication with the goal of helping the client, Fran. A counseling interview is only one of the many kinds of interviewing that human service workers do. Every intervention that a human service worker uses—whether counseling one client or mobilizing a group to take social action—requires interviewing. All our work is built on planned, careful communication: talking and listening, making nonverbal gestures, or writing. In this chapter, we will discuss the basic elements and skills of interviewing.

Because this book is for the beginning human service worker, we will not focus on long-term counseling or psychotherapy interviews or on specialized treatment of children. Nor will we discuss the skills specific to research interviewing (though many of the skills we will talk about also apply to this area). These topics require experience and training beyond the beginning level.

We define a human service interview as an interaction between people that has a consciously planned purpose, structure, and goal and requires specific communication skills.

Purposeful Communication

Social conversations need not have any conscious goal. When we are having a casual chat with a friend, we generally don't have a fixed agenda about what we discuss. The conversation often ambles at a leisurely pace from one topic to another: the weather, what happened on the way to work, how we feel, the party we went to last night, gossip about friends, and so on. You talk because you enjoy being with each other.

An interview, on the other hand, has a purpose and a goal. You may engage in some small talk with clients to establish rapport, but they usually come to you for a specific service, or you reach out to them.

Focus and Structure

Each person involved in a conversation expects more or less equal attention. But in an interview, the focus is on the needs of the client. We would feel neglected or angry if a friend talked endlessly about his or her problems without bothering to listen to us in return. In an interview, however, skilled workers know how to stay in the background and encourage clients to say what is on their minds. This does not mean that interviewers never reveal anything about themselves; in fact, research suggests that it is useful to share a moderate amount of information about one's own life (Hepworth & Larsen, 1987, p. 998). Of course, the interviewer is responsible for keeping the interview focused on the client.

The structure of an interview varies according to the context in which it takes place, the individual client, and the phase of the helping process. Each interview is unique, but initial interviews always include (1) the beginning process of establishing rapport (which continues to some degree throughout the helping relationship), (2) opening the interview and making the contract, (3) exploring the issues, and (4) closing the interview and looking forward to the next steps in the helping process.

SPONSORSHIP

The **primary purpose** of the social agency shapes the focus and content of the interview. The focus of the Department of Welfare, for example, was broader before 1974, when workers were called "social workers" and could offer help for problems beyond financial need. Now workers are called "investigators" or "eligibility workers." Their function is narrowly focused on a client's financial situation. However, a multifunction agency, such as Child and Family Services, can have a broader focus in an interview because it is authorized to offer counseling for a broad spectrum of clients' needs. When an agency has a narrow focus, the worker can refer a client whose needs fall outside its scope to one that serves those needs.

In agencies that work with involuntary clients, interviewers need to be particularly skilled in helping people express anger or resentment, yet they must be able to stay on course with the

primary purpose
The main goal of an agency that determines the work it does.

main purpose of the interview. A worker also needs to be skilled in sorting out the issues inherent in situations that limit self-determination and in dealing forthrightly with those issues.

image of an agency
The reputation that a social agency has established in its community.

The public support and **image of an agency** also influence interviews. For example, because welfare benefits are kept low and the agency is chronically underfunded and understaffed, a Department of Welfare office often does not provide the privacy that people should have when discussing their personal affairs. Understaffing means that clients must often wait long periods for an interview, and sometimes an interview is more rushed and mechanical than it should be. Such working conditions can be demoralizing to both clients and workers. Even though a dedicated worker can conduct a superb interview in a stigmatized or underfunded agency, the pressure of the work and the drabness of the surroundings can encourage joyless and dehumanizing treatment of claimants. As a general rule, agencies that serve the poor are understaffed and poorly housed and do not give as much privacy or time to the clientele as do agencies that serve more affluent people.

SETTING

The focus and content of an interview are affected by the setting in which it takes place. Interviews can happen anywhere—in a locker room, on a street corner, or in a living room. Ideally there should be a logical relationship between what you are going to talk about and the place where you do the talking. For example, if you are chatting with a member of a women's basketball team in a locker room after a basketball game and she blurts out that her father beat her mother the night before during an alcoholic binge, you might suggest she go with you for a cup of coffee or a walk so you can talk in privacy.

Sometimes interviews take place in the home of a client with the television set blaring and the children within earshot as the parents talk about them. Even in our offices, we must often ask personal questions with little more privacy than a room divider. Although we can try to improve these conditions as a long-range strategy, we must deal with them from moment to moment the best way we can.

The following suggestions can help make an awkward situation more private and comfortable for the client:

- Try to assess the emotional state of the client to see what behavior would be appropriate. Lower the tone of your voice, lean forward, and listen intently so the client does not have to shout his or her information.

- If you are in an office with no privacy, apologize to the client or comment that you know he or she might feel uncomfortable in such a setting. Say that you're sorry about it and wish there were a more private space.

- Move your chair to the side of the desk so that it doesn't separate you from the person you are talking with. Have at your desk a plant or some objects that make it as attractive and personal as possible.

Skill and Awareness

Conversations and interviews differ in the level of skill each requires. It is true that people vary enormously in their interpersonal skills, and therefore some people carry on more creative conversations than others. Yet, as long as we can make ourselves understood, most of us don't think we must train ourselves to carry on social conversations. In order to become skilled interviewers, however, we need to learn a great deal about how people interact with each other. We need to assess behavior—to listen carefully not only to words but to shadings and nuances of tone, pitch, and volume—and to communicate our understanding of what we have seen and heard in a clear and concise way that shows we genuinely care about that person. Indeed, much of the skill in interviewing comes from awareness:

- Awareness of your own personality and the personality of the interviewee
- Awareness of your own expectations and those of the interviewee
- Awareness of your own cultural background and that of the interviewee
- Awareness of your own attitudes and values

We will discuss each of these separately, but remember that, in practice, no one factor can *really* be separated from all the others.

AWARENESS OF PERSONALITY AND STYLE

Because each interviewer and interviewee has a unique personality and style, there is no magic formula for interviewing. An outgoing person may be a more assertive interviewer than a quieter one, but both can be equally skillful. Fortunately, people are not programmed robots. Precisely because of our human capacity for spontaneity, there is always an element of uncertainty in what we will say and what others will say to us. Therefore, interviewing, depending as it does on words and gestures, can never be totally systematized in a scientific way and will always remain—to some extent at least—*an art*. We believe, however, that we can all learn to become more sensitive to others through studying our interactions and ourselves and through continual practice in self-discovery and effective communication techniques.

Self-discovery continues for each of us until we die. Unquestionably, however, some people are more sensitive than others, and a certain level of sensitivity is an absolute requirement in human service work.

Certain kinds of interviewers' behavior that could create barriers to communication include:

- Focusing on weaknesses rather than strengths
- The need to "rescue"
- Overly passive behavior
- Discomfort with emotion
- Anger
- Condescension

Focusing on Weaknesses

Some interviewers see the glass as half empty rather than as half full. These interviewers are less helpful than those who look for strengths. *At the core of mental health is self-esteem*, so we look for genuine ways of enhancing the interviewee's self-esteem. Sometimes we can find an interviewee's positive intentions even in undesirable actions. Then we can emphasize the intentions, not the undesirable actions. For example, you might say to a man who stole money in order to feed his family: "Although your stealing gets you in trouble, I understand that you are very worried about your family and want to help them. Let's discuss ways of supporting your family that won't get you into trouble."

Need to "Rescue"

An occupational hazard of human service workers is their need to rescue people, whether or not the clients want to be rescued. *We are supposed to be "doing with," not "doing for."* "Doing for" implies that the helper is superior and knows what is best for the helpee. "Doing with" implies a mutuality and equality.

rescue fantasy
A fantasy that envisions saving someone from his or her fate.

Children and extremely dependent adults are especially likely to evoke **rescue fantasies** in us. We often have strong feelings about what is acceptable parenting, and when working with children, we must curb any tendencies to be in rivalry with the children's parents.

Overly Passive Behavior

The amount of the interviewer's verbal activity will vary from one situation to another. Some interviewees talk easily and with little prodding; some need help in limiting or structuring their verbosity; others do not talk easily and need more encouragement from the worker. A worker who sits like a bump on a log gives the appearance of being uninterested in the interviewee or of having no structure or goal for the encounter.

Discomfort with Emotion

Some interviewers are uncomfortable with emotions, which makes it harder for the interviewee to express powerful feelings. This characteristic can show itself whenever the interviewee cries or expresses anger. To avoid dealing with the emotion, the interviewer changes the subject, talks about superficial things, gives false reassurance, intellectualizes about the problems, or becomes emotionally detached.

Anger

Because an interview is a human encounter, there will be times when the interviewer will feel angry with the interviewee. There could be many reasons for the anger. Perhaps something the interviewee says triggers some old resentment, or perhaps some personality trait annoys the interviewer. An articulate, assertive interviewer may become impatient with a passive interviewee; a laid-back interviewer may feel annoyance at an interviewee who is a compulsive talker.

Whatever the reason, it is important for interviewers to be aware of their anger and come to terms with it. When this happens, anger can be a useful tool. It is not helpful to express the anger impulsively and thoughtlessly to the interviewee, but anger can be used helpfully if the interviewer understands it. One author recommends recognizing "the inward side of a feeling":

> If the counselor feels bored with or angry toward a client, rather than express these feelings (the outer edge) that imply criticism or blame, he seeks to determine and to express deeper aspects of the feelings by asking himself, "Why do I feel this way?" In seeking the answer, he will discover that behind the boredom lies a positive desire to hear more personal and relevant information that can facilitate progress. Likewise, behind the anger lies disappointment in being unable to be more helpful to the client.

If we similarly analyze such feelings as impatience, irritation, criticism, or disgust, we will discover that the inward side of these feelings will consist of a desire that the client have a better and more fulfilling life, a desire that can be shared safely and beneficially. (Hammond, Hepworth, & Smith, 1977, p. 224)

Condescension

Condescension implies that the worker feels superior to the client. Workers are generally unaware of these feelings, but clients have their antennae attuned to them. A condescending attitude gives the message, "I know what is good for you. The fact that you are a client automatically guarantees that you don't know as much as I do about human behavior in general and your behavior in particular. You came to me because you want my expertise, and I intend to give it to you."

AWARENESS OF MUTUAL EXPECTATIONS

When two people come together for an interview, they bring with them the sum total of their past experiences and current expectations. This is their mental set. They bring anxieties, knowledge, misinformation, and hopes to the interview. They may be from different social classes, races, or ethnic backgrounds. Their ages, gender, physical capacities, or sexual orientation may be different. All these qualities have shaped their attitudes and will help shape the interview. Each might have a drastically different agenda for the interview. A depressed person may hope for a pill to cure the depression immediately, and the worker may have been trained to believe that medication must be supplemented by a lengthy counseling process.

A study of working-class clients who came to a family service agency in England revealed that clients and workers had differing expectations of each other. Some clients who were having trouble with their husbands expected the worker to give the husband a good talking to straighten him out. Some resented personal questions and answered only when pushed continually to do so. Some assumed that workers asked personal questions because they were nosy, interested in gossip, or trying to annoy (Rhodes, 1989, p. 71).

The researchers were amazed by the mutual lack of awareness of the reasons for the other person's behavior (Mayer & Timms, 1970). Workers and clients seemed sometimes to be in two different worlds. The solution to such divergence between client and worker expectations is to clarify expectations and bring them into convergence by changing either the worker's or the client's expectations or by changing the treatment methods. At times, perhaps all these changes may be necessary.

Both the interviewer and interviewee come to the interview with anxiety, particularly if they are meeting for the first time. Everyone feels anxious in a new and untested situation. For example, remember how you felt at the beginning of a semester during the first session of your classes. Perhaps you wondered how the teachers would treat you or what they would expect from you. You might have wondered whether the teachers would be tough or easy graders. Would the classes be boring or interesting? Would the teachers humiliate you or be sarcastic if you gave a wrong answer? Would the teachers respect your individual needs and ideas?

Remember, too, how you felt when you were about to be interviewed by a prospective employer. You probably wondered whether you would measure up to the employer's expectations. Would you say the right things? Were you dressed correctly? Would the employer like you? Would you be asked questions you'd rather not answer? What parts of your experience and personality should you emphasize, deemphasize, alter, or conceal?

Inexperienced workers usually wonder whether they will ask the right questions: What if I ask the wrong question? Will it send the client into a tailspin? What if the client doesn't talk? What if the client talks too much? What if the client talks about the wrong things, or what if I talk about the wrong things? How can I keep the interview on target? Will the client like me, or will I like the client?

To move the interview along toward its goal, the anxieties of both the interviewer and the interviewee need to be dealt with. The interviewer can practice certain techniques through role-playing and can deal with personal anxieties through supervision and peer support.

AWARENESS OF CULTURAL BACKGROUNDS

Cultural issues are related to expectations because people from various cultural backgrounds might have different expectations of each other and might even literally speak different languages. Even when the language *seems* to be the same, people who belong to a subculture within an English-speaking culture will probably have developed their own language variations.

Sometimes words convey different meaning to different people. Slang is one example of this: *straight* means "very proper" in one person's vocabulary; to another it means "not crooked." To another it means "heterosexual." In a discussion of the relative merits of surplus foods, someone said, "The cheese was smokin'!" He was not referring to smoked cheese; he meant it was a very tasty cheese. We should try to use language that the interviewee understands, which means that we have to learn the interviewee's particular idiom if it differs from ours. However, we should not use slang that is unnatural or uncomfortable to us. Trying to act hip in a forced way with a teenager in order to be part of the gang is more likely to reap ridicule than trust.

Learning about a Client's Culture

Anthropologists have a lot to teach human service workers about interviewing and about how to relate to people. Their job is to learn how a culture works, how people relate to each other, what kinds of organizations they create, and what their strengths are. When anthropologists do ethnographic interviews, they are the students, and the interviewees are the teachers. The anthropologists make some decisions about how to structure their interviews, but they have no preconceptions about people's problems or the way to solve the problems. The anthropologists are curious about people's lives and their relationships to others in the family and the community.

Human service workers are more likely to think they need to be in control of an interview and to have some thoughts about the nature of the problems and ways to solve these problems because they believe that they are the experts. Anthropologist James Green (1982) challenges social workers' emphasis on empathy, openness, and getting in touch with feelings. He suggests that social workers could develop a deeper understanding of their clients if they think less about those emphases and strive instead to develop real knowledge of the client's worldview. He says:

> The real trick in cross-cultural social work, as in any kind of cross-cultural learning, is to comprehend what it is that the client knows and how that knowledge is used in the

mundane traffic of daily meaning, client meaning, and not contrived, a priori "caring responses." What clients say—literally—is a crucial source of data, which must be carefully gathered, using such simple ethnographic interviewing techniques as will elicit in the client's own terms . . . the meanings attached to personal, family, or other problems typically brought to social workers. (p. 74)

Although Green downplays the importance of empathy, the seriousness of an anthropologist's respect for the client's view and the intensity of his or her search for understanding can result in genuinely empathetic understanding. The worker who glibly responds, "I know how you feel," without actually having any idea how the client feels pays only lip service to the concept of empathy.

Social work professor Irene Glasser uses these ethnographic methods in teaching students interviewing techniques. She considers any situation to be cross-cultural when the worker

is working with someone who views the world, defines reality, and organizes behavior differently than the worker does. This means that practically all of my social-work students are engaged in cross-cultural work whether they are working with poor people, young parents, people on probation, children in a class for emotional problems, or shelter residents. (Glasser, 1989, p. 5)

Glasser suggests that students become the "learner" of each person's culture. Some questions that might be helpful are to ask people to talk about:

- Their daily routine
- A critical period in their lives
- Their childhood
- Common expressions and jokes friends tell each other

Listen carefully to people's words and ask for clarification when necessary. Don't be too quick to "understand." An admission of ignorance might be more productive than a facile claim to understanding. Look for recurring themes in people's conversation or behavior (Glasser, 1989).

James Spradley (1979) gives guidelines for ethnographic interviewing that emphasize three skills: (1) asking global questions, (2) identifying "cover terms," and (3) eliciting descriptors for the terms they choose to explore.

Global Questions   **Global questions** are "general, open-ended questions about some aspect of the interviewee's life, something personally or professionally puzzling to the worker and potentially salient to the presenting problem" (Green & Leigh, 1989, p. 8). A worker interviewing a Native American knows little or nothing about this group but knows that the Native American is newly arrived to a large city from a nearby reservation; the worker asks (after preliminary introductions) the following global question: "I don't often meet people from the American Indian community in this office; can you tell me why some of the people you know leave their reservations to live in this city?" (Green & Leigh, 1989, p. 8).

The worker does not start with the "presenting problem" or by taking a social history. While he is partly concerned with warming up and establishing rapport, he is also

global questions
General, open-ended questions about some aspect of an interviewee's life.

inviting the person to volunteer information about his experiences and his culture. The way the question is phrased puts the interviewee in the role of expert—a cultural guide. The goal is to generate discourse and to understand the context of his behavior, to see how normative it is in terms of his own reference group. The goal is not to jump right into a person's problem, as would the question, "Why did you leave the reservation?" The ethnically competent interviewer takes the interviewee's language seriously rather than "reading through" language to see what is really behind what is being said (Green & Leigh, 1989).

cover terms Terms that describe some aspect of culturally significant meaning and experience.

Cover Terms   **Cover terms** subsume, or cover, some aspect of culturally significant meaning and experience. In the previous example, the interviewee's response might be: "A lot of people leave. They need money, some kind of work, and they have families to help. But I know several who just wanted to see Seattle, to get away from it all, you know" (Green & Leigh, 1989, p. 8). There are at least six cover terms in this response:

1. "a lot of people"
2. "some kind of work"
3. "families"
4. "to help"
5. "just wanted to see Seattle"
6. "get away from it all"

The worker could choose one that seemed significant and might ask: "You say 'a lot of people'; does everyone you know leave at some time, or just some people?" By asking such global questions, the worker would in time elicit the cultural context of an interviewee's behavior, information that would also be applicable for work with future clients of similar background.

descriptors Blocks of descriptive information, systematically collected, used to build a composite portrait of selected cultural characteristics more or less shared by a set of clients.

Descriptors   "Descriptors are simply blocks of descriptive information, systematically collected, used to build a composite portrait of selected cultural characteristics more or less shared by a set of clients" (Green & Leigh, 1989, p. 8). Compiling **descriptors** requires careful recording, which could present a problem to workers already pressed for time. Green and Leigh suggest that the process of recording that agencies use to train workers could also be used to compile ethnographic descriptions of even a few paragraphs in length, which could then be used as training aids and for staff discussions. Green and Leigh (1989) list the following areas for focusing on the interviewee and his or her presenting problem:

1. The client's own definition and evaluation of an experience as a problem.
2. The semantic elements of the client's discourse in reference to the problem.
3. Indigenous strategies of problem resolution, including the identity and procedures of indigenous healers and advisers.
4. Culturally based criteria of problem resolution.
5. Contrasts in worker–client and agency–ethnic community views of the problem and articulation of how those contrasts can be positively used in problem solving (p. 8).

More and more inmates are being sent to prisons, faster than new ones can be built. Very little rehabilitation is offered to them. Because of prison gangs, overcrowding, harsh public attitudes, and budget cutbacks for programs, many inmates exit prisons the same as they entered, or worse.

AWARENESS OF ATTITUDES AND VALUES

Interviewers set the stage for a worthwhile interview by their attitudes of active observation, physical attentiveness to the interviewee, and active listening. These attitudes are essential to productive interviews.

Active Observation

The 1950 Japanese movie *Rashomon* tells the tale of a bride and her samurai bridegroom who were traveling through the woods when a bandit set upon them and may have raped the bride and murdered the bridegroom. We say "may have" because the only thing the film tells us for certain is that the bridegroom is dead. A woodcutter was the only witness at the scene. During the trial of the bandit, the audience hears four different versions of the incident: the bride's, the woodcutter's, the bandit's, and (through a clairvoyant speaking to the husband's ghost) the husband's. All the witnesses dispute the bride's alleged rape and the manner of the husband's death; each saw the events differently. This movie is a vivid reminder that each of us brings our selective filters to every event we observe.

Active observation is different from the kind of looking we generally do in our everyday life. It is like the difference between being a passenger on a bus and the driver. The driver is aware at every moment of the conditions of the road, the traffic, the passengers, and the fare box. But although they might glance casually about, noting some people and incidents with mild interest, the passengers are generally preoccupied with their own thoughts.

Observing Nonverbal Messages

Interviewers get clues about the people they are listening to from people's nonverbal messages. Suppose, for example, you are a human service worker in a nursing home. A middle-aged couple comes to see you about placing the husband's mother in this home. As you show them through the halls, you notice that they get quieter; their voices drop; their speech slows; they glance significantly at each other as they look at the seriously ill residents in wheelchairs, walking with walkers and canes, staring into space. They look away from you and decline your invitation to see the wing of the home where the more seriously ill residents live. Observing their behavior and knowing how much stress people are under when making decisions about their sick or aged parents, you'd want to help this couple talk about their feelings about placing their mother, as well as their impressions of what they have just seen.

Interviewees can give nonverbal clues about feelings: rigid posture, trembling, yawning, wringing hands, sweating palms, trembling voice, blushing, a sad look, moistening of the eyes, sighs, clenched jaws and hands, pursed lips, lowered head, and other gestures. Workers also communicate with clients through nonverbal behavior. They can express warmth with a handshake, by leaning toward the interviewee rather than sitting back, and with facial expressions. Workers can also express disapproval, contempt, or disinterest by glancing off into space, fidgeting, coming to an interview late, looking at their watches, forgetting important names or facts about the interviewee's situation, and interrupting the interview to answer the phone or talk to others.

There is disagreement in the field about how much physical contact is appropriate between an interviewer and an interviewee. Although we cannot go into a full discussion of this issue, we do believe that touching can send both positive and negative messages. When either the interviewer or the interviewee sexualizes touching, it can be abusive. Some people's natural style of relating to others involves touching. However, before you touch a client (except for a handshake), you should ask permission. Even if it is natural for you to touch people, it might make some interviewees uncomfortable. It takes experience and skill to know when, how much, and with whom physical contact will help build rapport. Few doubt, however, the usefulness of using some reassuring touch when it seems appropriate.

To illustrate this, we return to the case of the elderly woman whose son and daughter-in-law were choosing a nursing home for her. The woman was terrified of going into this institution, imagining it was a type of prison, even though her son and daughter-in-law saw it as a gracious, well-run home. During the intake interview, the worker in the nursing home took the woman's trembling hand in her own. Afterward, as the elderly woman recounted the interview to her children, she said, "She put both of her hands around mine and made me feel not so alone."

Looking for nonverbal clues to feelings is not a parlor game. Some people jump to quick, simplistic conclusions based on one gesture. Yet you can't tell much about the significance of a gesture if you don't know what a person's typical body stance is like. A crying child may tell you, when you ask, that nothing is wrong, but his or her uncharacteristically sad face and quietness tell you that something is upsetting this usually bouncy youngster.

Although intuitive understanding is important, your first reaction to a scene may not always give you accurate information. For example, you might see able-bodied men hanging around on a street during working hours and assume that they are shiftless or chronically unemployed. In fact, the men might be construction workers who have just been laid off because a project is finished and are looking for a new job. Or perhaps they might be migrant workers waiting for the grape harvest to begin. To arrive at any valid understanding, your observations of any one person or incident must be put in social and historical context.

Active Listening

Much as we long for perfect nonverbal understanding, we communicate our thoughts and feelings through language. Yet our attempts to communicate with one another often seem doomed to failure. Why is this so? One reason is that language itself is too frail to carry our full meaning. In the novel *Madame Bovary*, nineteenth-century French author Gustave Flaubert expressed his tragic awareness of this fact. Madame Bovary had told her lover Rudolph that she loved him, and she meant it sincerely. Rudolph, however, felt the words were being used in a phony way, perhaps because he himself had used them that way so often that he no longer believed them. Madame Bovary could not get through to him. This is what Flaubert (1856/1959) writes:

> He [Rudolph], this man of great experience, could not distinguish dissimilarities of feeling between similarities of expression . . . as though the fullness of the soul did not sometimes overflow into the emptiest phrases, since no one can ever express the measure of his needs, his conceptions or his sorrows, and human speech is like a cracked pot on which we beat out rhythms for bears to dance to when we are striving to make music that will wring tears from the stars. (p. 165)

In many of our conversations, we are faced with the awareness that our words may not carry our full meaning. Perhaps it is because we have not chosen the right words or because the listener is not really receiving our message or because we are not sure of what we mean ourselves.

An interviewer needs to master the crucial skill of active listening to be able to grasp the complex personality and the complex situation of each person. In order to "read" the emotion behind the words of the speaker and get closer to the real meaning, we must listen carefully to each word and then remember what has been said. Careful, active listening is not a usual occurrence.

Try to remember the last time someone gave you his or her absolutely undivided attention and listened to you talk about your concerns, without interjecting any of his or her own. Few people are capable of giving their undivided attention to everyone they meet. Most of us are preoccupied, worrying about a test, a dentist's appointment, or a troubled friendship.

Although some people reveal themselves easily, most of us do not pour out our innermost thoughts to total strangers. In fact, we have been taught caution. Even with good friends, we are often reluctant to speak about what is on our minds. Many people feel a special reticence when they must ask for help, embarrassed to admit that they can't handle some aspect of their lives without help. Many people raised in the United States have learned the individualistic "pull yourself up by your own bootstraps" ideology. So when a person comes into an interview at a human service agency, we need to be alert to any feelings of anxiety about asking for and receiving help.

Recurrent references to a subject may indicate great concern about that topic. The way ideas are associated with each other can give hints about feelings. For example, if a woman tells about her daughter's beauty and then shifts to her own concern about her appearance, we might wonder if the woman's feelings about herself are mixed up with her feelings about her daughter. Sometimes people conceal their meanings by saying the opposite of what they mean. A man whose fiancee has broken the engagement may say angrily that he's glad it's over because his ego is too injured for him to admit the opposite.

Core Values of the Interviewer

Many counselors and psychotherapists regard the values of empathy, warmth, respect, and genuineness as essential for a successful helping relationship. However, although everyone probably agrees that it is essential for a helper to respect a helpee, not everyone agrees about empathy.

EMPATHY

Empathy is the capacity to identify yourself with another person's feelings and thoughts, to suspend your own judgment for the moment and feel with another. It differs from sympathy, which involves feeling sorry for someone but not necessarily suspending one's own feelings to try to identify with another person.

Research indicates that the capacity for empathy may be based in biology. Italian neuroscientists studying monkeys were amazed to discover that the brain has a system of neurons, or nerve cells, that specialize in a sort of "walking in another's shoes" function. These neurons become active when a monkey actually makes a movement and when it is only watching another monkey, or even a human, make that same movement. "It is as if the monkey is imitating—or mirroring—the other's movement in its mind" (Goldberg, 2005, p. C1).

This may help researchers understand autism:

> The discovery of mirror neurons was important for basic brain science, but now it is also proving medically relevant: Researchers are reporting . . . that malfunctioning mirror neurons appear to play a central role in the social isolation of autistic children. (Goldberg, 2005, p. C1)

Empathy is an ongoing process rather than a state that is achieved once and for all. Some people object that because it is not measurable or observable, one should concentrate on training helpers in skills of communication that can be demonstrably improved. Others argue that empathy is not important when a helper is dealing with environmental concerns, such as helping someone to find housing.

We believe that empathy without knowledge of how to work the system would be useless in helping people with environmental concerns. Yet it is also essential to identify with people's feelings about their environmental concerns in order to understand fully how to help them. For example, a person may need to file a complaint against a landlord in order to get the heat turned on. The helping person needs to understand that person's personality in order to know whether he or she will actually file the complaint or be too frightened to do so.

In working with a welfare rights group of TANF recipients, the prime goal may be to increase the TANF grant; yet, on the way to doing that, we must feel the linkages between the personal and the political. We must be able to:

- Identify with the recipient's rage against an arbitrary system or a mean-spirited worker
- Identify with feelings of powerlessness
- Understand a recipient's need to identify with the oppressive welfare system when he or she acts superior to other recipients
- Stretch our capacity to understand when, as club treasurer, the recipient is tempted to steal the club funds
- Plumb the depths of the recipient's feelings of deprivation
- Understand the female recipient's feelings of frustration when the welfare functionaries watch her like a hawk to try to suppress her sexuality
- Understand the recipient's capacity to fight the system in order to know how to buoy that capacity

Empathy springs out of our common humanness. Although no two people have precisely the same experiences, we all go through the same life cycle and share similar feelings. This could be considered as a kind of universal kinship. Kinship is not only relatedness to one's family, but "also a type of connection—biological, spiritual, emotional, social, between people" (Cottle, 1974, p. xii). Using our imagination, we form connections to our interviewees that help us experience what they are experiencing. Empathy requires a finely tuned intuitive sensitivity to other people.

Empathy may be essential for survival, according to Dr. Steven Hyman, professor of neurobiology at Harvard Medical School. He says that "from an evolutionary point of view, we're probably hardwired for empathy, which confers 'elective advantage,' allowing the young—and the species—to survive" (Foreman, 2003). An infant is at increased risk of perishing if the parent is not empathic.

For people in the caring professions, there are potential pitfalls when experiencing another person's pain can lead to "empathic over-arousal," according to Nancy Eisenberg, a psychologist at Arizona State University. "In this unpleasant state, the focus then becomes one's own feelings of stress rather than the other person's need. The over-aroused person may have to leave the room or emotionally withdraw to feel better" (Foreman, 2003). Human service workers need to learn how to empathize with a client's feelings without drowning in those feelings and without accepting the person's assumptions that led to those feelings.

RESPECT

Respect is a quality that most people understand in their social relationships. It involves regarding others as important and being concerned about their welfare. It acknowledges their uniqueness and their rights to feelings and needs. Respect requires that a helper be **nonjudgmental** when trying to understand a helpee.

nonjudgmental An attitude that withholds moral judgments on another person's behaviors, attitudes, or values.

Amy.
17.

All we do is listen. 800.252.TEEN. The Samariteens.
There are a million reasons to feel alone. Call us if you want to talk about any of them. Teen to teen.

The teenage years can be very stressful, leading to anxiety and depression. The Samariteens, part of a suicide prevention program, trains young adult volunteers for its hotline, which lets young people discuss problems in total anonymity.

GENUINENESS

Genuineness is also a quality that people understand in their day-to-day relationships. When people use slang expressions such as "He's a stuffed shirt," or "She's a pompous . . .," or "White men speak with forked tongues," they are expressing contempt for a person who puts on airs or is hypocritical. We want to know that the person to whom we entrust our thoughts and feelings actually cares. This quality has come to be more highly valued by many helping professionals than it used to be. Classical Freudian psychoanalysis established a helping model in which the therapist acted as a "blank slate"—sitting passively behind the patient, seldom interjecting an opinion or showing strong emotions. This model was always inappropriate for helping people who had concrete environmental problems and is increasingly seen as inappropriate for most therapeutic relationships. Counselors and therapists today are more likely to express appropriate feelings openly. "By being willing to discuss personal feelings, the helper encourages the helpee to respond similarly. The helpee opens up and learns to be genuine, too" (D'Augelli, D'Augelli, & Danish, 1981, pp. 58–59).

Genuineness also involves "being non-defensive and human enough to admit errors to clients. . . . [Practitioners] must be models of humanness and openness and avoid hiding behind a mask of 'professionalism' " (Hepworth & Larson, 1987, p. 998).

Jean

A woman named Jean was out of money. Her husband had been unemployed for many months, and their relatives were equally poor and couldn't help. She set out for the welfare office to apply for TANF for herself and her two small children.

SPONSORSHIP AND SETTING

The welfare office had once been within walking distance of Jean's apartment, but because of fiscal cutbacks, the intake departments of several neighborhood welfare offices had been consolidated and centralized in a downtown office. Jean borrowed the $5 round-trip transit fare from a friend and, with two young children in tow, set out in the pouring rain for an address that rang no familiar bell in her memory. Asking her way as she went along, by trial and error, she finally found the office, marked by a sign chiseled into the stone facade: OVERSEERS OF THE PUBLIC WELFARE

Jean entered the lobby and winced as she saw a security guard with a gun in his holster. Because it was Monday morning, the lobby was filled with people, many of them standing, since there were not enough chairs. The once-white paint on the walls and ceiling was peeling, and it was hard to see what color the floors had been, as they were threadbare in many spots. Faded posters describing long-defunct job programs lined the walls.

The receptionist sitting behind a thick glass partition ignored Jean, continuing a conversation with the other receptionist about a party she had gone to the night before. Finally she shoved a piece of cardboard with the number 20 scribbled on it and an application form to fill out through the half-moon in the glass. Jean filled out the form and waited, and waited, and waited. The children whined, and whined, and whined. There were no toys for them and few diversions.

PERSONALITY AND STYLE OF THE INTERVIEWER

After about an hour, an assistance payments worker came into the hall and shouted, "Number 20!" Jean meekly followed the worker into a room, where four other workers sat at their desks, a room as dingy as the lobby, devoid of any of those objects that personalize an office.

There was a shaky coat rack, but the worker didn't suggest that Jean hang her wet coat there, so Jean simply left it on. Although the worker did not invite her to sit down, Jean assumed she was expected to do so. The worker did not smile, nor did she introduce herself. Jean remained "Number 20" in the worker's mind, and the worker was simply an animated function in Jean's mind. These two people were to talk with each other for at least half an hour, perhaps longer.

CLIENT EXPECTATIONS

Jean had been raised to believe that any interchange that took this long called for an exchange of names. Feeling that some deep social taboo was being violated and wanting to set it right, Jean introduced herself and made a few comments about the driving rain outside. The worker looked up briefly from the application form, which had been absorbing her attention since she sat down and mumbled, still unsmiling, "I'm Marie Klausner."

ATTITUDES AND VALUES OF HELPERS

The interview could have been conducted by a computer. In fact, Jean amused herself by turning Marie into a blinking, chiming computer in her fantasy as the questions and directives flew at her:

- How much money do you have in the bank?
- What is your bank account number?
- What is your Social Security number?
- What are your children's birth dates?
- Bring in verification of their birth dates.
- Bring in bank statements for the past twelve months.

And so on.

The worker was annoyed by the children's interruptions. After she filled out the intake form and listed the many verifications that Jean would have to bring back before Jean could be accepted for TANF, the worker finally asked if Jean was in immediate need. On hearing that she was, the worker gave her an EBT card to get food. Frantic and depressed, Jean went back home in the rain, the children begging to stop for a hamburger each time they passed a fast-food restaurant.

Jean lived in a large city, and her welfare office reflected the poverty of the inner city. Jean's friend Marian, however, had a very different experience.

CASE EXAMPLE

Marian

Marian lived in a smaller town, where most people knew each other and the director of public welfare had some personal contact with many of the clients or their families. The director was supportive of workers' efforts to experiment with innovative ways of getting the job done. Although the department had limited funds, the workers pooled their resources and found volunteers to set up a modest child care center in the lobby. They brought in plants to create a more cheerful atmosphere, and when they couldn't convince the town council to paint the office, they held a raffle to buy paint and organized a painting party. Workers, clients, and members of the welfare advisory board painted the lobby themselves.

On the same rainy morning that Jean visited her welfare office, Marian came to this office to apply for TANF for herself and her child. The receptionist smiled at Marian when she came in and pointed out the rack where she could hang her coat. She took the children to the volunteer who cared for clients' children, and in a short time, she escorted Marian to a worker's office. After introductions and a sociable comment about the weather, the worker asked Marian how she could help her and learned that she had come to apply for financial assistance because her husband had died recently.

ACTIVE LISTENING, EMPATHY

As she explained what benefits Marian was entitled to and what the application process involved, the worker, having learned that Marian's husband had died only a week ago, kept her emotional radar tuned to Marian's distress signals. The worker knew that her main job was to process an application for TANF; she also knew that a human being was in pain and might need solace on the way to getting financial support. She obtained the same kind of information that Jean's worker had gotten; yet she led Marian gently into the application process, taking time to let Marian talk about her grief when she needed to.

Why did Jean and Marian receive such different treatment from their respective workers? A comparison of Jean's and Marian's encounters illustrates some of the factors that shape a human service interview.

FOCUS

The focus of both interviews was to find out if the applicants were eligible for benefits and, if they were, to start the process of obtaining them. Both workers were clear about their primary purpose and did not allow other issues to distract them from the task. In that respect, they were on target. Marian's worker was skillful enough to achieve the primary goal while not ignoring the other needs of her client. Jean's worker, in her single-mindedness, accomplished her goal but with a high cost to her client's sense of self-worth.

CLIENT EXPECTATIONS

Jean's attitude about applying for welfare was shaped by all the negative publicity she had heard through the media and the grapevine. She came to the welfare office with a mental set of shame. The dingy, crowded, impersonal setting of the office heightened it. The interviewer was in no mood to reach out to Jean and put her at ease.

SPONSORSHIP OF THE INTERVIEW

Jean's worker was burned out. The entire office seemed demoralized. Demoralization is not inevitable, even in an organization with limited resources. The welfare office Marian went to was able to treat clients with respect and dignity because it was located in a small community where there was no sharp social division between the affluent and the poor. Most people knew each other, and the director and workers lived in the community and regarded their clients as "one of us" rather than as "one of them." The director was a warm and imaginative person who, working with limited resources, tried to bring out the best in workers and clients.

Both Jean and Marian were entitled to dignified treatment. Yet Jean went home with a hollow, angry sensation in the pit of her stomach. She had gone through what one sociologist has termed a "successful degradation ceremony" (Garfinkel, 1965). Marian, although still worried about a future with a diminished income and scared of loneliness, did not feel such degradation. She felt less alone and was reassured that the worker at the welfare office would process her claim as quickly as possible.

Interviewing skills are needed for many aspects of group work as well as for ongoing individual relationships. Before she began the school bully project, the worker described below interviewed teachers, parents, children, and the principal.

During the interview with a new client, we try to learn about the network of family and friends that surrounds him or her. The concept of "aging in place" has recently gained much attention. This wife, although also old, is able to care for her husband at home, with supports from a nearby health center.

INTERVIEW

Madeleine K. Jacobson, Director of a Bully Project

Madeleine Jacobson, a licensed social worker in private practice, directed the Bully Project at an inner-city Catholic elementary school. Two senior students in the Regis College social work program did their internship with her in the project.

Madeleine has an MSW degree from the University of Chicago and has completed training at the Boston Psychoanalytic Institute. She started her private therapy practice when she had a family, because it gave her flexible hours so that she could combine family responsibilities and work. Yet the work is isolating, and she felt the need to get into some work that broadened her contact with the world. She became a part-time field instructor at Regis College, where she supervised two students.

Bully programs with school children began in Norway, under the direction of Dan Olweus, who made major theoretical contributions to the program. Madeleine uses his theories, as well as behavior modification techniques, John Bowlby's attachment theory, and object relations theories.

In the wake of the student shootings at Columbine High School in Colorado and shootings at other schools, bully programs have been initiated in many schools in the United States. The two boys who did the shooting at Columbine had been bullied themselves.

The kind of bullying that children engaged in at the Catholic school where this project took place did not involve violent behavior such as carrying guns, sexual harassment, or physical assault. Catholic schools tend to expel children for that kind of behavior. The behavior that Madeleine observed was psychological bullying. Sometimes it involved a clique of children taunting a vulnerable child. The girls used gossip, exclusion, isolating, and rumor spreading as their method of bullying. They would direct this behavior at girls whom they viewed as more vulnerable. The boys made fun of each other openly.

Children cannot learn unless they feel safe. Unfortunately, many of our children do not come from positive, safe home environments and communities and therefore schools need to be safer than homes. The presence of bullying indicates that a school is not a safe environment.

While school administrators may see the bully problem as a problem of several individual children, this program identifies the school as the client and looks at the whole system first. Everyone must be involved—the administration, teachers, parents, and even the custodial staff. All members must be committed to working toward a bully-free environment, which is then declared through posters, letters home, and within each class. The children need to know that bullies will not be tolerated.

After involving the entire system, the second phase of the project is for the social worker to go into each class on a continuous basis, ideally once a week. The goal is to inform the students about bullying and to distribute questionnaires about the existence of bullying. Writing assignments are then assigned on a variety of topics such as:

- Describe a bully situation that you have observed.
- Who are your heroes?

- What are your goals for the future?
- Describe your family and country of origin.

Children are told that privacy will be respected. The social worker can communicate with individual children via their written work, which leads to many students asking to talk with the social worker. Thus, children become self-referred clients. Of course, parental permission is required.

Students read their papers on a volunteer basis only. As they read, some of the other students engage in bullying behavior through taunts, snickers, and rudeness. The social worker uses this "in-the-moment" aspect of the process to help children see for themselves their own behaviors. The social worker maintains a position of neutrality and acceptance. She does not express disapproval, but tries to help the children explain their feelings behind their actions. Many of the children are impulsive, have never been spoken to about "how they feel," and welcome this new and strange opportunity. Many come from homes where bullying behavior is encouraged as manly, and an "eye for an eye" retribution is encouraged.

Bullies lack empathy. Therefore, there are many lessons about empathy and what they can do about developing it. Obviously, in the lower grades, these techniques are modified in accordance with developmental needs.

Once information about bully patterns is established, the social worker is free to use her creativity in devising smaller groups. For example, Madeleine developed a group of bullies from the seventh grade and told them they were to be in charge of explaining bullying to the lower grades and acting as a tribunal in which they could "hear bully problems" from other classmates. These bully children wanted to be the center of attention but lacked the necessary social skills to know how to channel their needs.

If racism appears to be behind many bully problems, the social worker can create programs to encourage awareness of cultural differences. In the school where Madeleine worked, there was some tension between the Haitians, Latinos, and whites. Both children and staff tended to deny racism. When asked about racism, one child said what she thought adults wanted to hear, "We're all God's children, and the color of our skin doesn't make any difference."

One exercise that the children enjoyed was a "Chicken Festival." Madeleine had asked the children to name some of the things that people say about Haitians or about white people. One child said, "White people can't cook chicken. Their chicken is all bloody." With the consent of the parents, Madeleine asked each child to bring in the best chicken that their parents cook. Children enjoyed tasting each other's chicken, and of course the white-cooked chicken wasn't bloody. Madeleine used this as an example of how people hold false ideas about each other. However, one white parent was furious at the assignment and wrote a scathing letter, saying the idea was stupid and ridiculous.

Madeleine said the project was sometimes frustrating but rewarding. When children develop some awareness of their emotions and feel secure and contained in their environment, they will have positive attachments with the school and their friends. Children who can develop a thinking process that includes self-awareness and empathy for others have less chance of becoming either victims or bullies.

STRUCTURE OF AN INTERVIEW

Like a story, an interview has a beginning, a middle, and an end. It takes place within a specific time frame. The span of interviews varies enormously, from a ten-minute hotline conversation, to the more traditional "fifty-minute hour" at an agency, to an interview that could take an entire day (e.g., when a worker places a child in a new foster home). There are various ways of looking at the stages of an interview. From a broad view, the interview has three stages: (1) opening the interview, starting to build rapport, and making a contract; (2) exploring the issues and making an action plan; and (3) closing and reviewing the actions to be taken. In actual practice, these phases blend together, and elements of each phase can be found in the others.

If someone is applying for a benefit, such as food stamps, the purpose of the interview may be self-evident (although not necessarily; there may be other needs that the person is hesitant to admit to or other help for which he or she might be eligible). Once it is established, for example, that obtaining food stamps is the most pressing need, the beginning of the interview consists of the interviewer asking a few questions to establish whether the interviewee is potentially eligible. If, for example, the interviewee says that she is a college student, then the interviewer will save time for both of them by asking right away if the student meets a set of criteria. If not, there is no point in continuing. The interviewer then should politely explain the requirements, and ask the student if she would like to be referred to some other resource (or, if the student is interested, to some group that is seeking to improve food stamp benefits). Workers should also tell clients that they have the right to appeal the decision the worker has made.

Although most of us recoil from long, complex official forms, some forms are necessary. Yet an interview need not become machinelike. Sometimes the claimants already filled out the form while waiting to be interviewed. Then the interviewer can go over it, helping the interviewee provide additional answers. The worker can further explain the program, finding out if the interviewee needs other kinds of help.

If the form is to be filled out during their time together, an interviewer can use it as the basis for a structured conversation rather than as a script for a third degree. If information pertaining to a particular question on the form has already come out in the opening conversation, the question need not be asked again. If, however, the interviewer's time is limited and there are others waiting, then the interview will probably have to be more constricted. In general, workers should ask questions precisely as written only when the answers are needed for a very structured research project or for a medical history.

Consider how a food stamp application might be taken. Here is the beginning of an interview using the mechanical approach.

> Name?
> Address?
> Who is in your household?
> How much money do you have in the bank?
> Do you have a checking account?
> Do you have any insurance?
> Any boats, camping trailers, land?

The following interview uses the more human approach. After the initial pleasantries, the interviewer says to the applicant, Guy LeBlanc:

> Mr. LeBlanc, the food stamp program has a lot of rules about who can get food stamps and who can't. I hope you qualify, since you must need them or you wouldn't be asking for them. Yet I have to know a lot about your living arrangements and your resources before I can determine if you are eligible. Could you tell me about who you live with, how you make your living, and things that you own, such as a car, bank account, and so on?

This question is broad enough to set Mr. LeBlanc off on a discussion of his circumstances, from which you will probably be able to get most of the information you need. You can ask questions about the things he left out, but you have given Mr. LeBlanc initiative in the interview rather than making him feel as if he were on a witness stand.

The following two principles are useful guidelines for all stages of the interview: seeking concreteness and focusing on the here and now (immediacy).

Seeking Concreteness

Someone once said, "God resides in the details." It is life's details that are important, and a good interviewer knows how to go after those details. This is called *seeking concreteness* or *specificity of response*. When someone says, "She's an awful parent," you could ask the person to clarify exactly what she does that is awful. In this way, you help the client to be clearer, get details about significant interactions and events, and make sure that you and the client understand each other's meanings.

To help an interviewee be more concrete, the interviewer can ask about specific examples or stories as a follow-up to a general response. If the interviewee says, "I really liked it when I first got here," you can ask, "Can you give an example of something you really liked?" Or, "What was most surprising about . . .?" "What was the worst disappointment in . . .?" (Martin, 2001).

Immediacy

An interview should focus on the present concerns of the interviewee rather than on past or future events or concerns. This characteristic is called *immediacy*. The concerns may involve the interviewee's life situation or something happening in the relationship between interviewer and interviewee. Evans et al. give the example of the former:

> INTERVIEWEE (separated from her husband for three months):   When he first told me that he was going to leave me, I was very angry, but now I'm managing by myself without his help.
>
> INTERVIEWER: You're really proud that you have managed by yourself.

This response focused on the interviewee's present feelings of pride in her ability to manage her life, the most important issue at the moment. If the interviewer had chosen to focus on the past, she might have said, "You were really angry when he first told you." Or, if the interviewer had chosen to focus on the future, she might have said, "In the future, you'll be glad it worked out this way" (Evans, Hearn, Uhlemann, & Ivey, 1979). Both of those comments would have deflected the interviewee's attention from her main concern at the moment.

Questions That Help People Talk

open-ended questions
Questions asked in such a way that they allow for a variety of responses.

The techniques of the ethnographic interview, such as asking global questions, are useful in helping people to explore problems. **Open-ended questions** begin conversations but leave the choice of direction to the client.

If an interviewer asks a lot of closed-ended, or yes/no, questions, the interview becomes a question-and-answer period in which the interviewee passively responds. Experienced interviewers try to avoid asking too many questions, which can destroy a client's initiative. Asking the right question at the right time is an important interviewing skill. Beginning workers sometimes take refuge in the question-and-answer format as if it were a security blanket, perhaps fearing loss of control with a looser structure. One guideline to use in deciding how to ask a question is: The question should help to further the process of discovery, either of an interviewee's inner self or the outer world.

Even a question aimed at finding out if a person is eligible for a government benefit can, if combined with information, help interviewees understand the program and their place in it:

> INTERVIEWER (to a TANF recipient who has applied for the job training program): Mrs. Leavitt, the job training program doesn't require a parent to enroll in it if she has a child age 2 or under. How old are your children?
>
> MRS. LEAVITT: I have a one-year-old.
>
> INTERVIEWER: Then you don't need to apply, but you still can if you want to. How do you think the job training program might help you?

Some kinds of questions keep control in the hands of the interviewer; others give more freedom to the interviewee. The closed question allows for few options and gives minimal information:

> CLOSED: Do you like your teacher?
>
> OPEN: What's your teacher like?
>
> CLOSED: Do you shop for bargains and use dried skim milk?
>
> OPEN: It's hard to make a TANF grant stretch. How do you manage?
>
> CLOSED: Do you get enough sleep with the new baby?
>
> OPEN: How is the baby's schedule affecting you?

Another controlling question that is hardly ever helpful is the question "why?" Think about how your parents, teachers, and other authority figures frequently scolded by saying, "Why did you do that?" You probably answered, quite honestly, "I dunno," and the conversation ended. It is almost always perceived as a threatening question.

The **indirect question** gives the interviewee more options and elicits more insight than the direct question. It is phrased like a statement, without a question mark, but actually asks a question. Here are some examples:

DIRECT: What jobs have you held in the past?

INDIRECT: I'd be interested to hear about your previous jobs.

DIRECT: Has your new foster child adjusted well?

INDIRECT: I imagine a lot has happened since I placed Billy here. What kind of a week did you and he have?

Door openers, a term coined by Thomas Gordon (1970), are an invitation to say more about something the interviewee has brought up. Although sometimes done by questioning, door openers are best done in the form of an open-ended request for more information:

Tell me more.

I'm interested in hearing about that.

The concept of funnel sequences is another way of looking at ways to encourage interviewees to talk (France & Kish, 1995). Funnel sequences begin with a broad probe or question, continue with reflection and possibly some open questions, then end with closed questions to fill any gaps in information you must gather.

> **indirect question** A question or statement that encourages the fullest possible expression of an interviewee's thoughts and feelings.

> **door opener** An invitation to say more about something that an interviewee has brought up, preferably in the form of an open-ended request for information.

A counselor working with the parents of this family of six living crammed into a one-room "apartment" in a San Francisco Chinatown hotel would be challenged to find a relaxed space and the time needed to conduct a meaningful interview.

Inverted funnel sequences take the opposite path. They begin with easily answered closed questions, then move to broader responses such as reflection and open questions. This technique is a good way to encourage a client to talk when the person is reluctant to speak with you. Here is an example of an inverted funnel sequence, used in an interaction with a sixteen-year-old who was hospitalized following a drug overdose suicide attempt. In response to an initial open question of "How are things going?" the patient said nothing and turned away from the interviewer. But he started to talk when the interviewer used the following inverted funnel sequence:

INTERVIEWER: Did Dr. Matthews see you this morning?

CLIENT: Mmhmm.

INTERVIEWER: Have they brought you breakfast?

CLIENT: Yeah. (Turning toward the interviewer with a disgusted look.)

INTERVIEWER: You didn't like the food.

CLIENT: It was awful. Everything was cold, and the fried eggs were all runny. It was almost as bad as that stuff they had me drink last night to make me throw up. I just want out of here.

INTERVIEWER: You'd really like to go home.

CLIENT: But they're making me stay, even though I've told them I want to go home. This place is terrible. It's boring and there's nothing to do.

INTERVIEWER: What do you think would need to happen in order for Dr. Matthews to discharge you?

Initially, this client was reluctant to talk. But two easy-to-answer closed questions evoked short responses. Then two reflections elicited animated descriptions of thoughts and feelings. Finally, an open question led the interaction toward a discussion of positive change (France & Kish, 1995).

Furthering Responses

A number of techniques can be used to explore a problem. Often they can be used in combination. One skill, called **furthering responses**, encourages clients to continue talking (Hepworth & Larsen, 1987). These include:

furthering responses
Responses that encourage clients to continue talking.

1. *Physical attending.* This is part of active listening and involves being there physically.

2. *Silence* (when used to indicate thoughtful attention).

3. *Minimal verbal or nonverbal responses.* A minimal response such as an attentive look of interest, a nod of the head, or a verbal "uh-huh" is often all the encouragement the interviewee needs. Whatever is natural to the listener is usually appropriate as long as it does not interfere with the interviewee's message.

4. *Accent responses.* This involves repeating, in a questioning tone of voice or with emphasis, a word or short phrase that the client has just said. For example, "if a client says, 'I've really had it with the way my supervisor at work is treating me,' the practitioner might respond, 'Had it?' to prompt further elaboration by the client" (Hepworth & Larsen, 1987, p. 1000).

Verbal Following Responses

A number of responses let clients know they have been heard and understood and provide immediate feedback (Hepworth & Larsen, 1987). These are called *verbal following responses* and include paraphrasing or restating, clarifying, and reflecting.

PARAPHRASING OR RESTATING

Paraphrasing or restating what the interviewee has just said is similar to a minimal response in that its purpose is to let interviewees know their messages have been understood. They encourage clients to continue. There is literal restatement, such as:

INTERVIEWEE: I felt terrible.

INTERVIEWER: You felt terrible.

But there is paraphrasing or summarizing, such as:

INTERVIEWEE: The baby cried a lot, and I've never taken care of a baby before. I just didn't know what to do.

INTERVIEWER: It was a new experience and you were confused.

paraphrasing or restating   Putting an interviewee's words in another form without changing the content in order to encourage the interviewee to go on.

CLARIFYING

Clarifying goes beyond a minimal response. The interviewer now seeks further understanding of what has been said or tries to clarify for the interviewee something hard to express. A question designed to help the interviewer understand might be (1) I don't understand that very well. Could you explain it again? (2) Are you saying that . . . ? or (3) Do you mean . . . ?

The following is an example of clarification used to help interviewees articulate their thoughts:

INTERVIEWEE: When the baby cries, I feel like I'm falling apart. I don't know what to do, I'm so mixed up. I want to be a good father, but I don't know how to. It's all so confusing . . . .

INTERVIEWER: The baby's crying seems to scare you. You feel mixed up and unsure of how to care for your baby.

clarifying   Seeking further understanding of what has been said in an interview.

REFLECTING

Compared with restating, which deals with what the interviewee said, **reflecting** deals with what an interviewee feels. Adding nothing of their own, interviewers say what they empathically sense the interviewee might be feeling:

INTERVIEWEE: There's sure a lot of red tape I have to go through to apply for welfare, isn't there? Why can't you people get together? I go from one person to another answering the same old questions all over again.

INTERVIEWER: I guess you feel like you're getting the runaround, don't you? Are you pretty mad at us by now?

reflecting   An interviewer response that puts into words what the interviewer thinks the interviewee might be feeling.

Other Ways of Responding

Some responses are not specifically geared to drawing the client out but can be useful when timed correctly and given sensitively. However, some of them are controversial. They include giving information, encouraging and reassuring, suggesting, advising, confronting, and interpreting.

GIVING INFORMATION

Clients need to know everything we can tell them about the services and benefits to which they are entitled. This information should be given when clients are ready for it, in a way that doesn't overwhelm or confuse them.

ENCOURAGING AND REASSURING

encouraging and reassuring
Providing a message of hopefulness in an attempt to inspire confidence, sometimes without regard to what a person is actually feeling.

Encouraging and reassuring responses are too often used insensitively. In our everyday relationships, we often encourage our friends by saying, "Oh sure, you can win the race," " . . . you can get that job," " . . . you can get her to go out with you." Such statements may not always be helpful, especially if they are not true. We say such things because we can't think of anything else or because we don't have the time, emotional energy, or courage to explore the real possibilities.

Such seemingly reassuring statements can actually leave clients feeling even more frightened if they don't feel strong or qualified. We all need permission to feel weak and vulnerable and to anticipate failure, and sometimes we need someone to remind us of our strengths. It takes a great deal of sensitivity, however, to recognize when encouragement is appropriate.

The following is one example of helpful reassurance given by a foster parent to a biological parent:

BIOLOGICAL PARENT: I always felt low. Like I was kind of an outcast. I don't know why. This is just my nature. . . . I know people think I'm a drunkard. I was in a mental hospital for two weeks, and this had a bad effect on me. So I felt both insane and poor. I had no money. And you don't look nice, and you don't feel nice, you don't perform well.

FOSTER PARENT: . . . anybody who has done what you did and let your children go is a big person.

BIOLOGICAL PARENT: Well, I'm glad you feel this way.

FOSTER PARENT: And you yourself said you felt this way.

BIOLOGICAL PARENT: I don't think my child would have ever made it to college. At least she has the chance. . . . (Mandell, B., 1973, pp. 167–168)

The following is an example of reassurance that definitely can't help anyone cope with reality:

INTERVIEWEE: I'm feeling awful about my job. Nothing seems to work right.

INTERVIEWER: Oh, don't worry. We all have job problems. It will work out all right.

SUGGESTING

Suggesting is a mild form of advice. If a suggestion is made tentatively, without any coercion, it can pose alternatives that the interviewee may not have been aware of:

> INTERVIEWER (to a college student):   Since you are a junior with a 3.0 average and need money, you might consider the co-op program, where you could work for a regular salary and get six credits.

suggesting Giving a mild form of advice, generally made tentatively.

ADVISING

Giving advice assumes that one person knows what is best for another, and that is a risky assumption. An interviewer should be cautious when **advising** a client. When an interviewee asks for advice, the interviewer should first find out what the interviewee already thinks about the problem and what alternative paths are being considered. This process by itself may help the interviewee to clarify his or her problem.

Although many experienced interviewers try to avoid giving direct advice, when they feel it is appropriate, they do so tentatively. They make it clear that their feelings won't be hurt if the interviewee rejects it. Then they ask for feedback on what the interviewee thought about it. The following is an example of an interviewer talking with a student who is considering dropping out of college because he finds his workload too heavy and boring:

> INTERVIEWER: Maybe next semester you might want to take a lot of courses in your major with teachers whom you like and pick up the rest of your required courses later. You seem so discouraged about school that some "fun" courses might get you interested again. What do you think?

advising Telling a client what to do. Used with caution, if at all, in interviews, because it incorrectly assumes that one person knows what is best for another.

CONFRONTING

One of the most emotionally loaded debates about interviewing centers on the issue of the usefulness and timing of confrontation. **Confronting** is a tactic used to call interviewees' attention to discrepancies, inconsistencies, or self-destructive tendencies in their words or behavior. It aims to help interviewees view their behavior in a different light, perhaps unmasking distortions, rationalizations, or evasions. Confrontation can be used gently, with a great deal of empathy, or it can be used in a cruelly assaultive way. There are many gradations along the gentle-to-harsh continuum. Here is an example of a gentle confrontation:

confronting A tactic used by an interviewer to point out to interviewee discrepancies or inconsistencies in the interviewee's words or behavior.

> INTERVIEWEE: I don't mind that my husband insults me and says I look like a fat pig [tears in her eyes].
>
> INTERVIEWER: You say you don't mind, yet you have tears in your eyes. Most people I know mind a lot when someone insults them. I know I do.

This is a mild confrontation, pointing out the discrepancy between the client's words and behavior. It was followed by a supportive statement, which gives permission to be upset and is concrete and descriptive ("You have tears in your eyes") rather than abstract and judgmental ("You must be a masochist"). It "universalizes" the issue by helping the client realize her feelings are common to many people.

Some counselors routinely use a high level of confrontation and intrusiveness, justifying it as a high-risk but high-yield method. One study, however, declared that this justification is a myth (Lieberman, Yalom, & Miles, 1973). It found that highly challenging and confrontational encounter group leaders were destructive in their impatient pressuring of clients to change and ignored the need to individualize treatment. Another researcher warned against the assumption that everyone benefited by "letting it all hang out." Some may, indeed, need help "tucking it all in" (Parloff, 1970, p. 203).

Another study showed that counselors whose confrontations focused on the clients' weaknesses were less effective than those who focused on strengths (Berenson & Mitchell, 1974). It also showed that more effective counselors initiated sensitive confrontation more than did less effective ones.

Some human service workers who work with street people report that a more confrontational style is expected and appreciated on the streets. A human services professor in Minneapolis says, "On the streets here, it is known as 'tough love.' . . . Many of our students are street people. They understand 'tough love,' and they believe it works" (D. Foat, personal communication, 1982).

INTERPRETING

interpreting A form of response that speculates on the meaning of an interviewee's statement or behavior.

Interpreting is one of the most controversial responses. It originated in psychoanalytic practice. Client-centered, gestalt, and some existential theories avoid this technique. Ethnographic interviewers would also not use it because it puts the interviewer in the position of being the expert:

> Whatever information the client offers must be taken at face value, even if it seems outrageous or even false. Careful follow-up of the cover terms offered will quickly reveal if this is the case. It will also demonstrate to the client that the interviewer takes the discussion seriously, almost literally, and that dissembling will be difficult to sustain. (Green & Leigh, 1989, p. 9)

Others believe that interpretation is essential. They argue that it "encourages clients to see their problems from a different perspective, with the desired effect of opening up new possibilities for remedial courses of action" (Hepworth & Larsen, 1987, p. 1008).

The other responses we've described, if done correctly, do not go beyond what the interviewee says or feels. Interpretation, however, *speculates* on what the words might *actually* mean. If the interviewee accepts a response as an accurate interpretation, it can be helpful. However, the "expert's" interpretation is often rejected with irritation or, worse, swallowed whole without reflection. The interviewee's response is the best guide to deciding whether a worker's interpretation has been helpful. The following is an example:

INTERVIEWEE: I don't know why the baby's crying makes me feel so helpless. My mother always knew what to do when my baby brother cried.

INTERVIEWER: When you compare yourself to your mother, you feel inferior to her.

INTERVIEWEE: Maybe that's what it is.

Self-Disclosure

Interviewers often have a hard time deciding when they should reveal elements in their personal lives and attitudes. At one time, that was considered strictly a no-no. Now, most researchers and helpers believe that appropriate self-disclosure can be supportive to the interviewee and creates a more honest relationship. Most of us find it easier to share thoughts and feelings with someone who is willing to risk similar sharing. When the interviewer does this, he or she is modeling desirable sharing behavior and showing that he or she, too, is human.

The guideline for deciding when the worker should disclose something about his or her personal life is the extent to which it brings clarity rather than burdening the client with the interviewer's concerns. *Sharing can illustrate the universality of human concerns.* The interviewers who spend too much time discussing their families, hobbies, or worries are obviously more interested in themselves than in the client. The following are two examples of an appropriate use of sharing personal experience:

INTERVIEWER: You seem to be wondering if I can understand the problems you're having with your foster child. My wife and I cared for a friend's child for a couple of years while she was ill. I know that's not exactly the same as your situation, but the child did show some of the same problems you're having. I'm not sure that means I can understand the problems you're having, but I'd like to try.

INTERVIEWER: I just listened to you telling how hard you worked on the paper—reading books on research and style, spending days in the library, and doing everything in your power to do a good job. Then you described how the teacher scribbled sarcastic comments all over the paper and ridiculed it in front of the class. You apologized for doing such a bad job and say you feel like a failure. Yet, while listening to you, I found myself feeling indignant about the teacher's behavior. Didn't you feel some anger yourself?

Rather than pretend to an interviewee that you have no values or that you agree with the interviewee's values when you don't, it is better to be honest. This leaves both you and the interviewee free to hold on to values that are important without needing to impose them on each other. The following is an example of an appropriate use of disclosing values:

COUNSELOR: Can you try to tell me what you see as the worst problems in this marriage?

HUSBAND: Yes, that's easy. She's out fooling around with her art groups all the time and the house is a mess. I don't have clean socks and underwear in the morning and dinner is never ready on time.

WIFE: You never say anything nice to me, you never talk to me, and now that I finally, after twenty years, found interests and friends of my own, you resent it and you're continually carping at me.

COUNSELOR (to husband):   It's important to you that your laundry be done, the house cleaned, and dinner prepared when you come home.

HUSBAND: Damn right it is! That's what wives are supposed to do.

COUNSELOR: I have a hard time with this because I do not agree with your definition of a wife's obligations. However, I do see that in your view, she is not meeting the terms of the marriage contract under which you are operating. (Okun & Rappaport, 1980, p. 185)

The counselor expressed her views without deriding or punishing the husband. This seemed to help both husband and wife begin to acknowledge and evaluate some of their own values and beliefs about sex roles and marriage.

Authoritarian Leads and Responses

Although giving advice may *sometimes* be helpful, authoritarian leads and responses in interviewing are never helpful. They are generally harmful because they do not take the feelings and thoughts of the interviewee into account. They assume that the interviewer is superior, which makes the interviewee feel inferior. These leads and responses include:

- Urging
- Threatening
- Moralizing
- Contradicting
- Arguing
- Commanding
- Scolding
- Punishing
- Criticizing
- Denying
- Disapproving
- Rejecting
- Ridiculing
- Putting words in someone's mouth

When the interviewer takes a high-and-mighty moral tone, the interviewee has a choice of mindless submission or stubborn defiance. Either way, the interviewee has not been helped to grow in awareness or independence. We have all been lectured to or preached to at some time in our lives, and it's a safe bet that we have resented it! The following are some examples:

INTERVIEWER: I thought you were smart enough to know you should use birth control.

INTERVIEWER: Stealing is wrong, so the teacher had a right to suspend you.

RECORDING

Many workers would much rather spend their time on interviews than on recording interviews. Yet, because memory is notoriously unreliable, human service agencies would be in deep trouble if they did not require workers to record interviews:

1. Recording provides continuity from one worker to another and from one session to the next. Suppose as a worker in a halfway house you learned from Mary that she planned to go home next week and needed to be driven to a job interview from her

home on Wednesday of that week. If you did not record this, the staff member who came on duty after you might not learn of these plans, and Mary would not get to the interview.

2. Recordings of interviews can document progress or lack of it in each particular situation. If you are working with a woman in a nursing home who is losing her memory, your periodic notations about her mental state help to assess whether her memory loss is getting worse over time, staying about the same, or getting better. Or suppose you need to show your funding source the quality and quantity of the services you have given clients. Only if you have kept careful records of referrals and interviews, can you do that.

3. Recording provides documentation of a client's eligibility for service. If done according to previously agreed on and uniform procedures, recording can also be used for research and evaluation of programs and for researching the history of programs.

4. Recording can provide important evidence in legal suits. Workers who have been accused of negligence in child abuse cases have been able to prove, through records of visits and phone contacts, that they had done everything in their power to prevent the abuse.

5. Recording is used by some agencies as a therapeutic tool. In a few states, patients and ex-patients of mental hospitals are permitted to read their own records. "One state mental hospital in Washington has for several years allowed all patients to examine their own records and has found that policy to be therapeutic" (Ennis & Emery, 1978, p. 177).

Recording and Privacy

Even when an agency does not allow clients to read the record, a curious and ingenious client may sneak a look. A poignant example of the devastating effect this can have on a person's self-esteem is given in a *New Yorker* account of a mental hospital patient, Sylvia Frumkin:

> On March 20th, Sylvia Frumkin started therapy with Dr. Sheila Gross, a child psychiatrist at the Jamaica Center. That afternoon, when she arrived to see Dr. Gross, she saw a sheaf of papers on the doctor's desk. The top piece of paper was the first page of Mrs. Schwartz's report. Sylvia has always been able to read upside down. She was stunned by the first line on the page—the one that read "She is a tall, unattractive girl." She decided to test Dr. Gross, and asked her to read the page to her. Dr. Gross glanced at Mrs. Schwartz's report, read aloud, "She is a tall girl, not unattractive," and then changed the subject. Although Sylvia went to see Dr. Gross once a week from the end of March to the end of June, she didn't trust her, because the doctor hadn't been honest with her. (Sheehan, 1981, p. 66)

When workers know that interviewees can read their records, they are likely to be more careful about what they write. They are much less prone to make global evaluative statements such as "The child is in danger of neglect" and more likely to make concrete descriptive statements such as "The fourth-floor windows do not have window guards and the mother has four small children to look after so cannot always keep watch over each child to prevent them from falling out the window. The landlord has not provided enough heat, so the mother turns on the gas stove for heat. This is a fire hazard."

Instead of saying, "The child appeared malnourished," a more verifiable statement would be: "Medical exam showed the child to be fifteen pounds below the normal weight for that age and anemic."

You should strive in your recording to let a future reader see what you saw. Concrete, descriptive statements are not only more accurate, but they also force workers to be more precise, avoiding moralistic, judgmental statements. Some workers discuss with clients what they think should go into a record, using this as a tool to help clients articulate their problems and progress.

SUMMARY

1. An interview is defined as an interaction between people that has a consciously planned purpose, structure, and goal and requires specific communication skills.

2. Important elements of all interviews include the location or setting; the personality, expectations, cultural background, and style of both the interviewer and the interviewee; agency sponsorship; and the attitudes and values of the interviewer. All these are interrelated.

3. The structure of an interview includes three stages: opening, exploring the issues, and closing.

4. During the opening phase, the interviewer and interviewee work out a formal or informal contract to plan their work together.

5. Interviews should focus on a person's strengths rather than weaknesses.

6. Attitudes that are essential for good interviewing include active observing, physical attention, and active listening.

7. Important values include empathy, warmth, respect, and genuineness.

8. Interviews about benefits such as food stamps can be personalized and human rather than rote and bureaucratic.

9. An occupational hazard of human service workers is a need to rescue people and do things for them rather than with them.

10. Some roadblocks to good interviewing are overly passive behavior, discomfort with emotions, and condescension.

11. Open-ended questions help people to talk about themselves.

12. Confrontation can be used gently or in an assaultive way, and should be used sparingly.

13. It is important to observe nonverbal messages.

14. Personal disclosure should be used only to bring clarity rather than to burden the client with the worker's problems.

15. Authoritarian leads and responses are never helpful.

16. Recording interviews is important for continuity of work between workers, for helping the worker remember essential facts, and for legal reasons.

17. Concrete descriptive statements in recording force workers to be more precise.

DISCUSSION QUESTIONS

1. *Humanizing the eligibility interview.* Obtain an application form for food stamps or TANF and study the form with the goal of humanizing the interview. How can you ask questions that will give the interviewee some initiative in the interview? How can you keep some warmth and genuineness in the interview? How can you get the information you need and, at the same time, make the clients feel that they are important and deserving of respect? After studying the questions and deciding on your strategy, role-play the interview with someone, and complete the application form. After the interview, ask the interviewee for feedback on the strengths and weaknesses of your interview.

2. *Active observing.* With one other student, go to a railroad station, a store, the street, or around the campus with a notebook. Observe for fifteen minutes. Then write up a one-page summary of the observation. Bring it to class without conferring with each other. Note the differences in the pair of observations.

3. *Analyzing an observation.* In the presence of several other people—on a bus, in a subway, in a waiting room, or at a party—observe people's behavior closely. Note the relationship of elements in the environment to behavior and the interrelationships among people. Make notes on your observations, write them up, and discuss them with other students.

4. *How well can you listen?* Form a group with two other students. One student takes the role of listener and another of talker, and a third student observes. For three minutes, have the talker speak about any topic she or he chooses. Then the listener should repeat what has been heard. The observer should judge how accurately the listener has heard the speaker. Switch roles until each has had a chance to be talker, listener, and observer.

5. *Asking questions.* Decide on some information you want from another person. First, ask the person six controlling or closed-ended questions and write down the answers. Next, ask six noncontrolling or open-ended questions about the same subject and write down the answers. Which questions gave you more information? Talk to the interviewee about how he or she felt about the two kinds of questions.

6. *Learning to deal with anger.* Form a group with two other students. Two students should role-play, and the other student should observe an interview in which the interviewee imagines being very angry with the interviewer, feeling the anger as genuinely as possible and expressing it heatedly. For two or three minutes, the interviewer should react defensively; then for two or three minutes, the interviewer should react empathically. Both interviewer and interviewee should observe and contrast the difference in reactions to the two kinds of responses. The interviewer should note how he or she felt about the angry attack and how the two different responses felt. The interviewee should note how the two interviewer responses felt. The observer should note carefully the nature of the feelings expressed by the two role-players, as well as nonverbal behavior that gives clues to feelings. Change roles so that each person has an opportunity to play all the roles (Hammond et al., 1977).

7. *Dealing with a "helpless" person.* In a group, ask a volunteer to play the role of Mrs. Jones, an interviewee. All but Mrs. Jones should close their eyes and imagine that they are in an office and Mrs. Jones is seeing them for the first time. Their job is to help Mrs. Jones. She sits down (adopting a slightly helpless tone of voice and a dramatic presentation): "I am so glad you have time to see me. You are absolutely my last hope! I can just tell you will be able to help me. I've been to four other places, and they all have waiting lists, or no time, or just were not interested. I am feeling absolutely desperate and I was so relieved when you could see me right away! The others did not understand me at all; they didn't even take the time to listen to my difficulty; I only need someone to help me sort out the problem and I am sure you can do that. I am grateful that you are spending time with me." Change roles so that each person has an opportunity to play all the roles (National Center on Child Abuse and Neglect, 1979).

WEB RESOURCES FOR FURTHER STUDY

Social work interviewing
http://pages.prodigy.net/volksware/socialworkworld/questions/htm

A social worker discusses how she uses her social work interviewing skills to interview job applicants.

http://www.questia.com/library/sociology-and-anthropology/social-work/interviewing-in-social-work.jsp

Full-text books, journals, articles at the Questia Online Library

Chapter 10

Case Management/Counseling

Reading this excerpt from a human service student's journal is a very appropriate way to begin a discussion of case management/counseling:

> I was having a real hard time studying and I was sure I was going to flunk my courses. I couldn't concentrate because my family was going through a divorce. I felt like I was being pulled apart by my parents. Who was I supposed to be loyal to? I knew I was getting to depend on cocaine too much. I was stoned most of the time. I figured I better talk to someone soon before I blew my stack. I started asking my friends and my dorm supervisor for the name of a good therapist. People would ask me if I wanted to see a psychiatrist, a psychologist, a social worker, a family therapist, a drug and alcohol counselor, or what. I'd ask what the difference was but no one gave me a clear answer. So they didn't know and I didn't know! I felt more confused than when I began looking for help.

Thus far in this book you have met many human service workers. The majority of them were delivering direct services and spending most of their day working one-on-one with clients. Although doing similar work, they were likely to be referred to variously as:

- Case workers
- Social workers
- Counselors
- Advocates
- Therapists
- Case managers
- Clinicians
- Therapists

All this semantic fuzziness can be confusing to a client who must figure out whom to go to with a problem. And a worker searching the job listings in the newspaper or a web site can never tell from the title of the position exactly what tasks or problem areas it will include. The general public, accustomed to name brands, finds it difficult to understand how a middle-aged woman with a doctorate in psychology and a young man with an associate's degree in human services can both assert that they do "counseling."

In an effort to make job titles uniform, some professionals in the human service field have suggested that a distinction in title should be made according to how much a human service worker deals with highly charged emotional material rather than with the ordinary problems of daily life. They might say

> A social worker or therapist who has an advanced degree helps clients deal with deep-seated intrapsychic problems. A case manager or counselor (a less academically trained person) helps clients make decisions and then use social resources to implement them.

But we don't think that is a sensible distinction! All human service workers, regardless of their backgrounds, job titles, or their clients' problems, must inevitably deal with inner emotions as well as external pressures. Of course, with more study, experience, and training, a clinician can work more effectively with the deep emotions that surround problems.

Human service problems stem from the interaction of biological, emotional, and environmental stresses. If we ignore one set of forces, we get a lopsided view of a problem. And lopsided views lead to inadequate interventions.

For example, Timothy, a counselor in a residential prison-diversion program, has been asked by Barry, one of the residents, for a change of roommates. Before Timothy began to juggle rooms to accommodate Barry's request, he encouraged Barry to clarify the problem he was having with his present roommate. Timothy asked Barry about:

1. Barry's expectations of his present roommate and what he thought his roommate's expectations were of him
2. The similarities and differences in their habits, routines, and lifestyles
3. The extent to which they both tolerated differences in styles
4. The methods of conflict resolution they had already tried when they had a disagreement
5. The stresses of study, family, work, or social life that may have been aggravating their problem

After several conversations with the two men, some separately and some together, Timothy suggested that the tension between them might lessen if they set up a more workable system for cleanup. He offered to help them design a chore chart. They also agreed to make some mutually acceptable rules about playing the radio and going to bed. Through their sessions, one of the young men realized that some of his anger at his roommate probably stemmed from his past irritations with his brother and that, in fact, there were many parts of living together that he enjoyed. They agreed to try to use the chore chart and a few rules they both could agree on for two weeks. They also agreed to check in with Timothy for ten minutes each day. Thus, both young men found possible solutions to a relationship problem that at first seemed insurmountable.

There might have been other root causes for the tension. Perhaps Barry brought home a great deal of anger from his job and that was the primary source of tension between the roommates. If that had been the case, Timothy could have referred him to a vocational counselor and a youth employment agency to help him change jobs or cope better with the one he had.

Although the counseling assignment of beginning human service workers might involve helping clients find and use resources, they should never lose sight of the fact that a client's unexplored feelings can subtly sabotage even the simplest solution.

ALL PROBLEMS ARE SERIOUS YET ORDINARY

Some people assert that the differences in the roles of professional helpers lie in the gravity of the problems they are assigned. But this is also an oversimplification. Human problems can never be divided up on a scale ranging from very serious to less serious and then be parceled out to different workers.

All problems appear overwhelming but Epstein and Brown (2001), in discussing the concept of **task-focused casework**, argue that just the reverse is true. In reality, most human problems are mundane and ordinary. No one goes through life without facing many serious, painful problems. Someone we love will die or become disabled, someone we need very much might leave us, and barriers will be thrown up in our paths at many junctures. In making this surprising assertion, the authors do not mean to trivialize human problems or suggest that they are easily overcome. To the person struggling against a barrier, the pain and frustration are very real. They are, however, pointing out that all human service problems have similar characteristics:

> **task-focused casework** A method of helping a person with a problem by focusing on the immediate priorities of the client and the small steps involved in realizing, or seeking to realize, the ultimate goal.

- The person lacks the specific resources to alleviate a painful situation.
- The person lacks the skills to cope with or overcome a painful situation.

The difficulty of a problem-solving process depends on how well the necessary techniques and resources can be mustered. All human service workers are likely to encounter a variety of life's problems. On a first fieldwork assignment, for example, you might be coaching a basketball team in a suburban after-school program. That might seem like a pretty simple assignment until the day you take one of the youngsters home and are told that her mother has just been critically injured in a car accident.

We will resist the temptation to offer simple definitions for the titles and roles human service workers carry, and we urge you to tolerate a certain amount of confusion in the titles and roles themselves. In the rest of this chapter, the term *case manager/counselor* will be used. But everything we say could apply to any mental health worker, regardless of the title a particular agency chooses to use.

Let us listen in on a conversation with a counselor named Carmen Mejia. In the eleven years since she graduated from college, she has been employed by three different agencies. In each, she has been assigned a different title and has worked with a different population. First we will read about her current position. Then she will re-create a scene from each of her two previous jobs.

I N T E R V I E W

Carmen Mejia, Family Resource Worker, Coordinated Approach to Partnership in Parenting (CAPP)*

I'm really excited about talking about my current job. I've been here for four years, but my position keeps changing. I was hired as a foster care worker on a special grant from the Community Council Foundation. The child-protection social workers at the

---

*For further insights into permanency planning projects, see Hampton, Senatore, and Guillotta (1998); Kelly and Blythe (2000); Kinney, Happala, Booth, and Leavitte (1998); Lloyd and Bryce (1984); and Schneider (1991).

Department of Social Services (DSS) designed my position and then fought to get it funded. There were never enough appropriate places to send children when they had to be taken out of their homes on a temporary basis.

My first assignment was to recruit more foster parents, especially for Latino children. When children can't speak English or they are dark skinned, it is especially hard to place them. This county has a rapidly growing population of immigrants from El Salvador, Nicaragua, Panama, and the Dominican Republic. The families come here to escape discrimination and poverty but find a whole new set of problems. They have difficulty obtaining the "green cards" from the federal government that permit them to legally stay here. Even when they have the legal status, jobs are hard to find and pay very little. The housing they can afford is very run-down. They get frustrated from all the pressures and they lack the family support they were accustomed to in their countries. Frustration can turn outward into violence or inward into drug and alcohol abuse.

Before I started, they often placed Latino children in any home available. The kids weren't understood, the food was strange to them, and they were often ridiculed or rejected. They went from one bad situation at home to another in foster care.

For months I went around the community speaking at churches and meeting with residents at their social clubs. I had to explain about how someone applied to be a foster parent and reassure them they wouldn't be rejected because they didn't speak perfectly. I recruited a lot of new foster families. But it was obvious that just putting kids in foster homes isn't enough. It was often like a revolving door. Either the foster parents didn't get enough help from us, or their situations changed and they had to move to another town or focus on their own children.

No matter how good their foster parents were, the kids still suffered from having too many transitions in their lives. Most of the time they wanted to return home and their folks wanted them back. Both the foster and the birth parents were pretty much ignored by the system. Sometimes children did get sent back, but it would tear your heart out to hear stories of how nothing had changed; the same abuse or neglect would start all over again.

I think both the birth parents and the foster parents felt unsupported by DSS. The social workers felt they were being unfairly pressured by lawyers and the media. Nothing seemed to get resolved and children lived in limbo year after year. Every once in a while there would be a big newspaper article about some terrible mistake we made when we took children out of their homes or returned them to a dangerous situation.

permanency planning   An attempt to create, in a timely fashion, a plan for a child that will return him or her safely to the family of origin or legally free the child to be adopted.

I was about to leave the agency from sheer frustration. Then a new program was initiated. It's called CAPP, Coordinated Approach to Partnership in Parenting. It grew out of the mayor's task force on **permanency planning** and **family preservation**. The aim is to reunite families when that is possible or to free children for adoption and a new permanent home. All along the way it offers help to all the parties.

I am now called a family resource worker. I am part of a team composed of the foster parents, the birth parents, and the social worker. If the child is old enough and is able, he or she is included also. The first step in CAPP was a ten-session training program for workers. They also invited prospective foster parents to join so they could be trained and screened at the same time. We did role-plays and guided imagery and talked about our own childhoods and parenting styles. We discussed child development and alternative discipline techniques. We learned how to look for signs of learning disabilities, mental illness, depression, drugs, and sexual abuse.

family preservation A commitment to provide the resources and supports that can hold together or reunite a family unit, especially to provide stability to the children.

This wasn't the first time there has been training, but this was special. For once, we were all sitting down together. Maybe some of the presentations were a little elementary for the social workers with master's degrees, but for me it was eye-opening. I think that the morale and the understanding of this new batch of foster parents is better than most of the older ones. For the birth parents it is very supportive. They are encouraged to think of us as helpers, not as snoops who are punishing them. Some of them had pretty rough treatment when they were kids. They need new models of discipline and more understanding of children's needs.

One of the big parts of my job is to visit the birth parents and foster parents on a regular schedule. I ask them to make an agenda—topics they want to talk about so we can be sure to cover what is going on and what they need from me. Whenever there is a crisis—a child runs away or a parent goes off the deep end—I hang in with the family for as long as it takes to get the situation ironed out.

I had one case of a father who was removed from his home because he sexually abused his two sons. He was attending counseling regularly, so the team suggested that he be allowed to come home for visits as long as the children could be protected. I worked with the whole family on this. First we put locks on the younger children's door. Then I arranged for respite care—a child care worker was assigned so the mother didn't have to watch the children all the time. I spent a lot of time with the family, talking about what was okay touching and what is sexual or physical abuse. I go back often and monitor the arrangement. If our plan works, the father can stay in touch with his family while he continues his individual counseling and group therapy. He needs to figure out what drove him to be an abuser and how he can stop. Some people disapprove of this plan, but our goal is to reunite this family and extinguish the destructive behavior that led to its breakup.

The program is still new, and there is never enough time and energy. We do endless paperwork. Every contact has to be documented, partly for the research but mostly in case there is a legal problem down the road. We have to prove that we did everything possible if we recommend that parental custody be terminated. We have to keep records so that we don't just keep trying the same things over or lose track of something important.

I still get frustrated by the lack of resources for the kids despite the fact that research shows that most clients benefit more from things like day care or homemaker services than just counseling alone. But we are always hustling to obtain summer camp placements, transportation to school tutoring programs, and competent therapists, especially ones who speak Spanish. With all the talk about family preservation, child-welfare agencies spend only 10 percent of their budgets on concrete services for the families. It makes you wonder how serious they are about keeping families together.

Carmen Mejia as Case Manager/ Counselor for Youthful Offenders

The following is a scene from Carmen's previous case manager/counselor position at St. Joseph's Home, a program for youthful first-time offenders:

On a blustery, cold winter afternoon, Carmen drove up to the courthouse on Beel Street, parked her car, and rushed in to keep her 2:00 P.M. appointment with Mr. Creavey, a youth probation officer. As an advocate employed by St. Joseph's Home, she implements service plans for juveniles convicted of serious but nonviolent crimes.

She carried extensive notes on Sal, a fifteen-year-old boy found guilty of car theft. His case file included reports from the house parents at St. Joseph's where he had been living since convicted, from the guidance counselor at his high school, and from the therapist who worked with him and his family. During the next half hour, Carmen and Mr. Creavey reviewed the progress Sal had made toward the goals they had all agreed on three months earlier. Toward the end of their time together, she stated her arguments in favor of Sal returning home to live with his parents. They agreed to continue his family therapy; Sal had promised to attend school regularly. He was to get special-education services, which would hopefully make school a more successful experience than it had been in the past. He also would be enrolled in a teenage violence prevention program to help him learn more constructive ways of expressing his angry feelings with his peers and his family. The course used a curriculum developed by a public health expert (Prothrow-Smith, 1987).

That evening at St. Joseph's, Carmen met with Sal, his family, and the therapist to report on the meeting with Mr. Creavey. They reviewed the Individual Service Plan (ISP) agreed to by the probation officer. Carmen answered their questions and encouraged them to see this as a new start under better conditions.

Carmen Mejia as Case Manager/Counselor for the Elderly

The following is a scene from Carmen's first case manager/counselor job at Elder Care, a private, for-profit agency that helps to arrange supportive life services for aged infirm adults:

Carmen had been on the phone for almost an hour, calling local geriatric agencies to find out what services they offered and if they had space available. She looked over her notes and heaved a sigh of satisfaction. She had finished just in time and had located several resources. She placed them in her **referral file**.

referral file An updated list of all available resources in a human service area, with notations about the special characteristics or qualifications of each.

In ten minutes, she would be meeting with Mr. and Mrs. Knopf, who were coming to consult about Mr. Knopf's elderly aunt. They were concerned about her living arrangements and wanted to make some plans for her future. She lived alone, and they checked on her every few days. She had begun a rapid slide downhill in her ability to take care of herself. She could no longer feed or dress herself adequately or keep her apartment in reasonable order. They were planning a long trip to England and were her only close relatives. They wanted the agency to help them find a nursing home or assisted-living facility or perhaps a reliable personal-care attendant who would visit regularly.

In this first interview, Carmen wanted to understand the medical and social background of the aunt. She would find out what kind of services the Knopfs had already used and how those had worked. She would explain the services her agency offered and would strongly suggest that the next visit include the aunt. If the aunt was not able to come into the office, Carmen was prepared to set up a meeting in her home. Carmen was convinced that any referral she made would fail unless the client was involved in making the decisions about her care.

Carmen sees herself as a matchmaker, a person who brings people together with the services they need and then makes sure they are right for each other. She now understands how painful and stressful it can be for the whole family when a loved elder enters institutional care (Peek, 2000).

GOALS OF THE CASE MANAGER/COUNSELOR

Carmen has the same goals and employs the same skills, whether she is talking with a foster mother at her kitchen table, reporting to the young man and his family after the conference with the probation officer, or interviewing the couple who are planning care for their elderly relative. She asks questions and gives information and support in a way that allows the clients the space and time to clarify their situation and explore alternative courses of action. Because she believes in client self-determination, Carmen does not tell people what to do or how to do it. She knows she might be able to influence or manipulate a pregnant teenager into giving up her child; she knows she could pressure a young offender into going back to school. But she also suspects that as a result of that kind of worker interference, the teenage girl is likely to carry around a heavy emotional burden of loss for many years, and the young man coerced back into school is likely to drop out.

Often Carmen must set aside her own convictions. When she is working with the criminal justice system or the child-protective systems, her actions are dictated by certain rules and regulations that conflict with her concept of the importance of self-determination. Whether the clients come to her agency on their own initiative or are mandated to do so, she works to accomplish four outcomes:

1. The clients will be able to express or change a negative emotional state.
2. The clients will increase their understanding of themselves and their situation.
3. The clients will be better able to make important decisions.
4. The clients will be better able to implement a decision once it is made. (See Kennedy, 2001; Loughary & Ripley, 1979.)

Releasing or Changing a Negative Emotional State

As Carmen encourages her clients to express their negative feelings, she assures them that there are no right or wrong feelings. When fourteen-year-old Kim is angry at her foster mother for not allowing her to go to a party, Carmen does not tell the youngster that she should or should not feel angry. Feelings are valid and need to be respected. Well-meaning people often say to someone who is in a rage or a deep depression:

> You should be ashamed of yourself for being so angry (or depressed) when you have so much to be thankful for.

or

> You think *you've* got problems; let me tell you what happened to me.

These kinds of responses are likely to make the person feel worse! People do not want to be told that their feelings are trivial, self-pitying, or irrelevant. Carmen knows that when Kim is in pain, she desperately needs someone to listen. Sometimes she does not even need anyone to agree with her. Later, as the intensity of the feelings lessens, Carmen can discuss the problem in a more objective way.

Workers should not try to talk people out of their feelings. Their job is to help people figure out why one particular issue provokes emotion. After Kim is allowed to express her feelings, perhaps then she can figure out how to avoid another confrontation. And if her rage at her foster mother causes her to get into a fight with her teacher at school, Carmen needs to help her find a less destructive way to express her feelings.

Understanding of Self and Situation

After Kim expresses her feelings, Carmen tries to get her to put herself in the role of her foster mother or teacher. It is not easy for Kim, or any other high school students struggling to find their own identity, to tap into the feelings of powerlessness a caretaking adult might have. Perhaps her foster mother is immersed in a midlife crisis, job transition, or a marriage problem. Perhaps her desire to protect Kim is an expression of love. Empathy is a difficult skill for a client to develop. It is, however, the cornerstone of communication. Carmen has participated in workshops to learn how to utilize role-play techniques to increase her clients' ability to empathize with the other actors in their family dramas.

Carmen also tries to provide Kim with insights into the nature of her specific life crises, developmental issues, and social problems. She encourages Kim to ask questions. Together they might explore:

- What is alcohol really doing to my body or mind?
- How realistic is the notion that I'm going to flunk all my courses, or does it just feel that way at the moment?
- What are the phases most kids go through when they lose their home and parents?
- How much am I similar to other people who have faced this? In what ways am I unique?
- Why are adults so controlling?

Carmen helps clients gain perspective on their fears, hopes, and plans by sharing what she has learned from other young people and from college courses.

Carmen is always adding to her storehouse of information. From each of her jobs, she has learned information to take to the next one. She knows a great deal about the ins and outs of the juvenile justice system from her time at St. Joseph's Home. She received a crash course in special-education services as a foster care worker. And because of elder care, she knows about Meals on Wheels and different levels of nursing homes.

It is easy to assume that everyone knows the services available in this area for the unemployed, handicapped, elderly, depressed, or alcoholic. But often low-income as well as more affluent people do not know precisely how to connect with an agency once they have found it (Haas, 1959; Hall, Smith, & Bradley, 1970). Currently, those people who have access to a computer—their own or in a work place, school, or library—can turn to networking sites such as Facebook and Twitter. These sites may contain conflicting views (and even misinformation) but can also make approaching a social service a less mysterious task. Most social agencies now have created their own web sites that can prepare people for their first visit.

Making Decisions

When people are in crisis, they often desperately need to make a decision. Yet that is precisely when they are immobilized. Any actions they take are bound to have negative as well as positive consequences. To make the best possible decisions, they need to sort out inaccurate or conflicting bits of information about each possible choice, get in touch with their feelings, anticipate possible consequences, and then try to decide what is in their best interest. Solving problems and making decisions can be a reasonably systematic process or a frustrating and chaotic one.

Carmen works with her clients to help them make one specific decision and to develop decision-making skills that can be used again and again as new problems arise.

Implementing Decisions

BREAKING A BIG TASK DOWN INTO SMALL STEPS

The most carefully thought out decision is little more than an exercise in futility if action does not follow. When a decision is made, Carmen helps her clients break a big decision into small steps. Then each small step is discussed, practiced, and evaluated.

Carmen has been working with Lila Parsikian, a mother recently released from a drug rehabilitation program. Lila seems stuck. She has said that she wants to eject her abusive lover from her home. But even thinking about confronting him with her decision makes her break out in a cold sweat. Implementing a decision involves personal risk. The possibility of failure lies close behind each new move. Carmen and Lila have been rehearsing what she will say. They have also discussed her sources of protection. Lila thinks that her brother would be willing to stay with her for a few days. Carmen encouraged Lila to finish the paperwork for Transitional Assistance so she could get immediate financial support and break her economic dependency on her lover.

GIVING EMOTIONAL SUPPORT

Carmen has to be careful as she treads the fine line between reasonable encouragement and false reassurance. She can encourage her client to feel that she is a worthy person and does not deserve to be beaten. Carmen can explain to the young woman that she has the right to get a legal restraining order that prohibits her boyfriend from harassing her. She can promise to call her each day and refer her to a shelter if she wants to go that route. But she also must be honest about the fact that a restraining order does not guarantee her safety. Women have been battered and even killed by violent mates as they clutched a restraining order in their hand.

MODELING BEHAVIOR

When they discussed Lila's growing frustration with her very aggressive child, Carmen found out about the discipline techniques Lila uses. After suggesting some methods that avoid physical punishment, she visited Lila's home to work with her and her child. By modeling a disciplining behavior, such as a short "time out," and then staying there as the parent tries it, Carmen teaches while giving emotional support (Kernberg et al., 1991; Webster-Stratton & Martin, 1994; Zeilberger, Sampen, & Sloan, 1973).

MAKING REFERRALS

Sometimes Carmen refers clients to support groups or training programs. Assertiveness training helps hesitant young women put their good sense into action. Perhaps she will tell Lila about a parenting group at a local mental health center or at a shelter for women who are in abusive relationships. She might make the phone call with her to find out when it meets.

Carmen's clients' needs for hand-holding, reassurance, and rehearsing vary enormously. Sometimes a little push in the right direction can set the top spinning on its own. But sometimes, resistance to taking the next step masks real discontent about a decision. If Lila is not ready to take the first step to go back to school, maybe Carmen needs to spend more time working on building her self-confidence through taking some small steps with a high probability of success. Maybe attending a one-day workshop on career choice or opportunities in computers would be a good start.

OVERCOMING BARRIERS

Clients often get stuck moving a plan into action because barriers block their path. Kevin, a young man who is blind, is ready to graduate from a residential school and attend college in his community. But the college does not provide up-to-date Braille texts, special library equipment, and enough note takers. He will not be able to succeed without those supports.

When barriers keep her clients from getting the services they are entitled to, Carmen uses her organizing skills. She suggested that Kevin file a complaint to the dean and to the department in the state bureaucracy that oversees special educational services. If that does not work, he might need to go to court. Carmen is with him every step of the way. She might refer him to an agency that does legal advocacy on behalf of students with disabilities.

THE PROCESS OF CASE MANAGEMENT/ COUNSELING

Getting Prepared for the Client and the Problem

Even before clients walk into her agency, Carmen has begun working with them. Perhaps she has spoken to them briefly over the phone or a worker from another agency has sent a written referral about their situation.

Even though she never has enough time in her day, Carmen always takes a few moments to quietly and systematically think about her next appointment before the client arrives. During the initial encounter (and each subsequent one), she will face many unknowns, but the more carefully she has prepared herself, the more she will be able to meet the challenge of each unique personality and situation. She prepares herself by tuning in to the clients and their problems both emotionally and intellectually.

preparatory empathy An attempt to put oneself in the shoes of another person, to feel or think of a problem from another perspective, even before encountering a client, to sensitize the worker.

USING PREPARATORY EMPATHY

We have already stressed the critical importance of empathy, putting oneself into the shoes of another person and seeing the world out of the other person's eyes. Now we introduce the concept of **preparatory empathy** (Gitterman & Shulman, 1994; Shulman, 2008; Summers, 2005).

Of course, it would be arrogant to think that we can ever predict what another human being will feel. We can, however, sensitize ourselves to listen and watch intently for the emotions that might lie below the surface of a client's words and actions. Tuning in helps us to respond accurately to the garbled, often ambivalent messages that people send when they are experiencing a high level of stress.

To sharpen her preparatory empathy, Carmen collects and then sifts through all she knows about the emotional baggage that often accompanies a particular set of problems. Carmen has been preparing for a home visit to Laurel Schultz, the mother of a five-year-old girl who is enrolled in a day care center affiliated with a large teaching hospital. She has never met Ms. Schultz but was asked by the center director to try to get her to agree to having her daughter evaluated. The director suspects that the youngster has attention deficit/hyperactivity disorder (AD/HD), a biological condition that makes concentrating and following rules very difficult (Barkley, 2005; Wender, 1987). Because so few people understand this disability, children like Ms. Schultz's daughter are likely to be high-risk students when they go on to public school. They appear to not care, not listen, or not be trying hard enough, so they are frequently punished by authority figures and rejected by their peers.

The following "Q and S" section shows how Carmen prepared herself for her meeting with Laurel Schultz. "Q" stands for Carmen's questions, and "S" stands for her speculations. Some of this preparation she role-played with her supervisor.

Q: What kind of emotions might I anticipate from a parent at this day care center?

S: Well, I will be visiting the mother of a preschooler, so I'll need to review what I've learned about the parents of toddlers in general and about the parents in this particular center. One thing that stands out is that many of the parents feel that they are being blamed by the staff when their child has a problem. Most parents, especially of small children, have dreams for their youngsters. It can be devastating to be told that the experts suspect there is something that isn't quite normal.

I find most of the day care staff very supportive. They don't usually sound the alarm until they have a strong sense that the problem isn't going to work itself out.

Many of the parents have a love–hate relationship with the doctors at Morgantown Hospital, which works with the center. Some parents are so intimidated by experts that they don't question the experts about anything. Others are suspicious and bitter toward them. Many feel that the doctors use their kids as guinea pigs to train interns, who graduate and then practice in more affluent communities.

There are so many drugs around this community that the very mention of a medication such as Ritalin, which is sometimes used for ADHD, may be met with instant resistance.

Q: What kind of emotions might I anticipate from this family?

S: The staff has told me that the Schultzes have already asked them for help in figuring out how to cope with their daughter's impulsive and oppositional behavior. So they might really welcome the evaluation. They have three other children who have not had problems in school, so they are not likely to feel that they are being singled out unfairly. They can be reminded of how successful their parenting has been. Both of the Schultzes have attended meetings and potluck suppers at the center, so the staff thinks they are very motivated.

When I phoned Ms. Schultz, she sounded welcoming, but she did indicate that her husband thought his daughter's problem is due to the school's permissive discipline. She might be feeling pulled between him and the teachers. I'll need to try to engage his cooperation.

Q: What are my own feelings about this situation? How would I feel if a worker from my child's day care center came to visit me to tell me about a potential learning problem with my child, especially one that might not be easy to deal with?

S: I remember my mom would complain about my younger brother but hated it when anyone else said anything negative about him. I know she felt guilty about having a job. Ms. Schultz works outside the home. I wonder if she might have some of the same feelings?

I hate it when my supervisor is too critical about something I've done; it's hard to be told that things are not going well. But I appreciate it when she starts by talking about all the good things I do.

Q: What do I know about impulsive and oppositional behavior in young children?

S: I'd better call a therapist at the School Function Clinic at Children's Hospital and get some clues about techniques and referrals. I'll need them.

ANTICIPATING MISUNDERSTANDINGS AND TENSION BETWEEN WORKER AND CLIENT

Preparatory empathy is not a parlor game in which the worker tries to outguess the client. Rather, it is a process that alerts a worker to issues that might turn out to be important. If feelings are not brought up by the parents, then Carmen sends up a trial balloon. She might say:

> Some people have heard a lot of conflicting information about hyperactivity and attention deficit disorder. I'm wondering what you might have heard and if you have any feelings about the way it is diagnosed and treated.

If Ms. Schultz shrugs off the question, Carmen lets it drop. Perhaps she has no questions or isn't ready yet to ask them.

In the following, Shulman (1979) describes a home visit that goes sour very quickly because the worker did not use preparatory empathy:

> A young human service worker visits a parent in her home. This is their first meeting. The parent, a middle-aged mother of seven, had been struggling for years with a multitude of serious problems with her children. Over the previous several months, the mother had developed a good relationship with her last case manager/counselor. She was a woman close to her own age who was suddenly transferred to another office. After a few minutes of rather tense introductory chatting, the parent interrupted the worker and asked in a brusque tone of voice: "You got any children of your own?"
>
> After suppressing a gulp and an internal "Oh my goodness, what do I say now?" the young worker answered: "No, I don't have any children, but I have had child psychology courses in college and I know a lot about parenting." The client laughed derisively, and essentially ended the interview by withdrawing into silence. (p. 15)

Shulman states that if the worker had anticipated this question, she might have been prepared to respond to the mother's possible feelings of:

- Defensiveness
- Fear of being judged a "bad" parent
- Fear that this new worker couldn't understand how hard it is to parent when one is poor, lonely, and lives in a neglected neighborhood
- Anger at being abandoned by her former worker
- Sadness for the loss of a relationship that was helpful

If the worker had tuned in to these feelings, she could have answered with a more supportive, less defensive statement. She might have said:

> No, I don't have any children, but I'll try very hard to understand what your family situation is all about.

or

> No, I don't. I also have wondered if this will get in the way of my fully understanding you and being of help. I hope you'll tell me what it is like for you and what kind of help I can give.

or

> No, I don't. I wonder if you're worrying if this will make it hard for us to work together? Let's talk about that. (Shulman, 1979, p. 15)

Reading and Evaluating Referral Materials

When Carmen starts working with a client, she usually has some background information about the person and situation. Sometimes it is a bulging file; often it is just a brief note or verbal statement from another worker. When she worked with young people who had trouble with the law, a file was likely to contain some of the following:

- An official record of the arrest and a description of the precipitating incident
- A report prepared by the probation officer on the youth's school achievement, family background, and work history
- A summary of tests that the public school administered and the school transcripts
- The results of a vocational test administered by a rehabilitation agency that was working with the youth before the arrest
- A medical report on the youth's physical condition
- Notes taken at a family interview with the court social worker

Some of this information is **objective data**. It states facts such as the dates of events, medical findings, court dispositions, work history, or any public benefits that have been received. Other pieces of data might appear objective but are open to judgment and bias.

objective data
Data based on unbiased facts, not affected by personal feelings or prejudice.

For example, the results of a battery of personality tests, although useful, are open to varied interpretations according to who administered or scored them.

subjective data
Personal opinions about the client's attitude, situation, and behavior that may or may not be objectively true.

Other documents are filled with clearly **subjective data**. They state opinions about the client's attitude, situation, and behavior. Carmen is always careful to be a little skeptical of this kind of data. In the Shulman (2008) example of lack of preparatory empathy, the worker might have written that the client was "aggressive" or "hostile." But if Carmen had been the worker and had tuned in to the client's feelings, she might have interpreted her behavior as "appropriately anxious." Emotions are often in the eyes of the beholder.

Reports can be riddled with diagnostic labels that do not have hard data to support them. Phrases such as *mentally disturbed child, overprotective parent, hyperactive child,* or *juvenile delinquent* will frequently crop up in a client's file. We have no way to evaluate the credentials, skills, or sensitivity of the people who affixed the labels. These terms are often used imprecisely and should not be automatically accepted as an accurate depiction of a client's personality or background.

referral statement
An initial verbal or written statement that explains the reasons a client is being sent to or has chosen a specific resource, person, or agency.

As long as Carmen is a bit skeptical, the **referral statement** can still be very useful. She learns about the client's previous experiences, which might give clues to his or her expectations. If it is not clear from the referral statement exactly why the client is coming to the agency, a few direct questions early in the first interview may bring clarity.

POINTS TO KEEP IN MIND WHEN REVIEWING REFERRAL MATERIALS

1. *Background records generally exclude the views of the client.* The reports on a client's attitudes, behavior, or progress are written only from the perspective of the workers. To round out the picture, we need to hear how the clients evaluate their experiences. Unfortunately, their reflections, even when included, are often given little credence.

2. *Background records can lead us to prejudge clients.* Carmen tries to guard against tunnel vision. However, she may not realize it, but another worker's opinions can color her initial judgments, which might have been different if she had started from scratch.

3. *Background information can lead to shaping the client's behavior.* Once we have formed preconceptions, we might slip into a pattern of treating a client in a certain way. Treated that way, clients might reciprocate by acting as we assumed they would. That is called a *self-fulfilling prophecy.*

4. *Background data can be based on dubious measures.* Through the years, professional opinions about various test measures have shifted, and many questions have been raised about the extent to which some instruments unwittingly reflect only the ideas or styles of the test designer or the dominant cultural group. Intelligence tests, vocational tests, and even reading tests are believed to give inaccurate assessments of women and members of ethnic minorities. In addition, when clients are tested against their will, they are not at their sharpest or most optimistic, and thus inaccuracies may occur.

Methods of Collecting Additional Data about a Case

When we review the file of a new client and evaluate the quantity and quality of material in it, we appreciate the critical importance of careful recording. When records are well organized, including all the pertinent information about critical events, Carmen starts out many steps ahead. When records are vague and inaccurate, Carmen wastes valuable time hunting down the details of a hospitalization, an application for a program that was refused, or a court sentence that was suspended under specific conditions. Clients understandably resent telling their story again and again.

Information gathering must be focused. Human service workers often fall into the trap of assuming that more is better. Yet, random information gathering can muddy the waters. Although it is often true that the sources of current problems lie in past experiences, the case management/counseling process generally focuses on the here and now. Worker and client need to systematically gather data about the times, places, and circumstances surrounding the client's most immediately pressing problems.

The client should be told what information is needed and how it will be gathered and used. Many human service agencies have standardized procedures and time lines for gathering information. For example, if Carmen is helping a young mother apply for health care or for subsidized day care, she explains what documentation will be needed to support the request. She also explains why it is needed. She tells clients whether the law stipulates a time frame or an appeals process if they are denied benefits.

With all the explanations workers give, clarity and honesty coupled with sensitivity are vital. When Carmen calls to set up a visit, she might say, for example:

> Mrs. Tryforo, the social worker from school, has called me to say that she is very concerned about the bruises on your son's face. I need to visit with you, preferably in your home, and talk about those bruises. I will then have to visit his school and talk to his doctor and your neighbors. I have to submit my report to my supervisor within three days.

There are many ways we go about collecting data. Here are some of the methods we use.

INTAKE INTERVIEWS

In the CAPP program, all the counselors take turns doing initial **intake interviews**. They write up the information gathered and decide whether the person's needs fit in with the agency services. If they do and there is room in the agency's caseload, the worker decides which staff member might work best with that client. For example, one worker may have a reputation for being especially effective with angry teenagers and another worker may be known to do well with very shy, inarticulate people.

intake interview
An interview (form) that solicits relevant information before the delivery of a service begins.

The intake interview zeros in on the immediate problem situation—how it came about, what has already been done to deal with it, and what specific actions the client wants to or is required to take. Though intake is usually conducted on a one-on-one basis, CAPP has experimented with group intakes both for efficiency and to provide prospective clients with emotional support.

HOME VISITS

CAPP includes a home visit as an integral part of its regular data-gathering process. The home visit provides an opportunity to gain greater understanding of the patterns of interaction, support, and stress that daily confront clients and their family systems. Carmen has a few clients whom she sees regularly in their homes. Many clients welcome the less formal atmosphere, but others resist and resent it. Perhaps it makes them feel intruded upon.

This young girl was born with life-threatening food allergies. Her family joins with others who share a similar challenge, in order to raise research money and public awareness. Food allergies impact both the health and self-esteem of the children who must cope with them.

Carmen usually has the flexibility to let clients choose the interview setting. When clients have little choice because they are mandated to receive services in their home, she helps them express any negative feelings they might have about her visit. She reassures them that their angry or apprehensive feelings are understandable.

Client resistance usually lessens if a counselor makes advance appointments, sticks to a time schedule, has a clear sense of the purpose of each encounter and explains it clearly, encourages expression of feelings, and is respectful.

STAFFINGS OR CASE CONFERENCES

Often several different workers and agencies are involved with the same client or family. For example, Lila Parsikian has been seen by:

- A hospital staff person who evaluates her youngster's behavior problem
- A recreational specialist who works with her child in the after-school play group
- The teacher and guidance counselor who work with her child at school
- A rehabilitation counselor who runs an AA-type postrelease group
- The family therapist who meets with Lila, her boyfriend, and her child one evening a week
- The foster parent who provides respite care on the weekends

Carmen tries to weave all the strands into one supportive rope. All these people need to sit down together (preferably with the client) and pool information and ideas. CAPP organizes a conference when a new case is opened or when a new worker is assigned to an ongoing case. Conferences are also convened periodically throughout the service period as action plans are reviewed and revised. Carmen, the generalist among all the specialists, is the logical worker to chair these sessions.

An evaluation or information-sharing conference may be required under the mandate of a legislative act. Under Public Law 94.142, which governs the services given to pupils with special learning needs, a formal time schedule dictates how often staffing conferences are to be held. Everyone who attends must sign a form to show he or she participated. These reports are monitored by the regional or state education agency.

DIRECT OBSERVATIONS

Observations are usually informal. Carmen might visit the recreation room of an institution, drop into a child's classroom, or go on a trip with a client or foster parent. Here, too, she tries to be sensitive to signs that the client might be feeling invaded or spied on. It is important that she has a clear idea of what behaviors to observe and has formulated questions for which answers are being sought. The clearer the focus of the observation, the more useful the data she gathers will be.

BUILDING SUPPORTIVE RELATIONSHIPS

As we have stressed, the vital work of building a trusting relationship with each client starts immediately after Carmen has been assigned to a case. When she schedules the appointment for the initial interview and greets the client for the first time, she knows that her words, tone of voice, and facial expression all communicate. Through her warmth, openness, humanness, and honesty, she shows her clients that she respects them and considers their problems important. She continues to cement the relationship by:

- Listening, observing, and accurately reflecting back feelings and thoughts
- Encouraging the full expression of emotions and ideas by helping to put them into words
- Keeping clear about the purposes of each encounter
- Raising questions for thought and suggesting alternative actions, resources, and services
- Admitting the limits of her own expertise and seeking additional help
- Protecting confidentiality or being clear about why it cannot be kept

No matter how competent she is, Carmen's relationships with her clients are likely to be stressful and volatile. At no point can she sit back and say, "Well, that's done. Now we have a trusting relationship!"

At times, a particular relationship may seem very strong, but within minutes, it can swing to mistrust or conflict. Carmen has to keep reminding herself that frustration, anger, and tension are inevitable when people grapple with difficult decisions.

Carmen's ability to pay close attention to details strengthens her relationships. Returning phone calls promptly, being on time for appointments, remembering the details of what has been said, and following through on promises are all concrete demonstrations of the verbal caring that she professes. Leaving a client's record carelessly lying on a desk where it can be read by anyone or missing a special event in a client's life without telephoning are actions that communicate just the reverse. Being able to count on caring that is consistent with their cultural backgrounds can give clients that extra measure of emotional support they so desperately need when facing overwhelming personal distress. (See Ariel, 1999; Okun, Fried, & Okun, 1999.)

Negotiating and Refining the Working Contract

When Carmen begins an encounter with a client, she does not make any assumptions about who knows what or who wants what. All the parties in the process—client, worker, family members, or other professionals—must negotiate and then refine their own special mutual working agreement. Although contracting has long been part of the business and entertainment world, it has been widely used in casework and counseling only within the past few decades (Epstein, 1980, 1992; Kravetz & Rose, 1973; Schwartz, 1971; Shulman, 1979, 1993). Perhaps it was the civil rights struggles of the 1960s that made clients aware that they should be included in making the significant decisions that affect their lives.

Contracting grows out of the basic principle that the case management/counseling process is a collaborative endeavor between client and worker. Through mutual agreements and joint commitments, the worker tries to minimize the helpee's fear of being *caseworked, psyched out,* or *manipulated* by a powerful, controlling professional.

If clients do not acknowledge problems or are not convinced that they have the strength to overcome these problems, any change effort is likely to prove futile. According to the tenets of AA, no change effort can begin until the person with the problem stands up and says, "I am Susanne, and I am an alcoholic. I am an alcoholic, and I want to stop drinking." Yet some issues must be raised because they will have an impact on the successful outcome of the casemanagment encounter. Health issues are particularly difficult for the worker to bring up. For example, the worker might see that the client sitting across from her (or her child) is not just a little overweight, but is obese. Research indicates that many debilitating problems are likely to emerge from a body that is simply too heavy to function well. If health problems have not already been a source of client concern, they most certainly will be in the future. So, even if the client doesn't raise "losing weight" as one of his or her priority issues, the worker, with tact and sensitivity, might introduce a discussion about it (Heron, 2010; Robertson, 2010).

The word *negotiating* implies that Carmen and her clients might disagree on the work that has to be done. Sometimes they start out agreeing on all aspects of their working contract, but as they gain new insights, they are likely to change their initial contract. If there are many issues to be worked on, they must set priorities.

The word *refining* acknowledges that our goals and tasks are very imprecise. They must be broken down into many smaller components with specific meaning. If, for example, Carmen and Ms. Schultz agree that they will work together on her daughter's problems in school, that still leaves the parent unclear about what she is expected to do and what services Carmen can offer her.

PROBLEMS WITH CONTRACTS

No matter who has started the ball rolling, the goals of an encounter always need to be clarified. When workers fail to do so, the relationship can begin with tension. Shulman (1979, p. 26) illustrates this in the following passage about a hospital social service worker who visits the bedside of a woman who recently had a hysterectomy. The worker introduces himself by saying, "Good day, Ms. Tunney. I'm Mr. Franks from the social service department. Your doctor asked me to find out how I can help you."

Although the worker thought that was clear, the patient did not have the foggiest notion of what a hospital social worker had to do with her. Her first terrified thought was that the social worker was softening her up for some bad news. She wondered if she was sicker than the doctor had told her or if her husband was neglecting their children.

To reassure herself, the woman asked the social worker if he routinely visited all patients. But the worker, still not realizing that he was making her anxious, kept on talking in generalities about giving help. He asked her many questions about her family situation. She answered in a guarded fashion, wondering how her answers would be used.

Actually, the doctor had told the social worker that although the operation had been completely successful, Ms. Tunney required a long period of bed rest. Because she had several children and a working husband, she might need some referrals for homemaking and child care assistance. Shulman suggests that phrases such as *giving help* or *offering services* are so unclear that they have little meaning to most people.

By being very specific and giving an example of what help might mean in this particular situation, it could have become clearer. The worker might have said:

> Your doctor told us you have several small children at home, and your husband works long hours. He wondered if perhaps your husband needed some additional help in keeping your household running smoothly while you're away and when you're recovering. Sometimes people ask us for help in locating homemakers or in arranging for temporary day care. I'm wondering what concerns you have at this time.

In this example of contracting, the worker not only proposes some items for the contract but also tries to determine the client's priorities. Perhaps she has enough assistance from her neighbors for child care and housecleaning but is very confused about how to apply for disability compensation. Helping her file the proper forms would then become task number 1 in their working contract.

TASKS THE WORKER WILL DO

Some clients resist working with human service workers, but others do just the opposite: They impute magical powers to the workers. Without being cold or rejecting, we need to be honest about what actual activities we can undertake as well as our limitations. If it turns out that the client's needs are greater than our time or resources, we try to refer them to other agencies.

In the example of the hospital encounter, it is important that the worker let the patient know from the start that the hospital does not actually provide homemakers or day care. He can, however, refer patients to community agencies that do. Perhaps he is willing to make phone calls to these resources. But if he has a ward full of patients with urgent needs for postrelease planning and cannot realistically do the phoning, then he must say so.

TASKS THE CLIENT WILL NEED TO DO

Many of Carmen's cases are mandated by the courts or DSS. Agency regulations dictate what each party is expected to do. Carmen always makes sure that these regulations are discussed and understood early in the encounter. If clients are required by law to attend a counseling session, find a job, or do some other activity, it is important that they know what the consequences will be for them if they choose not to do so.

When clients are voluntary referrals, they should know that they have the right to shop around for social services and that it is best that they do. That is what an alert consumer does when choosing a home or buying a major appliance. If the agency employs a particular theory or philosophy of helping or if it uses behavior modification, psychoanalysis, or group therapy, certain demands will be made. The client needs a chance to say "No, thank you" without feeling guilty.

If the worker is aware of programs that use other approaches, clients should be encouraged to consider them. Then, hopefully, their decision to choose a particular helping process or social program will be made with the conviction that it suits their needs. Unfortunately, these choices are not as available in social service programs as they are in consumer products. The sad reality is that our finances usually determine the nature of our choices. This might be fair when choosing a couch or TV set, but it might be disastrous when picking a physician or nursing home.

DECIDING ON THE RULES OF THE ROAD

Early in their encounter, worker and client must agree on the following rules that will govern their working together:

1. A reasonable projection of how much time or how many sessions the overall process will entail and which special activities it will include (e.g., testing, home visiting, or a case conference)

2. A schedule for sessions, visits, and so forth

3. The names and addresses of places where the encounters will occur

4. A decision about the kind of note taking or recording the worker will do and the rules of confidentiality

5. Information about the client or the worker that might help or hinder their working together

6. Information about fees and how they will be billed and should be paid

Deciding on Problems and Priorities

Human service workers have often been criticized for having goals so grandiose that they can never be achieved (Richan & Mendelsohn, 1973). It is certainly true that it is an unrealistic aim to "save a marriage" or "improve someone's self-concept." Those goals are too global and diffuse for case management/counseling. We can, however, help a person with marital problems or low self-esteem figure out how to find better ways to settle arguments with a spouse, find a job or living situation that makes life less stressful, try out a new support group, or practice a form of self-relaxation.

Critics have long accused workers of choosing clients' goals for them rather than with them. To avoid that trap, Epstein and Brown (2001) stress that the skill of workers lies in their ability to help clients articulate their priorities. They assert that even very troubled people can be helped to state their most pressing problems in action-oriented, concrete terms. To do this, the worker helps the clients decide on the priority of their needs, ranking them by importance or feasibility.

By working on the problems that the client defines as critical, the worker captures the client's positive energy. If a definition of the problem is made primarily by the worker, client energy can be squandered in resisting the worker and protecting against being controlled. There are no right or wrong priorities in this task-centered and client-focused approach.

Conducting an Assessment Study for an Agency

Most often, the extensive data that the worker has been collecting is in preparation for the work the client and case manager/counselor will undertake together to work through a specific problem. But sometimes the data gathering is an end in itself or the major role the worker will play in a casework/counseling encounter. For example, if Carmen were employed by the department in her agency that arranges foster homes for children, her role would be to gather data that could be used by the agency to assess the suitability of a potential foster home. In order to do this, she would seek answers to a specific set of questions. She would use a form designed by the agency, which would be used as the basis of a final placement decision and an after-placement plan.

Some of the data collected will be factual information; much of it will be the applicant's feelings and thoughts. Some of the material in the assessment report will require Carmen's professional judgment of this applicant's capacity to parent and the kind of help they will need in order to thrive as a foster family.

QUESTIONS A WORKER MIGHT SEEK ANSWERS FOR
IN A FOSTER CARE ELIGIBILITY ASSESSMENT

Part I   In this section of the form (or interview schedule), Carmen seeks specific information about each member of the family—their ages, occupations, health status, ethnic background, schooling, and so on. Questions are also asked about their neighborhood and its accessibility to schools, churches, hospitals, its level of safety, and so on. The worker probes to establish what kinds of people constitute the support network of the family—their neighbors, extended kith and kin. She tries to ascertain what changes they might need to make in their employment and other life arrangements in order to foster a child.

Part II   In this section, the potential foster parents are presented with a checklist of the types of children they would accept—what gender, ages, disabilities, or past history (perhaps of abuse or neglect) they feel they could work with, and, most importantly, why they have made those choices.

Part III   In this section, Carmen asks questions that help assess the relationships among family members, the way decisions get made in the family, and the type of discipline used on their own children or with other foster children. She probes to clarify their attitudes toward people of different ethnic backgrounds and their exposure to people with physical handicaps or emotional problems.

Part IV In the final phase, Carmen estimates how open this family is to further training and to seeking out resources and support from the agency. Finally, Carmen would give her judgment of how successful she thinks this family can be with the type of child they have expressed a willingness to parent and with the resources the agency can offer.

The assessment process is not solely about establishing suitability for foster parenting but is also concerned with providing the potential parents with information and helping them decide if and what type of fostering would be right for them. (For further resources on conducting an assessment, see Holland [2004] and Jordan and Franken [1995]. A useful resource for preparing the final assessment or case study report can be found in Papadoupoulos, Bor, Cross, and Cohn-Shertok [2003].)

Creating the Action Plan

All the work we have done so far has prepared the soil for our action plan. Now the worker and client use the following techniques.

DIVIDING MAJOR PROBLEMS INTO THEIR SMALLER COMPONENTS

When they were negotiating their working contract, the most challenging task facing Carmen and the client was to state, in action terms, the exact nature of the problems and the hoped-for outcomes. When people are overwhelmed by life's demands and feel buffeted by circumstances, it is hard to see the small stumbling blocks that contribute to their overall problems of poverty, rage, or depression. Understandably, clients are impatient to tackle the problem head-on. In the action plan, we take the goals and figure out how to get to them one step at a time.

For example, Ms. Lugo is a recently widowed mother who complains of profound depression. She is overwhelmed by the prospect of parenting alone. Carmen helped her decide which component parts of her current situation troubled her the most. Then they could begin to work on the parts one at a time. Together, they reviewed her:

- Financial situation
- Social situation
- Living arrangements
- Work role
- Parenting role

Every widow experiencing the loss of a mate has different priorities, depending on her socioeconomic status, interests, age, location, and support system. All problems can, with skill and patience, be broken down into smaller parts.

VISUALIZING ALTERNATIVE PATHS, STRATEGIES, AND RESOURCES

Once the larger problem is seen in its component parts, we move on to choosing one piece of that larger problem to work on. Carmen encouraged her client to articulate exactly what she needed in order to cope with her sense of financial deprivation. They agreed that

Carmen would meet with her at home. Beforehand, the widow would gather all the bills and receipts she could find. Carmen would go over them with her, and together they would construct a budget. Once they figured out the family finances, Ms. Lugo might need to visit a legal services center or a consumer credit counselor to deal with any debts, inheritance, or documents that needed to be transferred into her name.

The second high-priority problem identified was the burden of parenting her little girl who had serious emotional upset. They began working on finding:

- Specific programs, social agencies, or "people resources" that would give her some time off from parenting and give her daughter additional adults to relate to

- Appropriate agencies or benefits that could pay for some respite care, camp placements, and so forth

- A counselor, support group, and network of family and friends who could be a sounding board for her questions about discipline now that there is no other adult in the home to talk things over with

CONSIDERING THE CONSTRAINTS

After thinking creatively about the many possible strategies and resources they could tap into, Carmen and Ms. Lugo reviewed the options to see how feasible each one was. For each possible program or resource, they had to find out its:

- Location
- Costs
- Availability
- Eligibility requirements

Together they weighed the pros and cons of each.

CHOOSING THE ACTION ALTERNATIVES

After the pros and cons of each option were analyzed, it became apparent that some action plans had more chance of success than others. For example, if enrolling in a support group for widows seemed helpful but the meetings were held in a building that was far away from public transportation, Ms. Lugo would not be able to use that resource.

Often, as resources are examined and found to be inappropriate, Carmen is able to identify significant unmet service needs in the community. Although she might not be able to single-handedly start a new support group that is accessible for inner-city residents, perhaps some other agency or worker might have the expertise to start one or obtain a van to drive people to one. (The chapters on program planning and systems change describe the skills workers need to undertake these tasks.)

MAPPING OUT STEPS IN AN ACTION PLAN

Once major problems have been broken into smaller issues and likely strategies have been chosen, Carmen and her client must put a time frame on each step. If Ms. Lugo's daughter is to enroll in a summer camp, they must find out when the application and medical forms need to be turned in. Then Ms. Lugo will have to find time to gather camp clothes, label them, and arrange the time off from her job to take her child to the bus depot. Ms. Lugo might decide that she wants to find a smaller apartment now that her income is reduced. Before rushing out to look for one, she needs to decide which steps in the apartment-hunting process must be done first; how long each will take; and where she will get the extra money for moving expenses, security deposit, and the last month's rent.

Implementing the Action Plan

Often Carmen's major contribution to the problem-solving process is to act as a sounding board. As she listens to the client's plans, she plays devil's advocate, raising questions to think about. At other times, she is like a coach, helping to recharge someone's emotional batteries. Worker and client can divide up the work. Ms. Lugo will find out about the town day camp while Carmen finds out how much money her agency might be able to contribute to the fees. They can share the work that needs to be done so that the client will not be overwhelmed. Yet Carmen should not infantilize Ms. Lugo by solving all her problems for her. Each time Ms. Lugo takes one small step, she begins to feel more confident about her capacity to successfully raise her child without her husband. Because she has worked with so many families, Carmen is frequently asked to suggest a specific program. Linking a person to such a resource is called the process of *making a referral.*

MAKING REFERRALS

Making a successful referral is a much more complicated process than simply supplying the name of an agency and trusting that the client will connect with it. Research has indicated that many clients fall through the cracks after being referred by one agency to another (Kirk & Greenley, 1974). Perhaps the client's needs and the agency's services were mismatched. Or perhaps the client and the agency failed to make a solid bond with each other. To avoid this, workers try to obtain accurate data about agency services and entitlements. They also need to learn to build firm linkages with both the client and the prospective agency (Feltham & Horton, 2000).

CREATING A RESOURCE FILE

Referrals can fail when a worker's information about an agency or a service is wrong or incomplete. There are often vast differences between the official description of an agency in a resource directory and the actual service it is able to deliver. Anticipating this kind of discrepancy, Carmen has constructed her own personal resource file. Alongside the official facts about the agency's fees, waiting period, and eligibility requirements, she notes her own observations. Perhaps the agency brochure states that all clients are seen within a two-week period, but she has heard from many clients that the waiting time is more like two months. She jots this down so she can warn the next client. Optimally, she has seen the agency in action. If that has not been possible, she relies on feedback from other workers and clients.

When Carmen has not taken the time to double-check on her referrals, she has sent clients on wild-goose chases. Once she sent a client to a legal services program for assistance in obtaining a legal separation from her husband; the agency had run out of rent money two years before. The client making that futile trip was rightfully annoyed and she then missed her next appointment at CAPP.

To build a supportive relationship, we try to find common ground. We work on developing trust according to the age and abilities of each client. Even the smallest child will hesitate to reveal a painful feeling until the worker has created an atmosphere of acceptance and safety.

If Carmen finds out that there is a long waiting list for a service, she warns clients about it. Armed with an accurate understanding of its limitations, clients can then decide whether to wait their turn or shift gears.

Carmen's referral file also includes resources that she has simply read about or heard of. Though they are potentially useful, the client needs to be warned that these resources are unknown quantities. A client who decides to use those services should be armed with a host of questions to ask. Role-playing the questions in advance prepares a client for an ill-defined encounter. Soliciting impressions after the client visits feeds valuable data back to Carmen's resource file.

CEMENTING A REFERRAL

After reviewing the official and informal data about a resource and deciding to suggest it, several acts can prevent the client—especially a very troubled or disorganized one—from falling through the cracks. Weissman (1976) has identified worker acts that constitute what he calls **linkage technology:**

1. *Write down the referral for the client.* Carmen always takes an extra moment to write down an agency's address, how it can be reached, when it is open, and any documentation that must be brought on a first visit. Then she hands the paper to her client. In the midst of an emotionally intense session, it might be hard for the client to take accurate notes or remember details.

linkage technology
The acts involved in referring a client to another agency, worker, or resource.

2. *Connect the client to a particular person at the agency.* If possible, Carmen tries to find out the name of the worker at a referral agency whom the client will be seeing. She often writes or e-mails an introductory note preceding the visit. This can build a valuable bridge for the client. Sometimes the referral can be set in motion by the client's phoning for an appointment from Carmen's office.

3. *Determine who might accompany the client.* In certain cases, Carmen might decide to go with her client to a referral agency. If she cannot go but thinks that extra support is necessary, she helps clients think about who in their own network of friends and relatives might be able to accompany them.

4. *Determine what other resources the client needs in order to use the referral.* Sometimes Carmen's clients need money for transportation, a specialized vehicle, child care, or another resource in order to use a referral. She helps them to think through potential stumbling blocks and negotiate them in advance. If left to chance, these stumbling blocks can undermine a referral.

5. *Check back on how the referral went.* Carmen always asks her clients for feedback. She often arranges an interview after their visit to an agency so they can talk it over. Then she can find out if there were any unanticipated obstacles that need to be dealt with.

6. *Advocate for high-quality service.* As she solicits feedback from her clients, Carmen discovers instances of inadequate service. Because of red tape, bureaucratic inertia, worker turnover, or misunderstanding, clients often do not get the services they need. Clients need encouragement to take the next step to overcome obstacles. That might entail switching to another resource or finding ways to pressure that agency to meet their needs.

It is best if clients advocate on their own behalf, but if they cannot, then an outside advocacy group, Carmen, or her supervisor can push a complaint higher up the power structure of the agency. If Carmen does not follow up on complaints, all her future referrals to that agency might be similarly undermined.

Evaluating the Work and Deciding on the Next Step

INFORMAL EVALUATION TECHNIQUES

There are many moments during a counseling session when both Carmen and the client step back and review the work they have done. If Carmen has just finished explaining the complex steps involved in applying for a job-training program—or if they have role-played a job interview—she does not move on to another issue without making sure that the client has understood the process. Carmen might say,

"I know this red tape can be hard to figure out,"

and

"Are there any steps in the application process that aren't as clear as they should be?"

or

"If any questions come to mind, I'd be glad to review what I've said."

Each time Carmen asks the client for feedback or shares her own reflections on their work together, she is evaluating. In addition to doing these moment-to-moment evaluations, she sets aside five minutes at the end of each session to review the progress that has been made in the last hour. If the session runs too long, and there is no time remaining for thoughtful evaluation, she phones the client before the next session.

Carmen has found that it is not easy to get honest feedback. Many of the foster and birth parents she works with are accustomed to doctors, lawyers, or school principals who rarely solicit or welcome client opinions about their services. When the clients have complained to authorities, they might have been ignored or punished for doing so. To convince them that she really wants to hear their opinions—negative as well as positive—and will seriously consider what they say, she needs to reassure them again and again. She might say:

> I really appreciate it when you stop me and ask me to explain a term or an abbreviation. I am so accustomed to using them that I forget that most people haven't a clear idea what they mean. Please stop me again if I forget, okay?

Carmen demonstrates how much she values feedback by trying, whenever possible, to act on criticism. If she has kept a client waiting for a long time, she not only apologizes but makes a point of rearranging her schedule so it is less likely to happen again. She also demonstrates the value of criticism by not becoming defensive when clients point out something she has said or done that upsets them. That does not mean that she accepts and acts on every evaluative comment, but it does mean that she listens attentively and thinks seriously about any she receives.

FORMAL EVALUATION TECHNIQUES

In addition to ongoing informal feedback, CAPP undergoes a yearly formal evaluation of its services by an outside consultant. The public who fund this agency have a right to know if their tax money is being used effectively.

The field of human service evaluation is very challenging. It is almost impossible to verify success or failure of case management/counseling encounters. Optimally we should be able to measure the progress of our programs by charting changes in the mental health or functioning of our clients. But rarely are we able to make cause-and-effect conclusions with a high degree of scientific accuracy.

When Carmen works to keep a family functioning, her efforts are only one factor in a vast constellation of shifting pressures. There are so many variables at work that her best efforts can be wiped out by forces well beyond her control. A poor economy makes job placement almost impossible for her low-skilled clients, so money pressures mount. Money pressures often lead to increased family tension, and so it goes.

Most personal and social problems resist arbitrary definitions of cure. How can we be sure that the improvement in the way the parents cope with their child is permanent? How can we know if any improvements we observe are a direct result of our work?

Recognizing the obstacles that keep us from fully evaluating our work should not, however, stop us from trying to do so. On a day-to-day basis, Carmen can see enormous changes in a few of her families and a little bit of change in most of them. The outside evaluation has helped to reshape the CAPP program by stimulating staff members to think about how they could do their jobs better.

CRISIS INTERVENTION

The word *crisis* is used frequently in daily conversation—so often, in fact, that it has lost precise meaning. In human services, however, both the terms *crisis* and *crisis intervention* apply to a specific condition and techniques of coping with it.

Defining a Crisis

Counselors assert that there are several types of potentially hazardous events that can precipitate a total upheaval in a person's life, such as:

1. An unanticipated situational event, such as hospitalization, sudden death, rape, robbery, or loss of a job.

2. An unusual widespread cataclysmic event, such as a flood, war, hurricane, or plane crash. The destruction of the World Trade Center and Hurricane Katrina in the United States and the tsunami in Southeast Asia are recent examples of such events. But of course there are hundreds and hundreds of less-well-known crises occurring every day in every part of the world.

3. Unusually severe reactions to normal developmental stages or events, such as the birth of a child, the onset of adolescence, retirement from work, or the emptying of the nest or the return of adult children to the nest (Frisch & Kelley, 1996; Golan, 1978; Hendricks, 1995).

Distinct periods mark a crisis. First there is the vulnerable state coming right before or after a hazardous event such as those listed earlier. People in a vulnerable state feel a heightened sense of stress and tension and a threatened loss of balance. They might experience a threat to their personal integrity and the fulfillment of their needs. Perhaps they fear the loss of an ability or a challenge to survival, growth, mastery, or self-expression (Golan, 1978).

The second period is the precipitating factor, the proverbial straw that breaks the camel's back. When the weak link in a chain of stresses is reached, anxiety rises to a peak, shattering one's sense of normalcy, well-being, and predictability.

Finally, there is the active state of crisis. Each of us reaches it at a different time and expresses crises in a unique manner. But generally we experience both emotional and physical turmoil. The head throbs or the belly knots in pain. There may be aimless activity, loss of cognitive functioning, and too much or too little eating and sleeping. There may be suicidal thoughts.

Helping a Person in Crisis

Crisis intervention draws on some basic theories about the way all of us maintain our balance, or homeostasis. It assumes that we are all mutually dependent on each other for support, nurturing, guidance, and communication. Our day-to-day behaviors are influenced by responses and feedback we get from others in our environment. All of us are part of many interdependent groups: family, friends, class, or work group. Each of these is a system of relationships.

This crippled, homeless man represents a series of crises that never got dealt with. Perhaps the loss of a job, a crippling accident or illness and unsupervised release from a hospital have combined to put him where he is today and might well be for many tomorrows.

A change in any one part of a system reverberates and can change everyone else in the system. Sometimes this change comes in unexpected ways. Sometimes the change comes in very negative ways. The case of the Knowles family that Carmen worked with helps to illustrate this.

The Knowles family, consisting of George and Myra Knowles, a couple in their mid-forties, and their three teenage daughters, was referred to her by a guidance counselor at one of the children's schools. Carmen found out in the first interview that Myra Knowles, who had long been a chronic alcohol abuser, had recently stopped drinking. But now that Ms. Knowles was assuming her parenting and homemaking role, the girls, who had become used to managing the household themselves, were suddenly doing poorly in school. At home they were surly and disrespectful, just as the family seemed to be pulling itself together.

Carmen worked with a consultant to her agency to understand what might be going on in this family. She realized that in order to maintain their family balance, the Knowles children had organized their behaviors around coping with the mother's addiction. The sudden move into sobriety changed the way the whole system functioned.

This case illustrates one way in which a disturbed system copes with change, even when it is for the better. In this case, perhaps the Knowles children, dealing with sudden unpredictability, developed more negative patterns, scapegoating their mother and each other. Perhaps they were able to be strong when it seemed important to be strong, and now they could let out their rage at all the years of tension. Perhaps they resisted believing that this change would last, in order to protect against the pain of more dashed hopes. The whole family needed to achieve insights and develop new, more appropriate coping mechanisms, perhaps taking some risks and experiencing success.

Carmen felt intuitively that if they did not integrate their mother's positive changes into their family system, she might become so discouraged that she would return to drinking. Life would be once again in balance, but everyone would suffer in the long run.

Lee Ann Hoff (Hoff, 2001; Hoff & Kazimiera, 1998) suggests that the following acts help people move to a new integration (see also Greene et al., 2006; Greenstone & Leviton, 2002; Hendricks, 1995; Van Ornum, 1990; Wright, 2003):

- Spend time listening actively and tuning in to feelings.
- Encourage freedom of expression, no matter how painful the feelings or memories are.
- Help the client make connections between the active state of crisis and the events that have led up to it.
- Move toward a realistic understanding of the situation.
- Encourage ideas and suggest new ways of coping.
- Find the sources of immediate support within the client's social network and community.
- Review progress frequently and point out positive developments.

EXAMPLE OF A SITUATIONAL CRISIS

Karen Siloe is a counselor at a community college. She had just started eating her long-deferred lunch when the receptionist phoned to say that a very agitated student wanted to talk with someone immediately. Karen put down her sandwich and went into the reception room to escort the student to her office.

The young woman slumped down in a chair opposite Karen and dissolved into tears. Little by little, she told her story. Over Christmas vacation, her boyfriend of two years was killed in a car crash as they were driving home from a party. She received minor bruises, which have now healed. But she finds it impossible to study, has bouts of nausea, and cannot sleep at night or pick up the threads of her life. She has a vial of sleeping pills in her hand and says she feels like taking them all.

Karen moved closer to the young woman and put her arms around her, holding her for a few minutes as she sobbed. Gently, Karen began to ask some questions, searching to discover the people who could give her some immediate support. She obviously needed help getting through the rest of that day and night. So she phoned the people the young woman told her she was close to. A sister said she would leave work and pick her up. Karen also called and left a message for a professor, stating that the young woman would not be in class that afternoon. Karen suggested that her family doctor might also be a resource if she needed some medication to get through the next few days.

They made an appointment to meet first thing the next morning. They would begin the process of grief work, sorting out her feelings of loss and guilt. Karen also knew of a support group she might refer her to. And she would also suggest a full physical examination to make sure that the young woman was not suffering from any undetected physical problems as a result of the accident (France, 1996).

9/11: The Human Service Response to the World Trade Center Crisis

There are many human service agencies—both public and privately financed—whose primary job is to respond rapidly when disasters occur that destroy a significant amount of property and cause widespread human suffering. Typically, the events that propel these agencies into action have been airplane crashes, shipwrecks, wars, and crime sprees, as well as natural disasters such as hurricanes, tornadoes, floods, and fires. Crisis response teams rapidly arrive on the scene of disasters with temporary food, shelter, and medical resources, as well as with financial and mental health assistance.

But the events of September 11, 2001, when the World Trade Center and four airliners went up in flames, taking thousands of lives and impacting many more thousands of relatives and neighbors, were surely the most complex of all the events the crisis management agencies in our country have ever had to cope with. It is impossible to imagine what the aftermath of such an event has been on the people left physically impaired by the blasts, the occupants of the buildings, and the families, neighbors, and spectators. All these people are likely to spend years restructuring and rebuilding their careers, families, and sense of security. Almost equally as difficult, all of us must find a way to cope with the memories of the human suffering 9/11 engendered. Words such as *posttraumatic stress disorder (PTSD)*, *flashbacks*, *sleep disturbances*, and *survivor guilt* crop up in discussions of the mental health aftermath of this unique episode in American history.

Two major constellations of groups have taken on the gigantic task of providing mental health assistance to those who were directly or indirectly traumatized by this disaster. One program, Project Liberty, is the federally financed agency that offers, free of charge, short-term crisis counseling for anyone experiencing distress related to 9/11. It is intended to help individuals return to their predisaster levels of functioning, especially to regain their sense of security. The project offers individual and group counseling. It also sends human service workers into schools and workplaces to offer educational services. One of its workers, for example, might visit a New York City day care center to help its children and staff talk about what they experienced during the blasts, what they have seen on TV, and what their fears are now about their own sense of safety. The counselors work primarily in the community, but they also meet with people in their homes. They operate a toll-free phone line that connects the caller (in English, Spanish, and several Asian languages) to a counselor with whom they can ventilate feelings while perhaps choosing to remain anonymous. Callers can also obtain referrals to mental health services that can work with them in more long-term or face-to-face counseling processes.

The other major group offering a wide range of mental health services is the 9/11 United Services Group (USG). USG is a coordinating body composed of more than thirty-eight social agencies that supplement what Project Liberty can offer. Member agencies represent a wide range of existing nonprofit groups, including the American Red Cross (traditionally the largest and most experienced of crisis management agencies in the country) as well as smaller special-interest agencies, such as Filipino American Human Services, Inc., the Hispanic Federation, the Jewish Board of Family and Children's Services, and the Council on Adoptable Children.

As time passes and there are fewer governmental resources available to meet 9/11-related needs, the USG services will become more critical to the long-term recovery process. USG has energized and coordinated the crisis counseling work of its various constituent agencies, and it has also trained hundreds of service coordinators who can help guide people through the complex maze of 9/11-related services and benefits. Most importantly, USG is recording all that has been learned from this disaster, so it can, in a systematic way, pass on this wisdom to hundreds of other social service agencies in other parts of the country and the world.

PROBLEMS THAT HAVE OCCURRED WITH THE DELIVERY OF 9/11 MENTAL HEALTH SERVICES

Only 642,710 people affected by 9/11 had asked for short-term, one-on-one counseling through March 2003 (Hoffman & Kasupski, 2007), while officials had expected 2.5 million people to use the services they offered. Surely many New Yorkers continue to suffer from the trauma of 9/11. Opinions vary as to why this number is low compared to the one predicted.

Of course, no matter how well-intentioned, there are always gaps between the services that human service agencies offer and those the clients feel that they need. There are also wide gaps between what human service workers plan to offer and what they can actually deliver. One major problem with the short-term immediate approach offered by Project Liberty may be that many of those affected by the trauma of 9/11 might require many more counseling sessions extending over several years. Symptoms of depression, aggravated grief, severe anxiety, phobias, alcohol and drug abuse, family disintegration, and so on may not occur or be recognized until years after the traumatic event. In addition, often the people who most need the help resist using it, held back by cultural and social resistance to counseling or the illusion that their adjustment has been fine.

The traditional crisis model of short-term therapy might be effective after earthquakes and floods, but living under the threat of future terrorist attacks tends to cause more prolonged psychological problems that cannot be addressed through quick interventions. Recognizing these problems, the government has recently allocated more money and extended the deadline of its own efforts. Private agencies that will be around for many years to come have tuned up their services to meet what is bound to be a growing need. In the human services, we are always evaluating our work and making informed guesses about how best to fit our model of crisis intervention with the needs of those we are counseling.*

---

*For a thoughtful analysis of crisis intervention strategies used to help law enforcement first responders in both crises, see article by Castellanano and Plionis, (2006). The journal Brief Treatment and Crisis Intervention, published by the Oxford University Press, in which this article was appeared, is also a very useful source of more information.

The Human Service Response to Hurricane Katrina, the Worst Natural Disaster in U.S. History

After the terrorist attack on the World Trade Center and Pentagon and the incredibly negative impact it left in its wake—the ongoing grief and stresses for the individuals and families who lost family and friends in the 9/11 blast as well as the wars in Afghanistan and Iraq begun in its name—it is hard to believe our country could face a worse crisis. But on August 29, 2005, Hurricane Katrina made landfall on the Gulf Coast of the Unities States, destroying thousands of lives through death, disease, and unimaginable stress. This time, the disaster was caused by natural forces rather than by a handful of diabolic suicide bombers, but its reverberations were even more widespread than those of the 9/11 tragedies. When the New Orleans levees gave way and many cities and towns were flooded, many people died, and thousands of survivors were left without homes, without jobs, and without the community institutions they depended upon for emotional support, often searching in vain for relatives and friends who had fled the region seeking refuge. It was the greatest displacement of Americans in our history, rivaling that caused by the Civil War.

The following are among the issues that human service workers are still attempting to help the storm's victims cope with. For each of the victims, this list would have a different set of priorities:

- The death of loved ones, especially the most vulnerable—young children, the elderly, and those with chronic illnesses or other compromising conditions
- The spread of disease complicated by the lack of accessible doctors, hospitals and clinics
- Separation from family members, friends, neighbors, pets, and community leaders, often exacerbated by not knowing whether they survived or where they are located
- The loss of community, institutions, such as houses of worship, firehouses, and social clubs
- The total or partial loss of their homes, resulting in widespread homelessness
- The lack of insurance or savings to rebuild their homes
- The loss of all their possessions, including important documents
- The loss of their businesses or jobs, impoverishing many and leaving them with few prospects
- The frustration of complex red tape and paperwork to receive benefits their taxes have paid for
- Unfilled promises of help and needless delays in receiving it, especially from the Federal Emergency Management Agency (FEMA)
- The sense of vulnerability to the vagaries of nature and to the lack of commitment from the political establishment
- Increased crime resulting from the lack of security and hope

Coupled with these very obvious problems, many of the residents who have fled Gulf Coast towns, especially New Orleans, face the daunting tasks of adjusting to life in their new towns and cities, most of which are very different from the places they came from. In addition, many of these towns that at first welcomed the refugees from the floodwaters now find that their own resources are strained by the influx, and "donor fatigue" has set in.

Finally, there is the feeling among many residents and observers that the often cumbersome and shockingly inadequate rescue and recovery efforts were to some extent the result of racism and classism because many of those affected were black and poor (Brinkley, 2006; "The Storm That Changed America," 2005).

Legions of professional human service workers as well as volunteers and, of course, the residents themselves have rallied to help rebuild the infrastructure of Gulf towns and assure the citizens that they are able to come home. In a later chapter we will describe the work of a Red Cross disaster worker, a role that readers may someday choose either as primary work or as community volunteer opportunities with national programs such as Habitat for Humanity or local ones, such as Boston Cares.

CASE MANAGEMENT/COUNSELING IN THE ERA OF MANAGED HEALTH CARE

At a recent public forum on managed health care, audience members lined up in front of the microphone to tell their legislators what was on their minds. A local real estate agent came up to the microphone and said:

> I had a blocked valve in my heart and they had to do extensive surgery. I was in the hospital three times, the last time for seven days. When I was released, they put me in cardiac rehab. I see a physical therapist and do stress management three times a week now. My bills must come to thousands of dollars but I have paid almost nothing out of my pocket. Without my managed health care plan, I would be dead or totally bankrupt. I am so damned grateful for the plan.

An elderly man faced the audience and stated with strong emotion:

> I absolutely refuse to give up my regular Medicare and be forced into a private managed health plan, even though I could probably get some financial help with my prescription costs. I have a friend who died waiting while his plan argued about whether he needed a certain procedure. My internist is very independent and doesn't belong to any of the plans. I won't give him up! He knows me and my health conditions so well. And I want to go to the specialists he recommends, not be forced to choose a doctor from some impersonal list.

Health care delivery is a much debated subject that no reader of this book can afford to ignore. It is vital—for both your personal and professional life. But if you are a young person whose parents have reasonably high incomes and jobs that offer them health insurance, paying medical bills probably hasn't been much of a worry. If you are in college now, although you may not be thrilled with its services, your school most likely has a free health clinic funded by the fee you paid along with tuition.

But if you took time off between high school and college, worked at an entry-level job, and turned 19, you might have been surprised to discover that you had been dropped from your parent's health insurance, and your entry-level job didn't offer any medical insurance. As a young person—with the illusion of invulnerability—that probably wouldn't have bothered you very much until:

- You came home from a camping trip with a strange rash that wouldn't heal

- You broke your leg in a waterskiing tumble

- You faced the stark reality that you needed help controlling your drinking or drugging behavior or your starving and binging behavior

- You wanted to try some new techniques such as acupuncture or hypnosis for an intractible sports injury (Becvar & Pontious, 2000)

Recent Developments in Health Care Delivery

Throughout most of the last century, medical care has been delivered by independent private doctors along with a mix of private and for-profit hospitals. The bills for medical care have been paid by the patient who received the treatment. Only very poor people (or those who are currently in or have served in the armed services) received free or subsidized care in clinics.

During the second half of the last century, hospitalization insurance, paid for by individuals, sometimes with the help of their employers, became part of the funding picture. As early as the 1920s, there were a few scattered small-scale experiments that offered prepaid doctor visits with a panel of medical practitioners. But it was not until the Depression that a large-scale innovative program, the nonprofit Kaiser Permanente—the grandparent of all **health maintenance organizations (HMOs)**—came into being (Lowman & Resnick, 1994). This early HMO had a populist flavor to it. The designers of the plan wanted to deliver accessible, high-quality care to a large portion of the neglected population. This experiment and others patterned on it were enthusiastically received years later, as health care costs and the demands for services spiraled out of control. Congress passed the Federal Health Maintenance Organization Act (PL 93-222) of 1973, which established nationwide standards and offered financial incentives to fledgling HMOs.

While employer-supported and private health plans expanded their reach, social activists have long been prodding Congress to pass health care legislation that would cover everyone in the country and be paid for from income taxes—the kind of universal coverage that Canada and several European countries have had for many years. After much acrimonious debate between the social service establishment and organized associations of medical doctors, Medicare, prepaid health care for those sixty-five years of age and older, was finally passed by Congress in 1965. It still wasn't universal coverage, but it represented a beginning.

health maintenance organization (HMO) A health care institution or an association of doctors that contracts with its members to collect a fixed sum of money monthly or yearly in exchange for doctor visits, tests, medications, hospital care, and preventive services, as needed.

steve@greenberg-art.com

www.greenberg-art.com

THE NEW COLOSSUS
(or, "Obesity Appalling the World")

Give me your doughnuts,
 your chips,
Your huddled nachos
 yearning to be cheesed,
The greasy refuse of your
 deep-fry vat,
Send these, the super-sized,
 by delivery van to me.
And give me fries with that.

GREENBERG VENTURA COUNTY STAR 2005

Even though we are not health care workers, we need to understand the impact that serious health problems, such as obesity, have on our clients. We try to help them anticipate and avoid these problems.

The Rise of For-Profit Managed Health Care

During the first two years of President Bill Clinton's administration, tax-supported universal health insurance looked as if it had a good chance of passing. But it suffered major political and public relations setbacks. Fearful of more "big government," Congress wiped it off its agenda.

However, it was clear to everyone that health care options were multiplying along with health care costs and that some type of managed system was vital. As these private plans for both medical care and prescription drug coverage grew in number, they formed what is now admiringly referred to by stockbrokers as the health care industry, the fastest-growing sector of the economy. The number of people enrolled in these plans continued to rise (Dee, 2007; *Psychotherapy Finances*, 1998; Vallianatos, 2001).

Some Problems with the Expansion of the Health Care Industry

Although more people had prepaid health care coverage than ever before and many were receiving care they never dreamed of in the past, both human service practitioners' and the public's attitudes about for-profit care have been conflicted (Corcoran & Vandiver, 1996; O'Neill, 2001). There is an odd mix of negatives and positives; there have been more medical options available; people are living longer, but health plans still need to turn a profit.

As one anonymous critic summed it up, "The doctor's credo of 'Do no harm!' sometimes seems to have evolved to 'Do no harm—to the stockholders!'" A review of the issue published by the National Association of Social Workers, titled "Humane Managed Care?" suggests that those words might be an oxymoron (Schamess & Lightburn, 1998). The following are some of the criticisms that have been discussed in human service agencies, by patient advocacy groups, and even the medical establishment:

- Some plans offer doctors financial incentives to keep costs down by not recommending expensive tests or procedures that might be of critical importance.

- Panels of approved health care providers are not necessarily screened for quality but simply for their willingness to accept the **fee for service** stipulated by the company. Often a limited list of providers means long waits for medical procedures or visits.

- Many plans have been accused of rationing or denying requests for respected experimental or complementary medical procedures.

- Most plans have **gatekeepers** (often untrained in the particular medical specialty) who have the power to veto a doctor's choice of a treatment plan.

- When a requested service is rejected, some plans have no genuine appeal mechanism for the consumer's protest.

- Mental health practitioners are often forced to affix a diagnosis or label to persons seeking help. They might not believe it is accurate but must do so in order to obtain approval for counseling sessions with a person in crisis.

- Computerization of personal health and mental health information might be used to reject a prospective enrollee or it might be divulged to a current employer without the patient's knowledge or consent.

- Some plans have routinely rejected applicants who have "pre-existing conditions" such as diabetes or cancer. Other plans have cancelled coverage of already enrolled people who develop serious health problems that need costly treatments.

> **fee for service** A prearranged amount of money that will be paid to a health care provider each time he or she delivers a specific service to a plan member in accordance with the plan's criteria for that service.
>
> **gatekeeper** A person in a health plan organization who decides whether a prescribed medical service will be paid for, based on its set of criteria for care.

The Current Status of Health Care Coverage

In 2010, in a very narrow, and mostly partisan vote, both houses of Congress passed a sweeping health care bill. It was carved out of many compromises but is not the universal coverage that many hoped for. In addition, many Congresspersons who voted against it have vowed to overturn the legislation or make it very ineffective by denying funding. As the eighth edition of this book goes to press it is anyone's guess what will happen to the new Health Care Bill. Whatever happens, it will affect you and the people you work with.

**"I'm learning how to relax, doctor —
but I want to relax *better* and *faster!*
I want to be on the cutting edge of relaxation!"**

In our current era, speed has become the new normal. Clients often cannot understand why there are few "quick fixes" for human service problems.

EMPLOYEE ASSISTANCE PROGRAMS (EAPs)

The terms *EAP* and *employee assistance program* may not be as familiar to most people as the terms *managed health* or *HMOs*, but EAPs are becoming increasingly more important in the provision of mental health services, often for people who have no other resources. EAPs have actually been in existence about as long as managed health plans, and as both types of program expand, it is often hard to tell where one begins and the other leaves off.

EAPs are structured, separate plans (independent from health insurance) provided by employers (usually of midsize to large nonprofit and profit-making businesses) that provide employees with referral and counseling services covering substance abuse, mental illness, marital difficulties, financial and legal problems, and the like (Sciegas et al., 2001; U.S. Department of Labor, 1998). These are all problems that could adversely affect the productivity of employees. In Chapter 1, we discussed a worker from a human resource department of a brokerage firm who made a referral and even arranged payment so a man could enter an alcohol rehabilitation program. His employers didn't want to lose this employee, who had many years of service and in whom they had invested the time it took to train him to do his work well.

If you attend a large university, it is likely that there are EAP personnel available to help a staff member who is in serious crisis. They might provide services in the personnel department or counseling center or contract with a local mental health agency, hospital, or other social service program.

There are scant hard data on the effectiveness of EAPs, but because they continue to proliferate, one might assume that employers find them a useful tool to cut down on the attrition, absenteeism, and distraction of employees, especially those in the upper echelons of the enterprise.

Yet EAPs, like managed health plans, have downsides, also. In a study of several companies, Ian Butterworth (2001) found an interesting paradox. On the one hand, there was consistent support among participants for the services provided. But, unfortunately, this enthusiasm appeared to apply only when it related to a fellow employee or a supervisor's problem, not their own. Butterworth found that many employees attached a great deal of stigma to using the services the EAP provided. They feared that supervisors or colleagues would lose respect for them if they admitted having a problem. They felt that they would be embarrassed to be seen, for example, walking into an AA meeting.

Not surprisingly, many employees who had previously avoided the "stigma" of EAP services embraced them gratefully after the attacks at the World Trade Center on September 11, 2001. Whether that will have a permanent effect on worker receptivity to their firms' EAP services in the future is open to conjecture.

Implications for Human Service Workers

The news from the financial sector is that many of the for-profit health care companies are merging, forming a few megacorporations, which will exert more and more decision-making control over which patients will receive what kinds of services.

Although all issues of a client's well-being are of concern to human service workers, it is the cutbacks in the area of mental health services that affect us the most. Many mental health workers complain that reimbursement for the "talking therapies" is becoming almost impossible to obtain. Routinely, patients are offered only the more economical, quick-fix medication solutions. While medication can be vital for a person in a psychological crisis, many causative factors in a person's depressed or addicted behavior require exploration and conversation (Hoyt, 1995; MacKenzie, 1995; Schreter, Sharfstein, & Schreter, 1994).

What Can an Individual Human Service Worker Do to Improve Health Care Delivery?

1. Keep yourself informed about the issues of patients' rights in health care by reading periodicals and professional articles. Share this information with your clients.

2. Write to your own legislators, encouraging them to support consumer protection legislation in health care.

3. When a client has a choice of health care providers, help him or her review questions to ask about the benefits and procedures of each plan that will lead to an informed decision.

Legacy of an Adopted Child

Once there were two women
Who never knew each other.
One you do not remember
The other you call mother.

Two different lives,
shaped to make yours one.
One became your guiding star
The other became your sun.

The first gave you life
And the second taught you to live in it.
The first gave you a need for love
And the second was there to give it.

One gave you a nationality
The other gave you a name.
One gave you the seed of talent
The other gave you an aim.

One gave you emotions
The other calmed your fears.
One saw your first sweet smile
The other dried your tears.

One gave you up
It was all that she could do.
The other prayed for a child—
And God led her straight to you.

And now you ask me through your tears
The age-old question through the years
Heredity or environment—which are you the product of?
Neither, my darling—Neither.
Just two different kinds of Love.

—Anonymous

This poem is a powerful reminder to counselors that parents can be defined both by biology and by the nurturing role they take in a child's life. It also poignantly asserts that neither guilt nor blame should be attached to a birth parent who cannot raise a child she has conceived. Most people are doing the best they can!

If necessary, make a phone call with them or for them, according to their language fluency and general capabilities.

4. If you believe that a client is being denied a necessary service, encourage him or her to get a full explanation (in writing) of the grounds for the refusal and the qualifications of the person who made the decision. If it seems warranted, file an appeal on the decision

and alert others in the agency about the appeal. If all other channels fail, the client usually has the right to go to arbitration.

5. If a particular company routinely denies appeals, it might be necessary to notify the state agency that oversees insurance carriers and health plans as well as your local legislators. This is especially important if there is a pattern of egregious practices that come to light.

All these actions might seem very difficult for the beginning worker. But when you read the chapter on organizing strategies, you will discover that most beneficial changes happen when a lot of people get together, do their homework, and mobilize public opinion (Jarmon, McFall, Kolar, & Strom, 1997; Urdang, 1999).

SUMMARY

1. Terms such as *case manager, counselor,* and *advocate* are often used interchangeably. There are no universally agreed-on definitions of their roles or training. We use the term *case manager/counselor.*

2. Arbitrary distinctions might be made on the basis of a worker's academic degree, the gravity of the problems he or she deals with, or whether the worker deals with emotions or resources. We do not think that this kind of distinction is useful. All workers deal with emotions and resources.

3. All case manager/counselors work to help clients
   a. Release negative feelings
   b. Increase understanding of themselves and their situations
   c. Make plans and decisions
   d. Implement plans and decisions

4. A case manager/counselor performs seven steps in each case process. He or she does the following:
   a. Prepares for an encounter by using preparatory empathy and evaluating referral data. (Referral data are both objective and subjective.)
   b. Gathers information in a planned and focused way through conducting intake interviews, home visiting, holding case conferences, and doing direct observation. This is often called the *assessment* phase.
   c. Builds supportive relationships.
   d. Negotiates a written or verbal contract with each client.
   e. Creates an action plan that translates overall problems into smaller ones, visualizes alternative paths, considers constraints and consequences, sets priority tasks, maps out steps, and sets time frames.
   f. Implements the action plan through giving emotional support and making referrals to resources.
   g. Evaluates the process through informal requests for feedback and through more formal surveys and questionnaires.

5. Crisis intervention is built on systems theory. The worker must quickly help mobilize a person in crisis and his or her resources until the immediate danger period passes. Long-range work on the precipitating problem can then begin.

6. A brief discussion of the human service issues, services, and problems in two major catastrophes—the destruction of the World Trade Center and Hurricane Katrina—are presented.

7. Case management in the era of managed health care offers both assets and liabilities. It can provide many more physical and mental health services now than in the past, but HMOs and insurance companies often arbitrarily ration or limit that care. Caseworkers must learn strategies to assist clients in choosing and navigating health care programs. The recently passed Health Care Reform Bill is under strong attack via the courts and state governments. Human service workers must stay in touch with its most current provisions and problems.

8. Employee assistance programs (EAPs) are sources of mental health services for workers in many businesses and nonprofit organizations. The stigma involved in using these services in the workplace needs to be openly acknowledged and worked with. Following the widespread trauma of 9/11 and Hurricane Katrina, this stigma may have lessened, as many employees, residents, and family members touched by these crises have sought help.

DISCUSSION QUESTIONS

1. Think back to when you have been in a dispute with your parents over issues of spending money, curfew, use of the car, your choice of friends, and so forth. In what ways have you tried to understand their point of view? How might you apply the concept of preparatory empathy before embarking on what might be a very tense encounter with your parents or in the future with a client who presents a very troubled picture of perhaps child or spousal abuse?

2. When you think about a class that you are now taking (either this one or another) as a form of human service encounter, with the student as a client and the instructor as the worker, try to visualize the contract between the parties. What are the rules of the road in that class, both the formal ones and the informal ones? How clear are the expectations the students have of the instructor and those the instructor has of each of the students? How might this contract be made clearer or more realistic, if you think it needs to be changed?

3. What kind of health care arrangements do you and your family have right now? What kind of comments have you heard your parents make about their coverage situation? Would you be willing to pay higher taxes if it meant that every citizen would be given health insurance through the government (just as Medicare now covers most people over age 65)? What are the upsides and downsides of a government-sponsored, universal health care program as opposed to the current free-market approach, where coverage depends on your employer or your ability to buy a private plan?

4. The new Health Reform bill requires that all citizens have a health care program. Some argue that this is a violation of a person's rights, while others assert that if a person does not have health care insurance other citizens will, in the long run, have to pick up his or her tab for medical services. What do you think of this very controversial requirement?

WEB RESOURCES FOR FURTHER STUDY

Health Care and Education Reconciliation Act of 2010

http://en.wikipedia.org/wiki/Health_Care_and_Education_Reconciliation_Act_of_2010

This explains the details of how the Act was passed, and what provisions it contains.

Children's Bureau, U. S. Department of Health and Human Services

www.acf.hhs.gov/programs/cb/

As the oldest federal agency for children within the Administration for Children and Families, the Children's Bureau has primary responsibility for administering federal child welfare programs. It seeks to provide for the safety, permanency and well being of children through leadership, support for necessary services, and productive partnerships with states, tribes, and communities.

Child Welfare Information Gateway, U. S. Department of Health and Human Services

www.childwelfare.gov

Connects child welfare and related professionals to comprehensive information and resources to help protect children and strengthen families. They feature the latest on topics from prevention to permanency, including child abuse and neglect, foster care, and adoption.

Substance Abuse and Mental Health Services Administration (SAMSHA)

www.mentalhealth.samsha.gov

SAMHSA was established in 1992 and directed by Congress to target effective substance abuse and mental health services to the people most in need and to translate research in these areas into the general health care system. Over the years SAMHSA has demonstrated that prevention works, treatment is effective, and people recover from mental and substance use disorders.

Healthinfo

www.healthinfo2000.com

Healthinfo provides viewers with a comprehensive list of available health and medical web sites on the Internet. It maintains a user-friendly environment that makes finding health and medical web sites just a click away.

For information on **managed care**, see www.healthinfo2000.com/managed_care.htm.

Chapter 11

Facilitating Groups

WORKERS AS GROUP MEMBERS

Few people have neutral feelings about being in a group or working with one. Group meetings elicit strong feelings, both negative and positive.

"Oh, no, not another meeting!" groans Arlene, an overworked drug abuse counselor. "All we do when the staff gets together is waste time arguing. We listen to dull reports or the administrator asks our opinion about decisions she has already made. I'd rather be at my desk catching up on my paperwork or be out in the field visiting a client!"

"Although I never have enough time in my day, I look forward to our agency meetings," says Ernesto, a family worker in an early-intervention program for developmentally delayed preschool children. "When we get together, we pool our ideas, share information, and really encourage each other. Sure we argue sometimes, but at least when a decision finally gets made, I know that I put my two cents' worth into it."

It is not surprising that there are such sharp differences of opinion about the usefulness of working in groups. When members are interacting productively, a group can be an invaluable tool for solving problems, receiving and offering emotional support, and building self-confidence. When conflict rages or goals and procedures are unclear, a group can be a seething cauldron of tension and inefficiency.

Regardless of how you feel about groups, as a staff worker in a human service agency, you will probably spend a large percentage of time interacting in groups. You will be expected to be an active participant in workshops, case conferences, and staff meetings. Eventually you might find yourself:

1. Facilitating a meeting of new staff or prospective clients
2. Leading a support or training group
3. Mediating a staff gripe session
4. Chairing a committee that is planning the agency open house
5. Becoming active in your agency union or professional association

norms Mutually acceptable rules, regulations, and standards of behavior.

After your workday ends, it is likely that you will interact with members of your family, the nuclear unit as well as your extended network of relatives and intimate friends. At some time in our lives, all of us have been members of peer groups: the Scouts, a 4-H club, the "Y," a sorority or fraternity, a church, a choral group, a civic association, or a sports team.

Some groups are formal organizations conducted according to by-laws, rules, and codes of conduct. Friendships, cliques, or gangs are informally organized, but they also develop a structure and unwritten rules called **norms**. Both types of groups play a role in our early socialization, and some will continue to influence us throughout adult life.

primary reference groups Groups in which a person is intimately involved, including family and friends who influence one's attitudes and values.

Groups are sources of emotional support and help shape each member's attitudes and behavior. Sociologists call the ones that influence us the most profoundly our **primary reference groups**.

Group Leadership Roles Have Been Increasing

In the past, workers who felt uncomfortable assuming group leadership roles used to be able to keep them to a minimum. As counselors in a hospital or a mental health agency, they traditionally conducted most of their work on a one-to-one model. The person coming for help was seated across the desk from the "expert" human service worker, who knew the resources. Because workers rarely interacted with clients in groups, the skills of group leadership received scant attention in the mental health literature and in college courses. But now the need for skilled group leaders has risen dramatically. Several factors have accounted for this increase. Let us review these, as they will undoubtedly continue to exert pressure to expand the use of group interventions.

THE IMPACT OF THE "WAR ON POVERTY" PROGRAMS

As noted in Chapter 2, Congress passed a landmark piece of legislation in the 1960s, the Economic Opportunity Act, which launched the War on Poverty. This bill mandated that all programs for the unemployed and underemployed must include the "maximum feasible participation" of the client population. For the first time in our history, poor people were not to be seen as simply the recipients of services. They were recognized in federal legislation as resources who had ideas about what they needed in order to improve their life chances. No longer would they be considered passive supplicants while professionals were the sole experts. The legislation assumed that clients and mental health professionals, by collaborating, could solve the pervasive problems of poverty.

The War on Poverty programs stressed the need to search out and eradicate the social roots of personal problems. During this period of energy and creativity there was a growing use of the "each-one-teach-one" model of helping. Community activists were encouraged to organize, inspire, teach, and assist their neighbors at religious institutions; in recreation centers; and at the meetings of tenants, unions, and hometown clubs.

Many of these activists were hired by neighborhood-based **grassroots programs**. The styles of these indigenous workers grew out of neighborhood life. They talked, ate, and lived like the client population. They felt at home with the pace and closeness of group interaction, which felt much like that of their extended families.

Although most of these programs have long since been terminated and maximum feasible participation is fast disappearing from the scene, the informal group interventions it birthed left an imprint on the field. The concept and style of client participation still persist in the ethical codes of most human service workers.

> **grassroots programs** Programs started by people who do not hold the official decision-making positions within a system but have a stake in the outcome of its services or policies.

THE RISE OF SELF-HELP SUPPORT GROUPS

During the past five decades, the self-help group model, pioneered by Alcoholics Anonymous (AA), has grown tremendously. The support group, in which members use each other as resources for problem solving, has spread from one area of addiction and dysfunction to many others. The twelve-step model of recovery designed for alcohol abuse has been adapted to help people who smoke, overeat, gamble too much, or use physical violence in relationships. It has grown at such a tremendous pace that there are now self-help groups for virtually every social and medical problem one can imagine (Gitterman & Shulman, 2005, Riessman &

Gartner, 1977, 1980; Wuthnow, 1994). They have proliferated all around the world (Madara & Meese, 1998; White & Madera, 2004).

A variation of this self-help model has been used to further the work of the civil rights movement and for the liberation struggles of feminists, homosexuals, and people who are physically and emotionally handicapped. Unquestionably, support groups will continue to spread in response to the increasing disintegration of the traditional extended family and workplace, as well as the decreasing role of many religious, civic, and fraternal associations.

THE IMPACT OF DEINSTITUTIONALIZATION

The community mental health movement, begun at the end of World War II, has continued to gain momentum and has firmly lodged itself in the field. It was propelled by the belief that mental patients and developmentally delayed adults were being made even more dysfunctional by being segregated in impersonal institutions. The road to health lay in moving them out of the wards of state institutions and back into community life.

Small community residences or group homes were opened to receive them and integrate them into the mainstream. There, the residents began to perform many tasks of daily life together. These groups became natural arenas for emotional support and behavioral change. Group leaders had to be recruited and trained to staff these houses. The need for staff continues to this day, and many students are likely to do their internships and accept employment in these programs.

After being deinstitutionalized, some former patients moved back to their family homes. To avoid isolation and stagnation, day-activities programs and sheltered workshops were organized. In these settings, group interaction is prescribed as a vehicle for acquiring socialization and independent-living skills.

THE DEVELOPMENT OF SYSTEMS THEORY

The development of systems theory has spurred interest in groups. Systems theorists assert that when any member of a group—a family, for example—has a serious emotional, physical, educational, or vocational crisis, all members of the group are intimately involved. They are part of the problem and thus must be part of its solution.

The group member who is identified as the troubled person might be acting out tensions that can be traced to the faulty interaction patterns of the whole family. A mother who drinks too much, for example, might be either the scapegoat or safety valve who keeps other family members from facing the seriousness of their own problems (Burnham, 2004; Okun, 1996, Okun & Rappaport, 1980). Systems theorists warned us that working with one family member in isolation from all the others is pointless. All of the members must struggle together to deal with the problem and readjust to a new way of interacting. The extensive use of family and network therapy (the web of significant people in one's life) plunged human service workers into the center of groups (Nelson & Tripper, 1998).

THE IMPACT OF BUDGET CUTS

After most periods of expansion, there is belt tightening. Downsizing budgets in the social services began in earnest in the 1980s and continues to this day. By working with people who share similar problems in groups, rather than in a series of one-to-one encounters, agencies try to use the shrinking time and energy of trained staff more efficiently. In schools, for example, as education budgets are trimmed, the guidance counselors and social workers are the first to experience a reduction in force. That lone counselor, facing a case-load of hundreds of teenagers and their families with many special needs and life transitions, is forced to utilize group meetings and orientations. In many settings, the one-on-one interview has become a rare luxury.

Thus, from both professionally sound considerations about the utility of groups as well as from practical necessity, the group model of problem solving continues to expand. Let's look at some moments in the life of the residents of a group home by reading the journal entries of one worker.

Example of a Human Service Worker in a Community Residence

Beth Soline is a night-shift counselor at Transition House, a community residence for ten adults who were released from a state mental hospital (after spending many years vegetating on the back wards). Transition House's primary goal is to provide a supportive home environment in which life survival skills can be strengthened. It is hoped that the residents will eventually rejoin their families or move into their own apartments and perhaps into the workforce. The residents have Individualized Service Plans (ISPs) that describe in detail the life skills they need to work on. For example, these are the priorities for two of the residents:

1. For Eileen, it is travel skills: learning to locate the correct buses, making change, and staying calm during the rush hour.

2. For Miriam, it is improving her social skills and learning to express feelings with words rather than through withdrawal or verbal abuse.

The counselors at Transition House spend the last hour of their shift carefully recording what transpired on the job. In the agency log book they note any commitments they have made to clients. They describe problems that occurred on their shift and any unusual circumstances that might have future repercussions.

The log book maintains continuity from one shift of workers to the next. By reviewing the logs periodically, the agency director assesses the progress of both the clients and the staff. Troubling episodes or behaviors that are described in the log book often become agenda items at weekly staff meetings. These notes also help the director decide on topics for their monthly staff training sessions.

Beth records in more detail than many of the other staff members because this position is her human service internship. By reading these recordings, her supervisor helps her expand her understanding of what is going on in the group and how she can best use her skills.

Transition House Log Book

Worker: Beth Soline
Time: Night Shift
Date: Tuesday, May 3

Arrived at 4:10 P.M. Found Miriam, Carlos, Michael, and Viet in the den, trying to decide where to go for their social activity that evening. Helped them sort through the choices. Movies, bowling, and eating out were their first three. Got them to consider the costs, time schedule, dress requirements, and behavioral demands of each.

Carlos, Viet, and Michael wanted to eat out, but Miriam kept insisting on going bowling. She got pretty agitated when they wouldn't budge, raised her voice, and began pacing. Viet started mimicking her. I stopped the action and tried to get them to talk about what was going on. Everyone finally agreed that if we ate out tonight, we'd go bowling next Monday. Miriam accepted that, but she got very quiet, curled up on the couch, and looked tense. I'd like to use that episode as a role-play for the house meeting next week. We need to help them all talk about what it feels like when you're on the losing side. Let's see what ideas folks have about why this always seems to happen when those particular four people try to plan an event together.

Went to dinner at Charlie O's Tavern. Atmosphere got more relaxed. In fact, it was so easygoing that ordering food, eating, and conversation came naturally. I began getting that old feeling of how-am-I-earning-my-salary? But then I remembered the time Carlos threw up on the waiter the evening he changed medications. I reminded myself that I never know when I'll be needed, so that's why I'm there. Decided to enjoy myself and skip the guilt trip.

Spent the next hour sitting in on group therapy session led by Dr. Kreger. Michael, Viet, Yolanda, Tricia, and Vikki were discussing last weekend. They had each gone home, and they needed to get a lot of stuff off their chests. I didn't say much. Afterwards I spent a half hour with Dr. Kreger comparing notes on what we'd both seen and heard. I feel like he appreciates my observations. Sitting in on these sessions helps me understand the moods of the residents much better. I hope we decide to make co-leading the group a permanent arrangement.

At 8:00 P.M. I went into the living room to visit the meeting of the Mental Patients' Liberation Front (MPLF). They are using the house for their meetings for the next three months on a trial basis. Made sure they had enough chairs, a working DVD player, and the coffee fixings. Talked for a while with Viola who was running the meeting that night. She complained about poor attendance. I suggested she write an article for the local newspaper about MPLF. She thanked me for the coffee and suggestions but said she'd prefer it if I didn't stay through the meeting. She thought my presence might intimidate some of the participants. They have several serious complaints about conditions at Twin Oaks Hospital and are preparing to testify at the State House hearings. I wished them well and left.

I think one of our staff should also give testimony. We have been hearing about problems at Twin Oaks for a while. I have been given the runaround several times when I've tried to get in touch with staff members about medication prescriptions for some of our residents. I am scared to speak in public, but I need the experience. If the other staff agree, I'm willing to represent the house.

At 8:30 P.M. I got together with the four residents who are employed at the sheltered workshop. We went over the schedule for the morning and decided who would cook breakfast, do wake up, and call in any absentees. There have been problems getting out on time, so we're going to try a new system for speeding up breakfast and cleanup. Tyrone worked out a plan for getting breakfast things ready the night before. He got a lot of support for his idea. We agreed to try it for a week and reevaluate next Tuesday.

Spent the rest of the evening in the lounge, helping ease in the two new work-study students from Ryder College. Gloria Nywand brought in a cake for Terry's birthday.

Terry played the recorder and a bunch of us had a cutthroat game of Scrabble. Evening ended with everyone but Carlos pitching in with cleanup.

When I went to Miriam's door to say good night, she wanted to talk about the blowup at dinner. She wondered if being the only woman in the group was why she was never listened to. She wanted to talk more about the male–female tension. I suggested she bring it up at house meeting. She asked me if I would do it for her. Do you think I should? Maybe we could have a discussion group for the women residents. Would it make for more or less division? Let's talk about it. Left at 11:45 P.M.

ESTABLISHING AND FACILITATING A GROUP: TEN KEY QUESTIONS

It might seem from Beth's journal that she was simply doing what comes naturally. But establishing and facilitating a group is not a random process. Before starting out and at many junctures along the way, Beth, the residents, and the self-help group leaders of the MPLF must ask ten key questions about their proposed or functioning group. The answers guide their actions as they organize and conduct the group meetings. These are questions that you will need to ask before you start a group. Each of these questions will be discussed in more detail:

1. What positives and negatives should we anticipate before beginning to work together as a group?
2. What phases or cycles is the group likely to pass through?
3. Why is this particular group needed? What is its central purpose? What are its secondary purposes?
4. What kinds of activities will help this group accomplish its goals?
5. Who should be included in this group? What kinds of people and how many?
6. What kind of structures will help this group do its work?
7. What will be the role of the designated leader? What other kinds of leadership roles will the group need?
8. In what kind of environment will this group flourish?
9. What kind of interaction will the members have with the leader and with each other?
10. In what ways can we keep evaluating how well the group is doing?

What Positives and Negatives Should the Group Anticipate?

After a long discussion at staff meeting and then at the residents' council, Beth decided to start a women's discussion group at Transition House. She will need to think about the positives and negatives of her plan. Should she be dealing with issues of gender and role in a group, or might it not be better to talk things out with individual members? Would a mixed gender group be more useful? Would the women speak up if the men were present? Even though she might be comfortable interacting in a group, she knows that groups can be enormously intimidating places. Each member will need protection and there is no guarantee that the group will be productive.

Before they get started, Beth and the other women need to sketch a well-rounded picture of potential **trade-offs**. What might they have to give up for the benefits they get in return?

trade-offs   Those things that must be sacrificed to obtain another hoped-for benefit.

During one of the early sessions, Beth and the members will review the pros and cons of working together as a group. Through sharing their past successes and failures in groups, they may be able to figure out traps to avoid. Although every group is a unique entity, we learn by analyzing our past experiences.

Here is a list of the positives and negatives of working in a group format rather than in the traditional lecture-hall format. It was composed by the members of Beth's human service class at their first session.

Positive Factors	Negative Factors
1. In a group interaction class you are figuring things out by getting involved. You learn a lot about how you react when dealing with different people and moods.	1. It's hard to do solid work in a group. People use the group for their own needs rather than for learning about the subject. When a few people take over, the person in charge can lose control.
2. You hear a lot of opinions and relate to many different personalities. You can pick and choose the people and ideas that are helpful.	2. It's hard to stick to the topic or task. There's a lot of side conversation and people go off on tangents, especially if they don't have much in common.
3. When you work in a group, sitting in a circle, you feel an emotional linkage with the other members, not just with the leader (teacher). You can see that you are not the only one who thinks a certain way.	3. People can make you feel a lot of pressure. If they disagree, you can read it all over their faces. It's hard to speak when everyone's eyes are on you.
4. The attention of the person in charge isn't always focused on you; yet, it's easy to get into the discussion when you are ready.	4. People can avoid responsibility in a group. They can sit back and complain about the others who talk too much or won't cooperate.

What Phases or Cycles Is the Group Likely to Go Through?

If you were to reconstruct the history of any group you have been in for a long time, you would discover that just like a human being, the group has gone through childhood, adolescence, adulthood, old age, and, inevitably, retirement. Researchers who study group behavior in experimental situations and in natural settings have tried to describe and put labels on the most typical phases or cycles through which most groups are likely to pass. Like their counterparts who study the growth and development of humans, they do not all affix the same labels to each phase or agree on where one ends and the next begins. Some do not even think it is useful to label them at all. But most agree that basic tasks must be worked through at different points in a group's maturation. Earlier stages often reoccur, particularly when new members join the group.

Two models often used to describe these stages were created by Tuckman (1965) and Garland, Jones, and Kolodny (1965). Even though they use different terms, they are similar. The focus of the Garland et al. model is on how intimate the group members are willing to get with each other. Tuckman focuses on the interaction of the group as it goes about its business. Here are the phases they each describe:

Phases of Group Life	
Tuckman	**Garland, Jones, and Kolodny**
Forming	Pre-affiliation
Storming	Power and control
Norming	Intimacy
Performing	Differentiation
Adjourning	Separation

FORMING, OR PRE-AFFILIATION

As it is being born and moving through infancy (forming), every group must, of course, work on negotiating its contract. Decisions need to be made about its purpose. What activities will implement its goals? Who should be a member? What type of structure, environment, and leadership will it need? Essentially, the "baby" is being named and is exploring the nursery and getting to know the rules of its own family. This is a period of tentative questioning. Members are probably asking these kinds of questions:

What's in this for me?

Is this group going to be worth the investment of my time?

Who in this group might be my friend, ally, or adversary?

How much can I share with these people? What about the leader?

Whom can I trust?

At the end of this pre-affiliation stage, members are beginning to feel fairly safe in the group and are willing to make a commitment to it. The leader gives the members freedom to explore, gently invites trust, and helps the group set up activities and group structure (Zastrow, 1993).

STORMING, OR POWER AND CONTROL

In the storming stage, members are struggling to carve out their territory in the group. Each member seeks power, both for self-protection and to get the most he or she can from the group. Members want the approval of the leader and may vie with each other to get it.

As soon as a new issue surfaces as a problem for several members, this human service agency explores whether a new group is needed and estimates how many people might want to join.

Cliques may form. Members begin to figure out ways to accomplish tasks. They test the leader and each other. Sometimes they become rebellious. Perhaps a few members decide the group is not working for them and they leave. This is the stage at which members are most likely to drop out. Some of their thoughts and questions might sound like this:

- Damn it, I seem to be the only one who gets here on time. Why shouldn't I come late also?

- We said we would throw people out if they missed three meetings, but is that fair?

- Boy, is that a relief. We agreed we could say anything we wanted, and when I told them I was gay they didn't seem to be blown away. But can I continue to trust them?

The group has to discover how well it can handle tension and resolve conflicts. During this tumultuous period, the group is beginning to establish rules. If members keep coming in late, for example, they can decide to be realistic and change the meeting time. If the bonding of the group members has developed well and they find ways of resolving conflicts, the group will be much stronger for having weathered this turmoil. If the group cannot achieve adequate **conflict resolution**, it probably will never be very productive.

For the worker, this is a particularly difficult period as his or her role, compared with those of other members, goes through much transition. The worker should help members understand the power struggle they are going through, give them emotional support, and assist them in establishing norms that are productive.

conflict resolution
The way in which a group handles sharp differences in opinion or digressions from accepted standards.

NORMING, OR INTIMACY

In the **norming**, or intimacy, stage, the group becomes more like a family, complete with sibling rivalry. Members are more able to discuss feelings about the group and their place in it. They are more comfortable with the rules they have carved out and they begin to work on group tasks together. They see the group as a place where they can grow and change. "There is a feeling of oneness or cohesiveness within the group. Struggle or turmoil during this stage leads the members to explore and make changes in their personal lives, and to examine what this group is all about" (Zastrow, 1993, p. 164).

norming A process of arriving at mutually acceptable rules, regulations, and standards of behavior.

PERFORMING, OR DIFFERENTIATION

Having had a few successes and having survived disagreements and personality clashes, in the performing, or differentiation, stage, the members should now be able to spend less time on organizational tasks and on testing each other and the leader. Now the group is able to devote more energy and skill to program activities—to performing. It should be ready to take on more challenging tasks. Members recognize individual rights (differentiation), and leadership is more evenly shared.

If Beth starts a women's group and it gets this far, members may now be ready to take on more leadership in the residence. Instead of withdrawing from disputes, they might support each other during a house discussion, reminding the men that their needs have equal importance. Miriam might take a risk and agree to coordinate a celebration for Women's History Month.

If Beth does start a women's discussion group, she also may discover that her thinking about the phases of group life outlined by Garland et al. (1965) needs to be readjusted. Linda Yael Schiller (1995, 1997) suggests that there are special qualities in the phases of development of groups composed solely of women. If the group is composed predominately of African American women, she would be wise to read *Images of Me: A Guide to Group Work with African American Women* (Pack-Brown & Whittington-Clark, 1998). This is one example of why we always do research before beginning any intervention or when trying to understand why an intervention is not going as well as anticipated.

As the group moves through its adulthood, new activities or shifts in membership might provoke other periods of tension and reorganization. But the group should be able to fall back on a reasonably workable structure, an appropriate division of labor, and some mutual trust. Now, the group has a history and a shared vision of its capacity to survive and perform.

ADJOURNING, OR SEPARATION

As the group comes to an end, hopefully its purposes have been achieved "and members have learned new behavioral patterns so they can move on to other social experiences" (Zastrow, 1993, p. 164). Ending is not always easy. Some members may not want to move on, and some go back to earlier behavior patterns to try to retain the feeling of safety of the group.

To help the members let go, the worker must be able to let go. Workers can help the members evaluate the experience, express their ambivalence, and take pride in the progress that they have made. If members need other sources of support, the leader can make a referral or bring in a guest facilitator.

How long any group will keep working together and whether it will need to change its direction will depend on its unique circumstances. Some groups never survive the storming stage, and some perform for a while and then enter old age, becoming stagnant and eventually dying. If, for example, the women's issues group needs to reorganize or decides to go out of business, it is not necessarily a negative outcome. Perhaps it served its purpose and to keep going would be an exercise in hollow ritualism. It is always better to terminate a group on a high note than to let it simply wither away.

THE NEED FOR AWARENESS OF THE PHASES OF GROUP LIFE

Being aware of the phases of group life keeps everyone alert to their impact. Often, group members and counselors like Beth are unaware of the patterns of growth and renewal that groups are likely to go through. Each group moves at its own pace "and may eventually arrive at the same destination. Groups that skip stages or whose development is otherwise thwarted will often return to a previous stage where business is yet unfinished" (Zastrow, 1993, p. 165). A wise worker will allow the natural process to evolve and not try to force it.

It takes time and patience to build a solid group, and, once a group is built, it may need to be frequently "renovated." Although deciding on a contract and negotiating conflicts can be very stressful, workers and members can be buoyed up during those hard times by realizing that periods of struggle are often precursors to periods of productiveness. The expression "no pain, no gain" is true for many human service interventions; it is especially true for groups.

Why Is This Group Needed? What Is Its Central Purpose? What Are Its Secondary Purposes?

All of the strategies we employ in the human service field have a definite purpose. When a collection of people join together to form a group, they need to articulate their goals and commit themselves to a shared purpose. This is easier said than done. Perhaps you can remember the feelings of annoyance and frustration that churned up your stomach when, after you had hurried to be on time to a meeting of your sorority or social club, someone asked:

"Hey, does anyone know what we're supposed to be doing here?"

Mild feelings of annoyance turn into rage when, after an hour spent working out the details of an event, someone says:

"Hey, wait a minute, it's not our job to do that. It's the job of the program committee."

Beth has noticed that when the members are not clear about the work their group is supposed to be doing, the members drift off, some to the coffee table, others to the restrooms and a few taking short naps. They start chatting with each other and arguing about trivial issues.

Each time a new activity or organizational arrangement is proposed, everyone should be able to answer the question:

"In what way will doing this activity bring us closer to our group goal?"

SECONDARY PURPOSES OR GOALS

A mutually agreed-on purpose is the cornerstone on which a worker begins to build a group. But even after the group has articulated its central purpose, members might still come to a meeting with some different agenda items. Tyrone attends this meeting of the MPLF because he is genuinely angry about the over prescribing of psychotropic medications, which have left many of his friends with facial tics. But he is also hoping to get a date with a young woman who captured his fancy at the last meeting.

Socializing can be a legitimate secondary purpose of this social action group. Recognizing this, Beth provides name tags and refreshments. A few minutes at the end of the meeting are always left for informal chatting. But socializing cannot fill too much of the time of this group. If it does, their goal of improving the mental health system will get lost in the shuffle.

In order to blend the group's central purpose with all those other purposes members bring with them, we need to remember two rather contradictory principles: (1) A group must be able to convince its members to put their own individual purposes aside to advance the central purpose of the group and (2) a group will be most effective if it is able to work on its own central purpose while still helping to meet some of the other needs of its members (Benson, 2009, Knowles & Knowles, 1959; Rose & Edelson, 1990).

Sometimes the secondary goals for joining a group are so important to some of the members that they cannot simply be put on the back burner. Tyrone's desire to expand his social contacts is perfectly legitimate. If the MPLF is not helping him meet that purpose, Beth might suggest two alternative pathways. Tyrone could try to get the group to expand beyond its political action goals by organizing some purely social events where members could get to know each other better. Or he might get together with some of the members who share his priorities and start another group whose main goal is socializing. Many new groups have begun as spin-offs from previous ones.

Experienced group leaders often begin a meeting by devoting a few minutes of time to the members' own immediate concerns. One welfare rights group always starts its meetings with a quick go-around in which everyone can tell the group about a tragedy or triumph that happened since they last met. The members of the Society of Friends (the Quakers) begin their religious gatherings with a group participation time they call "goods and news." Participants are invited to share with each other a brief thought before the formal meeting agenda begins.

GROUPS CAN BE CLASSIFIED BY THEIR CENTRAL PURPOSE

Although we are once again warning the reader that categories in the human services always have fluid boundary lines, it is useful to know the basic types of groups that can be organized to deal with an issue. Then, when you are in an agency and identify a new problem area, you can carefully think about which type of group seems most appropriate to deal with it. Of course, we would all like to choose the model that seems most immediately important, but we might end up having to choose the model that is within our ability to deliver. For example, you may be able to organize a task-focused social action group for Tyrone and his peers, or you may be able to help them organize a purely social club, but you are not likely to have the skills to be able to lead a therapy group. Here are brief descriptions of each of the basic group formats.

Therapy Groups

Beth looks back with great satisfaction at the camping trip she went on with the residents of Transition House. The director commented on the sense of self-worth and competence that radiated from the campers on their return. In the fullest sense of the word, all successful group experiences can be **therapeutic or rehabilitative** for their participants.

therapeutic or reha-bilitative Groups whose members usually have in common a mental or physical problem of some magnitude; usually led by a professionally trained leader.

But when we use those terms to describe a mental health group, we apply it more precisely. The term *therapy group* describes a group that is composed of people who have specific emotional and/or physical problems that seriously interfere with their work, education, or social relationships. At Transition House, for example, therapy groups are led by two trained professionals using a specific model of intervention. One of the psychologists describes herself as a behaviorist. She focuses on concrete methods of helping members extinguish nonproductive behaviors and create more positive ones. The other psychologist is more of an eclectic, using a variety of different psychological techniques, including art and music therapy, to stimulate insights that ultimately might change the members' behaviors.

Although the content of each therapy session grows out of the current and past experiences of the members, the focus of this type of group is in the hands of the counselor or therapist. The professional leader selects the participants and sets the ground rules. Most counseling or therapy groups encourage a great deal of interchange among the participants, but the leader is responsible for encouraging change in the attitudes or actions of each member.

These groups are usually quite small—six to ten members is most typical—and they frequently continue meeting over long periods of time (although current members might leave and new ones take their place) (Feltham & Horton, 2000; Jacobs, Masson, & Harvill, 2009).

Support or Self-Help Groups

Members who participate in a support or self-help group usually share at least one characteristic or experience that is troubling or challenging them. In Chapter 1 we saw Kathy's family becoming involved with AA (Alcoholics Anonymous) for those who drink too much, Al-Anon for their families, and Alateen and ACOA (Adult Children of Alcoholics). Within the mental health field, there are many similar groups, some based on the specific AA twelve-step program and others that develop their own unique pattern.

Beth helped George and Irma Castro, Yolanda's parents, to start a family support group that meets at Transition House once a month. The relatives of several of the residents of Transition House share their pain, disappointments, hopes, and resources. They call each other between meetings when a crisis looms large and in many ways act as an extended family for each other. The group is very member focused. Leadership rotates among the members. Every aspect of it is shaped by its participants.

Sometimes support groups are led by a professionally trained worker in their start-up phase. Beth withdrew after this group was launched. It has gone from being a support group to being a genuine self-help group with an indigenous leader and a self-generated agenda.

Support groups frequently form in response to the sense of alienation or dissatisfaction that many people encounter when enmeshed with faceless bureaucracies or unresponsive schools or social agencies. They provide desperately needed human services in the least threatening, most flexible manner. Through informality and dependence on each other, members vividly experience their own power to heal.

Both support and self-help groups typically meet in a wide range of settings, including hospitals, schools, religious institutions, women's centers, shelters, living rooms, parks, and individuals' kitchens.

Groups range in size from a handful of people to fifty or more members at one meeting. They are low cost or free, easy to get into and out of, and have few screening mechanisms. Like the parent support group at Transition House, some are homegrown. Others, like AA and its offshoots, are chapters of worldwide organizations.

Although most of the AA-type groups stick to a narrow focus, others, such as the MPLF, offer emotional support and engage in advocacy activities. Many support groups find these two goals compatible. For example, you may know someone who is a member of a DES support group. This countrywide network of groups is composed of women whose mothers took a drug called diethylstilbestrol (DES) to prevent miscarriages. Many of these women are now infertile. In small groups, they help each other cope with the deep feelings of loss engendered by not being able to conceive a child. They also plan strategies for their class-action lawsuit seeking monetary compensation from the drug manufacturer that marketed DES.* In *The Self-Help Sourcebook: Finding and Forming Mutual Aid Self-Help Groups*, Madara and Meese (1988) offer valuable insights on the nuts and bolts of organizing this type of self-help group. Simply putting in the word *support groups* in a Google search will yield a large number of very specific ideas for forming a variety of groups around hundreds of different problems and issues.

Training and Orientation Groups

Training and orientation groups have a clearly stated purpose and content that is established before any members are recruited. Although their goal is to educate participants and perhaps to change their attitudes and actions, they are different from traditional classes. They use experiential learning techniques. Participants can test new attitudes and behaviors in the safety of the group.

Transition House regularly conducts training groups for its new volunteers and staff. It has also organized workshops for the police department and for counselors of the local family service and vocational placement agencies. Through role-plays and other simulations, participants try to understand the barriers of self-doubt and discrimination that the Transition House residents must cope with. Workshop members also receive accurate information about mental illness that punctures their stereotypes about this population.

Transition House staff members use the same techniques to train residents in job-hunting strategies, interviewing, and on-the-job survival skills. Training groups are usually time limited but intensive. They might meet every Tuesday afternoon over a period of six weeks, last for a whole weekend, or occur several days in a row.

Beth's roommate, a graduate social worker, is employed by a private nonprofit adoption agency. Because there are so many complex issues to ponder before an individual or a couple can decide to start down the often torturous path to sharing their home with a child, her agency requires that all prospective parents attend an eight-week orientation/training course. Psychologists, social workers, medical personnel, and adoptive parents share a wealth of information on what to expect and strategies to deal with problems. They provoke the

---

*DESaction.org/desdaughters—law suits have continued over the course of several years as new and troubling health problems have emerged for the DES daughters.

participants to think realistically about the potential problems of taking on a child who is likely to be older, handicapped, of another race, or from another country.

These groups have proliferated in the last several years because many Americans have expressed a desire to adopt children from the former Soviet Union and eastern Europe. Some of these children, who have been virtually abandoned to warehouse-style foundling homes for the first years of their lives, have great difficulty bonding to their new families. There have been an alarming number of disrupted adoptions, a tragedy for parents and children. Responding to this, the social workers have organized many post-adoption groups providing information on the cultural background and sociopolitical situation the children came from and offering emotional support and referrals.

In highly focused training workshops, the leader sets up the tasks, assigns exercises, and runs the discussions. In more generalized human relations training—sensitivity or encounter groups, for example—the leader frequently sits quietly and challenges the members to carve out their own learning methods and find ways to resolve conflicts.

Task-Focused or Problem-Solving Groups

A task-focused or problem-solving group has both a clearly specified purpose and an end product. Staff, board members, and residents at Transition House volunteer (or are drafted) for these groups on the basis of their interests or special skills.

Committees, task forces, and study groups are formed when there is a job to be done. They disband when the task is completed, perhaps to be called back into action as needed.

Keeping members informed is an ongoing challenge for every group. Bulletin boards, both actual and electronic, can do that. They must be kept up to date and relevant.

Right now, one group of staff and board members is writing grant applications to obtain money to expand the job-training capacity of the residence. Once they have written the program proposal, they will begin sending it out to foundations and corporation executives.

Last year Beth worked on the committee that obtained funds to send five of the house residents to a special camp program. Now she serves on another ad hoc committee to recruit and screen applicants to fill a counselor position. An ongoing task-focused committee of staff and residents publishes a monthly newsletter, *Transition Times*. Another group is organizing a holiday fund-raising event.

Task-focused groups work best when kept small so that everyone can share a portion of the work and keep moving at a brisk pace. Once formed, these groups select a leader, or one person is asked to coordinate. Coordinators help to delegate work and keep track of the group's progress.

Although task groups can be therapeutic and supportive to their participants, that is not their primary focus. Because they have highly specific output goals, they are ultimately judged by how close they come to accomplishing what they set out to do (Fatout & Rose, 1995).

Social or Recreational Groups

While task groups have very specific goals, social and recreational groups tend to have quite diffuse goals, stating their original purpose in broad generalities: to have fun, play a sport, socialize, encourage moral development, or do good works.

After working together for a while, some groups carve out a series of smaller purposes—putting on plays, conducting tournaments, sponsoring concerts, giving awards—and each event has a specific goal and tasks.

Social groups at Transition House, like those at neighborhood community centers, Ys, or residences for the elderly, might be led by paid workers, college students, or volunteers. The activities or programs that these groups conduct vary enormously, depending on the interests of the members, skills of the leader, and resources available. For example, there used to be a bowling club at Transition House, but the neighborhood bowling alley closed and now the nearest one is too far away.

What Activities Will Help This Group Accomplish Its Purpose?

Every group, regardless of purpose, sophistication, or stage in its organizational life cycle, must plan and carry out two kinds of activities: *maintenance activities* and *program activities*.

MAINTENANCE ACTIVITIES

Maintenance activities are the housekeeping chores that keep the group functioning so that it can accomplish its goals. These activities include:

- Finding and setting up a meeting space
- Sending out notices
- Electing officers
- Arranging for child care, transportation, or refreshments
- Raising money and keeping financial records and distributing minutes

Although these activities might seem like tedious chores to the impatient residents at Transition House, Beth has learned that if a group ignores these tasks, it rarely progresses beyond the initial stages. When maintenance tasks are taken care of, the group is free to pursue its primary reasons for being.

PROGRAM ACTIVITIES*

Program activities are, of course, the primary reason for a group to exist. They include trips, plays, speakers, discussions, role-plays, and other special tasks or events through which members accomplish their goals. When Beth first began working with the residents' house council, she was not clear about what activities would be appropriate. Her supervisor told her that the acid test of any program activity was its logical connection to the primary and secondary purposes of the group. If the members could not explain in a few words why they voted to work on a particular task, it probably did not make sense to undertake it.

This advice came in handy when Beth was assigned to the World of Work Orientation group. When she took over from a previous worker, she discovered that the members had done little more than socialize and complain about their lack of jobs. They enjoyed coming to the meetings, but none of them had gotten much closer to their stated purpose of making money and moving toward independent living.

Beth suggested that they construct a long-range plan of activities to help them find work and keep a job. They could get started by inviting a speaker from the Downstate Rehabilitation Service to their next meeting. The employment specialist, Lionel Parker, could videotape them role-playing typical job interviews. When Beth first suggested it, they groaned, but she assured them that they would still have time for socializing if they started the meeting a half hour earlier. With that assurance, they agreed.

Beth learned, in her course on group work, that even programs that are very important to the lives of the participants might not be enough to ensure their regular attendance. Rose and Edelson (1990) suggest that group sessions, especially the initial ones, include high-interest activities, such as games, sports, dramatics, photography, and trips, in combination with the activities directly related to the more specific goals of the group. Beth has learned that delicious refreshments, especially made by one of the members, also make a group meeting so memorable that participants eagerly anticipate the next session.

COHESION

group bond or cohesion A complex set of forces that weld each member to the group and to each other.

Cohesion is vital to accomplishing a group's purposes. In addition to their maintenance and program activities, effective groups must develop trust among the members and between members and leaders. Trust leads to the development of **group bond or cohesion**. This is the glue that keeps members coming to the group even when the going gets rough.

Trust and cohesion are not built through any single activity. They grow out of the accumulated good feelings that come from weathering small challenges and successfully completing activities and tasks. The key to building them lies in the choice of activities.

*Articles on many activities that help in organizing and maintaining a group can be found in the *Journal of Small Group Research*, published by SAGE publications. Its web site allows the reader to access articles from the 1970s until the present.

The skillful worker tries to assess accurately where the group is at any point in time. Both program and maintenance activities are chosen to be challenging without being over-whelming.

Failures that result because the group bit off more than it could chew hinder the development of trust and cohesion. The choice and pacing of activities is a matter of trial and error followed by careful reflection.

Who Should Be Included in the Group?

Most of us have a vague feeling that there is some perfect formula for the composition of a group, some numerically correct mix of males and females, introverts and extroverts, leaders and followers. Even if such a formula could be found, circumstances beyond our control usually determine the composition of our groups. The nature of the setting most often dictates exactly who will be recruited and who will be excluded. For example:

> The Orientation group at Transition House is composed of all the new staff and volunteers who have started there during the month.

> The MPLF and the World of Work Orientation groups are self-selected.

> New members of the Transition House board of directors are chosen for their political clout, economic resources, expertise in mental illness, and willingness to give up time and energy for scant tangible rewards.

With membership chosen by administrative fiat, chance, or self-selection, all the groups at Transition House have imbalances. One week the MPLF had only one woman out of eight participants and no racial mix. The Parent Support Group had a preponderance of aggressive, outspoken people during its first year and the shyest of people the next.

When the family therapy group has several names on the waiting list, Dr. Kreger, the consulting psychologist, is able to make some thoughtful decisions about which members he thinks would do well together. Most of the time, though, he accepts any of the residents' families who are willing to attend.

In some groups in the community, members are voluntary participants; in others, members are mandated to attend. Perhaps a judge requires participation in a program as an alternative to a monetary fine or jail sentence. Or perhaps a spouse has dragged his or her partner to the meeting. There is profound disagreement in the field as to whether a human service worker can or should work with a group member who has not freely negotiated a contract. In any event, there are bound to be resistance, anger, and preconceived notions brought to the group by members who are forced to attend. These resistances must be brought out into the open.

STARTING FROM SCRATCH

Occasionally workers have the opportunity to start a group by selecting its members. Then they can test their hunches about the optimal composition for that particular group. First, they will have to decide if in this instance it would be better if "birds of a feather flock together," or if "opposites might attract each other."

They will need to decide if the more articulate members should be spread among all the subgroups and committees to stimulate discussion, or if the more assertive members should be kept together so that they can stimulate and challenge each other (and keep from overwhelming the shyer members).

Whatever choices are made, the elusive quality of personal chemistry will ultimately play the most decisive role in how well the group will click. Effective working together can be encouraged through a careful matching of people and activities. But just as in setting up a blind date, chemistry between people can never be predicted or guaranteed.

When deciding on the optimal size for a particular group, we are on firmer but still not solid ground. The sociology of numbers, long a fascination of sociologists (Simmel, 1955), as well as the practiced wisdom of experienced group leaders, provide some guidelines (Bales & Borgatta, 1955; Gitterman & Shulman, 2005, Hare, 1976).

Generally, when the tasks of a group are emotionally intense and highly focused, size should be kept small. Typically such groups have four to eight members. If they are much larger than that, members can be frustrated waiting a turn to speak. With too many opinions, decision making is cumbersome. When group purpose and tasks are less focused or the membership is transient, it is best to include more members. An open-ended support or social group might lack stimulation if it is too small.

Decisions about the composition of a group must also be related to the characteristics of the members. Age, past group experience, and communication disabilities are important factors in deciding on the optimal size of the group.

What Structure Does This Group Need?

group structure
The sum total of rules and regulations that govern how a group organizes itself to do its work.

Whenever people assemble to achieve a common purpose, a **group structure** or a way of working together evolves. Even a very transient group—for example, a collection of volunteers who come together to rescue flood victims—quickly develops a division of labor and a leadership pattern. If the group stays together for any length of time, the routines and rules they initially establish will probably undergo change.

No matter how small or unbureaucratic the group is or how diffuse its purpose, all groups should decide on basic elements of structure. If they do not articulate their structure, one will emerge anyway. But if it has not been planned and acknowledged, it will be unclear. Lack of clarity creates terrible tensions. Freeman (1972) aptly termed this the *tyranny of structurelessness.*

Over time, all groups develop rituals and norms, which are the rules, regulations, and methods of going about their work. The meetings of twelve-step groups like AA and NA (Narcotics Anonymous), for example, usually begin with the reciting of the Serenity Prayer. The meetings of the Transition House board of directors always start with the reading of the minutes of the previous meeting and a preview of the agenda for that meeting. The Parent Support Group never starts until a certain pivotal member arrives or until someone finally shouts, "Hey, gang, settle down!" The starting time in that group is officially 8:00 P.M., but the insiders know that they never begin before 9:00 P.M.

The structure that a group evolves must be reviewed from time to time. Sometimes members realize that a particular rule or norm stands in the way of getting their work done. Hopefully, they can then change either the rule or the way it is being administered.

Group purpose also determines structure. Training and task-focused groups often have a prearranged format that has proved workable in the past. Mutual-support groups and social clubs create their own. Counseling or therapy groups often have a structure dictated by the leader's psychological or theoretical orientation.

The secret of carving out a useful structure is to find a middle ground between mindless rigidity—"We start at 8:00 P.M. no matter who is here"—and total chaos—"Who was supposed to bring the key to the clubhouse this week?"

What Kind of Leadership Does This Group Need?

Over many years, the study of leaders—the kind of people they are, and what they do to mobilize others—has captured the imagination of sociologists, historians, political scientists, philosophers, and biographers (Andrews, 1995; Bertcher, 1994; Stogdill, 1948; Stogdill & Coons, 1957, Towson & Rivas, 2008). The nature of leadership is an intriguing topic.

Three different perspectives on leadership have held sway at different historical periods. All are still around today.

THE TRAIT THEORY OF LEADERSHIP

What historians call the "great man/woman theory" assumes that the unique, often **charismatic**, qualities needed to lead others lie within the character and personality of outstanding individuals. Gifted with natural capacity to inspire and organize others, these leaders will, in virtually any situation, leave their imprint on a group. Implicitly accepting this trait theory of leadership, many people in the United States believe that the economic reverses and national drift of the past decades result from the lack of outstanding leaders and statesmen. They indulge in the always-intriguing "what if" game: "What if President John F. Kennedy and Martin Luther King, Jr., both outstanding charismatic leaders, had not been assassinated?" or "What if the Supreme Court had decided in favor of Gore instead of Bush in the closest presidential election in our history?"

The house counselors at Transition House who accept this view of leadership keep their antennae out, looking for "natural" leaders among the residents. When they spot a likely candidate, they encourage him or her to take a position of responsibility on the house council.

charismatic leader
A person who profoundly influences others through the dynamism of his or her personality.

THE SITUATIONAL THEORY OF LEADERSHIP

Proponents of the situational theory of leadership argue that dependence on a natural or charismatic leader encourages passivity in other members. It denies them the chance to develop their own leadership capacities. Eugene Debs, a founder of the American labor movement, told his co-unionists that he would not lead them into the promised land even if he could. He warned them that if he led them in, someone else could surely lead them out!

Nichols and Jenkinson (2006) assert that some of the behaviors thought of as desirable in a leader of a governmental or business enterprise may be counterproductive in a support group. For instance, a firm insistence that one's view is the correct one is not always helpful, nor is the tendency to take control.

Situationalists assert that it is not so much the great leader who shapes the times but rather the times that make the situation ripe for the emergence of a gifted leader. They point to studies of temporary crisis situations when people who had never been viewed as leaders emerged out of the crowd. They took command during the flood or airplane crash, blending back into the background when the crisis abated.

Situationalists would argue that the Montgomery, Alabama, bus boycott was not so much the result of the charismatic leadership of Rev. Martin Luther King, Jr., but that the situation following World War II was ripe for the emergence of a civil rights movement. Reverend King and Rosa Parks, the tired black woman who refused to give up her seat on the bus to a white man, were instruments of change, the situationalists say. They expressed the widespread discontent and a readiness to take action that already existed in the black community. Ms. Parks's refusal to yield to an unjust law ignited a spark that galvanized others. Had the times not been auspicious, the anger they expressed about racial segregation on public buses would have fallen on deaf ears.

Beth has a mostly situational view of leadership. She consciously varies the activities at the house so that each member has an opportunity to become a leader at a particular time in the group's life. Each resident has some unique capacity. She tries to set up a situation in which each member can gain status by teaching or exhibiting that specialness.

THE FUNCTIONAL OR TASK-CENTERED VIEW OF LEADERSHIP

leadership acts and roles Influential behavior (feelings, acts, or words) that move a group toward its primary purposes and/or maintain the group.

The functional or task-centered theory of leadership does not focus attention primarily on the leadership person selected but concentrates on **leadership acts and roles**. It assumes that there are a series of leadership acts that are necessary for a group to maintain itself and achieve its goals. These tasks can be achieved by all the members working together. This concept of shared leadership focuses attention on the ways in which members interact with each other in pursuit of the group purpose.

Bales (1950), Bass and Stogdill (1990), and other group dynamics researchers have carefully studied many groups, both in laboratory settings and in real life, in order to describe specific leadership acts. Typical leadership acts they have identified include:

- Giving information
- Offering suggestions
- Seeking support
- Releasing tension
- Clarifying
- Elaborating
- Energizing
- Compromising
- Opening channels of communication
- Orienting
- Reminding the group of constraints

Bales and others visualized leadership as a series of functional acts. Thus, a group need not rely too heavily on outstanding personal qualities or auspicious circumstances.

Leadership acts can be taught, practiced, and strengthened in an intentional way in virtually any group.

Although human service workers find the functional theory the most useful to their work, all three theories help us understand and nurture leadership. By utilizing the task-focused concept, the staff at Transition House can help the group members understand that no one member, even the president or chair, should feel responsible for the successes and failures of the group.

The counselors at Transition House view themselves as **facilitators**, helping each of the group members improve their constructive leadership skills. Thus, when Brian loudly complains about members who consistently arrive late to meetings, they do not react as if he is a negative force. They assume that he is performing a constructive leadership act by trying to get others to live up to the group contract or to change it if it is not working.

facilitators People involved in helping to move group members in the direction of their goals.

This perspective encourages workers to design program activities and training exercises that increase teamwork and cohesion. The role of the counselor/leader is constantly changing. If someone else is clarifying a point or asking a useful question, there is no reason for Beth to intervene. She jumps into the discussion only when no one else in the group seems able to. Hopefully, everyone's leadership skills will improve as the group matures. The worker's role thus becomes less and less active over time.

Many members might be fearful if told that Beth's aim is to share the leadership of the group with everyone in it. They need reassurance that their worker will be there when they get stuck and will help them grow into leadership roles. Each time a worker encourages members to analyze critically what needs to be done and figure out why some things have not worked, he or she demystifies the group process. When Beth helps the members reshape a rule, routine, or activity to better meet their needs, she models a problem-solving method that can be transferred from this setting to any other.

THE NEED FOR A VARIETY OF LEADERSHIP STYLES

Classic group dynamics research has shown that a democratic group leadership style is more satisfying and productive in the long run than an authoritarian or **laissez-faire style** (Lewin, Lippett, & White, 1939). But the nature of the situation will modify Beth's usual democratic leadership style. In the middle of the night, when a sudden storm threatened to overwhelm the members on a camping trip, they had to quickly pack up and move into a shelter. It was not the correct time for shared decision making. Beth assumed an appropriately authoritarian "you-do-this and you-do-that" style.

laissez-faire style A leadership style in which the worker allows the process of the group to flow with a minimum amount of leader direction.

After the storm ended, everyone sat down and pooled their thoughts on what to do next. Should they stick it out another day as planned or go back to the house to dry out? During that discussion, Beth sat back, in laissez-faire style, letting the group make it or break it on their own. Switching styles is a matter of subtle timing that develops with experience.

What Kind of Environment Will This Group Need?

Flowers must be planted in soil that has the right nutrients. Although the surroundings are not the critical factor in deciding whether a group will flourish, they can significantly impede or encourage communication, trust, and cohesion.

Try to visualize a meeting of your college's student council being held in a 300-seat lecture hall. Thirty students are spread throughout the hall, and the president is on the stage behind the lectern. Trying to form committees or conduct an open discussion about school problems in such an atmosphere would challenge the skills of the most experienced leader. If the council president is sensitive to the impact of environment, he or she is likely to invite everyone to come up to the first two rows or sit on the stage.

It would probably be better to meet in a medium-size room with comfortable chairs arranged in a circle or horseshoe shape. A meeting place does not have to be beautifully furnished, but it should encourage members to talk easily without having to overcome barriers of space or noise.

Setting a good atmosphere entails common sense. If child care is provided at a parent meeting, the room for it should be convenient but not so close that group members can hear the noise of children at play. If the group is doing a long-range project, it needs a safe place to store materials between meetings.

When Beth thinks about choosing a place to hold a meeting, she anticipates the problems each site presents. Then she tries to overcome all the problems. Unanticipated obstacles are bound to emerge because every place has limitations. The challenge is to find a creative way to manipulate the obstacles we find in the spaces that are available.

What Kind of Interaction Will the Members Have with the Leader and with Each Other?

All of us communicate our thoughts through our words (verbal communication) and our body movements (nonverbal communication). Even during silences, something is always going on. Whether she is interviewing a client or leading a group, Beth attempts to see and hear everything that transpires.

When Beth was talking with Miriam, for example, there was a pattern to their communication. Miriam spoke about how she felt when she lost the vote, and Beth reflected back her feelings or made a suggestion. But in the group meeting earlier in the evening, the ebb and flow of communication was so fast moving and complex that Beth could barely keep track of what was happening and often could not react before the topic changed. It was like a fast volleyball or basketball game without any rules.

Communication flows in all directions during a meeting, as members look at and talk to the worker, whisper to their neighbor, or address their words to the whole group while staring intently at one particular person. While the worker is responding to a question that one member has asked, the others are out of her line of vision. The grimace on the face of one and the smile on another are messages that she probably has not received and cannot respond to.

As we get more experienced, we begin to discern the subtle patterns that have emerged among a particular group of people. We notice them and respond to the many barely audible messages crisscrossing the group. As the residents get to know each other, they will (if they have practiced their interaction skills) begin to take on more of the responsibility for responding; they, too, will pick up a look of distress or another sign that help is needed. Then, Beth need not be in every place at once.

After working for a while with a group, Beth begins to identify alliances and antipathies that emerge whenever the group is making a decision or working on a task. Protective relationships emerge also, and so do destructive patterns, such as scapegoating.

In many ways Beth is both a member of the group and its designated leader. She is distanced from it by virtue of the professional relationship. But she continues to play a central role in helping the members figure out which interaction patterns help or impede them as they work toward their goals. If no one else brings the issue up, she might say, "How come we can never make decisions without someone storming out of the room?" or "Does it bother you, Candice, that George always seems to disagree with you?"

The following are some of the acts the worker performs to help members understand and improve their interaction:

1. The worker watches to make sure that all members are part of the flow of ideas and opinions and are included in the activity if they want to be. If they are not, the worker helps members figure out what is blocking them. Perhaps the worker starts a discussion on how things might be organized better so people can move in and out of the action when they want to.

2. When conflict or confusion seems to be immobilizing the members, the worker helps them figure out where the trouble is, why it is there, and how it might be overcome.

3. The worker supports verbally and nonverbally those acts that increase cooperation, acceptance, and group bond.

4. Workers teach a repertoire of successful communication techniques drawn from previous groups they have interacted with.

These politically active young people are staffing a table for a voter registration drive.

Some surprisingly simple techniques can help a group get over seemingly insurmountable communication blockages. At the start of the women's movement, for example, many consciousness-raising groups experimented with ways to encourage members to participate equally. Some tried a system in which all the members began the meeting with the same number of poker chips. They had to use all of them by the end of the meeting. They spent one chip each time they spoke. Although the method seems very contrived, many groups found that it helped the more aggressive women to sit back while the painfully shy ones took a larger role.

Similarly, breaking one large group into several subgroups of four or five members for a particular activity or discussion helps people speak more easily than they would when watched by twenty sets of eyes. Subgroups also permit members to experience working with everyone in the group at one time or another. Increased comfort in communication leads to more productive or satisfying meetings.

Beth has gained insight into group processes and patterns by co-leading groups with a peer or supervisor. Through their lively postmortem discussions, she has learned more than any group process course can teach.

In What Ways Can We Keep Evaluating How Well the Group Is Doing?

feedback Both positive and negative critical comments on particular actions, statements, or other factors.

Every group needs a **feedback** mechanism so it can keep correcting its course. If feedback is left to chance, it develops like a fast-growing vine filled with the distortions typical of one-way communication. An informal grapevine rarely includes everyone, so complaints are never aired fully enough to be acted on in a rational manner.

By using open-ended questions, which do not constrict or channel the members' reactions, Beth tries to elicit useful feedback on how each member views group interactions and activities. Examples of open-ended questions are:

- What worked best for you in the meeting this evening?
- What were some of the things that may have gotten in your way this evening?
- What parts of this meeting were most and least useful for you?
- To what extent did we include everyone in the discussion this evening?
- How much progress do you think we made on listening better to each other?
- What are two or three tips you have for Beth on how she might run the meeting even better next time?

PRINCIPLES OF CONSTRUCTIVE FEEDBACK

Before asking for feedback, it is important that the members discuss and accept these five basic principles:

1. With enough help, every member is capable of changing a specific pattern of behavior. All groups are capable of changing a rule, regulation, or routine if it hinders their work.

2. The goals of a group should be important enough for members to risk exposing themselves.

3. Criticism is not intended to provoke guilt but to help plan strategies for change.

4. Members need reinforcement for positive behaviors and help in changing less positive ones. Positive feedback should always come before the less positive.

5. It is important to criticize yourself constructively. It is also okay to give yourself a pat on the back.

These basic principles also apply to human service workers. As they evaluate their roles in a group's process and progress, workers need to constantly grow in their capacity to sensitively facilitate the development of the members and the accomplishment of the group goals (Fetterman, Kafterian, & Wandersman, 1996).

TECHNIQUES OF GIVING FEEDBACK

- *Be concrete.* Give feedback only on specific sorts of behavior that were exhibited during the meeting of the group. When our whole personality or character is judged, we become understandably defensive. Members cannot be expected to suddenly change their style of acting and reacting. They can, however, change small bits of behavior in little steps. Compare:

    I found it very disruptive to our work when you didn't show up for the meeting with the paper we needed to make the banner.

  to

    You're the kind of person who always takes on a task and leaves others holding the bag.

- *Describe feelings or opinions in "I" statements rather than in "you" statements.* Most of us automatically interpret other people's behavior. Yet, we really do not know for sure what they meant; we know only how it felt to us. When we start a criticism with "You did . . . ," we can put people on the defensive. Compare:

    You ignored me!

  to

    I really felt ignored when you spoke to George and didn't say anything to me.

  The "I" message in the second sentence gives message recipients a chance to explain why they acted as they did or to explain that they did not intend to do it. Often we do not want to hurt someone's feelings and welcome being given a chance to clear the air. It takes a bit of practice to use "I" sentences in place of "you" sentences, but it is worth the effort if it stimulates honest communication.

- *Offer suggestions for change.* When something makes us feel bad or we sense that things are not going well, most of us have an alternative vision of what we would like to have happen. It is not always easy to find a concrete suggestion that puts that vision into words, but we need to try. When discussing that thorny issue of meetings not starting on time, the following sentences capture the spirit of the search for the constructive change of a negative behavior:

> I think if we all brought our coffee into the meeting room, perhaps we could start on time.

or

> Maybe it just isn't possible for Gloria to be here at 8:00, so how about starting the meetings at 8:15?

- *Make sure you have heard a criticism correctly.* When we hear a criticism, no matter how hard we try to be receptive, we may still feel embarrassment, anger, or defensiveness. As the flush rises on the cheeks and the belly tightens, it is easy to misunderstand what someone is trying to say. So, after he or she finishes, it is helpful to put what was just said into one's own words. This is the process of "reflecting" back.

For example:

> I think what you're saying is that several of us didn't do our committee work and that messed up the dance.

or

> Are you saying that you actually heard me say those things about you or that you heard from someone else that I said them?

- *Keep reminding members that change is difficult and slow.* Even if we follow the techniques listed here meticulously, there are no guarantees that feelings will not be hurt. Some of us are bound to feel attacked and defensive. We are not used to giving and getting constructive feedback. It is important to remind the members that everyone is probably doing his or her best and can expect the process of feedback to improve as group trust and cohesion increase. Of course, if over time a group cannot improve its feedback mechanism, it has little chance of maintaining itself.

When she first started working with groups, Beth had a hard time soliciting criticism from group members about her own behavior. When she listened to people who had mental illness talk critically about the way she conducted an activity, it threatened her professional self-image.

Beth has begun to work herself out of the rut of self-doubt and recrimination that each criticism would plunge her into. Now she can take each critical comment, examine it, and, if she thinks it has validity, design strategies to overcome it. If someone says, for example, that she took over too much of the leadership at a meeting, she tries to think of specific parts of the next meeting in which she can delegate a task or ask for opinions.

Beth's group strategies must be constantly evaluated and redesigned. By sharing her efforts to act positively on criticism with the group, she demonstrates a model of self-growth. The process also shows them that human service workers are fallible creatures who, just like everyone else, struggle to improve their skills and insights.

SUMMARY

1. Groups can be powerful arenas for problem solving, giving emotional support, and building self-confidence. Groups can also be filled with tension and frustration.

2. In both professional and personal life, reference groups help to shape our behaviors and actions.

3. Workers are both group participants and leaders. Group work has expanded in the wake of the War on Poverty, civil rights movements, community mental health and self-help movements, and deinstitutionalization. Systems theory, family counseling, budget cutbacks, and managed care companies withholding resources make the use of group interventions a practical necessity.

4. Organizing and facilitating groups is a systematic process built on asking and answering ten key questions.

5. The positives and negatives of a particular group need to be anticipated.

6. Groups have phases or cycles of growth.

7. Members must share a central or primary purpose as well as a limited number of individual secondary purposes.

8. The five categories of group purpose are:
   Therapeutic or rehabilitative
   Mutual support and self-help
   Training and orientation
   Task-focused or problem solving
   Social/recreational

9. All groups must work on maintenance activities and program activities. They must develop trust and cohesion, or group bond.

10. Group size and composition are not dictated by a formula. The more intense and focused the goals of a group, the fewer members the group can accommodate. The more diffuse the goals, the more members the group can absorb.

11. The structure of a group must be articulated clearly and reviewed from time to time.

12. The three theories of leadership are the trait theory; the situationalist theory; and the functional, or task-focused, theory. All have validity, but the functional theory is the most useful for human service workers.

13. A group needs a system of evaluation to receive and utilize ongoing constructive criticism. Feedback must be phrased in "I" rather than the more accusatory "you" statements.

DISCUSSION QUESTIONS

1. Beth Soline, the counselor at the residential treatment house whose log you read, is planning to have a support group for the women members. Do you think that is a good idea? Do you think it is fair to the men to be left out of the discussions? Do you think it might increase communication among the male and female house members or create a wider gulf between them?

2. In a small group with four or five other students, give your personal reactions to the May 2004 decision by the Massachusetts Supreme Court to issue marriage licenses to couples of the same sex. If there is no disagreement among the members (an unusual situation, given the American public's very split opinions on this subject), the group members should assume roles, with two students arguing for the rightness of the Supreme Court's action and two students arguing that the action is wrong and should be stopped, perhaps by the passage of the proposed amendment to the Constitution that defines marriage as between one man and one woman. After a certain amount of time, the group is required to reach a joint decision. One or two members of the group should remain out of the discussion and take notes on how the discussion proceeded and how the joint decision was reached. Referring to the leadership acts described in the text, see if you can pinpoint who performed each of them. The whole group should then assess the kind of job each member did at articulating his or her position and how well they listened to each other.

3. How do you think a worker should handle episodes of scapegoating in a group of teenagers? What about bullying? Do you think a young person needs to find his or her own ways to combat being a victim—which would make him or her stronger in the future—or do you think an adult should intervene and put an end to the situation? Did you see episodes of scapegoating or bullying in your own high school? What did adults do about it?

WEB RESOURCES FOR FURTHER STUDY

American Self-Help Clearinghouse

www.selfhelpgroups.org

A keyword-searchable database of over 1,100 national, international, model and online self-help support groups for addictions, bereavement, health, mental health, disabilities, abuse, parenting, caregiver concerns and other stressful life situations. Also lists local self-help clearinghouses worldwide, research studies, information on starting face-to-face and online groups, and a registry for persons interested in starting national or international self-help groups.

Alcoholics Anonymous

www.aa.org

Alcoholics Anonymous is a fellowship of men and women who share their experience, strength, and hopes with each other that they may solve their common problem and help others to recover from alcoholism. The only requirement for membership is a desire to stop drinking. There are no dues or fees for AA membership.

National & Community Service: The Resource Training Briefs

www.nationalservicereources.org/resources

Tools and training for volunteers and service programs.

Strategies in small groups

See www.mindtools.com for a variety of techniques for group leadership, decision making, and conflict resolution.

Chapter 12

Program Planning

A human service worker who was conducting a workshop on planning for several managers of group care facilities started the day with this anecdote:

> Years ago when I worked with after-school groups at a recreation center, I was cornered in the game room by an eight-year-old boy insisting that I try to guess the answer to his favorite riddle. Knowing when retreat was impossible, I graciously yielded.
>
> "What is the most important fish in the ocean?" he asked me. After a few feeble guesses, I gave up. With a triumphant grin he announced, "The most important fish in the ocean is the porpoise, because no one goes anywhere without one!"
>
> Out of the mouths of babes come words of wisdom! This silly riddle has stuck with me all these years because it is true for most things, and especially for the planning process. It gives us a good rule of thumb with which to begin this chapter. The human service interventions we plan and implement—all our words and actions—must have behind them a clear purpose. Planning is the process that helps us accomplish these purposes in a rational way. It is a systematic method of thinking through our words and actions so that they move clients and workers along in the direction of their goals.

Planning is an activity that is already very much a part of our daily lives. Think back to the last time you moved into a new apartment, looked for a summer job, or hosted a party. Before you started packing books into cartons or sending out resumes or invitations, chances are you had already decided on a plan of action. You might not have written down a step-by-step plan, but you must have had some overall map in your mind that would take you from point A to point B.

You probably gave some thought to which of the tasks needed to be done right away and which could be put off until later. You estimated how much time each task would take and figured out whom you could ask for help. If you are a good instinctive planner, you probably thought about what you would do if the apartment did not have enough closet space, if the job you were offered did not pay enough, or if the guest of honor could not make it to your party on the date you had chosen.

Without consciously realizing it, you probably evaluated your planning process after your goal was reached. Once you had settled into the apartment, you might have looked around your living room and said, "What a mistake I made stripping the floors before I painted the walls," "I should have checked with the neighbors before I moved in; then I'd have known that this landlord really scrimps on the heat," or "Next time I move into a new apartment, I'm going to start packing boxes two weeks in advance rather than leave everything to the night before."

When urged to think back over a major planning endeavor in our lives, most of us will confess we have made some monumental blunders.

> I can remember at least one hot summer day when, after reminding myself over and over again to fill up the gas tank, I realized I had neglected to do it when I stalled on a lonely highway miles from the nearest garage.

or

> I designed and printed a great advertisement for the big concert of the year. Then I stuffed and sealed 600 envelopes and brought them to the post office. On the way home, I showed one to a friend. He noticed immediately that I'd left the date off my fancy flyer. What a disaster!

At a party it may sound winsome to say, "Oh, I never can remember anyone's name!" But a human service worker cannot afford to forget. Behind each name left off a list stands a flesh-and-blood child left alone on a street corner, waiting for a bus that will never arrive to take him or her to an after-school program. Behind each forgotten name is a parent stung by your apparent indifference when you are not sure just which boy is her son Joshua, even though he has been coming to your recreation group for two weeks.

It is hard to imagine a human service job that does not require **problem-solving skills** and systematic planning. In his book on management in social agencies, Robert Weinbach (2002) asserts that even caseworkers, therapists, or social workers who spend most of their day in direct services still will be required to spend some time on management functions. Central to all those management functions is the skill of planning. He goes on to say that it is not true that managers manage, supervisors supervise, and caseworkers should be left alone to see clients. It is not "us" versus "them."

Even in an agency that uses the one-on-one, direct-service model, a worker might be assigned to:

- Compile a list of agencies that assist people with AIDS
- Design an outreach campaign to recruit volunteers
- Help clients put on a holiday celebration
- Assist clients who are starting a support group for eating disorders
- Organize an open house
- Plan a staff retreat
- Prepare a public information campaign
- Set up a child care corner in the waiting room
- Gather data to be used in an application for a grant to buy new computers

Although planning is a common act of daily life, a human service worker does it in a more disciplined fashion than the ordinary citizen is likely to. In this chapter we will start by describing the basic tools and attitudes of the **program design** process. Then we will describe some of its models, which can be adapted for use in an infinite number of situations.

BASIC TOOLS OF THE PLANNING PROCESS

problem-solving skills Systematic techniques that aid in achieving a goal in the most efficient and effective manner.

N o plumber or carpenter would go to a job without a bag of tools. Program planners also have their essential tools of the trade. The major ones are:

- Pencil and paper
- Computer, scanner, photocopier, e-mail, and planning software
- Directories, schedules, and other resource materials
- Calendar or memo book and a clock
- Large sheets of newsprint, a chalkboard, or an erasable board.

program design The thoughtful mapping out of a program so that it includes an analysis of tasks, strategies, resources, responsibilities, schedules, a budget, and an evaluation plan.

Pencil, Paper, and a Computer

Proposing that traditional writing instruments are the basic tools of the planning process seems like a very simplistic statement. Yet, surprisingly, many people do not approach planning tasks with these in hand. Lakien (1989), an organization development specialist, asserts that systematic planning is an act of writing, not simply one of thinking. We heartily concur.

When engrossed in planning an event, we think about it almost constantly. Before falling asleep at night or when waiting at a bus stop, the mind races, buzzing with details. But although our thoughts may be profound, they are often fleeting insights, half-forgotten when we wake up the next morning. Details of plans that are not committed to paper (or to a computer with a backup disc) and later double-checked for accuracy have a way of drifting out of our grasp. One supervisor we know lamented,

> When I supervised graduate community organization students in a large public agency, I lost count of the number of times I had to stop a staff meeting in the middle of a sentence to point out that I was the only one in the group taking notes on the decisions we had just made. Knowing they lacked their own personal record of what happened at the meeting, I found myself constantly calling them during the week to make sure they remembered the details of the task they had been assigned.

In the course of our busy lives we cannot depend simply on our memories. Our heads are filled with the conflicting demands of home, school, and job. A worker who is careless about the details of tasks, names, times, dates, locations, or costs often fails to accomplish the overall goal of the helping encounter despite other excellent skills.

When conducting a meeting, even the most enthusiastic beginner can forget to circulate a lined pad or have a lap top computer at the ready, with the words: NAME, ADDRESS, PHONE NUMBER (work, home, and cell), E-MAIL, and FAX NUMBER written across the top of the page. Lacking an accurate list of who attended the meeting and where those people live or work, the organizer cannot send everyone the minutes of that meeting or the notice of the next event. Without accurate records, it can take several days of diligent detective work to track down the person at the meeting who volunteered to print the flyers or staff the food booth for the neighborhood fair. All the people who do not receive the next mailing or phone call confirming their assignment are left to wonder why they were neglected. A minor omission can snowball into a major problem.

Pencil, paper, and a computer actually accomplish much more than simply guaranteeing that we remember important names, addresses, or commitments; they are also analytical tools. By forcing ourselves to write out hunches about our problems and our proposed solutions, we visualize the planning process as it might unfold. Each time we write a list of tasks that must be done, the amount of time each should take, who will do what, and what help they will need, we fill in more details in the road map of our journey to a goal. Although the shortest distance between two points is a straight line, we often need to construct a visual image to see exactly where the straight line lies. The sorting and listing process also gives us some level of predictability, alerting us to potential roadblocks we might encounter along the way.

It is a good practice to keep a small notebook (or computerized organizer) in your pocket, purse, or knapsack. Into it you can list fleeting ideas that occur to you at unexpected times, and each time someone hands you a business card or tells you his or her phone number, you have a ready receptacle for it.

Computer, Internet, and Planning Software

Although some of us still rely on the old-fashioned pen and pencil to help us remember bright ideas, commitments, and bits of information we have collected as we go about our work, computers, Internet, and several types of planning software are also becoming vital tools in the planning process. In fact, it is difficult to remember how we managed to go about our jobs before these modern aids became widely available.

The computer should be the trusty repository for the jottings you made in your pocket notebook when the machine was not available. If notes are transferred at the end of each day to your computer, placed in the proper file folder on the hard drive, and, of course, backed up on discs, they guard against the loss of the notes you have taken. They also change your scribblings into solid bits of data that can be used now or in a future project and easily shared with other planners.

We do not need highly sophisticated computer equipment to order our notes into logical categories and help us build a database of people, agencies, suppliers, and so forth. Even in the most resource-poor agency or group, at least one person is bound to have access to a computer, if not in his or her home, then perhaps at a workplace or public library. In many towns, there are stores that sell time on a computer, and most public libraries have computers that can be used by local people.

Later in the chapter we will describe several charts that assist us in moving through each step of the planning process. These charts are also available on several software programs.

When available, e-mail and the Internet are invaluable tools for networking with others who are working in similar areas of the human services to generate ideas, secure resources, and build support. Through the Internet we can cast our net wide, bringing in ideas from diverse communities. E-mail (and the fax machine as well) is a marvelous tool for keeping members in touch with the progress of each piece of the plan and for sending out a request for assistance when a planner has hit a roadblock.

Directories, Schedules, and Other Resource Materials

The telephone book for your town and specialized directories of services and brochures are the planner's trusty companions. In the words of the advertising department of the phone company:

> Let your fingers do the walking!

Perhaps you are working with a group of teenagers at a mental health center. They are trying to decide whether to go on a camping trip or to a country music concert in the next town. You suspect that both activities are too expensive. Before they get too deep into planning the details of either outing, you suggest they pick up the phone (or go to an appropriate website) and obtain answers to some key questions:

- How much will each of the activities cost?
- Are camping sites or tickets available?
- How can they get there?
- How long will it take to get there?

Armed with facts rather than speculations, they can then go on to discuss whether they will be able to obtain the time, money, transportation, and permissions they will need. Then you can help them weigh the trade-offs of each option—what they might have to give up in order to get something they want.

One worker described how she used this technique of matching facts with wishes with a group of teenagers she worked with on a summer work camp:

> Several years ago I took a group of twenty older teenagers to Mexico on an eight-week work project. The members were very mature but they often pushed against the limits of their independence and my sense of caution. During the first few weeks several of them made requests that frankly overwhelmed me. "We've been invited to a wedding next weekend three towns away. Please can't we go? Some people have asked us to join them in an expedition to climb a mountain. Is that okay?" Although many of their requests seemed risky, I didn't want to arbitrarily say "no." After a while we arrived at a program planning technique that worked wonderfully for the rest of the trip. At a group meeting we hammered out a set of basic questions: how, what, where, when, and what if? They were not to come to me with a request until they had the facts to back up their answers to those questions.
>
> If, for example, they planned to travel by bus, I wanted to know the exact schedule and the exact cost, where it left from, and how they would get there. Many grandiose schemes were quickly put to rest after a call to the bus station made it clear that in this country you simply couldn't get from point A to point B in two days on a shoestring budget. By the time a request actually came to me, it was quite feasible and I was likely to agree to it.

Another worker reported using this same kind of reality-testing technique with a much younger age group:

> When I ran a day camp in an inner-city housing project, the telephone was my best friend. On cold and rainy mornings the littlest children would crowd around me begging

to go swimming even though I knew it probably wasn't going to be warm enough. Finally, one of the camp counselors taught her group members the phone number for the local weather report and how to look up the weather on the office computer. If WE6-1212 or checking the computer screen—said it was above 70 degrees and it wasn't going to rain, they went swimming. If it was going to rain and was below 60 degrees, we went to a movie, to the bowling alley, or planned an indoor crafts activity. It wasn't *me* making the decision. It was the objective fact of the weather forecast.

In each of these experiences, clients practiced systematic problem-solving skills that helped them to formulate current plans and equipped them to plan in the future. If the worker had access to the Internet, this would be a wonderful opportunity to show the children a practical way in which information retrieval can be done easily and used wisely. Yaffe and Gotthuffer, in their book *Quick Guide to the Internet for Social Work* (2000), describe a multitude of ways in which the Internet can help us in every intervention we make.

Calendar/Memo Book and Clock

Watch a group of human service workers at a case conference trying to arrange a date for their next meeting. All of them will dig into a briefcase, handbag, or back pocket and produce a well-thumbed appointment book or PDA. In it will be listed daily meetings and all the details surrounding them: who is to be seen, where the encounter will take place, and any driving or public transportation directions needed. Human service workers often list the home and work phone numbers of the people with whom they have made appointments. Then if they must cancel a meeting because of an emergency, even from home at 6:00 A.M., they are prepared (another opportunity to demonstrate our caring for clients and colleagues!).

A calendar book right at hand also helps a worker visualize what needs to be done, define priorities, and fit them in. Thus, "Stop by and see me sometime about those new regulations" and "We'll have to get together and talk about the Kramer child some day soon" become definite half hours on a specific day. If a worker cannot make an appointment with the foster parent who mentioned she was having a hard time with the Medicaid office, a note in the calendar book is a reminder to phone her the next day and arrange a time to talk.

Most human service encounters require some type of follow-up activity. The calendar book is a logical place to list the many small tasks that will need to be done before the next interview with a client or before a deadline expires on an application for an entitlement.

Finally, a calendar book can be a device to set self-limits, guarding against burnout. It should help workers to space out their tasks at realistic intervals, with times in between for reflection or paperwork.

A watch or an unobtrusive desk clock can also help set a realistic pace. Although sensitive workers do not mechanically follow arbitrary time limits, they rarely have the luxury of unlimited time. Other clients are waiting for them, groups must begin on time, forms have to be submitted by deadline dates, or clients must be reminded to get to their jobs or interviews on time. Because every method of intervention has its own rhythm and flow, we need to establish and confirm with the clock an adequate time for a beginning, middle, and end to each encounter. Endings of meetings and interviews often sneak up on us, robbing us of the time we need to decide on subsequent steps, evaluate, or wind down emotionally. Setting a comfortable pace for our interventions is both an art and a skill.

Large Sheets of Newsprint, a Chalkboard, and Markers

To prod our memories or map out our ideas about a project, a pocket or desk pad or computer will do quite well. But when we are planning in concert with colleagues or clients, it is more helpful to use a large writing surface. A chalkboard, an erasable board, or large sheets of newsprint propped up on an easel work well. As members suggest an idea or take on an assignment, these can be written large enough to be seen by everyone. If there are disagreements about specific points, they can be quickly noticed and clarified.

An erasable surface communicates the message that ideas are to be played with. They can be listed, rubbed out as the members reject them, and raised to the top or dropped to the bottom of a list of priorities. This encourages experimentation and the free flow of ideas. Newsprint sheets lack that kind of flexibility, but they can be kept intact after a meeting ends. When a group is involved in a planning process over a protracted period, members can save the sheets with their initial ideas. Looking back at the sheets, they can analyze how far they have progressed or notice initial ideas that were forgotten in the flurry of activity.

Black felt-tip markers, as opposed to regular pencils or pens, are part of the standard tools of the planner. They can be easily read from a distance. Thus, members of the planning group are not excluded from considering an idea simply because they cannot read it. Markers used for attendance lists, name tags, and meeting notes have the additional advantage of being easy to photocopy, avoiding excessive clerical work.

Clearly Focused Questions

When planning an intervention, you might be able to manage without a pad and pencil, a computer, a calendar, a directory, a clock, newsprint, a chalkboard, markers, and a phone, but you could not function without these questions:

- Who?
- Where?
- How?
- Why?
- Why not?
- How else?
- What if?

Planning is first and foremost a process of asking and answering questions. Sometimes the questions workers ask have definite answers. Often the questions are more speculative and have several alternative answers. Workers anticipate an interview with a client or a meeting with a budget committee by asking themselves and everyone else logical, hard questions about the topic under consideration.

Keith, a staff worker at the Larkin School, which provides services for children who are deaf, blind, and have emotional problems, has designed an expanded summer camp program. Now he is preparing himself for the much anticipated but equally dreaded moment when he must appear before the annual meeting of the board of directors to justify his plan. To prepare his answers to the questions the board members are likely to ask, he puts himself in their shoes (he uses his capacity for anticipatory empathy). Then he rehearses his answers to the questions that he would ask if he were a member of the board. He makes sure that he has the data to back up his answers. Most board members receiving a proposal for a new program are likely to ask the following questions:

- Why isn't our existing summer program adequate?
- What did you find the problems to be in last summer's program?
- How do you know that the parents want a more extensive camp program?
- What have you done to make sure there will be sufficient enrollment to cover most of the costs?
- What makes you think that this new program can fill in some of the GAPs (necessary services or programs that are lacking) in the last one?
- How safe and adaptive is the facility you plan to use for the program?
- How much will the whole program cost the agency?

Keith knows there will be many more questions. The board of directors has a right to ask these questions, and he must be prepared to answer the questions well. The meeting will be like a tennis or fencing match with questions flying at him from all quarters.

Asking questions is like shining a flashlight in a dark cellar instead of simply stumbling around looking for the fuse box. Questions direct our thinking and protect us from jumping to wrong or incomplete conclusions. Even after he has designed his action plan, this process of asking, finding answers, acting, and then raising more questions continues. It creates an information loop that looks something like Figure 12.1.

Before we look at the specific techniques for moving a plan into action, we present the following interview with a young human service worker who has a great deal of experience in using these tools and techniques. Raquel Fenning is the program coordinator of the Volunteer Services Office at a large urban university.

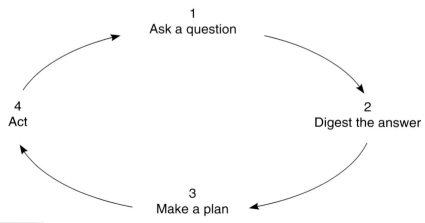

FIGURE 12.1   The information loop

INTERVIEW

Raquel Fenning, University Volunteer Coordinator

I have worked at the university doing volunteer placement for five years now. The first three years I was a student on work-study stipend and then for two more years after graduation, I was hired as a full-time employee to lead the office of Volunteer Placements. When I worked at the Fenway Project, I found volunteer jobs for students. I was responsible for making contact with neighborhood social service agencies and finding out what their volunteer needs were. Then I would draft a paper outlining the agency, its mission, its funding, and so on and finally write a job description for the prospective volunteer. I would check it out with the agency and begin to recruit students who were able and willing to fill it. Most of the volunteers were human service or criminal justice majors or were from some of the more socially conscious fraternities and sororities on campus.

The university put a low priority on student involvement in the neighborhood, so the Fenway Project was sort of an "add on" to the Human Service Program. We placed a few dozen volunteers each semester but mostly we involved classes and clubs in one-shot events in local agencies. We hosted bus trips for senior citizens, a friendly visitor program for seniors who were not able to leave their rooms, after-school recreation clubs for youngsters and teen dances. I couldn't imagine a better way to learn planning skills than this job. When I worked as the senior citizen coordinator, I met with a senior advisory committee composed of representatives from the seven senior residences in the town. The members suggested trips and activities. Then I would recruit the sororities, fraternities, and other clubs on campus to run them. I'd get the nursing or physical therapy students to conduct exercise classes. I'd try to find a political science or government major to run a current-events discussion group or maybe a seminar. The Fenway Project still exists and is run by students but now they pretty much stick to hosting special events for kids and senior citizens, leaving the regular volunteer placements to our office.

Now that I am a full-time employee, reporting to the Provost's office, I have a regular budget and a staff of six paid interns and a full-time secretary. The number of students using the program has gone from dozens each term to hundreds. And the students now are from all the majors on campus. Working as a volunteer in a community group for a certain number of hours each year is now a graduation requirement. Many faculty members facilitate the volunteerism by including appropriate community work as an integral part of their courses. So the student not only does the fieldwork but also has to analyze it for a research or concept paper. I still visit agencies, put out recruitment materials, screen students, and ultimately make sure they are evaluated. I also troubleshoot if something goes wrong on the placements either from the student's point of view or from the supervisor's point of view. But my staff does a lot of the legwork that permits me to get involved in other mental health issues on campus.

An important part of my job description is to participate in a variety of faculty/staff committees that grapple with "hot button issues" that affect the mental health and well-being of the student population. Since I had been a student here just two years ago and am now a trained human service worker, they place a lot of value on my input. I work on committees that deal with issues facing gay, lesbian, and **transgendered** students, the uses and abuses of alcohol and drugs on campus and on the committee that oversees political demonstrations and the like.

I have just been handed a challenging assignment! I will participate in a newly formed committee which is charged with creating programs, guidelines, and policies to deal with the hottest button issue of recent times: Recently there has been a lot of media coverage of **cyberbullying** in high schools. Newspapers have carried stories about high school kids (and even some younger children) posting nasty things about each other on websites or in widely distributed text messages. Some high school students have hosted on-line contests to choose the "ugliest girl in school"; they've posted messages about who hates whom, which person cheated on an exam, and other really hateful messages. They've tricked people into revealing their passwords and have posted photos of victims taken on cell phones without their permission. (See Harris Interactive Research Report on Cyberbullying, commissioned by the National Crime Prevention Council, 2006). This isn't just kids harmlessly fooling around. Serious consistent teasing, whether in person, or more likely through the anonymity of the web, has resulted in several teenage suicides and nervous breakdowns. In one high school district in Ohio, four students committed suicide in a year; each had undergone serious harassment.

To everyone's horror, this has moved from high school students—who one can assume are rather immature and might not know better—to college students. In one horrific incident, Tyler Clementi, a Rutgers University freshman, jumped to his death off the George Washington Bridge after a sexual encounter he had in his dorm room was secretly filmed by his roommate. After violating his rights by filming the encounter, the roommate then posted the video on the web (Foderato, 2010; McKinley, 2010). Several of these suicides, like Clementi's, were of persons who were or were assumed by others to be gay.

The committee has been told by the president of the university to develop programs to deal with all forms of the misuse of technology to harass members of the student body and staff. We are exploring the use of computer software that documents and stores offensive messages, that immediately notifies prespecified recipients of an online threat, and so forth. This way messages can be documented so that perpetrators can be located. We are also planning to hold dorm talks on the misuse of texting, social network sites, videos, and so on. In the spring we will hold a campuswide teach-in aimed at educating students on ways to protect themselves and most importantly, on the serious nature of what might be seen as harmless teasing, especially when done anonymously. We hope to build a community spirit that will make such behavior unacceptable. Of course, the first line of defense is always education but we will also have to draft a set of penalties for abuse when education is not enough. This is a particularly tricky issue since we will have to struggle to find the line where free speech ends and bullying begins.

So my position is very challenging but satisfying. I am so glad I took a course that helped me learn the steps in mounting a program. I will probably stay in this position for a few more years but then I hope to take a degree in public health. I like the idea of being a health educator; it builds on many of the skills I am practicing.

transgendered Appearing, acting, or actually becoming (by means of medical procedures) the opposite gender from that which a person is born.

cyberbullying The use of cyber communication technology to spread information about a person or group, which spreads deliberate, repeated, and hostile opinions or other data intended to harass a targeted victim.

PHASES AND STEPS IN THE PLANNING PROCESS

troubleshooter A person who is alert for signs or symptoms that indicate the existence of an actual or potential problem.

Planners wear many hats, a different one for each phase of the planning process. In the first phase, donning the peaked cap of a Sherlock Holmes detective, the planner is a gadfly, or **troubleshooter**. He or she runs around finding problems and noticing when the emperor has no clothes on. In the second phase, the planner replaces the peaked cap with a cowboy-style, ten-gallon hat and takes a giant step back from the problem, looking at the big picture. In the last phase, the peaked cap and ten-gallon hat are put aside for the green visor of the accountant. Now, the planner looks at each part of the plan in depth, figuring out exactly what must be done. Now he or she is a nitpicker, a list maker, and a rule maker and keeper.

In the following section we will look more closely at each of these three phases of the planning process: troubleshooting, magnifying, and microscoping.*

Phase 1: Troubleshooting

STEP 1: IDENTIFYING A GAP

As shown in Figure 12.2, the planning process begins as soon as Raquel or another Fenway Project staff member says:

> Something is wrong with how that is done!

or

> Something is missing from. . . . !

or

> Wouldn't it be wonderful if. . . . !

or

> There oughta be a law about. . . . !

GAP A necessary service or resource that is lacking in a program or in services that might help solve a problem.

Often we identify a **GAP**, without realizing we are doing so, when we are having a good gripe session. Listen in as Lowell, a human service student, complains about the difficulty he had finding the appropriate social services for his elderly aunt:

> Over Easter break I spent a lot of time with my Aunt Elsie, who is 82 years old. She's in the hospital with a broken hip. I knew she would need some homemaking help and

---

*To read more about the steps involved in the three phases, see American Association of University Women (1978); Dale, Magnani, and Miller (1979); Dale and Mitiguy (1978); Frame (1995); Kettner, Moroney, and Martin (2007); and Schram (1997).

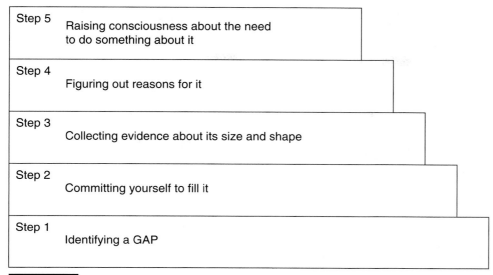

Step 5	Raising consciousness about the need to do something about it
Step 4	Figuring out reasons for it
Step 3	Collecting evidence about its size and shape
Step 2	Committing yourself to fill it
Step 1	Identifying a GAP

FIGURE 12.2   The process of trouble shooting a problem

maybe some emotional support when she returned home. She lives alone in a small house. I don't know my way around this city. The social worker at the hospital was either too busy with more serious cases or really didn't know much about the resources for elderly people. Boy, was that frustrating! There really ought to be a place where elderly people or their relatives could go to get current information on home-care services. Even more important, I could use someone to steer me to the good programs and warn me about the ones to avoid.

Lowell was describing what *now exists* and then visualizing what *ought to happen*. In between the two, "the what is" and the "what ought to be," there is a yawning cavern that a person is likely to fall into. We call that hole a GAP.

Sometimes a GAP is identified by a person who has a desperate need for a resource that he or she cannot locate, that does not exist, or that is functioning poorly. At other times a professional human service worker notices an unmet need and brings it to the attention of his or her supervisor or board.

In Figure 12.3 we have listed a few examples of people describing "what is" and visions of "what ought to be." In between the "is" and the "ought" lies a GAP that needs to be bridged by social service planning.

Example: A Professional Identifies a GAP

A doctor working in rural Alabama was surprised at how few patients came into the hospital to be treated for AIDS or HIV. Although AIDS is often thought of as an urban phenomenon, she knew that was not accurate. She had a hunch that people in southern rural towns, where everyone knows everyone else's business, were afraid to even ask for AIDS testing. The strong fundamentalist religious values of the region attach an especially noxious stigma to AIDS, with its implications of homosexual behavior. So, dipping into her

WHAT IS	THE GAP	WHAT OUGHT TO BE
This Is What Exists Now		**This Is What *Ought* to Happen**
"Every Sunday as I sit in church, I notice this group of people who are obviously retarded sitting in the last few rows. They don't bother anyone, and they leave right after the service. But they seem so lonely and out of it."	**GAP**	"These people are newcomers to our church and ought to be welcomed by the congregation. It would be nice if they could stay for the hospitality hour so members and their children could get to know them. That's what our church is supposed to be all about."
"Every week the hospital in our town releases people who have emotional disturbances to live on their own in the community. A lot of them have lost contact with old friends or relatives. They're just drifting. They live in cheap boarding houses, often on skid row, where they have nothing to do and little to look forward to"	**GAP**	"There ought to be some place they could go during the day if they are not working or on weekends if they are. They need to be with other people, especially ones who can understand what they've been through and know how hard it is to adjust after years spent in and out of an institution."
"Every year the YMCA has a junior olympics for the kids who attend gym classes. This year, because they've removed a lot of the architectural barriers, my son who is wheelchair-bound attends the sports program. He's going to feel very left out if he's not included in the big event, but everyone seems too worried about problems of safety and insurance to include the kids with handicaps."	**GAP**	"We ought to offer the kids with physical handicaps a chance to have the same type of activities all the others enjoy."

FIGURE 12.3   Examples of social service GAPs

own wallet for start-up funds, she began a public education program called ASK, which stood for **A**IDS **S**upport through **K**nowledge. These are some of the outreach strategies she used:

- She set up an anonymous information telephone hot line.

- She convinced a popular disc jockey to play a rap song about AIDS over the local radio station.

- She placed ads in newspapers.

- She sponsored a group of high school students, who performed a play about AIDS at schools and churches.

Eventually, many people who worried they might have contracted AIDS found the courage to come to the hospital for testing and care.

In *Designing and Managing Programs: An Effectiveness Based Approach*, Kettner et al. (2007) point out that many people who might need services seek them out only when the possibility of actually receiving them exists. Because people have such low expectations, they often do not even perceive that their GAP is a legitimate one or that they deserve to have it filled.

After a rape crisis center opens in a town, instead of seeing a reduction in the rape statistics, we are likely to see them increase. It looks as if the situation is getting worse, but what might actually be happening is that victims, especially of date rape, who used to feel that there was no possibility of getting justice and who endured their pain in silence, are finding the courage to come forward and report the crime. Now there is a chance that they might be protected and that the abuser might be punished.

STEP 2: COMMITTING OURSELVES TO FILLING THE GAP

Once it has been stated that a GAP exists, someone has to commit himself or herself to the long, painstaking, often thankless planning tasks that can fill it. Unfortunately, gripe sessions too often end with little to show for them but shared frustration. Often people will say:

What can I do? I don't know anything about starting up a program.

or

But it has always been that way!

These statements express widespread feelings of powerlessness, but they do not reflect reality. Many programs have grown out of an informal discussion in someone's living room. Park benches in schoolyards where parents gather to talk about their children, their families, and their hopes for the future are often fertile fields for new program ideas. For example, the widely translated, best-selling book *Our Bodies, Ourselves* (Boston Women's Health Book Collective, 2006) grew out of a small women's **consciousness-raising** group that met informally in the 1970s. The women began asking each other questions about their special issues of health and sexuality. Discovering how little any of them knew, they started doing research. Finding the books limited and written mostly from a male perspective, the women decided to write their own book. That first book (revised many times) was followed by *Ourselves and Our Children* (1981) and *The New Ourselves, Growing Older* (1994), among many others, and translated into several languages.

Programs designed to fill GAPs do not necessarily need vast sums of money and expertise. They grow out of someone's capacity to keep plugging away, aided by a fertile imagination, self-confidence, and a good **support network**.

Example: Members of a Church Commit Themselves to Filling a GAP

Several years ago, one of the authors of this text was visiting a friend who had just returned from delivering a paper on "supervised visitation" at a professional conference

consciousness raising The process in which people are provoked into giving an issue serious thought, perhaps through suggestion of new points of view to be considered.

support network The people and places in our lives that offer ongoing practical as well as emotional help.

(Speigel, 1992). Surprised that she had never heard that term, because she thought she "knew everything about social programs," the author admitted that she had no idea what supervised visitation was. Her friend explained that the supervised visitation program she directed was the brainchild of a member of a local church. Her minister had told the congregation of the problems that families face when an incident of abuse or neglect made it impossible for one of the parents to be left alone with his or her child. But, hoping that the abuser would have the incentive to change his or her behavior, so the family unit could eventually be preserved, the court did not want to sever their relationships. Judges mandate that the abusing parent can visit with the child only if a neutral, trained observer is present to guarantee safety during the visit. However, this arrangement is almost impossible to manage for most noncustodial parents. State social workers are overburdened, and private therapists charge high fees.

So this woman had the idea of using the church as a place for supervised family visits. By having several families come at one time in groups, more people could be served for a low cost. Also, families would realize that there were others who grappled with similar problems.

No event, no matter how often it is repeated, is ever taken for granted. Getting a message out to the public takes great imagination and attention to detail. These students are sponsoring a recruitment drive for volunteers.

The following is the program she designed:

- Each Saturday, eighteen families gather at the church, nine in the morning and nine in the afternoon.

- The custodial parents bring their children to the church, where they are met by volunteer facilitators and go off for a snack.

- The custodial parents gather in another room for a support-group session.

- The noncustodial parents then arrive, and the facilitators and children join them at a table in the social hall. The table is set with age-appropriate games and craft materials.

- The noncustodial parents and children interact for an hour while a facilitator sits a few feet away, unobtrusively monitoring the contact. The observer intervenes only if a child is in immediate danger or an inappropriate question is being asked or comment is made.

- The children and their custodial parents leave.

- The noncustodial parents go into a mandatory support-group meeting.

- The facilitators get together to review how things went and make suggestions.

- In the afternoon, the program repeats with the second group of parents and facilitators.

The role of the professional social worker, the only paid staff member, is to keep all the balls in the air: training and recruiting the volunteers, most of whom are students, church members, and interested citizens. The worker keeps in contact with the courts and the Department of Social Services.

The program is overseen and the funds are raised by church members as a tangible expression of their convictions about the importance of family values. Because the space is free and all the facilitators are volunteers, the yearly cost of the program is primarily the professional's half-time salary. So far, they have been able to raise this amount through a variety of fund-raising campaigns. Often it is easier to raise money for a very specific program such as this one than for a more amorphous general appeal.

Some people accurately define a problem and immediately propose solutions. But if they start to act too quickly, they run the risk of becoming a general without an army. Along with her commitment to act, this woman at the church did careful research before she proposed her idea. She understood that without solid data about the problem, she would never have been able to solicit the support of the congregation, the courts, the Department of Social Services, and the thirty-two volunteers who give up their Saturdays to help their neighbors.

STEP 3: COLLECTING EVIDENCE ABOUT A GAP

Remember the difficulties encountered by Lowell, the human service student, as he tried to find services for his elderly aunt? Although Raquel agreed with Lowell that there appeared to be an information GAP about services for the elderly in his hometown, she knew that they had to be *sure* it existed. Maybe Lowell simply couldn't find the information he needed. She decided to help him collect evidence to support (or perhaps refute) his assertion that information about geriatric services is not readily available.

They begin their research by collecting data in the public library. They look through directories (both hard copy and online) to find social services for the elderly, especially those that help maintain elderly persons in their own homes during a recovery period.

COLLECTING EVIDENCE ABOUT THE EXTENT OF A GAP
Services to the Elderly in Aurora

I. Questions to ask organization staff workers:

1. How many senior citizens do you have contact with, either in person or through newsletters?

2. What strategies do you use to get information out about available services to the elderly population and to social agencies?

3. What written guides do you have on elderly programs? Which of them seem most useful? What obstacles stand in the way of reaching some of the elderly?

4. Which groups of elderly citizens and their families do you feel are not being reached?

5. How great a need do you think there is for some type of information service for geriatric programs? What are your suggestions?

II. Questions to ask individual senior citizens or their families:

1. How did you hear about this particular organization (housing project, nursing home, recreational center, or whatever) you attend?

2. If you needed home care, a senior shuttle bus, meals on wheels, day care, or a nursing home, to whom would you turn for that information?

3. How easy is it to get information when you need some kind of services? If it is difficult, why do you think that is so? What are your suggestions to increase knowledge of resources?

FIGURE 12.4   Sample interview questions on services for the elderly

They plan to interview people at some of these agencies to get information straight from the source. Before they interview anyone, though, they write up a list of questions to ask, examples of which are shown in Figure 12.4. This way they can make sure that they get the same type of information from each interview. Of course, every GAP one is researching will need specially tailored questions. But these are samples of questions that might be asked.

It is important that the people Raquel and Lowell interview represent a cross-section of elderly service workers and consumers. They need to know in whose eyes the GAP exists. The people (and their programs) they interviewed are listed in Figure 12.5. Notice that their hunt for evidence about the GAP also included census data and other library resources.

From their interviews and reading, Raquel and Lowell decide that their initial hunch was correct: Information about available services is not getting to everyone who needs it, especially when they are in crisis. Both consumers and professionals agree that some central source of updated information is sorely needed. Raquel and Lowell's review of the census data reveals that the elderly population in this area has risen by 20 percent in the past ten years. The articles they read predicted that it will continue to grow.

Now Raquel and Lowell have evidence to show that outreach to the elderly and to the general public about the full range of elderly home care services is a legitimate GAP. Some agencies call this data-gathering process conducting a **needs assessment**. Once they are

needs assessment
Methods used to find out precisely what one particular person, group, or community needs to solve its problems and expand opportunities.

COLLECTING EVIDENCE ABOUT THE EXTENT OF A GAP
Services for the Elderly

I. *People we will need to talk to:*

1. Citywide council on elderly affairs in the mayor's office

2. Local chapter of AARP (American Association of Retired Persons), National Council of Older Americans, or OWL (Older Women's League)

3. Nursing Home Director's Group and some residents of local nursing homes

4. The Homecare Corporation

5. The Gray Panthers (a self-help elderly social action group)

6. Project manager and residents at the Susan B. Anthony Elderly Housing Project

7. The Methodist church's friendly visitors program

II. *Publications we will need to read:*

1. Citywide and community newspapers (large-print version, if there is one)

2. Newsletters of any senior citizen clubs or groups

3. Directory of services for the elderly

4. Census data for the area

FIGURE 12.5 Sources of information about services for the elderly

---

sure they have a legitimate GAP that needs to be filled, they must find out for what reasons it exists. To do this, they move on to the next step.*

STEP 4: FIGURING OUT CAUSALITY—THE REASONS FOR THE GAP

As Raquel and Lowell were collecting evidence about the size and shape of the GAP in referral services, they were constantly asking their informants "why" questions such as:

- Why do you think the public has so little knowledge about your program?

- Why do the booklets you publish seem to reach one group of professionals or elderly citizens more than another?

- Why haven't you tried using other media to inform them?

The answers to these questions begin the difficult process of estimating the reasons for the GAP. Reasons will suggest remedies. Although we can never be absolutely certain about the reasons for a problem, the process of identifying possible causes and then ranking them in importance is a vital one. It creates the foundation upon which the whole planning process is built.

---

*A useful resource Lowell could have used to generate ideas about agencies to look for is the book *Making Aging in Place Work* (Pastalan, 1999).

POSSIBLE REASONS FOR A GAP
Referral Services for the Elderly

Information about elderly services is not reaching enough people because:

1. The directories of services that do exist are all in the English language, and the print is often small and hard to read.

2. Directories of services for the elderly are not distributed widely enough. They are available only at social agencies or hospitals.

3. Directories of services for the elderly seem to be very specialized, concentrating on only one type of service. Often they don't mention alternative services available at other agencies.

4. The elderly are often homebound and use television and radio more frequently than books and newspapers to get information.

5. Often the elderly and their families don't prepare for emergencies and must do their planning when a crisis occurs, when they are least able to seek out resources rationally.

6. Many people assume that all service programs for the elderly are charity and resist exploring resources that might have a social stigma.

7. Programs change so often that staff are unaware of new ones or those which have been discontinued.

8. The best referrals are made by knowledgeable people, not directories; however, agencies are short of experienced staff.

FIGURE 12.6   Possible reasons for a GAP in referral services

Figure 12.6 shows the list of reasons Raquel and Lowell created after studying the interviews and reading journal articles on the subject. See how program ideas seem to flow logically from each of them! There is no way, of course, that they can design one program that deals with all the reasons. So they rank the listed items, giving some a higher priority than others. Finally, they will have to decide which reasons to deal with first.

Now the two young planners are ready to go public, looking to find others who will join them in filling this unmet need.

STEP 5: RAISING CONSCIOUSNESS ABOUT A GAP

Even after a GAP has been identified, evidence about its size, shape, and causes has been marshaled, and some possible reasons for it have been outlined, the demand that it be filled can fall on deaf ears. Lots of other people must agree that it is a problem before it can move up to the top of the agenda for the client, the agency, the bureaucrats, and the legislators.

Raquel and Lowell, enlisting the assistance of the students in a class on aging at their university, conduct the following consciousness-raising activities to spread concern about their GAP:

1. They write up a brief report, presenting their evidence that there is a lack of information about available resources and giving examples of the havoc it wreaks on the elderly homebound.

2. They meet with the president of a senior citizen center to solicit his or her group's support.

3. They meet with the chairperson of the Council on Aging and get his or her enthusiastic support.

4. They get themselves invited to speak about the problem at two local churches, a temple, and a mosque.

5. They convince the editor of the local newspaper to write a feature story about the plight of elderly homebound people who cannot find support services.

6. They speak on the local cable TV station about the GAP.

Phase 2: Magnifying

Having gathered evidence and marshaled enthusiastic support, Raquel and Lowell are now ready to begin **magnifying**. During this phase, they will collect, sort, and then choose concrete program ideas—vital components of the program design process. Figure 12.7 shows the steps they follow.

magnifying
Looking at a program or problem within the larger context of the community, laws, professional field, and so forth.

Now, Raquel and Lowell's imaginations can work overtime. Although looking for innovative ideas, they do not simply dismiss as old hat program ideas that already exist. Actually, few really new ideas are ever born. Most program concepts are variations on a few central themes. They borrow a technique from here, an approach from there. They recombine basic program interventions, giving them a new twist, one that is especially suited to this population, problem, and town.

Before they design their plan, Raquel and Lowell need to be reassured that although we strive for a perfect solution, in the real world, one will rarely be found. Program designs

Step 5	Drafting a plan and making an alternative one
Step 4	Doing a force-field analysis of alternative ideas
Step 3	Collecting and ranking ideas
Step 2	Brainstorming ideas
Step 1	Inventorying other programs

FIGURE 12.7   The process of magnifying the problem

have to be flexible and responsive to constant feedback. As soon as they have planned the program, they will want to start redoing the design. Programs are organic, living creatures with unpredictable demands and personalities.

STEP 1: CONDUCTING AN INVENTORY OF OTHER PROGRAMS

Throughout this book, we have stressed the critical importance of obtaining firsthand knowledge of program resources in the local community. But when designing an action plan, we look within and far beyond the boundaries of our own town because program ideas cross-fertilize from one region or country to another. For example, the concept of the ombudsperson—a red-tape cutter—now found in many U.S. city halls, universities, and hospitals—was borrowed from Scandinavia. The program design for the Samaritans, a volunteer suicide hot line, was imported from England. Creches—overnight shelters for young children whose parents have to leave them in emergencies—originated in France.

After visiting a poor developing country in Latin America, a social planning student observed:

> On this trip I was impressed by the way in which ideas flow in all directions. When I visited the country's only residential school for the blind, staff members told me how much they wanted to study in the United States. They wanted to learn about the newest Braille machines and mobility training techniques. Their country is very far behind us in special needs programming. I noted with regret that all their new public buildings are being constructed with complete disregard of the architectural barriers that exclude people who are physically disabled. In the future, when they become more conscious of integrating people with special needs, they'll have to spend thousands of dollars replacing steps with ramps and modifying bathrooms.
>
> Yet, surprisingly, they had some very innovative approaches that far outdistanced ours. For example, to meet the needs of urban, two-worker couples with elderly disabled relatives, they have constructed nursing and old-age homes. Yet, wanting to keep the traditional, extended family as intact as possible, they arrange to transport the elderly residents back to the homes of their relatives for weekends and holidays. I've not heard of many homes for the elderly doing that in the United States. Because we are concerned about the increasing isolation of the elderly, I suspect that idea will eventually catch on here.
>
> This was a good lesson for me. Although we are advanced in some areas, we still have plenty to learn from a developing country.

Sometimes program approaches are transplanted whole from one place to another. At other times, however, new program ideas leapfrog off each other. For example, in the travel section of our newspaper several years ago there was an article about a travel agency that arranges for tourists to stay in elegant castles and manor houses when visiting foreign countries. A few years later, other tourist companies began arranging accommodations in more humble kinds of homes in both Europe and Latin America. Eventually this commercial travel idea reached the human services. It changed from a profit-making enterprise into a nonprofit support network for a special population. A senior citizen council in a Midwestern city set up a vacation home-exchange program for elderly citizens on limited incomes. In this plan, older people living in modest homes can arrange a low-cost holiday trip. For only the cost of transportation, they can explore the countryside or a big city by exchanging their apartment for that of another elderly person. Because improving the quality of life for our elderly is an increasingly important concern, this innovative idea is likely to spread. Perhaps as a logical extension there might be a home-exchange program for physically challenged people and so on.

Program ideas also leapfrog from one problem area to another. The GAP in referral services for the elderly that Raquel analyzed has been filled in one local community by a program called the Geriatric Resource Center. Two years before it was begun, a divorce resource and mediation center was started in a nearby town. Several years before that, a child care resource center was begun. We cannot be sure that each was the ancestor of the next, but the program format of specialized resource centers that help a specific population has certainly spread.

Once you see yourself as a planner, you are likely to get new program ideas almost every time you read a newspaper, watch a television show, or attend a lecture or seminar. You will not be able to act on all of them, but you can store program designs away for future use.

STEP 2: BRAINSTORMING IDEAS

Brainstorming is a very simple yet elegant planning technique that quickly produces a great many ideas, some mundane and impractical, a few marvelously creative (Michaiko, 2006, Osborn, 1963). It energizes the staff member of the Office of Volunteer Services, freeing them of their usual reserve by sweeping them into the contagion of shared problem solving. They do it at staff meetings in groups of three. Everyone can easily be heard and is encouraged to participate. A brainstorming assignment must be very clear. It begins with a question, for instance:

> If we had $1,000 more in our budget, what programs would we initiate?
>
> If you were made dean of this college, what are the ten most important changes you'd make?
>
> If we open up this program to persons who are blind, what parts of it would have to be changed? In what ways?

A time limit of five or ten minutes is set for each session. The time pressure encourages members to keep throwing out ideas. The group leader begins the creative juices flowing by suggesting a few ideas of his or her own—the more innovative the better. Participants are told that there is a premium placed on far-ranging thinking. There are a few simple rules for brainstorming (Coover, Deacon, Esser, & Moore, 1985; Dale & Mitiguy, 1978; Siegel, 1996):

- Do not censor your ideas; let them flow. Even if they sound silly, impractical, or naive, they can be sorted out and discarded later.

- Do not censor anyone else's ideas by judging them or by communicating distaste, scorn, or ridicule.

brainstorming
A technique in which people generate ideas under time pressure and without judgment so that their most innovative thoughts can flow.

- Give encouragement and support to others and expect it from others.
- Build on each other's ideas, use them, and change them.
- Move quickly and try to get as many ideas out as possible.
- List ideas on paper so that they are not lost in the flow of talk.

STEP 3: COLLECTING AND RANKING IDEAS

At the Fenway Project quarterly retreat, the student staff members were asked to brainstorm ways to spend the grant they were awarded by the Office of Student Affairs. The ideas they came up with were listed on a chalkboard and then divided into categories:

1. Senior citizen programs
2. Youth after-school programs
3. Programs for developmentally delayed adults
4. Teenager programs
5. Special one-time work projects
6. Community fairs

Then they divided the categories according to the following criteria:

- Programs we can do ourselves
- Programs we can try to get other groups to sponsor

and according to still another dimension:

- Programs that do not cost money
- Programs that do cost money

Then the student staff edited the lists, discarding ideas that seemed impractical or that evoked little interest. They put check marks next to those that excited almost everyone. These lists will be carried over from one quarter to the next. As new ideas come up, they will be added. If a human service major wants to do a special internship at the Fenway Project, he or she can look at this list to see what program ideas are waiting to be developed.

The Fenway Project also keeps a *wish list*. Staff members suggest equipment or funding they would like to obtain if there is any money left at the end of the fiscal year. Three weeks before the budget closes, they review the auditor's printouts. They see how much money they were allocated and how much they have spent and then pick and choose what they can still afford to buy. If any individuals or organizations offer to make monetary donations, they refer to their wish list and suggest an item. The current wish list of the Fenway Project looks like this:

- A laser printer, a scanner, and a digital camera
- A paint job for the office

- Slides to use for class presentations
- A catcher's mitt and a left-handed fielder's mitt
- A new coffee urn

STEP 4: DOING A FORCE-FIELD ANALYSIS

After a program idea has survived the sorting and ranking process, it is time to analyze its chances of success. To do this the students use a simple but effective technique called **force-field analysis**. They first look at the forces that might help the program get started and the barriers that are likely to stand in its way. They gain confidence by reviewing the positive factors but are also alerted to the barriers posed by the negatives. They look at how they balance out.

force-field analysis
A systematic way of looking at the negatives and positives of an idea or event in order to understand it fully, anticipate problems, and estimate chances of success.

Some Fenway Project youth staff are working with Hi-Teens, a club of adolescents who live in the local public housing project. The staff has decided that the group needs a really good activity to pull the members together into a cohesive unit. They brainstormed with the teenagers and analyzed their list of ideas, and everyone agreed that they wanted a weekend camping trip. Now they must think through how likely it is that they will be able to plan and successfully carry out the idea. Systematically, they list the positive and negative forces, as in Figure 12.8.

If the negative forces are too overwhelming, the youth staff will move on to the next idea. Many of these inner-city teenagers have already experienced too much frustration and failure in their lives. They need a program that is grounded in reality and success. Their force-field list looks reasonably balanced. It will take a lot of work to turn those negatives into positives, but they think they can do it. If ignored, the negatives might sabotage their best planning efforts.

FORCE-FIELD ANALYSIS
Topic: Hi-Teens' Weekend Camping Trip

The Positives +
(What we have going for us)

1. We have been on several one-day trips, and they've worked out well.

2. It's January now, so we have lots of time to make a reservation at a camp site for the spring.

3. We all get along very well.

4. Our group leader has a lot of camping experience.

5. Because most of the members voted for this idea, we should get good cooperation from them.

The Negatives –
(What might get in our way)

1. We have no money in our treasury.

2. Some parents may refuse to give permission, especially if it's boys and girls together.

3. The camping sites are pretty far away, and we don't have any transportation.

4. Carlos, our group leader, has finals at college in the spring and may not have the time to take us.

FIGURE 12.8   A sample force-field analysis

FORCE-FIELD ANALYSIS STRATEGY PLANNING

The negative force	Strategies to overcome the negative force
Some parents may refuse to give permission, especially if it's boys and girls together.	1. Ask one or two parents to chaperone the trip.
	2. Go in two separate groups of boys and girls; combine for some activities.
	3. Have the overnight at the house of one of the members.
	4. Have the parents who are likely to give permission talk to the ones who are against it.
	5. Have the group leader meet with all the parents to discuss the trip.

FIGURE 12.9   A sample of force-field analysis strategy planning

After completing the force-field analysis, the teens brainstorm strategies that might overcome or neutralize those negative forces. Figure 12.9 lists the strategies to overcome one negative force listed in Figure 12.8, "parents' resistance to a coed trip." Now, they need to construct an action plan, making sure that potential obstacles to their plans are dealt with and that everything they have decided to do is clear to all the members.

STEP 5: CREATING A PROGRAM PROPOSAL AND MAKING A WORK PLAN

No matter how informal the group, it is imperative that the program plan the group hopes to implement be written down so that everyone can review it fully and those who become involved later on can be accurately oriented to it. The program proposal will be the road map. It keeps folks on course and invites others (especially funders) to come on board. Figure 12.10 lists what the proposal should include. A book the teens found useful was *Proposals That Work* (Locke, Spirduiso, & Silverman, 2007). As a first step in drafting the plan, we need to look back at our negative forces. How can we overcome the negative forces? In the minutes of the teenagers' meeting (prepared by Carlos, the college student volunteer), you can see how they began that process:

> We voted eight to one that we would have a two-day camping trip in the country in the late spring. We want the trip to include both boys and girls. We will schedule it for a weekend after Carlos's finals. We will have a meeting with all the parents this month to try to convince them to let us go and see what help they can give us. Some of the boys worried that the parents would resist. So then we spent more time figuring out what to do to get the parents to say okay.

In Figure 12.9 you can see some of the strategies they came up with.

The proposal should include:*

1. Title page—with name of program, who it is being presented to and by whom.

2. Abstract—a brief overview of the agency, problem (GAP) program activities, funding request, and planners. No more than one scant page, the abstract should be very tight and clear. It may be all that is ever looked at if many proposals are in a pile in a funder's in-box.

3. Table of contents—each part of the proposal should be numbered for each reference when the program is being discussed.

4. Problem statement—What (GAP) is this program trying to fill? How did the problem get identified, how long has it been going on, what are its consequences? This part would include backup data, surveys, professional articles, anecdotal evidence.

5. Background to the problem—brief information about the agency or persons making the proposal, who does it serve, how, when did it begin, staff, funding, facility, and geographic area.

6. Goals of the program—this includes hopeful outcomes spelled out very operationally and in very specific terms.

7. Proposed activities—Exactly what are you planning to do, when, and how? What staff will be needed, what facility, what equipment? This should also include a work plan or time line in this section or a separate one.

8. Budget—How much money will be needed for exactly what, and how much will need to be raised for the new program, and what in-kind donations are expected?

9. Evaluation—What methods will you use to assess how successfully your program activities have met your goals or hoped-for outcomes, over what period of time?

10. Additional supporting documents—this section would include bibliography if applicable, charts, and letters of support or concern.**

* Many funding agencies will have their own special format to follow.

**For a sample program proposal, see Schram (1997, pp. 220–226).

FIGURE 12.10   Writing a program proposal

They ended their meeting by deciding that they would raise the money through a car wash. It would be held on Saturday from 11:00 A.M. to 4:00 P.M. in front of the local housing project. Tiger and Arnie agreed to be in charge of it.

That plan may sound pretty clear, but it needs to be spelled out in greater detail, and it needs an alternative. "The best-laid plans of mice and men (and women) often go astray." Every planner knows Murphy's Law:

IF ANYTHING CAN GO WRONG, IT WILL!

Whether you are asking for extra funding or have the funds but need permission from the director or staff to embark on a new program, it is critically important that all the details of the proposed plan be set down on paper. In the process of doing this, the planners themselves will become much clearer and ultimately more persuasive. The proposal shows that you have done your homework and that you have a feasible plan and credible planners.

If Murphy's law is correct, the young people better plan the camping trip and car wash with some fallback arrangements. There must always be plans A, B, C, and D. Perhaps they cannot get a majority of the parents to approve the co-ed overnight trip, which is plan A, and, therefore, plan B might be that they will try to get the parents to agree to a one-day co-ed trip. Plan C could be separate overnight trips, one for the girls and one for the boys.

Because it might rain on the weekend they choose, they will book an alternate date for the next weekend. If Carlos cannot go because of his schoolwork, they will ask Mr. Devon, the gym coach, if he would be willing to go.

Of course, we can never anticipate all the twists of fate, but good planners try to cover as many bases as they can. Clients do not need workers to protect them from all possible failures. Rather, they need workers who encourage them to plan realistically.

Creating a sensible contingency plan is a problem-solving skill that is valuable in every phase of work, school, and social life. Parades are often rained on, but good planners bring umbrellas!

A vital part of the process of drafting a plan is estimating how much money it will take and how much money the group has or can raise. Although all of us resist making a budget, it is surprising how much clearer every part of a plan becomes when we have finished the budget-making process. Finances are always the bottom line. That does not mean that everything must cost a lot of money. As we get more skillful, we find many ways to get donations and make do with very little.

Phase 3: Microscoping

microscoping
Looking at a program or problem and seeing within it all the component parts and steps of action needed.

For the **microscoping** phase of the planning process, we take off our creative, think-big hat and put on the green visor of the accountant. Now we must focus all our attention on the minute details of our specific plan. We must make sure that it will work as smoothly as possible. The steps we follow are listed in Figure 12.11.

Step 4	Evaluating and following up
Step 3	Establishing time schedules
Step 2	Specifying and assigning tasks to be done
Step 1	Building a resource bank

FIGURE 12.11   The process of microscoping a problem

In this phase, we must nail down vague ideas. Using pad and paper, computers, date-books, clocks, and web sites and directories of resources, the teenagers make checklists (and double-checklists). The mindset of the microscoper is neat and orderly, leaving little to chance.

Many experienced workers have adopted the anxious stance of the microscoper after failing several classes in the "school of hard knocks." A student intern at the Fenway Project wrote the following about his fieldwork:

> I still carry with me the vivid memory of facing sixty disappointed, angry adults and children on a hot street corner. Although I had booked the buses for their annual family picnic at Riverside Amusement Park, I had neglected to double-check the bus company's arrangements. The buses never showed! Many of these folks had planned their vacations around this yearly outing. Few have the cars or money to take their own trips to the country. They counted on my planning ability, and I hadn't come through for them. Now I've learned to double- (or even triple-) check every time I lease a bus.

Every human service worker can recount a story of a catastrophe that destroyed a program. Perhaps the DVD for the cartoon show for little kids did not work, or the CD player for a dance was broken, or the staff member in charge of food bought only half the number of frankfurters needed for the barbecue.

Mistakes creep into our work in subtle and not-so-subtle ways. Chances are you will find in your own mail at least one advertisement for a conference, a meeting, or an open house that has the wrong date on it or fails to note that baby-sitting is provided or that there are special rates for students and senior citizens. Perhaps you have encountered the frustration of receiving an invitation mailed so late that the event has already passed.

With charts, graphs, checklists, and yellow stick-on papers on the refrigerator door, the microscoper tries to minimize small errors that can destroy months of hard work. Although there are no guarantees against errors, if we share the work of planning with others, we tap a large reservoir of energy and skills. This offers some protection.

The following anonymous poem hangs on the wall of the Fenway Project as a reminder of Murphy's Law:

I have a spelling checker

It came with my PC.

It plainly marks four my revue

Miss stakes I cannot sea

I've run this poem threw it,

I'm sure your please to no.

It's letter perfect in its weigh,

My checker toll me sew.

Now we will look at each of the steps in microscoping that can turn proposed programs into solid realities.

STEP 1: BUILDING A RESOURCE BANK

resource bank
People, places, services, or written materials that help people meet needs and reach goals.

Every action plan must draw on its own **resource bank**. Planners need to figure out what is needed and what resources are readily available. Each of us is an integral part of a network of friends, family, peers, and work associates. They share many of their resources with us, and we reciprocate. We turn first to them when looking for resources. No person or group, no matter how poor or troubled, is totally devoid of resources. By asking questions, we stimulate people to think about their own and others' resources.

After exploring all their contacts, the members of the teen group did a resource analysis so that they could see what they were still missing and how they might fill any GAPs (see Figure 12.12 for a chart of some of the resources they needed). All the ideas about where to find resources had to be carefully checked out—some materialized and some fell through. The creative hustling continued. The teens were surprised to find that most of the people they asked to help them said "yes." Generally people are very willing to lend a hand if asked to donate a specific resource or service that suits their capacity and time schedule. They are more likely to continue helping if their

Sitting at a computer is much less glamorous than other parts of the planning process, but when a file or report is missing, the cost in human energy and pain can be great.

```
┌─────────────────────────────────────────────────────────────────────┐
│                      RESOURCE ANALYSIS                                │
│                      Hi-Teens' Camping Trip                           │
│                                                                       │
│  Resources we need      Resources we have    Status    Possible sources│
│                                                                       │
│  lantern (3)            John has 2           ok                       │
│                         Carol has 1                                   │
│                                                                       │
│  stove (1)              Veronica's dad has 1 ok                       │
│                                                                       │
│  tents (to sleep 14)    Flora has tent for six;  need tent  • check out YMCA │
│                         Don can borrow one       space for            │
│                             for six              2 more    • Althea will ask her│
│                                                              camp director │
│                                                                       │
│                                                            • check Boy Scout│
│                                                              troop     │
└─────────────────────────────────────────────────────────────────────┘
```

FIGURE 12.12   A sample resource analysis

contribution is acknowledged (Ries & Leakfield, 1998; Shore, 1995). We can never say "thank you" too often.

STEP 2: SPECIFYING AND ASSIGNING TASKS

Most of us feel totally overwhelmed at the beginning of any new action plan—perhaps we are anticipating putting on a carnival, forming a tenant committee, or returning to school after twenty years of homemaking. New staff members or volunteers inevitably experience that initial panicky question:

Can I speak in front of a room full of faculty members?

Can I take fifty screaming kids to the circus?

Can I walk through that neighborhood?

Most workers quickly learn, however, that the most important part of creating an action plan is breaking down the big tasks into a series of smaller tasks. Thus they will not be overwhelmed or immobilized by the enormity of what they have been assigned. When a goal is broken down into many small tasks, rank ordered by immediacy, and then delegated to different people, the end seems attainable. Logically, each task depends on the successful completion of the one that came before. In Figure 12.13, you can see the task list that was constructed by the Hi-Teens. It demonstrated to their parents that they had done their homework and understood how much work the trip would involve.

The meeting with the parents of the Hi-Teens convinced most of them to let their children go on the overnight co-ed camping trip. Once that barrier was overcome, the teenagers

---

TASKS THAT NEED TO BE DONE
Hi-Teens' Camping Trip

1. Get a campsite
2. Round up camping equipment
3. Get signed permission slips
4. Organize transportation
5. Plan food
6. Shop for food
7. Practice camping skills
8. Get first-aid supplies
9. Practice first-aid skills
10. Make a budget*
11. Raise money
12. Plan schedule and activities for weekend
13. Decide on rules of trip

FIGURE 12.13   A sample task analysis

*Budgeting is a major human service task. A book such as *Financial and Strategic Management for Non-Profit Organizations* (Bryce, 2000) can provide the needed guidance.

could concentrate on the specifics of planning the weekend. With the help of a Fenway Project youth worker who was an experienced backpacker, they delegated each item on their task list. Figure 12.14 shows a sample of the way they did it.

Although all this list making can seem needlessly bureaucratic, especially for a group of teens, it is an absolute rule of planning that if definite assignments are not made or are

---

JOB ASSIGNMENTS
Hi-Teens' Camping Trip, Major Tasks

Tasks:	Coordinated by:	Assisted by:
1. Get the campsite	Carlos	Ron, Flora, & Jefferson
2. Round up camping equipment	Anita	all members
3. Get signed permission slips	Jefferson	all members

FIGURE 12.14   A sample job-assignment list

made but not put in writing, the morale of the group can deteriorate as a result of needless bickering or wasted effort:

"But I thought you were responsible for the paper goods!"

"Well, whose job was it to bring the matches?"

"They say they never received our reservation form for the campsite!"

Every committee needs task specifications and a coordinator. Even though a committee of four teens agreed to do the food shopping, one person had to be the "coordinator," "key person," or "honcho." Accountability is the key to moving an action plan along to completion. Each of the coordinators had to make a list of the smaller tasks that are the components of each job. Then these had to be assigned, as in Figure 12.14. In Figure 12.15 you can see the small tasks within each job and the assignments.

Every task must be thought about and followed up. At this stage, the accountant's compulsion to keep track of every penny and make the books balance comes into play. As we figure out and execute the tasks of each job, nothing can be left to chance. At the risk of being a nag, we must, hopefully with charm and humor, keep after everyone and everything. It is never enough simply to mail a letter or wait patiently for people to return our phone calls.

SMALL TASKS WITHIN A JOB
Getting a Campsite for the Hi-Teens' Trip

	Who will do it
1. Call Girl Scouts, Boy Scouts, 4-H headquarters, state park. Get names of camp sites between here and Nesoba County.	Ron & Flora
2. Call (or look up) each one of them and find out the following: • Location—Where they are located and are they on a public transportation line? • Costs—What do they charge for one night? Any extra costs? What do they require for deposit? Is it refundable? • Facilities—Do they have an indoor shelter, swimming area, grills, picnic tables, hot showers, parking lot, tent bases, others?	Ron & Flora
3. Choose one site and one alternative.	All
4. Try to arrange a visit or find someone who has been there and has firsthand information.	Jefferson
5. Send deposit and reservation form; make rain date.	Carlos
6. Make sure to get back a confirmation in writing.	Carlos
7. Call two days beforehand to double-check arrangements.	Carlos

FIGURE 12.15 A sample list of subtasks

When the Hi-Teens wanted to make sure that their parents' meeting would be well attended, they did more than simply send a notice to each family. This is what they did: They sent reminder cards a few days before (or e-mail, when possible); the club leader phoned or visited each family; if the parents were hesitant about coming, the group leader asked what he could do to make it possible for them; if the time was inconvenient, for many of them, he rescheduled the meeting or he asked parents if they needed a baby-sitter and he tried to get a volunteer to help out; if parents were worried about not speaking or understanding English, he tried to locate a translator.

STEP 3: ESTABLISHING A TIME FLOW CHART

time flow chart A diagram of the tasks that need to be done in a certain period of time by specific individuals.

Once tasks are broken into component parts and delegated, they must be put into a time framework called a **time flow chart**. Some tasks need to be done before others; some need more time than others. For example, if the teenagers use up most of their meetings planning their menu or arguing about curfew before they get around to booking the campsite, there may be no place available for the trip. First things come first! Drawing a picture of a logical sequence of events helps to visualize what lies ahead. It also gives some benchmarks along the way. If someone asks, "How's it coming along?" they can say, "Fine, everything seems to be moving on schedule," or "We seem to be getting bogged down by X, Y, or Z."

Nothing dooms a planning process as much as unrealistic time expectations. As we look over the chart, we notice possible stumbling blocks. We readjust our time line to avoid those problems. If the public schools' spring vacation falls in April and all the fund-raising is planned for then, we may be set up for defeat. If we are counting on outdoor sales and fairs to raise money, we have to remember they do best in warm weather. Few of us, clients or workers, are superpeople. We cannot manage to complete a task in too small a time period. Anxiety and immobility can be the prices we pay for pushing too hard. In Figure 12.16 you can see the time flow chart the group constructed.

For the days of the overnight, the group will need several more flow charts, resource lists, and agendas. If they are going to have a campfire, someone needs to build it and put it out. A talent show needs a time frame and, if prizes will be given, someone has to obtain them. And so it goes. A time flow chart can use units of hours and even minutes during the actual events.

Try making a time flow chart the next time you have a term paper due. See how close you can come to avoiding the night-before-the-deadline stampede to the library or the problem of a last-minute discovery that your printer is broken. But be honest with yourself. If you are a habitual late starter, do not try to begin three months before it is due; you will only feel guilty and unsuccessful when you do not stick to your unrealistic schedule. But perhaps you can start one or two weeks before you normally would. Pat yourself on the back for utilizing a planning technique that improves your chances of success and can aid clients in the same way.

Of course, there are very few action plans that actually proceed as written, but a flow chart helps people organize their efforts in the best possible way. In fact, it is a general rule of thumb that everything is likely to take twice as long as you think it should.

STEP 4: EVALUATING THE PLAN AND FOLLOWING UP

Evaluation is always the final act that closes the information loop on the old plan and sets the stage for a new one. In order for the teenagers and the youth workers to learn and grow, they need a feedback system. Are they on schedule and are things progressing well?

TIME FLOW CHART
Hi-Teens' Camping Trip

TIMES

	December	January	February	March	April	May 9	May 12–30
TASKS	Hold parents' meeting	Look for campsite Give out permission slips Make budget	Reserve campsite Slips due back Plan fund-raising	Hold fund-raising events Practice camping skills Practice first aid	Reconfirm campsite Funds all collected Plan menu Plan activities and daily schedule Decide on rules Gather equipment	Shop Leave at noon	Return equipment Send out thank-you notes Write up report on trip

FIGURE 12.16   A sample time flow chart

Because the Fenway Project volunteers turn over frequently, program continuity and growth are hard to achieve. Before leaving, the program student coordinators must store their knowledge in accessible form to orient the next year's workers.

Record keeping and report writing are especially critical when a group has just finished a large-scale planning effort such as an annual neighborhood fair or conference. Lists of prices, the names of the bands and supply houses, and copies of receipts and permits are invaluable documents. That information, plus comments on the quality of the goods and services that were used, will help next year's staff hit the ground running. Each worker should be able to learn from his or her predecessor. Financial management of a program can be a vital part of its success or failure (Martin, 200).

Process and Product Evaluations

In addition to factual records, we must also evaluate two dimensions of the activity we have planned, both the process—how we planned it—and the product—how it turned out. Sometimes the two can be different (Clifton & Dahms, 1993; Martin & Kettner, 2009).

The Hi-Teens had a wonderful time on their trip. The experience helped build group cohesion, the members learned new skills, and they gained a greater appreciation for the outdoors. They rate the outcome very highly. But in the planning process, many of the young people did not keep their commitments. Carlos, the group leader, is annoyed at them. He ended up getting most of the equipment for them, checking up on the reservation, and filling in for absent members at their fund-raising car wash.

The group needs to improve its process. They must meet together in a debriefing session and discuss what went wrong with the way they delegated work and double-checked their assigned tasks. Of course, they should also be reminded to take credit for all the things they did do well.

To systematically review the process they used, members will ask each other:

- How accurate was their original list of tasks?
- Did they think of everything that was needed?
- Did they set realistic time limits?
- What would they repeat and what would they do differently next time?

The techniques used to evaluate an intervention depend on the nature of the program: how complicated it was, how many people were involved, and what the evaluation will be used for. For a camping trip with a group of teens, a good discussion and brief report including comments of supervisors and parents is plenty. But if we are evaluating a large conference or the first few months of operation of a community residence for

Helping high school students work through the details of running a food booth at a community fair results in donating money to a worthy cause while sharpening their planning skills.

teenagers, staff must conduct in-depth interviews with clients and collect statistics, questionnaires, and the opinions of outsiders (Alter & Evans, 2001; Mark, 1996; Marlow, 2005; Smith, 2004). Almost any technique used with an open mind and a genuine desire to learn from experience will offer some insights.

We must be especially careful not to turn our attention away from an event before all the closure work is completed. Thank-you notes have to be written, bills have to be paid, and lost or damaged equipment must be replaced or fixed. Groups also need to spend some time saying good-bye, sharing their photos, or writing an article for a newsletter. There are always next steps to be taken.

SUMMARY

1. The planning process used in organizing events in our personal lives is similar to, but less formal than, the one used by human service workers.

2. The basic tools of the planning process include a pen and pencil, computer, internet and faxes, calendar/memo book, clock, resource directories, and many thoughtful questions.

3. When planning within a group, large paper sheets or a chalkboard ensures widespread understanding. Minutes keep members informed about decisions and commitments that have been made.

4. Question generation forms an information loop that leads to action, reflection, and new action.

5. The techniques of the planner include troubleshooting (defining the problem), magnifying (seeing it with its background context and complexity), and microscoping (attending to all the details of the plan).

6. To plan successfully, we separate events into their component parts, identify the small tasks in each, set up time frames, and assign responsibilities and coordinators.

7. Evaluation of a program focuses on the product (the outcome of the intervention) as well as the process (how it was conducted from inception on).

8. Planning is both a people skill and a technical skill. Functioning within a clear structure that has a logical system brings out the best in everyone, enabling the most limited or troubled people to make whatever contribution is possible and preparing them for an event.

DISCUSSION QUESTIONS

1. There is an old proverb that says, "He has half the deed done, when he has made a beginning." What do you think this proverb is trying to convey? Do you agree with it, or do you think that it is an exaggeration? What does it have to do with planning an event or program in a social agency?

2. How much emphasis is placed by your college on volunteer service in your community? How fair is it to require volunteer service as a requirement of graduation, especially for nonhuman service majors. What do you think a chemistry or math major might contribute to a social agency in the community? What do you think they might gain that would help them be a better worker in their particular fields of interest?

3. What do you see as a major GAP in the services provided for students at your college? What kind of program(s) do you think might fill that GAP? What evidence would you have to gather to convince the person in charge of that area or division that it is a GAP that must be filled with a new program or strategy? Do you see any evidence of cyberbullying on your campus?

4. What do you think is meant by the saying, "Life is lived forward but understood backward"? What do you think that saying has to do with the process of program evaluation?

WEB RESOURCES FOR FURTHER STUDY

Strategic Planning

www.mapnp.org/library/plan_dec/str_plan/str_plan.htm

Additional information on the strategic planning process.

National Council of Nonprofits

www.councilofnonprofits.org

Provides service to and advocacy for nonprofits.

Foundation Center

http://fdncenter.org

A national nonprofit service organization connecting non-profits and the grantmakers supporting them. Its audiences include grantseekers, grantmakers, researchers, policymakers, the media, and the general public. The Center maintains the most comprehensive database on U.S. grantmakers and their grants.

Chapter 13

Organizing and Changing Systems

GETTING TO THE SOURCE OF THE PROBLEM

We can think of no better way to start this chapter on organizing and changing systems than by retelling a parable attributed to the late Saul Alinsky, who was one of this country's most imaginative and dedicated community change agents (Alinsky, 1969, 1971).

A Parable

A woman is taking a stroll along a riverbank. Suddenly she hears a cry for help and jumps into the water to rescue a drowning man. After saving the first man, she is forced to jump back into the river to save another and then still another. After she has dragged four men from the river, she looks around in disgust and starts to leave. An onlooker says, "Hey, I see another guy in the water, where are you going?" She replies, "I can't hang around here all day long rescuing drowning victims. I'm going upstream to stop the son of a bitch who's pushing them all in."

Stopping Problems at Their Source

The point Alinsky is making is that it is never enough to just rescue victims from their troubles, important as that is. We have to try to change the situations that are creating their problems. Then, hopefully, we can cut off the problem at its source so that new victims are not constantly being produced.

For those of you who are mechanically inclined, visualize a machine that makes Ping-Pong balls. Every once in a while, it goofs and produces one that is not round enough. A worker tosses the defective balls into a bin. Later on, another worker takes the odd-shaped balls out of the reject pile and tries to round them off. But it would save time and money in the long run if they fixed the machine so that it did not make so many mistakes.

To translate this analogy into human service work, we will describe the case of Marty, a young adult of Mexican American background. He was raised on a run-down farm on the wrong side of the tracks in a rural community. He attended a substandard elementary school that did not stimulate him. When his mother needed surgery and his family lost their farm because they could not pay the mortgage, Marty was forced to drop out of high school and seek work. He soon discovered that the few jobs available in his town were given to people who had more skills or education than he did. He found that luck and chance and connections played a part also.

Marty had always tinkered with old cars and was a natural mechanic. But the garage owner held stereotypes about people from the Mexican American community—he was convinced that all Chicanos were lazy and dishonest. As a result, when a job at the garage became available, Marty was rejected.

Marty became depressed about his bleak future and found momentary relief in drugs. Once he became so frustrated that he lashed out, vandalizing the garage. He got caught and was then enmeshed in the criminal justice system. He spent two months in jail, where he was brutalized by both his cellmate and a guard. By the time the probation worker encountered Marty, he needed a whole series of direct-care and counseling strategies to overcome his addiction and rehabilitate his shattered self-esteem. Now he also had a jail record holding him back.

This young man's problems might have been prevented if there had been:

- Decent housing in an integrated area
- Adequate education, both academic and vocational
- Affordable health insurance
- Mortgage assistance to save family farms
- Drug and alcohol education
- Job-training and placement programs
- Protection from discriminatory employment practices
- A criminal justice system with the resources to protect and rehabilitate offenders

The lack of these basic services helped create and maintain Marty's situation. Like a snowball rolling down a hill, his problems kept getting bigger. In their book *Social Welfare: A History of the American Response to Need*, Axinn and Stern (2007) conclude that poor people too often come off as second best—scapegoats for circumstances beyond their control.

Human service workers cannot change all the dysfunctional systems that impinge on the Martys of our country. Nor is it likely that they can change one system in a massive way. But all of us can, in our daily work, create small yet significant improvements in the social systems that surround our clients.

What Can One Worker Do?

When working with Marty, we might find that helping him file a complaint against a discriminatory employer has two major outcomes. First, it gives him the feeling that he can take some control over his destiny. Second, if he succeeds in winning the case, not only will he get a badly needed job, but other Mexican Americans who follow him may also find it possible to work there. If this young man joins a group of citizens who succeed in bringing bilingual and multicultural programs to the local elementary school, that might improve the life chances of his neighbor's children also.

Filing a grievance when you believe a law or regulation is not working properly and drafting a proposal and lobbying for funds to start a program to fill an unmet social need are examples of strategies for organizing and changing systems. They support our efforts to deliver direct services to people.

These strategies rely on the same activities and skills as do direct-service strategies. They start with carefully collecting data, contracting, and building a trusting relationship. Worker acts flow out of well-designed and well-monitored action plans and are refined through reflection and evaluation. Although there are many similarities between direct-care and systems-change interventions, there are, of course, some significant differences in emphasis.

CHECKING ON THE MENTAL HEALTH QUOTIENT (MHQ) OF A SYSTEM

A counselor trying to help a child who is experiencing difficulty in school begins by seeking information about the child's health, family situation, and scores on achievement and IQ (intelligence quotient) tests. Many stop at that point, only seeking out the causal factors within the child and the family. But we believe that the hunt for relevant insights cannot stop there. The competent worker must go on further, to look at the system in which the child is functioning. The worker must gather data about the MHQ (mental health quotient) of that student's classroom and school. We must always look at both the internal and the external sources of stress. Ultimately we will need to intervene in both sets of forces.

Traditionally, workers in this field have often neglected the second step, looking at the system. It was the community mental health movement, with its focus on integrating institutionalized people back into the community that alerted us to the need to seek causality beyond the client. The civil rights struggles of the 1960s also convinced us that the problems individuals face could be made better or worse by forces exerted by their environments.

You can grasp this concept of the "system-as-problem-producer" if you think back to a time when you watched people rudely shoving each other in order to grab a cab at the airport—tempers flared, and anxiety levels rose as each person struggled to outmaneuver the others. Clearly, the environment with its chaotic method of allocating benefits exerts a negative impact on otherwise reasonably polite people. If a sensible airport manager inaugurated a system in which numbers are assigned to passengers in some equitable way, everyone could relax. It might take time to get a cab, but each person would be sure that his or her turn was coming. A passenger could risk leaving the line for a moment to carry the luggage of an elderly man or to help a harried mother with a toddler in a stroller and a heavy suitcase.

The airport analogy holds true for the bakery, the baseball game, the classroom, and any other environment in which people seek services or goods. All of us have the potential to act in a variety of negative and positive ways. What is it in an environment that brings out the best and worst in you?

Human service delivery systems—their rules, routines, and personality conflicts—all need to be examined. We must develop our personal method of measuring the MHQ of a system. For example, before we begin to plan counseling interventions for the little girl who runs around her classroom fighting with her classmates, we should check the organizational climate of her classroom and school. Some places are so disorganized or mindlessly rigid that they encourage disruptive behavior in a child who has some tendency in that direction. In a more sensibly organized environment, she might behave quite appropriately.

After we observe a client in a classroom or in a hospital ward, we might conclude that certain characteristics of the environment seem to be producing problems rather than solving them. Thus the *system*, rather than the *client*, should be the major focus of our change efforts. Yet despite recognition of this fact, research indicates that workers often continue to try to change the client by counseling, rather than change the environment by using organizing interventions (Brager, 2002, Brager, Specht, & Torczyner, 1987; Kahn, 1995).

Ryan, in his classic book *Blaming the Victim* (1976), asserts that focusing change efforts on the client rather than on the system that is malfunctioning leads us to design social programs that are at best irrelevant and at worst deceptively cruel. Why are so many human service workers unable to confront honestly the primary causes of a client's problem? We think one reason is that workers tend to accept society's negative attitudes toward social activism, even though social activism is required if systems are ever to change for the better.

ATTITUDES TOWARD SYSTEMS-CHANGE INTERVENTIONS

As we grew up, many of us might have heard adults in our families declare:

> You can't fight city hall!
>
> It's not what you know but who you know!
>
> Good guys finish last!
>
> Well-brought-up people (especially females) don't make waves or rock the boat!

These homespun bromides encourage us to believe that working for change in a rational way is virtually impossible. Stereotypes of **change agents** encourage us to shy away from that role. One prominent stereotype depicts change agents as cartoon-character 1960s activists and bomb-throwing anarchists, bearded, grubby, and deranged. Or they are depicted as naive Don Quixotes, futilely tilting at windmills. On the other side lie the stereotypes that depict change agents as saintly crusaders—Joan of Arc or Mother Teresa. Perhaps you have assumed that change agents must be charismatic leaders like the Rev. Martin Luther King, Jr., or President John F. Kennedy. That, too, is a stereotype.

change agents Workers who use their skills to bring about change in an unhealthy agency or situation, either alone or in concert with others.

When people see human service workers walking a picket line or speaking out at a school board meeting, they are often shocked by such aggressiveness. Activists are often accused by their own colleagues of behaving unprofessionally (Reeser & Epstein, 1990).

The social critic George Bernard Shaw has given us a fitting answer to that accusation. He often declared that reasonable people adapted themselves to the world as it was. Only the unreasonable ones persisted in trying to get the world to change. Thus, all progress depends on unreasonable people! We agree with Shaw and hope that there will be times when you decide you must take a strong stand on behalf of a client, despite an accusation that you are being "unreasonable."

Bertha Reynolds (1963), one of the outstanding leaders in the history of the profession of social work, argued that it is the obligation of social workers to take partisan political stands and work for structured change in the socioeconomic system.

To paint an accurate picture of change agents, we must discard all our preconceptions of who they are and what they do. We need to explore our ambivalent attitudes toward social change. Then we will need to replace the unrealistic attitudes with the conviction that each of us should use our skills to bring about change in a system, just as we do in a counseling intervention.

Working to change an unhealthy system raises unique value dilemmas for the human service worker, especially for one who is accustomed to delivering direct services to clients. The following is a look at what can happen to some of our basic attitudes and values when a worker takes on an adversarial or confrontational role. As you read about the day-to-day tasks of a human service worker who uses all the techniques we will be discussing in this chapter, see if you can spot the moments of potential conflicts.

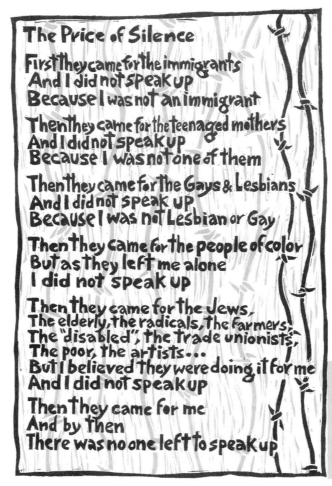

The Price of Silence

First they came for the immigrants
And I did not speak up
Because I was not an immigrant

Then they came for the teenaged mothers
And I did not speak up
Because I was not one of them

Then they came for the Gays & Lesbians
And I did not speak up
Because I was not Lesbian or Gay

Then they came for the people of color
But as they left me alone
I did not speak up

Then they came for the Jews,
The elderly, the radicals, the farmers,
The "disabled", the trade unionists,
The poor, the artists...
But I believed they were doing it for me
And I did not speak up

Then they came for me
And by then
There was no one left to speak up

This statement is adapted from one written by a pastor who was imprisoned in a Nazi concentration camp. It eloquently warns us that if we do not try to stop injustice when it starts, it will spread and eventually engulf each of us.

INTERVIEW

Ed Wong: Staff Worker for Citizen Action for the Environment (CAFTE)

Citizens Action for the Environment (CAFTE) is a citywide, citizen-based environmental advocacy organization. We combine independent research projects, practical ideas, and tough-minded advocacy to overcome the opposition of powerful special interests and the lack of knowledge (and often low commitment) of the average town resident.

These are the main tasks in my job description:

- Build coalitions with local, state, and national environmental, labor, farming, and consumer organizations; identify and mobilize concerned citizens; and reach out to new constituencies to build our base of support in this town and state-wide.

2007 Clean Water Champion Award

The Honorable Russ Feingold

We applaud your leadership in defense of the Clean Water Act
and your dedication to protecting all our nation's waters

Presented by the Clean Water Network
during Clean Water Week
February 27, 2007

While it is important for Edward and other environmental activists to confront those who pollute our air, water, and soil, it is equally as important to honor those who strive to undo past damage and protect our planet for future generations.

- Generate media attention and build public awareness. Organize at least one major news conference per month; meet with reporters throughout the town and the region; conduct TV and radio interviews, update our blog and conduct workshops with various groups, including schools, chambers of commerce, other merchant groups, religious institutions, and civic organizations.
- Lobby decision makers and expand our political base by building relationships with elected officials and candidates and demonstrate broad public support for our positions through letter-writing drives, e-mail activism, appearing at campaign events, and conducting meetings with decision makers.
- Build the organization by increasing membership and recruiting and orienting volunteers and other small grassroots groups that share our mission.

This looks like an overwhelming job description, but as with every other job in the human service field, you take it one step at a time, and of course I don't work alone.

Although I am the only paid staff member of CAFTE, we have an active board and an advisory committee. Both of these groups include professors from the local colleges, engineers and architects who specialize in environment issues, sympathetic politicians, and merchants and other leaders of groups in town who really care about what is happening not only to the town of Riverside but also to the whole world.

You probably wonder how a recent college graduate who majored in human services ended up in this kind of job. Well, I have to admit I am also amazed at times by my choice. When I was a student intern and in fact during most of my teenage years, I was involved in issues of homelessness. I volunteered for a food pantry and did overnight shifts at a shelter for men and women who had no place to sleep. Some of my friends were involved in environmental issues, and frankly I thought those activities were a way to avoid dealing with the more important problems of poverty, racism, mental illness, disability, and so forth.

green Those products, services, or other kinds of activities that exert no negative impact on the health of people and on the environment.

I have since learned that mine was a pretty typical response to the word **green**. For many years the term *green* was defined—probably by folks like me who disparaged it—as "ultraliberal," "elitist," "tree-hugging," "sissy," a "girlie-man issue," and alarmist. In an article in the *New York Times* titled "The Power of Green" (2007), Thomas Friedman argues that the wars in the Middle East revolved so much about the supply of oil; documentary films like *An Inconvenient Truth* (Gore & West, 2006) as well as popular books by Bill McKibben (2007a, 2007b) have pushed the terms *green*, *global warming*, and *climate change* onto Main Street. The reality is that the earth's weather is changing with some alarming consequences, and the supply of natural resources, such as fossil fuels, is not endless. In some parts of the world, there isn't enough water to sustain agriculture, thereby increasing famine, and in other places, the waters are rising and threatening to flood islands. The implications of these changes are not just on a few people but on the whole world. It might be that civil unrest will rise if these consequences continue.

On a more individual level, the evidence of climate change and its impact is reaching home. I read in a small-town newspaper that the maple syrup harvesters in Vermont are complaining that with the increasingly warmer weather in the fall, the yield of maple syrup has gone down by as much as 10 percent. Most of us couldn't help but notice with surprise that within the last few years in the United States, we have experienced some of the hottest winters on record. Once very skeptical, Americans in large bi-partisan numbers now say that the heating of the earth's atmosphere is having a serious effect on the polar ice caps now or will soon, and they think that it is necessary to take immediate steps to reduce its effects (Broder & Connelly, 2007).

My coming to understand the gravity of the situation was a result of joining the Sierra Club and the Appalachian Mountain Club because I love to hike with others. Both organizations publish magazines for members. I began to realize that although all human service issues are vital, our need to protect our forests and rivers is not "elite." It is a matter of keeping the air pure enough so we can continue to breathe and so our kids will have a livable planet.

Although my job description sounds monumental and I do work hard, it is not overwhelming. I take my job one step at a time and day by day. The members of my board set the priorities. This keeps me from being spread too thin and ultimately not accomplishing anything. Since I cooperate with a host of other groups, their programs often determine where I will invest my energy for a period of time.

These are some of the things I have worked on in the past few months:

- Helped publicize and recruit volunteers for a town-wide park cleanup day.
- Wrote an article and held three forums on ways to cut down on energy consumption both in stores and in private homes.
- Spearheaded a campaign to get the local big-box retailer to cut back on packaging on some of its products and to promote the sale of low-energy light bulbs.
- Wrote a proposal that gained funding for the town to plant 400 trees in parts of town that are noticeably not very green. (Naturally, these were in the more economically disadvantaged areas.) This isn't just for beauty; it helps the air we breathe and creates shade in summer months.
- Wrote an article for the local newspaper on new technologies for solar and wind power. Many people don't realize that the costs of these technologies are decreasing, and other countries are doing major projects using the sun and wind.
- Attended a benefit screening of *An Inconvenient Truth* to raise money for Earth Day activities in six different locations in town.
- Participated in a demonstration by the local biking advocacy group to try to convince the town to set aside a bike lane each time they have to do construction on the streets.
- Organized a panel for the homeowners' association on ways to insulate homes and on the use of programmable thermostats.
- Participated in a successful campaign to convince the supermarkets to make paper bags more available to shoppers and to have the checkout clerks suggest them as the first choice in bagging (instead of the plastic bags that don't biodegrade).
- Attended board meetings of the town-wide recycling committee to represent our group and lend support to their efforts to increase recycling of cans, plastic, and paper.
- Gave a talk at the high school on our need to cut carbon emissions, highlighting the plans already proposed by a few cities in the United States. This was an effort to let the future generation know that the problems are not insurmountable and to encourage the students to start a green club in their school—and maybe choose environmental studies if they go on to college.

I use all the strategies I studied in college, but of course it is the organizing ones I use the most. Skills like active listening come in handy when I am in a meeting with a company executive. I also use preparatory empathy when I am in a situation where I know I will be up against resistance. (I tried to go in prepared with answers to questions I thought they would ask when we lobbied for the bike lanes.) Proposal-writing skills and research are vital in this job.

I am not sure what I am going to be doing in the future, but for now, I could not be more excited about the job I chose. I feel that I am working in a small way on a very monumental problem. And I still have the time and incentive to hike in the woods on the weekends.

DILEMMAS OF THE CHANGE AGENT

Very Often, the Worker Must Choose Sides

If we believe that the needs of one group are being neglected and the needs of another are given an unfair advantage or that one of our clients is being punished by an unjust rule or an unresponsive bureaucrat, we are making a judgment of *right* and *wrong*. When, for example, a human service worker helps a group of tenants who have been living with inhuman conditions organize a rent strike, he or she is taking sides in the struggle between landlords and tenants. Although he or she might realize that the landlord will have a temporary cash-flow problem when rent money is withheld, if he or she is convinced that the tenants are being exploited, he or she cannot expend much of his or her energy worrying about the landlord's problems. But he or she has been trained to be empathetic and caring to *everyone!*

Of course, such adversarial situations can also occur when a worker is counseling or doing recreation work. But in an organizing advocacy job, they occur with alarming regularity. The pull between competing needs and outlooks is painful. It is often impossible to find a compromise. In Ed's professional role, he often feels more like a lawyer than a human service worker. Having chosen to represent the interests of the town residents for a clean environment, he advocates for them with tenacity. He becomes adversarial when dealing with a factory owner who will not acknowledge that he has dumped industrial waste into a local stream, even though that is not Ed's usual inclination. It is a difficult balancing act.

Frequently, Workers Must Choose among Competing Values

In addition to choosing sides between adversaries in a dispute, Ed is often forced to make almost impossible choices between competing values. This is frequently the case for social change agents.

For example, in writing about their experiences as welfare rights organizers in the rural South in the 1960s, several idealistic young human service workers described how they found the maintenance needs of their organization conflicting with the service needs of individual clients (Kurzman, 1971). In order to recruit new members to the Welfare Rights Organization, they would offer to accompany clients into their eligibility interviews, coaching them right in front of the welfare investigators. They were especially interested in recruiting articulate, energetic clients—most often, young single parents—who would be the most likely to give their time and energy to expanding the welfare rights group. Yet, it was frequently the elderly, infirm clients who begged them for help with their welfare and disability applications or appeals. Though desperately needy, they were also bound by the old traditions and fears engendered by experiencing a lifetime of segregation. They were sometimes the least likely to sign a petition, attend a rally, or become leaders in the welfare reform movement. Striking a comfortable balance between giving services to the most needy and building up the social change group gave many workers sleepless nights.

Workers Must Overcome Resistance to Change with No Guarantees of Success

Most interventions encounter resistance. But social change efforts exert a special kind of drain on our time and energy. They follow unpredictable courses down twisting, perilous roads that lead to many dead ends. There are dubious rewards at the end of the path, and both client and worker can burn out from their seemingly futile investment of time and energy. Lodging a complaint of environmental abuse or neglect, for example, can involve endless postponements and legal maneuvers, resulting in years of waiting for a trial date. By the time the trial rolls around, the litigants in the dispute have probably moved away; and even if they win the case, the current laws provide for few sanctions. Often it is cheaper for a store owner or factory owner to pay the fine than it is to clean up garbage he or she is dumping in our streams.

The laws that prohibit housing or job discrimination also have few penalties for those who flaunt the laws. Many times, in these kinds of disputes, the clients back off from pursuing complaints, even when it looks as if they might win, because they fear that their landlords or employers would retaliate. The threat of eviction or shutting off their heat in the winter and other forms of harassment often abruptly terminate protests. An organizer cannot in good conscience promise people that he or she can protect them. When a person files a discrimination complaint against an employer or agency, for example, the citizen litigant can fear being blackballed by other employers that now view him or her as a troublemaker. Of course, direct-service interventions also carry risks, but they are rarely as consistently perilous as those in advocacy situations.

Given Ed's slim chances of winning most of the protests his agency is involved with, one wonders why he continues with so much goodwill. But he feels that though the risks of failure may be much greater in his kind of job, so too are the rewards for success. When CAFTE wins one reform in the way industrial wastes are disposed of, or when he convinces one company to lower its energy consumption, the eventual improvement in the quality of the lives of many people is incalculable.

Historically this has proved to be true. With the stroke of a pen, President Franklin Delano Roosevelt signed the Social Security Act in 1935 and, since then, millions of elderly people have been able to look forward to some measure of financial security in their retirement years. An army of counselors working with each of those older people, one person at a time, could not possibly have achieved such positive changes in their emotional lives. To live in fear of being destitute in one's old age is surely a gateway to depression.

Yet, surprisingly, remains much resistance after a new policy has been enacted. Often nothing changes until informed consumers rattle the cages of the bureaucracy. Implementation should be a rational process, but barriers of community indifference, lack of information, and bureaucratic rigidity often slow down real progress (Bobo, Kendall, & Max, 2010). Social Security is still, after all these years, under attack by some political groups that believe it would be a sounder plan to have the elderly depend on private pensions and investment schemes.

Workers Lack Models

Systems-change skills can be difficult to learn because we lack role models in our personal and professional lives. There is also a woeful lack of written material about successful social change efforts. Not surprisingly, workers who thrive on the unstructured, rough-and-tumble nature of social change often resist sitting down and putting their thoughts on paper. Many excellent change efforts go undocumented and unrewarded (Rivera & Erlich, 1998). However, there are some written materials, and we urge students to seek out those books that give first-hand accounts of systems-change efforts (Bobo et al., 2010; Boyte, 1986; Greenberg, 1969 reprinted 1990 Kahn, 1995; Kurzman, 1971; Miller, M., 2009, Russell, 1990, Shaw, 2001).

Children of the St. Mary Center in Oakland are sheltered by a massive puppet of Dr. Martin Luther King, Jr., created by a group of senior citizens as a tribute to his memory. MLK, Jr., brilliantly employed the three escalating strategies of organizing to overturn many of the practices of racial segregation.

CHANGES ARE GENERATED FROM THE TOP DOWN AND FROM THE BOTTOM UP

Change flows in two directions. Like a giant waterfall, it flows from the top down, dragging the stones and sand along in its wake. Just as often, like a volcano, it simmers beneath the surface and then bubbles up from the bottom, engulfing everything in its path.

When change starts from the top of a system, it usually comes in the form of an administrative or legislative fiat. A board of directors, a supervisor, or an administrator announces a new policy or reduces or expands a budget item. It occurs when new legislation is passed. It can happen when the courts rule on a landmark case. Change can be propelled by the writing of a memo banning discrimination against one or another class of tenants or the passage or repeal of a housing or zoning ordinance. Sometimes seemingly benign words inserted in or deleted from an official policy dramatically change the course of life for many human beings.

Clients, workers, and students usually lack the formal authority to change destructive policies. But they can force change from the bottom up through the weight of their numbers and the power that weight can mobilize. Sometimes bottom-up change comes through the ballot box. Often it comes from citizen initiative or agitation. When homeless squatters break into a building that is boarded up and demand that city officials rehabilitate it, they are attempting to create change. The movement to accelerate the testing of new AIDS medications was spurred on by public demonstrations by citizen activists. Although these AIDS protests seemed to be unruly and angry, they were a catalyst in forcing the Food and Drug Administration to speed up the approval process of new medications.

Case histories of change efforts reveal that most of the time, struggles to create change and resistance against change are going on simultaneously, at both the top and bottom of the system. In the history of public welfare, for example, positive changes in benefits emanating from the top of the bureaucracy have often been initiated only after it looked as if the bubbling up from the bottom, from the grass roots, would spill over into uncontrolled disruptions. A fascinating analysis that links protest to reform was written by Piven and Cloward (1993).

The recent congressional actions that dramatically scaled back the social welfare system were spearheaded by many angry conservative legislators. Whether there will be effective grassroots opposition to these cutbacks as the U.S. economy slows down will depend on how accurately the elected officials have read the mood of their constituents. In any event, we can expect much ferment at the top and bottom of the society as the shifting away from post-Depression entitlements and the rise of **Tea Party Movement** accelerates.

Change efforts must be directed at all points of a system—the top, the bottom, and in between. But rarely can any one group or person spread thin enough to cover all the bases. Even if that were possible, however, different styles of organizing are needed to confront different parts of a system, for different issues, and to keep up with the changing public mood and world events.

Change agents come in two basic models: the *in-fighter* and the *outside agitator*. Infighters are legitimate members of the established authority who work for or administer a particular system. They might be directors of hospitals, supervisors of social service agencies, judges, or politicians. Outside agitators are neither employed by nor beholden to any of the established systems.

Tea Party Movement The Tea Party is a political movement in the United States that has sponsored locally and nationally coordinated protests since 2009 and is generally recognized as conservative and libertarian. It endorses reduced government spending, lower taxes, reduction of the national debt and federal budget deficit, and adherence to an originalist interpretation of the U.S. Constitution.

Ed is an example of an outside agitator. He stands outside the bureaucracy of the public sector and private corporations. He dresses, talks, and acts differently than he would if he were working for the Department of Energy, Environmental Protection Agency, or Mobil Oil Corporation. But sometimes Ed and a worker at a state agency or an employee of a corporation may share a similar change goal. Their techniques are different because they work on different rungs of the change ladder. If they build a coalition around a common goal using different change strategies, they can create powerful momentum for change (Seaver, 1971).

In the civil rights era, it was often said that the agitation of militant grassroots groups, such as those led by Malcolm X and Stokely Carmichael, provoked the established authorities into dealing with the more moderate groups such as the National Association for the Advancement of Colored People (NAACP) and the Urban League. Malcolm X stirred the pot of protest in the streets of Harlem, and Martin Luther King, Jr., organized nonviolent marches, while the NAACP filed one lawsuit after another.

It is important to realize that if they work alone, neither enlightened leaders at the top of a system nor masses of angry people at the bottom of it are likely to create major, permanent changes.

Guarding Change

Change must be guarded after it has been won. Once instituted, it must be constantly monitored. If left unattended, a new law or policy can turn out to be totally ineffective. It can be "business as usual" unless an organized constituency monitors the process of implementation. The Supreme Court desegregation decision of 1954 is a good example of this. Although the decision made in *Brown v. Board of Education* outlawed racial segregation in every public school in the land, it has taken hundreds of individual lawsuits and the constant watchfulness of citizens' groups to achieve even the modest amount of school desegregation we now have, over six decades later. If a school is segregated and no one complains about it, it is likely just to stay that way (see Ehrlander, 2002; Patterson, 2001).

The Targets of Change

Changes such as the Supreme Court school desegregation decision or the Americans with Disabilities Act must have two thrusts. First, change agents must create new structures composed of rules and regulations that translate the vision of change into the new reality. But that is never enough. For change to take root in a system, it must also become an integral part of the consciousness of the people involved.

For example, when parents are committed to overturning racial segregation in the local school system, they need to marshal the evidence that it is segregated and bring it to court. They must persuade a judge to order the school board to draw up an integration plan. If the parents, school administrators, or some other organization do not like the plan or the way it is being implemented, they return to court to negotiate adjustments. If the school board continues its opposition, the schools might be taken over by the courts, as they once were in Boston.

However, no matter how good a plan is on paper, on the day a desegregated school opens, the attitudes of the school and town officials, parents, and teachers determine whether the elaborate plans have any chance of succeeding. Ultimately, a new law is only as effective as the feelings that swirl around it.

If women, former mental patients, immigrants, or people with disabilities do not use the protection of the laws that guarantee their rights, those laws are worth nothing. On the reverse side, if a law is routinely circumvented by large numbers of people, it cannot be enforced. This was the case with the prohibition of alcohol in the 1920s. This law was consistently violated by the usually law-abiding general public. Alcohol was legally banned, which was a major structural change, but the desire (consciousness) of the population to use liquor as a means of pleasure or escape never changed. Today we face a similar situation with marijuana. Though it is illegal, both a Supreme Court judge and a two-term president, among other high-ranking officials, admit to having tried it when they were younger.

Learning a lesson from the failure of prohibition, antismoking advocates proceed on both fronts—structure and consciousness. They have changed the structure of smoking by prohibiting cigarettes from being advertised on television and passing smoking bans in government buildings and in many public spaces, such as movie theaters, workplaces, restaurants, and airplanes and colleges. They have succeeded in placing warning labels on cigarette packages. The antismoking change efforts have also moved into courtrooms. In high-profile lawsuits, the attorneys general of several states have sued the major tobacco companies to recover the money the state health care systems have expended caring for citizens who have sickened or died from smoking-related illnesses. In many cases, they have garnered large cash settlements for both individuals and states. But, after the legal victories, alert citizen groups have had to make sure that the cash is used for public health purposes, not to fill in budget gaps in unrelated areas.

And antismoking advocates continue to target the hearts and minds of smokers through smoke-awareness seminars and "I quit" days. Although many Americans still smoke, by targeting structure as well as consciousness, antismoking advocates have begun to tip the balance. Now it is often the smoker who is on the defensive, shivering outside the doors of office buildings and restaurants, puffing away almost furtively.

The feminist movement pioneered the use of consciousness-raising techniques. Out of this movement have come step-by-step procedures for conducting consciousness-raising groups in which members examine their current situation by thinking about the impact of current structures and by suggesting necessary structural changes (Culbert, 1976).

Feminist organizers have long understood that laws redressing gender inequality were a necessary first step but would not be enough to bring about major changes. Many women had to be convinced that they had a legitimate right to demand equal pay for their labor. They also needed to build up courage and group solidarity in order to press for remedies when equality was withheld from them.

The struggle of American women for liberation, social justice, and self-development has been waxing and waning for 160 years yet, not surprisingly, pioneers of social work and community organizing were women. They included Jane Addams, Dorothea Dix, Julia Lathrop, and Florence Kelley. Yet, despite this rich heritage, men came to dominate the field of community organizing as they did other fields.

In general, feminist organizing tends to be concerned with the quality of interaction between the members of the group and with their individual concerns, rather than focusing only on results. With a single-minded focus on results, leaders might be tempted to view members as faceless creatures who can be manipulated to achieve outcomes. Trying to avoid this trap, Ella Baker, who organized the Student Nonviolent Coordinating Committee (SNCC) during the civil rights movement, always started each meeting by asking if members had any personal concerns that needed to be dealt with before they settled down to planning organizing strategies. Only after they dealt with their own pressing issues would their minds be free enough to turn to the needs of the movement.

Now, on college campuses, both administrators and student activists work to change the definitions of appropriate sexual conduct. Policies defining date rape and sexual and gender harassment, with stiff penalties for transgressions, have been drawn up. And seminars and workshops are conducted to sensitize students and staff to new definitions or their rights and to inform them about the way to protest if they think their rights are being abridged.

METHODS OF ORGANIZING AND CHANGING SYSTEMS

Change methods fall into roughly three categories of escalating intensity: *educating*, *persuading*, and *pressuring*. We always start out by trying to educate the public and the powers that be about the need for change. If that is not sufficient to bring about change, we try to persuade them. Finally, if change is still resisted, we resort to pressure.

Educating to Create Change

When a change effort begins, we point out the problems (the GAPs), systematically document them, and suggest solutions. Ed spends a large amount of his time compiling statistics about the increasing incidence of certain diseases in areas with a great deal of industrial pollution. He reads journals and checks out web sites from all over the country and goes to conferences to find out what other groups are doing to solve the problems of carbon emissions and overdependence on fossil fuels. He digests the material and helps produce a monthly newsletter that is sent to members, politicians, and businesspeople.

Whenever a new ordinance or program is proposed, a committee from CAFTE reviews the plan to make sure it protects the interests of ordinary people. Then they testify before the planning board or selectmen to give their opinions and suggest changes.

lobby An attempt to convince decision makers to support one's ideas or proposed actions.

Ed has learned the importance of having facts ready when he visits a legislator to **lobby** for change. Often he is competing with real estate developers who have assembled their own set of data printed in a fancy booklet. Although he complained about having to study statistics and research methods in college, he has come to appreciate their power and is grateful that he can read and interpret budgets, architectural plans, census data, and other weighty documents. The volunteer lawyers who work with CAFTE do much of the actual negotiating, but he needs to understand enough to explain the CAFTE position and answer questions about it.

Sometimes as a result of an educational campaign, people realize how destructive a certain rule, policy, or action is and agree to change it. If that happens, then the change effort is successful and it terminates. But many times, exposing an unhealthy situation and suggesting ways of dealing with it are not enough.

So the change agents turn to the second, more powerful change method.

Persuading to Create Change

Persuasion strategies use both the carrot and the stick. They reward constructive changes and threaten sanctions for continued negative practices. For example, if employers lack the resources but are willing to hire workers who have disabilities (as they are legally bound to do), they might be granted the "carrot" of tax reductions or be given loans to build the ramps or install the special phone and computer equipment they will need. Or, if developers are willing to build affordable housing in low-income communities, they might be given grants-in-aid, tax abatements, and special technical-assistance programs. Factory owners who agree to retro-fit old polluting equipment or restaurant owners who agree to eliminate trans fats from their food might be given technical assistance and even some funds to help in the switch. But even with incentives, change does not come about easily. Systems need money and technical know-how, but they also need goodwill to forge new ways of thinking and acting. It is always easier (and, sometimes, more lucrative) to do "business as usual," even if it results in harm to many.

If, despite all the incentives, change does not happen, then the "stick" might be threatened or used. Sanctions on this second level usually involve withholding money, denying

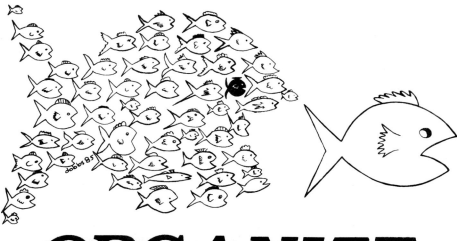

A little fish swimming alone can easily be gobbled up. But when lots of little fish get organized, it's amazing what they can accomplish.

permits, or causing public humiliation. For example, some towns list in the local newspaper the names of landlords and restaurant owners who have been cited for health and safety violations. There are lists on some post office bulletin boards of the names and pictures of noncustodial parents who have not paid their court-mandated child support payments.

CAFTE has used persuasion by organizing public rallies supporting or opposing a proposed housing plan or industrial complex, has collected signatures on petitions, and organized letter-writing campaigns.

Pressuring to Create Change

When education and persuasion strategies fail to bring about change, the CAFTE board resorts to using pressure tactics. They go into court to punish, restrain, or force compliance. If these formal channels of appeal are too weak or slow, the pressure tactics of **direct action** are used. They picket or boycott an office, or conduct a sit-in and refuse to move, or find some other way to disrupt "business as usual."

> **direct action** An action that interferes with the orderly conduct of a system that is the target of change.

Believing they answer to a higher code of ethics, the agents of change sometimes take the law into their own hands. The Reverend Martin Luther King, Jr., encouraged people to do this when Rosa Parks was arrested for refusing to yield her seat on a bus to a white passenger. In accordance with the laws of Montgomery, Alabama, she was wrong. But she and the other members of the black community believed that they had the right to disobey an unjust and morally repugnant law. In order to force change, they boycotted the buses for almost one year. Faced with the possibility of a bankrupt bus company as well as many bankrupt stores, the town officials capitulated, and the segregation law was changed.

Forty years later, those who believe that abortion, although legal, violates religious or ethical principles, formed Operation Rescue. They chained themselves to the doors of family planning clinics, blocking the entrances. They have intercepted people walking into the clinics and attempted to disrupt the functioning of these agencies to rescue the "unborn children." As the Supreme Court and state legislatures have debated the pros and cons of abortion, these activists have taken direct action on their convictions. The issue of stem cell research using human embryos has now taken center stage in public debate. The sides are shaping up on this issue. In the next few years, we will see many groups—pro and con—using all these change methods.

Choosing Which Method to Use and Who Should Lead the Struggle

We make no value judgments about which set of change strategies is better, more appropriate, or more professional. Obviously Ed, like other change agents, always hopes that exposing the facts about a problem will lead to solutions. But he knows that change comes slowly and often encounters a great deal of resistance. An elderly woman soon to be evicted from her apartment or a family whose baby is eating lead paint chips cannot keep waiting for help as the wheels of a bureaucratic grievance procedure grind on.

Thus, each strategy plays a role at a particular time with a particular problem in a change campaign. The important point to remember is that in order to maintain credibility, change agents must climb each step of the ladder before escalating to the final, most aggressive one. Each set of strategies must be carefully mapped out and executed, using the kind of planning models we have already described.

Frequently, visionaries or charismatic people take a prominent role in a change effort. They become identified with it. Mr. Pulashnik is an activist in a local housing group that is part of the CAFTE coalition. He is a recent immigrant from the Ukraine. He has the ability to rivet an audience with his eloquence and his rage. When a group of homeless families broke into a boarded-up apartment house, vowing to stay until the city made the apartments habitable, he was their spokesperson. It might have seemed to the public that he was the person who galvanized the city council into action. But that was not so. A phalanx of law students and their professor, a priest, a candy store owner, three housewives, and the members of eight homeless families all played significant roles. Before the news of the takeover made a front-page splash, many people had spent months collecting information, negotiating, and forging **coalitions**. If there had not been widespread participation and support for "Operation Move-in," it could have been swept aside with one quick police action or simply ignored until the squatters gave up and left. *All change efforts must be group endeavors.*

coalition   A loose amalgam of people or groups who support a similar idea or goal.

When he first began his job, Ed was brimming over with energy and enthusiasm. Occasionally those wonderful qualities got in the way of careful planning. At one point, he helped organize a rally to protest the mayor's deletion of money needed to fix up three local parks, which the city council had promised. To his great embarrassment, reporters outnumbered neighborhood residents at the demonstration, and one of the speakers never showed up. Ed did not realize then that he first had to prepare the ground very well before the seeds could grow into an effective intervention. He learned that preparation consists of:

- Learning about the history of the problem and the systems involved in it
- Locating the sources of **power** and estimating their potential for change
- Getting to know the local community through both formal and informal channels of information

power   The capacity to influence others to achieve certain desired ends.

And of course he needed to learn the "rule of three": double-check, double-check, and then double-check some more to make sure that everyone potentially involved knows the exact details of the mission and the strategy.

Learning about the History of the Problem and the System

Whatever the nature of the change we hope to bring about—more responsive routines in a day care classroom, more humane treatment for victims of domestic violence, changes in the governance of a recreation center—we need to learn about the full dimension of the problem. We accumulate the hard facts of the situation by asking questions such as:

- How widespread is the problem?
- How long has it been like this?
- How did this problem come about?
- Is it getting better or worse?
- What evidence backs up our estimate?

- Who benefits and who loses from this situation?
- What will happen in the future if the situation does not change?
- What solutions have others suggested? Which ones have been tried?

During a campaign to scale down a proposed development that would bring too many cars into an already overcrowded area, Ed located an investigative reporter who was also interested in the problem. Both of them believed there was corruption in the housing authority that had approved these plans without an environmental impact study. The reporter uncovered valuable information and brought it to the attention of the public. The developer's plans are still on hold while this situation is being further investigated by the attorney general of the state. Ed also recruited assistance from a business professor. He and his students studied the feasibility of creating bike lanes and employing shuttle buses to reduce the crush of cars (and carbon emissions) in the center of town.

Locating the Sources of Power and Potential for Change

Before CAFTE begins a change effort, the members need to know just where the power lies to make the proposed changes. Ed has discovered that this is more complex than it at first appears. When dealing with city government, several agencies, bureaus, and commissions have overlapping jurisdiction. Ed worked with a committee trying to clean up a vacant lot and turn it into a playground. He soon found out how Alice felt when she went down the rabbit hole into Wonderland. Everyone who answered the phone was eager to pass him along to another person. After many calls, he was right back with the first person again.

In trying to get that vacant lot cleaned up, he discovered that the health department was concerned about it only if he could prove it was rat infested (rat bites are health hazards). He discovered that the sanitation department could not clean it up because it was private property. They said they would be happy to clean it *after* it became a park. Finally, he discovered that the lot had been condemned for nonpayment of taxes many years earlier. In addition, no one at city hall could find a record of who held the title to the land.

With patience, time, persistence, and lots of help from friends, CAFTE finally unraveled the threads that led to the desk of the person who could cut through the red tape and say, "Okay!" A bit of green grass and trees now exists where only rubbish grew before. Ed often eats his lunch in that park and grins with pride (and scowls at children who try to pick the flowers).

FORMAL AND INFORMAL SOURCES OF POWER

Finding the genuine movers and shakers is complicated by the existence of two types of power hierarchies: (1) the formal power structure, which is composed of people who have the official authority to make decisions, and (2) the informal power structure, which is composed of people who actually make the decisions.

If you think about how decisions get made in your family system, in your college, or in a social agency you have worked in, you can grasp the complex reality of power. Locating the real decision makers in any system is a skill gained from many years of going down blind alleys and returning to try again. It develops out of having the courage to ask everyone involved with the system a lot of concrete questions, thinking about the answers, and then relying on your own intuition.

Ed has learned how to ask questions that might unveil the realities of power. Compare the following two questions. Which one is likely to yield the clearest picture?

Mr. Knight, who makes the policy decisions about hiring staff in your agency?

or

Mr. Knight, would you please describe exactly how the hiring of the project manager was done?

Of course, good questions do not guarantee accurate answers. But if you have ever watched a skilled television interviewer, you can appreciate the art of phrasing questions that elicit rich information.

POWER AND CHANGE

Ed has discovered that power is in a state of perpetual flux, and change is always possible. If he gets turned down on a request one day, he tries again later, as the situation or the cast of characters changes. An election, a turnover in staff, or a downturn in the economy can change a "yes" into a "no" and vice versa.

No system is ever totally closed. Every system, no matter how rigid it appears, is vulnerable to change. When Ed gets frustrated and begins to believe the looming threat of global warming will never improve, he reminds himself of the dramatic international changes of the recent past. Ed's mother describes signing petitions and demonstrating for nuclear disarmament. At that time, the world tottered on the brink of nuclear destruction, as the United States and the former Soviet Union faced each other from opposite corners. But almost overnight, the Soviet Empire came apart at the seams, and "Ban the Bomb" buttons became collectors' items. After seventy years of power, the "evil empire" became a supplicant, coming to the West for advice and loans. On the other hand, while Ed's mother is pleased to see that China, where she was born, has opened up its economy and now has a thriving middle class, she also fears that China is making all the mistakes we have made. The roads are clogged with cars, and many factories make the skies gray with the smoke from coal-burning furnaces, smoke that destroys cities and human lungs.

Getting to Know the Resources of the Community

Just as each client is rooted within a variety of systems—home, school, workplace, and peer groups—so too are systems rooted within communities. Before we attempt to change one part of a system, we must learn about its context. Communities are the sum total of their history, ethnicity, economics, geography, and relationships with the larger city or town.

The word *community* is often used in two ways. First, it is used to describe a physical entity. The Riverside community, where CAFTE's office is located, for example, has homes, shops, streets, and boundary lines. However, we might also use the term to describe a community of interest, a group with which we identify. It need not have a geographic boundary.

Perhaps we see ourselves as belonging to the gay community, the Christian community, the university community, or the macrobiotic community. In this section we will be dealing primarily with understanding the geographic community.

Understanding the physical layout of a community as well as its spirit helps us design strategies to cope with its problems. When Ed was a student, he helped conduct an attitude survey in Riverside. Crime and vandalism had been escalating, and one summer evening, a near-riot occurred when the police tried to disperse a group of teenagers congregating on a corner. When the surveys were tabulated, the researchers found that a major complaint of community members was the lack of decent public transportation. Because they could not get to the stores and factories of the nearby city, many residents had given up hope of ever obtaining steady, decent-paying employment. Hopelessness led to frustration, which then led to aggressiveness and destructiveness. When the Riverside Citizens Committee was formed, obtaining transportation was its major priority. Each community has its own agenda. Human service workers have to learn to read it.

When Ed takes a job in a new community, he will have to start learning about it from scratch. He will not be able to communicate with the people he works with if he does not have, at his fingertips, the details of their daily lives (see Kahn, 1995; Vollbracht, 2002). He will begin his education by creating a community profile. He does this by searching out answers to the following kinds of questions:

- Where does this neighborhood begin and end?
- What are the differences between what the map defines as the neighborhood and how the community describes its boundary lines?
- Which is considered a central location?
- Where do different age groups and interest groups congregate?
- Where is the "other side of the tracks"?
- Where are the significant dividing lines between the rich and poor and between one racial or religious group and another?
- What are the main industries and in what way does each impact the environment?

Before scheduling any meetings, Ed needs to know how the neighbors feel about coming out at night or entering certain areas. He needs to know if in this community parents are likely to bring their children to meetings. If so, he needs to arrange child care. He needs to know what significant events his meetings might conflict with (such as the local church bingo game or ethnic holidays).

Ed needs to find out what languages people speak so he can arrange for translators, if needed. In Riverside, many of the elderly speak English but cannot read and write it, having emigrated from Greece as adults. The newest residents are Chinese, whose primary dialect is Mandarin. Ed speaks a bit of Cantonese, the two dialects are almost totally different. He has to find some community activists to translate CAFTE's meeting notices into the languages of community residents. CAFTE has a phone message about upcoming activities it is sponsoring or supporting that is spoken in three different languages.

Even the refreshments Ed serves at meetings tend to mirror the preferences or dietary restrictions of the Greek and Chinese members. And their festivals and holidays are celebrated and acknowledged.

FORMAL CHANNELS OF INFORMATION

Even though Ed had volunteered in the Riverside community and helped to conduct its community survey, when he started this job, he still had much to learn. He found many valuable sources of information at the library and on the Internet (Kjosness, Barr, & Rettman, 2004). He looked up the census data, read reports written by different city agencies, and read the town budget. He even looked back over old copies of the *Riverside News*.

Then Ed made a list of the people in town he needed to meet. His list included politicians, school board members, clergy, directors of social agencies, and especially the local heroes and town characters. Although he did not formally interview each one, he did have a series of questions he tried to work into conversations whenever he got a chance to meet a person on the list.

INFORMAL CHANNELS OF INFORMATION

The formal channels of information were valuable, but Ed found that walking and driving slowly in and out of the community's streets was just as important. Often the official version of the economic or recreational life of the community contradicted what he saw with his own eyes.

The boarded-up stores he observed and the neighborhood park strewn with beer bottles and sleeping men and women told him more about its spirit and daily life than did the statistics on parks and unemployment. Through the use of the senses—looking, listening, feeling, smelling—human service workers can round out their profile and identify glaring GAPs in services.

Whenever possible, Ed drops into a service at a local church, attends a parents' association meeting, and stops by the American Legion fair or the police versus firefighters challenge baseball game. He makes a point of doing his laundry near the office because the Laundromat is a great place to chat with folks, and it has a bulletin board full of notices about events he might never hear of otherwise.

MAKING SENSE OF WHAT WE HAVE FOUND

After observing an institution or a slice of community life, we try to make sense out of what we have seen and heard. This process involves three steps:

1. *Observation*—What exactly did I see?
2. *Speculation*—What might it mean?
3. *Reaction*—How do I feel about it?

Observation We describe exactly what we have seen, with no interpretation or evaluation. This guards us from jumping to premature conclusions. As a famous television detective used to say, "Just give me the facts, Ma'am!" after a visit to a local public school, for example, Ed describes what he has seen:

> At the school I saw a lot of students milling in the hallways. There was a lot of noise, and some small fights broke out while I was there.

instead of

> I visited the public school, and it was a zoo.

Speculation   We propose alternative interpretations of what we have seen and heard. By observing a place or person for only a few moments, Ed cannot possibly know what might have led to whatever behavior he has observed. Later on, after learning more about that school, he may find out which one of these interpretations is more accurate. These are his speculations on his observations:

Observation	Speculation
At the school I saw a lot of students milling in the hallways. There was a lot of noise, and some small fights broke out while I was there.	1. The school usually has very poor discipline. 2. There was some kind of recess or break in classes. 3. Something had just happened that was upsetting the pupils 4. The hall monitor was absent that day so the students were reveling in this found freedom to cut up.

Reaction   Only at the end of an observation can we give our personal reactions. Now we express how what we have seen or heard strikes us emotionally—in the stomach (or gut) rather than in the head. Ed might conclude his discussion of the visit to the school this way:

Observation	Reaction
At the school I saw a lot of students milling in the hallways. There was a lot of noise, and some small fights broke out while I was there.	I felt a little apprehensive; the atmosphere was so tense. I got the impression of neglect and unhappiness.

PLANNING AND IMPLEMENTING A CHANGE EFFORT

*Reaching Out to the Public**

No matter how brilliant our ideas, they are destined to fail if we do not have active, broad-based support. We always seek coalitions with groups of clients and their families, influential community members, other human service workers, and the ordinary, not-to-be-ignored taxpayers.

Imagine that you were assigned the job of establishing a new family residential center in the Riverside community for mothers who have AIDS. First, you found the latest infor-

*For further step-by-step organizing techniques, see Dale (1978); Kahn (1995); Mitiguy (1978); Mizrahi and Morrison (1993); Morse (2004); Rivera and Erlich (1998); Russell (1990); Shaw (2001); Speeter (1978a, 1978b); Weissberg (1999); and Wharf and Clague, 1997. For organizing manuals, contact the Center for Third World Organizing, 1218 East 21st, Oakland, CA 94606.

mation on AIDS treatment and committed yourself to keeping current. (The *POZ* and *A+U* magazines are excellent ongoing resources.) For two years, you have been working with a citywide coalition to get funds. You gathered thousands of signatures on petitions. You went to the state capitol and spent days meeting with your legislators. You helped organize a sit-in demonstration on the steps of the capitol with people with AIDS. Finally, a bill was passed and funds were appropriated. Your group has written a program proposal. It wants to manage one of the three facilities that will be funded. Now you should be able to start the program. Well, not quite yet!

Assuming that you are lucky enough to find an affordable building in an accessible location, you still must negotiate a complex maze of obstacles. You will need to use all your understanding of the formal and informal power systems of the community to obtain the permits and licenses needed to transform a private house into a nonprofit group home. You will have to get permits from the building department to make renovations. You will have to meet the fire and health department regulations. The police department will probably be concerned about neighborhood safety and the extra cars the center will bring into a narrow street with limited parking.

You and your group (and your lawyer) will have to appear before the town zoning board to convince them to grant a variance to its usual rule that prohibits anything but a private home in a residential neighborhood.

Then you will have to face the members of the block association. They are planning to protest that the proposed center will lower the value of their houses. They are also terrified that their children might get AIDS from the children who will live at the house. At an emotional meeting, they pour out their fear and rage. Renting or buying a house for a community-based human service program is almost always a politically sensitive issue. Inevitably you will run up against the NIMBY syndrome—"I agree that those people need a place to live, but

NOT IN MY BACK YARD."

Anticipating all these obstacles, you and your board have carefully laid the groundwork to defuse the protests. For six months, you have been actively reaching out to everyone who might be an ally. You have been presenting accurate data about AIDS, hoping to show that the risk of contagion from the mothers and children who will live in the house is minimal. You have also been reassuring the community that the house will be so well maintained that it will add to the value of the neighborhood, not detract from it. These are just a few of the outreach activities your group might do:

- Speak at every church, mosque, and synagogue in the community
- Appear on a panel discussion about the proposed residence on local cable television
- Run public-service announcements on the radio
- Recruit an advisory committee of local influential people
- Set up an interview with the local newspaper
- Run a series of workshops at the local high school
- Speak at a parent–teachers association meeting
- Convince a famous sports figure who is HIV positive (and heterosexual) to speak at a neighborhood rally

- Organize a walkathon to raise money for AIDS research
- Speak to the Chamber of Commerce to assure them that the center will patronize local businesses
- Publish a monthly newsletter of your activities and progress
- Organize and keep current a web site about the house

Even after successfully working your way through red tape and most of the resistance, you will need to continue to stay in close touch with the community. Some of the typical ways social programs do that are:

- Have an open house
- Become members of the block association and other civic groups in town
- Offer free, anonymous AIDS tests or another benefit to the neighborhood
- Encourage the Boy Scouts, Girl Scouts, and other groups to use your backyard for their fund-raising events or to use your living room for meetings

By keeping the channels of communication open in both directions, you will be able to accomplish several of your goals. Your staff will:

- Receive constant, current feedback so that complaints can be dealt with before they explode into conflicts
- Recruit volunteers and obtain donations of materials and services to supplement the scanty budget of the program
- Obtain referrals of clients
- Mobilize supporters for your grant renewal or to protect the program when budget cuts are threatened

INVOLVING THE PUBLIC IN THE DECISION-MAKING PROCESS

The most potent vehicle for creating significant change in any sector of the community is the ongoing, genuine participation—the give and take of ideas—of those who will be affected. Psychologists and sociologists have found that when workers are asked to help design changes in their work routine, they tend to be receptive to innovation. When they feel excluded from decisions, they are likely to resist even positive change, subtly sabotaging and undermining it (Klein, A.F., 1953; Mondros & Wilson, 1994).

As change agents, we encourage people to articulate their complaints and visualize solutions. Yet some human service workers fear putting too much power in the hands of clients or citizens. This is especially so when the clients are emotionally troubled, physically handicapped, or burdened with the daily problems of getting food, clothing, and shelter. Although the professional's hesitations are understandable, there are at least three excellent arguments in favor of giving clients and citizens key roles in maintaining and changing systems (Fisher, 1997):

1. *Client and citizen involvement is efficient and effective.* Time and again, clients complain that social researchers spend needless time and money arriving at conclusions about social causation that the clients themselves could have supplied gratis. Although this is a pretty cynical view, it carries a kernel of truth. No matter how troubled or disorganized

they may be, clients do have enormous insights into their problems, aspirations, culture, and lifestyle. No matter how skillful we are at understanding systems, clients undoubtedly know their world better than we ever can.

Rather than sit in the office wondering why so few tenants attended a workshop on applying for fuel subsidies or replacing high-wattage appliances with energy-saving ones, a worker can visit the Laundromat, school playground, and local park and ask folks why they didn't come. Workers often find that one-shot research projects or twice-a-year open meetings are not enough to mobilize the ideas or energy of the neighbors. So community workers must constantly work at sharpening their program's ability to solicit ongoing client and community feedback. This feedback has to be a regular part of the planning of every workshop and the evaluating of it after the workshop is completed.

2. *Client and citizen involvement has therapeutic and protective value.* Many of the people who arrive at the doors of human service agencies have already been overwhelmed by bureaucracies, unresponsive cumbersome institutions, urban ghettos, and suburban isolation. Feeling alienated and vulnerable—one small ant on a very big hill—they desperately yearn to play a significant role in the systems that affect their lives. When we counsel clients, we carefully guard their right to choose their own path. We must also do that as we pursue change.

Viable decision making about the administration of prisons, mental hospitals, counseling agencies, community residences, day care centers, nursing homes, and the like helps release positive forces for change. These forces might have lain dormant, but they have not atrophied. Participation in change efforts as equals rather than as passive recipients guards clients against the further development of their sense of powerlessness. It also protects change efforts from the self-interest of entrenched leaders and workers who might perpetuate their own powerful roles. One of the few truths we know that has no exceptions is *power tends to corrupt, and absolute power corrupts absolutely.*

We always have to be careful of our capacity to manipulate. Brager, Specht, and Torczyner (1987) point out that client trust in us is shaken when the worker engages in manipulative acts.

3. *Client and citizen involvement in decision making is both a moral right and a legal obligation.* Juggling the rights of individuals and neighborhoods with the rights of the larger society requires the wisdom of Solomon. Advocates try to find answers for questions that probably have no definitive answers:

> Why should landlords be forced to abide by rent controls rather than charge whatever the traffic can bear, as in other nonregulated industries?

> Why should people who work hard and save money have it taxed by the government to support programs for mothers who have children and no ability to support them?

All sides of these controversial issues have strong proponents. Although social policy issues are perplexing, they must be decided in an open marketplace of ideas. In some towns, legislation constricts the size of new buildings and taxes businesses differently than homeowners. In some towns, in order to fund improvements to the green belt, each time a house is sold, a portion of the proceeds goes into a fund to purchase open space for parks. Some towns spend tax money on building subsidized housing units, and other towns do nothing and hope that low-income people will move away. Whatever the arrangement, it is always open to change. The public can vote to change policies, and they can vote for candidates who espouse their positions. Thus, participation is built into our system at every level, either directly or indirectly.

In public education, for example, the federal government leaves to local jurisdictions a great deal of freedom to teach the curriculum as they choose. But, with the passage of Public Law 94-142 (the Education for All Children's Act) in 1974, the federal government assumed a central role in deciding what kind of services must be offered to students with disabilities. The Education for All Children Act also mandates citizen participation. Every educational plan created for a child with special needs requires parental consent. If the parents withhold their consent, they can mediate with public officials, then arbitrate, and then finally go to court. If the lower court disagrees with them, they can go to a higher court. Currently there is a growing push for mandated academic testing and an effort to require passing a standardized test in order to graduate. Parent groups have mobilized on both sides of this hotly contested issue. Local school boards now grapple with federal legislation.

Many health and environmental laws require the approval of community planning groups. Social welfare and housing laws require advisory or review panels of citizens and consumers. These panels periodically review the work of public agencies and have some say in whether their funding is expanded or downsized.

Thus, whether or not human service workers are convinced that their clients can handle the responsibility or that participation has intrinsic value, they have no choice but to include it in most publicly funded programs. The challenge is to learn how to implement the mandate for participation so that it works well.

Decision Making and Participation

Citizen decision making is essential in a democracy, but both skeptics and supporters of participation agree that many barriers stand in its way. Citizens often lack time, self-confidence, specialized knowledge of resources and alternatives, articulateness, and objectivity. No less an authority than Thomas Jefferson, however, offered an answer to the public's unreadiness to assume power. In a letter to William Charles Jarvis, dated September 28, 1820, he wrote:

> I know of no safe repository of the ultimate powers of this society but the people themselves; and if we think them not enlightened enough to exercise their control with a wholesome discretion, the remedy is not to take it from them, but to inform their discretion.

An in-depth examination of several day care programs that had strong parental and citizen participation identified five crucial building blocks that help inform the discretion of citizens (Schram, 1975). Let's look at each of them (Figure 13.1). You can use them in the future when you are given the task of building a strong advisory committee, house council, or board of directors.

A. *Commitment.* After the third meeting in a row when a vote cannot be taken on a grant proposal to fund a solar panel installation in the neighborhood hospital because there

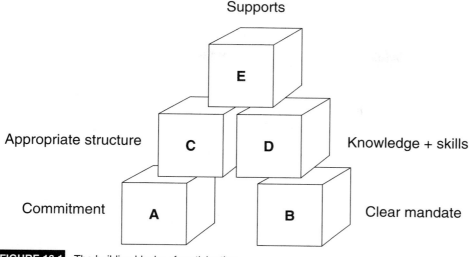

Supports

Appropriate structure

Knowledge + skills

Commitment

Clear mandate

FIGURE 13.1   The building blocks of participation

is no quorum, a legislator might be tempted to throw up his hands and yell, "Damn it, I'll decide myself!" But even if shared decision-making is not working very well, it still cannot be abandoned.

The agency director mandated to check out proposals with a citizen's advisory board must grit her teeth and try a new approach to solicit the opinions of the members. She could call each one and take a telephone poll, or she could write a letter (and enclose a stamped, self-addressed postcard) and ask for written feedback. She must continue to believe that six hesitant citizens will eventually make a sounder decision about the proposal than she could make alone. She understands that there are low points in every group's participation history.

Because of our deep commitment to the process of citizen input, we need to find ways to make it work. When it does not work (e.g., by not acting soon enough, they lose money the grant would have provided), we do not resort to blaming the members of the board. Their lives are complex, and we believe that they do the best they can. During the next funding cycle we will give them more advance notice, tack one meeting onto another, or take a telephone survey to obtain a vote. And there usually is a next time.

B. *Clear mandate.* Participation has the best chance of working when the contract governing the process is clear. Discussing each of the details of by-laws or personnel practices seems to most of us like tedious nitpicking. However, carefully written rules of the road are the backdrop against which rational participation can take place. Vague generalities doom shared decision making. Compare the following statements in the by-laws of two different community residences for adults who are in recovery from drug addition. The clarity of the second statement offers residents more of a chance of gaining significant participation than the generality of the first:

Residents will play an active role in running the house.

Compare that vague mandate with this very clearly specified process of decision making:

> Once a week, there will be a two-hour meeting during which activities for the next seven days will be planned. Each member will have one vote. All activities must get the majority of votes and must fall within the recreation funds allocated for that week.

C. *Appropriate structure.* Every participation effort needs a tailor-made participation structure. The format must be the right one for the mix of purpose, participants, and set of tasks. Unfortunately, most of us know of few alternative models of structure. We drift into the familiar, having elections for president, vice president, secretary, and treasurer. Then we establish a weekly or monthly meeting.

But not all groups need the same kind of officers, nor do they need to meet on a regular, arbitrary schedule. Some decisions need the face-to-face interaction of a meeting; many just need a polling of opinions in a variety of ways. Some tasks need not be done by everyone but can be delegated to committees. A neighborhood resident who recently returned to school was given the job of rewriting the *Recycling and Waste Disposal Handbook.* She sold ads to local merchants and churches. The proceeds from the ads and the small purchase price for the book covered her two-week salary. Once a year, CAFTE sponsors a citywide Earth Day conference. The fees from renting booths cover the small stipend paid to the member who does the secretarial work involved.

Some committees can be ad hoc, taking on one task and then disbanding when it is completed. Ed has found that it is much easier to ask a resident to take on a task if it has a beginning and an ending time attached to it. Although she turned down the job of chair of the fund-raising committee, for example, Ms. Kazantakis was willing to run two bake sales a year. That was a role that did not overwhelm her.

Carving out a structure is like sculpting a face. No two are identical. Experimentation and imagination are the keys to success. But if the structure is not designed, an informal one will evolve anyway, with all its attendant fuzziness and potential for conflict.

D. *Knowledge and skills.* Few of the citizens in Riverside have ever made the kinds of decisions that organizing a social change movement entails. Ed has often passed on to the members the knowledge and skills he has learned in college courses as well as the skills he has acquired from volunteering in local political campaigns.

When the board of CAFTE was hiring an architectural consultant and an engineer to help evaluate a developer's plans for a shopping mall in what is a wetlands area, Ed showed them how to use the role-playing he had learned in counseling classes to prepare for the interview. Ed has brought in sample budgets from other groups to show them what is usually included. When they wrote their by-laws, he invited a guest from an older, established neighborhood association who had already gone through the process. And now that they have been meeting for several years, they can reach out and help other fledgling groups.

E. *Supports that enable participation.* No matter what the issue—a tenant council is lobbying for legislation to control the spread of condominiums in a low-income area or a community residence for retarded adults is planning its first open house—some people will inevitably invest more time, energy, and enthusiasm than will others. Those who do the work need to be warmly thanked, whether with a letter of appreciation, a dinner, or a certificate of appreciation.

Less active people also need encouragement. Resources can support the growth of democracy. Perhaps if child care were provided during meetings, more people might come. Ed has found that if he rotates the locations and schedules of meetings, it becomes easier for some folks to attend. Sometimes he suggests to one member that he or she carpool with someone he knows is coming. He always makes it a point to offer rides to members because very few of them can afford to maintain a car, and walking long distances at night can be frightening.

Ed also tries to remember that as important as CAFTE is, each member and coworker has a personal life outside the organization, and *that* life also needs to be nurtured. Ed builds time into meetings so members can swap news of job openings or available apartments. The group often has potluck birthday or wedding celebrations. He takes the time to visit a sick colleague or member. It is these touches of warmth that provide tangible rewards for the members' investment of energy.

Because CAFTE is often on one side of a confrontation, it is especially important that the human service worker and participants form strong supportive relationships. They will need to shore each other up when they become discouraged or fearful. While social networking sites such as Facebook and Twitter are effective means for mobilizing large numbers of people to raise funds, attend a rally, or protest, they create only "weak ties" among people. Malcolm Gladwell (2010) points out that the people with whom you might engage in risky behavior, such as social activism, need to have strong, real (not virtual) relationships with you.

Changing the Rules, Rgulations, and Power Arrangements of a System

Just as every worker has a boss, so every public or private organization has some type of governing body. Decisions are generally made in a boardroom, courtroom, or legislative chamber. It is to these groups that the members of CAFTE turn when they become frustrated trying to cope with a problem that is not getting solved at the local level. After they determine where the next level of power lies, they try to educate those officials.

For many years, the citizens in Riverside had been complaining about garbage collection that was very sporadic. When garbage was collected, the empty cans were often thrown in the street, where buses would reduce them to junk metal. The smell of garbage, especially in the summer, hung over their neighborhood. Letters written to the manager of the sanitation department got polite answers but no improvement. A petition demanding regularly scheduled and more careful sanitation service was circulated. More than 200 people signed their names, but nothing changed. So, for three weeks, an elderly homebound CAFTE volunteer sat by her window, marking down the times the trucks arrived on her corner and what the sanitation workers actually did. She noted their numbers so drivers could be held accountable.

Armed with all these credible data, Ed helped to arrange a meeting with the regional director of sanitation who listened courteously and promised to discipline his staff. For two months the situation improved, but it drifted back to its original sorry state. Summer came, and the stench of garbage increased. The fear of rat infestation increased along with it.

APPEALING TO ELECTED OFFICIALS

Ed realized they had to go over the head of the regional sanitation director. One of the experienced members of CAFTE suggested that the group members appeal to their local town council. Ed panicked a little. Since his public school social studies lessons, the legislative process had always seemed very overwhelming. But, as he soon discovered, in day-to-day practice, social change agents must inevitably deal with local, state, and federal elected officials. And when taxpayers have complaints that are not being taken seriously, they have a right to expect that those who are paid by their tax money will respond to their legitimate requests.

Ed made the appointment with Councilor Irene Haupt, who represented the Riverside neighborhood. The committee members practiced stating their demands in

To remove the "Whites Only" signs in public accommodations in the southern states, advocates went all the way to the U.S. Supreme Court. Our society still must deal with the legacy of humiliation and resentment such segregation engendered.

a tense late-night session. They went in with a written agenda, with evidence collected by the homebound volunteer, and with their petitions. Ms. Haupt, anticipating an upcoming hotly contested reelection campaign, seemed very impressed with the 209 signatures. Each of those signatures represented a potential vote she might capture.

Ms. Haupt investigated the sanitation department's operations. Eventually the regional administrator was censured and put on probation. Ed was surprised to find that Ms. Haupt genuinely appreciated the feedback she got from the residents. She encouraged them to return to discuss their suggestions to improve the derelict park in their area and increase recycling efforts. She listened to their complaints about the lack of police foot patrols and promised to begin working on that GAP. Ed has found that legislators often depend on citizen groups. They cannot know everything that is going on in their districts, and the voters are their eyes and ears.

CAFTE is often consulted by a town councilor or by a state representative who wants to hear their ideas or solicit support when legislation that might have an environmental impact is proposed. The members have established credibility as people who do their homework. They have also built a reputation of having good memories, especially on election day!

Although they might think of themselves as apolitical, human service workers cannot be. They visit their statehouse when budgets are being discussed by legislators. If they do not lobby for the funding of social welfare programs, perhaps no one else will! The opponents of affordable housing, humane correctional programs, or shelters for battered women are likely to be there, telling their side of the story. They are demanding that money be diverted from social programs to fund their priorities. They too will have research documents and signatures on petitions. Thus, as Ed has learned, understanding how to present a case to a legislator is not a skill reserved just for community organizers. It is a skill he will take with him into every human service job he does. He will also use it in his personal life as a citizen of his own community.

TURNING TO THE COURTS FOR REDRESS OF GRIEVANCES

Although the sanitation complaint was resolved on the legislative level, at other times Ed has needed to follow the path to the courthouse. If he is convinced that an inequity in the wording or practice of a law stands in the way of citizens getting fair treatment, CAFTE either tries to get the law repealed or asks a judge to change the way it has been interpreted or implemented.

Lawyers from legal services programs (many of them initially funded by the federal poverty program), private attorneys doing pro bono work, and nonprofit groups such as the American Civil Liberties Union (ACLU), the Southern Poverty Law Center, and the Sierra Club carry these cases into court. They work on behalf of both individuals and communities, especially when they are convinced that their civil rights or health and safety are being violated. When homeless residents of Riverside were being routinely gathered up by the police and forced to go to shelters against their will, lawyers from one of these groups filed a suit on their behalf.

Although the volunteer lawyers do the actual juggling of the incomprehensible legal words and motions, Ed plays a role, too. Because he had met many of the homeless residents when they were working on getting the parks cleaned up, he was the one who talked to them about participating in the lawsuit. He provided them with information at every step. And he also gave them the emotional support that helped them hang on through the endless delays before their case was finally heard.

Rewards of Social Change Interventions

Most human service jobs do not require as much time, energy, and skill at social change as Ed's role at CAFTE. But all workers will, at some point, encounter an unyielding barrier that stands between their clients and the services they need. Then, even on a very small scale, the worker acts as a change agent. As the federal government continues to shift away from publicly funded programs and the slack is picked up by the private sector, human service workers will have to continually monitor the output of social programs. Would you stand by quietly if:

> . . . a disoriented elderly woman you counsel was being evicted from her home because the landlord wanted to sell her apartment as a condominium?

> . . . a young man just released from prison wanted to find work as an electrician, and the union representative told him the union would not take anyone with a prison record?

> . . . the mother of a Cambodian youngster was told that she would have to wait six months for an educational assessment because the school psychologist was too busy?

> . . . a person was running for office in your town on a platform of cutting out all the frills and was targeting the only teenage recreation center, a Meals-on-Wheels program for elderly shut-ins, and a van to transport adults who were physically disabled to their sheltered workshop?

We hope your answer is a resounding, "Of course not!" Walking a picket line and knocking on a stranger's door to explain a community problem can at first be intimidating. Licking stamps, stuffing envelopes, handing out leaflets, and making endless phone calls is tedious. And losing a struggle after months of hard work can be devastating. Ed does all these tasks and has faced many disappointments. Yet he has also had incredible highs when desperately needed services were begun or reinstated after being cut back. The day the first tenants move into the demonstration "green" housing development he has worked on for so long will be filled with indescribable joy.

Every organizer can tell stories about coworkers or citizens who, after experiencing a new sense of their own power, went back to school to finish their degree, took a more responsible job, conquered an addiction, or returned home feeling more hopeful about their children's futures.

Deborah Rosenfelt sums up the legacies of a social change campaign in her study of the aftereffects of a dramatic labor dispute in the mines of New Mexico in the 1950s. A group of poor Chicana (Mexican American) women defied years of their community's machismo tradition and the prospect of spending several days in jail and walked a picket line for months. Their husbands and sons had been forbidden to strike by a court order.

Thirty years later, Rosenfelt interviewed those women. That strike had been the most significant event of their lives. For most, the relationships with their husbands had changed dramatically when their roles reversed during the strike. But afterward, their roles in the family gradually regressed to the old inequality. The women's feelings of self-confidence had also gradually faded, they said, but not completely (Wilson & Rosenfelt, 1978).

Although it often appears as if the field of human services has, like the field of social work, moved away from social change and become enmeshed solely in clinical and direct-service practice, that might not be the full picture. With a shaky economy, questionable welfare reform, and a world community reeling from the impact of globalization, terrorism, and dramatic climate change we cannot afford this. Community efforts to work for positive change have never been more necessary. And they need not be gigantic efforts. *Stopping at Every Lemonade Stand* (Vollbracht, 2002) and *Deep Economy* (McKibben, 2007) describe the host of small acts all of us can take to build up a safer and more satisfying community, one that nurtures children—and everyone else.

Finally, one of our former students, remembering our oft-repeated injunction: *Don't Mourn, Organize!* sent us this obituary from her local newspaper. It seems to epitomize what we have urged beginning students to do, when there is a problem; join together with others and try to tackle it. More importantly, it illustrates an ordinary woman taking an active role in her community, and doing it for a lifetime!

Pat Cody, Bookstore Owner, Pioneering Feminist and Health Advocate

My First Teacher

October 5, 2010*

My mother, Pat Cody, passed away last Thursday, at 87 years of age. She was quite a woman. Here are some of the lessons she taught me over the years.

If you see something is wrong, speak up and try to change it. Join with others and raise your voices together. In the early 1960s she helped found Women for Peace, which took a stand against nuclear weapons and the slowly expanding Vietnam war. Years before protesters marched by the millions, my mother was marching every week at Berkeley's city hall, protesting the US advisors that would wind up leading the nation to war. The fact that most people had not heard of Vietnam did not stop her from speaking out. More recently, she helped found

a group called Grandmothers Against the War, to call for peace once again.

Respond to the immediate needs of those around you. In 1967 the summer of love blossomed around the world, and Berkeley became one of the places where youth gathered. Every week, hundreds of youngsters would arrive with their belongings on their backs, looking for a new scene. My mother and father had a bookstore in the midst of this scene on Telegraph Avenue. Some of the local business owners wanted to make life as hard as possible for the youth. But my parents helped found the Berkeley Free Clinic in 1969, and for many years my mother served as the treasurer for the organization. This clinic has been a lifeline for thousands of people, and operates mostly on volunteer labor. Much of the funds for the project came in the

*Used by permission of Anthony Cody, first published in the *Berkeley Daily Planet* on October 1, 2010, and then in a smaller version on his blog. With thanks also to Nora Cody.

form of spare change collected by young people on the street, who cajoled donations from passersby and split the proceeds with the clinic. My sisters and I did our part by counting and rolling the coins on the dining room table every Sunday night for years.

When personal tragedy strikes, build community with others and face it together. In 1971, my mother learned that DES, a drug she had taken to prevent miscarriages, actually caused reproductive damage to the children who were in utero. She discovered there were millions who had been affected, but there was very little public information available. She connected with others and started DES Action, a group devoted to informing people about the effects of the drug, advocating for research and support for those affected. This group grew to have chapters in more than thirty states and in other countries as

well. My mother was the linchpin of this group, and built a powerful network that included doctors, medical researchers, and the people affected by the drug. She personally responded to thousands of people seeking information and support, and was like a second mother to many. Finally after her husband died Pat realized that there were very few support groups for those living with devastating grief from losing a close family member. She founded the Grief Support Project and created a model that paired a trained counselor with a layperson who had coped with such a loss to lead groups for those recently widowed or otherwise grieving.

Don't preoccupy yourself with credit or awards or power. Just do what needs to be done, and enjoy the company of others while working towards common goals. She gave me the example by which I have lived my life, and I will miss her.

CRUSADERS FOR JUSTICE

HOWARD ZINN

© 2010
Lyons

"There is a tendency to think that what we see in the present moment we will continue to see. We forget how often in this century we have been astonished by extraordinary changes in people's thoughts, by unexpected eruptions of rebellion against tyrannies by the quick collapse of systems of power that seemed invincible...

To be hopeful in bad times is not just foolishly romantic. It is based on the fact that human history is a history not only of cruelty, but also of compassion, sacrifice, courage, kindness.

What we choose to emphasize in this complex history will determine our lives. If we only see the worst, it destroys our capacity to do something. If we remember those times and places—and there are so many—where people have behaved magnificently, this gives us the energy to act, and at least the possibility of sending this spinning top of a world in a different direction."

— **Howard Zinn**
Activist, historian, writer

SUMMARY

1. Individual problems are often caused by factors rooted in the social environment.

2. Changes in the social environment can help one troubled individual and, more importantly, they can prevent the development of similar problems in others.

3. Systems-organizing and systems-change strategies rely on the same basic activities and skills as the direct-service strategies. They begin with data collection and terminate with evaluation.

4. Before forming an action plan to counsel a client, a human service worker must check out the mental health of the systems within which the client lives and works.

5. Human service workers need to explore their ambivalent or unrealistic attitudes toward change agents.

6. Momentum for change generates from the top down through legislative or administrative fiat. It also generates from the bottom up through the actions of organized citizens and clients. Often it is generating from the top and bottom of the system simultaneously.

7. Human service workers attempt to change both the structure of an unhealthy system and the consciousness of the people in it.

8. The three escalating methods of organizing for change are education, persuasion, and pressure.

9. Before a change effort begins, organizers research the background of the problem and locate where the power to make change really resides. They need to prepare a community profile to assess resources and understand the lifestyles of the people involved in the organizing.

10. Organizers use outreach techniques to solicit public support and participation in generating ideas and making decisions and to overcome resistance to change.

11. Citizen participation depends on obtaining strong commitment, clear mandates, appropriate structure, knowledge, skills, and participation supports.

12. To change the rules, regulations, and power arrangements of a system, organizers disseminate information, rally support, lobby decision makers, and take direct action when other techniques have not worked.

13. Working to change systems is time- and energy-consuming, frustrating, and often fruitless. But even very small changes can result in dramatic improvements. The potential rewards of all our change efforts can have widespread ramifications that change many people's life situations.

14. Change efforts can be undertaken by anyone and can continue for a lifetime, bringing great satisfaction to both those who initiate and those who benefit.

DISCUSSION QUESTIONS

1. George Bernard Shaw, a social critic of his times, is reported to have said that only unreasonable people will not accept the world as it is and, therefore, all change depends on "unreasonable people." How do you feel about that statement? Does it make sense to you? Would you feel comfortable in the role of "an unreasonable person"? Can you think of some famous people who might fit that description?

2. What kind of change efforts have you been involved in within your own hometown or on your college campus? Who started them, what techniques did they use, and how did the effort work out? Remember that these change efforts need not be major campaigns. If you can't think of any change efforts in your own experiences, what kind of change efforts have you heard of or seen in your community or on your college campus? Have you seen or read about any groups that asserted their position for or against a woman's right to an abortion or for or against gun control? What kind of tactics did they use to influence the public or legislators?

3. Is there any form of student governance on your campus? Where would you go to find the sources of power that might be able to change a rule or regulation that you feel is unfair or not fairly implemented?

4. Who were your first teachers? What lessons did they leave with you?

WEB RESOURCES FOR FURTHER STUDY

Neighborhoods Online

www.neighborhoodsonline.net

This is an online resource center for people who work through grassroots organizations as volunteers, and in government. It provides fast access to information and ideas covering all aspects of neighborhood revitalization, as well as to create a national network of activists and people in government working on problems that affect us where we live.

Net Action's Virtual Activist Training Guide

www.netaction.org/training/reader.htm

A training guide for using the Internet to organize. It shows how to build and maintain a web site and become a virtual activist.

Websites on community organizing

www.nfg.org/cotb/Websites-4.pdf

Website listings including community organizing resources, toolkits, manuals, and an organizing game.

Nonviolent organizing

www.nonviolence.org/support

Many web sites on nonviolent organizing.

Write your Representative

www.writerep.house.gov/writerep/welcome.shtml

This service will assist you by identifying your Congressperson in the U.S. House of Representatives and providing contact information.

Writing to government officials

USA.gov

This web site encourages you to contact your elected officials and share your thoughts on current events and government policy. Links are provided to the president and vice-president, U.S. senators and representatives, state governors and legislators, how to tweet a message to your representatives, and how to contact government agencies.

COMM-ORG: The Online Conference on Community Organizing

http://com-org.wisc.edu/node/27

COMM-ORG conducts an e-mail list and a List-Serve to help connect people who are interested in community organizing, including organizers, scholars, and scholar-organizers, and to provide information about organizing. The e-mail list, with over 1,000 members across more than a dozen nations, is moderated by Randy Stoecker at the University of Wisconsin.

MoveOn.org

www.moveon.org

MoveOn organizes on the Internet as well as in communities. It has a Facebook page and it sponsors MoveOn Councils, local teams of committed members who organize in their community and build leadership among MoveOn members. They work on national campaigns to push for progressive change.

Chapter 14

Understanding Legal Issues

On October 5, 1994, the American Civil Liberties Union of Ohio filed a lawsuit against the City of Cleveland on behalf of four homeless plaintiffs and the Northeast Ohio Coalition for the Homeless. The plaintiffs allege that Cleveland police officers, under the direction of their superiors, engaged in "dumping" homeless people—a charge that the defendants flatly deny. The complaint sought injunctive relief to halt an unconstitutional practice under which police officers physically remove homeless and/or destitute individuals from certain sectors of the city, transport them against their will to various distant locations, and abandon them. (*Spare Change*, 1995)

LEGAL ISSUES THAT CAN CONFRONT A WORKER

The preceding case is one example of the many kinds of legal issues that a human service worker might deal with. It is impossible in one chapter to cover all the legal issues that affect human service workers. Not only can they seem overwhelming, but no human service worker knows the ins and outs of every issue. However, it is vital that we be sensitive to legal rights and dilemmas and that we seek further help when on shaky ground. Knowing where to turn and being willing to ask for help are strengths of a conscientious worker.

To begin your thinking about legal issues, take the following quiz. We would be surprised if you knew all the answers. Legal issues in the human services can be complicated.

Question 1: An eighteen-year-old high school student began to wonder just what her teachers had been writing in her record since she started school. She asked her homeroom teacher if she could look at her cumulative school record. The teacher said no because it would violate the confidence of all those teachers who had counted on some measure of confidentiality. Did the teacher break the law?

Question 2: In 1974 the State of Georgia set up a central computer bank to store mental health information about its citizens. State officials requested all clinics and community mental health centers to send in the following information for each new patient: background data, Social Security number, the nature of the patient's primary disability, previous mental health services, and diagnosis. A human service worker at a community mental health clinic asked all her clients to sign this medical release authorization, which read:

> The state wants to keep a record of name, Social Security number, and the type of problem of every person who comes for mental health services. The reason why the state wants this information is so that it can keep track of mental health services and clients throughout the state. If you sign this paper it means that you give us permission to send your name, Social Security number, and diagnosis to the state offices in the capital, where it will be placed in the mental health computer file. (Rosen, 1976, p. 285)

Question 3: Felicia, a twenty-three-year-old woman who had been adopted, wrote to the state registrar of vital statistics in New Hampshire to request a copy of her original birth certificate. After receiving it, she went to the agency that had placed her with her adoptive parents to ask their help in finding her biological parents, who were named on the birth certificate. The adoption worker agreed to help her with this search (Weidell, 1980). At the same time, Felicia's twenty-one-year-old brother Paul, who had been placed for adoption in Washington D.C. where his biological mother had moved from New Hampshire, wrote to the registrar of vital statistics for his original birth certificate, and they refused to send it to him. He went to the adoption agency, and they refused to help him.

Why did the adoption agency in New Hampshire help Felicia, whereas the agency in Washington, D.C., refused to help Paul?

If you knew the answers to these questions, you are better informed about legal issues than a good many experienced human service workers. One study found that a significant proportion of mental health professionals either are ignorant of or ignore their legal obligations (Swoboda, Elwork, Sales, & Levine, 1978, p. 448). Until recently, legal issues either have not been taught at all in human service training programs or have been dealt with superficially.

What Is Wrong with What the Worker Did?

Here are the answers to the questions:

Answer 1: Yes, the teacher broke the law. According to the Family Educational Rights and Privacy Act, often called the Buckley Amendment, educational institutions that receive federal aid must make students' records available to them if they are 18 or older and to their parents when they are minors (Bershoff, 1975, p. 367).

Answer 2: The State of Georgia, which requested this very personal information for its computer records, did not show sufficient concern for its citizens' right to privacy. Some states have adopted progressive privacy laws, and some states have constitutional provisions protecting the right of privacy. However, clients did not have to sign that medical release authorization in order to receive service from the clinic. The mistake the worker made was not telling clients this. A study showed that when clients were told the following in addition to the first part of the statement, the majority of them chose not to sign the statement:

> If you do not sign this paper, this identifying information will not be sent to the state offices in the capital and will only be kept locally. The services you get will not depend on your choice. In other words, if you don't sign you will get the same services from us as if you did sign. (Rosen, 1976, p. 285)

The principle of consent assumes that people are informed about what they are giving consent to and that it is freely given, without any real or implied threats. If people think they will be refused services if they don't sign the consent form, most will sign.

Answer 3: The New Hampshire agency helped Felicia in the search for her biological parents, whereas the Washington, D.C., agency refused Paul, because New Hampshire passed a law that allowed adoptees who are at least twenty years old to obtain their original birth certificate if the biological parents have consented to the search. Washington, D.C. law does not allow birth records to be revealed for such a search.

Variations in the Law

Notice as you read those questions and answers that some laws apply equally to everyone in the United States (e.g., letting students see their records), while other laws (opening adoption records) vary from state to state. As you read this chapter, some of the laws we discuss are probably already in the process of being changed by state or federal legislatures or by a court decision. Even lawyers must do constant research to keep abreast of current law in a particular field. Although most human service workers cannot know the law in the same way, they should strive to keep abreast of the particular body of law that applies to their agency population.

THE LAW AS RESOURCE

Laws can give people rights and resources, and therefore, workers need to know them. Suppose that a human service worker is helping a blind child and the child's family to find an appropriate school. If the worker did not know that the Education for All Handicapped Children Act requires that handicapped children be placed in the most nearly normal setting, the worker might try to find a placement in a residential school for the blind rather than in the local school system.

This process of finding information, evaluating it as it applies to a particular problem, assessing the needs of the person or group you are working with, and finding the correct fit between person and resource, is the same problem-solving process that human service workers use in all the interventions discussed in this book.

Street-Level Bureaucracy

street-level bureaucracy The way laws and regulations are implemented by human service workers at the level of direct contact with clients.

Although laws are passed at various government levels—federal, state, and local—most beginning human service workers will encounter those laws that affect their practice at the level of the agency in which they work. Michael Lipsky (1980) calls this **street-level bureaucracy**. Laws and policies are implemented on the streets where people live. A law sets the broad outlines of a program, but the face of the law that clients see is the face of the agency worker who delivers the service. Moving up the bureaucratic ladder, the worker sees the face of the law in the face of her or his supervisor and the agency director, who interpret how regulations shall be put in practice in that particular agency. In a large government agency, the state officials of that bureaucracy have written those regulations according to the way they interpret the law.

Regulations: Bureaucratic Interpretations of Law

After laws are passed, they cannot affect anyone's life until the money is appropriated and the regulations spelling out how to implement the laws are written. Agencies don't make laws, but their regulations define how the law will be put into practice. They end up having the same force as a law. For example, Congress passed the Rehabilitation Act for the Physically and Mentally Disabled in 1973. The regulations making key portions of it effective were not signed by the secretary of Health, Education, and Welfare (HEW) until 1977, when several disabled people protested the four-year hiatus by sitting in at the HEW office. The 1973 law stated, among other things, that barriers that prevent the handicapped from gaining access to various facilities should be removed. Yet the ramps replacing curbs at crosswalks to accommodate wheelchairs, the audiocassettes opening museum tours to the blind, or the captioned news for hearing-impaired television viewers did not appear until the secretary of HEW signed those regulations and set the procedures in motion.

Regulations are generally more specific than laws. For example, a law about licensing day care centers may say that the center shall be operated with "due regard for health and sanitation." But it is the regulations that specify a minimum number of toilets and the water temperature for dishwashing (Brieland & Goldfarb, 1987).

Sometimes, in order to save money, officials make regulations that do not conform to the law, or they break their own regulations. This happened in 1981, when the Reagan administration ordered accelerated reviews of Social Security disability cases using what a Minnesota federal district court called "arbitrary," "capricious," and "irrational" standards to evaluate applicants' eligibility for the benefits (National Association of Social Workers, 1983). Thousands of eligible people were terminated until Congress reviewed the process, slowed the rate of review, and provided for continuation of benefits during the appeals process. An attorney for the Mental Health Law Project, which brought suit in Minnesota on behalf of the disproportionate numbers of mentally ill people who were terminated, said,

> The court confirmed that SSA, in its eagerness to reduce the disability rolls, has been systematically violating both the law as spelled out by Congress and its own regulations. (p. 9)

In Massachusetts, doctors were reviewing these Social Security disability cases without giving physical exams, and 80 percent of their decisions were ultimately overturned by administrative law judges. A legislative commission that investigated this said, "the doctors are following Social Security Administration regulations, while the administrative law judges are relying on federal law when they overturn the doctors' decisions" ("The Law on Disabilities," 1983).

"CATCH-22" REGULATIONS

Regulations can put clients in a catch-22* a situation in which they are damned if they do and damned if they don't.

Catch-22 refers to a novel of the same name by Joseph Heller (1961) and describes dilemmas that are impossible to solve because of contradictory requirements.

Suppose that a toddler has outgrown his or her crib and needs a child-size bed. In the state where the child lives, the welfare officials who drew up the regulations decided that public money should not be spent on beds. Therefore, the three-year-old will stay crammed in the crib or sleep on the floor.

Or suppose that a woman has been told by her landlord that she must leave her apartment. She agrees and then asks welfare for money to pay a security deposit on another apartment. The officials who wrote the regulations, however, specify that she must show the worker a court eviction order or already be evicted before the welfare department can help her pay the security deposit.

CONFLICTING JURISDICTIONS AND REGULATIONS

The different levels of government involved in the same program may further complicate the picture. This catches the client in a web of conflicting jurisdictions and regulations. Fuel assistance for poor people is one such example. A federal program provides money that some states supplement. If a state requires a client to apply first to a federal antipoverty agency for fuel assistance before applying to the state welfare department, the client can get a bureaucratic runaround and perhaps live in a freezing home until the confusing tangle is unraveled.

States and localities often implement programs that are not federally mandated. Sometimes they even challenge federal regulations. For example, at one time a federal drug abuse program had a regulation that required all states receiving money from the program to put personal data on patients into a centralized computer. Massachusetts refused to do so on the grounds that it would violate patients' confidentiality. Some states have stronger privacy laws than does the federal government.*

If the foregoing discussion has been confusing, imagine what it feels like to be a client. You might have only a dim understanding of who gives the money and makes the regulations. When you complain, you are told, "We don't make the regulations. The 'feds' (state, county, city) make them." Local, state, and federal bureaucrats sometimes fight each other about policies and regulations, passing the buck from one to the other when clients complain. Advocating for clients in these situations requires patience, tenacity, and the concerted efforts of many people and organizations.

AMBIGUOUS WORDING

Regulations are sometimes worded so ambiguously that citizen groups or individual clients challenge them, claiming they give a false interpretation of the original intent of the law. Sometimes the laws themselves are ambiguous and loosely written. When a confusing regulation is stacked on top of a confusing law, conscientious workers are also caught in a bind. How can one interpret them? Many bureaucrats are becoming increasingly aware of the immobility caused by ambiguous intent or language, and now and then agency workers are pleasantly surprised to find on their desks a revision of agency regulations written in *plain, easy-to-understand English*. Sometimes these regulations give examples, which can make complex rulings easier to comprehend.

Some people argue that the ambiguity of regulations is intentional. When clients don't understand what they are entitled to, they are less likely to ask for those rights.

---

*The federal law regarding disclosure of drug information was later changed to prohibit it in all states.

Learning the Regulations

Few things are more frustrating to a consumer than being served by a poorly informed worker. Think of how you feel when you ask for information about housing, financial aid, or degree requirements from a college employee and are given the runaround! A worker who is confused by the full meaning of a regulation should discuss it with a supervisor or a colleague. If the confusion persists, it is best to turn to a lawyer who specializes in this area. Most large agencies, such as a Department of Social Services or a Department of Vocational Rehabilitation, have legal divisions. In addition, there are many public-service law groups that specialize in children's rights, welfare reform, the needs of the physically disabled or developmentally delayed, and so forth. When a new law is passed or a regulation promulgated, memos and newsletters are distributed and conferences are organized to help workers and consumers understand and use its provisions.

Without these forms of public information, none of us—human service worker, client, or lawyer—would be able to keep clear about the endless changes and refinements in social service law.

Unfortunately, the federal government has been cutting back on legal services for the poor since the Nixon administration. President Reagan tried unsuccessfully to eliminate them altogether. In 1995 the Republican-controlled Congress made cutbacks of over 25 percent in an already weakened legal services. The struggle continues today. Bureaucrats and public

Deciding exactly what are the limits of protests is a challenge for constitutional scholars and community residents. These members of the white supremacist KKK can march in Washington, D.C., but may no longer hide their faces behind their sheets.

officials resist protests against their rules and try to weaken organizations that challenge them. Because there are not nearly enough legal services for all the people who need them, human service workers will need to learn more than ever about the law in order to be able to help their clients.

THE LAW AS RESTRICTION

Laws provide resources and rights; they also limit them. City councils and state and federal legislatures create programs; they also cut them. Delinquency and correctional programs and agencies that investigate child abuse and neglect are examples of the government policing people's behavior. Human service workers in these programs need to be sensitive to the *stigmatizing* effects that such programs have on the clientele. They work to combat the **stigma** through social action and sensitive individual and group counseling. People may need to be stopped when their behavior is endangering themselves or others, but social stigma cripples rather than rehabilitates.

stigma Something that detracts from the character or reputation of a person or group; a mark of disgrace or reproach.

Human service workers work with many stigmatized clients:

1. When parents have been accused of child abuse and a child-protection worker goes to their home to investigate, the parents inevitably feel stigmatized, regardless of whether they actually abused their child.

2. When a child has been labeled a "delinquent," that label becomes a stigma that can create a self-fulfilling prophecy.

3. When patients in a drug or an alcohol abuse program have their names put in a centralized computer, they have legitimate fears about how this information will be used.

4. When people test positive for HIV, they have legitimate fears that they will be discriminated against.

Convicted sex offenders have had their mobility limited by laws restricting where they may live. One of the nation's most aggressive attempts to limit the mobility of sex offenders was struck down by the Georgia Supreme Court in 2007. The roughly 10,000 sex offenders living in Georgia had been forbidden to live within 1,000 feet of a school, playground, church, school-bus stop, or other places where children might assemble. The prohibitions placed nearly all the homes in some counties off-limits—amounting, in a practical sense, to banishment.

The case that led to the ruling was brought by Anthony Mann, 45, who in 2002 pleaded no contest in North Carolina to "indecent liberties with a child." On the state sex-offender registry, he is not listed as a predator. A year later, Mann married, and he and his wife purchased a home in Hampton, Georgia. At the time he and his wife purchased the home, there were no child-care facilities nearby. But one later moved within 1,000 feet of his property line, and, following the law, his probation officer ordered him to move. Mann sued.

The Georgia Supreme Court ruled that, by forcing a sex-offender from his home, the law violated his Fifth Amendment right to be safe from the government "taking" his property. The ruling said, "It is apparent that there is no place in Georgia where a registered sex offender can live without continually being at risk of being ejected" (Whoriskey, 2007).

LAWS EVERY WORKER NEEDS TO KNOW

These are some areas of law that all human service workers need to understand:

- Confidentiality
- Privileged communication
- Privacy
- Due process

Some laws affect one specific field of practice. For example, only those involved with the courts need a thorough understanding of the probation and parole regulations of that particular county or state.

Confidentiality, privileged communication, and privacy, however, affect all fields of service delivery. What do they mean as legal concepts to human service workers? To summarize, a human service worker promises confidentiality to a client in order to protect the client's privacy and develop trust between them. In a few human service relationships, the law treats those confidences as privileged communication, protected from being divulged in court. The only way that information should be shared with others outside the worker–client relationship is for the client to give informed consent. We shall discuss these concepts further in the sections that follow.

Confidentiality

Confidentiality is important in order to build trust. People are not likely to reveal anything embarrassing or intimate if they cannot rely on the helping person to keep secrets. *Confidentiality* means protecting a person's privacy and respecting that person's autonomy. Some people have such strong feelings against exposing their lives to public view that they will ask for help or reveal themselves only in dire circumstances.

Most people want the right to control information about themselves. People don't like having secret files about them that they can't look at or having credit records given out that might damage their ability to get a loan or buy a car. People get angry when they talk to someone in confidence and that person spreads their secrets to others without permission. We feel betrayed if a person violates our trust.

The psychotherapeutic relationship depends on confidentiality. People need to feel free to express their most private thoughts, feelings, and impulses. Some psychotherapists have gone to jail rather than testify in court about their patients. Some therapists have stopped including highly personal material in their notes to protect clients' confidences in case a court subpoenas the notes.

Social agencies usually have a specific policy on confidentiality, but these statements are often vaguely worded, containing many *ifs*, *ands*, and *buts*, which create many loopholes. In practice many agencies freely give out information about clients to other agencies, human services data banks, police or court officials, schools, employers, landlords, and researchers from both public and private groups. One experienced worker laments:

> It is not unusual for intake workers to have their new clients routinely sign a handful of blank consent forms "to make it easier for everyone." These forms authorize the agency

to seek or release information about the client to almost everybody at any time under any circumstances. With the client's signature already obtained, the worker can fill in the blanks later when a need arises to disclose data. This system doesn't allow the client to maintain any meaningful control over the content of his case record. Thus, many settings (and federal regulations) are requiring that the client's consent be "informed." (Wilson, 1980, pp. 189–190)

This violation of confidentiality is not ethical, but it is legal. Two lawyers who studied the daily practices of public agencies concluded that clients of welfare or other social service agencies have no legal right to privacy and no legal way to fight a breach of confidentiality except where the federal Privacy Act or a state privacy act covers the agency's operations (Hayden & Novik, 1980).

Privileged Communication

privileged communication Legal protection of confidences revealed in certain specified relationships.

Privileged communication gives legal protection to some human service workers against having to reveal a client's confidences in court, unless the client consents. It has historical roots in the privileged communication of the lawyer–client relationship, which held that confidences told to the lawyer must be kept secret to protect not only the client but, more importantly, to protect the right of all clients to be represented by counsel. Privileged communication is essential to ensure that clients will confide in their lawyers.

However, some states have freed lawyers to violate a client's confidentiality if they believe doing so could prevent injury or death to another person. California passed such a law in 2003, which states that the attorney–client privilege can be broken when a lawyer "reasonably believes" that disclosure is necessary to prevent a criminal act by any person, including a client, that could result in death or substantial injury. While disclosure is discretionary, not mandatory, the law was opposed by many lawyers and by the San Diego County Bar Association, which feared that it would "discourage clients from being forthright and complete" ("State Bar to Allow Lawyers to Break Confidentiality," 2004).

Privileged communication has been extended to other relationships in which trust is of the utmost importance—husband and wife, priest and penitent, psychiatrist and patient, journalist and source, and sometimes psychologist and client and social worker and client. Although it protects certain professionals from having to reveal confidences in court, it is not an absolute privilege. In fact, there is considerable disagreement and debate about this concept, even among lawyers. Some argue that privileged communication should be restricted when there is a threat to society, as when a client tells about a crime he or she has committed or is contemplating.

Human service workers are sometimes caught in an agonizing bind when they are subpoenaed by a court to testify. The worker may have promised clients that the information given them was confidential, honestly believing that he or she could guarantee confidentiality, but the state he or she works in does not provide the legal protection of privileged communication. The following are three examples of cases that have been contested in court:

1. *Director of a rape crisis center threatened with jail for refusing to give the court a rape crisis file.* Nassrine Farhoody, director of a rape crisis center in Worcester, Massachusetts,

refused to release records of a client's rape counseling, which put her in contempt of court. She faced a jail sentence but fought the case all the way up to the state's Supreme Judicial Court, which decided in her favor in July 1996 and tightened access to rape counseling records. The confidentiality of rape counseling sessions in Massachusetts is now as protected as the confessional with a priest. The woman whose records Farhoody refused to release during the rape trial came close to saying, "Turn over the records. I can't deal with this" (Coleman, 1997). But each time, Farhoody assured her she was willing to carry the burden. "She keeps saying she's only doing her job. . . . I love that woman," said Darlene, who doesn't want her last name used (p. D1).

2. *Rape victims' center defends confidentiality.* Erin Marie Ellis, the executive director of Washington County's Sexual Assault Resource Center in Oregon, was in court with her nine-year-old child, ready to be sent to jail for challenging a defense lawyer's subpoena seeking records on a rape victim whom the center counseled. A judge quashed the subpoena on a technicality on the eve of trial, but the case highlighted the ongoing effort by statewide advocates working for nonprofit sexual assault crisis centers to protect their clients and maintain confidentiality.

    "Once we start losing control of our records, it greatly diminishes our ability to do our work and do it well," Ellis said. Gina McClard, associate director of the National Crime Victim Law Institute at Lewis & Clark Law School in Portland, said, "This is a privacy issue for rape victims, but it's also a crime-prevention and a crime-fighting tool." "Rape is the least-reported crime. There's no reason we should put up another barrier" (Bernstein, 2004).

3. *Eighteen agencies refuse to turn over records to Department of Social Services.* In a successful court suit in 1982, eighteen agencies in New York City that had contracts with the New York City Department of Social Services were threatened with having their funds cut off if they did not turn over their clients' case records to that agency. A U.S. District Court judge ruled in the agencies' favor, saying the information in the records "may well be constitutionally protected in that it touches upon intimate personal and family matters and was disclosed in confidence with some reasonable expectation of privacy" (National Association of Social Workers, 1982, p. 3).

Women's crisis intervention agencies in Maine scored a victory for confidentiality in 2004, when the state enacted a law to protect victims of domestic violence attempting to elude their assailants. The law established a program that provides a designated address to individuals who have relocated or plan to move to a location unknown to their abuser. It also provides participants with a first-class mail-forwarding service and a designated address that has no relationship to the participant's actual address. As a result of the program, victims of domestic violence, sexual assault, and stalking are able to interact with businesses, government agencies, and other organizations without disclosing their actual address (Higgins, 2004).

A majority of state legislatures have enacted legislation privileging the communication between rape crisis counselors and sexual assault victims.

Some research projects have been charged with violating confidentiality. For example, a research project that involved drug testing of high school athletes in Oregon did not protect the students' confidentiality because students who refused to participate in the research or who tested positive for drugs came to the attention of coaches and principals were prohibited from engaging in school sports, and could be suspended from school:

> Considering the profound social and psychological importance of peer relationships among adolescents, the loss of confidentiality results in humiliation as well as the public airing of drug-using status, assuming that the test result is a true positive. Confidentiality requires that the consequences of trial participation not be subject to publicity of any form in which individuals are reasonably at risk of identification. (Shamoo, 2004)

Agencies sometimes invoke confidentiality as a way of avoiding public scrutiny of their failings. Child welfare agencies have legitimate reasons for assuring their clients that information will be kept confidential. Many people would not report child abuse if their identity were known; people who have been charged with abusing children do not want publicity. Yet when an agency is failing to protect the children who are in its care from abuse, it may not be possible to correct the agency's failings unless the public is informed and presses for change through the legislature. In 1999, two children ages 11 and 9, who had been in the custody and care of the New Jersey Division of Youth and Family Services (DYFS) for more than five years, brought a class action suit which alleged a systemic failure of the agency to protect them and twenty other children from harm "and to provide their families with support and services to maintain adequate health and safety".

Since then, the tragic death of a foster child, Faheem Williams, and the abuse of his siblings, who were known to DYFS, encouraged the plaintiffs and interveners to request a modification of the existing confidentiality order in the class action suit. They asked for public disclosure of materials pertaining to child fatality and near-fatality cases. The *New York Times* and the *Newark Star Ledger* joined the suit, requesting permission to publish the information. The U.S. District Court of New Jersey ruled that because DYFS is a public agency, the public has a right to know some relevant information regarding the health and safety of the children. The court gave the newspapers the right to review about 10 percent of the agency's files related to child death reports and other substantiated reports, but not identifying information about children currently in the custody of DYFS. The court attempted to "strike that balance between protecting the privacy interests with the public's right to know" National Center for Youth Law (2001).

PROFESSIONS AND PRIVILEGED COMMUNICATION

Although privileged communication protects both the client and the professional, the confidence belongs only to the client, and only the client can waive it. Some states grant the privilege to clinical psychologists and to social workers. Human service professionals try to get broader legal coverage and stricter laws.

The confidentiality of a patient's communications with a psychotherapist was guaranteed on a federal level in a 1996 Supreme Court decision, *Jaffee v. Redmond*. The Health Insurance Portability and Accountability Act of 1996 (HIPAA) required rules to be drawn up governing the privacy of health and mental health information. The rules were four years in the making, and in 2001 the Department of Health and Human Services announced them. The rules now:

- Require clients' consent in order to disclose health information for the purpose of treatment, payment, and health care operations.

- Preserve state laws' stronger privacy protections, where they exist.

- Recognize that psychotherapy notes require a greater level of protection than other types of health records (Moss, 2001).

- Prohibit employers from receiving personal health data, except for the administration of health plans.

- Subject people who misuse private medical records, such as selling them, to fines or imprisonment (O'Harrow, 2001).

However, the rules allowed doctors, hospitals, other health services, and some of their business associates to use personal health records for marketing and fund-raising. In response to customer concerns that the marketing provision in the law did not protect privacy, the Department of Health and Human Services modified the law in August 2002 to prohibit selling lists of patients or enrollees to third parties without an individual's prior authorization. However, marketing to doctors is still permitted.

The new rules also say that sick patients will not be required to visit a pharmacy themselves to pick up a prescription but can send a family member or a friend instead (U.S. Privacy, 2002).

The Act applies to medical records only if a health care facility maintains and transmits records in electronic form. A great deal of health-related information exists outside of health care facilities and the files of health plans, and thus beyond the reach of HIPAA (Privacy Rights Clearinghouse, 2010).

You have probably seen the effects of this law when your doctor or hospital handed you a "Notice of Privacy Practices" brochure and asked you to sign a form saying that you had read it. You may notice greater privacy in the reception room and changes in sign-in sheets so that patients can't see each other's names.

Despite this law, a national survey showed that an overwhelming number of Americans fear that their psychological health records are not kept confidential, particularly from their employers. And most people are not aware that many insurance plans require a diagnosis of mental illness to cover ongoing counseling. Many people are reluctant to seek psychological health care for fear their psychological health records may be shared with their employers or others. Two-thirds of Americans would not be likely to tell their employer they were seeing a mental health professional, and 70 percent would not tell their work associates. Half of Americans said they would hesitate to see a counselor if a mental illness diagnosis were required. To address these concerns and ease the strong stigma that is still prevalent in America, some health care professionals created a counseling service called OnMind Psychological Services, based in Kansas City, Missouri, which does not participate in insurance plans and does not require a diagnosis of mental illness for treatment. It charges fees directly, but its fees are at least 50 percent lower than national averages (*PR Newswire*, 2004b).

If human service workers do not have the protection of privileged communication, they must decide, with the help of their agencies, what to do if they are subpoenaed to appear in court with certain information. Even though a subpoena looks impressive, even frightening, you need not automatically comply with it. You can challenge its validity or relevance or the information it requests. You can contest it, with the help of a lawyer, by claiming privileged communication or other legal regulations. Most agencies have legal consultation.

LIMITS ON PRIVILEGED COMMUNICATION

There are certain legal limits on privileged communication. Privileged communication laws do not grant protection from reporting child abuse. All fifty states have passed some form of mandatory child abuse and neglect reporting law.

Some highly publicized cases of priests and church youth workers sexually abusing children have helped to create public demand for applying these laws to priests. In Massachusetts, a youth worker at a church pleaded guilty to dozens of child sex abuse and pornography charges, and a former priest was accused of repeatedly molesting children during a twenty-seven-year career in the church. Two dozen of the priest's seventy-seven alleged victims sued Cardinal Bernard F. Law for transferring the priest from parish to parish.

Some states have extended the reporting requirement to include reporting the abuse or neglect of people who are disabled or incompetent, particularly the dependent elderly (Gothard, 1995).

Most states have passed laws mandating that police arrest a person who batters another person and have also passed laws that mandate treatment programs for those convicted of domestic violence. Work with batterers poses dilemmas regarding confidentiality because counselors are required to report on the progress of the treatment to the court. Most treatment programs for batterers have a written contract explaining that because both the court and the agency want the victim to be safe, they will contact both the court and the victim to inform them of the batterer's progress in treatment. Participants are required to sign this contract before they begin treatment (Buttell, 1998).

Probation and parole officers and counselors who work with prisoners cannot assure their clients of confidentiality because they are required to report violations of probation, parole, or prison rules to the authorities. Clients should be informed immediately of the many limitations of confidentiality.

Workers in agencies receiving federal funds are prohibited by federal regulations from disclosing information about a client's substance abuse without the client's consent. But even the federal code of regulations allows disclosure of confidential information in cases involving such offenses as child abuse, homicide, rape, or aggravated assault (Landers, 1998).

PRIVILEGED COMMUNICATION AND INDIVIDUAL AND COMMUNITY RIGHTS

Laws often require a professional to break confidentiality if there is a possibility of a crime being committed. In a landmark 1974 case, *Tarasoff v. California Board of Regents*, an eighteen-year-old high school senior told the school psychologist in a therapy session that he planned to kill a girl when she returned from a midsemester vacation with her parents. The psychologist agonized over the ethical dilemma she was in. Should she break the confidence of the therapy relationship? Was the murder threat genuine? Convinced that it was, she called the campus police and asked them to take the student into custody for possible commitment. The police took him in, but convinced that he was rational, released him on his promise to stay away from the girl. The psychologist wondered if she should warn the young woman but, following her interpretation of the American Psychological Association

Toward hope and healing for America

Dave, Ruth and Margie Waterbury

We're living proof that families with lesbian and gay kids can be whole, happy and worthy of all that this great country promises.

Laws often reflect public opinion. This family is helping create a favorable climate for gays and lesbians so that laws will not oppress their lesbian daughter.

Code of Ethics,* did not do so. The student carried out his threat eight weeks after he had confided in the psychologist. The parents of the dead girl sued the psychologist, the school, the psychologist's supervisor, and the campus police. The parents charged them with negligence in failing to warn the girl of the student's threat. The court ruled that the psychologist was negligent in failing to warn the young woman.

*APA's Principle 4.01 Maintaining Confidentiality: Psychologists have a primary obligation and take reasonable precautions to protect confidential information obtained through or stored in any medium, recognizing that the extent and limits of confidentiality may be regulated by law or established by institutional rules or professional or scientific relation. Principle 4/02 Discussing the limits of confidentiality: Psychologists discuss with persons (including, to the extent feasible, person who are legally incapable of giving informed consent and their legal representatives) and organizations with whom they establish a scientific or professional relationship (1) the relevant limits of confidentiality and (2) the foreseeable uses of this information generated through their psychological activities. (*American Psychological Association*, 2010, Ethical Principles of Psychologists and Code of Conduct, http::/www.apa.org/ethics/code/index/aspx).

There are no easy answers. If you know that in an interview you will not be able to keep everything confidential, tell the client in advance. Discuss with the client what you must reveal. If you are a probation officer working with juvenile delinquents, you are legally required to tell the court if a juvenile has violated parole. If you are an assistance payments worker in the Department of Welfare, you are required to act if your client has broken welfare regulations. If your clients know these rules, they can make their own decisions about what to tell you.

Privacy

privacy   The right to be left alone.

Privacy can be defined as the "right to be left alone." In many state constitutions, it is defined as an individual's right to decide how much to share private thoughts, feelings, and facts of one's personal life. In other words, no one has a right to make public anything about a person that the person wants to be kept secret. Before a human service worker gives information about a client to someone outside the relationship, the client must give **informed consent**. This means that the client understands *exactly what the consequences of the consent will be* before giving it and that *consent is given willingly*, without any coercion or fear of reprisal.

informed consent
Agreement given with the understanding of the full implications of what one is agreeing to.

Most human service professional societies have codes of ethics that are intended to provide their members with guidance on how to protect clients' privacy. However, these codes are rarely revised often enough to keep up with changing circumstances. They are not always helpful guides to the legality of any one particular action. Here are two examples:

1. *Research project on drug use violates privacy.* In a junior high school in Pennsylvania, a consulting firm wanted to administer questionnaires for a study designed to identify potential drug users. The school psychologist, seeking guidance from the codes of ethics of the American Psychological Association and the National Association of School Psychologists, followed what she interpreted as their guidelines in requesting the consent of the research subjects. Some parents, however, sued the school to prohibit the research study, and the U.S. District Court (*Merriken v. Cressman*) agreed with them. The court concluded that even if the subject signed a release, it did not constitute *informed consent* because the students and parents were not given enough facts about the reasons for the test or the ways in which the test was going to be used to identify and counsel potential drug users. In balancing the right of an individual to privacy and the right of the government to invade that privacy for the sake of the public interest, the court struck the balance on the side of individual privacy, believing that "there is too much of a chance that the wrong people for the wrong reasons will be singled out and counseled in the wrong manner" (Bershoff, 1975, p. 367).

2. *Court says that state agencies giving records to each other violates privacy.* The question of whether state records in one bureaucracy should be made available to another without client consent was tested in Massachusetts in 1979, and the client won. Jose Torres, represented by the Juvenile Law Reform Project, was the plaintiff

in a class-action suit against the state's Department of Mental Health and Department of Education.

The suit was brought in an attempt to obtain services for Torres and other emotionally disturbed adolescents. In preparing the state's defense, the attorney general obtained information about Torres that was in the state's Department of Social Services files. When Torres and his lawyer contested this action, the Supreme Court of Massachusetts ruled that this disclosure of information about Torres amounted to "an unwarranted invasion of his privacy" ("Privacy and State Records," 1984). The attorney general was wrong to assume that you give up your rights when you sue the state ("Privacy and State Records," 1984).

Since the shooting massacre at Virginia Tech, all colleges have been on the alert to spot students who might pose a threat to other students. At Virginia Tech, a disturbed student gunman killed thirty-two people and committed suicide. There were several people who knew that student had problems, but because of privacy and other issues, they didn't talk to others about it. Seung-Hui Cho, the Virginia Tech gunman, was ruled a danger to himself in a court hearing in 2005 that resulted from a roommate's call to police after Cho mentioned suicide in an e-mail. He was held overnight at a mental health center off campus and was ordered into outpatient treatment. But he received no follow-up services, despite his sullen behavior and his violence-filled writings.

College officials had traditionally been reluctant to share information about students' mental health for fear of violating privacy laws. But since Virginia Tech, some colleges have initiated programs to deal with potential threats. At the University of Kentucky, a committee of deans, administrators, camps police, and mental health officials began meeting regularly to discuss a watch list of troubled students and

CASE EXAMPLE

Aspiring artist Quentin Wanham never imagined that some yellow scribbles on his pants would land him in the principal's office at Everett High School for questioning, with a police officer monitoring the interview. The 17-year-old senior was asked about a 6-inch-long logo, known as a graffiti tag, on his pants.

The trip to the office was equally alarming to Wanham's horrified mother, who said she learned of it only afterward from her son. Lorraine Wanham is furious that school authorities did not call her before they questioned her son, and she worries that the answers he gave to school administrators could come back to haunt him. At 17, if charged with a crime, he could be tried as an adult.

Courts generally do not consider questioning by a school official to be the same as questioning by police. School officials, often in the presence of school-based law enforcement officials, question students without the protection of Miranda warnings.* (Lazar, 2008)

*A *Miranda warning* refers to the warning that a person who is arrested has a right to remain silent, and the right to a lawyer. The U.S. Supreme Court in 2010 watered it down by ruling that a person has to ask for a Miranda warning before it is given.

decide whether they need professional help or should be dismissed from college. Patricia Terrell, vice president of student affairs, who created the panel said, "If a student is a danger to himself or others, all the privacy concerns go out the windows" (McMurray, 2008).

Virginia Tech has added a threat assessment team since the massacre there. Bryan Cloyd, a Virginia Tech accounting professor whose daughter Austin was killed in the rampage, welcomed the efforts to monitor troubled students, but stressed he doesn't want to turn every campus into a "police state." "We can't afford to overreact," Cloyd said, but "we also can't afford to underreact" (McMurray, 2008).

Schools are also dealing with issues of student rights and invasion of privacy. There is a growing conflict between administrators' goals of running safe schools and students' legal rights. Civil libertarians say that with police officers routinely assigned to many schools, the legal boundaries between schools and law enforcement have blurred. Amy Reichbach, an attorney with the American Civil Liberties Union of Massachusetts, said there have been reports of arrests being made for "stupid stuff, like disorderly conduct."

COMPUTER DATA AND PRIVACY

The federal Privacy Act of 1974 says that people have a right to control information about themselves and to prevent its use without their consent "for purposes wholly unrelated to those for which it was collected" (Massachusetts Civil Liberties Union, 1983). Yet, in their eagerness to find fraud, some welfare departments are routinely doing computer matches with bank records and records of other benefit programs, such as Social Security, unemployment compensation, and so forth, without the consent of the recipients.

In Massachusetts, for example, the Department of Welfare in 1982 gave the Social Security numbers of all welfare recipients to 117 Massachusetts banks. When the department received the list of people whose assets were over the allowable limit, it immediately sent out benefit termination notices to all the people on the list, without first discussing it with the recipients. John Shattuck, the national legislative director of the American Civil Liberties Union, pointed out that this was a violation of the Fourth Amendment to the Constitution, which prohibits unreasonable searches and seizures. Computer matches of unrelated files have generally been "fishing expeditions" directed against large numbers of people on the chance that something will turn up (Massachusetts Civil Liberties Union, 1983). Further, Shattuck says, they violate the legal principle on which law is based in the United States, that *a person is innocent until proven guilty.* Many of the people on the list were in fact innocent of fraud.

CRIMINAL RECORDS AND PRIVACY

Gelbspan says that a seven-year study of FBI criminal-history files gives us cause to worry about the use of records to invade our privacy. According to professor Kenneth Laudon, an expert in information systems at New York University who conducted the study, the persistently high error rate of these records makes them "a bigger blacklist than existed during the McCarthy period"* (Gelbspan, 1986, p. 15). Laudon warns that "today, there is a

---

*The *McCarthy period* refers to the years during the 1950s when Senator Joseph McCarthy conducted what some describe as a witch hunt against people whom he alleged to be Communists or Communist sympathizers.

gargantuan, runaway system of records on individuals which is unregulated and unaccountable" (Gelbspan, 1986, p. 15).

Criminal history files have kept thousands of people from:

- Employment
- Housing
- Loans
- Insurance
- Entrance to college
- Becoming guardians or foster parents. (Massachusetts Alliance to Reform CORI, 2007)

Private and government employers who screen job applicants increasingly use records. Because the records are often inaccurate, every year several million Americans are unjustly denied jobs. The most common flaw involves records that list arrests but fail to distinguish between people convicted of crimes and those who were never brought to trial or who were acquitted. The impact of this falls hardest on black and Latino men and the poor because they experience a disproportionate number of arrests that are later dismissed. Representative Don Edwards of California, chairman of the House subcommittee on civil and constitutional rights, said, "We are only perpetuating their disadvantages when we use those arrests to deny them jobs" (Gelbspan, 1986, p. 15).

Criminal records are used for screening even menial jobs. According to Diane Gordon, a political science professor at the City University of New York, "You can't even be a . . . janitor in a day care center if you have a criminal record of any kind" (Gelbspan, 1986, p. 15). How can ex-offenders stay out of jail if they can't find work?

This issue is particularly important for human service workers. People can be denied employment if they have a criminal record, whether or not the record is accurate. They may work in an agency that will not hire anyone who has a criminal record. People who have been denied employment include:

- A grandmother who has been caring for her grandchildren while their mother recovered from drug addiction, was discovered to have a criminal record. She had given the children excellent care, and the mother was not yet ready to take them back, but when the agency considered paying her as a foster parent, they discovered that she had a criminal record, and they removed the children. The grandmother's "crime" was to possess some marijuana in her youth.

- A black day care worker is stopped and arrested for DWB ("driving while black") and taken to the police station. The police discover that his car registration has expired. The charges are eventually dismissed, but it is still on his record, and he loses his job.

- Sandy, a homeless woman, was arrested when her boyfriend used her apartment to sell drugs to an undercover police officer. The judge in her case ruled that she was not involved in the drug transaction and therefore dismissed her case. The arrest, however, remains in her criminal record and has become the basis of her being denied housing and employment (*Rosie's Place Spring Newsletter*, 2007).

- Tina and her children lost their home due to a fire that left them homeless. Due to their income and housing situation, Tina's family was eligible for public housing.

However, when the housing authority performed a CORI (Criminal Offense Record Information) check, she was denied housing due to a fifteen-year-old arrest for public drinking, a misdemeanor. In the years since her arrest, Tina had taken charge of her life by becoming sober and eventually working two jobs, yet her CORI continues to haunt her (*Rosie's Place Spring Newsletter,* 2007).

The human service and social work professions are quite concerned about the criminal record checks because they sometimes prevent workers from doing good work. Schools of social work are debating how to handle these checks when they place students in a field-work agency.

Human service workers can join in efforts to reform the program. Some legal services agencies are helping people to correct their criminal records, and some states have reform movements to get their legislators to change the system.

CLIENT ACCESS TO RECORDS

In order to protect privacy, people need to know what has been said about them and have the opportunity to correct misinformation. Clients of human service agencies sometimes ask to read their records. Some states have privacy laws regulating this. The Privacy Act of 1974 and the Family Educational Rights and Privacy Act (Buckley Amendment) are the two main federal privacy laws.

The Privacy Act of 1974 gives certain rights of privacy to clients of federal programs, particularly the right to read and copy one's own record and to insist that it be corrected or updated if its accuracy is questionable. The client must give consent for the record to be used for any purpose other than that for which it was specifically compiled. The heaviest public demands for information have been made of the CIA, FBI, and Treasury Department. Federal social service agencies, such as the Veterans Administration (VA), are also subject to the Privacy Act.

When a program is partially or totally federally funded, as with Medicaid and the Title XX social services programs, clients who have appealed an agency action and have a scheduled hearing have a right to examine their case files before the hearing. The Privacy Act provisions for client access and correction cover any federally administered social service program, such as the Supplemental Security Income program.

OPEN ACCESS TO RECORD KEEPING

Some professional organizations, including the National Association of Social Workers (NASW), favor open access to records, but there is debate about this within all the human service fields. Our own position is that an open-record policy encourages honesty between worker and client. That makes for a trusting relationship. We like this guideline that one author offers:

> Pretend that your client is sitting beside you reading everything as you write in his record. Consider consciously what should and should not be documented, and figure out the most effective way of wording what has to be said. Be aware of things that might upset the consumer, but that must be recorded, and be prepared to deal with your client's reaction. (Wilson, 1980, p. 197)

PRIVACY FOR WELFARE RECIPIENTS

When people have been stigmatized and treated in a demeaning manner, they are also likely to have their privacy invaded; all of these things erode peoples' pride. Welfare applications, for example, ask detailed personal questions to decide if the applicant is eligible. The federal–state Parent Locator Service (PLS) of the Child Support Enforcement Program has been especially prone to use "police state" tactics in its zeal to track down fathers who don't pay child support:

> In some states PLS paternity investigations have required women to complete question-naires revealing all of their sexual relationships, including dates and places and the names of witnesses, and to take polygraph [lie detector] tests. (Hayden & Novik, 1980, pp. 68–69)

When people were examined for their suitability for workfare in New York City, interviews with recipients with psychological problems were conducted in public spaces and not by doctors. Recipients were not given the results of their exams unless they specifically requested them. Inside the waiting room, "waits are long, tempers short. People are moved in bunches by security guards through the crowds, off to have their blood drawn. One morning, the receptionist was observed openly mocking Spanish speakers" (Sexton, 1997, p. 17).

The privacy of welfare recipients in Michigan was invaded by mandatory drug testing of all state welfare benefit applicants. Michigan is the only state in the nation to institute a policy of mandatory drug testing of welfare recipients, although the 1996 Welfare Reform Act authorized (but did not require) states to impose mandatory drug testing as a prerequisite to receiving welfare assistance. This policy was opposed by physicians, social workers, public health workers, and substance abuse treatment professionals, who filed an *amicus curiae* brief with the U.S. Court of Appeals in January 2001. The brief argued that mandatory drug testing is a marked deterrent on the willingness of individuals, particularly pregnant and parenting women, to access essential medical and social services (Vallianatos, 2001a).

The brief stated that this invasion of privacy was not justified by any special need to protect public safety. It identified other shortcomings of the policy:

- The use of drug testing is narrow in scope and fails to detect obstacles to employment and problematic family relationships.
- Drug testing does not detect child abuse or neglect.
- Suspicionless drug testing erodes the trust between welfare recipients and benefit workers—such as by promoting the fear that drug testing will result in removal of children from the home (Vallianatos, 2001a).

A federal appeals court upheld the Michigan program in 2002, but in 2003, the ACLU reached a settlement with the Family Independence Agency of Michigan which states that the FIA can now require drug testing of welfare recipients only where there is a reasonable suspicion that the recipient is using drugs (American Civil Liberties Union, 2003).

In 2009, some Republicans in the Michigan state legislature put forward a proposal to do random drug testing for those who receive food and cash assistance, making college students who apply for a card show proof they can't be claimed as someone's dependent, and adding photo identification to the cards. Democratic Rep. Robert Dean said those bills are "partly election-year posturing that sounds good to voters," and some people cautioned those stiffer requirements could hurt those in need of help (Scott, 2010).

PRIVACY IN A TIME OF WAR

As we write, there are both domestic wars and a foreign war in progress. Both are affecting our right to privacy. Domestically, there is a war over the legal right to have an abortion. The Bush administration claimed in legal proceedings that it does not believe that there is any legal protection for the confidentiality of the doctor–patient relationship.

In 2004, the Justice Department demanded to subpoena the records of patients who had received abortion care at a Chicago hospital. A district court judge denied the Justice Department's demand to subpoena the records.

Shortly after September 11, the Justice Department submitted to Congress a law dubbed the "USA Patriot Act," an acronym for "Uniting and Strengthening America by Providing Appropriate Tools Required to Intercept and Obstruct Terrorism." It was rushed through Congress in several days, no hearings were held, and it went largely unread. The Patriot Act contains provisions that increase the ability of federal officers of the executive branch to enter and search a person's house, to survey private medical records, business records, library records, and educational records, and to monitor telephone, e-mail, and Internet use. It struck most heavily against noncitizens. It permitted the incarceration of noncitizens for seven days without charge, and for six-month periods indefinitely without access to counsel if the attorney general determines release would endanger either the country or individual persons. The Patriot Act imperiled democracy by invading people's privacy and promoting governmental secrecy.

In 2007, a federal judge in Oregon ruled that crucial parts of the Patriot Act were not constitutional because they allowed federal surveillance and searches of Americans without demonstrating probable cause. Shortly after that, however, President Obama asked to "make a slight change in a law to make clear that we have the right to see the names of anyone's e-mail correspondent and their Web browsing history without the messy complication of asking a judge for permission." A *New York* Times editorial said, "Yet the change he asked for was not slight, but would allow huge numbers of electronic communications to be examined with no judicial oversight" (*New York Times*, 2010).

The Patriot Act was set to expire in February 2011. The White House said that it "would strongly prefer" an extension until December 2013, noting that the longer timeline "provides the necessary certainty and predictability" that law enforcement agencies require while at the same time ensuring congressional oversight by maintaining a sunset (Sommez, F., 2011). As we go to press, both the House and Senate are working on proposals that would permanently extend three provisions of the bill or extend them through 2013.

Due Process

due process
Procedural mechanisms that secure or protect a person's legal rights.

Due process means that, under the Fifth and Fourteenth Amendments to the U.S. Constitution, individuals are entitled to "due process of law"—including notice of the charge, an open trial, and right to counsel—before they can be deprived by the government of life, liberty, or property. In recent years, due-process protection has been extended to include some social agency practices. This was done to curb "the broad discretion available to officials and employees of public agencies and institutions and the arbitrary or illegal acts that have sometimes resulted." (Dickson, 1976, p. 274)

If someone does something to you that you think is unfair, you naturally want to find out why, give your side, and rectify the wrong. You may want others to support you—perhaps a lawyer. Clients of human service agencies want the same. They often disagree with agency policy and workers' actions. They need some protection against arbitrary decisions.

FULL AND PARTIAL DUE PROCESS

There can be either full or partial due-process procedures. In situations in which a person might be seriously damaged by a decision, full due-process proceedings are usually allowed. These include representation by a lawyer, the right to present evidence and witnesses, the right to cross-examine witnesses, the right to a written statement of findings, and the right to a trial by judge and/or jury.

When there is less potential harm to an individual, or when a full-blown judicial hearing would be costly, laws provide partial due process. Generally they grant an administrative hearing and notice of charges and perhaps assistance in preparing and presenting the case (Dickson, 1976).

Most human service organizations give partial due process in a dispute with a client. Clients generally have a right to appeal an agency decision, and the agency holds an administrative hearing before an impartial examiner. Agencies sometimes allow legal assistance or an advocate from another human service organization, an advocacy support group, or even a well-informed friend. One of the authors of this book, (Mandell), does outreach at a Boston welfare office to help clients negotiate the bureaucracy and to protect their rights.

DUE PROCESS IN HUMAN SERVICE ORGANIZATIONS

Clients of most human service organizations had few legal rights to appeal an agency decision before 1970. In that year, the U.S. Supreme Court decided, in *Goldberg v. Kelly*, that the due-process amendments of the Constitution applied to welfare hearings. Eventually the same principles were applied to schools, prisons, parole proceedings, Title XX (federally financed) social services, mental hospitals and institutions for the mentally retarded, the physically disabled, juvenile delinquents, and other service consumers.

Soon after the *Goldberg* ruling, there was a sharp rise in administrative hearings. Many people who did not agree with this expansion of entitlements began to attack those procedures, saying they were going too far. There were demands for change, and certain due-process procedures were made less stringent. Welfare hearings were made more informal, and in the 1976 case *Mathews v. Eldridge*, the Supreme Court allowed disability benefits to be cut off before a hearing, although the *Goldberg v. Kelly* decision had stipulated that a hearing be held before adverse action was taken.

The Personal Responsibility and Work Opportunity Act of 1996, which began the Temporary Assistance to Needy Families (TANF) program, ended entitlement to welfare, and clients no longer had the due-process rights that they had when it was an entitlement. Welfare departments often use arbitrary means of denying TANF to clients, and clients often had no recourse to an appeal process. A number of states have "no entitlement" language in their TANF statutes. However, in 1999 a Colorado state court ruled that due process applies to TANF benefits despite the "no entitlement" language. The court challenged sanction notices as inadequate and in violation of federal and state due-process requirement. The court ruled that the plaintiffs have a property interest to which due process applies because under the state's welfare program benefits must be provided to those who meet the state's requirements, and does not allow unfettered agency discretion in determining who gets benefits (National Center for Law and Economic Justice, 2010).

In the Supplemental Security Income and Social Security Disability Insurance programs, the Social Security Administration often denies that a person is disabled. In a large number of such cases, an administrative law judge grants disability benefits to clients who appeal (Heller, 1981).

It is easier to appeal a decision in some agencies than in others. One person standing alone is always at a disadvantage when confronting an institution, but there are even more obstacles when that person lives in the institution and depends on it for food, clothing, shelter, and care (Handler, 1979).

Although children gained some due-process rights in the *Gault* case, they do not have the right to refuse institutionalization against their parents' wishes. The Supreme Court decided in the 1979 case *Parham v. J. L. and J. R.* that parents have the right to institutionalize their children without the children's consent. Justice Brennan, one of three dissenters, argued, "It is a blind assumption that parents act in their child's best interests when making commitment decisions" (Frank, 1980, p. 379). Should parents be given full control over their children? Until what age? Under what circumstances?

HELPING CLIENTS GET THEIR LEGAL RIGHTS

During the 1960s and early 1970s, clients' rights were greatly expanded through the organizing of grassroots groups, including:

- The Welfare Rights Organization
- The Mental Patients' Liberation Front
- Feminist health collectives
- Children's rights advocates

Although the rights they gained still don't necessarily fulfill all their needs, clients are slightly less powerless. In recent years, however, the government has been whittling down those gains. Federal legislation has cut out or weakened client-participation provisions that gave social service consumers a way to monitor and change programs that affected them.

Title I of the Elementary and Secondary Education Act, which provides enriched resources for educationally disadvantaged children, used to give parents a share in the schools' decision making. But recent legislation has weakened their role and only gives them a watered-down advisory role. Title XX of the Social Security Act, which provides for social services, has also weakened its consumer-participation provisions. Class-action suits, which represent an entire class of clients rather than just one individual, have been severely curtailed.

Due-process rights were significantly eroded in 1996 by both the Immigration Act and the Personal Responsibility Act. Immigrants who are deported or imprisoned have no right of appeal, and recipients of TANF are not guaranteed a right of appeal against unfavorable decisions by the federal law, although states may still allow it.

Strategies

Human service workers, on the frontlines with clients, must devise ever more ingenious strategies to help them secure their rights. Following is a description of some of these strategies:

1. *Human service workers need to be fully informed about their clients' legal rights, and they need to clearly inform their clients.* Reciting clients' rights at the beginning of your

working relationship is rarely enough. Clients are under stress when applying for benefits or services. They might not hear or understand your full meaning. They frequently need to be told about their rights again, in other contexts and with fresh emphasis.

Some advocacy groups publish booklets that spell out the rights of their constituents in clear, easy-to-understand language. If none exists in your area, consider helping your clients to write one.*

Legal services groups sometimes publish manuals, and welfare rights activists in several states are publishing newspapers to inform people of their rights. There are also nationwide advocacy groups that publish useful information about legislation and people's rights.**

2. *Even if you are convinced that you are correct in denying a particular benefit, you must remember that the client has the right to appeal a worker's decision.* A conscientious worker reminds the client of that right. Perhaps new evidence will come to light. Perhaps you made a mistake. An appeal is an opportunity to make sure a decision has been fair. If another agency has denied benefits to the client, the primary worker might investigate that denial, urging the client to appeal if there is a shadow of a doubt about the decision. The client may need help from a lawyer or an advocate to prepare or pursue the appeal. An updated resource file of legal services, advocates, and consumer groups is invaluable.

3. *The worker should encourage clients to learn as much as they can about their rights.* There are never enough low-cost legal services, so people will often need to defend themselves. Find out if there is a relevant self-help group that your clients can join. Welfare recipients, mental patients, adoptees, birth parents, adoptive families, divorced fathers, battered wives, people who are disabled, nursing-home residents, prisoners, families and friends of prisoners, and many others have advocacy groups that go to bat for clients.

4. *Human service workers can help in due-process hearings by interviewing participants, collecting evidence, and helping in the preparation of cases.* They also serve as **expert witnesses**, testifying in court on the basis of their specialized knowledge or experience in the field. If, for example, there is a question about whether a specific patient can

expert witness A person who is especially knowledgeable in a particular field and who is asked to give testimony based on that knowledge in a court trial.

---

*Survivors, Inc. (www.survivorsinc.org), a welfare rights group in Massachusetts, publishes a newspaper that includes a section called "Survival Tips," which gives information about benefits and rights.

**In the area of children's services, the Children's Defense Fund (www.chidrensdefense.org) publishes *CDF Reports*. The Gray Panthers (http://www.graypanthers.org) have been progressive activists in the field of aging and social justice since the 1960s. (This is actually an intergenerational organization.) The Older Women's League (OWL—http://www.owl-national.org) focuses on social justice issues affecting older women. Food Research and Action Center (http://www.frac.org) publishes information on food programs, including food stamps and school breakfast and lunch programs. The American Civil Liberties Union (ACLU—http://www.aclu.org) defends people and organizations against various kinds of injustice. The National Center for Law and Economic Justice (http://www.nclej.org—formerly the Welfare Law Center) focuses on economic justice for low-income families. Legal Momentum (www.egalmomentum.org) is sponsored by the Women's Legal Defense and Education Fund. They focus on women's poverty, immigrant women's rights, reproductive rights, the social safety net, and other women's issues.

manage his or her life outside the hospital, a worker in a community residence for the mentally ill could compare that patient with the residents he or she works with, establishing the likelihood of success or failure.

5. *Welfare rights advocates often advise welfare recipients to take someone with them to all their interviews at the welfare office.* A welfare recipient should take along a friend or advocate to lend support and to ensure fair treatment by the welfare worker.

6. *Workers who believe that an agency practice is harmful to a client must decide whether to challenge the agency or "go along to get along."* Often a professional organization will support the worker in challenging the agency. For example, the NASW gave a Whistleblowers Award and some legal assistance to a social worker who sued the U.S. Public Health Service (PHS). The worker, Donald Soeken, was forced to retire from PHS due to what he described as substantial animosity from his supervisors after he testified on behalf of a patient's family that the patient at St. Elizabeth Hospital was not treated in a timely fashion after the diagnosis of cancer ("Two Cases Given Legal Aid Grants," 2001).

In an innovative program called the Medical–Legal Partnership, lawyers have teamed up with doctors to help solve clients' problems. Dr. Barry Zuckerman, head of Boston Medical Center's pediatric department, started the program in 1993. It is now a national phenomenon, used in nearly 200 hospitals and clinics, with fifteen participating law firms.

Human service workers in a training session about legal issues and agency regulations.

The program first started in pediatrics, but it has expanded into cancer care and geriatrics, areas that involve extremely vulnerable patients.

For instance, cancer patients are legally entitled to less strenuous jobs when they are receiving and recuperating from treatment, but many are still forced to choose between their workday and their appointment for radiation. . . . Older people may be subject to abuse in nursing homes or by family members. (Weintraub, 2010)

The lawyers help in various ways. For example, lawyers connected to a hospital or clinic might write a letter encouraging a landlord to replace moldy carpeting that's triggering asthma attacks, assist families in getting food stamps and other government benefits, and obtain power of attorney for the parents of a severely disabled child who is turning 18. Dr. Peter Loewinthan Binah, a pediatrician at Dorchester House (a community center), said he used to send letters to landlords or a school district on behalf of patients. But when the law firm of Ropes & Gray sends out a letter, it gets more attention. He said, "If you're some landlord who isn't fixing up your apartment and get a letter from Ropes & Gray stationery, you know that one of the major law firms in Boston is going to stick it to you if you don't clean up." (Weintraub, p. 8)

SOME CURRENT LEGAL ISSUES

There are some hotly contested issues in the human services that, although they do not apply equally to all workers, have wide-ranging implications and should be thought about. These include the **right to treatment**, the right to treatment or education in the **least restrictive setting**, and the **right to refuse treatment**.

To help you visualize how a human service worker might be called on to deal with some of these issues, we present an interview with Donald Boucher, who worked in a mental hospital for adolescents while completing his undergraduate degree in social work.

> **right to treatment** Legal assurance that a person who is placed in an institution that purports to give treatment does, in fact, receive treatment.
>
> **least restrictive setting** The type of treatment and location that provide the greatest amount of freedom to a client (who often has a specific disability).
>
> **right to refuse treatment** Legal protection granted to a person who does not want treatment that is prescribed by professionals.

INTERVIEW

Donald Boucher, Mental Health Worker

Donald Boucher has worked as a mental health counselor at a private psychiatric hospital that has a seventeen-bed co-ed treatment program for youth ages 12 to 19 years. They stay from fourteen days to five or six months. The policies of the program are strict, based on firm limit and goal setting to modify behavior.

Donald's job was to help with the scheduled daily activities, to maintain the safety of the clients, and to enforce the rules. He believes that those rules are sometimes too strict and actually prevent genuine treatment. On two occasions, parents protested hospital practices because they believed that the treatment was harmful to their children. Donald describes these two situations:

1. A fourteen-year-old girl had a severe eating disorder called bulimia. She would vomit in front of staff and patients, sometimes at the dinner table. Because of her behavior, the other patients didn't want to be around her, and the staff was also repulsed by her actions.

The girl was placed in isolation in her room, with no contact with other patients and limited staff contact. She was not allowed to participate in group counseling sessions with her peers. She wasn't allowed to leave her room and had no individual counseling sessions while in isolation. She was punished in the hope that her negative behavior would be extinguished. Instead, she became more and more detached. She was kept isolated for about four months.

Her mother was outraged when she learned what was going on. She told the hospital that her daughter desperately needed to learn socialization skills, but instead she was isolated and ignored. She wasn't getting treatment she needed to overcome her illness.

The mother sent a letter to her hometown newspaper, and it was published. She also sent copies of the letter to politicians and others who she thought would be shocked to find out how the hospital is run. The newspaper called the hospital a "snake pit." This prompted an investigation, which resulted in some improvement.

2. The second case concerned a teenage girl who would behave violently even when no one provoked her. Once, for example, she began kicking a staff person in the head for no apparent reason. He just happened to be near her when she had this outburst. At other times, she was calm, rational, and very pleasant.

At this hospital, when clients behave positively, they earn more privileges. They climb a ladder of steps of increased privileges and freedoms, such as being able to go for a walk outside around the grounds. This particular client had climbed to a very high level. She was doing very well with her positive behavior. However, one act changed all this for her.

When the clients aren't actively involved in counseling sessions, they have to go to their rooms. They are not allowed to socialize with other clients outside supervised group sessions. One day this client, out of boredom, sat in the doorway of her room and was carrying on a conversation across the hall with another client. A staff person caught her doing this, reminded her of the rules, and told her to go inside her room and stop talking. Angry, she refused to move. She was then physically carried into her room. She kicked and screamed. She was then put in restraints and stripped of all the privileges it had taken her so long to earn.

Her family, who were very involved in her recovery, were upset by the punishment she received for such a small infraction of the rules. They wrote letters and made complaints, which resulted in an investigation.

One of the positive changes that came about as a result of both families' complaints was the creation of a common room where the clients can socialize and participate in recreational activities instead of staying isolated in their rooms. Also, the entire program became more humane, with less harsh punishment for minor infractions. Donald feels that the changes were a step in the right direction.

Right to Adequate Treatment

The patients' rights movement of the 1960s and 1970s asserted that mental hospitals and institutions for the retarded were more like prisons than hospitals. Patients, ex-patients, and their advocates turned to the courts for relief. The first "right to treatment" case,

Wyatt v. Stickney, was tried in Alabama in 1971. The court ordered the state social service officials to provide a specified quality of treatment for institutionalized mentally retarded people. The court argued that when a person is involuntarily committed without the same type of due process given even to criminals, that person has a *constitutional right to receive adequate treatment.*

A 1974 Florida decision, *Donaldson v. O'Connor,* asserted that if a person was dangerous, he or she could be committed involuntarily. But the state had a responsibility to give that person adequate treatment. Some other states followed suit, prohibiting involuntary commitment to a mental institution unless the person is a clear danger to self or others.

On June 18, 1982, the U.S. Supreme Court made a decision in *Youngberg v. Romeo* that established, for the first time, constitutional rights for people committed to institutions for the mentally retarded. It guaranteed a minimum level of training and development (Barbash, 1982).

The parents who protested the treatment their daughters received in the hospital where Donald Boucher worked probably knew they had a right to demand adequate treatment for their children. Their protest techniques succeeded in making the hospital more responsive, so they didn't have to go to court. The hospital knew that the parents had a legal basis for a suit if they chose that route. *Legal suits that establish precedents make it easier for people to bring about change without having to resort to costly and time-consuming suits.*

Right to Treatment in the Least Restrictive Setting

The right to be treated in the least restrictive setting means that the conditions should allow the most possible freedom. Implicit in the right to treatment is the constitutional issue of whether the state has the right to *force* treatment on people. The Fifth and Fourteenth Amendments to the Constitution specify that a citizen's liberty shall not be deprived except in accord with due process of law. When the state decides to provide a service for a particular group of disturbed or disturbing citizens, it must do so in a manner that restricts their basic liberties as little as possible.

In deciding what treatment to use, an agency and its workers must consider which treatment will do the least to restrict the client's full growth. Courts have applied this concept to residential mental health and mental retardation facilities, juvenile institutions, and educational facilities in the Education for All Handicapped Children Act. Perhaps you sat next to a pupil with a learning disability or physical impairment. It is this act that gave the student the right to occupy that seat.

The Education for All Handicapped Children Act requires that all children be "mainstreamed" into regular classrooms *whenever that is possible.* **Mainstreaming** means that schools must make every effort to put special-needs students in as normal a classroom setting as possible. Many hard-fought battles have raged between parents and their advocates and school systems, arguing about the definition of "the best setting" for a particular child. Teachers who aren't used to teaching children with disabilities have had to develop new skills. States and school systems have spent a great deal of money developing the facilities and expertise to incorporate children with special needs into public schools.

The Supreme Court ruled in 1999, in what is called the "*Olmstead* decision," that states may be violating the Americans with Disabilities Act if they provide care to people with disabilities in an institutional setting when they could be appropriately served in a home or

mainstreaming Putting people who have emotional or physical disabilities into the mainstream of society as much as possible. The Education for All Handicapped Children Act requires that all children be taught in regular schools and classrooms whenever possible.

community-based setting. This decision was made in regard to two women with developmental disabilities and mental illness who were residents of a psychiatric hospital, but it has been interpreted to extend to people with physical as well as mental disabilities, to those in nursing homes and other institutional settings in addition to psychiatric hospitals, and to those who live in the community and are at risk for institutionalization (General Accounting Office, 2001).

Right to Refuse Treatment

Efforts to force treatment on clients are problematic. Can the state insist on counseling as a condition for obtaining a divorce or retaining custody of a child, even though counseling requires trust and a readiness to change? There will be many court cases before this issue is resolved—if it ever is.

Mental patients have challenged the states' right to commit them to an institution and employ psychosurgery, shock therapy, aversion therapy, seclusion, restraints, drug therapy, or behavioral modifications that withhold food and privileges. Courts consider whether the patient was legally competent to be involved in a treatment decision, and if so, whether the institution obtained the patient's informed consent. Courts also consider whether the treatment is experimental or traditional and how intrusive and potentially dangerous it is. Psychosurgery, aversion therapy, and shock therapy, for example, are considered much riskier than other behavioral strategies.

The Importance of Written Plans

Written documentation of a treatment plan is often required. The Education for All Handicapped Children Act is very specific about such plans. Also, the Developmental Disabilities and Rights Act requires program plans for institutions and for individuals in community programs that receive federal funds. Whether or not law requires a written plan, it is helpful to have one because it ensures continuity of service (Burgdorf & Burgdorf, 1977).

SUMMARY

1. Many human service workers are unaware of their legal obligations. Human service training programs have often omitted such issues or have treated them superficially.

2. Federal laws apply equally to all states. Other laws vary from one state to another. Because laws change frequently, a human service worker needs to keep up-to-date on changes.

3. Laws are a resource; many human service programs were created by laws. In order to help clients obtain their entitlements, workers need to understand these laws.

4. After laws have been passed, a government agency draws up the regulations, which are the bureaucratic procedures that put the law into practice.

5. Some regulations are so restrictive that they make life very difficult for clients.

6. Some programs are governed by several government jurisdictions, and clients often get a bureaucratic runaround.

7. Some regulations are worded ambiguously, either intentionally or because bureaucrats are unable to

write clear English. If clients do not understand their rights, they are not likely to claim the rights.

8. People enmeshed in the legal system are often stigmatized. Human service workers need to combat this stigma.

9. There are some laws that every worker needs to know. These include laws concerning confidentiality, privileged communication, privacy, and due process.

10. In order to protect privacy, clients need to know what is said about them in records so they can correct the records if they want to.

11. Agencies comply with privacy laws to varying degrees. Those that are covered by federal privacy laws are more likely to allow open access to records, but they do not always comply with the law or inform clients of their right to read their records.

12. Open access to records causes workers to be more careful in their recording. There are pros and cons to an open-access policy. The authors favor open access.

13. Welfare recipients have few legal guarantees of privacy. The Parent Locator Service is particularly intrusive.

14. Privileged communication protects the confidences of the client–worker relationship in some cases, but it is not complete protection, nor is it extended to all professions in all states. The privilege belongs to the client, not to the worker.

15. The Patriot Act, passed shortly after 9/11, imperiled democracy by invading people's privacy and promoting governmental secrecy. President Obama asked for a change in the law that would allow the government to monitor people's web browsing.

16. Due process assures a client the right to disagree with a worker's decision. Most clients of human service agencies are granted only partial due-process procedures.

17. Human service workers should help clients appeal adverse decisions, which might be reversed on appeal.

18. Federal legislation is weakening or eliminating provisions that allow clients decision-making power in federal programs; therefore, self-help advocacy groups are increasingly important.

19. Workers should learn about clients' legal rights and inform clients about them.

20. Current legal issues that human service workers should be aware of include the right to obtain treatment, the right to treatment or education in the least restrictive setting, and the right to refuse treatment.

21. Written plans are often required by law, as is client involvement in writing them.

22. Criminal records frequently contain errors that make it impossible for people to get jobs and housing.

DISCUSSION QUESTIONS

1. Should parents be given full control over their children? If so, until what age? Under what circumstances?

2. What are the pros and cons of allowing clients to read their own records?

3. The state makes many intrusions into the privacy of welfare recipients but very few into the lives of children and their parents who receive Social Security. Why do you think this is? Do you think the state has the right to investigate the personal behavior of welfare recipients?

4. People with criminal records can be kept out of public housing and many kinds of jobs. They can also be prevented from voting. What do you think of this?

WEB RESOURCES FOR FURTHER STUDY

National Women's Law Center
http://www.nwlc.org
A staff of nearly sixty advances the issues that cut to the core of women's lives in education, employment, family and economic security, and health and reproductive rights—with special attention given to the needs of low-income women and their families.

Legal Momentum
www.legalmomentum.org
Legal Momentum is the nation's oldest legal defense and education fund dedicated to advancing the rights of all women and girls. Over the past forty years, Legal Momentum has made historic contributions through litigation and

public policy advocacy to advance economic and personal security for women.

Center for Law and Social Policy (CLASP)
www.clasp.org

CLASP seeks to improve the lives of low-income people. It develops and advocates for federal, state, and local policies to strengthen families and create pathways to education and work. Through careful research and analysis and effective advocacy, CLASP develops and promotes new ideas, mobilizes others, and directly assists governments and advocates to put in place successful strategies that deliver results that matter to people across America.

National Center for Law and Economic Justice
www.nclej.org

For the past forty-five years, the Center has led the way nationally in promoting economic justice, fairness and opportunity for those in need; securing systemic reform in the delivery of income support and related human services; and safe-guarding important legal and constitutional rights. The Center uses a coordinated strategy of impact litigation, policy analysis and advocacy, and support for low-income grassroots groups to: uphold the right to fair treatment; protect the civil rights of low-income people; and support community empowerment.

Find Law for the Public
http://consumer.pub.findlaw.com

Find Law for the Public offers extensive plain-English legal information, such as user-friendly articles, guides, forms, and FAQ pages to help people and businesses understand and deal with legal issues. Its resources include West Legal Directory, the Internet's largest directory of lawyers and legal professionals, as well as many resources for lawyers.

Chapter 15

Staying Current and Avoiding Burnout

The word *crispy* may not refer to crackers when human service workers use it; it may describe a burned-out worker. One of the authors first heard it at a college human service career day:

> I had invited two of my former students to talk about their human service jobs. The first, Kathie, was all fired up and spoke energetically about her work in child protection and foster care. Sure, she said, her job had its hard moments, but that did not stop her from doing a good job or figuring out ways to solve the problems.
>
> The second speaker, Brian, whom the teacher remembered as a bright and enthusiastic student, talked in a depressed monotone about the problems of his job that he felt were insurmountable. He droned on about his work as a probation officer in a juvenile court, complaining about large caseloads, ungrateful and manipulative clients, inadequate resources, coworkers who goofed off, other agencies that refused referrals, insensitive judges, and mountains of paperwork.
>
> After the speeches were over, I commented to Kathie about Brian's lack of enthusiasm. Kathie replied, "He's not just burnt out, he's crispy—for sure!"

Human service work draws on our deepest impulses to form important relationships and on our curiosity about what makes us think, feel, and act the way we do. It gives us a chance to laugh and play with people, to solve problems with them, to cry and grieve with them, to share the joy of their successes, to share their anger at injustice, and to work with them to change unjust systems. What job can be more important than that?

In fact, there is evidence that by helping others, people improve their mental health, their physical well-being, and even their longevity. A University of Michigan study of 423 elderly couples followed for five years found that the people who reported helping others—even if it was just giving emotional support to a spouse—were only about half as likely to die within those five years as those who did not. Another study of 2,000 Presbyterians found that improved mental health seemed to be more closely linked to giving help than to receiving it. A study of older people who volunteered in the Experience Corps to mentor elementary school pupils found that tutoring lead to measurable benefits for the volunteers, who showed improved physical activity and health compared with adults of similar age and demographics (Associated Press, 2010). However, when helping involves constant or exhausting demands, the toll it takes clearly outweighs any good it does (Goldberg, 2003).

Any work is exciting only as long as we are growing in it—expanding our self-awareness, learning more about the job, feeling good about our ability to do it, gaining more power over the conditions of work, and getting some measure of success from it. In order to grow, we need the following supports from our environment:

- Working conditions that make it possible to do our best
- Support and respect from our peers and supervisors
- Freedom from unconstructive criticism and control
- Ability to share in decision making
- Some stability

It is the same with flowers: They grow luxuriously only when they have the right conditions of sun, soil, and water; if those are lacking, they wilt and die. Continual change in the human service field brings excitement and adventure as well as tension. When the change is too rapid or when it brings a political climate that is unsympathetic, it is hard for workers to do their best work.

BURNOUT

The term *burnout* and the slang terms for its varying degrees of intensity have been coined to describe the mood that human service workers sink into when they have lost their spark. The concept has—to coin a pun—caught fire. Newspapers print articles about it, workshops and conferences are held on it, teachers' unions devote entire issues of their professional journals to it, books are written about it, and there are now "burnout experts." On January 3, 2011, there were about 13,600,000 references for "burnout" on Google.

Reed (1979) says that burnout "disproportionately strikes those in the helping professions—teachers, counselors, social workers. It's related to stress and can last for years. It's harmful physically to the individual and psychologically to all those around him" (p. 12).

Two terms that are related to and sometimes used interchangeably with burnout are *vicarious traumatization* and *compassion fatigue*. Vicarious traumatization is specific to trauma and results from empathic engagement with traumatized clients, and their reports of traumatic experiences. A worker may experience both vicarious traumatization and burnout, and each has its own remedies. *Compassion fatigue*, also known as a Secondary Traumatic Stress Disorder, is a term that refers to a gradual lessening of compassion over time. It is common among victims of trauma and individuals who work directly with victims of trauma (LPAC, 2006).

Symptoms of Burnout

Grey (1979) says these five symptoms of stress are common:

- Difficulty in sleeping
- Irritability
- Upset stomach

- Headaches
- Shortness of breath

Burnout may lead human service workers to stop caring about the people they work with, perhaps to sneer at them, laugh at them, label them, or treat them in derogatory ways. It causes workers to exaggerate differences between clients and themselves, seeing clients as "less good, less capable, and more blameworthy than themselves" (Maslach, 1978, p. 113).

Some workers escape their job by drinking or taking drugs or staying away from work—calling in sick or pretending to be at work when they are not. In place of enthusiasm, a sense of futility sets in. Some workers develop a callousness and cynicism to protect them from feeling anything. Behind this callousness may be an idealist who became overwhelmed by the job and stopped caring. Starting out with empathy for victims, the worker ends up being a victim blamer.

One woman who worked for the Save the Children agency during the war in Vietnam watched this process happen in herself. She said that when she went to Vietnam, she was fired up with enthusiasm about saving the victims of the war. But there was never enough medical staff, supplies, or equipment, and the destruction of war was too devastating for the staff to handle. In order to get even a few hours of sleep so they could start again the next day, they had to push the doors shut against the bodies of people screaming and pressing to get in for emergency medical treatment. She began to resent the people for their insatiable demands and for making her act like that. She never in her life dreamed that she would be slamming a door on people in such desperate straits. She had to go home to rebuild her sense of self.

CAUSES OF BURNOUT

There are at least two ways to analyze the phenomenon of burnout. One, based on individual psychology, emphasizes the emotional stress of working with problems that can reactivate the worker's unconscious childhood conflicts (Littner, 1957). The other approach, based on sociological theory, examines the social system in which human services are embedded and claims that the system itself creates the stresses. Karger (1981) argues that the very term *burnout* is misleading because it focuses on the subjective state of the individual. He would substitute the term **alienation**, a sociological term used to describe the way that the structure of a job distances people from their work, from each other, and from themselves. This would put the focus *on the organization and the larger society*. Both the psychological and the sociological points of view are correct, but they often ignore each other's insights.

alienation A sociological term used to describe the way the structure of a job or an organization distances people from their work, from each other, and from themselves.

Karl Marx used the term *alienation* to describe the process that happens to workers under the system of capitalism. His description matches closely the descriptions of burnout experts:

What constitutes the *alienation of labor?* The fact that labor is external to the worker, i.e., it does not belong to his essential being; that in his work, therefore, he does not affirm himself but denies himself, does not feel content but unhappy. Does not develop freely his physical and mental energy but mortifies his body and ruins his mind. The worker therefore only feels himself outside his work, and in his work feels outside himself. He is at home when he is not working, and when he is working he is not at home. His labor is therefore not voluntary, but coerced; it is forced labor. It is therefore not the satisfaction of a need; it is merely a means to satisfy needs external to it. Its alien character emerges clearly in the fact that as soon as no physical or other compulsion exists, labor is shunned like the plague. External labor, labor in which man alienates himself, is a labor of self-sacrifice, of mortification. (Tucker, 1972, p. 60)

Marx does not distinguish between skilled and unskilled workers. However, a worker who takes pride in her or his work because of its high quality is probably less likely to burn out than is an unskilled worker.

Alienation can affect anyone in any kind of work and with any status. One of the earliest researchers on it, Christina Maslach, says that today hedge fund managers are as likely to be burned out as any do-gooders. "In 21st-century New York, the 60-hour week is considered normal. In some professions, it's a status symbol. But burnout, for the most part, is considered a sign of weakness, a career killer" (Senior, 2007).

Psychological Conflicts

The powerful emotional stress and thorny problems that human service workers deal with daily often touch deep responsive chords in them: A worker who was neglected as a child may impute neglect when parents are merely casual in their parenting style; one whose parents were extremely strict may see the with fury at seemingly overdemanding parents. Many beginning workers are still dealing with their own issues of dependence and independence from family, mate, religion, and cultural group. Often it is difficult for them to sort out when their own struggles and those of their clients begin and end. For young workers, identification with the problems of teenagers or young adults can easily cross the line into **overidentification**.

Sometimes the goals of the work itself cause ambivalence and anxiety, even when the worker basically agrees with the agency's mission. You can feel strongly about the importance of protecting children from abuse, but accusing parents of perpetrating that abuse, and even removing children from their homes, can cause intense anxiety.

Workers in abortion clinics are also under emotional stress because of the nature of the work. Carol Joffe (1983) studied workers in one clinic and found that, even though the workers supported a woman's right to choose an abortion, they did not believe that abortion should be done as a method of contraception. They loved babies, were happy when a client decided to go through with her pregnancy, and were joyous when one of their own staff had a baby. They were more pro-choice than pro-abortion. Yet, in the embattled political atmosphere that surrounds abortion, they were forced to "cling, at least publicly, to a rhetorical pro-abortion position" (p. 318). The politics of abortion rights forced them into a rigidity they did not really feel, and this created stress.

overidentification
The process of relating so completely to another person's feelings and/or experiences that one cannot separate oneself from the other person.

Conflicting Social Values

Combined with these very personal stresses are the even more serious strains induced by the ambivalent values of our social system, which gives only grudging support to universal social services. Welfare workers are in the front line of this conflict. To illustrate how one worker deals with these conflicts, following is an interview with Rick Colbath Hess.

INTERVIEW

Rick Colbath Hess, Director of MassSERVE

Rick Colbath Hess is the founder of MassSERVE, an organization dedicated to improving the working conditions of human service workers. We present here an interview with him, conducted by a staff member of the Mass Human Services Coalition in October 2001 (Mass Human Services Coalition, 2001).

HSC: *We'd like to talk to you about the whole direct care worker crisis that's rampant throughout human services and in particular, what MassSERVE has been doing about it. So perhaps we could start by you giving a little background on the founding of MassSERVE.*

RC: Well, there were essentially a bunch of human service workers who came together who didn't feel like they had a voice in any other place. Their organizations were not unionized and they felt like they should have a voice in the political process and they came together and people were very upset about the working conditions and what was going on in the field and out of that came MassSERVE. That's the short version.

HSC: *Could you tell us a little bit about your own experience as a direct care worker? Or how you became involved in this cause and effort?*

RC: Sure. I've been in human services now for seventeen or eighteen years, I've worked with homeless people, I've worked with people with drug addictions, I've worked with people in food pantries, I've worked with program creation, and my last job was at Catholic Charities, and when I went around interviewing for that job, I went to many many different agencies and they were all dropping their personnel policies and going to "worker at will" provisions and I realized at the time that there was really a power shift in the dynamics of what was happening in the field and that people really didn't have much say at work because providers were also losing their say and it was trickling down to the workers. After working at Catholic Charities for three years I had children and—let me see how to say this—I was essentially demoted for trying to negotiate a child-friendly work schedule and there was really nowhere for me to turn for help, and out of that experience really came my organization. I ended up being laid off from that job and I started organizing MassSERVE and putting together a lot of people who had been talking around these issues.

Also in my internships at social work school, I saw how depressed everybody was. People were essentially responding the way they would respond to crisis, fight or flight. Half the staff was depressed in my internships and the other half was angry as hell and the energy was very misdirected. People did not seem to be able to respond to the political crisis at the time: the crisis of privatization, the degradation of human services, both at the service level and at the employee level.

HSC: *Well now MassSERVE has put forward a possible solution to the direct care worker crisis; the Human Services Worker Living Wage Bill. Could you tell us a little bit more about the genesis of the bill and what coalition has emerged in support of it?*

RC: Well, the bill came out of looking at the whole field, who was suffering the most, looking at research and seeing that when you push the bottom up, everybody else goes up too. And also following the Living Wage movement nationally and seeing what a success it's had and we had a number of goals at MassSERVE but we decided that wages were the most pressing at the time and we started working on developing a strategy around the living wage bill. And from that we were able to try to pull together—one of the advantages of the organizing that we're doing is that being a worker organization, we don't go directly after providers, we essentially view the state as the provider. Without moving the state you can't change much of the conditions in the work field. We were able to pull providers, unions and recipient groups together which has been a very hard thing and phenomenal kind of thing that came together.

HSC: *Well now there is a very large dollar amount attached to the Living Wage Bill, in the range of $100 million, what's it going to take to get the state to be willing to make that kind of investment? What do YOU think it's going to take to get that bill passed?*

RC: Well clearly . . . all salaries need to be upgraded, not just people at the bottom, there needs to be more training and possibly some kind of career ladder, [where] salary is tied to education and experience, that world view—I think there are many places in other parts of the world where it's a very professional field where you actually get trained and people get paid much higher. I think if it was looked at more professionally, then salaries would go up and that quality of care would go up. And I think that another one of the long-term strategies is essentially for the union providers and recipient groups to work together and to find their common ground to push for legislation to improve all their lots.

The Bind of the Double Message

As we discussed in Chapter 2, powerful forces are trying to dismantle most, if not all, government support for social welfare. As a result, "social workers are caught between the privatization of profits and the socialization of the costs from that profit making" (O'Connor, 1973, cited by Arches, 1991).

The human service profession is built on a **humanitarian ethos**, but everyone in our society does not fully subscribe to it. And therein lies the conflict. Communities rarely provide the full resources of money, time, and caring to allow the human service worker to do the kind of job that needs to be done. One writer says that the modern welfare state has converted the ideal of service into cynicism or self-serving **careerism** (building your career at the expense of other values). This has made some committed and idealistic workers so disillusioned that they leave public service. This in turn makes it less likely that agencies will change, because the most idealistic workers often leave.

Workers face many double messages in this country. They are continually in conflict about whether to help clients summon their energies for change or to make the client more

humanitarian ethos
A dedication to promoting the welfare of humanity, especially through the elimination of pain and suffering.

careerism   A single-minded preoccupation with getting ahead in a career to the exclusion of other interests or values.

obedient in order to fit better into the agency's way of "helping." They may want to advocate for their clients to get more services, but the agency, with an eye on the budget, probably wants to limit services. Workers may want to work with clients as allies in shaping the policies and practices of the agency, but the agency does not encourage input from clients or alliances between workers and clients. Although the agency proclaims its desire to "help," that help may merely mean manipulation. All of these contradictions mirror the ambivalence society has about its poor.

> It is the front-line worker who is called upon to broker these contradictions and rationalize them to the client and to her or himself. . . . Public defenders committed to the ideal of providing the indigent with legal representation find themselves in court without time even to interview the client, let alone prepare adequately. Teachers find that the more pressing the need for creative classroom instruction, the more likely is the school to be overcrowded, and the more inundated the teacher is with disciplinary and housekeeping chores. When welfare workers in Massachusetts are assigned the statutory maximum of 180 cases (and others stack up, uncovered), or when judges have dozens of cases to dispose of daily, the possibility of personalized assessment becomes submerged in the need to process the work.
>
> Although public agencies empowered under various legislative acts are required to serve everyone who is eligible, they often cannot do so with their limited resources. Some react to this imbalance by devising ways to keep people from applying for service and by delivering an inaccessible or inferior product. Public programs often cannot charge fees, but they can set "prices" by inflicting indignities such as requiring long waits or limiting information.
>
> Obviously, these techniques contradict the ostensible program goals. Yet a worker who provides superior service will be rewarded only with additional clients. Greater availability or quality of services like health care, or greater accessibility of effective counseling to families in crisis, simply attracts more customers and harder cases. Adding capacity fails to solve the worker's perennial problem of inadequate resources (although it may in fact extend mediocre service to more people).
>
> The worker in public welfare programs confronts the dilemma of the fabled highway planner of the congested Long Island Expressway. The engineers kept adding additional lanes on the theory that this would alleviate traffic jams. However, the increased capacity only attracted more drivers, so that congestion was perpetuated, albeit at higher traffic levels. (Lipsky, 1980a, pp. 33–34)

Agencies respond to this pressure by following the Peter Principle (which suggests that services expand until they reach the point of mediocrity). More people may be served, but they are not served well. Agencies often sacrifice their original service goals in order to meet their bureaucratic needs. For example, when the job market shrinks, vocational placement agencies change their objectives from finding people jobs to "job counseling."

The recession has resulted in cutbacks in human service programs. Many services have been eliminated completely, and some have had severe cutbacks in staff. A medical social worker in a hospital says that the most frustrating part of her job is the fact that there are so few services to refer people to when they are ready for discharge from the hospital.

Increased Bureaucratization

Bureaucracy has become pervasive within the past few decades, and social agencies too have followed that trend. Increased bureaucratization means more centralization, more hierarchical control, larger workplaces, and decreased autonomy for workers. "Authority and discipline imposed by sponsors undermine autonomous input. Rigidly enforced and scheduled work hours and quotas are common" (Arches, 1991, p. 202).

Butler studied 404 members of the Virginia National Association of Social Workers in 1986 to assess job satisfaction. Not surprisingly, she found that workers who had high levels of daily frustration and emotional intensity, excessive bureaucratic demand, and too much paperwork were less likely to be satisfied (Butler, 1990). Those who worked in large agencies were also less satisfied. Thirteen percent of the workers studied had a full-time private practice, and 17 percent had a part-time private practice. Butler says that small groups give better support to coworkers and have less bureaucratic red tape. Social work managers in large bureaucratic organizations need to find ways to organize their work units into smaller groups (p. 25).

Low Salaries and Decreased Satisfaction

A factor that caused discontent among some workers in Butler's study was low salaries, which was apparently one reason that some workers left agency work to go into private practice. Other studies show that in social work, men are more satisfied with their jobs than women. Men's salaries are consistently higher than those of women in both service and administration positions.

Insurance and Government Reimbursement

When insurance companies dictate the kind of treatment to be given and the way of giving it, workers no longer decide how the work gets done. This affects social workers in private practice as well as in agencies. Private insurance companies reimburse only for psychotherapy, diagnosis, and evaluation. They do not reimburse for marital counseling unless the client is given a diagnosis from what has become the "bible" of diagnosis, the *DSM-IV*—the *Diagnostic and Statistical Manual of Mental Disorders*, fourth edition (Text Revision) (American Psychiatric Association, 2000). Every request for reimbursement in any field of practice must be accompanied by a diagnosis from *DSM-IV*. This means that much of our work is not reimbursable, including nursing-home placements, foster care, client-related meetings, and advocacy.

Even when a practice is reimbursable, the insurance company sets the time limits. Workers make cynical jokes about "sixty-day miracle cures" for psychiatric patients. They are discharged as "cured" from the hospital when the insurance runs out, whether or not they act or feel cured. However, the Health Care Reform bill of 2010 includes a provision that people will no longer have a lifetime limit or "cap" on insurance coverage.

Workers may not be able to choose the treatment of choice because of insurance requirements. "For example, if only 12 visits are reimbursable, then planned short-term therapy is likely to be used whether or not it is deemed clinically the best treatment by the social worker"

(Ortiz & Bassoff, 1988, p. 116). Medicare establishes time limits for treatment of each diagnosis under its system of diagnosis-related groups (DRGs). Ethical dilemmas abound:

> In some agencies, social workers are encouraged to double-book clients so that the outside coverage will still pay for the worker's time if one of the clients does not show up. If both show up, someone is forced to cool their heels in the waiting room. In other settings, social workers are pressured to drop clients who do not show up for two consecutive appointments. (Arches, 1991)

Arches (1991) studied 275 registered social workers in Massachusetts in 1988 to assess their level of job satisfaction and burnout and found that one source of stress was that agencies have several financial sponsors, and each sponsor has different demands. The workers in her study "reported working in agencies with an average of five external sponsors" (p. 203). For example, a family agency might receive money from several insurance companies, Medicaid, Medicare, state contracts, and the federal government. The agency is responsible to each of these sources of money, and the worker must comply with their demands as well as the agency's demands.

Time Pressures

When there is not enough time, the helping impulse may become extinguished. Careful listening takes time and patience. In fact, according to a Princeton University study, time is one of the most important reinforcers of the helping impulse (Shenker, 1971).

In the study, three groups of theological seminary students were given a speech to read at a nearby building. On the way to the building, they encountered a man lying on the ground acting as if he were suffering (this was arranged by the researchers). One group of seminarians was told they had plenty of time; another, just enough time; and another, that they were already late. The ones who stopped to help most often were the ones with the

© 2003 Randy Glasbergen   www.glasbergen.com

"I'd like to schedule a time management seminar on my calendar...as soon as I find time to buy a calendar. "

most time (63 percent of "low hurry," 45 percent of "intermediate hurry," and 10 percent of "high hurry" men stopped). The researchers speculated that in the biblical parable of the Good Samaritan, the Samaritan, being a man of low public status, had little important business to attend to, so that he had the time to help. One could imagine the priest and Levite, "prominent public figures, hurrying along with little black books full of meetings and appointments, glancing furtively at their sun dials as they go" (Shenker, 1971, p. 25).

Lack of Resources Outside the Agency

Even if workers are lucky enough to be at an agency with enough money to hire competent staff, keep caseloads to a manageable size, and provide good supervision and a supportive environment, they are not home free. As long as other agencies are not as lucky, the impact is still felt by the clients and workers of all agencies. In the following narrative, Priscilla Shade (1981) tells of how state cutbacks in medical benefits to General Relief recipients affected her work in the welfare department:

> What this left workers like me to cope with were cases like the man who'd had surgery of the colon, who, with medical benefits cut, couldn't afford colostomy bags—life-sustaining medical supplies—because he got so little money on General Relief. He'd come in the office and get sick right there. Of course I was hysterically dumping him and clients like him back on City Hospital. At the hospital they went crazy from the patient overload. It also put the doctors there in the position of seeing a patient who may not have been disabled for the minimum of thirty days that was required for eligibility, but the doctor knew the patient would have nothing to eat if he didn't say he or she was disabled for thirty days. So all of a sudden, doctors were put in a position of having to lie for the client: they were caught right in the middle. (p. 28)

Shade goes on to describe how her work was affected when the state eliminated General Relief for the unemployed:

> Those clients who were merely unemployed and now cut off from General Relief began to reappear with a variety of illnesses related to their mental state. This meant an additional burden for caseworkers. In the end, clients got no "stopgap" assistance for unemployment, caseworkers were saddled with heavier "crisis" caseloads, the state footed a higher bill—and no one was helped. (p. 30)

Shade also describes how the housing shortage forced workers to do "shelter shuffling," sending deinstitutionalized mentally ill homeless people from one shelter to another because of the differing eligibility criteria of shelters, and how workers are caught in the middle of contradictory agency policies. She tells how at one point the state provided professional services to clients while ignoring their basic needs for food and shelter:

> When I worked in the services division I learned to beg, borrow, and steal. I got to know a lot of people and I got to know where I could beg this, where I could borrow that, and where I could get $5 for groceries. I depended on the private agencies. I went outside the system. It strained every resource I could ever think of—even my own pocketbook. I was broke every week. (p. 30)

Lack of Support from the Agency

A worker's frustrations in the face of inadequate resources can be eased when the agency goes to bat for its workers, helping them do the job despite problems. But if the agency *blames* the workers for its own inadequacies (as sometimes happens), workers are likely to feel angry, guilty, and depressed. Some government funding sources and agency bureaucracies have tried to deal with their workload problems by introducing management methods that stress **accountability** and speeded-up work.

accountability A requirement, usually imposed by a funding source, that an agency perform according to a certain set of standards.

Agencies are increasingly under the gun for accountability and effectiveness. This can cause anxiety that sometimes interferes with doing quality work because of the new concern with quantity and numbers. Although workers should always be concerned about their effectiveness, attempts to prove effectiveness in narrowly conceived mechanical ways can be useless at best and intimidating at worst. Workers may have to write down the way they spend every minute of the day in an efficiency study. New managers and management techniques come and go. The concern with numbers and quantification can lead people to adopt techniques they are not comfortable with and use them in absurd ways.

Buckholdt and Gubrium (1979) studied a children's residential treatment institution that had adopted behavior modification as its treatment method because its funding sources insisted on some numerical proof of effectiveness. Behavioral modification offered more precision than the psychodynamic strategies the institution had previously used. The actual treatment seemed to continue more or less as it had before—loving and caring and time-consuming, the days filled with activities. It was probably one of the best-run institutions in the area, perhaps the nation. Yet the workers, anxious to prove their effectiveness, became preoccupied with quantifying the children's behavior—how many temper tantrums, how many refusals to do homework, how many small thefts—in an effort to prove that they had solved these problems.

We return to Priscilla Shade's (1981) account of her work in the welfare department to illustrate how an agency can subvert a worker's desire to help people:

> The worst thing was that the worker was caught in the middle—caught in the contradictions of programs that provided, for instance, job counseling to clients when there was little hope of employment. Then, too, workers were faced daily with programs that provided preventive health screening for children; while other policies cut down on the amount and quality of food that could be purchased by the family. In effect, well-intentioned programs were being established while other policies undermined them. Those of us whose job was to help people found ourselves working in a system that did not allow it. (p. 30)

Pressures Exerted by Clients

Workers are not the only ones who become angry and frustrated when resources are inadequate or rules are restrictive. Clients feel the same but often express their negative reactions to the worker because that is the person who face-to-face denies them the resources they need. The legislators who voted the inadequate funding are shadowy figures. Today, the worker not only has to face clients' anger but also has to face continual value dilemmas.

In an effort to help their clients find the resources they need for survival, workers often devise their own methods of playing the system, or they look the other way as their clients do so. One British author describes the kinds of dilemmas that workers face daily:

> How many social workers, for example, ignore the illegal fiddling of some of their clients against the Department of Health and Social Security, an organization which social workers surely see as being unkind to themselves as well as to their clients? How many probation officers turn a blind eye to the breaches of the probation order by offenses of their clients? How many social workers simply do not care about the fact that a client earns a pound or so more than social security regulations permit by working behind a pub bar at night? These are questions to which we do not know the answers, and perhaps nothing more than discretion will prevent us from ever knowing. But our commonsense knowledge tells us, as insiders to the codes and signals of the profession, that the social worker sometimes serves the function of a . . . Robin Hood who, if he is not actually robbing the rich to feed the poor, is aiding and abetting the offense. (Pearson, 1975, p. 21)

A few welfare workers, on the other hand, regard bureaucratic rules with almost religious reverence and are on the lookout even during their leisure time for clients who are working part time without reporting their wages.

INVOLUNTARY CLIENTS

Some clients are angry because they never asked to be clients, and they fight their client status every step of the way. Such **involuntary clients** include parents accused of child abuse and neglect, juvenile or adult offenders who are imprisoned or on probation, involuntarily committed mental patients, some old people in rest homes or nursing homes, children in treatment programs, and people caught driving under the influence of alcohol. Through patient and empathetic work, many of these people can be encouraged to participate, and some end up being genuinely grateful for the worker's intervention. Some continue to resist even the most patient and caring of workers.

involuntary clients Clients who are forced to use a social service, usually by a court.

T. S. Szasz (1965), a psychiatrist who thought and wrote a great deal about the involuntary status of clients, argued that when the power differential inherent in the relationship is made clear and explicit, both you and the client can deal more honestly with each other. Some human service work is used for social control, so it is important to distinguish between social control and social service, both for theoretical clarity and to help us understand our relationships with clients. Clients of probation officers or parole officers may regard their workers as police officers who are not to be trusted. Child-protection workers investigating an abuse complaint should not be surprised if they are also regarded as police officers, because they are symbolically entering a client's home with the long arm of the law.

Stigma, Discrimination, and Status Ranking

The poor, the physically disabled, the retarded, the mentally ill, and the prisoner are often stigmatized by the larger society. People who work with them find that some of that stigma rubs off on them. Workers may often discover this when telling their friends or relatives about the nature of their jobs. Perhaps they have just gone on a home visit in a very poor section of town, or they have just gone to court with a youthful offender accused of a violent crime. People may say, "Aren't they dirty?" "Why do you want to help him?" Some people can brush off these remarks, which only reinforce their commitment. Yet such constant reminders of the low social esteem in which their daily tasks are held can be demoralizing.

The public often makes distinctions between and within groups of people, continuing the age-old stereotypes of "deserving" and "undeserving" clients. Among the least stigmatized are the more affluent clients who take their interpersonal problems to the offices of private psychiatrists. Among the most stigmatized are the drug addicts and alcoholics who live and socialize on the local skid row. Because human service workers are part of the same society that creates these stigmas, they also sometimes measure their clientele by the same yardstick.

A stigma is effective only if you believe it. Rick Colbath Hess and many other workers refuse to accept the stigma that society puts on clients and the people who work with them. Rick sees all people as equally valuable and does not divide his clients into "deserving" and "undeserving." Nor does he consider his social status diminished because he works with stigmatized clients.

Added to the stigma problem is the status problem. There are often sharp and painful status differences between professionals within an agency. A worker with an associate's degree from a community college may be doing exactly the same work and doing it just as competently as a worker with a Bachelor of Social Work (BSW) degree from a four-year college; yet the pay for the associate's degree worker will probably be less, the possibility of being promoted without further credentials may be nil, and—to rub even more salt into the wound—the BSW worker might even be insensitive enough to remind the worker with the associate's degree of the supposed superiority of the BSW degree.

Dealing with Danger

Human service workers usually work with poor people, and some of them live in neighborhoods that contain some violence. Naturally, a worker wants to avoid violence, yet needs to work in those neighborhoods. When a worker shows excessive anxiety about it, disproportionate to the reality, clients can interpret that as contempt or hostility toward all the people who live in the neighborhood. Yet some caution is realistic, and clients know that better than anyone else. They can give you good advice about taking precautionary steps. It is important to establish collegial relationships with neighborhood people so they trust you and show concern for your safety, just as you are concerned for their safety.

Human service workers have sometimes been assaulted by their clients, and even murdered. Health care and social services workers have a high incidence of assault injuries. Definitions of violence vary, depending on the person doing the defining. Some people consider a verbal threat to be violence, while others do not. The most prevalent form of violence is verbal threat (Kadushin, 1992). Physical assaults are not as prevalent. Research shows that young and relatively inexperienced staff are at greatest risk of client assault in community residential mental health programs (Flannery, Fisher, & Walker, 2000; Flannery et al., 2001).

Child-protection work is especially dangerous because parents sometimes react violently when a worker threatens to take away their children. In 2007 in Massachusetts, nineteen Department of Social Service workers reported that they had been physically assaulted on the job, and five of those assaults resulted in injuries: for example, when a client punched a social worker in the face in a courtroom, or when someone hit a social worker in the side of the head with a rock while that worker was knocking on a client's door (Badkhen, 2008).

Most agencies offer their staff strategies to stay safe. The Massachusetts Department of Social Services has installed fortified glass in the reception areas at most field offices. In one office, a police officer sits in the lobby once a week. Social workers schedule meetings with potentially threatening clients for the day the police officer is on duty. The department also instructs its workers to always go in pairs when they investigate reports of child abuse or neglect. If the workers believe that they are at risk, they can ask police officers to accompany them (Badkhen, 2008).

Workers often deny that they can become victims at the hands of their clients, thereby overlooking the potential for danger (Maier, 1996). This leaves them more vulnerable because they do not take realistic steps to protect themselves, and it also denies the agency information that they could use to help protect workers. Your agency has a responsibility to keep you safe and you should expect, even demand, practices that protect you from possible danger and that give you support when you encounter a threatening situation. You should expect support from your supervisor and from your colleagues. Sometimes colleagues are not as supportive as they should be because they want to deny that the same thing could happen to them. None of us is invulnerable, and we all need support.

Hazards of the Work

Most human service workers go into the field because they have ideals and a vision about helping people and optimism about the possibilities of change. This is an absolute requirement for the work; when ideals die and turn to cynicism, that is burnout. Yet an occupational hazard for human service workers is that the desire to be of help can turn into a rescue fantasy—a belief that they have to do it all, and if clients don't change in a desired way, the worker has failed:

> No matter how much you care, show concern, or even love, students will quit, inmates will mess up, patients will die, depressives will commit suicide, and parolees will violate the conditions of their paroles. It's natural to feel that a portion of the failure is your responsibility. Maybe you really did the best you could. If you had to do it over again, perhaps you would do some things differently. Perhaps that will help you with the next challenge. Failure is especially hard on the new staff member who is fired up with humanitarian zeal to help, to give, and to serve. Your own well being and sanity may be at stake if you accept more than your portion of any failures. (Russo, 1980, pp. 157–158)

Even workers who do not succumb to rescue fantasies or the need to be omnipotent in clients' lives can be dragged under by the sheer weight of people's problems, many of which may be essentially unsolvable. Sometimes the feelings of helplessness and of being overwhelmed come from the simple fact that life is often painful and that some pain cannot be removed, some problems cannot be solved, and the best you can do is simply reach out and show that you care. Here is an account of one student's feelings about the pain of the human drama in her fieldwork:

> Sometimes when I go into the home and I haven't been there for a while, I'm almost afraid to ask, "Well, how are things with you, Mrs. J.?" I know that she'll begin to catalogue all the things that are wrong with her. Her health is really in a terrible state, and it's hard for her to get used to all the tubes and bags and the feelings that she can't do anything by herself. And then she'll tell me that her son didn't show up after he swore he would. And, damn him, why can't he visit once in a while? She seems like she's such a decent person and she really cares about him. A visit would make such a difference in her morale, but I can't drag him in, and what can I say to her to make it okay—that he is just too busy with his own life to visit a sick old lady, the person who raised him and looked after him when he needed it?

For all of us, there is often a wide gap between what we wish we could do and what we can do. As human service workers, this gap can be particularly painful when we feel we are behaving differently with our clients than we were taught to behave in our college classes. Human service workers can lament, along with doctors, that no one comes to see them when they are feeling good. In some ways that is true. We often encounter people at their worst, when they are the most abusive, discouraged, depressed, overwhelmed, and angry. Frequently they have already had their problems for many years. Inadequate housing, poor schools, bad marriages, and destructive parenting patterns did not appear overnight and will not disappear overnight; so several things happen. Our clients often slip back into destructive patterns of behavior even after they see other possibilities. An alcoholic adult may make a hundred vows that will probably be broken and cover each with a hundred excuses—the same ones we ourselves use when we explain why we have abandoned our exercise program again or have broken our diets:

- I'm not really hooked.
- I'll just do it one more time to get me through this hard stretch.
- When things calm down, I'll stop drinking (overeating, taking dope, being beaten or beating).
- Just one more binge, and then I'll quit!

The parent council that quite justifiably complained that no one ever listened to their opinions before still has barely a quorum even though you are committed to not submitting the next budget without their approval. You really, really mean to share the power with them yet they still don't show up in any significant numbers. So here you sit, making the decisions for them!

Often when our clients are feeling better about their lives and possibilities, they take off, and we never know just how well they are doing and how well we did with them. Sometimes they even need to deny that we were of any help to them at all. Sometimes we encourage them to feel their own sense of power by minimizing the contributions we may have made. But being human and having our own needs for stroking, we can at times get angry at them when they fall back into old behaviors or seem to be rejecting us or putting down the help we have given them.

Living life fully as a handicapped person and as the parents or caregivers of handicapped young adults takes genuine courage. An array of tennis stars at a tournament celebrate two young people they dubbed, "the True Champions." The tennis players are McEnroe, Martin, Cash, Courier, Ivanisevic, and Wilander.

Some days being a human service worker can be a thankless task. You have to look in the mirror and say, "Hey, I just did a damn good piece of work!" You'll probably have a supervisor, coworker, or good friend who gives you strokes for your good work just in case you don't get them from anyone else. We shouldn't need to be constantly thanked and fussed over, but we are all human and need a small pat on the back from time to time.

SOME LESS-THAN-IDEAL REACTIONS TO STRESSFUL CONDITIONS

Some ways of reacting perpetuate feelings of powerlessness, and others help workers to gain power and autonomy for themselves and their clients. The following five common reactions illustrate the least creative ways of coping with job stress; they do not involve an active struggle to take charge and master one's work environment (Wenocur & Sherman, 1980).

Total Capitulation

A patient in the hospital where she worked asked Ginny, a social service aide, if he could look at his medical records. Ginny said she'd ask her supervisor, who promptly said, "No. Patients have never been allowed to look at their records. That's our policy. We've always done it this way." That made sense to Ginny. If things had always been done that way, that's the way she wanted to do them, too. All her life she had tried hard to do things the way other people did them. She had only to pick up a slight cue from her parents, her teachers, her minister to set her on the straight and narrow path; she never rocked the boat. Needless to say, Ginny never went out on a limb to fight for patients' rights to read their records or for anything else. She simply closed off whatever empathy she had brought to the job and spent a lot of time shuffling papers. She lasted a long time.

Total Noncapitulation

In the course of his twenty-two years, Rafael had variously been described as a "maverick," an "agitator," a "radical," "unrealistic," and "immature." In his job at the Department of Welfare, he was constantly furious at the bureaucracy, "the stupid regs," "the dumb supervisor," "the crummy welfare grants," and "the stupid, greedy, and corrupt legislators" (and he used other, less printable terms). He always agreed with his clients when they railed against the system; yet he never controlled his anger long enough to analyze the system or to help his clients understand it or work to change staff attitudes or regulations. His radical friends described him as a "rebel without a cause," not the kind of radical who got to the roots of problems. Rafael was fired after six months on the job; he had achieved little positive change but was well on the way to his first heart attack.

Niche Finding

After Bisi finished college, she got a job at the county Department of Child Welfare, where she was given a caseload of eighty foster children, plus their foster and birth parents. The workload overwhelmed her; she could never get on top of it. In the morning, she reached in her box to take out the telephone messages written on pink memo slips that had piled up when she was out in the field the day before. She held her breath as she read them, hoping she wouldn't find the dreaded message from a foster parent—"Take Johnny out today. I can't stand him a minute longer!" or "Susie's run away. Call the police!" As she reached the point of being unable to stand it anymore, the agency offered her a special intake job, with a lower caseload. One can certainly understand Bisi's finding a safe niche for herself—any one of us might do the same. Workers like Bisi find an area of expertise or a special position in the organization.

If workers concentrate only on their particular niche, they gain real but limited power in one small segment of an agency, but they have opted out of trying to change the entire agency. However, it is also possible that, having found a job that uses her full talents, Bisi will have more energy to devote to changing the agency.

Becoming a Victim Martyr

Following is a narrative by one worker who tried to do too much:

> We were so terribly understaffed when I first went to work at the recreation center that I found myself doing everything from running the dance to cleaning up afterwards. It killed me to have to keep saying "no" to the kids every time they'd come up with something they wanted to do. So, little by little, I'd give in—one weekend it would be a camping trip, another a disco party, and soon I realized I'd worked seven Saturday nights in a row. Well, my boyfriend was getting really annoyed. He's a computer programmer who works very hard but doesn't take his work home with him, so on the weekends he's ready to play. I dragged him with me when I took the kids places, and he was terrific with them, but he began resenting the fact that we were never alone.
>
> After a while I also began to miss the closeness we used to have. I got flak from other friends, too—they'd want to talk with me and I'd be falling asleep from sheer physical exhaustion. Suddenly I realized that at 23 I didn't have the stamina of my 14-year-old group members. I also realized that I still had to clean my apartment and do the laundry, and my world was getting messier and messier. Somehow I got through that summer, but in the fall I told the director that this center absolutely had to have more staff if it was really going to respond to the neighborhood kids. I knew I was falling apart and couldn't keep up the one-handed tennis match much longer.

This worker quickly fell into the trap of being a "victim martyr," believing that she had to fulfill totally all the tasks the agency claimed it was doing. The job was impossible to do by herself, but she believed the implicit message of the agency that she had to do it. This is sometimes called a double bind—a person is given two contradictory messages. She obeyed the part of the message that said, "You must do it because we say that's what we do" but was continually facing the other message: "But you can't do it—no one can alone." Until she faced that issue with the agency, she was unable to lead a well-balanced life of her own.

Some victim martyrs have the additional burden of working in agencies where the clients are angry and powerless. The victimized workers identify with the clients' anger and powerlessness, feeling the same themselves, but then get stuck in a powerless position and feel unable to change the system (Wenocur & Sherman, 1980).

It is easy to be sucked into the role of victim martyr, because most workers genuinely want to help and place high demands on themselves. Knowing our limits helps both us and the agency to face reality in a constructive way.

Withdrawal

Many workers withdraw from the overwhelming pressures of their jobs by quitting. This may sometimes be a move that is essential for the worker's mental health, yet, it doesn't change anything for the agency or the workers (Wenocur & Sherman, 1980).

Mixed Reactions

Although we have described these five reactions as "pure types," people are more complex than that and generally react in various ways to their jobs. Priscilla Shade, for example, fought valiantly for her clients for a time but finally felt that it was hopeless and quit the job to be a full-time mother. Here is her description of that process:

> I dealt with the welfare department's Wonderland-like working conditions by venting my anger. I raved a lot. I screamed. I called Legal Aid. I exerted political pressure. I went and testified in district and federal courts against rulings that affected clients. In the instance where medical benefits were cut from General Relief, I and a group of co-workers went to our state legislator. His assistant, who also had contacts in the human services department, had been told that people were dying for lack of medical benefits. So in six weeks the legislature—without going through the usual public hearings—restored medical benefits to people who were on General Relief. . . . In the end, though, the workers and clients were driven apart. This is what happened to me. Slowly I was going down. And no matter what I did, the policy makers were going to come up with some beaut tomorrow that would put me three feet behind where I was the day before. So when the baby sitter who was taking care of my child suddenly got sick, I decided I'd be a full-time mother again. . . . Even with the best of intentions, programs don't work when they're erratic, underfunded, and understaffed. And starting new programs while crippling others will not help. Ultimately, client advocacy is not an option for the line worker: it is a requirement. For only advocacy will enable workers to obtain the means to do their job, hopefully in a decent and humane way. (Shade, 1981, p. 31)

STAYING ALIVE—POSITIVE ADJUSTMENTS

The major responsibility for avoiding staff burnout rests with the administration: this is what administrators are paid to deal with (Weissman, Epstein, & Savage, 1983, p. 301). Just as workers are held accountable for their work, agencies too should be held accountable. Weissman (1973) believes that agencies avoid examining their own efficiency and effectiveness by focusing on the efficiency and effectiveness of their employees, and he recommends "bottom up" evaluations, that is, having workers evaluate their supervisors and directors as well as the other way around. We would add to this that clients should also be routinely asked to evaluate both their workers and the agency.

Combating Stress

The welfare department is particularly vulnerable to shifts and contradictions in social policy, and those of course are reflected in the workplace. However, even within the constraints imposed on them by the legislature, courts, and governor's office, managers of welfare offices have some options. They do not have to operate according to the "dixie cup—use them up and throw them away—school of management" (Bramhall & Ezell, 1991, p. 33). There are many things they can do:

1. They can take principled stands with the legislature and governor against policies that limit their ability to help people.

2. They can enlist workers in advocacy for clients and encourage alliances between workers and clients.

3. They can go to bat for higher pay and better working conditions for workers.

4. They can set up **support groups** in which workers can share their feelings and frustrations with each other and brainstorm to solve problems in the agency.

5. They can recognize the pressure that workers are under and give them encouragement and support.

6. They can involve the frontline staff as partners in decision making and create smaller and more intimate work groups.

7. They can pay attention to workers' stress levels and do whatever is necessary to keep them from burning out, including:
   Varying a worker's tasks
   Instituting flex time
   Limiting a person's work hours
   Keeping a roster of on-call workers to maintain client–staff ratios during periods of absenteeism
   Providing carefully graduated levels of responsibility for new staff
   Streamlining paperwork

8. They can make the workplace surroundings as pleasant and clean as possible. (Bramhall & Ezell, 1991)

9. They can set up child care space in the waiting room and enlist volunteers to care for children of waiting clients.

10. They can involve clients in decision-making bodies.

support groups
Groups in which members help each other to clarify or act on certain issues.

According to one study by psychologists, political activism can even make you happier. Two university psychologists, Malte Klar and Tim Kasser, interviewed two sets of around 350 college students, both about their degree of political engagement and their levels of happiness and optimism. They found that those most inclined to go on a demo were also the cheeriest. "The study flies in the face of the popular wisdom that happiness resides in creature comforts and relative affluence. Perhaps activism gives people a sense of purpose, or of agency, or just a chance to hang out with other people. Most likely it does all of the above" (Charkrabortty, 2010).

Problem Solving

Administrators are under the gun to save money and are responding to pressure. They often lose sight of both workers' and clients' needs. Everyone in an agency needs to be involved in solving its problems.

Many of the skills involved in solving work problems in an agency are the same analytical and change skills that workers have learned in dealing with clients. Workers who do certain kinds of work, such as in rape crisis or battered women's centers, no longer see these problems as just individual troubles. They involve their clients in a social and political analysis of their problems. It is a relief to clients to realize they are not alone. Using the same skills, workers can involve their colleagues in analyzing agency problems. This gets workers beyond incessant criticism of the agency that goes nowhere, and it helps them gain mastery of agency problems (Bramhall & Ezell, 1991).

If workers feel powerless and helpless, how can they help clients feel less so? Workers cannot provide models for growth for clients or help them gain mastery over their lives unless they are taking some control over their own work lives. How is that done? We have pointed out that when people analyze the reasons for their burnout, they tend to overemphasize either the personal or the organizational reasons, rarely balancing the two. The same dichotomy happens when people prescribe remedies. Although some can look at both personal and political issues as all of a piece, many prescribe only individual remedies (biofeedback, meditation, relaxation techniques, job rotation). Others insist that the only solution to worker stress is to change the whole agency and even the whole social system. Both sets of remedies have utility but they need to be combined. Certainly, a rigid and an authoritarian agency working with a stigmatized clientele on a shoestring budget can literally produce

NO PAID FAMILY LEAVE, SO—HERE'S THE FAMILY!

Meeting family responsibilities while working is stressful, and can contribute to burnout.

a pain in the neck, stomach, head, or gut of the worker, but even in a "good" agency, with a low caseload and lots of support, we still find ourselves under occasional stress simply because we are dealing with people's emotions and unmet needs.

Gaining Power through Knowledge

In order to get power in an agency, you need to understand the social and political economy of the agency and how it fits into society. As one sociologist put it, you need to break out of "occupationally trained incapacity to rise above a series of cases" (Mills, 1943, p. 171) in order to figure out what society *really* wants you to do with these clients, what society *really* expects of you, what is *really* known about the kinds of problems your clients have.

Your study of your own agency should begin with close observation, perhaps using your journal to document your observations and thoughts. Notice who does what and why, who is especially rewarded and why, what kind of behavior in both workers and clients is valued. Supplement your own observations by studying what others have said about these issues in books or at workshops, conferences, visits to other agencies, formal courses, and your own informal support group. Remember that *knowledge is power*, and if you do not understand what is coming down, you will be buffeted about by mysterious forces.

In order to understand our own position in an agency and intervene helpfully in people's lives, we need to see them and their environments as clearly as possible. For example, some of the "whys" that might occur to you in a foster care agency are:

1. Why are so many children being moved so often from one home to another?
2. Why do children stay so long in foster care?
3. Why is it so hard to find foster homes for adolescents?
4. Why don't some social workers and foster parents want the biological parents to see more of their children?
5. Why is my caseload so high and my pay so low?

In child-protection work, an area with a high rate of burnout, a study of the job should include an analysis of the structure of the worker's job. One expert on the child-welfare system maintains that high burnout is at least partly caused by the fact that the worker is asked to perform the two incompatible roles of policing and providing supportive help to families (Pelton, 1989). Pelton argues that, in order to develop the trust necessary to provide the supportive help that families need, families must voluntarily choose the help. Because workers often meet families with a real or an implied threat to invoke the state's power to remove their children, it is impossible for families to trust the workers. Pelton believes that the two roles should be separated, creating special police units to handle the coercive functions and freeing social workers to give help that families genuinely need and want.

Along with your independent study, you will need to join with others, both coworkers and clients, in seeking answers. One person working alone can conceivably change an organization, but that is rare, and it is a lonely road. We stress, again, that change comes about through people working together.

Getting Support

SUPERVISION

Social agencies have traditionally relied on supervision to train workers and to give them support in their work. The profession of social work has probably relied more than any other profession or trade on long-term, one-to-one supervision. Although it can have its benefits, not all human service workers are happy with the kind of supervision they interpret as enforced dependence for their entire career.

There are good and bad aspects to traditional supervision. The best part is that a supportive supervisor can help human service workers function at their full potential, often helping them discover creativity and strength they never knew they had. Such a supervisor can help prevent burnout and poor-quality service.

One research project (Berkeley Planning Associates, 1978) that evaluated child abuse and neglect programs concluded that the most important factor in keeping workers actively engaged was supportive program leadership. This was especially important to younger and more inexperienced workers. Workers functioned best when they were:

- Active participants in supervision
- Encouraged to be innovative
- Given clear communication and expectations from supervisors
- Not required to follow formalized rules rigidly when it was more helpful to the clients to bend the rules

Good supervisors:

- Took the work seriously
- Emphasized its importance
- Encouraged workers to get the job done
- Were neither passive nor authoritarian
- Provided support and structure
- Conveyed a sense of trust in staff
- Gave direct feedback to workers on their performance
- Helped workers find resources in the community
- Provided strong advocacy on behalf of the clients and workers within the agency

The same research report showed that workers who had poor supervision burned out at a much greater rate than did workers with good leadership.

IDEAL SUPERVISION

One of the most important qualities of a good supervisor is the ability to allow workers freedom and responsibility for their own work. An overcontrolling supervisor encourages dependence and childish subservience. Workers under the tutelage of such a person never develop their own creativity. The study on child abuse and neglect demonstrated that workers became seriously demoralized when they were not given autonomy.

Most of us would agree that we can, and need to, learn from more experienced and knowledgeable people both in our professional and our personal lives. In any job, a worker should expect good supervision at a regularly scheduled time—perhaps an hour or two a week set aside to talk about work-related problems and plan for future activities. Supervision need not be done only on a one-to-one basis. Informal peer supervision and formal group sessions, which are regularly scheduled discussion groups of agency workers and selected consultants, can replace or supplement it. In many human service agencies, most of the staff supervision is done through groups. Some people think this is better than one-to-one supervision because "the group has a way of maintaining honesty; the supervisor shares power with the group members, and they add their power to his. One result can be a lessening of the threat of the conference held behind closed doors" (Abels, 1979, p. 174).

OTHER FORMS OF SUPERVISION

Other forms of group supervision are **case conferences**, core evaluations, and staffings, in which the workers concentrate on one particular client's problem or on one key issue affecting groups of clients. A study of child abuse and neglect programs (Berkeley Planning Associates, 1978) concluded that work was more likely to be successful when the workers used multidisciplinary teams to review more serious or complex cases at intake and at some other point in the treatment process (at least once every six months). Using such teams, which might include teachers, homemakers, lay therapists, social workers, psychologists, nurses, and doctors, helped workers learn how to handle a particular case and similar cases in the future. Workers also did better in these projects when they had case conferences in which two or more workers reviewed their progress on a case once every three months and when they used outside consultants from different disciplines on more complex cases.

case conferences
Conferences about a particular client in which staff members pool their information and share resources.

SUPERVISION AS A PROBLEM-SOLVING PROCESS

A supervisor's broadly ranging knowledge is not enough, however, if he or she does not know how to pass the knowledge along. Supervision is a problem-solving relationship. A worker must feel safe in supervisory relationships before he or she will risk honestly admitting insecurities, mistakes, and ignorance. A supervisor who acts like a "snoopervisor," always checking up and looking over the worker's shoulder for mistakes, ready to mark them down on an evaluation sheet, is not someone with whom subordinates will willingly discuss problems. In fact, many will respond to this assault by playing games, telling the supervisor what he or she wants to hear while shoving their real problems under the rug.

If supervisors are secure, they can invite workers to tell what helps or hinders the workers about their way of working. Open discussion is the best way to work out problems in supervision. If the supervisor feels too threatened by this, or if it is impossible to change supervisors, one must look around for support elsewhere.

SUPERVISORS AND WORKERS' SELF-ESTEEM

Because human service workers "as a rule, are easily convinced that they are doing a poor job" (Feldman, 1979, p. 118), one of the supervisor's most important jobs is to help workers gain confidence in the effective work they are actually doing, often without being aware of it. For example, there are times in a working relationship with a client when he or she needs to express anger and be critical of a worker. Such an expression may be a sign that the worker has helped a client feel free enough to express anger. Yet anger is hard to take, and a worker may feel that he or she has failed. A supervisor, understanding the relationship more objectively, can help the worker understand the anger as a sign of progress and can also show the worker points at which the worker "felt empathy and was able to perceive her client's need and respond constructively—without herself being aware of it. . . . (Analyzing with workers their intuitively correct responses is the best way of teaching)" (Feldman, 1979, p. 124).

Formal and Informal Groups

Another study of worker effectiveness and morale showed that workers needed informal peer support (Maslach, 1966). In high-morale agencies, workers were encouraged to choose a consultant on their own, either a fellow worker whom they respected and trusted or someone outside the agency. Human service students or trainees in fieldwork placements often turn to a field supervisor from their college in addition to the one appointed at their field agency. This doubling up of supervisors can be an asset or a liability, of course, according to the skill and commitment of all involved.

INFORMAL NETWORKS

The informal conversations we have with our friends and coworkers are the most common way of sharing experiences. These take place during coffee breaks, over lunch, after work on the telephone, at each other's homes, and during shared entertainment. These conversations give us the emotional support to keep at our demanding jobs. They are one way to check out, add to, and revise our store of knowledge about our work. Sometimes they can improve our practice. We may share innovative ideas; but we may also share ignorance, prejudice, and stereotypes. If the conversation stays on the level of griping, it can increase anxiety and keep people mired in helplessness. One needs to gripe, but if one never moves on to analysis and action, complaining can be counterproductive.

Informal networks are essential for survival on the job. Sociologist Howard Polsky (1962) studied a residential treatment center for delinquent youths and found that the live-in cottage parents felt, and in fact, were the most isolated and vulnerable of all the staff members because they did not have a reference group—friends they could go home to and share ideas and feelings with. The social workers, on the other hand, commuting together back to New York City and spending evenings with family and friends, returned to work the next day emotionally replenished for their bouts with the rage, wisecracks, con games, and sadness of these youngsters who had been taken from their homes by the state. The cottage parents' lack of an alternative status reference group had a negative impact on the treatment they gave to the teenagers in their care:

> Lacking an alternative status reference group, the cottage parent becomes dependent upon, and conforming to, the boys' delinquent orientation and eventually adjusts to it by taking over and utilizing modified delinquent techniques. The extreme concern with cottage loyalty and the violent condemnation of "ratting" cement the cottage parent to the boys' subculture and perpetuate a vicious circle, which insulates the cottage from the rest of the therapeutic milieu. (Polsky, 1962, p. 135)

FORMALLY ORGANIZED SUPPORT GROUPS

A formally organized support group may or may not include one's friends. It may consist only of colleagues on the job, or it may be an explicitly political group that is open to people from other agencies who want to clarify their thinking about their work. They may be a study group that meets regularly, chooses readings to discuss, and perhaps invites specialists to discuss certain issues. A study group is most effective when people give it a high priority in their lives, meet regularly, and use the group to analyze the workplace: how it is affecting each member and how members can individually and collectively deal with their work-related frustrations. It can become quite an effective tool for collectively tackling problems in the workplace, and it can give enormous psychological support to its members. Wenocur and Sherman (1980) suggest a few important items to discuss:

- How the organization heightens the guilt of the workers
- The role of dependency in keeping workers in patterns of victimization
- How workers identify with the powerlessness of their clients
- The forms of accommodation the members have adopted in order to survive in the agency

Most of the literature on burnout emphasizes the crucial importance of support groups. One child-welfare agency held a support group for child abuse workers to deal with the severe stresses of the job (Copans et al., 1979). The group met for one and one-half hours once a week for six months to "examine the feelings aroused in workers by their work and to discuss how these feelings aided or interfered with effective delivery of care" (p. 302). During these meetings, ten major sets of feelings that often interfere with effective delivery of care were identified:

- Anxiety about the effects of a decision
- Need for emotional gratification from clients
- Lack of professional support
- Denial and inhibition of anger
- Feelings of incompetence
- Denial and projection of responsibility
- Difficulty in separating personal from professional responsibility
- Feelings of being victimized
- Ambivalent feelings toward clients and about one's professional role
- The need to be in control

In all these areas, workers got emotional support and helpful suggestions for dealing with the problem. Every group member suffered from feelings of incompetence:

> One very competent worker said that she felt professionally inadequate most of the time. Since she rarely received comments on her work, she assumed it was not good. It was a great relief to her to discover that others shared these feelings of failure. As a result of recognizing this problem in the group, many workers returned to their agencies and asked for critical feedback on their work. Most of them also felt much less incompetent, as they could see from case discussions that there is generally no "best way" or "right answer" in such work. (Copans et al., 1979, p. 305)

One of the reasons for this widespread feeling of incompetence among human service workers is that they are not sure whether their work is effective. Most researchers on burnout assume that when workers' morale is high, their work is effective and productive. Weissman and his colleagues (1973), however, believe that this is the wrong way to look at it. They assert that worker morale will improve when the agency is effective. They would shift the focus from the individual worker to the agency:

> There is nothing more satisfying to professionals than spending their work lives in an organization that they feel is effective. . . . The competence of the agency should be as high a priority to the profession as the competence of individual practitioners. If agencies are not effective, clients suffer, and workers suffer. (Copans et al., 1979, p. 331)

Researchers at the Wellesley Center for Research on Women studied stress in the service sector of the economy and found that "regardless of how demanding their jobs were, workers who felt they weren't making a contribution to the lives of others were more distressed." Their advice to employers in the service sector was to design jobs that permit individuals to be effective service providers, to make a difference to others. "This won't make the stress of a demanding service job any easier to bear, but it may prevent job-related distress from worsening" (Center for Research on Women, 1999/2000).

PROFESSIONAL ORGANIZATIONS

A professional organization forges links between people in the same field. Collectively, these people share their values and their knowledge and support each other in job searching and other concrete ways. Most organizations have at least one professional journal that provides a platform for workers to carry on their professional debates and to share their research and practice experiences. Most human service organizations have a code of ethical practice. Workers often derive support by holding on to their professional values, even though these may at times be in conflict with those practiced in the agency. The profession often uses the clout afforded by its numbers to improve agency practice and to lobby for better social services.

UNIONS

There is often no sharp distinction between a professional organization and a union; some professional organizations, such as the National Education Association (NEA) and the American Association of University Professors (AAUP), started as professional associations but have gradually taken on the traditional functions of a trade union. Generally, professional organizations do not engage in contract negotiations or in job actions such as slowdowns or strikes.

As the country's workforce has increasingly moved into service occupations, professionals such as teachers and human service workers are unionizing much more now than in the past. The greatest increase in unionization recently has been among professionals in education, government service, and nonprofit organizations. Public social agencies generally pay workers more than private agencies because they are more unionized.

Turning their pain into positive energy, AIDS activists organize fund-raising long-distance bike rides all around the country. They provide money for medical research while increasing their own fitness.

One of the most important reasons workers give for leaving human service agencies is their lack of control over their working conditions. Unions are often perceived as the most powerful tool to wrest some of that control from management. Some social service unions have a limited vision of their task, bargaining mainly for wages, hours, and fringe benefits, while others struggle for a greater worker role in decision making and for changes in systems. A spokesperson for the American Federation of State, County, and Municipal Employees (AFSCME), which has organized many human service workers, tells of his union's concern for those broader issues. Professionals often want representation at the planning or policy level. For example, social caseworkers, who are often overburdened with high caseloads, work for policies that lower their caseloads (Curtin, 1970, pp. 12, 15).

The organization that Rick Colbath Hess founded is one model for human service workers to improve their working conditions. This is especially important for direct care workers, who often have lower salaries and worse working conditions than others in the field.

If your agency is not unionized and the workers want a union, a group of you can work on it. Study all the unions that could represent you. Find out their track record on organizing and bargaining; check out what salaries their staff earn. (There's no reason union bureaucrats should be living in luxury while human service workers scrimp.) See what issues they are willing to take a stand on; ask how elitist or hierarchical they are in their own decision making. Do they believe the membership or the union staff should call the shots? How much are the dues? Do they have a fund to tide you over if it comes to a strike? Can they give you legal assistance and help in bargaining? Give ample time for everyone to share his or her concerns about what might happen to the clients if there was a work stoppage and what he or she is prepared to do if the organizing or contract negotiation gets sticky. Don't be surprised if the agency management is not happy about the prospect of workers organizing. Even human service supervisors can have serious misgivings and fears of turmoil and conflict.

Some organizations play on workers' fears in order to reduce union activity—fear of being fired, not promoted, or disapproved of. Sometimes the fears are justified. One reason for the recent decline in union membership is that employers have fired union organizers, which has made people more afraid to organize. Find out from the union leaders in your area whether this has been happening in the human service field and what you can do about it.

Often there will be resistance from some agency colleagues, who believe that it is unprofessional to organize. As the economic crunch hits more middle-class people, however, they tend to look for a union's protection. Finally, if workers are in a small private agency that contracts out work from the state, they may find they need to form coalitions with fellow workers in similar small agencies before unionizing in order to grow large enough to influence management.

Service Employees International Union (SEIU) has organized workers often considered "unorganizable," especially low-wage service sector workers, in what is often called "social movement organizing." Many of these service sector workers are minorities, immigrants, and women. Some of the union's organizing campaigns include:

- Justice for Janitors (janitors),
- Stand for Security (security officers),
- Invisible No More (home care workers),
- Clean Up Sodexo (outsourced services),
- National Health Care Workers Union (healthcare providers),
- SEIU Kids First (childcare),
- Quality Public Services (public workers), and
- Everybody Wins (public workers) (SEIU, Local 503).

A particularly significant organizing campaign for welfare recipients occurred in Milwaukee, Wisconsin, when SEIU organized 604 people who cared for their parents, employed by the nonprofit agency New Health Services (NHS). This was the first large-scale organizing in Milwaukee at the low end of the wage scale since the 1997 launch of "W-2," Wisconsin's welfare reform system initiated by then-governor Tommy Thompson. Many former welfare recipients are employed by NHS. These workers were paid at the rate of $7.10 per hour, with no benefits of any kind. After their union was certified, they went on to negotiate a contract for higher wages, improved training, health insurance, and pension benefits (Glenn, 2001b). Many feminists have long argued for paying wages to caregivers. This campaign is the first to organize people who care for their own parents.

Choosing Your Fights

After analyzing your situation and setting up your support groups, you then need to set priorities on what you want to change in your work situation. You can't change everything at once, so decide what it is that you simply can't live with any more. Say that your gripes include having to punch a time clock at 8:30 and carrying a caseload of 800 food stamp clients*—with inadequate secretarial staff to prepare documents, write letters, and do publicity. Which of these is most important? You will probably decide that the clock punching is least important, so you won't take on that fight just yet. There is no point in risking a major confrontation on a minor issue, especially one that doesn't compromise any basic principles, when there are other things much more crucial to your effectiveness or job satisfaction.

Make a cost–benefit analysis of your issue. How much might it cost you in terms of job risk, disapproval from the boss, and so on, and what are the possible benefits? Which side of the scale tips—risks or benefits? Don't overestimate the risks, especially if you have substantial support from your colleagues and advocacy groups. People tend to err on the side of caution when some risk might actually reap large benefits. The more people you have with you, the more you reduce your risks. It is harder to reprimand or even fire ten people than one. Watch out for divide-and-conquer tactics. Agency management may lay off the people with the least formal training first, and the others may assume that they have escaped. Later, management may pick off the trained workers or lower their salaries. The more people and advocacy organizations you include in your struggle, the better your chance of success.

Creative Ways of Working

One way of keeping the spark alive on the job is to experiment with new ideas. It may be hard to think of new ways to do your work when so many people are telling you, "but we've always done it this way." Yet well-thought-out experimentation is often worth the risks it might entail. Clearly, it keeps people enthusiastic.

Working with people in groups rather than as individuals can sometimes save time. You might make an overly large caseload more manageable through such devices as conducting group intakes for adoption applicants. Foster parents can be trained in groups to care for children; they can also help the worker to recruit other foster parents. Group counseling for unemployed people and support groups for parents, teens, families of alcoholics, and others can all be both time-saving and sometimes more effective than individual work. One study found that treatment of abusive and neglectful parents was most effective when parents were involved in mutual support groups such as Parents Anonymous and when parent aides were used (Berkeley Planning Associates, 1978). Encouraging and supporting clients to help themselves and each other cuts down on your caseload and pressures while strengthening your clients' abilities.

*In 2010, Massachusetts food stamp workers had 800 cases. Even after more workers were hired, they had 600 cases. Obviously, clients weren't served well and workers were burned out.

If you can get enough support from your colleagues, clients, and community, you might persuade your agency to change the way it does the work. One staff member of a sheltered workshop for retarded people said this in her letter of protest to the agency board:

> While I was told that teaching clients would be at least a part of my job, this has not been the case so far. In the weeks I've been at [the workshop], I've spent a total of half an hour working on money skills with a client, and that was only because I put other things aside and took initiative to do so. In reality, my job consists of fixing and counting chess pieces and mascara brushes, inspecting bathrooms, opening boxes of calculators. How about if I spend two hours a day teaching clients to do these tasks? I understand they must be done but think it is a ridiculous use of my skills. From 10:00–12:00 I could work on routine sorting tasks and from 1:00–3:00 hold a money management workshop. I'd like six weeks to stick with this schedule and then I'll report back on how it's working.

Programs that allow scope for creativity make space for workers and clients to grow. The ultimate goal of any human service work is the mutual empowerment of clients, workers, and the community. Workers can reach out to clients and the community to explore and discuss alternative modes of service.

Varying the Work

A good way to survive on the job is to vary the work by rotating duties with other workers, alternating between intense involvement with clients and less emotionally draining administrative work, or taking time out from regular tasks to do a special project or attend a course or conference. Workers often break a cycle of defeat by figuring out which clients are the most draining on them and making trade-offs with other workers who have different kinds of tolerances and bring a new insight to a stalled group or individual case process.

Sharing Ideas

One of the most important ways of enjoying your work is to know you are doing a good job. That is a good reason to continue to sharpen your skills throughout your career. It is stimulating to share ideas with others, both verbally and in writing. You can be part of the "community of scholars" at work, in the community, and in your profession by writing letters to the editor of your local newspaper, composing practice notes and accounts for your professional journal, and, if you have a bent for more formal research and theoretical speculation, producing articles that present your thinking and research.

CLARITY OF THOUGHT AND WRITING

Most human service concepts can be expressed in clear language. The beginning student should be wary of articles or lectures that are overly abstract or filled with labels, jargon, categories, and excessive complexity.

English writer George Orwell (famous for his political novel *1984*) warned us about pretentious diction in his classic essay, "Politics and the English Language" (1950). He illustrates his point by translating a passage from the Bible into "modern English of the worst sort." Here is the original passage from *Ecclesiastes*:

> I returned and saw under the sun, that the race is not to the swift nor the battle to the strong, neither yet bread to the wise, nor yet riches to men of understanding, nor yet favour to men of skill; but time and chance happeneth to them all.

Here it is in modern "jargonese" English:

> Objective consideration of contemporary phenomena compels the conclusion that success or failure in competitive activities exhibits no tendency to be commensurate with innate capacity, but that a considerable element of the unpredictable must invariably be taken into account. (Orwell, 1950, p. 92)

Clear thinking demands honesty, not pretentiousness, and in studying the field of human services, students should demand clarity of teachers and supervisors and should strive for honest expression in their own writing. Orwell's guidelines for writing can be helpful to all of us:

1. Never use a metaphor, simile or other figure of speech which you are used to seeing in print.
2. Never use a long word where a short one will do.
3. If it is possible to cut a word out, always cut it out.
4. Never use the passive where you can use the active.
5. Never use a foreign phrase, a scientific word, or a jargon word if you can think of an everyday English equivalent.
6. Break any of these rules sooner than say anything outright barbarous. (Orwell, 1950, p. 100)

Orwell tells us that our writing style will be clearer and more forceful if we speak in the active rather than passive voice. An active style forces us to take responsibility for our thoughts. When I say, "I think . . . ," I announce that I am the author of that thought and am willing to take both the praise and the blame for it. If, on the other hand, I want to duck responsibility for the thought, I might say, "It has been thought . . . ." A person who thinks and writes in the active voice is more likely to be actively engaged in dialogue that shapes practice.

AVOIDING ABBREVIATIONS

In addition to avoiding pretentiousness in our speaking and writing, we need to avoid the casual drift into speaking in human service abbreviations—the secret code of our field. It is very easy to say to a parent, "After your child has been cored, we'll apply to OCD for CHINS or Title XX money, and we'll find a less restrictive setting for your child," when what you want them to know is, "After the study and evaluation of your child's special needs are completed, we can apply to the Office of Child Development for money from the Children in

Need of Service fund or the Supplementary Security Act. We'll also find a school that will provide him with the best, most normal education."

If you are sure that the parent knows the jargon, then speaking in abbreviations or professional terms is, of course, acceptable. But we must always check to make sure we aren't speaking in a "foreign language." One of the authors [Schram] recalls an example of this in the 1960s, the time of the War on Poverty:

> When I was on the board of a poverty program funded by the Office of Economic Opportunity (fondly known as O.E.O.), we were always having one or another crisis with our funding and must have mentioned O.E.O.—cursing or praising it—at least twenty times in the course of one board meeting. At the close of one particularly dramatic meeting, I realized that one of the new board members, known for her militancy in neighborhood politics, was remarkably quiet, and in fact she had abstained from voting on several important issues. When I took her aside after the meeting and asked her why she was acting in this untypically laid-back manner, she explained that much of the meeting had been a jumble to her. "What," she asked me, "did oleo (the local word for oleomargarine, the butter substitute) have to do with the poverty program?" My heart sank when I realized that we unwittingly excluded through our use of "insider's" abbreviations the very person we most wanted to involve. It taught me a lesson I will not soon forget.

Of course, no matter how conscious we are, code words and initials will creep into our writing and speaking. If you as a new worker are plunged into a bowl of alphabet soup, the only way to keep from drowning is to interrupt the action politely and ask for an explanation.

Setting Limits on Self and Others

Finally, you need to know how to protect yourself from the unrealistic demands that people make on you. You need to learn to recognize your limits and let others know when you have reached them. Learn to say "no" without feeling guilty. Take time out when you're feeling drained. If you've just had a nerve-wracking experience with a client and your knees are shaking, let your supervisor know that you need to take a walk or talk it out. If you're exhausted after a few years on the job, try to take a leave of absence, if you can afford it. You may come back refreshed, with new ideas.

You need to learn how not to take your work home with you, and you need to take good care of yourself outside the job. There are lots of ways to do this. Our list would include good nutrition, regular exercise, rest, recreation, reading, and friendships. Some people find meditation, relaxation techniques, or biofeedback helpful. One psychologist in a teachers' stress counseling program talks of how some people neglect their health: "Many teachers subsist on coffee and nicotine. They don't eat breakfast, but they might drink coffee with sugar, or a Coke, with a doughnut. They get sugared up. It makes them sleepy, cranky, and inefficient" (Grey, 1979, p. 6).

However we manage to do it, we must keep our spontaneity and spirit of play alive. If we lose our joy, how can we bring joy and hope to our clients?

SUMMARY

1. Human service work can be one of the most exciting careers in the world, but only as long as one can grow in the job and feel successful in it.

2. Growth requires support from peers, supervisors, and the society that sponsors your agency.

3. If support is not forthcoming, a human service job can create stress, which leads to burnout.

4. Symptoms of burnout can include sleep problems, irritability, upset stomach, headaches, and shortness of breath. Workers may become cynical and hard-hearted, stop caring about the clients, and treat clients with contempt.

5. Burnout can be caused by both psychological and environmental stress.

6. The human service profession is built on a humanitarian ethos, but in practice that ideal sometimes turns into cynicism or careerism.

7. When insurance companies dictate the kind of treatment to be given and the way to give it, human service workers are restricted in their choices.

8. When there is not enough time, the helping impulse may become extinguished.

9. Government cutbacks in services restrict the kind of help that workers can give.

10. Agencies that serve the poor seldom have enough resources.

11. Pressure for accountability can cause agencies to take refuge in sorting and counting behavior, which may not reflect the true quality of their work.

12. Clients exert pressures on the worker when resources are restricted.

13. Work stress is increased when the client has not chosen to come to the agency, as in child-protection work.

14. Clients of agencies are often stigmatized by society. Those who work with them are sometimes included in this stigmatization.

15. Some human service work is dangerous, and workers need help from their agencies to protect themselves.

16. Hazards of human service work include workers' rescue fantasies, the fact that some problems cannot be solved, and the enormity of the problems.

17. Some of the less creative reactions to the pressures of work include capitulation, total noncapitulation, niche finding, withdrawal, and becoming a victim martyr.

18. Taking control of one's work situation involves understanding the social and political structure of the agency and its relationship to the larger society.

19. Support groups, professional organizations, and unions are important sources of support.

20. A supportive supervisor can help workers function at their full potential.

21. One of the most important qualities of a good supervisor is the ability to allow workers freedom and responsibility for their own work.

22. Individual methods of change include finding more creative ways of doing the work, varying the work, improving one's competence, and joining the "community of scholars" by contributing to the dialogue of the profession.

23. Unions can give workers more control over the conditions of their work.

24. Clarity of thought and writing help one to maintain a forceful presence in the human service profession.

25. Workers need to protect themselves from impossible demands and learn how to say *no* without feeling guilty.

26. Taking care of oneself includes good nutrition, regular exercise, rest, recreation, reading, and friendships.

DISCUSSION QUESTIONS

1. If you were in charge of a social agency, how would you structure it to avoid worker burnout?

2. Imagine that you are a worker who wants to form a union to improve wages and working conditions. The administrator of your agency calls a meeting to warn workers about the dangers of unions and makes a veiled threat that workers might be fired if they try to form a union. How would you respond to this?

3. What are some examples of federal and state laws that might contribute to worker burnout?

4. What are some examples of agency regulations that might contribute to worker burnout?

5. Describe what you would consider to be the ideal supervisor and the ideal method of supervision.

WEB RESOURCES FOR FURTHER STUDY

American Federation of State, County, and Municipal Employees (AFSCME)
www.afscme.org

AFSCME is the largest union for workers in the public service. AFSCME organizes for social and economic justice in the workplace and through political action and legislative advocacy. AFSCME represents a diverse group of service and health care workers in the public and private sectors, including nurses, EMTs, sanitation workers, bus drivers, child care providers, corrections officers, child care providers, human service workers, custodians, and librarians.

U.S. Department of Labor
www.dol.gov

This site provides information on government programs affecting workers, and on occupations.

Service Employees International Union (SEIU)
www.seiu.org

SEIU'S membership includes 2.2 million working people and retirees in North America. Counterparts around the world help ensure that workers, not just corporations and CEOs, benefit from today's global economy. SEIU includes the largest health care union, the largest property services union, and the second largest public services union. Some of the groups it organizes include human service workers, health care and mental health workers, home care workers, cafeteria workers, janitors, and security officers.

Employee Assistance Plans
http://www.dol.gov/odep/documents/employeeassistance.pdf (Employee Assistance Programs for a New Generation of Employees, U.S. Department of Labor 2009-01-01)

Employee Assistance Programs (EAPs) are employee benefit programs offered by many employers, typically in conjunction with a health insurance plan. EAPs are intended to help employees deal with personal problems that might adversely impact their work performance, health, and well-being.

Glossary

Accent response   Repetition, as a question or with some emphasis, of a word or short phrase that a client has just said.

Accountability   A requirement, usually imposed by a funding source, that an agency perform according to a certain set of standards.

Adult Children of Alcoholics (ACOA)   A self-help support group that runs on the model of Alcoholics Anonymous for adults whose parents were alcoholics.

Advising   Telling a client what to do. Advising is used with caution, if at all, in interviews, because it incorrectly assumes that one person knows what is best for another.

Ageism   The practice of discriminating against people because they are old; attitudes associated with the practice.

Aid to Families with Dependent Children (AFDC)   The title of the Social Security Act that authorized public financial assistance for parents of dependent children. It is now called *Temporary Assistance to Needy Families* (TANF).

Al-Anon   A self-help group for the families and friends of alcoholics.

Alateen   A self-help group for teenage children of alcoholics.

Alcoholics Anonymous (AA)   A self-help organization that uses a specific twelve-step program for recovery from addiction to alcohol.

Alienation   A sociological term used to describe the way the structure of a job or an organization distances people from their work, from each other, and from themselves.

Americans with Disabilities Act (ADA)   A congressional mandate that guarantees many rights to people with physical and mental disabilities, especially in the areas of employment and architectural access.

Anxiety disorder   A biological condition in which feelings of extreme fear, tension, and dread often overwhelm a person, even when there is no apparent threat to his or her well-being.

Assessment summary   A summary that analyzes the observations and information that a worker has obtained through interviews.

Attention deficit/hyperactivity disorder (ADHD)   A biological condition with early onset and often long duration that interferes with a person's capacity to focus and sustain interest, especially when the agenda is set by an outside authority, as in the school or work setting.

Aversive behavioral treatment   A form of behavior modification based primarily on punishment rather than reward.

Battered women   Women who have been physically abused.

Behaviorist   A theorist who believes that behavior can be shaped or changed by the systematic application of rewards for behavioral compliance with the demands of a caregiver or therapist.

Bicultural theory   A theory which asserts that although people are socialized into their minority culture through family and their ethnic community, they are also influenced by the dominant culture through social institutions and the mass media.

Brainstorming   A technique in which people generate ideas under time pressure and without judgment so that their most innovative thoughts can flow.

Bureaucratization   Increased organizational centralization, hierarchical control, larger workplaces, and decreased autonomy for workers.

Careerism   A single-minded preoccupation with getting ahead in a career to the exclusion of other interests or values.

Career ladder   A specific path of jobs that relates accomplishment and tenure to upward mobility.

Case conferences   Conferences about a particular client in which staff members pool their information and share resources.

Change agents   Workers who use their skills to bring about change in an unhealthy agency or situation, either alone or in concert with others.

Charismatic leader   A person who profoundly influences others through his or her dynamism of personality.

Charity Organization Societies (COSs)   The earliest professional social work agencies, organized first in England and later in the United States; they claimed to deliver "scientific charity" through case-by-case work of "friendly visitors."

Child-saving movement   A term used to describe the efforts of reformers in the late nineteenth and early twentieth centuries to rescue children from "unwholesome influences." The movement led to the development of children's institutions, foster care, and the juvenile court.

Clarifying   Seeking further understanding of what has been said in an interview.

Coalition   A loose amalgam of people or groups that support a similar idea or goal.

Co-dependency   A mutually destructive relationship between a person who is addicted and his or her significant other who helps to continue, rather than break, the addiction.

Community residences   Small living units, houses, or apartments located in communities that serve people who have disabilities or other special situations that render them unable to live on their own. (Also known as *halfway houses* or *group homes.*)

Comparable worth   Describing and paying wages for jobs according to their inherent difficulty and worth in order to help equalize women's wages with men's.

Confidentiality   Keeping information secret that a client reveals to a worker.

Conflict resolution   The way in which a group handles sharp differences in opinion or digressions from accepted standards.

Confronting   A tactic used by an interviewer to point out to an interviewee discrepancies or inconsistencies in an interviewee's words or behavior.

Contracting out   The process of an agency hiring another agency to do some of its own work.

Corporate restructuring   A process of shifting resources within corporations, resulting in lower pay for workers and higher pay for executives and in the laying off of workers. This is brought on partially by technological developments and investment decisions and partially by a decision to cut labor costs in order to maximize profits.

Consciousness raising   The process in which people are provoked into giving an issue serious thought, perhaps through suggestion of new points of view to be considered.

Cover terms   Terms that describe some aspect of culturally significant meaning and experience.

Cyberbullying   The use of cyber communication technology to spread information about a person or group, which spreads deliberate, repeated, and hostile opinions or other data intended to harass a targeted victim.

Deindustrialization   Changes in the U.S. economy in recent decades that have reduced the number of jobs in the manufacturing industry and increased the number of jobs in the service sector.

Deinstitutionalization   A large-scale reform movement that took people out of institutions and hospitals and returned them to their community with special services to aid their reintegration.

Deregulation   Ending government regulation of a program.

Descriptors   Blocks of descriptive information, systematically collected, used to build a composite portrait of selected cultural characteristics more or less shared by a set of clients.

Deserving versus undeserving   The discriminatory classification of people into higher and lower categories, considering some people to be more worthy of receiving benefits and services than others.

Dialectical   Refers to the principle that an idea or event (thesis) generates its opposite (antithesis), leading to a reconciliation of opposites (synthesis) and a continuation of the dialectical process.

Direct action   Interfering with the orderly conduct of a system that is the target of change.

Direct-service strategies (intervention, roles)   Worker actions that deliver services directly to clients.

Disabilities Resource Center (DRC)   An office that coordinates the academic support services that enable students with physical, mental, or educational disabilities to pursue their class work.

Door opener   An invitation to say more about something that an interviewee has brought up, preferably in the form of an open-ended request for information.

Due process   Procedural mechanisms that secure or protect one's legal rights.

Early intervention program   A program that attempts to deal with a person's (often a child's) problem at the first sign of difficulty.

Empathy   An attempt to put oneself in the shoes of another person, to feel or think of a problem from another perspective.

Employee assistance programs (EAPs)   Supportive services that deal with mental health or financial or legal issues that are offered directly to employees by their company or agency. Their goal is to reduce worker turnover and raise productivity.

Encouraging and reassuring   Providing a message of hopefulness in an attempt to inspire confidence, often without regard to what a person is actually feeling.

Entitlements   Benefits and services that people are legally entitled to, as compared to those that are given at the discretion of officials.

Ethics of helping   An ethical commitment to helping others rather than engaging in dog-eat-dog competition.

Euthanasia   Active intervention in hastening death, usually made by a doctor with the permission of the dying person or his or her family.

Expert witness   A person who is especially knowledgeable in a particular field and who is asked to give testimony based on that knowledge in a court trial.

External barriers   Barriers in the environment that make it difficult for a person to receive help.

Facilitators   People involved in helping to move group members in the direction of their goal.

Family preservation   A commitment to provide the resources and supports that can hold together or reunite a family unit, especially to provide stability to the children.

Fee for service   A prearranged amount of money that will be paid to a health care provider each time he or she delivers a specific service to a plan member in accordance with the plan's criteria for that service.

Feedback   Both positive and negative critical comments on particular actions, statements, or other factors.

Force-field analysis   A systematic way of looking at the negatives and positives of an idea or event in order to understand it fully, anticipate problems, and estimate chances of success.

Furthering responses   Responses that encourage clients to continue talking.

GAP   A necessary service or resource that is lacking in a program or in services that might help solve a problem.

Gatekeeper   A person in a health plan organization who decides whether a prescribed medical service will be paid for based on the organization's set of criteria for care.

Generalist   A worker who is knowledgeable about a wide range of resources and subgroups and who can use a variety of helping interventions.

Global questions   General, open-ended questions about some aspect of an interviewee's life.

Google search   Clicking onto a web search engine owned by Google Inc. which is the most-used search engine on the web, receiving millions of queries and postings each day.

Grassroots programs   Programs started by people who do not hold official decision-making positions within a system but have a stake in the outcome of its services or policies.

Green   Those products, services, or other kinds of activities that exert no negative impact on the health of people or on the environment.

Group bond (or cohesion)   A complex set of forces that weld each member to a group and to each other.

Group structure   The sum total of rules and regulations that govern how a group organizes itself to do its work.

Guest worker program   A program that contracts immigrants to work for a specified time in the United States for a particular job, but does not hold out any promise of citizenship.

Hate crimes   Also known as bias-motivated crime, is a criminal act in which a perpetrator targets a victim primarily because of his or her membership in a racial or religious group, his or her sexual identity, age, gender or disability.

Head Start   A federally funded preschool program that aims to increase the readiness for public school of children from low-income families. It was begun during the War on Poverty in the 1960s.

Health maintenance organization (HMO)   A health care institution or an association of doctors that contracts with its members to collect a fixed sum of money monthly or yearly in exchange for doctor visits, tests, medications, hospital care, and preventive services, as needed.

Hobbes, Thomas   A seventeenth-century English philosopher who believed that people need a strong authority in order to regulate their desires.

Homophobia   An unreasoning fear or loathing of a person who has an intimate sexual relationship with a person of the same sex.

Hot line   A telephone service that gives information or short-term counseling on a variety of human service issues.

Humanitarian ethos   A dedication to promoting the welfare of humanity, especially through the elimination of pain and suffering.

Human service networks (or delivery systems)   Programs and entitlements that offer help in dealing with different but complementary parts of an overall problem.

Image of an agency   The reputation that a social agency has established in its community.

Indirect question   A question or statement that encourages the fullest possible expression of the interviewee's thoughts and feelings.

Information loop   A circular method of constantly refining one's interventions on the basis of careful questioning and absorption of evaluative feedback.

Informed choice   A choice that is made after being given all the relevant information about the issue.

Informed consent   Agreement given with the understanding of the full implications of what one is agreeing to.

Institutional philosophy of social welfare   A philosophy that looks at people as being embedded in a social system and as having predictable developmental needs.

Institutional racism (sexism)   Discrimination against a racial group (or gender) practiced by an organization or an institution, usually perpetuated by an interconnected system of policies and practices.

Intake interview   An interview that solicits relevant information before the delivery of a service begins.

Internal barriers   Emotions or attitudes within a person that make it difficult for him or her to seek help.

Interpreting   A form of response that speculates on the meaning of an interviewee's statement or behavior.

Involuntary clients   Clients who are forced, usually by a court, to use a social service.

Laissez-faire style   A leadership style in which a worker allows the process of the group to flow with a minimum amount of leader direction.

Leadership acts and roles   Influential behavior (feelings, acts, or words) that move a group toward its primary purposes and/or maintain the group.

Least restrictive setting   The type of treatment and location that provide the greatest amount of freedom to a client (who often has a specific disability).

Legal services   Organizations, generally supported by state or federal governments, that provide legal services to low-income people.

Linkage technology   The acts involved in referring a client to another agency, worker, or resource.

Lobby   An attempt to convince decision makers to support one's ideas or proposed actions.

Locke, John   A seventeenth-century English philosopher and scientist who believed that if people followed their own self-interest, a rational, just society would result.

Magnifying   Looking at a program or problem within the larger context of the community, laws, professional field, and so forth.

Mainstreaming   Putting people who have emotional or physical disabilities into the mainstream of society as much as possible. The Education for All Handicapped Children Act requires that all children be taught in regular schools and classrooms whenever possible.

Managed health care   A prepaid system in which an individual must choose among the doctors included in a particular plan, such as a health maintenance organization. It generally stresses preventive health care but is often used as a cost-cutting measure.

Mandated treatment   Treatment that is legally required by the courts or by government officials.

Manipulation   Attempts to influence someone's behavior or thoughts by covert, unstated methods rather than open, explicit methods.

Means-tested programs   Programs that are available only to the poor, whose assets fall below a certain set eligibility level.

Medicaid   A program that pays for the medical treatment of poor people, administered by states and paid for by federal and state funds.

Mental Patients' Liberation   Front (MPLF) An organization of people who are or have been patients in psychiatric hospitals and who oppose many established psychiatric practices. MPLF has established support groups and alternative institutions.

Microscoping   Looking at a program or problem and seeing within it all the component parts and steps of action needed.

Minimal verbal or nonverbal response   A small response to an interviewee, such as a nod or a look of interest, to encourage the interviewee to continue.

Multicausality   The view that personal or social problems are caused by many interacting factors, often too complex to allow a precise assessment of causality.

Needs assessment   Methods used to find out precisely what one particular person, group, or community needs in order to solve its problems and expand opportunities.

Negotiate a contract   An attempt on the part of the helper and the helpee to forge an agreement about what will be included in their work together.

New Careers for the Poor movement   A movement that began in the 1960s to train workers who do not have extensive formal credentials for human service jobs.

Nonjudgmental   Refers to an attitude that withholds moral judgments on another person's behavior, attitude, or values.

Norming   A process of arriving at mutually acceptable rules, regulations, and standards of behavior.

Norms   Mutually acceptable rules, regulations, and standards of behavior.

Objective data   Data based on unbiased facts, not affected by personal feelings or prejudice.

Open-ended questions   Questions asked in such a way that they allow for a variety of responses.

Opportunity theory   The theory that people are prevented from getting out of poverty because of a lack of social opportunities rather than because of individual defects.

Overidentification   The process of relating so completely to another person's feelings and/or experiences that one cannot separate oneself from the other person.

Paraphrasing (or restating)   Putting the interviewee's words in another form without changing the content in order to encourage the interviewee to go on.

Permanency planning   An attempt to create, in a timely fashion, a plan for a child that will return him or her safely to the family of origin or that legally frees the child to be adopted.

Personal Responsibility Act   A bill passed by Congress in 1996 and signed by former President Clinton that ended federal entitlements to needy families. It replaced AFDC with Temporary Aid to Needy Families (TANF), which gave grants to the states to administer work-related and time-limited programs of aid.

Physical attending   Making oneself physically receptive to an interviewee.

Posttraumatic stress disorder (PTSD)   A common anxiety disorder that develops after exposure to a terrifying event or an ordeal in which grave physical harm occurred or was threatened. Family members of victims also can develop the disorder. PTSD can occur in people of any age, including children and adolescents.

Power   The capacity to influence others to achieve certain desired ends.

Preparatory empathy   An attempt to put oneself in the shoes of another person, to feel or think of a problem from another perspective, even before encountering a client, to sensitize a worker.

Primary purpose   The main goal of an agency that determines the work it does.

Primary reference groups   Groups in which a person is intimately involved, including family and friends who influence the person's attitudes and values.

Principle of less eligibility   The principle that the amount of welfare given to people should be less than the lowest wage so that people will not be tempted to take welfare rather than get a wage-earning job.

Principle of reciprocity   The principle that social relationships are based to some extent on an analysis of trade-offs that determines what each person must give to the relationship in order to get back certain benefits.

Privacy   The right to be left alone.

Privatization   Changing the funding and administration of social welfare programs from the public sector to the private sector.

Privileged communication   Legal protection of confidences revealed in certain specific relationships.

Problem-solving skills   Systematic techniques that aid in achieving a goal in the most efficient and effective manner.

Professional helping relationship   A relationship between a worker and client(s) that follows a pattern determined by the goals and ethics of the human service field.

Program design (or program proposal)   The thoughtful mapping out of a program so that it includes an analysis of tasks, strategies, resources, responsibilities, and schedules; a budget; and an evaluation plan.

Progressive taxes   Taxes that tax rich people at a higher rate than those who are less affluent.

Progressives   Members of the Progressive party in the early twentieth century who favored social reforms such as abolition of child labor, juvenile courts, and more individualized treatment of the mentally ill.

Psychosocial model of disability   A model that looks at the entire environment of a person, including social attitudes, attitudes of other individuals, and the society that the able-bodied have created.

Public-health approach   A preventive approach to social problems as opposed to a remedial approach. It implements large-scale programs to meet people's basic health and nutritional needs in order to prevent illness.

Racism   Hatred or intolerance of another race or other races. Belief that one's own race is superior.

Reassuring   Making statements that seek to restore someone's confidence.

Red-lining   The practice of restricting a particular living area to white people, excluding people of color.

Referral file   An updated list of all available resources in a human service area with notations about the special characteristics or qualifications of each.

Referral statement   An initial verbal or written statement that explains the reasons a client is being sent to or has chosen a specific resource, person, or agency.

Reflecting   An interviewer response that puts into words what the interviewer thinks the interviewee might be feeling.

Rescue fantasy   A fantasy in which someone envisions saving another person from his or her fate.

Residential treatment center   A facility that provides mental and physical services for a specific problem population which requires that the person being treated stay within its walls for a specified period of time.

Residual philosophy of social welfare   A philosophy that believes a problem that requires help is not a "normal" social need but arises because of special circumstances brought about by individual deficiency.

Resource bank   People, places, services, or written materials that help people meet needs and reach goals.

Respite care   Provision of a paid worker to relieve a person who is a primary caretaker so that the caretaker can pursue outside tasks or have some free time.

Restraining order   A document issued by a judge that prohibits a specific person from approaching another person who feels that he or she is being threatened.

Right to refuse treatment   Legal protection granted to a person who does not want treatment that is prescribed by professionals.

Right to treatment   Legal assurance that a person who is placed in an institution that purports to give treatment does, in fact, receive treatment.

Root causes   The critical causes of a particular problem that seem to have contributed most significantly to its emergence.

Rousseau, Jean-Jacques   An eighteenth-century Swiss-French philosopher who believed that people are good by nature but corrupted by civilization.

Self-determination   People's right to determine their own life plan without interference.

Settlement house movement   The movement of the late nineteenth and early twentieth centuries that established agencies in city slums of England and the United States, where professionals gave group services and engaged in social action on behalf of the slum dwellers.

Shift from industrial to service jobs   Changes in the U.S. economy in recent decades that have reduced the number of jobs in the manufacturing industry and increased the number of jobs in the service sector.

Social Darwinism   The application of Charles Darwin's theories of evolution to the human sphere by sociologist Herbert Spencer. The concept "the survival of the fittest" was used to justify accumulation of wealth and disregard of the needs of the poor.

Stereotype   To make generalizations based on little or no information about people or a subject. The generalizations are invested with special meaning and shared by a group of people.

Stigma   Something that detracts from the character or reputation of a person or group; a mark of disgrace or reproach.

Street-level bureaucracy   The way laws and regulations are implemented by human service workers at the level of direct contact with clients.

Subjective data   Personal opinions about a client's attitude, situation, and behavior that may or may not be objectively true.

Substance abuse   The misuse of substances such as alcohol and drugs.

Suggesting   Giving a mild form of advice, generally made tentatively.

Support groups   Groups in which members help each other to clarify or act on certain issues.

Support network   The people and places in a person's life that offer ongoing practical as well as emotional help.

Systems-change strategies (interventions)   Acts aimed at helping clients by creating or improving the organizations that are supposed to deliver services to them.

Task-focused casework   A method of helping a person with a problem by focusing on the immediate priorities of the client and the small steps involved in realizing, or seeking to realize, the ultimate goal.

Tea Party Movement   The Tea Party is a political movement in the United States that has sponsored locally and nationally coordinated protests since 2009 and is generally recognized as conservative and libertarian. It endorses reduced government spending, lower taxes, reduction of the national debt and federal budget deficit, and adherence to an originalist interpretation of the U.S. Constitution.

Therapeutic, or rehabilitative   Types of groups whose members usually have in common a mental or physical problem of some magnitude. Such groups are usually led by a professionally trained leader.

Third-party payment   A payment made by an insurance company or a government program for medical expenses incurred by an individual.

Time flow chart   A diagram of the tasks that need to be done in a certain period of time by specific individuals.

Trade-offs   Things that must be sacrificed to obtain another hoped-for benefit.

Trangendered   Appearing, acting, or actually becoming (by means of medical procedures) the opposite gender from that which a person is born.

Troubleshooter   A person who is alert for signs or symptoms that indicate the existence of an actual or a potential problem.

Twelve-step program   A program of healing activities designed by the founders of Alcoholics Anonymous.

Unintended consequences of reform   Events that occur as a result of reform measures that were not planned or anticipated by the reformers.

Universal programs   Programs that provide income supports and social services to both the affluent and the poor.

Value conflicts   Disagreements brought about by differences in values between people.

Value dilemmas   A situation in which competing values make it difficult, if not impossible, to determine the correct choice.

Verbal following responses   Responses that let clients know they have been heard and understood.

Victim blaming   Blaming a person for his or her own misfortune rather than considering the social forces that contributed to the problem.

Work participation rates   1996 TANF legislation that required states to have a certain percentage of TANF recipients working, or risk losing a portion of their state TANF allocation. The percentages were raised in 2005 legislation.

References

ABC online. (2007, May 24). McDonald's insulted by dictionary definition of McJobs.

Abels, P. A. (1979). On the nature of supervision: The medium is the group. In C. E. Munson (Ed.), *Social work supervision* (pp. 174–179). New York: Free Press.

Aber, J. L., Bennett, N. G., Conley, D. C., & Li, J. (1997). The effects of poverty on child health and development. *Annual Review of Public Health 18*, 463–483.

About.com Guide (2011, February 22). Census counts Katrina housing damage. About.com US Government Info

Abramovitz, M. (1986). The privatization of the welfare state: A review. *Social Work 31*, 257–264.

Abramovitz, M. (1988). *Regulating the lives of women: Social welfare policy from colonial times to the present.* Boston: South End Press.

Abramovitz, M. (1992, Summer). Poor women in a bind: Social reproduction without social supports. *Affilia 7 (2),* 23–43.

ACORN (2010). Home page. http://www.acorn.org.

Adams, M. (2002, November). Showing good faith towards Muslims. *Human Resources Magazine 45,* 11.

Addams, J. (1902). *Democracy and social ethics.* New York: Macmillan.

ADL Anti-Defamation League. (2009). Audit of anti-semitic incidents. http://www.adl.org/NRexeres/219DC361

Administration for Children & Families. (2009). Fact Sheet. http://www.acf.hhs.gov/programs/ocs/liheap/about/factsheet.html

Administration for Children and Families, U.S. Department of Health and Human Services. (2008). "Characteristics and financial circumstances of TANF recipients," http://www.acf.hhs.gv/programs/ofa/character/FY2008/tab08.htm. Accessed April 8, 2010.

Albelda, R., & Tilly, C. (1997). *Glass ceilings and bottomless pits.* Boston: South End Press.

Albelda, R., Withorn, A., & Navin, C. (1998, May). Poor timing: An analysis of welfare time limits. Boston Area Academics' Working Group on Poverty.

Albert, E. (1989). AIDS and the press: The creation and transformation of a social problem. In Joel Best (Ed.), *Images of issues* (pp. 39–54). New York: Aldine de Gruyter.

Alejandra, L. (2010, May). Alternatives to detention: Unaccompanied immigrant children in the U.S. immigration system. Pace University. http://digital/commons.pac.edu/honorscollege_thesis97

Alinsky, S. (1969). *Reveille for radicals.* New York: Vintage Books.

Alinsky, S. (1971). *Rules for radicals: A practical primer for realistic radicals.* New York: Random House.

All Things Considered. (1992, May 20). National Public Radio.

All Things Considered. (1995, November 21). National Public Radio.

All Things Considered. (1998a, January 5). National Public Radio.

All Things Considered. (1998b, April 7). National Public Radio.

Allard, M. A., Albelda, R., Cotten, M. E., & Cosenza, C. (1997). *In harm's way? Domestic violence, AFDC receipt, and welfare reform in Massachusetts.* Boston: University of Massachusetts Press.

Allen, S. (2006). Wide gaps in U.S. life expectancy. *Boston Globe,* p. A6.

Allport, G. (1954). *The nature of prejudice.* Reading, MA: Addison-Wesley.

Alter, C., & Evans, W. (2001). *Evaluating your practice: A guide to self-assessment.* New York: Springer.

Alter, J. (1994, February 12). The name of the game is shame. *Newsweek*, p. 41.

American Association of University Women. (1978). *Community action tool catalog: Techniques and strategies for successful action programs.* Washington, D.C.: Author.

American Civil Liberties Union. (2003, December 18). *Drug policy.* www.aclu.org/drugpolicy/index.html

American Civil Liberties Union. (2007). Education not incarceration. www.aclu.com/racialjustice/racialprofiling/index.html

American Civil Liberties Union (2005, March 15). Caught in the Net: The impact of drug policies on women and families. http://www.aclu.org/drug-law-reform/caught-net-impact-drug-policies-women-and-families

American College of Physicians. (2007). No health insurance? It's enough to make you sick—scientific research linking the lack of health coverage to poor health. www.acponline.org/uninsured/lack-exec.htm

American College of Physicians. (2010). Racial and ethnic disparities in health care, updated 2010. http://www.acponline.org/advocacy/where_we_stand/access/racial_disparities.pdf

American Friends Service Committee. (2001). *Everyone is deserving.* Philadelphia: Author.

American Friends Service Committee. (2007, March 23). Substantial gaps remain in proposed house immigration bill. www.us.oneworld.net/external/?url=http%3a%2f%2Fww.afsc.org%2Fnews%F2007%Fsubstantial-Gaps-Remain-immigration-Bill.htm

American Psychiatric Association. (2000). *Diagnostic and statistical manual of mental disorders* (4th ed.). Washington, D.C.: Author.

American Psychological Association. (1963). Ethical standards of psychologists. *American Psychologist 18*, 56–60.

Andrews, H. B. (1995). *Group design and leadership.* Boston: Allyn & Bacon.

Angus Reid Global Monitor. (2007). Another immigration myth bites the dust. www.latinalista.net/palabrafinal/2007/05/by_now_the_vast_majority.html

Anti-Defamation League. (1998, September) *Anti-Semitism in America, highlights from an ADL* survey. See www.adl.org.

Anti-Defamation League. (2003, September). *Conspiracy theories about Jews and 9/11 cause dangerous mutations in global anti-Semitism.* www.adl.org.

Appleby, G. A., & Anastas, J. W. (1992). Social work practice with lesbians and gays. In A. T. Morales & B. W. Sheafor (Eds.), *Social work: A profession of many faces* (pp. 347–381). Boston: Allyn & Bacon.

Applied Research Center (2009, May). Race and Recession: How inequity rigged the economy and how to change the rules. arc.org/recession.

Arches, J. (1991). Social structure, burnout, and job satisfaction. *Social Work 36*, 202–206.

Archibold, R., & Preston, J. (2007, May 20). Illegal migrants dissect details of Senate deal. *New York Times*, p. A1.

Archibold, R., & Preston, J. (2008, May 21). Homeland Security stands by its fence. *New York Times.* http://wwwnytimes.com/2008/05/21/Washington/21/fence

Ariel, S. (1999). *Culturally competent family therapy: A general model.* Westport, CT: Greenwood Press.

Associated Press. (2010, April 5). Tutoring found to help mentors, too. *Boston Globe*, p. A2.

Atkinson, L., & Kunkel, O. D. (1992). Should social workers participate in treatment only if the client consents to such treatment freely and without coercion? In E. Gambrill & R. Pruger (Eds.), *Controversial issues in social work* (pp. 157–172). Boston: Allyn & Bacon.

Axinn, J., & Stern, M. (2001). *Social welfare: A history of the American response to need* (5th ed.). Boston: Allyn & Bacon.

Bacon, D. (2007, March 30). The real political purpose of the ICE raids. *New America Media.* http://news.newamericamedia.org/news/view_article.html?article_id=e5a3be40balf338650f2c0f793dllc3d.

Bacon, D., & Edwards, B. (2010, May 1). Hungry by the numbers. *East Bay Express.* http://www.eastbayexpress.com/ebx/hungry-by-thenumbers/Content?oid=1725214.

Baker, C. S. (2001). *Charitable choice. The employment project.* www.nomorejobs.org/charitable.htm.

Baker, P. (2010, June 3). VICTORY!! More community college students in Mass to qualify for FS/SNAP benefits! Massachusetts Law Reform Institute. pbaker@mlri.org

Bales, R. (1950). *Interaction process analysis.* Cambridge, MA: Addison-Wesley.

Bales, R., & Borgatta, E. F. (1955). Size of group as a factor in the interaction profile. In A. D. Hare, E. F. Borgatta, & R. F. Bales (Eds.), *Small groups* (pp. 396–413). New York: Alfred Knopf.

Banfield, E. (1974). *The unheavenly city.* Boston: Little, Brown.

Bannerman, S. (2007, February). *Broken by this war.* http://progressive.org/mag_bannerman0307.

Barbash, F. (1982, June 19). Justices rule for mentally retarded. *Boston Globe,* p. 13.

Barker, R. L. (1995). Private practice. In *Encyclopedia of social work,* (19th ed., Vol. 3, pp. 1905–1906). Washington, D.C.: National Association of Social Workers.

Barkley, R. (1981). *Hyperactive children.* New York: Guilford Press.

Barkley, R. (1997). *Attention deficit disorder: A clinical workbook.* New York: Guilford Press.

Barlett, D. L., & Steele, J. B. (1992). *America: What went wrong?* Kansas City, MO: Andrews & McMeel.

Barr, M. (2010, October 8). Ohio school, 4 bullied teens dead at own hand. *San Francisco Chronicle.* Associated Press.

Barry, E. (2000, February 20). Stranded. *Boston Globe,* pp. A1, A26.

Barry, E. (2002, March 3). Group stirs debate over schizophrenia. *Boston Globe,* p. B1.

Bass, A. (1992, February 3). Illness coupled with stigma. *Boston Globe,* p. 16.

Bass, B. M., & Stogdill, R. M. (1990). *Handbook of leadership.* New York: Free Press.

Bassuk, E., Browne, A., & Buckner, J. C. (1996, October). Single mothers and welfare. *Scientific American, 275,* 60-74.

Battle, M. (1990). National Association of Social Workers. In *Encyclopedia of social work: 1990 supplement* (18th ed., pp. 232–233). Silver Spring, MD: National Association of Social Workers.

Baumberger, J., & Harper, R. E, (2007). *Counseling students with disabilities.* CA: Sage-Corwin Press.

Bazelon, E. (2010, July 14). "The new abortion providers." *New York Times.* http://www.nytimes.com/2010/07/18/magazine/18/abortion-t.html

Becvar, D. S., & Pontious, S. L. (2000). Complementary alternative medicine in health and mental health: Implications for social work practice. *Social Work in Health Care, 31* (3), 39–57.

Bell, W. (1965). *Aid to dependent children.* New York: Columbia University Press.

Bennhold, K. (2010, June 9). In Sweden, man can have it all. *New York Times.* http://www.nytimes.com/2010/06/10/world/europe/10iht-sweden.html?scp=2&sq=sweden&st=cse

Benson, J. (2009). *Working more creatively with groups.* New York: Routledge.

Berenson, B. G., & Mitchell, K. M. (1974). *Confrontation: For better or worse!* Amherst, MA: Human Resource Development Press.

Berkeley Planning Associates. (1978, August). *Evaluation of child abuse and neglect demonstration projects, 1974–1977* (Vols. 1 and 2, DHEW Publication No. (PHS) 79-3217-1). Hyattsville, MD: National Center for Health Services Research, U.S. Department of Health, Education and Welfare.

Berney, L. (1984, January 15). Social, moral issues in case of 96-year-old. *Boston Globe,* p. B4.

Bernstein, M. (2004, March 16). Rape victims' center defends confidentiality. *The Oregonian.*

Bernstein, N. (1996a, August 20). Criminal and welfare rules raise new issues of fairness. *New York Times,* p. A16.

Bernstein, N. (1996b, September 15). Giant companies entering race to run state welfare programs. *New York Times,* pp. 1, 26.

Bershoff, D. N. (1975). Professional ethics and legal responsibilities: On the horns of a dilemma. *Journal of School Psychology 13,* 359–376.

Bertcher, H. J. (1994). *Group participation: Techniques for leaders and members* (2nd ed.). Thousand Oaks, CA: Sage.

Besharov, D. (2004, March 6). *There's more welfare to reform.* www.nytimes.com/2004/03/06/opinion/06BESH.htm.

Best, J. (Ed.). (1989). *Images of issues.* New York: Aldine de Gruyter.

Bettelheim, B. (1950). *Love is not enough: The treatment of emotionally disturbed children.* Glencoe, IL: Free Press.

Bill of wrath. (1998, May 11). *The Nation 266* (17), 3.

Blau, J. (1992). *The visible poor: Homelessness in the United States.* New York: Oxford University Press.

Bobo, K., Kendall, J., & Max, S. (2010). *Organizing for social change* (4th ed.). Washington, D.C.: Seven Locks Press.

Bonds, M. (2006). Race and welfare reform: The Wisconsin Works W-2 experience. *Journal of Health and Social Policy 21 (3)*, 37–54.

Bornstein, D. (2010, December 20). A plan to make homelessness history. *New York Times* http://opionator.blogs.nytimes.com/2010/12/20/a-plan-to-make-homelessness-history/

Bosman, J. (2009, February 19). Newly poor swell lines at food banks. *New York Times*. http://www.nytimes.com/2009/02/20nyregion/20food.html

Boston.com. (2009, December 3). Correction agencies' budgets soaring. http://www.boston.com/news/local/massachusetts/artickes/2009/12/03/state_correction_budget_is_soaring_new_study_says/

Boston Globe. (2008, January 8). "$26.7m recovered in Medicaid fraud cases."

Boston Globe. (2010, May 14). US antifraud effort nets Medicare $2.5b. p. A2.

Boston Women's Health Book Collective. (1978). *Ourselves and our children*. New York: Random House.

Boston Women's Health Book Collective. (1987). *Ourselves, growing older*. New York: Simon & Schuster.

Boston Women's Health Book Collective. (2006). *Our bodies, ourselves: A new edition for a new era*. New York: Touchstone Books.

Boyd, J. A. (1990). Ethnic and cultural diversity: Keys to power. In L. S. Brown & M. P. Root (Eds.), *Diversity and complexity in feminist therapy* (pp. 151–167). New York: Harrington Park Press.

Boyte, H. C. (1980). *The backyard revolution: Understanding the new citizen movement*. Philadelphia: Temple University Press.

Brager, G., Specht, H., & Torczyner, J. L. (1987). *Community organization* (2nd ed.). New York: Columbia University Press.

Brager, G. (2002). *Changing human service organizations*. New York: The Free Press.

Bramhall, M., & Ezell, S. (1991, Summer). How agencies can prevent burnout. *Public Welfare*, 33–37.

Brawley, E. A. (1980, March). *Emerging human service education programs: Characteristics and implications for social work education and practice*. [unpublished report prepared for the Joint Board Committee of the National Association of Social Workers and the Council on Social Work Education].

Breggin, P. (1991). *Toxic psychiatry*. New York: St. Martin's Press.

Breitbart, V., & Schram, B. (1978, September). Rocking the cradle without rocking the boat: An analysis of twenty-four child-raising manuals. *Bulletin of the Council on Interracial Books for Children 9* (6 and 7), 4.

Brieland, D., & Goldfarb, S. Z. (1987). Legal issues and legal services. In *Encyclopedia of social work* (pp. 29–33). Silver Spring, MD: National Association of Social Workers.

Brinkley, D. (2006). *The great deluge: Katrina, New Orleans and the Mississippi Gulf Coast*. New York: William Morrow Co.

Broder, J. & Connelly, M. (2007, April 27). Public remains split on response to warming. *New York Times*. http://www.nytimes.com/2007/04/27/washington/27poll.html

Brown, C. (1965). *Manchild in the promised land*. New York: Macmillan.

Brown, D. (2007, April 23). Medicaid programs "severely challenged," report says. *Boston Globe*, p. A2.

Bryce, H. J. (2000). *Financial and strategic management for non-profit organizations* (3rd ed.). San Francisco: Jossey-Bass.

Buckholdt, D. R., & Gubrium, J. F. (1979). *Caretakers*. Beverly Hills, CA: Sage.

The budget politics of being poor. (2003, December 31). *New York Times*.

Burgdorf, M. P., & Burgdorf, R. L., Jr. (1977). Law. In P. J. Valletutti & F. Christoplos (Eds.), *Interdisciplinary approaches to human services* (pp. 111–134). Baltimore: University Park Press.

Burger, D. (2007, March 6). *We're all at Walter Reed*. moderator@portside.org Retrieved from http://lists.portside.org/cgi-bin/listserv/wa?Az= ind0703A&L= PORTSIDE&T=O&F=&S=&P=3171.

Burnham, J. (2004). *Family therapy* (rev. ed.). New York: Routledge.

Bustillo, M. (2007, March 4). Texas bill targets benefits of immigrants' children. *Boston Globe*, p. A12.

Butler, B. B. (1990). Job satisfaction: Management's continuing challenge. *Social Work 35* (2), 25–29.

Butler, R. N. (1975). *Why survive? Being old in America.* New York: Harper & Row.

Buttell, F. (1998, Spring). Issues and ethics in social work with batterers. *The New Social Worker.*

Butterworth, I. E. (2001). The components and impact of stigma associated with EAP counseling. *Employee Assistance Quarterly 16* (3), 1–8.

Cahill, S. (2000). *Tip of the iceberg or bump in the road: The initial impact of welfare reform in Dorchester.* Boston: Massachusetts Human Services Coalition.

Canada, G. (1998). *Reaching up for manhood: Transforming the lives of boys in America.* Boston: Beacon Press.

Carden, A. (1994). Wife abuse and the wife abuser: Review and recommendations. *The Counseling Psychologist 22,* 539–582.

Capazzi, D. & Gross, G. (2008). *Introduction to the counseling professions,* 5th ed. Boston: Pearson Educational.

Carkhuff, R. R., & Berenson, B. J. (1968). *Beyond counseling and therapy.* New York: Holt, Rinehart & Winston.

Carr, G. (2010, June 6). Jobless look to Feds to save homes. *The Courier News: Business.*

Carter, B. (1995, July). Looking at families through the gay lens: An interview with Betty Carter. *In the Family,* 12–15.

Casey, T. (2010, September 16). "New poverty data for 2009—some "highlights." endpovertynow@google.groups.com

Cass, C. (2004, May 28). 1 in 75 men were in prison or jail in 2003. *Boston Globe.*

Cassidy, J. (1997, July 14). The melting pot myth. *The New Yorker,* 40–43.

Castellano, C. & Plionis, E. (2006). Comparative analysis of three crisis intervention models applied to law enforcement, first responders during the 9/11 and Hurricane Katrina. *Brief Treatment and Crisis Intervention 6* (4), 326–336.

Cawthorne, A. (2008, July 30). Elderly poverty: The challenge before us. Center for American Progress. http://www.americanprogress.org/issues/2008/07/elderly_poverty.html

CensusScope.org. (2000). Population by race. http://www.censusscope.org/us/chart_race.html.

Center for Medicare Advocacy, Inc. (2007). www.medicareadvocacy.org/FAQ_QuickStats.htm

Center for Research on Women, Wellesley College. (1999/2000, Fall/Winter). *Research Report 20,* 1.

Center on Budget and Policy Priorities. (2007a, January 23). *New CBO data show income inequality continues to widen: After-tax-income for top 1 percent rose by $146,000 in 2004.* www.cbpp.org/1-23-07inc.htm.

Center on Budget and Policy Priorities. (2010a). Free tax help and asset development. The Earned Income Credit and Child Tax Credit 2010, p11. Washington D.C.

Center on Budget and Policy Priorities. (2010b). Free tax help and asset development. Child Tax Credit 2010. Washington D.C.

Chakrabortty, A. (2010, March 2). New research shows there is a link between being politically active and wellbeing. *The Guardian* (UK). http://www.guardian.co.uk/science/2010/mar/02/brain-food-activism-makes-you-happy

Chamberlin, J. (1998). *On our own.* London: RAP.

Chambers, C. A. (1980). *Seedtime of reform: American social service and social action* 1918–1933. Westport, CT: Greenwood Press.

Chandler, D. L. (1997, May 11). In shift, many anthropologists see race as social construct. *Boston Globe,* p. A30.

Chappell, D. (2004, May 8). If affirmative action fails . . . what then? *New York Times.* http://query.nytimes.com/gst/fullpage.html?res=980DE3D7171CF938A3575

Chen, M. (2010, May 29). Living wage fight revitalized in New York City. Working In These Times Blog. http://inthesetimes.com/working/entry/6044/living_wage_fight_revitalized_in_new_york_city

Chesler, P. (1972). *Women and madness.* New York: Avon Books.

Child Trends Databank. (2007). Adopted Children. http://www.childtrendsdatabank.org/?q=node/341

Children's Defense Fund. (2004a). Child health. www.childrensdefense.org/childhealth/chip/default.asp.

Children's Defense Fund. (2004b). Testimony of the Children's Defense Fund on the impact on children of proposed federal marriage initiative. Washington D.C.: Author.

Children's Defense Fund. (2005a, June 2). Over 13 million children face food insecurity. Washington, D.C.: Author

Children's Defense Fund. (2008, September). Invest in every child: Secure the future. www.childrensdefense.org.

Clifton, R., & Dahms, A. M. (1993). *Grassroots organizations: A resource book* (2nd ed.). Prospect Heights, IL: Waveland Press.

Cloward, R. A., & Ohlin, L. E. (1964). *Delinquency and opportunity: A theory of delinquent gangs.* New York: Free Press.

CMS. (2009). The Children's Health Insurance Program (CHIP). http://www.cms.gov/LowCostHealthinsFamChild/

CNN.com/U.S. News (2000, August 8). www.cnn.com/2000/US/08/08/teen.births.ap/.

Coalition of Battered Women's Advocates. (1988, November 1). *Position paper on child welfare* [unpublished manuscript].

Coleman, S. (1997, January 28). The woman who said no. *Boston Globe,* pp. D1, D6.

Coles, R. (1977). *Privileged ones: The well-off and the rich in America.* Boston: Little, Brown.

College Board 2005, as cited in Susan Dynarski and David Deming, *Into college, out of poverty? Policies to increase the postsecondary attainment of the poor,* NBER Working Paper, 2009. http://www.nber.org/papers/w153867

Collins, P. H. (1990). *Black feminist thought: Knowledge, consciousness, and the politics of empowerment.* London: Harper Collins.

Congressional Black Caucus. (2007). *African American members of the 110th United States Congress.* www.cbcfimc.org/About/CBC/members.html.

Congressional Record (1995, September 11). The Family Self-Sufficiency Act, #473, 104th Congress (1995-1996) http://thomas.loc.gov/cgl-bin/query/r?r104:phrase (post%62Boffice):

Conklin, M. (1997, March 26). Out in the cold: Washington shows drug addicts the door. *The Progressive,* pp. 25–27.

Cooper, M. (1997, June 2). When push comes to shove: Who is welfare reform really helping? *The Nation,* pp. 11–15.

Coover, V., Deacon, C., Esser, R., & Moore, P. (1978). *Resource manual for a living revolution.* Philadelphia: New Society Press.

Copans, S., Kress, H., Gundy, J. H., Rogan, J., & Field, F. (1979). The stresses of treating child abuse. In H. Weissman, I. Epstein, & A. Savage (Eds.), *Agency-based social work: Neglected aspects of clinical practice.* Philadelphia: Temple University Press 1983.

Corcoran, K. J., & Vandiver, V. (1996). *Maneuvering the maze of managed care: Skills for the mental health practitioners.* New York: Free Press.

Cornell University (2008). Percentage of people reporting a disability in 2008. Online resources for U.S. disability statistics.http://www.//r.cornell.edu/edi/disabilitystatistics/reports/acs.cfm?statistic=1

Cottle, T. J. (1974). *A family album.* New York: Harper & Row.

Crary, D. (2003, January 12). Prison moms fight termination of parental rights. *Los Angeles Times.* http://articles.latimes.com/2003/jan12/news,adba-prisonmom12

Crary, D. (2007, March 4). Military struggles to do right by bereaved. *Boston Globe,* p. A10.

Crisp, R. and Fletcher, D. R. (2008). A comparative review of workfare programmes in the United States, Canada, and Australia. http://www.scribd.com/doc/42443808/Workfare-Doesn-t-Work

Culbert, S. A. (1976). Consciousness raising: A five stage model for social and organizational change. In W. Bennis, K. Benne, & R. Chin (Eds.), *The planning of change* (3rd ed., pp. 231–245). New York: Holt, Rinehart & Winston.

Curtin, E. R. (1970). *White-collar unionization.* New York: National Industrial Conference Board.

Cyrus-Lutz, C., & Gaitz, C. M. (1972, Summer). Psychiatrists' attitudes toward the aged and aging. *Gerontologist 12,* 163–167.

Dale, D. (1978). *How to make citizen involvement work: Strategies for developing clout.* Amherst, MA: Citizen's Involvement Training Project, University of Massachusetts.

Dale, D., Magnani, D., & Miller, R. (1979). *Beyond experts: A guide for citizen group training.* Amherst, MA: Citizen's Involvement Training Project, University of Massachusetts.

Dale, D., & Mitiguy, N. (1978). *Planning for a change: A citizen's guide to creative planning and program development.* Amherst, MA: Citizen's Involvement Training Project, University of Massachusetts.

Dao, J. (2010, July 7). V.A. is easing rules to cover stress disorder. *New York Times.* http://www.nytimes.com/2010/07/08/us/08vets.html

D'Augelli, A. R., D'Augelli, J. F., & Danish, S. J. (1981). *Helping others.* Monterey, CA: Brooks/Cole.

Davis, M. (1998, July). The illegitimacy game. *Sojourner,* p. 10.

Davis, M. H. (1994). *Empathy: A social psychological approach.* Madison, WI: Brown & Benchmark.

Davis, M. (2010). Learning to work: A functional approach to welfare and higher education. *Buffalo Law Review,* Vol. 58, p. 157.

Deci, E. and Ryan, R. (2004). *Handbook of self-determination research*. Rochester, N.Y.: University of Rochester Press.

de Cunha, P. (1983, Spring). The feel of culture shock. *Bilingual Journal 7* (3), 15–17.

Delgado, G. (1986). *Organizing the movement, the roots and growth of ACORN*. Philadelphia: Temple University Press.

Dembner, A. (2001, September 21). Medicare waste raises cost of drugs by $1b. *Boston Globe*, p. A2.

DeParle, J. (1997, September 11). As rules on welfare tighten, its recipients gain in stature. *New York Times*, pp. A1, A28.

DeParle, J. (2007, April 12). The American prison nightmare. *The New York Review of Books*, pp. 33–36.

DeParle, J., and Gebeloff, R. (2010, January 3). Living on nothing but food stamps. *New York Times*. http://www.nytimes.com/2010/01/03/us/03foodstamps.html

DePass, T. (2003, April). Bay state votes to kill bilingual ed. *Resist*, p. 3.

Detention Watch Network. (2009). About the U.S. detention and deportation system. http://www.detentionwatchnetwork.org/aboutdetention

Di Giovanni, M. (1996, April 17). Speech at the New England Organization of Human Service Educators.

Dickson, D. T. (1976, July). Law in social work: Impact on due process. *Social Work 21*, 274–278.

Doten, P. (1991, April 20). Falsely accused, a mother fights back. *Boston Globe*, p. 31.

Dougherty, R. (2001, July 22). Overworked, underpaid, undercover. *Boston Globe*, p. D4.

Dowdy, Z. B. (1998, June 21). Who pulled the trigger? *Boston Globe*, p. E1.

Drug Policy Alliance (2003). *Race and the drug war*. www.drugpolicy.org/race/.

Dumont, M. (1992). *Treating the poor*. Belmont, MA: Dymphna Press.

Dunham, W. (2007, March 17) Lifespan gap between blacks, whites in U.S. narrows. *Boston Globe*, p. A1.

Dunlap, K. (2010, January 25). "Sex offenders after prison: Any place to call home?" Find Law. http://blogs.findlaw.com/blotter/2010/01/sex-offenders-after-prison-where-to-find-a-plce-to-call-home.html

Dutton, S. (2009, June 29). Polling shows support for affirmative action. *CBS News*. http://www.cbsnews.com/8301-503544_162-5122472-503544.html

Eckholm, E. (2007, June 8). Veterans' benefits system needs overhaul, panel says. *New York Times*. http://www.hytimes.com/2007/06/08/us/08vets.html

Economist's View. (2007, March 18). *Wage insurance*. http://economistsview.typepad.com/economistsview/2007/03/wage.

Edelman, P. (1997, March). The worst thing Bill Clinton has done. *The Atlantic Monthly*, pp. 43–58.

Edelman, P. (2009, Fall). "Welfare and the poorest of the poor," *Dissent*.

Edelman, P., & Ehrenreich, B. (2010, April 10). "What really happened to welfare," *Nation*, pp. 15–17.

Ehrenreich, B. (2001). *Nickel and dimed: On (not) getting by in America*. New York: Metropolitan Books.

Ehrenreich, B. (2007, May 31). *CEOs vs. slaves*. Alternet. www.alternet.org/story/52645/.

Ehrlander, M. F. (2002). *Equal educational opportunity*. Brown's *elusive mandate*. New York: Oxford University Press.

Elias, M. (2006, August 10). USA Muslims under a cloud. *USA Today*.

Ellis (2006). Gallup poll of 1,007 Americans reported by Ellis. *USA Today*.

The Employment Project. (1997). *No more jobs*. New York: The Employment Project.

English, B. (2007, May 19). Lawmaker cuts budget to $3 a day. *Boston Globe*, p. A1.

Ennis, B. J., & Emery, R. D. (1978). *The rights of mental patients: An American Civil Liberties Union handbook*. New York: Avon Books.

Ephron, D., & Childress, S. (2007, March). Forgotten heros. *Newsweek*, pp. 31–34.

Epstein, L. (1980). *Helping people: The task-centered approach*. St. Louis C. V. Mosby Co.

Epstein, L. (1992). *Brief treatment and a new look at the task centered approach* (3rd ed.). New York: Macmillan.

Equal choice for the disabled and seniors. *The Malden Advocate*, (2001, August 3). p. 12.

Esber, G., Jr. (1989). Anthropological contributions for social work education. *Practicing Anthropology 11* (3), 4–11.

Evans, D. R., Hearn, M. T., Uhlemann, M. R., & Ivey, A. E. (1979). *Essential interviewing.* Monterey, CA: Brooks/Cole.

Evans, W. P., Fitzgerald, C., & Frantz, C. E. (Eds.). (2000). *Shocking violence: Youth perpetrators and victims: A multidisciplinary perspective.* Springfield, IL: Charles C. Thomas.

Eysenck, H. (1971). *The IQ argument.* Freeport, NY: Library Press.

Ezorsky, G. (1991). *Racism and justice: The case for affirmative action.* Ithaca, NY: Cornell University Press.

Farragher, T. (2006, October 29). *The war after the war.* www.boston.com/news/nation/articles/2006/10/29/the_war_after_the_war?mode=PF.

Fatout, M., & Rose, S. (1995). *Task groups in the human services.* Thousand Oaks, CA: Sage.

Feeding America (2010). Hunger Report 2010. http:feedingamerica.org/faces-of-hunger/hunger-in-america-2010/hunger-report-2010.aspx

Fei, M., & Peter, L. (1998). *Financial management in human services.* New York: Haworth Press.

Feldman, S. (1998). Behavioral health services: Carved out and managed. *American Journal of Managed Care, 4,* SP59–SP67.

Feldman, Y. (1979). The supervisory process: An experience in teaching and learning. In C. E. Munson (Ed.), *Social work supervision* (pp. 118–124). New York: Free Press.

Feltham, C., & Horton, I. (2000). *Handbook of counseling and psychotherapy.* Thousand Oaks, CA: Sage.

Fetterman, D. M., Kafterian, S. J., & Wandersman, A., (Eds.) (1996). *Empowerment evaluation: Knowledge for self-assessment and accountability.* Thousand Oaks, CA: Sage.

Finder, A. (1998, April 12). Evidence is scant that workfare leads to full-time jobs. *New York Times,* pp. 1, 26.

Fisher, R. (1994). *Let the people decide: Neighborhood organizing in America* (updated ed.). New York: Twayne.

Fisher, W. (2010, May 17). U.S. Overflowing prisons spur call for reform commission. Inter Press Service. http://ips.asp?idnews=51453

Flanders, L., Jackson, J., & Shadoan, D. (1997). Media lies. In D. Dujon & A. Withorn (Eds.), *For crying out loud* (pp. 29–39). Boston: South End Press.

Flannery, R. B., Jr., Fisher, H., & Walker, A. P. (2000). Characteristics of patient and staff victims of assaults in community residences by previously nonviolent psychiatric inpatients. *Psychiatric Quarterly 71,* 195–203.

Flannery, R. B. Jr., Lizotte, D., Laudani, L., Staffieri, A., & Walker, A. P. (2001). Violence against women and the assaulted staff action program. *Administration and Policy in Mental Health 28,* 491–498.

Flaubert, G. (1959). *Madame Bovary.* New York: Bantam Books (original work published 1856).

Flaws in immigration law. (1997, September 29). *New York Times,* p. A1.

Fletcher, B. (2007, May 23). *Anti-immigrant in black face? Black Commentator.* www.blackcommentator.com/231/231_cover_anti_immigrant_in_black_face_fletcher_ed_bd.html.

Fletcher, M. A. (2000, June 8). Drug war targets blacks unfairly, civil rights group says. *Boston Globe,* p. A3.

Foderaro, L. W. (2010, September 10). Private moment made public, then a fatal jump. *New York Times.* http://community.nytimes.com/comments/www.nytimes.com/2010/09/30

Food Research Action Council. (2006). *Current news & analyses.* www.frac.org/html/news/fap/2006.12_FSP.html.

Food Research and Action Center (2010, January). *Food hardship: a closer look at hunger.* Food Research and Action Center. www.frac.org.

Foot, P. (1979). Active euthanasia with parental consent [Commentary]. *Hastings Center Report,* pp. 20–21. New York: Hastings-on-Hudson.

Foreclosure to Homelessness 2009. (2009). A joint report from the National Coalition for the Homeless, the National Health Care for the Homeless Council, the National Alliance to End Homelessness, the National Association for the Education of Homeless Children and Youth, the National Law Center on Homelessness & Poverty, the National Low Income Housing Coalition, and the National Policy and Advocacy Council on Homelessness. ForeclosuretoHomelessness0609.pdf

Foreman, J. (2003, July 29). A little empathy please! *Boston Globe Online* www.boston.com/dailyglobe2/210/science/A_little_empathy_please_tishtm/3.8.2003.

Forman, J., Jr. (1992, Summer). Fighting against the tide: Defending racial preferences. *New Politics 4* (1), 171–175.

Foucault, M. (1987). *Mental illness and psychology.* Berkeley, CA: University of California Press.

Fox News (2010, May 31). Census counts illegal immigrants in detention centers, may bring aid to towns, cities. Associated

Press. http://www.foxnews.com/us/2010/05/31/census-counts-illegal-immigrants

Fox News (2011, January 5). Census: Number of poor may be millions higher. http://www.foxnews.com/us/2011/01/05/census-number-poor-millions-higher/#ixzz1I1SFpfum

Foxman, A. (2003, December 7). Reviving hate: America is not immune to canards against Jews. *Chattanooga Times Free Press.*

Frame, D. J. (1995). *Managing projects in organizations.* San Francisco: Jossey-Bass.

France, K. (1996). *Crisis intervention: A handbook of immediate person-to-person help* (3rd ed.). Springfield, IL: Charles C. Thomas.

France, K., & Kish, M. (1995). *Supportive interviewing in human service organizations: Fundamental skills for gathering and encouraging productive change.* Springfield, IL: Charles C. Thomas.

Frank, C. C. (1980, June). Children's rights after the Supreme Court's decision on Parham, J. L. and J. R. *Child Welfare 59,* 375–380.

Freeman, J. (1972). The tyranny of structurelessness. In A. Koedt, E. Levine, & A. Rapone (Eds.), *Radical feminism* (pp. 285–299). New York: Quadrangle.

Freire, P. (1970). *The pedagogy of the oppressed* (M. B. Ramos, Trans.). New York: Continuum.

Fremstad, S. (2010, May 13). Written statement submitted on May 13, 2010 for inclusion in the record of the April 22, 2010 hearing on the role of education and training in the TANF program, Subcommittee on Income Security and Family Support Committee on Ways and Means U.S. House of Representatives.

Friedlander, W. A., & Apte, R. A. (1980). *Introduction to social welfare.* Englewood Cliffs, NJ: Prentice-Hall.

Friedlin, J. (2004). *Minnesota's Family Cap on Welfare Draws Fire.* www.womensenews.org/article.cfm/dyn/aid/2033/context/archive

Friedman, T. (2007, April 15). The power of green. *New York Times Magazine.* http://www.nytimes.com/2007/04/15/magazine/15green.t.html

Frisch, N. C., & Kelley, J. (1996). *Healing life's crises: A guide for nurses.* Albany, NY: Delmar.

Gallagher, C. (2003). Color-blind privilege: The social and political functions of erasing the color line in post race America.*Race, Gender & Class* 10 (4) 22-37.

Gallup Organization (2004, May 25). *Tuesday briefing.*

GAO report reviews state sanction policies and limited data on effects on families. (2000, July). *Welfare News,* p. 2.

Gardner, H. (1962). *A thousand clowns.* New York: Penguin Press.

Gardner, M. (2005, April 4). Bankruptcy reform hits women hard. *Christian Science Monitor.* www.csmonitor.com/2005/0404/p13s01-wmgn.html.

Garfinkel, H. (1965, March). Conditions of successful degradation ceremonies. *American Journal of Sociology 61,* 420–424.

Garland, J. A., Jones, H., & Kolodny, R. (1965). A model for stages of development in social work groups. In S. Bernstein (Ed.), *Explorations in group work.* Boston: Milford House.

Garrett, L. (2004, July 17–18). The politics and profit of AIDS. *International Herald Tribune,* p. 4.

Gary, L. T. (1991). Feminist practice and family violence. In M. Bricker-Jenkins, N. R. Hooyman, & N. Gottlieb (Eds.), *Feminist social work practice in clinical settings.* Newbury Park, CA: Sage.

Gehmlich, K. (2007, January 4). France endorses housing as a legal right. Boston.com. World News. http://www.boston.com/news/world/europe/articles/2007/01/04/france_endorses_housing_as_a_legal_right

Gelbspan, R. (1986, October 19). FBI's arrest files often do injustice. *Boston Globe,* p. 15.

Gellman, B. (2000, July 6). West refused to heed early warnings of pandemic. *International Herald Tribune,* pp. 1–2.

General Accounting Office. (2001). *Long-term care: Implications of Supreme Court's Olmstead decision are still unfolding.* Statement of Kathryn G. Allen at hearing before the Special Committee on Aging, U.S. Senate, Washington DC, September 24, 2001. Serial No. 107–15. Washington D.C.: U.S. Government Printing Office.

Gerth, R. H., & Mills, C. W. (Eds.). (1958). *From Max Weber: Essays in sociology.* New York: Oxford, Galaxy.

Gilder, G. (1981). *Wealth and poverty.* New York: Bantam Books.

Gill, J. F. (2007, April 1). *New York Times,* p. 1.

Gilligan, C. (1982). *In a different voice: Psychological theory of women's development.* Cambridge, MA: Harvard University Press.

Ginsberg, L. (1998). *Careers in social work.* Boston: Allyn & Bacon.

Gitterman, A., & Shulman, L. (eds.). (1994). *Mutual aid groups, vulnerable populations, and the life cycle* (2nd ed.). New York: Columbia University Press.

Gladwell, M. (2010, September 4). Why the revolution will not be tweeted. *New Yorker*, pp. 42–49.

Glasser, I. (1989). Techniques for teaching anthropology to social work students. *Practicing Anthropology 11* (3), 5–10.

Glasser, I. (1992, Spring). Talking liberties. *Civil Liberties 2*, 376.

Glenn, D. (2001a, September 3–10). Labor of love. *The Nation 273* (7), 30–34.

Glenn, D. (2001b, Summer). I thought you said she worked full time. *Dissent*, pp. 101–105.

Golan, N. (1978). *Treatment in crisis situations.* New York: Free Press.

Goldberg, C. (2003, November 28). For good health, it is better to give, science suggests. *Boston Globe*, p. B5.

Goldberg, C. (2005, December 12). We feel your pain. *Boston Globe*, p. C1.

Goldberg, C. (2007a, May 7). "No" to drug money. *Boston Globe*, p. C1.

Goldberg, C. (2007b, June 8). Mental patients find understanding in therapy led by peers. *Boston Globe*, p. A1.

Golden, D. (1990, November 11). Halfway to where? *Boston Globe Magazine*, pp. 49–50.

Golding, W. (1959). *Lord of the flies.* New York: Capricorn Books.

Gonnerman, J. (1997, March 10). Welfare's domestic violence. *The Nation*, 21–23.

Gordon, L. (1994). *Pitied but not entitled: Single mothers and the history of welfare.* New York: Free Press.

Gordon, T. (1970). *Parent effectiveness training.* New York: Peter H. Wyden.

Gore, A. & West, D. (2006). *An inconvenient truth.* [DVD]. Paramount.

Gornick, J. C. (2001, Summer). Cancel the funeral. *Dissent*, pp. 13–18.

Gorov, L. (1997, December 23). Affirmative-action ban alters terrain in California. *Boston Globe*, p. A1.

Gorov, L. (1999, January 22). Oakland council mulls spanking ban. *Boston Globe*.

Gothard, S. (1995). Legal issues: Confidentiality and privileged communication. In *Encyclopedia of Social Work* (19th ed.). Washington, D.C.: National Association of Social Workers.

Gottlieb, N. (Ed.). (1980a). *Alternative social services for women.* New York: Columbia University Press.

Gottlieb, N. (Ed.). (1980b). Women and mental health. In *Alternative social services for women* (pp. 3–22). New York: Columbia University Press.

Gowans, P. (2000, October 13). *Privatization out of control.* Retrieved from www.google.com/search?q=Gowanst%2B+privatization+out+of+control&hl=enclient=fivefox_ar&ls=org

Green, J. (1982). *Cultural awareness in the human services.* Englewood Cliffs, NJ: Prentice Hall.

Green, J., & Leigh, J. W. (1989). Teaching ethnographic methods to social service workers. *Practicing Anthropology 11* (3), 8–10.

Greenberg, M. (1993). *Beyond stereotypes: What state AFDC studies on length of stay tell us about welfare as a way of life.* Washington, D.C.: Center for Law and Social Policy.

Greenberg, P. (1969, reprinted 1990). *The devil has slippery shoes.* Los Angeles, CA: Youth Policy Institute.

Greene, P., Christ, G. H., Corrigan, M. P., Kane, D., & Lynch, S.F. FDNY crisis innovative responses to 9/11 firefighters, families, and communities. Hoboken, NJ: John Wiley & Sons, Inc., 2008.

Greenhouse, L. (2004, May 18). States can be liable for not making courthouses accessible. *New York Times*, p. A20.

Greenhouse, S. (1997, July 24). Nonprofit and religious groups to fight workfare in New York. *New York Times*, p. A1.

Greenhouse, S. (1998, April 13). Many participants in workfare take the place of city workers. *New York Times*, pp. A1, B6.

Greenhouse, S. (2007, October 24). Child care workers in New York City vote to unionize. *New York Times*. http://www.nytimes.com/2007/10/24/nyregion/24childcare.html

Greenhouse, S. (2010, September 23). Muslims say they face more discrimination at work. *New York Times*. http://www.nytimes.com/2010/09/24/business/24muslim.html

Greenstein, R., & Horney, J. (2000, July 7). How much of the enlarged surplus is available for tax and program initiatives? Washington, D.C.: Center on Budget and Policy Priorities.

Greenstone, J. L., & Leviton, S. C. (2002). *Elements of crisis intervention: Crises and how to respond to them* (2nd ed). Monterey, CA: Wadsworth.

Grey, N. (1979, October). Tucson teachers initiate stress counseling program. *NEA Reporter 18.*

Griffin, R. (2007, April 26). *Growing older.* Brookline TAB.

Grossman, H. (1984). *Manual on terminology and classification in mental retardation.* Washington, D.C.: American Association on Mental Deficiency.

Gruenstein, D., Li, W., & Ernst, K. (2010, June 18). Foreclosures by race and ethnicity. http://www.responsible-lending.org/mortgage-lending/research-analysis/foreclosures-by-race-executive-summary.pdf

Guetzloe, E. (Ed.). (1999). Violence in children and adults: A threat to public health and safety: A paradigm of prevention.*Preventing School Failure 44* (1), 21–24.

Gutierrez, L. M. (1990, March). Working with women of color: An empowerment perspective. *Social Work 35,* 149–153.

Haas, W. (1959, July). Reaching out: A dynamic concept in casework. *Social Work* 4, 41–45.

Hacker, A. (1992, April). Speech at the Socialist Scholars Conference in New York City.

Hall, J. C., Smith, K., & Bradley, A. K. (1970, April). Delivering mental health services to the urban poor. *Social Work 15,* 35–39.

Hallums, M, & Lewis, M. (2003, June). *Welfare, poverty, and racism: The impact of race on welfare reform.* Washington, D.C: Lawyers' Committee for Civil Rights.

Halmos, P. (1966). *The faith of the counselors.* New York: Schocken Books.

Hammond, C., Hepworth, D. H., & Smith, V. G. (1977). *Improving therapeutic communication.* San Francisco: Jossey-Bass.

Hampton, R. L., Senatore, V., & Guillotta, T. P. (Eds.) (1998). *Substance abuse, family violence and child welfare.* Thousand Oaks, CA: Sage.

Handler, J. F., & White, L. (1999). *Hard labor: Women and work in the post-welfare era.* New York: M. E. Sharpe, Inc.

Hankin, C. et al. (1999, October). Prevalence of depressive and alcohol abuse symptoms among women VA outpatients who report experiencing sexual assault while in the military. *Journal of Traumatic Stress,* Vol. 12, No. 4, 601-612.

Harcourt, B. (2007, January 15). *New York Times.* www.law.uchicago.edu/news/Harcourt-mentally-ill-prisoners/index.html.

Hard times for immigrants. (1997, April 4). *New York Times,* p. A34.

Hare, A. P. (1976). *Handbook of small group research* (2nd ed.). New York: Free Press.

Hare, A. P., Borgatta, E. F., & Bales, R. F. (1955). *Small groups.* New York: Alfred Knopf.

Harris, G. (2010, August 23). "U.S. judge rules against Obama' stem cell policy." *New York Times.* http://www.nytimes.com/2010/08/24/health/policy/24stem.html

Harris, G. (2009, May 13). Out-of-wedlock birthrates are soaring, U.S. reports. *New York Times.* http://www.nytimes.com2009/05/13/health/13mothers.html

Harris Interactive. (2006). Cyberbullying Research Report. Commissioned by the National Crime Prevention Council. www.cyberbullying.org

Hastings Center. (1979). *Hastings Center report.* New York: Hastings-on-Hudson.

Hayden, T., & Novik, J. (1980). *Your rights to privacy.* New York: Avon Books.

Heller, J. (1961). *Catch-22.* NY: Dell.

Heller, N. (1981). Unpublished manuscript.

Hendricks, J. E. (1995). *Crisis intervention: Contemporary issues for on-site interveners.* Springfield, IL: Charles C. Thomas.

Hepworth, D. H., & Larsen, J. A. (1987). Interviewing. In *Encyclopedia of social work.* Silver Spring, MD: National Association of Social Workers.

Hepworth, C., Rooney, R. H., Rooney, G., Strom-Gottfried, K., and Larsen, J. (2010). *Direct social work practice: theory and skills,* 8th ed. Florence, KS: Cengage Learning.

Herbert, B. (1996, July 23). Welfare "reform": Officially sanctioned brutality. *International Herald Tribune,* p. 2.

Herbert, B. (1998, June 14). Hidden agendas. *New York Times,* p. 17.

Herbert, B. (2004, June 11). Punishing the poor. *New York Times.*

Herbert, B. (2010, June 7). A very deep hole. *New York Times,* p. A27.

Heron, K. A. (2010, September 21). Doctors orders: Eat well to be well. *New York Times,* p. D1.

Herrnstein, R. (1971, September). I.Q. *Atlantic Monthly*, pp. 43–64.

Higgins, A. (2004, May 14). Program bolsters violence, victims' confidentiality. *Bangor Daily News*.

Himmelstein, D., Warren, E., Thorne, D., & Woolhandler, S. (2005, February 2). Illness and injury as contributors to bankruptcy. *Health Affairs* (2005). http://content.healthaffairs.org/content/early/2005/02/02/hlthaff.w5.63.full.pdf+html

HIV-related knowledge and stigma. (2001, March 14). Morbidity and mortality weekly report. *Journal of the American Medical Association 10*, 285.

Hockenberry, J. (2005, July 24). Yes, you can. *Parade Magazine*, p. 4.

Hoff, L. A. (2001). *People in crisis: Clinical and public health perspectives*. San Francisco, CA: Jossey-Bass.

Hoff, L. A., & Kaimiera, A. (1998). *Creating excellence in crisis care: A guide to effective training and program design*. San Francisco: Jossey-Bass.

Hoffman, B., and Kasupki, R. (2007) *The victims of terrorism: An assessment of their influence and growing role in policy, legislation, and the private sector*. Santa Monica, CA: RAND Corporation. http://www.rand.org/content/dam/rand/pubs/occasional_papers/2007/RAND_OP180-1.pdf

Holland, S. (2004). *Childhood family assessment in social work practice*. Thousand Oaks, CA: Sage.

Hollar, J. (2010, June) Wealth gap yawns—and so do media. *Extra!* http://www.commondreams.org/view/2010/06/02-10

Holmes, S. A. (1997, December 21). Thinking about race with one-track mind. *New York Times*, pp. 1, 12.

Hooks, B. (1997). Representing whiteness in the black imagination. In R. Frankenber (Ed.), *Displacing whiteness*. Durham, NC: Duke University Press.

Houston, L. P., & Cohen, A. C. (1972, Fall). The college for human services: A model for alternative professional education. *New Generation 54* (4), 22–23.

Hoyt, M. F. (1995). *Brief therapy and managed care: Readings for contemporary practice*. San Francisco: Jossey-Bass.

Hsu, F. L. K. (1971). *The challenge of the American dream: The Chinese in the United States*. Belmont, CA: Wadsworth.

HUD.Gov/Recovery (2009, February 17). HUD implementation of the Recovery Act. http://portal.hud.gov/portal/page/portal/HUD/recovery/about

Huezo, J., Mazher, A., Miller, B., Mwangi, W., & Prokosch, M (2009). The state of the dream 2009: The silent depression. United for a Fair Economy, 2009. www.faireconomy.org/dream.

Huffington, A. (2007, March 24). The war on drugs' war on minorities. *Los Angeles Times*. www.commondreams.org/archive/2007/03/24/63/.

Huffington Post, (2010). "Health Reform Bill Summary." http://www.huffingtonpost.com/2010/03/22/health-reform-bill-summary_n_508315.html#s75236

Human services referral directory of Massachusetts. (2004). Kennebunkport, ME: George D. Hall Co.

Hunt, A. (2010, July 26). Chief gains for disabled are attitude. *International Herald Tribune*, p. 2.

Hurley, R. (1969). *Poverty and mental retardation: A causal relationship*. New York: Vintage Books.

Indian Country (2006). *Fuel assistance program kicks off*. www.indiancountry.com/content.cfm?id=1096414145.

Ingram, R. (1992, April). When therapy is oppression. *Transactional Analysis Journal 22* (2), 95–100.

Inter-Religious Task Force for Social Ministries. (1979). *A parable of good works: Must we choose sides?*

International Herald Tribune. (2000, August, p. 3) Editorial.

Issues and controversies: Immigration update. (1997, October 10). Facts on File News Services.

Jackson, B. (2003, November 24). Poll of teens back Affirmative Action for college admission. *Rocky Mountain News*.

Jackson, D. Z. (1998, April 15). Women on welfare need education: Why deny them? *Boston Globe*, p. 23.

Jackson, D. Z. (2007, February 28). The politics of drug sentencing. *Boston Globe*, p. A7.

Jackson, D. Z. (2010, September 21). Apartheid in our schools. *Boston Globe*, p. A11.

Jacobs, E. E., Masson, R. L., & Harvill, R. L. (2009). *Group counseling: Strategies and Skills*. Belmont, CA: Thompson/Brooks Cole.

Janofsky, M. (2001, July 15). States pressed as 3 boys die at boot camps. *New York Times*, pp. A1, A13.

Jarmon, R. L., McFall, J., Kolar, P., & Strom, G. (1997). The changing context of social work practice: Implications and recommendations for social work educators. *Journal of Social Work Education* 33, 29–46.

Jay, J. & Jay, D. (2000). *Love first: A new approach to intervention for alcoholism and drug addiction.* Center City, MN: Hazelden Publishing.

Jenkins, S. (1981). *The ethnic dilemma in social services.* New York: Free Press.

Jenson, J. M., & Howard, M. O. (Eds.) (1999). *Youth violence: Current research and recent practice innovations.* Washington, D.C.: NASW Press.

Jesella, K. (2007, February 22). Mom's mad. And she's organized. *New York Times.* http://www.nytimes.com/2007/02/22/fashion/22mothers.html/

Joffe, C. (1983). Abortion work: Strains, coping strategies, policy implications. In H. Weissman, I. Epstein, & A. Savage (Eds.), *Agency-based social work: Neglected aspects of clinical practice* (pp. 62–67). Philadelphia: Temple University Press.

Johnson, D. (1996, May 19). Wisconsin welfare effort on schools is a failure, study says. *New York Times*, p. 6.

Jordan, B. (1998, March 18–25). The long arm of immigration reform. *Christian Century 115* (9), 15.

Jordan, C., & Franklen, C. (1995). *Clinical assessment for social workers: Quantitative and qualitative methods.* Chicago: Lyceum Books.

Journal of Small Group Research. Thousand Oaks, CA: Sage Publishers. (All issues from 1970 to present can be accessed on line.)

Kadushin, A. (1980). *Child welfare services* (3rd ed.). New York: Macmillan.

Kadushin, A. (1992). *Supervision in social work* (3rd ed.). New York: Columbia University Press.

Kagan, J. (1989). *Unstable ideas: Temperament, cognition & self.* Cambridge, MA: Harvard University Press.

Kahn, S. (1970). *How people get power.* New York: McGraw-Hill.

Kahn, S. (1995). *Organizing: A guide for grassroots leaders.* Washington, D.C.: NASW Press.

Kaminer, W. (1997, November/December). Unholy alliance. *American Prospect 35*, 54–55.

Kaminer, W. (2001). Religion, public schools, and gray areas. *Free Inquiry 21*, 3.

Karger, H. (1981). Burnout as alienation. *Social Service Review* 55, 271–283.

Katz, M. B. (1989). *The undeserving poor: From the war on poverty to the war on welfare.* New York: Pantheon.

Katz, N. L. (1997, December 28). California's Prop 209 clouds future of some programs. *Boston Globe*, p. 17.

Keefe, T., & Maypole, D. E. (1983). *Relationships in social service practice: Context and skills.* Monterey, CA: Wadsworth.

Keltner, D. (2009, February 28) "Darwin 2C: The evolutionary logic of kindness," Portside, http://www.sciam.com/article.cfm?id=kindness-emotions-psychology

Keith-Lucas, A. (1972). *Giving and taking help.* Chapel Hill, NC: University of North Carolina Press.

Keller, M. (2005, Fall). Abortion procedures ban ruled unconstitutional. National Organization for Women. www.now.org/nnt/fall-2004/pba.html

Kelly, S., & Blythe, B. J. (2000). Family preservation: A potential not yet realized. *Journal of Child Welfare LXXIX*(1), 29–41.

Kennedy, E. (2001). *On becoming a counselor: A basic guide for non-professional counselors and other helpers* (rev. ed.). New York: Crossroads Classics.

Kernberg, P. F. et al. (1991). *Children with conduct disorders: A psychotherapy manual.* New York: Basic Books.

Kettner, P. M., Moroney, R. M., & Martin, L. L. (2007). *Designing and managing programs: An effectiveness based approach*, 3d ed. Newbury Park, CA: Sage.

Kilborn, P. (1997, December 10). Mentally ill called victims of cost-cutting. *New York Times*, p. A20.

Kindlon, D., & Thompson, M. (2000). *Raising Cain: Protecting the emotional life of boys.* New York: Ballantine.

Kingston, M. H. (1977). *The woman warrior: Memoirs of a girlhood among ghosts.* New York: Alfred Knopf.

Kinney, J., Haapala, D., Booth, C., & Leavitt, S. (1988). The homebuilder's model. In J. K. Whittaker, J. Kinney, J. Tracy, E. M. Tracy, & C. Booth (Eds.), *Improving practice technology for work with high risk families: Lessons from the homebuilders.* Seattle, WA: Center for Sociological Welfare Research, University of Washington School of Social Work.

Kinsella, S., (2007, March 10). Personal communication.

Kinsey, A. C., Pomeroy, W. B., & Martin, C. E. (1948). *Sexual behavior in the human male.* Philadelphia: W. B. Saunders.

Kirk, S. A., & Greenley, J. R. (1974). Denying or delivering services? *Social Work 19,* 439–447.

Kirkpatrick, M., & Hitchens, D. (1985). Lesbian mothers/Gay fathers. In D. H. Schetky & E. P. Benedek (Eds.), *Emerging issues in child psychiatry and the law.* New York: Brunner/Mazel.

Kjosness, J., Barr, L. R., & Rettman, S. (2004). *Research navigator guide: The helping professions.* Boston, MA: Allyn & Bacon.

Klein, A. (2004, April 9). Affirmative-action opponents suffer setbacks in Colorado and Michigan. *Chronicle of Higher Education.* http://chronicle.com/article/Affirmative-Action-Opponents/32016

Klein, A. F. (1953). Society, democracy and the group. New York: Morrow.

Knowles, M., & Knowles, H. (1959). *Introduction to group dynamics.* New York: Association Press.

Koedt, A. (1971). The myth of the vaginal orgasm. In *Liberation now: Writings from the women's liberation movement* (pp. 311–320). New York: Dell.

Kowalczyn, L. (2001, August 6). Despite U.S. law, seniors click on Canada for drugs. *Boston Globe,* p. A1.

Kravetz, D. F., & Rose, S. D. (1973). *Contracts in groups: A workbook.* Dubuque, IA: Kendall-Hunt.

Krugman, P. (2008, February 18). Poverty is poison. *New York Times.* http://www.nytimes.com/2008/02/18/opinion/18krugman.html

Kurzman, P. A. (1971). *The Mississippi experience: Strategies for welfare rights action.* New York: Association Press.

Kuttner, R. (2004, April 21). The problem with outsourcing. *Boston Globe,* p. A19.

Kuttner, R. (2007, March 31). Comeback attempt for the labor movement. *Boston Globe,* p. A11.

La Botz, D. (2007, Summer). The immigrant rights movement: Between political realism and social idealism. *New Politics,* pp. 24–33.

Lacombe, A. (1997, June 2). *Welfare reform and access to jobs in Boston.* Boston: Bureau of Transportation Statistics.

Lahr, J. (2001, April 16). Been here and gone. *The New Yorker,* p. 50.

Lakien, A. (1987). *How to get control of your time and your life.* New York: The New American Library (Signet Division).

Landers, S. (1998, May). Balancing confidences, laws, and ethics. *NASW News,* p. 3.

Lasser, K., Himmelstein, D., & Woolhandler, S. (2006, July). Access to care, health status, and health disparities in the United States and Canada: Results of a cross-national population-based survey. *American Journal of Public Health, 96.*

LatinosVote.com. (2007). *Latino leaders.* www.latinosvote.com/index.php?section=leaders.

Latour, F. (2002, June 16). Marching orders: After 10 years, state closes boot camp. *Boston Globe,* p. B1.

Lauffer, A. (1997). *Grants etc.* Thousand Oaks, CA: Sage. The law on disabilities. (1983, February 23). *Boston Globe,* p. 18.

Lawrence, S. (2002). *Domestic violence and welfare policy: Research findings that can inform policies on marriage and child well-being.* New York, NY: National Center for Children in Poverty.

Lazar, K. (2008, March 27). When school needs counter student rights. *Boston Globe,* p. B1.

Lazarin, M. (2003, November/December). Children of immigrants dare to dream. *Network Connection,* pp. 8–9.

Lefferts, S. (1982). *People's guide to health care.* Stony Brook, NY: Social Services Interdisciplinary Program, State University of New York.

Legal Momentum (2009). The bitter fruit of welfare reform: A sharp drop in the percentage of eligible women and children receiving welfare. Available at http://www.legalmomentum.org/assets/pdfs/lm-tanf-bitter-fruit.pdf.

Lehrer, T. (1965). *Too many songs.* http://www.scribd.com/doc/21011329/Too-Many-Songs-by-Tom-Lehrer

Leichter, H. J., & Mitchell, W. E. (1967). *Kinship and casework.* New York: Russell Sage Foundation.

Leonhardt, D. (2007, May 30). Truth, fiction and Lou Dobbs. *New York Times,* p. 30 Business.

Lerner, M. & West, C. (1996). *Jews and Blacks: A dialogue on race, religion, and culture in America.* New York: Plume.

Lester, B. M., & Tronick, E. Z. (1994). The effects of prenatal cocaine exposure on child outcome. *Infant Mental Health Journal 15,* 107–120.

Lever, R. (2007, February 13). *Agence France Presse—English.*

Levi-Strauss, C. (1974). Reciprocity, the essence of social life. In R. L. Coser (Ed.), *The family: Its structures and functions* (pp. 3–12). New York: St. Martin's Press.

Lewin, K., Lippett, R., & White, R. K. (1939). Patterns of aggressive behavior in experimentally created social climates. *Journal of Social Psychology 10*, 271–299.

Lewis, J. A., Lewis, M. D., Packard, T., & Souflec, F. (2006). *Management of human service programs* (2nd ed.). Pacific Grove, CA: Brooks/Cole.

Lewis, N. A. (1997, April 2). With immigration law in effect, battles go on. *New York Times*, p. 1.

Lewis, O. (1961). *The children of Sanchez*. New York: Random House.

Lewis, O. (1966). *La vida: A Puerto Rican family in the culture of poverty—San Juan and New York*. New York: Random House.

Lieberman, M. A., Yalom, I. D., & Miles, M. B. (1973). *Encounter groups: First facts*. New York: Basic Books.

Lieberman, T. (2006, January 30). Part D from outer space, *The Nation*. http://www.thenation.com/article/part-d-outer-space

Lindblom, C. E., & Cohen, D. K. (1979). *Usable knowledge: Social science and social problem solving*. New York: Simon and Schuster.

Lipsky, M. (1980a). *Street-level bureaucracy: Dilemmas of the individual in public services.* New York: Basic Books.

Littner, N. (1957). *The strains and stresses on the child welfare worker*. New York: Child Welfare League of America.

Living Wage Resource Center (2007). *Acorn and Living Wage*. www.livingwagecampaign.org/index.php?id=2070.

Lloyd, J. C., & Bryce, M. E. (1984). *Placement prevention and family reunification: A handbook for the family centered practitioner* (rev. ed.). Iowa City, IA: National Resource Center on Family Based Services, University of Iowa School of Social Work.

Locke, I. S., Spirduso, W. & Silverman (2007). *Proposals that work* (5th ed.). Thousand Oaks, CA: Sage.

Lopresi, P., & Maag, E. (2009, May). Disabilities among TANF recipients: Evidence from the NHIS. Washington, D.C.: The Urban Institute.

Loughary, J. W., & Ripley, T. (1979). *Helping others help themselves: A guide to counseling skills*. New York: McGraw-Hill.

Lowman, R. L., & Resnick, R. J. (Eds.). (1994). *The mental health professional's guide to managed care*. Washington, D.C.: The American Psychological Association.

LPAC (Legal Profession Assistance Conference of the Canadian Bar Association). (2006, February). Compassion fatigue — Because you care. *St. Petersburg Bar Association Magazine.* http://www.lpac.ca/main/articles_bibs/vicarious_bib.aspx

LRP Publications. (2004, April 12). *Agencies seek to improve measurement of disability population*. http://www.ahead.org/aff/ctahead/doc.guidelines.htm

Lukes, C. A., & Land, H. (1990, March). Biculturality and homosexuality. *Social Work 35* (2), 155–161.

Luo, M. (2010, August 4). Out of work, and now out of jobless benefits. *International Herald Tribune*, p. 14.

Lyons, P., & Rittner, B. (1998, April). The construction of the crack babies phenomenon as a social problem. *American Journal of Orthopsychiatry 68* (2), 42–49.

Maas, H. S., & Engler, R. E., Jr. (1959). *Children's need of parents*. New York: Columbia University Press.

MacKenzie, K. R. (Ed.). (1995). *Effective use of group therapy in managed care*. Washington, D.C.: American Psychiatric Press.

MacQuarrie, B. (2007, March 14). Guardsmen in Kosovo may see pay cut, *Boston Globe*, p. B1.

Madara, E. J., & Meese, A. (1998). *The self-help sourcebook: Finding and forming mutual aid self-help groups*. Denville, NJ: The Self-Help Clearing House, Saint Clares-Riverside Medical Center.

Maier, G. J. (1996). Managing threatening behavior: The role of talk down and talk up. *Journal of Psychosocial Nursing, 34* (6), 25–30.

Malcolm X., & Haley, A. (1966). *The autobiography of Malcolm X*. New York: Grove Press.

Mancillas, J. (2001, September 3/10). Jorge Mancillas replies to "Changing to Organize." *The Nation 273* (7), 24.

Mandell, B. (1973). *Where are the children? A class analysis of foster care and adoption*. Lexington, MA: D. C. Heath.

Mandell, B. (1997, Winter). Downsizing the welfare state. *New Politics*, pp. 33–46.

Mandell, B. (2004a, Summer). Diminishing welfare: A review essay. *New Politics*, pp. 158–174.

Mandell, B. (2004c, Winter). *You've been well cared for*. New Politics, pp. 136–137.

Mandell, M. (1997, Summer). In defense of social security. *New Politics 6* (3), 21–29.

Mark, R. (1996). *Research made simple: A handbook for social workers.* Thousand Oaks, CA: Sage.

Marlow, C. (2005). *Research methods for generalist social work.* Pacific Grove, CA: Brooks/Cole.

Martin, L. (2001) *Financial management for human service administrators.* Boston: Allyn & Bacon.

Martin, L. L., & Kettner, P. M. (2009). *Measuring the performance of human service programs* (2nd ed.). Thousand Oaks, CA: Sage.

Martin, R. (2001). *Listening up: Reinventing ourselves as teachers and students.* Portsmouth, NH: Heinemann.

Maslach, C. (1966, September). Burned out. *Human Behavior,* pp. 16–22.

Maslach, C. (1978). The client role in staff burnout. *Journal of Social Issues 34* (4), 111–124.

Mass Human Services Coalition (2001). *State House Watch.* Boston: Author.

Massachusetts Alliance to Reform CORI (2007). *C.O.R.I.* www. unionofminorityneighborhoods.org/marc/whatiscori.html.

Massachusetts Civil Liberties Union. (1983, August). Computer matching serious threat to privacy. *The Docket 13.*

Massachusetts Coalition for the Homeless. (2000). *Home stretch support and action group: Voices of homelessness.* Boston: Self Published.

Massachusetts English Plus Coalition. (2003, April). *Resist,* p. 5.

Matchan, L. (1992, January 8). Once homeless, now in tug of war. *Boston Globe,* pp. 1, 9.

Maxwell, M. L. (1988, Fall). Empower. *Social Policy,* pp. 11–16.

Mayer, J., & Timms, N. (1970). *The client speaks: Working class impressions of casework.* Chicago: Aldine Publishing.

McClellan, M. (2004) "Faith and federalism: Do Charitable Choice provisions preempt state nondiscrimination employment laws?" *Washington and Lee Law Review.* http://litigation-essentials.lexisnexis.com/webcd/app/actor

McCourt, K., & Nyden, G. (1990). *Promises made, promises broken ... the crisis and challenge: Homeless Families in Chicago.* Chicago Institute on Urban Poverty and Travelers & Immigrants Aid.

McGowan, J. F., & Porter, T. L. (1967). *An introduction to the vocational rehabilitation process.* Washington, D.C.: U.S. Department of Health, Education, and Welfare, Vocational Rehabilitation Administration.

McHugh, D. (2007). US, Britain ranked last on child welfare. *Boston Globe,* p. A4.

McKibben, B. (1989) *The end of nature.* New York: Anchor Books, Random House.

McKibben, B. (2007). *Deep economy: The wealth of communities and the durable future.* New York: Times Books/Henry Holt & Co.

McKibben, B. K (2007). *Fight global warming now: The handbook for taking action in your community.* New York: Holt Paperbacks.

McKinley, J. (2010, October 4). Suicides put light on pressures of gay teenagers. *New York Times,* p. A9.

McKnight, J. (1992, April 22). Speech at Foundations Affecting the Future of Massachusetts' Communities Forum on Community Organizing.

McMurray, J. (2008, March 29). Colleges keep closer watch on students. *Boston Globe,* p. A2.

McNamara, E. (1991, December 26). "Last one over the wall": Battling youth crime with compassion. *Boston Globe,* p. 24.

McNamara, E. (1995, October 20). Where will your mother go now? *Boston Globe,* p. 28.

McRoy, R. G. (1990). A historical overview of black families. In S. Logan, E. M. Freeman, & R. McRoy (Eds.), *Social work practice with black families* (pp. 3–17). White Plains, NY: Longman.

McSwain, C., & Davis, R. (2007, July). *College access for the working poor: Overcoming burdens to succeed in higher education.* Institute for Higher Education Policy. http://www.cpec.ca.gov/CompleteReports/ExternalDocuments/College_Access_for_the_Working_Poor_2007_Report.pdf.

Mechanic, D., Olfson McAlpine, D. D. (1999). Mission unfulfilled: Potholes on the road to mental health parity. *Health Affairs, 18* (5), 7–21.

Meckler, L. (2004, October 16). 'Get tough' programs for youths criticized. *Boston Globe,* p. A3.

Medrano, L. (2011, April 1). Arizona march puts spotlight on shootings by border patrol. *Christian Science Monitor.* http://www.google.com/search?q=Arizona+march+puts+spotlight+on+shootings+by+border+patrol.

Michaiko, M. (2006) *Tinkertoys: A handbook of creative thinking techniques.* Berkeley, CA: Ten Speed Press.

Middleton-Mozm, J., & Dwinell, L. (2010). *After the Tears* (revised). Deerfield Beach, Fla: HCI Books.

Milgram, S. (1974). *Obedience to authority: An experimental view.* New York: Harper & Row.

Miller, J. B. (1976). *Toward a new psychology of women.* Boston: Beacon Press.

Miller, J. G. (1991). *Last one over the wall: The Massachusetts experiment in closing reform schools.* Athens, OH: Ohio University Press.

Miller, J. G. (2008, March 7). Who will look out for DYS inmates? *Boston Globe,* p. A14.

Miller, M. (2009) *A community organizers tale: People and power in San Francisco* Berkeley, CA: Ten Speed Press.

Miller, P. (1992). *The worst of times.* New York: Harper Collins.

Milligan, S. (2007, June 5). Fiscal lift, burden in immigrant legislation. *Boston Globe,* p. A1.

Mills, C. W. (1943, September). The professional ideology of social pathologists. *American Journal of Sociology 49,* 165–180.

Mills, C. W. (1959). *The sociological imagination.* New York: Oxford University.

Mink, G. (1998). *Welfare's end.* Ithaca, NY: Cornell University Press.

Miranne, K. B., & Young, A. H. (1998, June). Women reading the world: Challenging welfare reform in Wisconsin. *Journal of Sociology and Social Welfare 25,* 155–176.

Mitiguy, N. (1978). *The rich get richer and the poor write proposals.* Amherst, MA: Citizen's Involvement Training Project, University of Massachusetts.

Mizrahi, T., & Morrison, J. (Eds.). (1993). *Community organization & social administration.* New York: Haworth Press.

Moderator@portside.org. (2007, February 14). *New Orleans public housing residents issue urgent call for electrical support.* Retrieved from http://lists.portside.org/cai-bin/listserve/wa?A/=/nd0702BdL=PORTSIDE.Re/

Mondros, J. B., & Wilson, S. M. (1994). *Organizing for power and empowerment.* New York: Columbia University Press.

Moon, S., & Hegar, R. (2006, January 14). *Impact of TANF status and ethnicity on early school success: Implications for social policy.* Society for Social Work and Research. http://sswr.confex.com/sswr/2006/techprogram/P4188.htm.

Mora, J. (2010, May 2). Overstated optimist: Arizona's Structured English Immersion Program. A research paper presented at the annual meeting of the American Educational Research Association. Denver, Colorado. http://www.moramodules.com/documents/MoraFloresAERA5-10.pdf

Morales, A. (1978, July). Institutional racism in mental health and criminal justice. *Social Casework 59,* 387–395.

Moran, T. (2000, September). *Immigrants still hurting from welfare reform.* Boston: Massachusetts Immigration and Refugee Advocacy Coalition.

Morse, S. (2004). *How citizens and local leaders can use strategic thinking to build a brighter future.* San Francisco, CA: Jossey-Bass.

Mosher, L., & Berti, L. (1989). *Community mental health: Principles and practice.* New York: Norton.

Moss, M. S. (2001, May). HHS gets additional comments on privacy rules. *NASW News 46* (5), p. 4.

Moynihan, D. P. (1965). *The Negro family: The case for national action.* Washington, D.C.: U.S. Department of Labor, Office of Policy Planning and Research.

Murray, C. A. (1984). *Losing ground: American social policy 1950–1980.* New York: Basic Books.

Murray, C. A. (1994, October 29). The coming white underclass. *Wall Street Journal.*

Murray, C., & Herrnstein, R. (1994). *The bell curve: Intelligence and class structure in American life.* New York: Free Press.

Musto, D. F. (1988). Evolution of American attitudes toward substance abuse. *Annals of the New York Academy of Science 562,* 3–7.

Nader, R. (2007, April 16). *Outrageous words, outrageous deeds.* www.commondreams.org/archive/2007/04/16/564/.

National Alliance to End Homelessness. (2005). *Homelessness counts.* Washington, D.C.: Self Published.

National Association of Social Workers. (1982, September). Suit settlement favors confidentiality of records. *NASW News 27*(7), 7.

National Association of Social Workers. (1983, February). Congress, district court chop rate of disability cutoffs. *NASW News 28*(2), 9.

National Center for Health Statistics, (2008). Health, United States, 2008. http://www.cdc.gov/nchs/fastats/lifexpect.htm

National Center for Law and Economic Justice (2010). Colorado court rules that due process applied to TANF benefits despite "no entitlement" language. http://www.nclej.org/courts-resources-coloradocourt.php

National Center for Missing & Exploited Children. (2007). *Sex-offenders: History.* http://www.missingkids.com/missingkids/servlet/PageServlet?LanguageCountry=en_US&PageId=1545

National Center for Policy Analysis (2001). *Fraud in Medicare.* www.ncpa.org/health/pdh5.html.

National Center for Youth Law (2001). *Charlie, Nadine H., V. Whitman et al.* http://www.youthlaw.org/publications/fe_docket/alpha/charlieandnadineh/Chasnoff, I. J. (1989). Drug use in women: Establishing a standard of care. *Annals of the New York Academy of Science 562,* 208–210.

National Center on Child Abuse and Neglect. (1979, September). *Resource materials,* OHDS, Children's Bureau, DHEW, Publication No. 79-30221. Washington, D.C.: Department of Health, Education, and Welfare.

National Commission for Human Service Workers. (1982, July). *Registration and certification of human service workers.* Paper prepared and distributed by the National Commission for Human Service Workers (NCHSW). Atlanta.

National Conference of Catholic Bishops. (1986). *Economic justice for all: Pastoral letter on Catholic social teaching and the U.S. economy.* Washington, D.C.: United States Catholic Conference.

National Employment Law Project. (2004). Why Unemployment Insurance matters to working women and their families. An important tool in the work-family balance. http://nelp.3cdn.net/160e9cc27e3f2a6d6e_bwm6b5dz6.pdf.

National Housing Law Project. (2002) *False HOPE: A critical assessment of the Hope VI public housing redevelopment program. Supra note 54.* www.nhlp.org/html/pubhsg/FalseHOPE.pdf.

National Law Center on Homelessness & Poverty (2006). *Homelessness and United States compliance with the international covenant on civil and political rights.* Washington, D.C., May 31.

National Organization for Women. (2004a, March 26). *NOW fights right-wing assault on abortion rights, urges supporters to march on April 25th.* www.now.org/press/03-04/03-26.html.

National Public Radio. (2009, February 16). Foster care system unkind to black children. http://www.npr.org/templates/story/story.php?storyId=100694902

National Women's Law Center. (2010, April). Women's lower wages worsen their circumstances in a difficult economy. www.nwlc.org/pdf/lowerwageshurtwomen.pdf.

National Women's Law Center. (2010b, October 21) *Mothers Behind Bars: A state-by-state report card and analysis of federal policies on conditions of confinement for pregnant and parenting women and the effect on their children.* http://www.nwlc.org/resource/mothers-behind-bars-state-state-report-card-and-analysis-federal-policies-conditions-confin

Nelson, T. S., & Tripper, T. S. (Eds.) (1998). *101 more interventions in family therapy.* New York: Haworth Press.

New York Times. (2004, June 23). A blow to health plan patients.

New York Times. (2009, September 25). Medicare. http://topics.nytimes.com/top/news/health/diseasesconditionsandhealthtopics/medicare/index.html medicare

New York Times. (2010, May 6). Foreclosures. http://topics.nytimes.com/top/reference/timestopics/subjects/f/foreclosures/index.html

New York Times (2010, July 29), Breaking a promise on surveillance. http://www.nytimes.com/2010/07/30/opinion/30fri1.html?ref=usa_patriot_act

New York Times. (2010, October 17). Running against food stamps. Editorial.

Newman, B. (2001, August 29). Lost in America: Quirk in law creates health-care minefield for legal immigrants. *Wall Street Journal,* pp. A1, A16.

A new picture of poverty. (1997, November 25). *Boston Globe,* p. 11.

Nichols, K., & Jenkinson, J. (2006). *Leading a support group.* Berkshire, UK: Open University Press (McGraw Hill Co).

Nichols, K., & Potter, K. (1995, March 14). General assistance programs: Gaps in the safety net. Washington, D.C.: Center for Budget and Policy Priorities.

Nickerson, C. (1985, March 10). Reformers' dream that went astray. *Boston Globe,* p. 21.

Norsigian, J., & Newman, S. (2001, August 3). Ban human cloning right now. *Boston Globe,* p. A23.

Northeast Action. (2004, Spring). *Worldview and immigrant rights.*

NOW (2008, August 15). The Border Fence. PBS. http://www.pbs.org/now/shows/432/

Nussbaum, L. (2008, October 10). Charitable Choice and the 2008 presidential campaign. http://www.rothgerder.com/showarticle.aspx?Show=1057

Nystul, M. (2010). *Introduction to Counseling: An art and science perspective.* Upper Saddle River, N.J.: Pearson.

O'Connor, J. (1973). *The fiscal crisis of the state.* New York: St. Martin's Press.

O'Harrow, R., Jr. (2001, January 21). Medical Privacy: Exception to a rule. *Boston Globe,* p. A13.

Okun, B. (1991). *Effective helping: Interviewing and counseling techniques* (4th ed.). Pacific Grove, CA: Brooks/Cole.

Okun, B. (1996). *Understanding diverse families: What practitioners need to know.* New York: Guilford Press.

Okun, B., Fried, J., & Okun, M. (1999). *Understanding diversity: A learning-as-practice primer.* Pacific Oaks, CA: Grove/Brooks Cole Publishing Co.

Okun, B., & Rappaport, L. (1980). *Working with families: An introduction to family therapy.* North Scituate, MA: Duxbury Press.

O'Neill, J. V. (2001). MCOs hear practitioners' grievances. *NASW News 46*(2), 1–4.

Open Congress (2010). H.R. 4213 — Unemployment Compensation Act of 2010. http://www.opencongress.org/bill/111-h4213.show

Ortiz, E. T., & Bassoff, B. Z. (1988). Proprietary hospital social work. *Health and Social Work 13,* 114–121.

Orwell, G. (1950). Politics and the English language. In *Shooting an elephant and other essays* (pp. 84–101). London: Secker and Warburg.

Orwell, G. (1961). *The Road to Wigan Pier.* New York: Berkley Medallion Books, (pp. 88–89).

Osborn, A. F. (1963). *Applied imagination* (3rd ed.). New York: Scribner's.

Our Bodies Ourselves (2010, July 16). "'The new abortion providers'" and the old political dilemmas." http://www.our-bodiesourblog-org/blog/20/10/07/the-new-abortion-providers-and-the-old-political-dilemmas

Pack-Brown, S. P., & Whittington-Clark, L. E. (1998). *Images of me: A guide to group work with African-American women.* Boston: Allyn & Bacon.

Panaro, F. (2004). *September 11 doesn't justify discrimination against Muslims, Arabs, and others.* Bankers.online.com.

Pantoja, A., & Perry, W. (1992). Community development & restoration: A perspective. In F. G. Rivera & J. L. Erlich (Eds.),*Community organizing in a diverse society* (p. 71). Boston: Allyn & Bacon.

Papadoupoulos, L., Bor. R., Cross, M. C., & Cohn-Shertok, D. C. (2003). *Reporting in counseling and psycotherapy: A trainee's guide to preparing case studies & reports.* New York: Routledge.

Parker, L., & Eisler, P. (2001, April 6–8). Ballots in black Florida precincts invalidated more. *USA Today,* p. A1.

Parloff, M. B. (1970). Sheltered workshops for the alienated. *International Journal of Psychiatry 9,* 197–204.

Pastalan, L. A. (Ed.). (1999). *Making aging in place work.* Binghamton, NY: Haworth Press.

Patterson, J. (2001). *Brown v. Board of Education: A civil rights milestone & its troubled legacy.* New York: Oxford University Press.

Pear, R. (2003, December 7). Medicare plan for drug costs bars insurance. *New York Times,* p. 1.

Pear, R. (2004, April 26). U.S. finds fault in all 50 states' child welfare. *New York Times.*

Pear, R. (2007, April 1). Expanded health program for children causes clash. *New York Times,* p. 16.

Pear, R. (2010, April 10). In a tough economy, old limits on welfare. *New York Times.* http://www.nytimes.com/2010/04/11/us/11welfare.html?ref=us

Pearce, D. (2010, June). The self-sufficiency standard for New York State 2010. Center for Women's Welfare, School of Social Work, University of Washington.

Pearce, D. (2010, May). The self-sufficiency standard for Pennsylvania 2010-2011. Center for Women's Welfare, School of Social Work, University of Washington.

Pearce, D. (2010, June). The self-sufficiency standard for New York State 2010.

Pearl, A., & Riessman, F. (1965). *New careers for the poor.* New York: Free Press.

Pearson, G. (1975). The politics of uncertainty: A study in the socialization of the social worker. In H. Jones (Ed.), *Towards a new social work* (pp. 21–23). London: Routledge and Kegan Paul.

Peek, T. (2000). Families and the nursing home environment: Adaptation in a group context. *Journal of Gerontological Social Work 33*(1), 51–66.

Pelton, L. (1989). *For reasons of poverty.* New York: Praeger.

The perils of cutting Medicaid. (2004, April 17). *New York Times.*

Perlman, R. (1975). *Consumers and social services.* New York: John Wiley and Sons.

Pertman, A. (2001, May 20). Still illegal, but . . . *Boston Globe*, p. D1.

Pew Research Center's Forum on Religion & Public Life and the Pew Research Center for the People and the Press. (2009, July 15). Among U.S. religious groups, Muslims seen as facing more discrimination. www.pewforum.org

Pfeiffer, S. (2006, April 10). BMC to go national with legal aid program. *Boston Globe*, p. A1.

Pincus, A. H., & Minahan, A. (1973). *Social work practice: Model and method.* Itasca, IL: F. S. Peacock.

Pipher, M. (1998). *Reviving Ophelia: Saving the lives of adolescent girls.* New York: Ballantine Books.

Piven, F. F., & Cloward, R. A. (1966, May 2). A strategy to end poverty. *The Nation 202*(18), 510–517.

Piven, F. F., & Cloward, R. A. (1971). *Regulating the poor: The functions of public welfare.* New York: Random House.

Platt, A. M. (1977). *The child savers: The invention of delinquency.* Chicago: University of Chicago Press.

Pollitt, K. (2010, May 31). What ever happened to welfare mothers? *Nation*, p. 6.

Polsky, H. W. (1962). *Cottage six—The social system of delinquent boys in residential treatment.* New York: Russell Sage Foundation.

Portes, A., & Rumbaut, R. (1990). *Immigrant America.* Berkeley, CA: University of California Press.

Power, M. (2006, March). Fuel poverty in the USA: The overview and the outlook. *Energy Action* 98, pp. 1–2.

PR Newswire. (2004a, April 19). No cause for celebrating Equal Pay Day, says Michigan Pay Equity Network.

PR Newswire. (2004b, May 17). National survey finds confidentiality and forced mental health diagnoses are major barriers to seeking psychological care.

Press, E. (2001, April 9). Lead us not into temptation. *The American Prospect 12*(6), 20–27.

Priest, D., & Hull, A. (2007, February 18). Soldiers face neglect, frustration at Army's top medical facility, *Washington Post*, p. A01.

Prime Time Live. (1995, February 16).

Prinz, Joachim. (1963). Speech at the March on Washington. www.Joachimprinz.com

Privacy and State Records (1984, February 4) *Boston Globe.*

Privacy Rights Clearinghouse. Medical Records Privacy. Accessed October 4, 2010. http://www.privacyrights.org/fe/fs8-med.htm#8

The Progressive. (1997, November 8).

Project Bread/The Walk for Hunger. (1991). *Children are hungry in Massachusetts: A report of the Massachusetts community childhood hunger identification project.* Boston: Author.

Prothrow-Smith, D. (1987). *Violence protection for adolescents.* Newton, MA: Educational Development Center, Inc.

Psychotherapy Finances. (1998, May). P.O. Box 8979, Jupiter, FL 33468. Vol. 24(5), Issue 289.

Quaid, L. (2005, December 14). More children getting school breakfast. *Boston Globe*, p. A4.

Rachels, J. (1979). Active euthanasia with parental consent [Commentary]. *Hastings Center Report.* New York: Hastings-on-Hudson.

Rampell, C. (2010, July 8). For younger women, a smaller wage gap. *New York Times.* http://economix.blogs.nytims.com/2010/07/08/for-youner-women-a-smaller-wage-gap/

Raphael, J., & Tolman, R. (1997). *Trapped by poverty, trapped by abuse: New evidence documenting the relationship between domestic violence and welfare.* Ann Arbor, MI: University of Michigan Research Center on Poverty, Risk, and Mental Health.

Reamer, F. (2001, October 15). Social work values resonate, inspire in wake of recent tragedies. *Social Work Today*, pp. 22–23.

Reed, S. (1979, January 7). Teacher burnout a growing hazard. *New York Times*, p. L12.

Rees, S. (1979). *Social work face to face.* New York: Columbia University Press.

Reeser, L. C., & Epstein, I. (1990). *Professionalism and activism in social work.* New York: Columbia University Press.

Reich, R. (2001, May 21). No tax cut. Period. *The American Prospect 12*(9), 48.

Reich, R. (2010, October 18). America is becoming a plutocracy. http://robertreich.org/

Reinarman, C., & Levine, H. G. (1989). The crack attack: Politics and media in America's latest drug scare. In J. Best (Ed.), *Images of issues* (pp. 115–137). New York: Aldine de Gruyter.

Reynolds, B. (1963). *An uncharted journey.* New York: Citadel.

Rhodes, M. L. (1989). *Ethical dilemmas in social work practice.* Milwaukee, WI: Family Service America.

Richan, W. C., & Mendelsohn, A. R. (1973). *Social work: The unloved profession.* New York: Franklin Watts.

Richmond, M. (1917). *Social diagnosis.* New York: Russell Sage.

Ries, J. B., & Leakfield, C. G. (1998). *The research funding guidebook: Getting it, managing it, and renewing it.* Thousand Oaks, CA: Sage.

Riessman, F., & Gartner, A. (1977). *Self-help groups in the human services.* San Francisco, CA: Jossey-Bass.

Riessman, F., & Gartner, A. (1980). *A working guide to self-help groups.* New York: Franklin Watts.

Rivera, F. G., & Erlich, J. L. (Eds.). (1998). *Community organizing in a diverse society* (3rd ed.). Boston: Allyn & Bacon.

Roberts, Dorothy. (2002). *Shattered Bonds.* New York: Basic Books, p. 164.

Robertson, C. (2009, August 31). In New Orleans, recovery is not enough. *New York Times,* p. A8.

Robertson, C. (2010, August 9). First lady asks Congress to join childhood obesity fight. *New York Times.*

Rodriguez, C. (2001, June 7). Latino prison count called inaccurate. *Boston Globe,* p. A3.

Rogers, C. (1951). *Client-centered therapy.* Boston: Houghton Mifflin.

Rose, S., & Edelson, J. L. (1990). *Working with children and adolescents in groups.* Santa Fe, NM: Jossey-Bass.

Rosen, C. E. (1976, July). Sign-away pressures. *Social Work 21,* 284–287.

Rosen, F. (2001, July 8). The promise of stem cell research. *Boston Globe,* p. D7.

Rosenhan, D. L. (1973, January 19). On being sane in insane places. *Science 179,* 250–258.

Rosie's Place Spring Newsletter. (2007), p. 2. Rosie's Place, Boston, MA.

Rosenthal, M. (2007). Letter to the editor. *Boston Globe,* January 17.

Rossen, S. (1987). Hospital social work. In A. Menahan (Ed.), *Encyclopedia of social work* (18th ed., pp. 816–820). Silver Spring, MD: National Association of Social Workers.

Rothman, D. (1971). *The discovery of the asylum.* Boston: Little, Brown.

Ruben, D. H. (2001). *Treating adult children of alcoholics: A behavioral approach.* San Diego, CA: Academic Press.

Russell, D. M. (1989). *Political organizing in grassroots politics.* Lanham, MD: University Press of America.

Russo, J. R. (1980). *Serving and surviving as a human service worker.* Monterey, CA: Brooks/Cole.

Ryan, W. (1976). *Blaming the victim.* New York: Random House.

Sachs, J. (2010, December 27). America's political class struggle. *The Huffington Post.* http://wwwhuffingtonpost.com/jeffrey-sachs/americas-political-class_b_801663.html

Sack, K., & Pear, R. (2010, February 18). States consider Medicaid cuts as use grows. *New York Times.* http://www.nytimes.com/2010/02/19/us/politics/19medicaid.html

Sacks, O. (1989). *Seeing voices: A journey into the land of the deaf.* Berkeley, CA: University of California.

Sahagan, L. (2007, June 4). Illegal immigrant invokes church sanctuary. *Boston Globe,* p. A2.

Sainsbury, E. (1974). *Social work with families: Perceptions of social casework among clients of a family service unit.* London: Routledge.

Salem, G. (2010, August 17). George Salem, other Arab-American Republicans, push back on GOP rhetoric on Manhattan Islamic center. http://www.aaiusa.org/blog

Schamess, G., & Lightburn, A., (Eds.) (1998). *Humane managed care?* Washington, D.C.: NASW Press.

Schein, V. E. (1995). *Working from the margins: Voices of mothers in poverty.* Ithaca, NY: Cornell University Press.

Schiller, L. Y. (1995). Stages of development in women's groups: A relational model. In R. Kurland & R. Salmon (Eds.). *Group work practice in a troubled society.* New York: Haworth.

Schiller, L. Y. (1997). Rethinking stages of development in women's groups. *Social Work with Groups 20.*

Schmitt, E. (2001a, May 15). For first time, nuclear families drop below 25% of households. *New York Times,* p. 1.

Schmitt, E. (2001b, July 29). You can come in, you stay out. *New York Times,* p. 5.

Schneider, P. (1991). *Teamwork in the hierarchy: Sustained in the thick of organizational culture.* Unpublished doctoral dissertation, Northeastern University, Boston.

Schott, L., and Pavetti, L. (2010). Federal TANF funding shrinking while need remains high. Center on Budget and Policy Priorities.http://www.cbpp.org/cms/index.cfm?fa=view&id=3345

Schram, B. (1971). The conscious use of color. In P. Kurzman (Ed.), *The Mississippi experience: Strategies for welfare rights organization* (pp. 66–83). New York: Association Press.

Schram, B. (1997). *Creating the small scale social program: Planning, implementation and evaluation.* Thousand Oaks, CA: Sage.

Schram, B. (2011, Winter). Savior in the desert. *New Politics,* pp. 105–107.

Schreiber, L. A. (1993, January 17). What kind of abortions do we want? *New York Times Book Review,* pp. 13–14.

Schreter, R. K., Sharfstein, S. S., & Schreter, C. A. (Eds.). (1994). *Allies and adversaries: The impact of managed care on mental health services.* Washington, D.C.: American Psychiatric Press.

Schulman, L. (1993). *Developing and testing a practice theory: An interactional perspective.* New York: National Association of Social Workers.

Schwartz, W. (1971). On the use of groups in social work practice. In W. Schwartz & S. Zalba (Eds.), *The practice of group work* (pp. 3–24). New York: Columbia University Press.

Sciegas, M., Garnick, D. W., Hogan, C. M., Merrick, E., Goldin, D., Urato, M., & Hodgkin, D. (2001). Employee assistance programs among Fortune 500 firms. *Employee Assistance Quarterly 16*(3), 25–35.

Science Daily (2010, May 27). Despite food-assistance programs, many children experience food insecurity, hunger. http://www.sciencedaily.com/releases/2010/05/100527111337.htm

Scott, M. (2010, March 11). Michigan Republicans propose drug testing, other rules to stop public assistance fraud among Bridge Card users. *The Grand Rapids Press.* Mlive.com, http://www.mlive.com.politics/indx.ssf/22010/03/michigan_republicans_propose_d.html

Seaver, T. (1971). The care and feeding of southern welfare departments. In P. A. Kurzman (Ed.), *The Mississippi experience: Strategies for welfare rights organizing* (pp. 53–65). New York: Association Press.

Seever, F. S. (1987). (Review of the book *Professionalism and social change: From settlement house movement to neighborhood centers, 1886 to the present*). *Social Service Review 64*(1), 163.

SEIU, Local 503. (2010, April 14). Andy Stern, president of Service Employees (SEIU), announces retirement. http://www.seiu503.org/media/Andy_Stern_President_of_Service_Employees_International_Union

Seligman, L. (1996). *Diagnosis and treatment planning in counseling* (2nd ed.). New York: Plenum Press.

Sen, R. (2000, Fall). The first time was tragedy. *Color lines 3,* 3.

Senior, J. (2007). Can't get no satisfaction. *New York Times Magazine.* http://cantate-domino.blogspot.com/2006/12/jennifer-senior-can't-get-no-satisfaction

Sentencing Project. (2010). Incarceration. http://www.sentencingproject.org/template/page.cfm?id=107

Service Employees International Union. (1997, November). *Contracting human services: Recurring scandals and bad performance.* Boston: Author.

Service Employees International Union. (2006). *Houston janitors—part-time work doesn't add up.* www.houstonjanitors.org/problem/.

Sexton, J. (1997, October 12). Privacy and pride are submerged at busy workfare evaluation site. *New York Times,* p. 17.

Shade, P. (1981, Summer). Running to stay in place. *Public Welfare,* pp. 28–31.

Shamoo, A. (2004, Winter). Ethics of research involving mandatory drug testing of high school athletes in Oregon. *American Journal of Bioethics.* Vol. 4, No. 1. http://muse.jhu.edu/login?uri=journals/american_journal_of_bioethics/v004

Shaw, R. (2001). *The activists' handbook: A primer for the 1990s and beyond.* Berkeley, CA: University of California Press.

Sheehan, S. (1981, June 8). A reporter at large (Creedmoor-Part III). *The New Yorker.* http://www.newyorker.com/search/query?keyword=schizophrenia

Sheldrick, C. (1999). The management of risk in adolescence. *Journal of Child Psychology, Psychiatry, and Allied Disorders 40,* 507–518.

Shenker, I. (1971, April 10). Test of Samaritan parable: Just who aids the helpless? *New York Times,* p. 25.

Sherman, A., & Stone, C., (2010, June 25). "Income gaps between very rich and everyone else more than tripled in last three decades, new data show." Center on Budget and Policy Priorities. http://www.cbpp.org/cms/index.cfm?fa=view&id=3220

Shertzer, B., & Stone, S. (1980). *Fundamentals of counseling* (3rd ed.). Boston: Houghton Mifflin.

Shore, W. H. (1995). *Revolution of the heart: A new strategy for creating wealth & meaningful change.* New York: Riverside Books.

Shulman, L. (1979). *The skills of helping individuals and groups.* Itasca, IL: F. E. Peacock.

Shulman, L (2008). *The skills of helping individuals, families, groups, and communities* (6th ed.). Pacific Grove: Brooks/Cole Pub.

Siegel, G. B. (1996). *Mass interviewing and the marshaling of ideas to improve performance.* Lanham, MD: University Press of America.

Silk, L. (1981, November–December). A walk on the supply side. *Harvard Business Review.*

Simmel, G. (1955). The significance of numbers for social life. In A. D. Hare, E. F. Borgatta, & R. F. Bales (Eds.), *Small groups* (pp. 9–15). New York: Alfred Knopf.

Skinner, B. F. (1974). *About behaviorism.* New York: Alfred A. Knopf.

Smith, M. J. (rev. 2004). *Program evaluation in the human services.* New York: Springer.

Smith, P. (1993, February 16). "Queen" star McKee takes on role of bolstering black clout. *Boston Globe,* pp. 25, 30.

Social Security Administration. (2010). Fast Facts. http://www.ssa/gov/policy/docs/chartbooks/fast_facts/fast_facts08.pdf

Social Security Online. (2010a, July). http://www.socialsecurity.gov/pressoffice/factsheets/women.htm

Social Security Online. (2010b, June 30). http://www.socialsecurity.gov/OACT/FACTS/

Social Security Online. (2010c). Electronic Fact Sheet. http://ssa/gov/pubs/10003.html

Solomon, A. (2001, May 6). A cure for poverty. *New York Times Magazine,* pp. 112–117.

Somers, S. (1988). *Keeping secrets.* New York: Warner Books.

Sommez, F. (2011, February 8). House rejects measure that would extend key Patriot Act provisions through December. *The Washington Post.* http://voices.washingtonpost.com/44/2011/02/ahead-of-patriot-act-vote

Sourander, A., Helstela, L., Helenrus, H., & Pina, J. (2000). Persistence of bullying from childhood to adolescence: A longitudinal 8 year follow-up study. *Child Abuse and Neglect (The International Journal) 24,* 873–881.

Southern Regional Education Board. (1969, December). *Roles and functions for mental health workers: A report of a symposium.* Atlanta, GA: Community Mental Health Worker Project.

Spare Change. (1995, October). Homeless win legal battle in Ohio, p. 1.

Specht, H. (1990, September). Social work and the popular psychotherapies. *Social Service Review,* pp. 19–24.

Speeter, G. (1978a). *Playing their game our way, using the political process to meet community needs.* Amherst, MA: Citizen's Involvement Training Project, University of Massachusetts.

Speeter, G. (1978b). *Power: A repossession manual, organizing strategies for citizens.* Amherst, MA: Citizen's Involvement Training Project, University of Massachusetts.

Speigel, B. (1992). *The supervised visitation program at the New York Society for Ethical Culture.* Paper presented at the Vermont Child Study Association's Conference on Supervised Visitation Programs, 1992.

Spock, B. (1946). *Common sense book of baby and childcare.* New York: Meredith Press.

Spock, B. (1976). *Baby and child care* (4th ed.). New York: Hawthorn Books.

Spock, B., & Morgan, M. (1989). *Spock on Spock. A memoir of growing up with the century.* New York: Pantheon Books.

Spradley, J. (1979). *The ethnographic interview.* New York: Holt, Rinehart & Winston.

Squires, G. (2006, Winter). Reintroducing the black/white divide in racial discourse. *New Politics,* p. 111.

Stack, C. (1974). *All our kin: Strategies for survival in a black community.* New York: Harper & Row.

Staples, R. (1988). The black American family. In C. H. Mindel (Ed.), *Ethnic families in America* (pp. 303–324). New York: Elsevier.

State bar to allow lawyers to break confidentiality. (2004, May 14). *The Recorder.*

Steele, C. M., & Aronson, J. (1995, August). *Stereotype vulnerability and the intellectual test performance of African-Americans.* Paper presented at the American Psychological Association.

Steinberg, S. (2005, Summer). Immigration, African Americans, and race discourse. *New Politics,* p. 45.

Stern, A. L. (2001, September 3). Andrew L. Stern replies to "Changing to Organize." *The Nation 273* (7), p. 23.

Sterngold, J. (2001, October 7). Legal residency hopes of millions dashed. *New York Times,* p. A20.

Stoesz, D., & Karger, H. (1991, April). The corporatisation of the United States welfare state. *Journal of Social Policy 20,* 157–171.

Stogdill, R. M. (1948). Personal factors associated with leadership: A survey of the literature. *Journal of Psychology 25,* 37–71.

Stogdill, R. M., & Coons, A. E. (1957). *Leader behavior: Its description and measurement.* Columbus, OH: Bureau of Business Research, Ohio State University.

Stolberg, S. G. (2001, May 13). Shouldn't a pill be colorblind? *New York Times,* pp. 1, 3.

The storm that changed America. (2005). New York: Time, Inc.

Story, L. (2007, April 28). Rewriting the ad rules for Muslim-Americans. *New York Times.*

Story, L. (2010, August 23). Does income gap presage crisis? *International Herald Tribune,* p. 15.

Student Loan Blog. (2010). Quick school search. http://www.studentloaninfo.org/blog/student-loan-forgiveness-social-workers

Sue, D. W., Ivey, A. E., & Pederson, P. (1996). *A theory of multicultural counseling and therapy.* Pacific Grove, CA: Brooks/Cole.

Summers, N. (2005). *Fundamentals of case management practice: Skills for human services.* CA: Wadsworth Press.

Svonkin, S. (1998). *Jews against prejudice: American Jews and the fight for civil rights.* New York: Columbia University Press.

Swarns, R. L. (1997, December 8). Denied food stamps, many immigrants scrape for meals. *New York Times,* pp. B1, B4.

Swarns, R. L. (1998, April 14). Mothers poised for workfare face acute lack of day care. *New York Times,* pp. A1, A21.

Swoboda, J. S., Elwork, A., Sales, B. D., & Levine, D. (1978, August). Knowledge of and compliance with privileged communication and child abuse reporting laws. *Professional Psychology 9*(3), 448–457.

Szasz, T. S. (1961). *The myth of mental illness.* New York: Harper & Row.

Szasz, T. S. (1965). *Psychiatric justice.* New York: Macmillan.

Szyndrowski, D. (1999). Impact of domestic violence on adolescent aggression in the schools. *Preventing School Failure 44*(1), 9–11.

Talk of the Nation. (2004a, January 15). National Public Radio.

Talk of the Nation. (2004b, April 15). National Public Radio.

The StandDown Texas Project. (2010, May 17). Supreme Court rules in juvenile sentencing. http://standdown.type-pad.com/weblog/2010/05/supreme-court-rules-on-juvenile-sentencing.html

Toner, R., Elder, J., Thee, M., & Connelly, M. (2007, March 2). Most support U.S. guarantee of health care. *New York Times.* http://www.nytimes.com/2007/03/02/washington/02/poll.htm

Townsend, P. (1992, April 25). Speech at the Socialist Scholars Conference, New York.

Towson, R. W. & Rivas, R. F. (2008). *An introduction to group work practice.* Boston: Allyn & Bacon.

Toy, V. (1998, April 15). Tough workfare rules used as way to cut welfare rolls. *New York Times,* pp. A1, A27.

Trillin, C. (2001, September 3). New grub streets. *The New Yorker,* pp. 42–48.

Trimmer, S. (1964). The economy of charity (1801). Cited in D. Owen, *English Philanthropy 1660–1960.* Cambridge, MA: Harvard University Press.

Truax, C. B., & Carkhuff, R. R. (1967). *Toward effective counseling and psychotherapy.* Chicago: Aldine.

Truax, C. B., & Mitchell, K. M. (1971). Research on certain therapists' interpersonal skills in relation to process and outcomes. In A. E. Bergin & S. L. Garfield (Eds.), *Handbook of psychotherapy and behavior change.* New York: Wiley.

Tucker, Robert, C., (Ed.) (1972) "Economic and Philosophic Manuscripts of 1844: Selections." *The Marx-Engels Reader.* New York: W.W. Norton, p. 60.

Tuckman, B. (1965). Developmental sequence in small groups. *Psychological Bulletin 63*, 384–399.

Two cases given legal aid grants. (2001, February). *NASW News 46*(2), p. 12.

Uchitelle, L. (2010, July 9). Optimistic but unemployed: A generation adrift. *International Herald Tribune*, p. 18.

UNICEF, (2007). An overview of child well-being in rich countries. UNICEF Innocenti Research Centre, Florence, Italy.

United Nations. (1948). *General assembly resolution 217A (III)*. www.un.org/Overview/rights.

United Nations Children's Fund. (2007). An overview of child well-being in rich countries. *Innocenti Report Card 7*. UNICEF Innocenti Research Centere, Florence. The United Nations Children's Fund.

United Press International. (2004, April 26). Welfare kids staying longer in foster care.

United States Department of Agriculture (2009) Food and Nutrition Service. http://www.fns.usda.gov/fns/recovery

Universal Living Wage. (2010). Home page. http://www.universalminimumwage.org

Urban Institute. (2000, October 24). *America's families better off today than in 1997, but not all share equally in economic gains*. www.urban.org.

Urbina, I. (2009, October 27). For runaways, sex buys survival. *New York Times*.

Urdang, E. (1999). The influence of managed care on the MSW social work student development of the professional self. *Smith College Studies in Social Work 70* (1), 3–25.

USA Today. (2009, June 29). Thousands remain in FEMA trailers.

U.S. Census Bureau. (2009a). Current Population Survey. People in families by relationship to householder, age of householder, number of related children present, and family structure: 2008. Washington, D.C.: Government Printing Office.

U.S. Census Bureau. (2009b). Homeownership rates by race and ethnicity of householder: 2006 to 2009. Washington, D.C.: Government Printing Office.

U.S. Census Bureau. (2010a). The 2010 Statistical Abstract. http://www.census.gov/compendia/statab/cats/population.html

U.S. Census Bureau. (2010b). The 2010 Statistical Abstract. http://www.childwelfare.gov/pubs/factsheets/foster.cfm

U.S. Conference of Mayors. (2009, December 6). U.S. cities see sharp increases in the need for food assistance: decreases in individual homelessness. Washington, D.C.: U.S. Conference of Mayors.

U. S. Department of Agriculture. (2009a). Women, infants, and children program. WIC-Fact-sheet.pdf

U.S. Department of Agriculture. (2009b). National school lunch program. NSLPFactSheet.pdf

U.S. Department of Commerce. (1995). Statistical abstract of the United States 1995. Washington, D.C.: Bureau of the Census.

U.S. Department of Health and Human Services. (1997). *AFDC total caseload*. www.acf.hhs.gov//programs/ofa/casekiad/afdc/1997/fycytotal97.htm.

U.S. Department of Health and Human Services. (2001, March 31). *The AFCARS Report, for the period ending March 31, 2000*. www.acf.dhhs.gov/programs/ch/publications/afcars/apr2001.htm.

U.S. Department of Health and Human Services. (2007). *TANF recipients as of 1/10/2007*. www.acf.hhs.gov//programs/ofa/caseload/2006/tanf_recipients.htm.

U.S. Department of Health and Human Services. (2010, April 29). Race and disability discrimination complaints in Wisconsin TANF program to be resolved by statewide agreement. http://www.hhs.gov/news/press/2010press/04/20100429b.html

U.S. Department of Health and Human Services. (2010b, July). The AFCARS Report. http://www.acf.hhs.gov/programs/cb/stats_research/index.htm

U.S. Department of Housing and Urban Development. (2007). *Hope VI: Community building makes a difference*. www.huduser.org/publications/pubasst/hope2.

U. S. Department of Justice. (2001). Americans with Disabilities Act. www.usdoj.gov.80/cit/ada/pubs/10hrpt.htmlanchor 30598.

U.S. Department of Labor. (1998, August). *Glossary of compensation terms*. Washington, D.C.: Bureau of Labor Statistics.

U.S. Department of Labor Employment and Training Administration. (2007). High growth industry profile: Health care. www.doleta.gov.

U.S. Department of Labor. (2011, March). Disability employment statistics released. Office of Disability Employment Policy.http://www.dol.gov.odep/

U.S. House of Representatives Committee on Ways and Means. (2010, April 15). Chairman McDermott announces hearing on the role of education and training in the TANF program. Press release. http://waysandmeans.house.gov/press/PRArticle.aspx?NewsID=11134xs

U.S. National Coalition for the Homeless. (2006, January 15). *U.S. National Coalition for the Homeless Report—A Dream Denied: The Criminalization of Homelessness in U.S. Cities.* www.alterinfos.org/spip.phb?article185.

U.S. Privacy: Health Insurance and Accountability Act 1996: Synopsis. (2002). www.gpit.ie/presentations/Gregg%Palmer.pdf.

Valentine, P. (1997, February 5). Maryland suspends licenses over child support: Thousands of parents lose the right to drive. *Washington Post.*

Vallianatos, C. (2001a). Association backing given in two cases. *NASW News 46*(14), 11.

Vallianatos, C. (2001b). Managed care is faulted. *NASW News 46*(17).

Van Ornum, W. (1990). *Crisis counseling with children & adolescents: A guide for nonprofessional counselors.* New York: Continuum.

Vicini, J. (1999, March 9). Justice Department attempt to speed deportations is set back. *Boston Globe*, p. A5.

Vogel, R. (1979, November 11). Teachers' colleges shift their focus to 'related fields.' *New York Times*, p. 32.

Voices heard, lessons learned: Progress and evolving challenges for practice, research, and policy. (2006). *Journal of HIV/AIDS & Social Services 5.* Available at http://jhaso.haworthpress.com.

Vollbracht, J. (2002). *Stopping at every lemonade stand: How to create a culture that cares for kids.* New York: Penguin Books.

Vonnegut, K. (1991). *Fates worse than death.* New York: G. P. Putnam.

Wacquant, Loïc, (2009) *Punishing the Poor: The Neoliberal Government of Social Insecurity.* Durham, NC: Duke University Press.

Wagner, D. (2005). *The poorhouse: America's forgotten institution.* New York: Rowman & Littlefield.

Walker, R. (1995, January–February). California rages against the dying of the light. *New Left Review 209*, 42–74.

Ward, P. R (2008, October 26). Residency restrictions for sex offenders popular, but ineffective. *Post-Gazette.* http://www.post-gazette.com/pgo8300/922948-85.stm

Warner, R. (1989). Deinstitutionalization: How did we get where we are? *Journal of Social Issues 45* (3), 17–30.

Washington, W. (2004, May 31). Bush takes spotlight off Medicare drug benefit. *Boston Globe*, p. A1.

Webster-Stratton, C., & Martin, H. (1994). *Troubled families, problem children.* New York: John Wiley.

Weidell, R. C. (1980, February). Unsealing birth certificates in Minnesota. *Child Welfare 59*, 113–119.

Weil, M. (1986). Women, community and organizing. In N. Van Den Bugh & L. Cooper (Eds.), *Feminist vision for social work* (pp. 126–134). Silver Spring, MD: National Association of Social Workers.

Weinbach, R. (2002). *The social worker as manager: A practical guide to success* (4th ed.). Boston: Allyn & Bacon.

Weintraub, K. (2010, May 10). Putting lawyers on the case. *Boston Globe*, p. B6.

Weissberg, R. (1999). *The politics of empowerment.* Westport, CT: Praeger.

Weissman, A. (1976). Industrial social services: Linkage technology. *Social Casework 57*, 50–54.

Weissman, H., Epstein, I., & Savage, A. (1983). *Agency-based social work: Neglected aspects of clinical practice.* Philadelphia: Temple University Press.

Weissman, H. H. (1973). *Overcoming mismanagement in the human service professions.* San Francisco: Jossey-Bass.

Welfare reform's uncounted failures. (1998, April 2). *Boston Globe*, p. A22.

Wen, P. (2010, December 12). A legacy of unintended side effects, *Boston Globe*, p. A1.

Wender, P. (1987). *The hyperactive child, adolescent and adult.* New York: Oxford University Press.

Wenocur, S., & Sherman, W. (1980, March). *Empowering the social worker.* Baltimore: University of Maryland School of Social Work and Community Planning.

Western Regional Advocacy Project. (2006). *Without housing: Decades of federal housing cutbacks, massive homelessness, and policy failures.* San Francisco, CA.

Wharf, B., & Clague, M. (Eds.). (1997). *Community organizing: Canadian experiences.* Toronto, Canada: Oxford University Press.

White, B. J., & Madera, E., compiled and edited, web version updated by Kerrin, M. E., & Rothblatt, A. (2004). *American self-help clearing house, 1993–2004*. Mental Help Net. www.mentalhelpnet/selfhelp/.

Whoriskey, P. (2007, November 22). Ga. Court rejects sex offender law. *Boston Globe*, p. A28.

Wilkinson, R. (2010, Summer). "Reviving the spirit of equality." *International Socialism*, pp. 67–79.

Williams, C. J. (2010, March 18). Court tightens definition of cyber-bullying. *Los Angeles Times*.

Williams, J. C. (2003). *A roof over my head*. Boulder, CO: University Press of Colorado.

Williams, L. (1997). *Decades of distortion: The right's 30-year assault on welfare*. Somerville, MA: Political Research Associates.

Williams, R., Jr. (1966). Prejudice and society. In J. P. Davis (Ed.), *The American negro reference book* (pp. 727–730). Englewood Cliffs, NJ: Prentice Hall.

Wilson, M., & Rosenfelt, D. S. (1978). *Salt of the earth: Screenplay and commentary*. Old Westbury, NY: Feminist Press.

Wilson, S. (1980). *Recording: Guidelines for social workers*. New York: Free Press.

Withorn, A. (1994, October 3). Personal communication.

Wolff, R. (2007). *The decline of public higher education*. http://mrzine.monthlyreview.org/wolff170207.html.

Wolvin, A., & Coakley, C. G. (1992). *Listening* (4th ed.). Dubuque, IA: William C. Brown.

Woodside, M., and McClam, T. (1990). *An Introduction to Human Services, 2nd ed.* Florence, KY: Cenage Learning/Brooks/Cole.

Women Veterans' Network. (2007). *25 frequently asked questions from Massachusetts' women veterans*. www.mass.gov/veterans.

Workfare's missing link. (1996, October 21). *New York Times*, p. A31.

Wright, N. (2003). *The new guide to crisis and trauma counseling*. Ventura, CA: Regal Books.

Wright, T. (1997). *Out of place*. New York: State University of New York Press.

Wuthnow, R. (1994). *Sharing the journey: Support groups and America's new quest for community*. New York: Free Press.

Yaffe, J., & Gotthuffer, D. (2000). *Quick guide to the Internet for social work*. Boston: Allyn & Bacon.

Yenkin, J. (1992, September 10). 30 million Americans go hungry, report says. *Boston Globe*, p 3.

Yin, S. (2008, March). How older women can shield themselves from poverty. Population Reference Bureau. http://www.prb.org/Journalists/Webcasts/2008/olderwomen.aspx.

York, R. (2009). *Evaluating Human Services: A practical approach of the human service professional*. Upper Saddle River, N.J.: Pearson.

Young, L. (2002, February 6). *Women and aging: Bearing the burden of long-term care*. Testimony at Joint Hearing before the Special Committee on aging of the committee on Health, Education, Labor, and Pensions of the U.S. Senate. U.S. Government Printing Office: Washington, D.C., p. 37.

Zastrow, C. (1993). *Social work with groups* (3rd ed.). Chicago: Nelson-Hall.

Zayas, L., & Katch, M. (1989, January). Contracting with adolescents: An ego-psychological approach. *Social Casework* 70(1), 3–9.

Zeilberger, J., Sampen, S. E., & Sloan, H. N., Jr. (1973). Modification of a child's behavior in the home with the mother as therapist. In J. Fischer (Ed.), *Interpersonal helping* (pp. 224–236). Springfield, IL: Charles C. Thomas.

Zimbardo, P. G., Haney, C., Banks, W. C., & Jaffe, D. (1982). The psychology of imprisonment. In J. C. Brigham & L. Wrightsman (Eds.), *Contemporary issues in social psychology* (4th ed.). (pp. 230–245). Monterey, CA: Brooks/Cole.

Index